Bonds of Civility

Aesthetic Networks and the Political Origins of Japanese Culture

In this path-breaking book, Eiko Ikegami uncovers a complex history of social life in which aesthetic images become central to Japan's cultural identities. Combining sociological insights on organizations with prodigious scholarship on cultural history, this book explores such wide-ranging topics as the central role of networks in performing arts, tea ceremony and *haiku*, the politics of *kimono* aesthetics, the rise of commercial publishing, the popularization of etiquette and manners, the vogue of androgyny in *kabuki* performance, and the rise of tacit modes of communication.

Eiko Ikegami is Professor of Sociology at the New School for Social Research. She is the author of *Taming of the Samurai*.

CW00952574

"[This book] is as brilliant a description of the stratification of Japanese culture as *Bourdieu's Distinction* is of French culture... Ikegami's work opens up the social history of Japanese culture in the way that the past two generations of social historians from Elias to Darnton have done for European culture... This is as fine a work as we have for any part of the world on the long-term shaping of culture, and on the political consequences of cultural institutions."
– Randall Collins, University of Pennsylvania

"In a world in which the social order was theoretically rigid, Ikegami demonstrates how people in medieval and early modern Japan carved out spheres through a variety of aesthetic associations to bring 'beauty' into their lives. Using sociological and anthropological tools and with the extraordinary training of a historian, Ikegami brings this world to life."
– Joshua Fogel, University of California, Santa Barbara

"In this fascinating and illuminating study of the politics of civility in Japan, Eiko Ikegami discusses the way that politeness and politics are inseparable... [S]he shows persuasively that what in Western cultures is normally separated, like art and politics, has been, and is, closely interwoven in Japan. It is an amazing society that rises before her audience's eyes, and, since Ikegami presents this astonishing story with enviable lucidity, her book is as accessible to the reader innocent in the ways of Japan as it is to the specialist."
– Peter Gay, Yale University

"Eiko Ikegami has made excellent use of her sociological insights and her command over Japanese history to present a highly original interpretation of Japanese society. This is an important contribution in exploring the interrelations between culture and politics in one of the most intriguing civilizations in the world."
– Amartya Sen, Harvard University

"Ikegami shows how the brilliant colorings of Japanese history were mobilized in and through what she calls 'aesthetic publics,' each reflecting a dynamic interplay among social networks that elicit, even as they shape, tacit cultural practices. She induces this highly original vision from a dazzling array of evidence across centuries. A fresh and powerful mode of network theorizing."
– Harrison White, Columbia University

Structural Analysis in the Social Sciences

Mark Granovetter, editor

The series Structural Analysis in the Social Sciences presents approaches that explain social behavior and institutions by reference to relations among such concrete entities as persons and organizations. This contrasts with at least four other popular strategies: (a) reductionist attempts to explain by a focus on individuals alone; (b) explanations stressing the causal primacy of such abstract concepts as ideas, values, mental harmonies, and cognitive maps (thus, "structuralism" on the Continent should be distinguished from structural analysis in the present sense); (c) technological and material determination; (d) explanation using "variables" as the main analytic concepts (as in the "structural equation" models that dominated much of the sociology of the 1970s), where structure is that connecting variables rather than actual social entities.

   The social network approach is an important example of the strategy of structural analysis; the series also draws on social science theory and research that is not framed explicitly in network terms but stresses the importance of relations rather than the atomization of reduction or the determination of ideas, technology, or material conditions. Though the structural perspective has become extremely popular and influential in all the social sciences, it does not have a coherent identity, and no series yet pulls together such work under a single rubric. By bringing the achievements of structurally oriented scholars to a wider public, the Structural Analysis series hopes to encourage the use of this very fruitful approach.

– Mark Granovetter

Other Books in the Series

1. Mark S. Mizruchi and Michael Schwartz, eds., *Intercorporate Relations: The Structural Analysis of Business*
2. Barry Wellman and S. D. Berkowitz, eds., *Social Structures: A Network Approach*
3. Ronald L. Brieger, ed., *Social Mobility and Social Structure*
4. David Knoke, *Political Networks: The Structural Perspective*
5. John L. Campbell, J. Rogers Hollingsworth, and Leon N. Lindberg, eds., *Governance of the American Economy*
6. Kyriakos Kontopoulos, *The Logics of Social Structure*
7. Philippa Pattison, *Algebraic Models for Social Structure*
8. Stanley Wasserman and Katherine Faust, *Social Network Analysis: Methods and Applications*
9. Gary Herrigel, *Industrial Constructions: The Sources of German Industrial Power*
10. Philippe Bourgois, *In Search of Respect: Selling Crack in El Barrio*
11. Per Hage and Frank Harary, *Island Networks: Communication, Kinship, and Classification Structures in Oceania*
12. Thomas Schweizer and Douglas R. White, eds., *Kinship, Networks and Exchange*

Series information continues after the index.

Bonds of Civility

Aesthetic Networks and the Political Origins of Japanese Culture

EIKO IKEGAMI

CAMBRIDGE
UNIVERSITY PRESS

CAMBRIDGE UNIVERSITY PRESS
Cambridge, New York, Melbourne, Madrid, Cape Town, Singapore, São Paulo

Cambridge University Press
40 West 20th Street, New York, NY 10011-4211, USA

www.cambridge.org
Information on this title: www.cambridge.org/9780521809429

First published 2005

Printed in the United States of America

A catalog record for this publication is available from the British Library.

Library of Congress Cataloging in Publication data
Ikegami, Eiko.
Bonds of civility : aesthetic networks and the political origins of Japanese culture /
Eiko Ikegami.
    p.   cm. – (Structural analysis in the social sciences)
Includes bibliographical references and index.
ISBN 0-521-80942-8 – ISBN 0-521-60115-0 (pbk.)
1. Japan – Civilization.   2. Aesthetics, Japanese.   3. Japan – Social conditions.
4. Social networks – Japan.   I. Title.   II. Series.
DS821.I437   2005
952–dc22   2004046574

ISBN-13   978-0-521-80942-9 hardback
ISBN-10   0-521-80942-8 hardback

ISBN-13   978-0-521-60115-3 paperback
ISBN-10   0-521-60115-0 paperback

Supported by the Japan Foundation.

For my mother, Kiyoko Ikegami

Contents

ix

Illustrations

xii   *Illustrations*

Color Plates

Color plates follow page 258.

Acknowledgments

I have been fortunate in forming connections with a number of intellectual and scholarly institutions and resources. Parts of this book were written in one of the pleasant studies in the Center for Scholars and Writers of the New York Public Library, which awarded me a year-long fellowship in 2000–2001. I would like to thank Peter Gay, who was hosting an unusual mix of Fellows that included both academic scholars and creative writers. John M. Lundquist, from the Oriental Division, and Robert Rainwater, from the Spencer Collection, helped my research at the Library. I also wish to thank the Waseda University Library and the Kaga Archive of the Tokyo City Library, whose excellent collections of Tokugawa manuals were the starting point of my research. Matthi Forrer helped me to examine the valuable collections at the Rijksmuseum voor Volkenkunde in Leiden.

The basic idea for this book came to me while I was working on the manuscript of my previous book, *The Taming of the Samurai: Honorific Individualism and the Making of Modern Japan*, when I was a member of the Institute for Advanced Study in Princeton. I am grateful to Clifford Geertz, as well as Michael Waltzer, Joan Scott, and Albert O. Hirschman, for their hospitality and inspiration. Natalie Davis, who was director of the Davis Center at Princeton University at that time, suggested to me that the project merited a book-length investigation. A grant from the joint program of the Social Science Research Council and the American Council of Learned Societies and a senior faculty fellowship from Yale University, in addition to grants from Yale's Whitney Humanities Center, Yale's Sumitomo Fund of the Council of East Asian Studies, and the Center for Studies of Social Change at the New School for Social Research, helped me complete different phases of this research project.

The colleagues and friends who have influenced my understanding of the history of Japanese aesthetic civility are many: David E. Apter, Andrew Arato, Tsuneo Ayabe, Karen Barkey, Richard Bernstein, Scott A. Boorman, Randall Collins, Giles Constable, Veena Das,

xiv   *Acknowledgments*

Deborah Davis, Diane Davis, Paul DiMaggio, Benjamin Elman, Priscilla Ferguson, Joshua Fogel, Rebecca Frey, Takashi Inoguchi, Haruko Iwasaki, Kazuhiko Kasaya, William Kelly, Roger Keyes, Orlando Patterson, Alessandro Pizzorno, William Roseberry, Gilbert Rozman, Amartya Sen, Haruo Shirane, Allan Silver, Henry D. Smith, Charles Tilly, Ezra Vogel, Haruko Wakita, Harrison C. White, R. Bin Wong, Aristide R. Zolberg, and Vera L. Zolberg. As the series editor for *Structural Analysis in the Social Sciences* at Cambridge University Press, Mark Granovetter has been the unflagging supporter of this book project. He has been very generous with his time, giving me valuable feedback that has helped to shape this manuscript at a number of critical points. I also thank Kiyoshi Asai, Nōichi Imoto, and Seiji Tsutsumi, who trained me in their intensive four-year program in classical Japanese literature at Ochanomizu University in Tokyo. Without this undergraduate education, this book could not have been completed as it is.

This book is dedicated to my mother, Kiyoko Ikegami, a practical businesswoman and an accomplished tea ceremony practitioner. She has always been a constant source of encouragement while I pursued my career outside Japan. Although she and her two late sisters, Hatsuko Ikegami and Hideko Sakurai, were not living in privileged circumstances while growing up in wartime Japan, they showed me through their personal examples how to bring the pleasure of beauty into our lives. My husband, Piet Hut, has provided me with moral support throughout this project, and I happily look back to many inspirational conversations about our mutual intellectual concerns.

Section One

A Social Theory of State, Civility, and Publics

Introduction

Aesthetic Japan and the Tokugawa Network Revolution

In 1969, a thin, elderly novelist with eagle eyes made an important presentation in Stockholm. The official Nobel Prize lecture given by Kawabata Yasunari, the first Japanese novelist to win the Nobel Prize in Literature, was titled "Japan, the Beautiful and Myself." Sounding the depth of human feeling elicited by the poetic beauty of snow, moon, and blossom, he declared his personal solidarity with the Japanese aesthetic tradition. Kawabata's lecture was a singularly powerful representation of Japan's cultural identity in aesthetic terms. Two and a half decades later, the novelist Oe Kenzaburo, Japan's second Nobel laureate in literature, delivered a provocative critique of Kawabata from the same podium. His Nobel lecture had a challenging title: "Japan, the Ambiguous and Myself." Oe implied that Japan's uncritical celebration of its aesthetic traditions had resulted in the overvaluation of an ambiguous mode of communication that proved to have strongly negative consequences for modern Japanese democracy – this cultivation of ambiguity in the last analysis represents a distrust of rational linguistic articulation as a means of communication.[1]

I cite these two Nobel laureates' views on "Japan and the beautiful" not to adjudicate their views but rather to use their words as pointers to the presence of unsettling cultural questions. Their critical exchange at one of the most prestigious public forums in the world reminds us of the political significance of Japanese aesthetic culture. This book does not explain their views, but I focus on an element that is missing in their discussions. I place their questions in historical context by presenting a detailed survey of the social history of an aesthetic – namely, how the people of Japan actually incorporated the world of the beautiful within their social lives. There were many individuals, both professionals and very serious amateur artists, who loved to share the world of beauty. To that end, they formed incredibly robust and vibrant networks with the sole goal of practicing traditional forms of Japanese arts and poetry. I maintain that the history of the ways in which people develop their

3

aesthetic lives in close connection with their cultures of sociability offers a key to deciphering the social complexities of the Japanese world of beauty.[2] Consequently, this book examines the historical process through which aesthetic socializing became a central component of pre-modern Japanese civility and associational life.

Although the realm of the beautiful is usually understood as separate from the political arena, this notion does not necessarily hold true for every society. Japan offers us a case in point. The pre-modern Japanese approach to poetry and other arts stands in sharp contrast to the modern notion of artistic and literary appreciation as produced primarily by isolated individuals in private studios or studies. The greater part of artistic and literary endeavors in pre-modern Japan consisted of group activities in which the participants were at once producers and recipients of aesthetic productions. This reflects the fact that Japanese people appreciated the interactive *process* of creating an art through an intense emotional rapture of synergy at the site of production. In other words, the Japanese artistic and poetic traditions were highly social as well as intensely aesthetic.

One curious aspect of tracing the history of Japanese organizational experiments is that one finds the Japanese search for horizontal and voluntary social associations intersecting at a number of points with the cultivation of beauty. The arts and poetry associations began to organize people into networks that extended beyond their immediate territorial and status affiliations. The most critical element of this pattern of artistic production was the formation of a common spatial/cognitive sphere for aesthetic socialization among the participants – the sphere that I will call the *aesthetic public*. These sites of aesthetic appreciation constituted enclaves of free socialization in which people could temporarily suspend the application of feudal norms. By forming connections among people from different economic and status backgrounds, the art and poetry circles and associations of early modern Japan began to play roles functionally similar to those of civic networks in Western political history. In fact, I have found that a focus on the social dimension of aesthetic life in early modern Japan offers a new perspective on the relationships among the distinctive trajectories of Japanese state formation, associational politics, and the emergence of nationwide market networks.

Consequently, this book is about politics as well as aesthetics. The analysis that follows presents a sociological examination of the transformation of Japanese aesthetic cultures and its unexpected role in the invention of Japanese styles of civility and cultural identities.[3] A closer look at the history of Japan indicates that aesthetic patterns of socializing have been closely intertwined with the political and associational life of the Japanese people. For this reason, an investigation into aesthetic socialization offers a telescopic view of historical discoveries that goes well beyond the realm of the aesthetic alone.

Contemporary Japanese, as well as outside observers, often associate Japan with distinctive aesthetic traditions in the arts and literature. From local goodwill volunteers in the Rotary clubs who receive foreign visitors with the tea ceremony and flower arrangements to Kawabata's Nobel Prize lecture, contemporary Japanese draw on this image continually when they are required to introduce their country to outsiders. It is not only on the level of cultural identities and images that one can still encounter some distinctive cultural practices in contemporary Japan. For example, Ōoka Makoto, a poet and critic, has estimated that modern Japan probably has the highest density of amateur poets in the industrial world – in such traditional shorter forms of poetry as *haiku* and *waka*.[4] The high level of enthusiasm for traditional forms of poetry is evident from the fact that almost all major Japanese popular newspapers have weekly poetry pages that usually feature winning poems selected from several thousand entries submitted each week by readers. And the association of the realm of the beautiful and Japan is so much taken for granted that it can be put to use for commercial purposes. One recent magazine advertisement that exploited this well-established cognitive association conveys the flavor of the present situation. The advertisement featured two forms of "the beautiful" on two facing pages. On the left-hand page is a picture of a woman bowing slightly in an elegant but dignified manner accompanied by copy that reads *"Hito ga, utsukushi kuni"* ("As people, we form a beautiful country"). The facing page has a picture of an automobile and Mount Fuji with the words *"utsukushii kuni no merusedesu,"* which can be translated as "Mercedes fits the beautiful country" (Figure 0.1).

These contemporary applications of the Japanese aesthetic tradition reflect the interplay among various contemporary actors with widely differing motivations and interests. At the same time, the image of Japan as a nation with a long history of aesthetic accomplishment has definite historical roots. This book sheds new light on one of these roots, namely the political and organizational origins of Japanese aesthetic culture. I maintain that this taken for granted aspect of Japanese cultural identities was invented and formulated through the dynamics of Japanese organizational developments. The study of the emergence of Japanese collective identity, in particular with regard to its evolution into a modern nation-state, requires an examination of historical contingencies. I examine a critical period in the genealogy of the rise of a Japanese aesthetic by focusing on the early modern era, the period of the Tokugawa shogunate (1603–1867).

This book does not focus on any specific group or class of people. The aesthetic associations touched a variety of people in Japan, from emperors, warlords, samurai, merchants, and farmers to courtesans, outcasts, and other marginal groups of people. And it was these people who also continuously experimented with various ways of socializing with one

Figure 0.1. Japan the Beautiful. An advertisement based on Japan's reputation for beauty. On the left-hand page, a woman bowing, with the legend "*Hito ga, utsukushi kuni*" ("As people, we form a beautiful country"). On the facing page, an automobile and Mount Fuji with the words "*utsukushii kuni no merusedesu,*" "Mercedes fits the beautiful country."

another. The majority of individuals who appear in this book are undistinguished men and women who left barely identifiable traces on Japanese aesthetic and literary history. For example, there were lowly monks, warriors, and courtiers in the medieval period sitting excitedly together under the cherry blossoms, creating chains of verses. There were male and female amateur poets who traveled extensively across Japan and corresponded incessantly; their activities unintentionally produced a remarkable complex of private networks outside the control of the Tokugawa state. There were also samurai who enjoyed singing popular songs so much that they considered their artist identities within their music circles to be much more important than their formal feudal titles. There were also groups of people who exhibited a contentious solidarity against the established feudal order by showing off outlandish tastes in *kimono* fashion. Although these uses of aesthetic activities look quite different from one another, they have one thing in common. The people who were involved in aesthetic socialization had great capacities for networking across social barriers, and the multiplication of their network connections often yielded unexpected social results. When networks based on aesthetic activities intersected the rapidly expanding social, political, and economic networks of the Tokugawa period, a set of unforeseen complex social and cultural dynamics emerged in Japanese society.

As I examined the transformation of Japanese associational life from the medieval to the early modern periods, I came to realize the importance of incorporating the notion of *publics* – the spheres of interactions where cultural activities take place – into sociological theories of cultural change and identity formation. As I use the term as a technical word, publics are communicative sites that emerge at the points of connection among social and/or cognitive networks. As I see it, identity, culture, and meanings as such are "emergent properties" arising from the interplay of human subjectivity in actors involved in network relationships at the communicative sites of publics.[5] In this way, my sociological accounts of history take the social sites of interactions as focal points of analysis.

Interestingly, pre-modern Japan developed a distinctive form of arts whose practices crystallized the importance of sites of gathering and the interactive process of artistic production. During the medieval period, a style of arts and literature that emphasized the importance of collaborative interactions emerged. This style of arts emphasizes interactions at a site of aesthetic production as the centerpiece of their aesthetic theories. Unlike an individualized modern notion of arts and literature, these arts took interactive processes as their most meaningful aspect. In these forms of performing arts, which some scholars called *za* (seated) arts and literature, the sites of aesthetic productions were consciously regarded as spaces distinct from the social order. This deliberate theorizing of the dynamics of collaborative synergy in spheres of interactions made this style of arts not only a distinctive aesthetic form but also an important means of sociability. A form of linked poetry known as *renga* and the tea ceremony most eloquently advocated the spirit of such aesthetic theories. The rise of the *za* arts represented the emergence of an important cultural resource in Japan. Although not all art forms in pre-modern Japan took a distinctively collective approach, an aesthetic ideal that considered the sites of art gatherings as free associational activities had a lasting influence on the social role of arts in general.

The Tokugawa Popularization of Aesthetic Knowledge

The rise of this distinctive aesthetic style alone would not have made aesthetic publics so central to Japanese social life. Politics played a significant role as well. To understand the process in which aesthetic publics became so important as sites of communicative activities, we have to step back to examine the history of Japanese social organizations. In particular, the distinctive relationship between two important factors, the trajectory of Japanese state development and the development of horizontally organized associations significantly influenced the social role of aesthetic publics. During the medieval period, the samurai warlords continuously fought each other while attempting to reorganize the social order based on the model of hierarchical samurai vassalage. However, unlike the popular image of feudal Japan, medieval Japan also experienced the development of political forces that organized people in relatively horizontal forms. The activities of various trade guilds (also called *za*), corporate villages, and a form of horizontal alliances called *ikki* were most vigorous during the medieval period. Although not political by nature, the aesthetic associational networks that developed during this period incorporated the same free spirit of horizontally organized associations. Eventually, however, at the end of centuries of struggles, it was the vertical reorganization of the samurai's national hierarchies that became a unifying principle for the early modern political order. To protect this order, the unifying rulers severely suppressed the political power of various social associations.

The tension in the relationship between the state and associational networks influenced the structures and interrelationships of various communicative sites. Because the formation of horizontal associations was severely restricted under the Tokugawa shoguns, it was difficult to form active communicative sites of publics based on voluntary political alliances of people. At the same time, artistic networking became surprisingly vital as it was already an established method of civic sociability. Under the rules of Tokugawa shoguns, aesthetic publics became unofficial but valuable and lively sites of social interactions outside the formal hierarchical order of the state.

The rise of aesthetic images of Japan was a path-dependent phenomenon formulated through successive phases of political and cultural developments since the ancient period. Clearly, the close association of beauty and political power did not enter Japanese history with the Tokugawa shogunate. Nor did the construction of Japanese cultural identities centering on aesthetic idioms originate in the early modern period. Some specific genres of high culture – which produced such masterpieces as "The Tale of Genji" and *waka* poetry – had flourished in the milieu of the ancient imperial court. And, as discussed earlier, the medieval period saw the emergence of various distinctive forms of performing arts and literature. Given all that, what role did the Tokugawa period play in the formation of aesthetic identities in Japanese society? During the pre-Tokugawa period, cultural resources of outstanding merit were still largely produced, patronized, and consumed by an elite circle of courtiers, priests, and higher-ranking samurai. Although medieval Japan developed a prototypical form of aesthetic socialization, the body of cultural knowledge rarely functioned as an imagined link with the space called Japan in the minds of the Japanese population at large.

In contrast, the early modern period was a critical phase in Japanese cultural history because it witnessed the popularization of many elements of what we now consider Japanese traditions. Long before the rise of the contemporary nation-state, Japan was ruled by Tokugawa shoguns who officially upheld a policy of strict status distinctions and territorial segmentation. For the first time in history, a large portion of the Japanese population began to assume the existence of objective cultural standards that should be met by those aspiring to gentility. Socialization through the aesthetic circles became an important part of Tokugawa styles of civility. Furthermore, the book trade of the Tokugawa period supported a growing sense of symbolic community among the Japanese through the objectification of a collective consciousness, the accelerated formation of communication networks, and material additions to the fund of common knowledge. The fact that a plane of commonality evolved primarily within the realm of the beautiful in Tokugawa society, which was otherwise decentralized and divided, holds some suggestive implications for the post-Tokugawa development of the modern Japanese nation-state.

Aesthetic practices in Tokugawa Japan had their roots in the ancient and medieval cultures that developed in and around the emperor's court in Kyoto. As a result, in the Tokugawa civilizing process, images of Japan were presented from the viewpoint of the supposed center, ancient court life, while Japan's periphery was neglected. The implied process of exclusion extended not only to the cultures of people living in territorial peripheries such as the Northern Uteri (Ainu) and people in Okinawa but also filtered out diverse cultural traditions of various marginal subpopulations. However, the story of the rise of aesthetic Japan was not that of a top-down enforcement of national solidarity. Tokugawa Japan was ruled by feudal rulers whose acute concern was to divide and subjugate the population. The rise of aesthetic Japan is also not simply the story of elite intellectuals who created a national myth. Rather, it was the accumulative effect of largely unplanned actions of originally unrelated people who began to network with each other. They did this in order to search for ways of socializing with each other and, in doing so, to trespass feudal boundaries and limitations. People explored horizontal and voluntary ways of associating and found genuine joy in immersing themselves into aesthetic group activities while thus escaping from the tedium and the constrictions of the hierarchical feudal state structures. Another force was comprised by the merchant-publishers, who were eager to popularize aesthetic knowledge for profit.

Consequently, the central focus of this book is the fluid dynamics and unexpected consequences of what might be called "the Tokugawa network revolution." As I see it, a critical moment of cultural history in any society occurs when communicative networks suddenly expand in scale, density, and complexity. The resulting patterns of communication influence both the form and the content of the discourse conveyed through the networks. The kinds of cultural resources that are available at the time of network expansion will determine the range of content in the resulting cultural identities of that society. Thus, the extension of a society's communicative networks and the alteration of its cognitive maps are reciprocally influential.

A network revolution can occur within a variety of social-structural circumstances and phases of development. Although a network revolution may appear to be a politically neutral organizational transformation, it never occurs in a power vacuum. Network multiplication is likelier to result from the unequal distribution of power among intersecting network systems. An example of such inequality would be the forceful incorporation of the political structure, economic system, and aesthetic standards of a suzerain state within the cultures of its colonial possessions. Another example of a rapid cognitive revision is a society's collective incorporation into the conceptual framework of a world religion. The power differential between the indigenous cognitive network and the external cultural force affects the formation of new associational maps, as do timing and socio-political contexts. Together with the available cultural resources and the structural patterns of emerging network relations, the effects of hegemonic power relations at the critical moment of rapid network multiplication are important influences on the new collective cultural identities of a people.

It is in this sense that I consider that Tokugawa Japan arrived at a critical moment of cultural history at the time of its network revolution in the early modern period. To summarize my argument, I maintain that this revolution consisted of the simultaneous development of four kinds of social networks: (1) a phase of territorial state-making at the beginning of the seventeenth century involving the construction of decentralized but well-integrated political networks; (2) the formation of nationwide trade routes and commodities markets together with the remarkable growth of urban consumption centers; and (3) the development of such knowledge-based networks as aesthetic circles and associations. Furthermore, as derivative effects of the rise of the integrated state and nationwide market systems, there emerged (4) the development of infrastructures for communication networks, including improvements in sea and overland travel as well as commercial publishing. These four conditions of possibility provided the socio-economic backdrop for the vibrant informal spheres of civic cultures that emerged within Tokugawa society.

In terms of the kind of information diffused through these networks, Japan had already developed a wealth of aesthetic knowledge ripe for popularization by the time of the Tokugawa network revolution. For example, classical Japanese poetry and novels that had circulated only in manuscript form during the medieval era provided available resources that could be readily modified for popular commercial publications. In addition, the organizational prototype for the aesthetic associations had already been established before the Tokugawa period. The aesthetic associational networks thus benefited from organizational innovations by absorbing certain commercial structures. Their operations began to intersect with those of the commercial publishing industry, which in turn hastened the rapid diffusion of cultural information. The commercial trading networks also brought beauty closer to the people in the form of such commodities as beautiful *kimono*.

The fact that the aesthetic circles became centers of civilized socialization was closely connected with the idiosyncratic nature, trajectory, and structure of the Tokugawa neo-feudal state. The main governing strategy of the Tokugawa state can be described as the institutional segmentation of its population through a decentralized, indirect control system. The Tokugawa shoguns repeatedly issued edicts prohibiting the formation of horizontal alliances and parties because they feared that private networks of horizontal alliances among individuals that cut through carefully prescribed segmented boundaries would eventually threaten the Tokugawa system. This prohibition made private aesthetic associations even more important for civic life. It was in this situation that what I call the Japanese proto-modern network revolution revitalized art and poetry circles as centers of communicative activity. The Japanese culture of sociability was inevitably colored heavily by aesthetic traditions and standards.

In this environment, Tokugawa Japanese from all age and status groups formed numerous associations, found personal enjoyment and satisfaction in them, and produced some remarkable cultural achievements. If Alexis de Tocqueville, the perceptive analyst of Andrew Jackson's America, had been able to visit Japan during the same period, he would have been both impressed and puzzled by the phenomenon of voluntary organizations thriving within the framework of a feudal rather than a democratic polity. Tocqueville noted that the flourishing associational life of the young republic was one of the most important organizational and cultural foundations of its democracy. "Americans of all ages, all stations in life, and all types of dispositions are forever forming associations. There are not only commercial and industrial associations in which all take part, but others of a thousand different types – religious, moral, serious, futile, very general and very limited, immensely large and very minute."[6] In contrast, the subjects of a supposedly authoritarian regime engaged in vigorous discussions within these aesthetic enclaves of free communication, which were characterized by liveliness, sensuality, and laughter. The stereotype of pre-modern Japanese people as submissive doormats trodden beneath the heel of militaristic despots fails to convey the vitality of Japanese communicative activities in this period – not to mention modern Japanese cultural practices.

Civility and Tokugawa Proto-modernity

New sensibilities arose within this environment in the consciousness of individuals as well as in Tokugawa social life. In spite of the Tokugawa policy of institutional segregation, people were no longer confined to localized clusters of networks defined by the political order. They were connected by a number of new types of social ties that were flexible, loose, and voluntary in nature. Consequently, a cultured person who participated in a number of different aesthetic groups might well have several artist or literary names. The use of artist names reflected the emergence of private social spaces in which the formal hierarchical norms of the Tokugawa state were irrelevant. For example, the cultural circles of the period constituted a tradition of aesthetic publics that was specific to Japan but functioned in a manner partially comparable to the cafes, salons, and reading circles of eighteenth-century Europe. In the early eighteenth century, for example, the city of Edo alone had more than 130 *haikai* circles.[7] In addition, the Tokugawa cultural circles were incorporated into the trading networks of a thriving nationwide economy.

The aesthetic publics had the ability to create alternative realities by intermittently injecting an element of unconventionality into the lives of Tokugawa people. By recurrently joining the sites of aesthetic publics, people temporarily decoupled from their existing ties and switched their identities from those of a dutiful samurai or wealthy merchant to those of poets or artists. Frequent participation in the aesthetic circles quietly transformed personal identities as well as the quality of individual social relations. Usually, people could join and leave these hobby circles rather casually. Compared to feudal political ties or primordial territorial and kinship ties that enforced heavy obligations and lifelong commitment – that is to say strong ties – these hobby circles represented more or less weak ties in the sense of Mark Granovetter's usage.[8] The strength of "weak ties" – as Granovetter demonstrates in his case study of a job search – lies in their ability to spread information quickly and extensively. The reader may be surprised not only to see the extensive scale, complexity, and robustness of the hobby circles but also their openness and flexibility, as I will analyze in this book. In contrast to highly localized cohesive networks, the operation of these collective arts and poetry circles brought an important degree of openness to Japanese society.

The historical study of associational life, in particular the voluntary formation of horizontal associations, has recently gained renewed interest in social scientific literature because of its positive implications for the qualities of civil society.[9] Nonetheless, so far, too little attention has been given to the importance of weak ties in this context and of casual, flexible, and ephemeral human voluntary associations, which have historically provided society with increased flexibility by providing open circuits to social relations.

Although I share a view that emphasizes the importance of structures of associational life, focusing only on the "firmness" of horizontal associations has a limitation in terms of understanding the qualities of associational life. When strongly cohesive horizontal associations gain hegemonic power, they may impose suffocating disciplinary effects on their members while excluding others. In contrast, a society with network connections that allow relatively casual forms of shifting and reconnecting empowers its citizens and can be described as more open and flexible in nature. While both types of networks entail voluntary connections between people, in the former case the lack of open circuits may have a suffocating effect on the citizens.

For the last fifteen years after the collapse of the Soviet bloc, intellectuals around the world have shown a renewed interest in the notion of civil society because this was supposed to be a necessary condition for building a properly functioning democracy. Continuous violent conflicts in the Middle East and elsewhere in the world recurrently bring the issue of civil society to center stage in global political discussions. The supposed historical absence of civil society in these regions is often identified as the root problem for their difficulty in building democracies.

While researching indigenous forms of associational life, I have come to the conclusion that the broadly used Western-centered notion of civil society does not shed sufficient light on the positive aspect of non-Western experiences. The neo-Toquevillian focuses on voluntary and horizontal associations are indeed helpful to some extent, but such an approach alone does not illuminate qualities of social life that are often distinctively vibrant in pre-modern non-Western societies. Even in regions with highly divided multi-ethnic or religious communities, it was not unusual to find the existence of various cultural and social mechanisms that produced spheres of communications in which individuals of various backgrounds could safely communicate with each other. To be sure, these indigenous developments of civility did not directly produce a modern notion of democracy based on the equalizing principle for the members of the state. Yet, an important step in a parallel direction was made by the creation of a variety of indigenous mechanisms that helped to facilitate communications beyond the confinement of primordial social ties.

For example, the critical feature of Tokugawa organizational developments was that they supplied individual citizens with occasions for exchanging their feudal identities of obligation for identities otherwise defined. Thus, the Tokugawa network revolution was characterized not only by an increase in scale and density of network intersections but also by a qualitative difference in the increase in the number of weaker ties that connected clusters of people in unexpected ways. The implications and ramifications of this revolution in subsequent Japanese social, political, and cultural developments are so extensive that it is impossible to discuss the making of modern Japan without touching in one way or another on the organizational transformations of Tokugawa society resulting from the network revolution.

It is in this context that I propose to focus in this book on the notion of civility rather than civil society. I maintain that civility implies a grammar of sociability that is most suitable for less committed social relationships, that is to say, interactions mediated by weak ties. Across a whole range of interactions, from encounters with acquaintances in the marketplace to meeting passersby on the street, the effective cultural grammar of sociability allowed Tokugawa individuals to interact safely and confidently with those individuals whose backgrounds were unknown or apparently different from their own. Although pre-modern Japan under the shoguns' rule did not allow people to form political parties and autonomous civic organizations, this society was endowed with shared codes of manners and expressions that facilitated transactions among people from different categories. Furthermore, the tradition of aesthetic methods of socialization generated extensive spheres of communications in which aesthetic sociability provided a method for creating and sustaining civility distinct from the hierarchical order of the Tokugawa shogunate. There were numerous casual, flexible, and ephemeral private associations that took the shape of various forms of aesthetic hobby groups. Even though the society was officially segmented and hierarchically divided by the shogunate system, "bonds of civility" thus loosely united the people in the plane of commonality built on the aesthetic images of Japan.

These observations lead me to conclude that prior to Japan's intensive period of Westernization following the Meiji restoration in 1868, the country was moving toward its own version of *proto-modernity*, or "modernity before modernization." As I see it, proto-modernity as a cultural phenomenon emerges when a society acquires a simultaneous endowment of social and cultural capital – not only among its elites but also among the general population. Proto-modernity in the area of sociability develops when individuals are able to socialize through participation in groups that they choose to join and to form voluntary ties with others in those groups. The aesthetic associations of Tokugawa Japan were not civic political ties in the modern sense of the word, but they were neither primordial relationships (such as kinship or religious ties by birth) nor politically enforced ties. Japanese people in this period were able to enjoy cultural activities that were not limited by official regional and status boundaries through participation in amateur artistic and hobby networks. These popular networks created open circuits within the social life of the Tokugawa period.

To be sure, the form and content of Tokugawa proto-modernity were very different from those of Western modernity, whose ideological foundations were laid by Enlightenment rationalism and the methodologies of post-Cartesian science.[10] The popularization of tacit modes of communication through participation in the performing arts was one of the distinctive characteristics of Tokugawa proto-modernity. In the following historical survey, I articulate the ways in which these proto-modern features emerged in various aspects of Tokugawa life.

My use of the term proto-modernity is influenced by the concept of *proto-industrialization*, which was used to describe the first phase of Europe's development of industry on a large scale. Since the 1970s, economic historians have generally used the concept of proto-industrialization with reference to "... the type of industry – the traditionally organized, principally rural handicrafts – [that] barely fits the image that one has of a modernizing economy," in the words of Franklin Mendels.[11] Industrial revolution better describes the subsequent second phase of modern machine-based industrialization. Although the term *industrial revolution* conveys an image of abrupt discontinuity, the introduction of the factory system in the nineteenth century built upon the earlier proto-industrialization of the European countryside. The evolution of cottage industries in rural Europe not only helped to expand trading and commodities networks but also brought numerous significant changes in "... a life experience faced by ordinary people."[12] Following the introduction of the term proto-industrialization into the European historical literature, Japanese economic historians began to apply it to eighteenth-century Japan.[13] They maintained that the Tokugawa shogunate underwent a similar process of rural industrialization, although tillage rather than herding was the basis of the cottage industries of the Japanese countryside. In the eighteenth century, these industries included the manufacture of cotton and silk textiles, production of dyestuffs and indigenous ceramics, and the brewing of *sake*. The expanded availability of commercially produced goods and services brought beauty into the everyday life of Tokugawa people, even those citizens who were neither wealthy nor politically influential. The activities of the aesthetic groups became the center of Tokugawa associational life only against this social and economic background.

The study of Tokugawa proto-modernity will illuminate the fact that phenomena associated with so-called modernization in non-Western societies did not appear suddenly at the beginning of Westernization. Many non-Western societies had developed indigenous processes prior to their incorporation into a world system under the hegemony of the Western powers. Although these various forms of proto-modern development were interrupted or profoundly altered during their societies' incorporation into the global community, nonetheless these earlier patterns affected the trajectory and timing of the second stage of these societies' modernization.

Lastly, the method and structure of this book also require some comment. This book makes extensive use of primary and secondary historical materials drawn from a number of subspecialties in historical and literary studies of pre-modern Japan. The central purpose of this book, however, is not to make technical contributions to these subspecialties but rather to draw connections between them and a number of other historical themes. For example, there is a rich accumulation of scholarly studies of Japanese literature and such performing arts as the tea ceremony. What is missing is a study of the systematic connections between these various aesthetic activities and the political history of Japan. In addition, the common elements linking different artistic and literary genres have not been clearly identified and analyzed. Scholarship in the fields of political and institutional history usually takes developments in literature and the arts as peripheral matters compared with such important topics as the history of state formation, class divisions, and collective actions. In contrast, the present work provides a new vantage point for observing the long-term dynamics of Japanese history by making the connections between the realms of statecraft and aesthetics central to its analysis.

One of the important tasks of historical sociology is to contribute to theoretical understandings of human society. This commitment sometimes requires a sociologist to engage in philosophical contemplation of social theories. At the same time, I also am committed, as a historian, to prove my theoretical points through historical evidence. In particular, because the central role of group activities in arts and literature and their main aspect of voluntary horizontal associations are sufficiently unusual in world history, it is necessary to give detailed and nuanced historical accounts. On the other hand, my historical inquiries that follow do not address an established theme in the scholarship of Japanese history. Rather, I cover themes and subjects of several subspecialties of cultural and social history to decipher the complexity of the interconnections. Specifically, I use sociological theories of complexity and networks as tools to guide my inquiry while traveling through theoretically still unmapped territory. In the process, these guiding tools themselves will undergo constant reevaluation and elaboration. In this way, my historical inquiries will be shaped by and, in turn, shape sociological theories.

Consequently, this book unfolds leisurely through a process of interweaving theories and history. Chapters 1 and 2 address theoretical concerns and questions fully. One important theoretical concern is an ongoing dialogue with other theories of civil society and publics. Thus, Chapter 1 opens with a comparative sociological overview of "Tokugawa civility" while paying particular attention to the complex relational dynamics of the three dimensions of macro-structures, namely state, associations, and market. The idiosyncratic relations between those three dimensions gave rise to the emergence of what might be labeled "civility without civil society," which was also profoundly marked by the tradition of aesthetic socializing. As a centerpiece of my analysis, I employ the idioms of network analysis and complexity in Chapter 2 to lay the theoretical groundwork for my approach to issues of structures, publics, and identity. My investigation into the culture of sociability in Japanese society forced me to confront the theoretical question of how to connect culture with a structural analysis in historical sociology. Rather than simply regarding culture as coherent ideas and generalized morality, I analyze how culture arises out of the interactions in publics. This foundational task necessitates a temporary leave of absence, so to speak, from the historical context in order to deepen conversations with other social theorists. The reader who is interested primarily in the historical development of Japanese aesthetic social life could skip this chapter without losing the main thread of the historical arguments.

The structure of Section Two, from the Prelude through Chapter 9, is more straightforward. After an introductory analysis regarding aesthetic associations in the Prelude, the subsequent seven chapters consist of historical essays placed in rough chronological order for the purpose of tracing the medieval origins and early modern development of what I call aesthetic publics. My focus is the relationships among political developments, the formation of voluntary associational networks, and the evolution of aesthetic life from the medieval to the Tokugawa period. I demonstrate how the transformation of the Japanese state was intimately related to this process. Following this presentation of my major arguments and supporting evidence, Section Three moves in a different direction. Section Three consists of three long essays that address the dynamic of categorical politics by focusing on the complex side effects of the nationwide market economy that developed within the feudally segmented society of Tokugawa Japan. I show in detail how the distinctive state–market relationship and Tokugawa styles of communicative life were mutually influential. My exposition centers around the politics of *kimono* fashion, the rise of commercial publishing, and the popularization of etiquette manuals. In the concluding section, I return to the question of the image of Japan as an aesthetic treasure-house that grew out of the Tokugawa network revolution.

1

Civility without Civil Society

A Comparative Overview

"You cannot study Japanese art, it seems to me, without becoming much gayer and happier."[1]
> (from a letter by Vincent Van Gogh talking about his impression of *ukiyo-e* woodblock prints)

The following study of the formation of Japanese collective cultural identities will center on the issue of what I call "Tokugawa civility." This term may immediately raise questions, since "civility" in Western usage has come to be associated with the historical emergence of "civil society" in Europe. Civil society implies a domain of private citizens that has a certain degree of autonomy from the state. The empowerment of civil society has been closely associated with the historical development of modern democracy. By contrast, Tokugawa Japan experienced the emergence of a form of civility that flourished within a neo-feudal political structure. Under the firm hand of the Tokugawa shoguns, Japan did not develop a civic associational domain that fit the Western notion of civil society. However, if we define *civility* as the cultural grammar of sociability that governs interactional public spaces, then the widespread practices and sophisticated characteristics of Tokugawa sociability would certainly be deserving of the term civility. This seemingly paradoxical combination of "civility without civil society" provides a useful starting point for our attempt to articulate the distinctive path of Tokugawa cultural development that created much of what we now perceive as "Japanese tradition."

Japan: A School of Civility and Good Manners

Before proceeding with our investigation, however, let us listen to a voice from the late seventeenth century. When Engelbert Kaempfer, a German physician attached to the embassy of the Dutch East India Company,

19

arrived in Nagasaki in 1690, Japan had been enjoying a century of peace and prosperity as a result of its self-imposed withdrawal from foreign affairs under the Tokugawa shoguns. Following pacification, the new regime had imposed a policy of strict isolation that prohibited Japanese citizens from traveling abroad.[2] Although the shoguns permitted closely supervised trade relations with Korea and China, their only concession to the West was some limited transactions with the Dutch East India Company. To be sure, the shoguns' isolationist policy did not mean that the Japanese were cut off from information about the outside world. Although they had only limited and selective interactions with outsiders, they remained intensely curious about the outside world, maintained a keen interest in international relations, and quietly formulated their own cultural identities while comparing themselves with the strangers from overseas. Kaempfer recognized the presence of this combination of fervent pride and inquisitive interest in the Japanese that he met, including the fifth shogun, Tokugawa Tsunayoshi (1646–1709), himself.[3]

As Kaempfer traveled from Nagasaki to Edo (the original name of Tokyo), the shogun's castle city, he was deeply impressed by the Japanese people and their "apparent civility."[4] In his *History of Japan*, Kaempfer described Japan in the following manner: "as civil, as polite and curious a nation as any in the world."[5] The German visitor was impressed by the fact that the cultivation of proper behavior extended throughout the society: the "behavior of the Japanese, from the meanest countryman up to the greatest Prince or Lord, is such that the whole Empire might be called a School of Civility and good manners."[6] Because of the Western conceptual distinction between "barbarism" and "civility" (barbarism, non-Christians, and oppression vs. civility, Christians, and liberty), Kaempfer's recognition of civility in a non-Western society was a decidedly unconventional view for the time and indeed might have been difficult to accept in some quarters. Yet, it was precisely because of this contradictory image that Kaempfer's "discovery" of the Japanese as civilized barbarians was so intriguing for European intellectuals. In spite of this unconventionality, the book was widely read in Europe and went through many editions in several different languages. A number of prominent intellectuals, including Kant, Goethe, and Montesquieu, cited Kaempfer's book in their own works.[7]

After the opening of the country in the mid-nineteenth century, many European visitors to Tokugawa Japan also wrote about the exquisite politeness embodied in stylized elegant movements of the body. In November 1858, for example, the *Times* (London) featured a column by a special correspondent who covered Lord Elgin's official visit to Japan. At one point, the visitors enjoyed an excursion of some 10 miles from the city of Edo. According to the anonymous correspondent, "one opinion prevailed with respect to the extraordinary evidence of civilization." The party enjoyed the beautiful scenery and admired the neatly kept cottages, temples, and gardens, but their admiration peaked when they arrived at a teahouse where the English visitors were served tea by "fair damsels, who glide rapidly and noiselessly about, the most zealous and skillful of attendants."[8] For them, the manners of maids in a teahouse symbolized the presence of a civilization more than anything else.

Interpreting foreign observations such as Kaempfer's certainly calls for care. It is, of course, easy to point out the romantic bias in the *Times* article and other Western journalistic accounts of the time, as they were eager to locate an Arcadia in the East.[9] Praise for civilized Japan from Kaempfer, as well as other nineteenth-century travel writings by Western visitors, re-flected the contemporaneous Orientalist stereotypes held by Westerners, as amply revealed in Yokoyama Toshio's pioneering work on Victorian travel writings.[10] Obviously, the subjects of Victoria under the sober of-ficial morality of the time had ample reasons to be amazed at Tokugawa Japan. Yet, did such gushing testimony simply repeat the established bias without contributing sociological views or cultural appreciation of any substance? Watanabe Kyōji, who extensively surveyed nineteenth-century foreigners' travel writings, criticized Yokoyama's stance as being overtly influenced by the scheme of Orientalism as held by Edward Said. In con-trast, Watanabe found that some travel writings indeed revealed the world that was lost, something forgotten even by the modern Japanese.[11] I do not seek to adjudicate this debate because both viewpoints are in fact complementary. European observations could not be understood with-out taking into account the social-historical context of the time, which influenced the Western mentality. At the same time, it does not dismiss European observations as totally unfounded romanticization.

Concrete evidence presented in this book reveals that Tokugawa Japan was indeed building its own style of cultural socialization, replete with elaborate codes and styles. The differential attitude was enforced partly by the shogunate's strict policy of rule by status. Yet, the elegant styles of politeness went beyond the observation of politically enforced codes. Besides expressing and acknowledging stratified relationships, beauty was a central mechanism of control in the culture of sociability. Polite arts of the time included not only the learning of etiquette and manners but various performing arts that taught students aesthetic ways of socializing and communicating.

Civility and Civil Society

Kaempfer was fortunate to observe Japan during a critical moment in its cultural history, when the townspeople and even some rural dwellers were availing themselves of new opportunities to learn the polite arts. By the late seventeenth century, when the development of commercial publishing gave rise to the phenomenon of "print-as-commodity," the average literate citizen could choose from a wide assortment of commercial guidebooks to answer his or her questions about the complexities of proper conduct. Popular illustrated manuals of etiquette treated a range of topics, including the conventions of proper letter writing, table manners, and gift giving.

Coincidently, at the time of Kaempfer's visit to Japan, variations of the term civility were entering the standard vocabularies of the European vernaculars. The appearance of the notion of civility in early modern Europe has usually been understood as an index to a social transformation in which, as Roger Chartier noted, "the traditional rules of chivalric society were gradually yielding before the new demands that arose from a denser social life and a closer interdependence among men."[12] Chartier's emphasis on "a closer interdependence" stemmed from the relational sociology of Norbert Elias. Elias, in *The Civilizing Process*, stresses the significance of one particular turning point in early modern European society: the point at which the concept of *courtesy*, a term reflecting the aristocratic values and attitudes derived from court society, was gradually replaced by the notion of civility.[13] The advent of civility marked the bourgeoisification of European culture, in which etiquette and manners defined by the royal court gradually yielded to a new code emerging from the rising civil society.

The emerging notion of civility reflected the transfiguration of the idealized image of society moving toward a more democratic realm. The French notion of *civilité* acquired a double connotation as Roger Chartier explains:

> [Civility] is inscribed in the public space of the society of citizens, and it stands opposed to the barbarity of those who have not been civilized. It thus appears closely linked both to a cultural heritage that connects the Western nations to the history of ancient Greece, the first source of civilization, and to a form of society that presupposes the liberty of the subjects in relation to the power of the state.[14]

The rise of the Western concept of civility was closely linked to the normative development of new social and historical identities for the populations of these states. Underlying the new understanding of collective identities was a new sensibility of sharing – a sense that a public space existed for the expression of the ideal of civility among citizens. We can assume that there existed a close affinity between civility and the development of concrete as well as imaginary communicative sites that required civilized behavior from their inhabitants.

Thus, the rise of civility was closely connected with the emergence of new types of publics that were supported by associations of citizens. The rise of citizenship as the right for political representation arose in this context as a process of constructing an imagined community of citizens. The construction of citizenship as a political relationship between a polity and its members rests upon a shared yet often contested understanding of the social identities of the polity's members as well as of the polity itself (e.g., statehood) coupled with the simultaneous categorification of "others" not included in the political community (e.g., barbarians, enemies, social outcasts, minorities, women).[15] In Europe, civility and the rise of citizenship were thus historically connected to one another.[16] It is at this point that Elias's and Chartier's definitions of civility overlap with Habermas's theory of the emergence of the bourgeois public sphere, which occurred when the late eighteenth-century civil society developed into "the genuine domain of private autonomy that stood opposed to the state." Habermas traced the origin of bourgeois public spheres to the development of social institutions that fostered open debates, such as the European salons, coffeehouses, and reading societies.[17] The empowerment of communicative spheres that were distinct from the sphere of the state entailed a historical context in which modern democracy arose.

In contrast to Europe, as we have seen, the civility that Kaempfer praised so highly in Tokugawa Japan did not reflect the emergence of a civil society. In fact, it signaled the opposite. Early modern state formation in Japan did not result from the decline of a feudal warrior society; on the contrary, it took its own distinctive path, revitalizing and reinforcing the exclusive domination of the Japanese warrior class, the samurai. This paradoxical situation – that the lengthiest period of peace in Japanese history resulted from political domination by an elite still officially defined as a warrior class – was the defining condition of Tokugawa cultural development. Unlike many European absolutist states that made concessions to the power of money – such as allowing merchants some access to political power through parliamentary representation or the purchase of offices, estates, or titles – the Tokugawa shoguns effectively quashed mercantile influence on the political process for two and a half centuries. Tokugawa "civility without civil society" grew out of this distinctive pattern of political economy.

Thus, we conventionally define civil society as the democratic associational domain that reflected the rise of political power of the bourgeoisie; in this view, Tokugawa society certainly did not develop a tradition of civil society. For two and a half centuries until the late nineteenth century, the Tokugawa state thus retained the original form of the samurai dominance, while European states were transforming themselves into modern nation-states.

In spite of this difference, the civilized behavior of Tokugawa people was not simply imposed or enforced by political superiors; rather it was disseminated and popularized by the vital forces of the marketplace and associational activities of private citizens. Though it was hardly recognized as a democratic polity, Tokugawa Japan embraced a vast array of communicative spheres that were not easily controlled by the state. It was not robustness of communicative activities that was the problem in Tokugawa Japan. Armed only with the Western notion of a public sphere as a unitary sphere of democratic political discourse based upon civil society, we cannot comprehend the robustness of Tokugawa communicative activities.

The difficulties involved in attempting to define Tokugawa civility reflect the importance of the need to reconstitute social theories of sociability in social-scientific terms. As a first step in this direction, I have already redefined civility as an emerging grammar of sociability in the interactional space of publics. This redefinition of civility brings us to an important point of discussion, namely the relationship between publics and civility. In this book, I define the term *publics* as interactional and communicative spaces; put somewhat differently, publics are the imagined or actual realms in which different social and cognitive network connections meet and intersect. Publics as interactional spaces within network connections are the sites of cultural productions and subsequently of the rules of civility. In the next chapter, I discuss in greater detail the theoretical implications of this definition of publics as a social-scientific term. At this point, it is sufficient to point out that rules of sociability cannot exist without an imagined space of reference. When individuals are concerned for their reputation within that space, they create the preconditions for the emergence of a code of sociability. Thus, civility is not only suitable for communication in public space, but with practices of civility, people are also engaging in the process of constructing public space.

We also should not idealize the history of the term civility in Europe as singularly representative of a move toward a construction of democracy. In reality, when the concept of civility was insinuating itself into the common European vernacular around the seventeenth century, European society still took its predominate political lead from the aristocracy. During the seventeenth and eighteenth centuries, with the bourgeoisification of European culture, books on manners evolved into literature intended to teach the rules of polite conduct to a wider segment of the European population. In France and elsewhere around this time, the aristocracy maintained hegemony in societies given their first glimpse of the rise of commercial societies. Civility rose in Europe, where commercial societies coexisted side by side with the prevailing mentality of aristocratic courtly societies. In fact, the political and cultural power of aristocratic society was pre-eminent in many European societies well into the nineteenth century. The resulting situation was one of prolonged ambivalence, as Peter Gay described it: "[I]n the Victorian decades, the name bourgeois was at once a term of reproach and a source of self-respect."[18]

It therefore was natural that in the late seventeenth century, when Kaempfer visited Japan, the content of European teachings of *civilité* held that the manners and postures to be assumed depended closely upon the status of the parties involved and the relations existing between them. Chartier offered a view that "civilité, like all other behavior in polite society, takes on the mask of a courtesy that is mere falsehood and trickery."[19] The situation in which the *ancien régime* and the aristocracy still held hegemony – while spheres outside the control of aristocratic forces were on the rise – profoundly influenced this ambiguous stage. In short, a transition from courtesy to civility did not sweep European manners in a more democratic direction. Rather, relying on the older version of aristocratic codes of politeness as cultural resources, new versions of social norms gradually developed along with the expanding new spheres of publics outside the court societies. In this aspect, Tokugawa hierarchical manners of civility were not too different from the actual practice of European civility at around the same time.[20] Furthermore, Tokugawa civility was manifested in the social field in which lively civic associational activities and market-oriented cultures were blossoming outside the direct control of the state.

Moral Requirements in the Age of Interdependence

On top of the prior development of medieval court societies, early modern Europe and Japan shared other common macro-structural conditions. During the early modern period, social communicative networks grew rapidly under the influence of the simultaneous expansion of political and economic networks. If such a critical phase of expansion coincides with the rise of commercial publishing, which not only mediates and promotes the new discourse but also encodes, objectifies, and standardizes it, the resulting symbolic plane of commonality is often commemorated in the public imagination as "tradition." This same developmental coincidence was present in both Tokugawa Japan and early modern Europe.

On the other hand, the increased flow of people and information with the rise of commercial society brought with it a new sense of anxiety. Unlike old modes of the patron–client system under feudalism that constituted personal and long-term hierarchical relationships, social relations born from the expansion of a capitalistic economy tended to be more temporary, insecure, and impersonal. Money uniquely defined and structured the social relations of individuals in the marketplace.

Kaempfer's European contemporaries were keenly aware of the moral requirements of the great social transition facing Europeans. The conversion of the honor-seeking passion of the aristocratic mentality into calm reason and calculation based upon commercial interests was a point taken up by Albert Hirschman in *The Passions and the Interests*.[21] He describes convincingly how European intellectuals of the seventeenth and eighteenth centuries struggled with such processes to devise moral prescriptions for emerging new political communities in which commercial activities enlarged their social functions. Within this general intellectual context, notions of politeness and refinement came to embrace a special meaning during the first half of the eighteenth century, "with Montesquieu as not the first but an authoritative exponent," as J. G. A. Pocock noted in *Virtue, Commerce, and History*[22]: "[The] passion was moderated in history by the progress of commerce and politeness."[23]

The writers of the Scottish Enlightenment in particular were acutely aware of a new universalistic norm of sociability that this increased interdependence and communication entailed. They were especially concerned with the effect of a rising commercial society on the ways of sociability and attempted to provide the social transformation with a theoretical base by focusing on what might be called "strangership" (in the words of Allan Silver) in the public domain. In the historical imagination of such Scottish thinkers as Smith, Hume, and Ferguson, Silver observes that "the space between friend and enemy was not occupied, prior to commercial society, by mere acquaintances or neutral strangers, but was charged with uncertain and menacing possibilities."[24] In pre-commercial European society, aristocratic codes of honor divided others into two basic categories – foes or allies – and incorporated this distinction into political and military calculations. In contrast, the new commercial society offered individuals more opportunities to interact with indifferent strangers, with persons who fit Adam Smith's category of "impartial spectators." In commercial society, a stranger is someone who is neither friend nor enemy but simply uninvolved with oneself on a personal level. In this new strangership of commercial society, "impartial spectators" exercised mutual social control over one another's behavior. This new situation led people to conduct themselves better in public spaces in an age of interdependence. Smith's moral theory of the impartial spectator was amazingly consistent with his main theme in *The Wealth of Nations*, in which he upheld the development of the division of labor as the main force for economic growth.

We cannot assume in the optimistic manner of Adam Smith that an infinitely large number of social interactions in commercial society will inevitably lead people into a universal community of sociability. Smith went astray in assuming that a high numerical level of social encounters would per se guarantee a correspondingly high degree of social polish. The average airport or subway station with its throngs of hurrying passengers is not the best laboratory for the study of civilized behavior – particularly at rush hour. By contrast, we would have higher expectations of courtesy and mutual concern among the members of a parish church in a small town who live in the immediate neighborhood and want to preserve their good names among their neighbors. People are more likely to concern themselves with maintaining social reputations and credentials in settings in which they assume a long-term duration of social interactions. With due respect to Adam Smith, we cannot expect that strangership will emerge automatically from the category of impartial spectators in a commercial society.

With the rise of an integrated state and nationwide market economy that resulted in what I call the communicative network revolution, the moral challenge of strangership was certainly present in Japan. People started to have more chances to interact with others outside their immediate social ties, such as in kinship networks, territorial communities, and occupational social relations. When such network density and complexity increased more radically, a certain qualitative difference in the quality of life started to emerge. Yet, the direction of such a change is unpredictable. The increased complexity of social interactions may produce a new culture of civility only when there is a certain effective structure of control. In the search for such a mechanism of control, we should widen our scope beyond the increase of interdependence and complexity.

Elias's Model of Civilizing

Norbert Elias's study presented a more complex explanation of the rise of civility in early modern Europe. For Elias, the emergence of civility was the popularization of good manners that replaced medieval aristocratic court-centered notions of courtesy; it simultaneously represented the spread of the deepening of self-control, strict control over bodily desires, and the segmentation of personal space to protect a zone of privacy. His explanatory model of this transition was twofold. Elias believed in the "natural" force of social differentiation on human mentality. "[T]he most general answer to this question [of civilizing] . . . was," Elias claimed, that "social functions have become more and more differentiated under the pressure of competition. . . . The individual is compelled to regulate his conduct in an increasingly differentiated, more even and more stable manner."[25] Unlike Adam Smith, however, Elias offered a second explanatory variable, the impact of political pacification through state formation.

He pointed out the importance of the effect of internal pacification concomitant with the rise of territorial states in early modern Europe. With territorial pacification, the individual was largely freed from the burden of constant self-defense of the state's monopoly on physical force. Simultaneously, the individual learned to suppress passionate impulses.

When Elias analyzes the impact of state formation, however, he tends toward the speculative, summoning a universalistic psychological explanation for the rise of self-regulation. With a strong debt to Adam Smith, Elias claimed that "the web of actions grows so complex and extensive, the effort required to behave 'correctly' within it becomes so great, that besides the individual's conscious self-control an automatic, blindly functioning apparatus of self control is firmly established."[26] Although the increased complexity, scale, and density of network connections may pose a new challenge in the moral requirements for sociability, increased interdependency on its own does not direct individuals to a civilized behavior. To offer an obvious example, the large commercial urban centers of the twenty-first century, such as New York and Chicago, can hardly be regarded as models of civility compared with their eighteenth-century European counterparts.

Elias developed his image of modernity from data supplied solely by the Occidental pattern of modernization. Elias's work was originally published in the 1930s and "rediscovered" through English translation in the 1970s, and it constituted a major pioneering contribution to the sociology of social change and culture. Elias was a man of his time and presumed a unitary model of civilization that other societies would eventually follow.[27] In the case of Tokugawa Japan, however, we can see how a different pattern of state formation could result in a different style of civility.

To observe the dynamics of the Tokugawa culture of sociability further, however, we have to look at the practice of their social life in a historical contingency. Furthermore, we have to articulate institutional mechanisms that more thoughtfully facilitate different styles of sociability. At this point, however, let us consider the notion of civility from a slightly different angle to enrich our view toward the culture of sociability.

Civility and the Emotional Cost of Transaction

Sociologically, civility may be thought of as a ritual technology of interpersonal exchanges that shapes a kind of intermediate zone of social relationships between the intimate and the hostile. Civility tends to govern non-intimate interpersonal relations because it provides a common ground for transactions between persons from different backgrounds with different interests. For example, civility is particularly evident in the case of business etiquette, which provides transactional rules for workplace colleagues, strangers, or even strategic competitors. A person who observes the accepted codes of civility in the business world is able to interact with others with reasonable confidence and thereby creates an acceptable social persona. Because civility provides a basis for communication between persons who may otherwise be very different, its codes also help to establish a quasi-trust in the routine actions of impersonal social relations. In these modes of exchange, civility decreases the level of "the emotional cost of transaction" in social situations. Transaction cost is a notion from economic analysis.[28] In market activities, prices and immediate benefits of commodities and services in trade are not the sole factors determining actors' behaviors. Various costs of transaction, such as the possibility of cheating, must be taken into account. The operation of market activities functions effectively when laws, norms, and other institutional frameworks enforce trustworthy behavior among actors in a market; the cost of transaction will consequently be reduced. Civility in human interactions works in a similar way to reduce the cost of exchange on an emotional level.

Civility, as I observe it, has an aspect of reducing emotional transaction cost by supplying external criteria of evaluating the transaction partners' trustworthiness. This is what makes civility particularly pragmatic, as the safest mode of social interactions in casual and temporary social relations mediated by weak ties. This aspect of civility – strangership as we have called it – is not the only aspect of civility, but it is an important function of the established culture of sociability. A society endowed with a widely accepted code of behavior would decrease unnecessary frictions in social interactions. From this perspective, civility and social trust are closely related in constructing a temporary psychological cocoon for social interactions.

In early modern Europe as well as in Tokugawa Japan, prior developments of aristocratic modes of sociability were used as a cultural resource – in this case, in response to a new social challenge – in constructing a new culture of civility. The aristocratic origin of hierarchically differentiated codes of politeness can be easily translated into patterns of social interactions in commercial society. For example, in the case of an obvious difference of power among transactional parties in the marketplace, acknowledging hierarchical codes of politeness enables each party to decrease the emotional costs of human interaction. At the same time, when each party's position is not transparent (such as in the case of strangers), it is always safest to use reasonably polite expressions. When a citizen of this commercial society can "size up" a stranger and locate him or her within the social universe on the basis of hierarchical standards of measurement, encounters with strangers lose much of their potential to trigger anxiety. From this perspective, the culture of civility served as a means of reducing the emotional cost of transaction by assimilating new-comers through controlling uncertainties. Although I do not assume that civility was intended solely for business relationships, considering this assimilative function and the value of reducing the emotional costs of transaction, historically civility and commercial society have enjoyed an intimate relationship.

Having observed such aspects of civility, I am not asserting that civil-ity emerges automatically in commercial societies. Rather, the opposite seems to be true. In this sense, some recent work by economic historians on the rise of trustworthy behavior in the marketplace is suggestive. Their work has shown that the rise of the market economy in European history was not a natural result of economic growth. Through an examination of European economic history, Douglass C. North and Robert P. Thomas conclude that growth hinged on the construction of efficient economic organization. The state's involvement in institution-building to yield a means of enforcing property rights significantly reduced the "cost of transaction."[29] "Ultimately, it is the state that is responsible for the effi-cacy of the property rights structure."[30]

Yet, the state was not solely responsible for establishing the institu-tional infrastructure for market activities. For example, economic histo-rian Avner Greif presented a revisionist contribution that elucidated how private institutions such as coalitions of medieval long-distance traders created a mechanism that enforced contracts and trustworthy behavior. In his historical analysis of the medieval Maghiribi traders, he found that a strong concern for reputation among long-distance traders enforced contracts. Although cheating was always an economically feasible option for overseas agents, a bad reputation, once gained, would jeopardize the chance of doing business with other Maghiribi traders.[31] The work of economic historians on the enforcement of trust in a market economy il-lustrates that the formation of trustworthy conduct was not a natural and inevitable outcome of civilizing; rather, there were always political, social, and cultural institutions that encouraged or enforced trustworthy behav-ior by individuals.

These studies were suggestive in the notion that civility and trust are closely related. Enforcement of trustworthy behavior in a temporal di-mension requires a certain stability in long-term transactional relation-ships. For example, Maghiribi traders assumed that they would continue to transact with multiple market players in the community of traders who shared the reputation of trustworthiness. However, the mechanism of enforcing trustworthy behavior in long-term exchange relationships is not necessarily limited to socio-political means for enforcing contracts and ensuring property rights. Culture plays an important role. In *The Taming of the Samurai*, I pointed out that the prevailing culture of honor among Japanese samurai warriors in the medieval period functioned to reduce the uncertainty of human interaction by supplying internal principles of integrity and predictability in action.[32] The samurai's vassalage (master–follower relationships) in the medieval period was essentially a military alliance built on the premise of providing military service in times of emergency. However, with the rise of the stable Tokugawa state, the culture of the samurai was urged to transform because the quality of vassalage was completely altered. In contrast to the picture presented by Albert Hirschman in *The Passions and the Interests*, the samurai's glory-seeking honor culture was not replaced by the alternative paradigm of discipline arising from a capitalist mentality of rational calculation; the samurai culture of honor was retained and put to use on behalf of the ruling class, albeit in a significantly altered form. No longer a glorious presentation of military might, the samurai's honor was internalized as a principle of virtue and self-control for those who had to sustain their sober devotion to their organizational duties as stipendiary quasi-bureaucrats.

Although the transformation of the samurai disciplinary culture was an important aspect of creating the civic culture of Japan's proto-modernity, the rise of civility also played an important role by not only affecting the samurai elite but involving a larger segment of the population. As I will discuss in this book, the arts and poetry played important roles in generating spheres of civility in pre-modern Japan. While Japan's aesthetic ways of socialization may seem unusual, we can appreciate the advantage of forms of sociability that unfold in the spheres of practicing and sharing an art in that they can reduce the emotional cost of a transaction. In a society equipped with civility, skillful ways of sociability develop that positively create "a comfortable zone of distance" in social relations. In the spheres of such social interactions that feature not too intimate but still friendly relations, there should be reasonable shared rules that regulate the emotional states and behavior of the interacting parties. However, when the grammars of sociability become too strict, people feel uncomfortable due to the suppression of their instincts for expressing their emotion. In contrast, socialization mediated by the rules of the arts satisfy the emotional needs of individuals to express themselves not by suppressing their emotions but rather by redirecting them by following the procedure of an art while avoiding the direct facing-off of the participants' assertive selves. For example, the sharing of a cup of tea following the aesthetic procedure of the tea ceremony would achieve the aim of civilized sociability. Thus, along with the development of such an aspect of civility as etiquette and manners, the development of spheres for aesthetic socialization greatly improved the culture of sociability in Japanese society. This development, in which civility mediated through the arts became a major character of the Tokugawa culture of sociability, was the product of complex historical contingencies. What made arts and poetry circles so central to Tokugawa social life? Why, as Kaempfer observed, did Tokugawa Japan exhibit a particularly hierarchical style of politeness?

Civility, the State, and Associational Networks

The study of Tokugawa cultures of sociability upholds the view that effective human transactions need a certain structure but that the configuration of such a structure of control can vary widely among societies. In our inquiry into the Tokugawa culture of sociability, we also expect to observe that Japan took a distinct route to the formation of civility. This route involves relationships between (1) the state and associational domains and (2) the state and the market. These relational contexts of associations, markets, and politics gave certain structures to the development of the Japanese culture of civility.

The State-Association Relationship

In the process of exploring why such a distinctive form of aesthetic activities occupied a central place in the civic life of pre-modern Japanese people, I realized the importance of articulating the intimate relationship between the trajectory of Japanese state formation and the transformation of associational networks. The question remains, however, how the distinctive structure and trajectory of Japanese state formation affected the structure of associational life and, conversely, how the distinctive characteristics of various social networks condition and characterize the route of early modern state developments.

The domination of the samurai state for two and a half centuries without permitting formal political representation of other classes certainly distinguished the Tokugawa political experience. Historically, however, during the pre-Tokugawa period, various associations and groups had exhibited a much larger degree of autonomy and self-defense abilities, relatively speaking. However, with the establishment of the national hierarchy of the samurai class as part of the process of Tokugawa state formation, the Tokugawa state wisely tamed and reorganized existing regional, status, and occupational associations (e.g., villages, trade associations, outcast groups) to better serve the ends of the state. The shogunate claimed a position of supreme public propriety. Having little choice but to accept the framework of the shogunate, these various organizations reduced their exercise of publicness while retaining their self-governing abilities. As entities supporting self-governing and discipline in everyday life, these organizations served as the most accessible sites of communicative activities for the people.

The main governing strategy of the Tokugawa state was thus institutional segmentation and segregation of its population through a decentralized, indirect control system. Institutional segregation was critical to the stability of the Tokugawa system because the feudal authorities in medieval Japan often felt threatened by horizontal alliances of various people and groups. The state provided a system of jurisdiction and adjudication whose involvement in civil disputes, however, was kept to a minimum. The state preferred that those disputes occurring within villages, trade groups, and other associations be taken care of internally. The state also did not develop direct institutions of social control, such as police, because such mid-range social institutions could effectively provide discipline and enhance trust in this society. The shogunate's basic principles of control, such as status distinctions and indirect control, were unshakable throughout two and a half centuries. The state and samurai elite made it abundantly clear, through various legal and disciplinary measures, that the status rules of distinction formed the most basic principle of governing in this society.

Note the fact that these mid-range organizations connecting individuals with the larger polity were neither primordial kinship organizations nor modern voluntary associations of citizens. Simply because the authorities granted these organizations some apparently generous self-governing activities, the polity was far from democratic in that there was no official participation of the "lower-ranking entities" in the formal political process. Furthermore, the state established clear limitations for associational activities. Since networking activities were traditionally very vigorous in the society, the shogunate and the *daimyo* lords were rightfully suspicious of the formation of private alliances beyond the officially recognized semi-autonomous groups and associations. The formation of political parties and alliances was thus strictly prohibited.

The expansion of aesthetic and literary activities became an important locus of Tokugawa social life in this situation. Organized social life based upon the arts and literature became a safe haven for voluntary associational activities. Unlike political alliances, authorities did not bother to meticulously control the numerous networks of cultural circles and associations. Furthermore, unlike regional or status organizations, these artistic and literary circles and associations were purely "voluntary associations" that were formed privately; members of aesthetic associations joined of their own free will as private individuals.

State–Market Relations

The second institutional venue that linked politics and the Tokugawa culture of sociability was its distinctive state–market relationships. Charles Tilly has defined them as "coercion and capital" relationships that form the key combination to explain great variations in the type of European states from the medieval to the early modern periods.[33] The varied combinations of the reservoirs of political power produced institution-yielding power that also affected the cultural fields. I would argue that the extensive development of nationwide commercial networks within a unified neo-feudal Tokugawa state constituted a condition of possibility for the emergence of communicative activities and a collective cultural consciousness among the Japanese people in this period. Tokugawa's idiosyncratic state–market relations facilitated the emergence of vibrant yet hierarchical and also aesthetic forms of civility.

Commercial trade encouraged the flow of people and commodities, often in unexpected ways. When a thing becomes a commodity in the market, it generates a chain of exchange from production site to consumer as it contacts commercial workers such as traders, wholesalers, and retailers. When a commodity travels – through the hands of producers, traders, retailers, and consumers – it hosts and generates sites of communicative actions along the way. The establishment of a far-reaching network of horizontal economic dependencies under the Tokugawa expanded the horizon of people's communicative lives.

Although the Tokugawa state developed the distinctive organizational structure of a decentralized polity, the state's existence also hinged upon the expansion of a nationwide market economy. Although the samurai regime remained essentially feudal in nature, it could not prevent or oppose wide-ranging changes in commerce and agriculture because the financial well-being of the samurai houses depended upon income from the grain tax, primarily paid in rice, which required the open vicissitudes of the marketplace. Unlike in the previous period, the samurai no longer lived in villages as military feudal lords but had moved to the castle towns of the *daimyo* lords. The samurai relied on significant incomes to support their urban lifestyles. Thus, the operation of the Tokugawa state depended upon a well-organized market economy.

During the seventeenth century, the shogunate constructed major road and sea links connecting the larger cities, as well as standardizing coinage and measurements. The institutionalization of the alternate residence system for *daimyo* lords, which required regular travel between the capital city of Edo and their local domains, promoted a nationwide flow of people, goods, and institutional innovations. As a result, the Japanese economy by the late seventeenth century was profiting from a thriving nationwide exchange of commodities.

To be sure, medieval Japan was already enriched with thriving commercial networks that often cut across feudal territorial boundaries.[34] However, starting in the late sixteenth century and continuing into the seventeenth, the Japanese economy entered a phase of expansion that surpassed that of any previous period. During the sixteenth century, the provincial *daimyo* lords became seriously involved in the expansion of their territories' basic productive capacities. In the final stages of the Warring States period, in particular, in order to finance their increasingly expensive war machines, the *daimyo* were eager to construct large-scale irrigation facilities to maximize their revenue. It is estimated that the arable acreage in Japan almost tripled during the course of the sixteenth and seventeenth centuries. The Tokugawa nationwide market economy was founded on this dramatic economic growth. However, this remarkable agricultural expansion was slowing down in the late seventeenth century and reached its plateau around 1700.[35] At the same time, the Japanese population grew from about eighteen million in 1600 (at the outset of the Tokugawa period) to some thirty-one million by 1720.[36] Although the population stabilized at the beginning of the eighteenth century, the aftereffects of the earlier surge, combined with rapid commercial development, brought about a profound social transformation of eighteenth-century Japan.

Furthermore, as Gilbert Rozman has remarked,[37] the sudden increase in Japan's urban population "in the century and a half prior to the early 1700's may well have had no parallel in world history before industrialization." By 1700, Japan had become one of the most urbanized societies in the world. John Hall has estimated that by 1700, 10% of the Japanese population lived in cities larger than 10,000, while some Japanese scholars have estimated this fraction to be even larger. Only the Netherlands and England/Wales could boast of urban concentrations greater than Japan's in the same period.

Therefore, before the genesis of the Tokugawa state, there certainly existed market, city, and society. Yet, we should not miss the point that the market system under the Tokugawa had a qualitative difference from its predecessor, just as the medieval associations and groups were very different from the Tokugawa versions. The mature form of the Tokugawa market system developed into the nationwide system of exchange based upon the institutional field molded by the Tokugawa state. The market structures resembled the integrated but decentralized Tokugawa state system itself as it connected the nationwide centers (located first in Osaka and then in Edo) and local markets of the *daimyo* territories.

The question is posed: In spite of the ongoing expansion of the market economy and urbanization, why was the shogunate able to maintain its original form of the samurai-dominated feudal polity for two and a half centuries? We can speculate that if domestic pacification had not been coupled with the shogunate's intentional withdrawal from international competition, the *daimyo* and their samurai vassals would most likely have continued to invest in the upkeep of their military efficacy. International trade and diplomatic relations had been on the increase by 1600; nevertheless, the Tokugawa shogunate's deliberate decision to withdraw from international trade and military competition discouraged the growth of politically powerful merchant houses. Merchants could not become politically powerful as suppliers of military materiel – unlike the case in European societies in which armed competition for territorial redefinition continued during the same period – since the samurai ceased to function as warriors after 1615. To be sure, the merchant class was the primary economic beneficiary of Japan's commercial boom during the seventeenth century; moreover, merchants were less heavily taxed than the agricultural population. This combination of factors meant that Tokugawa merchants prospered economically at the same time that they were classified as social subordinates whose success depended upon the favor of the ruling class.

Two additional institutional constraints prevented the Tokugawa merchants from acquiring any real political influence. First, most major Japanese cities, despite the impressive speed of urbanization during the late sixteenth and seventeenth centuries, originated as castle towns for the provincial *daimyo* during the process of unification. This rapid urbanization of Japan was largely politically driven, as most of these cities had originated as castle towns or administrative centers of provincial or local governments rather than as centers of commercial activities. The city administrations continued to be staffed solely by samurai bureaucrats, who were vassals of the *daimyo* or the shogun. These governing bodies were created in response to the shogunate's need for regional or national political centers, unlike the medieval European pattern of urban self-government. As a result, the cities of Tokugawa Japan did not develop official representative bodies reflecting the interests of the townspeople themselves. In contrast, the medieval and early modern cities in Europe developed a measure of autonomy, and citizenship in these cities conveyed certain political privileges. Although medieval municipal citizenship differed from modern citizenship rights, the tradition of municipal citizenship was an indispensable ingredient, socially and ideologically, for the expansion of civic and political rights of the non-aristocratic population in the nineteenth century.[38]

Second, the shogunate never formally introduced a system of selling public offices comparable to the French pattern, which allowed the *haute bourgeoisie* to purchase admission to the formal power structures of the Bourbon monarchy. In the late Tokugawa period, the sons of wealthy commoner families were occasionally allowed to buy their way into the ranks of the lesser samurai. This practice, however, was largely limited to positions of lower samurai status; it was never widespread, nor did it open up formal regular channels for access to political power through commercial distinction and prosperity. The Tokugawa rulers maintained a policy of status demarcation that formally segregated the non-samurai population from the political process. Thus, although the merchant class became powerful in the economic arena and was connected with the fiscal dimension of the state's operations, its influence was not formally represented in the government.

In Tokugawa Japan, the strong hegemony of the samurai state was firmly established prior to any thoroughgoing commercialization of the economy. The growth of the commercial market economy became conspicuous only after the samurai class had firmly reestablished its hegemony through the reconstitution of its internal hierarchy. The Tokugawa nationwide market system rose within that framework. The system of the Tokugawa state prescribed one's location according to the hierarchies of formal status categories. As a result, the emergent relational patterns in the economic domain were deeply affected by the prescribed requirements of the Tokugawa state. It was in this uneasy matrix of conflicts that a hybrid of capitalistic and neo-feudal cultural characteristics emerged in Tokugawa Japan.

Civility and Multiplicity of Publics

The hierarchies of communicative spheres of publics that emerged under the Tokugawa shogunate were highly idiosyncratic. In the "official" arena of social interactions, which might be called *dominant publics*, the formal code of social interactions predictably emphasized the maintenance of existing social hierarchies. Political rituals underscored the various status rankings through physical and linguistic expressions. The basic principle of hierarchical civility was also used for addressing "strangers" since it was the safest way to perform an interaction; neglecting an apparent status difference was the surest route to emotional friction.

Hierarchical Civility in Dominant Publics

A famous Tokugawa scholar of formal rituals and manners, Ise Sadatake (1717–1784), elaborated the ideology of hierarchical civility in his commentaries on good manners: "[T]he way of manners (reihō) is nothing more than respect for superiors.... A just action is in correspondence with your own status; it is important that it not be too servile and that it not be less deferential than it should be; a just action can be called rightful manners."[39]

Though scarcely a groundbreaking insight, it served as a sensible reminder to the Tokugawa people that they were living in a society of hierarchical order in which specific forms of good manners were determined by recognizing one's relative social status in the context of a socially interactive occasion. Sadatake's interpretation was but one telling passage in a crowded catalogue of commentaries on the hierarchical grammars of sociability. The resulting "common sense" logic of Tokugawa good manners resembled an obsession to find one's relative position within any specific social setting. The other side of this coin was that people naturally became extremely concerned with being treated inappropriately as per their status.

To recapitulate, the rise of a hierarchical aspect of civility may therefore be considered a cumulative result of state development coupled with expansion of the Japanese market economy. Its emergence was facilitated by the interactional networks among samurai bureaucrats in government administration and by capitalist trade conducted through the newly formed commercial networks. Once a capitalist model of commerce was introduced into this highly stratified society defined by a unified political structure, it necessitated more frequent social interactions between people of different classes and regional backgrounds, giving rise to extended interactional networks. The changed social situation of those previously confined to relatively localized networks created a new awareness and curiosity regarding the ways and manners of the privileged classes. Simultaneous with these communicative developments, the samurai bureaucrats' political and cultural hegemony was affecting the shape and norms of network construction and operation. The result was the emergence of feudal-capitalist social institutions that defined the framework for Tokugawa cultural developments in dominant publics.

The net result of hierarchical civility was a curious social paradox. On the one hand, Tokugawa people were segregated from one another by the institution of status differentials codified in the practices of formal civility; on the other hand, the same code of formal civility brought together individuals who had been previously compartmentalized (if not isolated) in localized networks of knowledge.

Aesthetic Sociability in Enclave Publics

However, the situation becomes even more convoluted. Remember the fact that the formation of political parties was strictly forbidden in this society. Nonetheless, as long as the general population accepted the "inferior" status of the private sphere, and as long as individuals carried out their assigned public duties and generally followed the framework of formal status distinctions in the formal arena, the authorities refrained for the most part from interfering with people's private lives. Even the samurai (who were officially defined as persons obligated to devote themselves to public affairs) were not closely monitored when they were "off duty," so to speak. Due to the Tokugawa indirect control system, wide enclaves of free discursive spheres emerged outside the boundaries of the formal public world. These spheres of communicative activities can be called *enclave publics* since they were officially unconnected with the hierarchical order of the dominant publics.

It was at this point that aesthetic publics entered the center stage of Tokugawa social life as a version of enclave publics. The Tokugawa shoguns repeatedly issued edicts prohibiting "the formation of parties" because they feared that private networks of horizontal alliances among individuals would lead eventually to collective action against their regime. This prohibition made private aesthetic associations even more important for civic life during the Tokugawa period. Circles for sharing the arts and literature were well-accepted; they were safe ways to organize voluntary associations open to people from different social backgrounds. The result was the evolution of civility centered on aesthetic pursuits. From the samurai to merchants and farmers, in cities as well as in villages, people found enjoyment and realized a sense of self-improvement in joining these circles, which were a rare social space populated by private persons regardless of their status background. Various ritual technologies developed to nullify formal requirements of hierarchical social codes in these circles. For example, people introduced themselves and addressed one another by their artist names in the Tokugawa poetry groups or other amateur circles. Although these aesthetic publics were not dominant in the official hierarchy of publics, they were much more attractive than official dominant publics largely because participants could choose to join by their own will and preference. Unlike the official world institutionally segregated by status distinctions, private associations were active and lively spheres of socialization. Tokugawa people installed an amazing and extremely extensive aesthetic network, rich in its variety of arts and literature, as well as robust activities.

Furthermore, Tokugawa townspeople produced even more radical *counter-publics*, the lifestyle of the so-called floating world (*ukiyo*). Aided by the rising commercialized material culture and new commercial media such as commercial printing and publishing, as well as commercial theaters, the typically disseminated image of the floating world consisted of light-hearted, cheerful representations of the sensual pleasures of urban sophisticates and was diametrically opposed to the image of Tokugawa citizens as compliant subjects of an oppressive regime. The culture of the floating world had two popular versions of court societies with their own lifestyles and codes of sociability: the space of the so-called *akusho* (literally, "the bad place," or the courtesan quarter) and the space of *Kabuki* theaters. Courtesans and *Kabuki* actors were treated as celebrities and sold many *ukiyo-e* woodblock prints that illustrated their portraits, while their fashions and lifestyle attracted the popular imagination. *Kabuki*'s gorgeous theatrical performances and idealized beauty of courtesans also invited the people to temporarily forget about their formal duties and to indulge themselves in a moment of sensual pleasure.

The impressive aspect of this enculturation was that it did not stay in the level of the elite but went to a large segment of society, the common people. For example, circle activities of making *haikai* poetry included farmers and craftsmen, while learning dance and *shamisen* music became common for daughters of small shopkeepers. The employees of large merchant shops were allowed to learn some performing arts. Although their formal codes of civility dictated the observation of status hierarchies, the culture of sociability cannot be understood from only that viewpoint.

Under the policy of institutional segregation and its distinctive state–market relationships, Tokugawa Japan thus developed idiosyncratic hierarchies and interrelationships of multiple publics. One can plausibly describe Tokugawa civility as having multiple modes of operation according to the nature of the publics in which interactional communications took place. In more formal modes of interaction in which individuals had to negotiate with one another based on "official" identities, the precise observation and acknowledgment of minute status differentials was essential to proper conduct. Nevertheless, in communicative spheres of a more private nature, the adoption of enclave identities permitted interactions governed by different rules of sociability associated with publics of a different sort. By officially confining the official public sphere to the activities of the Tokugawa state system, however, the shogunate maintained the system in such a way that private associational activities evolved as a unified public forum for political discourse. On the other hand, many samurai and urban commoners alike were able to enjoy participation in communications in private circles set apart by aesthetic ritual technologies, provided that these enclaves were strictly defined as inferior spheres of discourse. People switched between different modes of interaction as they socially, physically, or cognitively shifted their network connections over time.

With multiple publics, therefore, just which version of voices from Tokugawa Japan best epitomizes the culture of the age is hard to answer. It was the period of cultural diversity since the institutionally segregated population produced a rich diversity of tastes, temperaments, and cultural practices. The spirit of the age required individuals to skillfully switch network connections and to change modes of sociability accordingly. Yet, the spheres of enclave publics, particularly aesthetic publics – those sites of communication centering on shared artistic and literary hobbies – require particular attention for further investigation. In between the formal and counter-publics, enclave publics provided a middle ground for socialization for various private citizens. The fact that a middle ground for socialization in this highly segregated society was built upon the realm of arts and literature made a lasting influence on the formation of Japanese cultural identities.

Cultural Mobility through Enclave and Formal Identities

The study of Tokugawa Japan highlights a basic human feature of communication, namely the constant switching of our social functions, roles, and identities as we move from one communicative site to another. However, the political situation of Tokugawa Japan – that of a long-lasting regime dominated by a single status group (the samurai) – made this aspect of human nature much more apparent.

Tokugawa aesthetic publics were based upon an assumption that entering into these sites of aesthetic sociability required the temporary leaving of feudal official identities. There were, to be sure, always many individuals who would try to impose their self-importance in the hierarchies of the outside world on these private occasions for aesthetic socialization. Yet, such an attitude of self-importance was generally regarded as unrefined and unstylish in the world of beauty.

This social aspect of Tokugawa aesthetic publics characterizes both the strength and weakness of Japanese aesthetic civility. Tokugawa people could enjoy the benefits of an impressive degree of cultural popularization and mobility – though not exclusively – through the enclave identities that they assumed in their leisure-time cultural pursuits. The cultural mobility that existed in the enclave publics, however, had no explicit or external connection to promotion or upward mobility in the participants' public/official identities. For example, learning arts in these circles may sometimes have enhanced the prestige of a merchant among peers and may have allowed him to socialize with respectable samurai. However, such cultural upward mobility was not institutionally connected to his promotion in the official world.

The distinctive features of early modern Japanese cultural mobility may perhaps be better understood in contrast to the cultural mobility of the early modern British elites. Modern British political development is usually characterized as the product of an alliance between the landed gentry and the bourgeoisie that allowed for social mobility, as compared with the more confrontational relations that marked the two equivalent groups in early modern France. The social encounters between landowning gentry and bankers or merchants in the London clubs were not confined to cultural fraternization within the confines of the clubs but were linked to wider political alliances. Concrete institutional developments that gave official sanction to this socio-cultural transformation facilitated the process.

One such institutional development was the body of credentials acquired through attendance at an English public school. J. V. Beckett has pointed out that public schools allowed the sons of bankers to rub shoulders with the sons of aristocrats in the process of receiving the same education. "[I]t was accepted that in itself this made them gentlemen. Instead of their having to earn gentility through acquiring landed acreage, it was possible for them to obtain it via the public school. As a result, the public schools helped to maintain the quasi-hereditary elite, and at the same time to fulfill the status hopes of professional and some business families."[40] A common understanding of the qualities of elite culture thus supported communicative interactions taking place in the emerging British liberal public sphere. In this way, it gained the superordinate position in the hierarchy of discursive spheres. The legal backdrop of this development was that by the eighteenth century adult males in Great Britain had acquired the basic civil rights essential to personal freedom – including freedom of religion, thought, and speech – as well as the right to hold property. This early legalization of civic rights in Britain can be interpreted as a definition of the public/official identities of members of the state derived from universal aspects of citizenship. The cultural merger of the aristocratic and moneyed elites unfolded in this legal context.

In France, the construction of the formal and legal equality of public/ official identities of the members of the state was a relatively late by-product of the violent synthesis of antagonistic social forces following the revolution of 1789. Even so, in comparison with the experience of early modern Japan, the French road to the construction of an egalitarian public/official identity for the country's inhabitants underwent a long period of preparation prior to the late eighteenth century. Even under the *ancien régime*, the institutionalized sale of public offices allowed the sons of wealthy mercantile families to take the first step toward eventual acquisition of noble rank. When individual achievement of higher cultural status is linked to plausible upward social mobility, we can consider it a type of cultural mobility through formal identity.

In contrast, cultural mobility in the enclave publics of Tokugawa Japan had no apparent connection to the formal promotion of the public/official identities of the amateur poets, artists, and tea ceremony enthusiasts. A samurai in good standing, on the other hand, could indulge himself in popular art forms and literature that had originated as entertainment for the commoners without much risk of becoming *déclassé*. Members of the elite were permitted a certain amount of cultural deviation in their enclave identities, under the thin disguise of artist or pen names, provided such excursions did not interfere with their "official" duties. Toward the end of the Tokugawa period, in the late eighteenth and early nineteenth centuries, the trespassing of status boundaries in the cultural sphere was sufficiently frequent to make such limits ambiguous. This boundary confusion, however, should not be equated with the upward mobility in formal identities. The cultural mixing of the late Tokugawa period still occurred within the institutional field of the Tokugawa state, which – in principle at least – continued to uphold status distinctions. Therefore, it cannot be said that this particular development led to a new paradigmatic disciplinary culture for an emerging elite substantially similar to the British fusion of aristocratic and bourgeois cultures.

Enchanting and lively as it may have been, the culture of the Tokugawa urban commoners did not create an alternative model of formal civility reflecting the commoners' sensibility and political empowerment. More accurately, rather than developing a coherent dominant culture of civil society, Japan under the shogunate produced a loose collection of cognitive networks comprising multiple identities and cultural styles. Although the Tokugawa social configuration might be problematic from a liberal political perspective, its concessions to cultural mobility through the adoption of enclave identities allowed for a high degree of cultural diversity and creativity. Once the aesthetic publics were accepted as important components of the private life in Tokugawa Japan, they quietly produced individuals who considered their aesthetic enclave identities to be more profoundly rooted to their true selves than were their feudal categorical identities. In spite of the apolitical nature of aesthetic activities, the emerging new mentality thus quietly eroded the ideological foundation of the Tokugawa state that segmented people through hierarchical status categories.

2

Culture and Identity as Emergent Properties in Networks

Using the characterization of Japanese rules of sociability as "civility without civil society" as an entry point, I have offered a broad outline of the distinctive patterns of the Tokugawa civilizing process and its socio-political environment. In this chapter, I set aside the Japanese historical experience and examine some theoretical and methodological issues regarding the foundation of a public-centered perspective and its relation to studying collective cultural identities and social stratification.

Publics as Negative Space

Since the 1990s, many social scientists have engaged in projects intended to bring the aspect of culture back into sociological research. The resurgence of cultural analysis in social change that asserts the constitutive role of culture is one such endeavor. This effort has been productive and provides a necessary correction to the reductionist tendency to collapse culture and discourse into the category of social organization. Researchers have revealed the dynamics in which culture is not only influenced by social forces and organizations but is itself a force capable of enacting change in society. In other words, culture is an *agent*, to use a sociologist's own term. At the same time, we cannot neglect the fact that culture depends on specific kinds of social organization that undergird cultural production. On the other hand, when a view of culture as an agent of change takes us only as far as the simplistic discussion of an essentialized national culture or moral values as the cause of social change, we are in danger of falling into the trap of modernization theory. The predictable result reduces culture to a watered-down version of morals and values or popular impressionistic arguments such as "the Japanese (or any types of "others") are inherently and intrinsically different." Then

44

the question becomes: Where and how do the webs of culture and social networks overlap?

It was in the context of these theoretical questions that I arrived at a public-centered perspective. I consider the location and sphere of cultural production as the primary locus for understanding the mechanisms of cultural change and identity construction. Social-structural constraints influence cultural production primarily through structuring publics and influencing their interrelationships. At the same time, publics are spheres in which individuals interact and networks intersect with other networks. In my view, the identity of a person or collectivity is not a fixed, pre-existing entity but is fluid and revisable through interactions with others in the space of a public. Publics, in this sense, are sites that usher change into social life. I will elaborate on these points shortly. However, to give the reader an image of my view of publics, let me introduce an analogy from the typical academic approach to drawing.

In a drawing class, the instructor often asks new students to draw oranges and apples on a sheet of paper. An amateur student usually tries to draw the contour of each apple and orange as accurately as possible. In other words, he or she attempts to essentialize the "orangeness" of the orange and the "appleness" of the apple by drawing a boundary. The instructor then encourages the students to attend to their objects more carefully by focusing on the negative space, or the space between the objects' solid or material contours. The novice art student usually regards this space as simply nothing, or as empty space. An untrained student's perception often cannot recognize empty spaces because it cannot match them with stored essential images or categories. But, to the artist with trained perception, it is clear that the negative space and the object work together to create the picture. Thus, the skilled draftsperson can render the contours of oranges and apples on the surface of the paper merely by filling in the negative spaces surrounding them.

Negative space is a metaphor for a public in which the identities of oranges and apples take shape. The negative space is in fact not empty at all, nor is it simply a background. The space is filled with relationships – that is, the spatial relationships among the objects. More precisely, we could say that the negative space is the condition of possibility within which the shape of the fruit emerges. In other words, the objects and the negative space emerge only *co-dependently*. I have used the example of negative space to illustrate the importance of the location of cultural production and the context of identity formation. Furthermore, negative space illustrates the *relational* existence of identities; appleness or orangeness in fact consist not only of the contours of the object but emerge simultaneously with the negative-space, relational contexts of being. In a phrase, publics are spheres full of potentiality for generating and revising identities.

To be sure, the metaphor of negative space has only limited utility because it is a static example. Our daily life is more complex and fluid than the example of drawing a fixed object. In real life, individuals are constantly switching from one public to the next through connecting to and decoupling from their network intersections. In other words, an individual's identity is not a fixed, structured entity but rather has been formed, revised, and shifted constantly through contacting actual or virtual "others" in publics. In fact, what I attempt to sketch is a fluid worldview that manifests in dynamic relations. Identity as such cannot be understood as a pre-constituted structure but only as a process of constant flux and alteration. Furthermore, publics and identities can be described as continuous *co-dependent emergence*. For the sake of further articulating the relationship between publics and identities, I now turn to the metaphor of networks.

Networks as Phenomenological Realities

In this book, I frequently draw upon the imagery of networks in describing the relational underpinnings of important subjects, including the formation of new publics, the rules of sociability, and collective Japanese identities. In the social sciences, network analysis has developed into a powerful mathematical instrument for articulating and measuring the concrete relational patterns of social structures. However, as I use the term, *networks* implies not only concrete external and measurable social ties, such as political-power relations, economic transactions, communicative relations, affectional relationships, and social-interactive ties (that is to say, "networks out there"), but also includes shifting cognitive associational maps perceived inwardly in the form of narrative "stories." The unit of analysis in networks is not restricted to relational settings among individuals, groups, or organizations that can be plotted on a map of physical space. The present discussion is chiefly concerned with the phenomenological complexity of networks rather than their measurable aspects.

Narratives, particularly when they are stored and reproduced as stories – which are *temporally and spatially structured cognitive associational networks* – allow human beings to address the ontological problems involved in "translating knowing into telling," to borrow from Hayden White; stories also offer a solution to "the problem of fashioning human experience into a form assimilable to structures of meaning."[1] Because stories can "store" network relationships, these networks then exist in a very real sense within us. For example, when the ancient Japanese animistic *feeling* (which was, of course, their way of knowing the world, or worldview) was translated into myths, legends, and poetry, their fluid feelings received more stable forms of meaning structures. Once these feelings transformed into more stabilized cognitive networks, they were more widely shared by others and more easily passed to the next generation. From a phenomenological perspective, what we now perceive as "collective cultural identities" emerge as stories when they begin to yield a relatively coherent network of meaning shared by a collectivity.

Categorical identities (the identities of a person, or any categories of collectivity) articulate themselves better when they retain stories. Having stories helps an individual sort out the internalized multiplicity of networked identities with a certain sense of consistency. When these stories are held within the collective memories of an "imagined community" called a *nation-state*, to use Benedict Anderson's term, the members of that community, as well as outside observers, consider them as "national cultures." My inquiry concerns the formation of such networks of meanings and symbols as well as the concrete social-structural networks that undergird them.[2]

If we use the term network in an extended sense, however, we should justify its usage as preferable to more established terms, such as *social relations* for individual links, *social structures* for relatively stable systems of stratification, and *values and norms* for cognitive associations or economic transactions. However, using different terms for various relational settings can sometimes be quite misleading since such a usage tends to reify them: instead of more fluid relational concepts, their specific naming tends to freeze them into fixed conceptual notions. For example, I am working on a hypothesis that holds that a critical moment of cultural history in any society occurs when network relationships undergo sudden expansions in scale, density, and complexity. To understand a critical moment of this type, one should refrain from reducing it to a single social, political, economic, or communicative structural factor. It is rather the *aggregate* effect or synergistic energies of different kinds of relational contexts intersecting or colliding with one another that enable qualitatively different results in cultural domains. On the other hand, many relational settings are multiplex networks that include more than two types of transactional relationships. For example, a market network represents not only economic transactions but also communicative and cultural exchanges. The use of common network imagery underscores the aggregate nature of these effects.

Redefining Publics

Armed with this phenomenological understanding of networks, we are ready to redefine publics. As I use the term, *publics* are communicative sites that emerge at the points of connection among social and/or cognitive networks. Each individual carries with him or her an amalgamation of cognitive, social, and symbolic networks. The public is the sphere – actual–physical and/or imagined–virtual space – in which the actions of switching/connecting and decoupling of networks take place. Understood phenomenologically, a public emerges on the smallest scale as the site of a temporary intersection of two "network domains," which may be represented by two individuals. These network domains carry unique configurations of social and cognitive ties. Harrison White has suggested the term *Goffman public* for this type of ephemeral micro-public.[3] Erving Goffman was an American sociologist who studied the symbolic dynamics of small-scale interactional rituals. Goffman considers a micro-public as an almost magical device that briefly frees the participants from their restrictive embedding in existing networks.

A more sustained public may emerge as a micro-public within a community. To give a specific example, displays of personal consumption often stimulate the emergence of numerous micro-unofficial publics. Consider the ways in which the inhabitants of a modest neighborhood might react to one person's "upscale" house renovations or the acquisition of an expensive car. A conspicuous purchase often triggers the formation of active micro-publics in the neighborhood. These micro-publics may bring about a variety of reactions to the stimulus – for instance, the fortunate family may throw a housewarming party for friends and neighbors, while others may spread gossip about the source of the money behind the upgrade. Within these micro-publics, people will discuss, evaluate, and critique the tastes and spending habits of those who stand out from the rest of the neighborhood. Through participation in publics of this type, residents of the neighborhood may revise their own evaluation of the better-off neighbor; their tastes may be influenced by the higher standard of consumption, or they may feel compelled to "keep up with the Joneses" by competing for status in the neighborhood through comparable or greater consumption.

In its larger and more organizational form, a public may emerge on the basis of concrete institutionalized associational networks and communicative infrastructures that facilitate and sustain durable mechanisms for bringing interacting agents into the condition of a public. Habermas's examples of publics – cafes, salons, and reading circles – are examples of more institutionalized forms of publics that regularly hosted intersections of various individuals and information. However, union rallies, the rituals of religious worship, and political demonstrations can also be seen as cases of publics more institutionalized than Goffman publics. Schools and business firms are also examples of institutionalized sites of publics that provided regular organizational and physical environments for recurrent communicative activities. Prescribed network structures – the formal organizational structures of a school or firm – would by their very nature influence the structures of publics that occurred there.

Actors participating in discursive and non-discursive communication within the interactional space of a public will experience a temporal suspension of the social and cognitive networks that existed prior to their participation. Of course, the degree of such a suspension can span the range from a non-committed or habitual interaction to an enlightened experience. Regardless of the degree, however, such a suspension can potentially create a source for revising one's perception of the self, the other, and the world. Active participation in public communications can effect significant changes in people's feelings, opinions, and perceptions. The continuous participation of actors in different types of publics results in an ongoing revision of both the identities of the actors themselves and the ways in which these actors are perceived by others.

In the ontological dimension of the human being, however, an individual can be perceived as having internalized publics at the points where different cognitive associational networks intersect. A person's mind is constantly involved in internal dialogues while processing and cross-sectioning various thoughts and pieces of information. After all, it is easy to enter into a dispute with others because one is always getting into disputes with oneself. The popular assumption that a "person" is an integrated and consistent entity is a myth. In other words, the subjectivity of a person as such can be considered a *collection of loosely networked multiple identities* in which exchanges with an internal otherness are necessary to maintain selfhood. A person's categorical identities are thus necessarily changing all the time, with his or her connections constantly shifting in multiple ways. In sum, there are many forms of publics that an individual encounters in everyday life. They are, in their various levels, sites of shifting and switching network connections. An individual moves internally, externally, and multidimensionally from one public to another in his or her daily life.

Publics in Motion: Switching and Agency

At this point, we have the notion of publics as spheres for change. A human being is not simply a passive emergent entity arising out of network intersections. Whereas the flow of water in a given direction is bound by physical laws, a human being makes choices of network connections along the way consciously or unconsciously.

I consider that the power of human agency lies in people's creative ability to form meta-cognitive connections between separate or even radically different kinds of network domains. The human capacity for connectivity includes the temporal shifting of connections within various network settings, combining or intersecting them, and forming boundaries by shifting and decoupling among different sets of connections. People also leave behind pre-existing network connections – sometimes intentionally, sometimes unconsciously. It is in a public that such a shift of network connections occurs. In this sense, publics are spheres for action, the location in which changes, evolution, and shifting of identities take place.

The most common conscious practice is the evaluation of relative preferences and values by intersecting multiple networks that differ widely in type, level, content, and strength. Only human beings are able to form judgments ranging from the relative importance of career or economic interests to the values of family and affectional life or the importance of commitment to a religious community. Daily contact with a range of people, organizations, institutions, and events compels us to make constant adjustments in our connectivity with different relational settings. In addition to our circumstantial fine-tuning, we can purposefully select, evaluate, or intersect various relationships. We do more than simply make decisions regarding conflicting network requirements in everyday life, however; we also make creative connections among them or even invent new sets of cognitively perceived relational meanings in order to settle conflicts. The repeated action of connecting and switching allows structures to become embedded over time and affect social processes.[4]

The identity of an individual, group, or nation – which I prefer to call a "categorical identity" – results from a series of experiences of alternating among multiple publics. In an instance of network switching in a public, the agent's identity is revised and reconfirmed through experiencing an act of suspending one's pre-existing identity. To be sure, we may often fail to make our network transitions smoothly and effectively in social settings, like an older car whose gears need lubrication. In spite of a certain built-in preference for established behavior patterns, however, people are pushed toward continual revision of their pre-existing chains of cognitive associations by numerous daily exposures to the interactional spaces of different publics. Their "career paths" of switching, suspending, and revising their identities in turn create an "imagined public" in our minds to which we internally refer in assessing our behaviors. When we try to sustain our "integrity" or make radical decisions, we often get into disputes with ourselves in our internalized so-called imagined publics.

By involving us in many different micro-publics, modern life compels us to switch continuously without conscious attention to the process from one domain to another and among multiple sets of ties. The identity of a person engaged in interactions emerges and reemerges phenomenologically through frequent conscious and unconscious switching among different social roles. Therefore, I define *publics* as interactional spaces of discursive or non-discursive communication emerging through the actions of shifting network connections.

Identity in Motion

Given this definition of publics, I consider an identity and a public to emerge co-dependently. As in the analogy of negative space, the boundary of identity is revised and drawn only in the relational context in a public. Instead of constructing a theory upon the notion of "person" as a category of pre-existing atoms, Harrison White proposed an analytical model predicated on the emergence of identity from behavior – from action and counteraction. The formation of categorical identities, according to White, is "triggered from contingencies," which are nested in contexts of social relationship. The construction of a clear categorical identity with an articulated boundary is often not the result of deliberate social actions but rather an interdependent and incremental agglomeration of unplanned social interactions. Thus, identities are not only relationally but also path-dependently formulated. The content of a categorical identity can be better understood as loosely coupled cognitive networks of multiple identities. According to the kind of public you encounter, a particular element in the network of identities might manifest in the process of interactions.

Yet, contradictory as it may seem, however fluid an identity may inherently be, it always tends to want to reify itself. In order to maintain its coherence over time, it is continuously on the lookout for ways to construct stable structures with which to identify itself. This form of essentialism seems to be almost inescapable for any identity dealing with itself as a subject. Interestingly, we even encounter a linguistic pun when we summarize this tendency as "each identity tries to keep its identity over time." Our whole sense of human integrity is based on this ideal of clinging to one's values, and to one's promises made, over time. Furthermore, categorical identities by nature attempt to essentialize other identities by creating stories (e.g., labeling another's essential nature through gossiping). Such attempts at essentializing other people's identities occur partly because of the need to discern epistemological others (i.e., other groups, other individuals, and other societies) in order to construct a coherent subject. The process of identity formation thus compulsively engages in misrecognition and approximation of others in the context of power struggles. It is in this process that identities emerge to control other identities. This sociological–phenomenological view of identity formation resembles the view of some physicists toward the material world. "We live in a world of verbs," said astrophysicist Piet Hut, noting that "nouns are only shorthand for those verbs whose actions are sufficiently stationary to show some thing-like behavior. These statements may seem like philosophy or poetry, but in fact they are an accurate description of the material world, when we take into account the quantum nature of reality."[5] Likewise, in spite of the fluid quality of identity in motion, by creating relatively stable boundaries of self and otherness, the identities of a person, group, or nation may show "thing-like" behaviors. How do we conceptualize this seemingly contradictory dynamic?

"More Is Different"

Furthermore, since I conceptualized the notion of publics as the sphere of intersections among cognitive and social networks, the relationship between intersecting networks, as well as the identity and culture that emerge in a public, must be articulated. My definition of publics as points of intersecting network domains logically assumes that an expansion in the scale and density of political, economic, organizational, and communicative networks would engender conditions for increased possibilities for the emerging sites of publics. With active interactions and shifting of network connections in these publics, this development in turn results in changes in the realms of discursive life, cultures, and identities. It follows that a major expansion of communicative networks often marks a critical moment in cultural history. A sociological argument of this type begs a question concerning the relationship between the concrete bases of social structures and the discursive quality of communicative life. It is not helpful to collapse culture and discourse into the category of social organization; at the same time, we cannot neglect the fact that the production and social efficacy of discourse depend on specific kinds of social organizations.

The relationship between increases in scale, density, and complexity of social networks and cultural-discursive outcomes can be better understood in the light of P. W. Anderson's finding that "more is different."[6] Anderson, a Nobel laureate physicist, noticed that in every situation he studied, significant quantitative changes invariably resulted in qualitative changes. For example, if you have only a few water molecules, their mutual interaction is relatively uninteresting. When you combine a large number of such molecules, however, new phenomena emerge: at low temperatures, the ensemble of molecules forms solid ice crystals; increase the temperature, and the ice melts to form water; and further heating will produce steam at a different transitional temperature. Likewise, the human body offers some striking examples of "more is different," or what might also be termed *emergent properties*. The body contains many different levels of emergence: at a single location in the body, we can focus on the organization that is present there on the level of organs, tissues, cells, organelles, molecules, atoms, quarks, or vacuum fluctuations. A human body thus entails not just one complex network but an intricate assemblage of many complicated networks, each of which displays many different emergent properties. For example, every human cell contains roughly 100,000 genes that are continuously involved in intricate patterns of switching each other on and off in an unimaginably bewildering interactive network.

These so-called phase transitions between different states of matter are examples of emergent properties – phenomena that can be understood retrospectively based on the properties of the individual molecules but that are very hard to predict from those properties alone. To complicate matters, the details of emergent properties are often sensitively dependent on historical trajectories and as such are unpredictable even in principle. In the case of a phase transition from water to ice, the orientations in space of the individual ice crystals, as well as their sizes, are dependent on the most minute perturbations that take place during the process of freezing. In principle, each of these interactions can be explained in terms of detailed molecular behavior, even though we are still far from a detailed descriptive form of understanding. The same holds true for the exponentially more complicated behavior of the molecules in living tissue. But, if and when we achieve a complete molecular description, will that mean that we have "explained" the workings of a living cell, and that we thereby fully "understand" what the living cell is "all about"? Clearly not: the paradoxical aspect of emergent properties lies precisely in the fact that they are at the same time "nothing more" than what is already given at a lower level of description, yet simultaneously "completely different" and in that qualitative sense "far more" compared with the lower level.

Emergent Properties

The notion of emergent properties as indicators of separate levels of meaning applies everywhere, in nature as well as in cultural artifacts. A computer, for example, can replicate a photograph of a human face with remarkable fidelity. In the memory of the computer, the brightness and color values of each of the picture elements are readily accessible. But nowhere in its memory is there any information as to whether the picture does indeed represent a human face rather than something completely different, such as a rock or even a meaningless pattern. And even the most powerful computer cannot yet distinguish reliably among these different interpretations, given the complete picture. Even young children, of course, have no trouble answering the question of human identity, and in doing so provide this extra information. Again we see that what seemed to be a "complete" description was merely complete on one level, the level of the picture elements, and totally incomplete with respect to another level, the interpretation of the picture as that of a human face.[7]

As I see it, meanings and representations as such are emergent properties arising from the interplay of human subjectivity in actors involved in network relationships with institutions, technologies, and changes in the political and economic climate of their society. From this perspective, what I have called early modern network revolutions in Japan or elsewhere – simultaneous expansions of political, economic, and communicative networks – were significant turning points in cultural history, occasions that ushered in qualitative differences in the cultural realms.

At the same time, individual actors are not simply passive members of publics. Individuals have the ability to create new associational networks and to make a choice of publics in which to participate. Individuals do not ordinarily confine themselves to participation in a single public but switch from one to another. In other words, an individual actor or group's purposeful action can make a significant difference in social structures by intentionally generating the sphere of a new public. Students of collective actions have been acutely aware that the robust action of organizing actors was critical for the creation of a new public that could make a significant impact on the direction of a social movement. For example, organizing a rally is an occasion that does more than physically mobilize a number of people into the space of public discourse. In a successful rally, the action of participation creates and strengthens the degree of engagement among participants because they are temporarily decoupled from their pre-existing cognitive and social networks. It may effectively allow them to liberate themselves from pre-existing "prejudice." There are various methods for mobilizing a public to enact change. Traditional ways include publishing, as well as organizing rallies, demonstrations, ceremonies, and petition movements. Mobilization in cyberspace has also become increasingly popular. Modern life not only forces us to alternate among various publics but also offers us more resources and means for the purposive generation of publics.

Social-structural networks are conducive to the structuring and creation of networks for publics; they also affect the hierarchical interrelationships among publics. It is primarily through this process of affecting the structures of publics that social-structural networks influence the process of cultural production and identity formation. Social organizations that affect the formation of publics might not by themselves directly govern the course of cultural developments. For example, an elementary school is a stable form of institution that seeks to regulate the process of learning among children. The school system regulates the ways in which children encounter new information and influences how they interact with others. In other words, schools shape the types and structures of the publics in which the children live and grow. It is, of course, true that the design of the educational system of a school can never "determine" the structures of publics; it can only influence them. As we all know, children often "hang around" informally with "unexpected" (from the viewpoint of teachers and parents) friends and may also acquire information not deemed worthwhile by the school system. Yet, the school program can still heavily influence the children's learning processes and ways of interacting with other individuals. This degree of influence explains why many parents spare no effort to help their children get into "better" schools.

Once they are manifested as an emerging property, however, cultural outcomes – including religion, value systems, literature, arts, and various forms of popular culture – can exercise a "thing-like" independent influence over the course of socio-cultural developments insofar as individuals use the repertoire of cultural resources and idioms to their own ends. Norbert Elias insightfully asserted that:

> [S]tanding by a river we see the perpetual flowing of the water. But to grasp it conceptually, and to communicate it to others, we do not think and say, 'Look at the perpetual flowing of the water'. We say, 'Look how fast the river is flowing.' ... This reduction of processes to static conditions, which we shall call 'process-reduction' for short, appears self-explanatory to people who have grown up with such languages.[8]

Here, Elias points out the dual nature of human perception – the ontological understanding of a process-oriented worldview and the human actuality that requires understanding the world through essentializing the nature of phenomena. Furthermore, as Charles Tilly noted, once categories are formulated and sustained as relatively coherent identities, they perpetuate durable inequality when combined with social hierarchies.[9]

Culture and Agency as an Ocean Liner and Its Captain

To be sure, individuals cannot form their own cultural practices in isolation from other human beings. Cultural practices, insofar as they embody conscious human experience, do not occur in a social vacuum. They occur in spaces in which the phenomenological property of social relations is instantiated. From this perspective, the metaphor of culture as a "tool kit" reveals obvious limitations. The metaphor of a tool kit, as proposed by Ann Swidler, has been influential in sociology because it neatly underscores the agency of actors – in particular, in the area of political action.[10] As originally devised, the metaphor can be of great use as long as we recognize its limitations, a task we face when using any metaphor. In this particular case, there is a danger that we can get the impression that actors can use cultural tool kits freely for their own ends regardless of their cognitive network contexts. This is not the case. For example, an organizer of a union rally may be able to introduce a new symbolic metaphor for mobilizing others, but he or she cannot completely neglect the linguistic associational contexts of the metaphor. Another danger of taking the image of a tool kit too literally is when we consider the tools to be ready-made and unchanging once they are produced; such a view fails to do justice to the fact that the social effectiveness of cultural messages depends upon the collaboration of others in the agent's network connections.

This is a particularly important consideration in explicit verbal communications. Getting one's message across with any effectiveness in most societies requires the cooperation of many others. It is also true that a specific person's situationally advantageous position in network relations often makes a difference in enlisting such cooperation. We might say that an actor with situational advantages resembles the captain of an ocean liner, who requires the collaboration of other crew members but who can still exercise considerable control and initiative in pursuit of his or her goal. The metaphor of an ocean liner was used by Hilary Putnam in the context of reviewing the debates in philosophy in terms of the function of language during the second half of the twentieth century.[11] He concluded that:

> [T]he familiar comparison of *words to tools* is wrong, if the "tools" one has in mind are tools that one person could in principle use in isolation, such as a hammer or a screwdriver. If language is a tool, it is a tool like an ocean liner, which requires many people cooperating (and participating in a complex division of labor) to use. What gives one's words the particular meanings they have is not just the state of one's brain, but the relations one has to both one's non-human environment and to others.[12]

This situation is not limited to the use of languages but extends to cultural symbols in general; they exist on two levels of associations or networks. First of all, they are "cognitive associations" within an individual subject's mind. As such, they are "tools" created in internal cognitive networks. The process of creation is only partly free and spontaneous, however, since the subject cannot neglect existing cognitive associations that were partially made of their own personal history and partially dictated by their own culture. Second, cultural symbols were enacted through association with others. Culture relies on communications among individuals to achieve a certain end. For the purpose of gaining collaboration from others, individuals have to consider the effectiveness of pre-existing chains of meanings.

Nonetheless, it is equally clear that a cultural product emerging out of network relations often has an unpredictable and autonomous impact on subsequent socio-cultural developments. This dynamic, in my opinion, requires not only in-depth examination of narratives and representations but also the focus of an examination into the functioning of publics and switching because it is the latter that introduces human agency into our analysis. In other words, it is a mechanism in which an individual who was born into and is living the webs of pre-existing cultural and linguistic networks is able to exercise some freedom in his or her choice. Individuals cannot be reduced to slaves of the structural requirements of network relationships. People can create their own cultural practices and cognitive networks by drawing on the idioms and resources available to them and combining them in their own ways. Unexpected or unpredictable connectivity often results in cultural innovation or qualitatively different emerging cultural properties.

In spite of this caveat, however, the emergence of cultural practices cannot be understood without articulating the developmental trajectories of network complexity. Organizational network structures include political and economic networks that affect the connections among individuals, social organizations, materials, and information in a variety of ways. This epistemological understanding of the relationship between social-structural and cultural-discursive domains governs my historical analysis, with particular respect paid to the dynamic interactions of these two types of network domains.

The increasing density, scale, and complexity of various kinds of network relationships in specific historical contexts – including Tokugawa Japan – create conditions of possibility for new cultural emergent properties to arise. While such an increase in network complexity in and of itself does not directly produce or formulate new cultural items, it may lead in that direction. In each case, the increase in the density of intersections between networks intensifies communication and in the process produces increasingly varied publics. These publics, in turn, can provide opportunities for cultural innovation. Yet, once a culture has arisen as a manifestation of complex network systems, the culture as an emerging property retains its own qualitative distinctiveness and social dynamics that cannot be exhausted by or reduced to the network relations that gave rise to it. In this respect, culture is comparable to subjective experiences of consciousness that cannot be fully described in purely biochemical terms, even though consciousness as such is a manifestation of physical systems of enormous complexity in the human brain.[13] When internal cognitive associational maps are translated and codified into narrative forms, or when cultural practices create a concrete social-institutional or physical or representational presence, these entities also produce independent social effects that cannot be simplistically reduced to the network relationships that called them forth.

Categorical Stratification of Publics

Having sociologically reconceptualized the notion of publics, my view of publics is necessarily plural. In contrast, Jürgen Habermas's normative concept of "the public sphere" defines it as an integrated and unified realm of discursive interactions in which citizens deliberate about their common political concerns through discussions and debates. In his *The Structural Transformation of the Public Sphere*,[14] Habermas focused on a particular aspect of the historical and institutional development of European civil society by analyzing the emergent conditions of the category of the public sphere during the eighteenth century. He emphasized the role of social institutions that fostered open critical debates within Enlightenment society. The new sociability that unfolded in the salons, cafes, and other places relied heavily on a rational-critical mode of argumentation rather than on the social status of the actors involved.

Habermas's idealized picture of the eighteenth century bourgeois public sphere has, however, met with serious criticism on both empirical and theoretical grounds. Recent revisionist scholarship on public spheres has criticized Habermas on this issue by pointing out that a number of social groups (e.g., women, racial minorities, political or religious dissidents, outcasts, and others defined as deviants) are excluded from the "official" bourgeois public sphere. These excluded groups then often form "counter-public" spheres of their own in order to have some influence on the political process.[15]

Although this revisionist view presents a more realistic picture of the political dimension of different publics, it is still lacking in one important aspect. To extend Habermas's model, it is not sufficient to point to the plurality of publics. We have to probe deeper, to the level of ontological reconstitution of identities and cultures. I have already discussed that a plurality of publics exists because multiplicity is inherent in human cognitive functioning and sociability. Furthermore, the social field of multiple publics is always charged with the dynamic of power. And the power of an individual or a group often stems not simply from the possession of material or military forces but from the *relational position*

that one occupies in networks. Therefore, the interrelationships and hierarchical structures of publics must be analyzed to understand the efficacy
of communicative messages produced in these spheres. The efficacy of the
message that flows from communicative actions is also influenced by the
way in which that public is positioned in the field of multiple publics.
Consequently, the concept of the multiplicity of publics brings us to another important question: If publics are necessarily multiple, what are the
interrelations among them?

Obviously, the structure of interrelationships among publics differs
greatly in society. Just as in the smallest-scale instance of a Goffman public, in which a powerful individual can dominate an interactive space, a
hierarchy of multiple publics may emerge in a social field in which the
dominant public claims the highest authority of "publicness." Often, the
decline and exclusion of older types of publics underlies this hegemonic
process of celebrating the dominant public sphere. The hierarchical power
relations among publics thus affect the social impact of the discourse produced in these public spheres.

My conclusion is that Habermas's historically informed analysis of the
public sphere in the West is in fact a case study of this hegemonic process
in which one category of the liberal bourgeois public sphere gained normative authority in the West. The category of publics in various natural
languages also reflects the underlying struggles for creating the "dominant public." It is not uncommon in many societies for a certain category
of public to attain a normative authority to the degree that it demands
sacrifice of the members of the collective group under the argument of the
public good. Historical changes in the perception of categories of public
are thus reflected in the way that the term "public" is used in different
historical periods in the same natural language. In this way, the struggle to
attain authority over the dynamic of publicness leaves behind a linguistic
equivalent of archeological strata in a living language. (I will refer to the
history of Japanese terms for public from this perspective in Section Two.)
On the other hand, it is important to keep in mind that the emergence
of a dominant public does not imply or entail the disappearance of other
communicative spheres. For example, the rise of public formal education
through schooling may decrease the social role of the parents, relatives,
and neighbors in passing knowledge to the next generation. Nevertheless,
schools would never think of replacing the roles of family and community.

The field of multiple publics in society is always categorically stratified. Yet, the categorical stratification and interrelation among publics are
constantly shifting. The emergence of new types of publics often brings
about the decline, stagnation, or delegitimization of older forms. For example, with the increased number of women in the American workforce,

feminist publics (e.g., women's employment networks, journals, telephone hot lines, bookstores, research centers, festivals, and local meeting places) have grown considerably, while older types of women's networks, such as housewives' informal gatherings and neighborhood "kaffeeklatsches," have declined. On the other hand, a move toward hegemony on the part of one public may encourage the proliferation of new counter-publics that maintain oppositional discourses of resistance. When the state tightens moral regulations on sexual expression such as pornography, it sometimes makes underground expression more attractive to consumers.

As seen in the case of a radical religious millennium movement, when a counter-public can mobilize strong loyalty from participants, the existence of such a sphere of alternative discourse can threaten the authority of the dominant public. Sometimes, when a counter-public commands the public authority, it can form a dominant counter-public capable of countervailing the authority of the dominant public. When the balance of power is well-achieved among dominant and counter-dominant publics, it may encourage the development of a democratic tendency in the field of communicative actions.

The hegemony of a public may also encourage the formation of ritual enclaves in which the authority of the discourse in the dominant public is temporarily nullified. This form of escapist reaction may or may not produce an explicit counter-message but rather creates enclave publics. Like the Tokugawa aesthetic circles and associations, enclave publics may encourage participants to suspend their formal identity and temporarily assume the identity of a lesser public. The existence of such enclaves by itself may sometimes threaten the authority of the dominant category of the public. However, they also could functionally support the existing order as safety valves.

Whether or not certain messages and cultural practices become influential in a society depends, in part, on its actors' strategic use of opportunity structures within network relationships. The social efficacy of a message is determined within a given domain, which itself is nested within other domains within a network of hierarchical relations. A person or group that tries to construct an effective social reality cannot ignore this structure of social hierarchies. From this perspective, individuals and groups in the upper tiers of social hierarchies may enjoy some advantage in refining their message through their control of public hierarchies.

However, the complexity of the dynamics of interrelationships among publics is that their relationships cannot be grasped only from a viewpoint of power, authority, and hierarchy. It is not always true that those who have ideological, social, and economic power can control the communicative action of society at large. The axis of *cultural appeal* is also important.

For example, the ruling class may hold cultural hegemony/authority, but it may not be able to formulate attractive cultural productions. To put it bluntly, although snobbish high culture may hold sway, it may not prove attractive or lively to the popular mind. Cultural innovation and vitality often come from publics located on the periphery of society rather than from publics closer to the centers of power. Therefore, the public at the top of the hierarchy of multiple publics in terms of authority is not necessarily the most influential site of communicative actions. This is an important consideration for understanding the dynamics of Tokugawa culture because the most lively sites of communicative activities were unauthorized townsmen cultures – such as the culture of the floating world – that had a subversive and pervasive influence on Tokugawa mentality.

Furthermore, publics that emerge on the basis of intersecting "weak" ties are often more conducive to spreading information. Consider the cases of casual contacts among strangers at parties and in bars, informal gossip networks in workplaces, or teenagers absorbed in television programs. Participants in such publics are less responsible for the consequences of communicative actions, less committed to the intersecting networks in their publics, and consequently more prone to spread information, gossip, and rumors. These casual publics usually exert only weak authority, but they are often influential in spreading hearsay, fashion trends, and lifestyles. However, "the strength of weak ties," as Mark Granovetter calls it,[16] is observed not only in these marginal fashions. For example, it comes with experience that useful information for getting a job often comes from unexpected persons with casual contacts. Likewise, discourse in unauthorized publics through casual contacts, gossip, and rumor often threatens those in power. Acquaintanceships, made through participation in artistic and literary gatherings, also constituted weak ties in comparison with social ties requiring stronger commitment. Strong ties, such as those formed in close circles of friends, among co-workers in an office, or among members of a kinship group in a community, may represent a higher level of commitment among the persons involved; but these persons are more likely to circulate within the same cluster of people, and they repeatedly share the same information. On the other hand, such weak ties as casual relationships formed through artistic gatherings can serve as bridges to new worlds of thought, new information, and new clusters of networks. The consumption of commodities mediated by commercial markets often also exhibits the strength of publics based upon intersecting weak ties.

In short, it is not enough to recognize the multiplicity of publics; rather, one must examine the dynamics of interrelationships of publics in a social context in order to understand the dynamics of emerging cultural properties. The transformation of the definitions of the word "public" in a natural language in a given society reflects underlying social struggles. It is through the interactions of discourse produced in categorically stratified multiple publics that the emerging property of collective cultural consciousness is spelled out.

The State, Associations, and Publics

To return for a moment to Habermas's project, his explanatory model of the rise of the liberal public sphere in eighteenth-century Europe relies on two historically specific social-structural variables as conditions of possibility for the emergence of the bourgeois public sphere. The first of these was the establishment of a far-reaching network of horizontal economic dependencies that increased the traffic flow of commodities, people, and information among the countries of Western Europe. The second variable, which received considerably less emphasis in Habermas's account, was the process of overt political change in the formation of modern nation-states that gave rise to depersonalized state authorities. This combination of economic and political factors resulted in the development of new institutions for public discourse. To be sure, the multiplication of social network relations as a condition of possibility for emergent publics can result from different causes and means other than the effects of markets and the state. Yet, it is also true that these macro–socio-political factors provide a critically important impetus for generating and extending network relationships.

Between these two factors, market and state, the impact of market networks on encouraging the development and expansion of horizontal social networks and alliances has been well-discussed in the literature on civil society and public spheres. In fact, the relationships among capitalistic developments, civil society, and democratic discourse have been explored often and ideologically promoted. In contrast, Western scholarship on public spheres and civil society, or on any exploration of the connections between the state and publics, has been relatively tentative. The literature on publics and civil society arose in the normative context of evaluating communities of citizens that organized themselves apart from the state. As a result, scholars interested in the topic of public spheres tend to concentrate their efforts on exploring cultural domains outside the state; there is little discussion of the state per se or of the crucial interconnection between these two realms. Similarly, those who approach the question of civil society from the viewpoint of associational structures often avoid discussing the relationships between state structures and associational patterns. This omission is clearly regrettable from the viewpoint of sociological exploration since *the patterns and kinds of civil associations and the structure and trajectory of state formation historically have proven mutually influential.*

On the other hand, the study of comparative state formation emphasizes regional variations in early modern state-making in Europe and the subsequent various patterns of development in different Western societies. The works of Barrington Moore, Charles Tilly, Perry Anderson, Michael Mann, Anthony Giddens, Douglass North, and Immanuel Wallerstein have proposed a number of persuasive theories regarding the impact of social transition from the medieval to the early modern period in Europe. Yet, to date, the relationships between the structure and stratification of publics and state formation have not been directly addressed by these theorists. The growing literature on the comparative study of state formation in Europe has yet to engage fully the question raised by students of public spheres and civil society.

Having reformulated the concept of publics with the help of network language, I propose the hypothesis that *the structure of the institutional field of publics in a society is profoundly affected by the organizational structure of the state. The types, shapes, and hierarchies of publics in turn affect the contents of the emerging discursive and cultural properties.* The state's most significant effect on cultural spheres is its indirect influence on the shaping and sustenance of a durable organizational–institutional field that affects the structures, hierarchies, and interrelationships of publics. For example, the state and associational networks affected each other mutually and simultaneously: the structure of the state limited the kind of associational networks that could arise in society, while in turn the variety of existing social networks affected the route of state development. Publics as interactional spaces emerge within this relationally structured field.[17] I will soon illustrate these mutually determining relationships between the process of state formation and the transformation of associational networks in the Japanese case by focusing on the transformation of aesthetic networks. However, at this point it is important to remember the critical role of associational networks in enabling recurrent interactions among actors. The ways that people self-organized themselves by forming various types of associational networks intimately affected the location, types, and structure of publics and thus influenced the process of cultural production.

Multiple publics continue to speak in different voices even when a dominant public commands the highest authority. According to the different structures and patterns of the political structure, however, the "grip" of the public on the top rung of the hierarchy over the communicative actions taken in lesser publics may differ. For example, consider the case of an authoritarian state equipped with the direct means of social control (e.g., police, bureaucracy, and a state-financed education system) coupled with a teleocratic nature (i.e., the government has secular or religious missions to fulfill, such as fostering nationalism, the moral growth of its subjects, religious righteousness, expanding its wealth, etc.). Such a state may attempt to force moral conformity on the population by disciplinary measures. In this state, marginal or "alternative" publics may be obliged to go underground.

On the other hand, even in an authoritarian state, if there is no effective infrastructural means of direct social control, the communicative actions at the top of the hierarchy of publics may exert only a weak symbolic hold on the population. In such a case, there could be larger communicative spheres not closely supervised by the officials. Consequently, rather than being forced underground, proponents of unofficial communicative activities might be officially tolerated, though segregated as "private publics" not connected to the official public. Avoiding stigmatization while crossing the boundary between official and unofficial publics may be easier in a regime of this type. These scenarios are meant only to suggest the possible links between state structures and the patterns of publics.

The organizational structure and trajectory of the Tokugawa state influences the types, shapes, and hierarchies of the institutional field of publics in a society. The formation of the Tokugawa shogunate influenced the structures of associational life, and its influence over the workings of markets influenced and shaped the field of publics in this society. The result was, for one thing, an extremely hierarchical structure of publics in which the shogunate declared itself as the supreme authority of the public. However, because of its indirect and decentralized control system without a direct means of disciplining its subjects, Tokugawa Japan developed numerous enclave publics outside the control of the state.

Further actual articulation of the relationships among the state, associations, market, and publics must be studied in relation to concrete historical contexts. In the case of Tokugawa Japan, it was the colorful processes of cultural production in which the prototype of Japanese civility and cultural identities was formulated. For this reason, I invite the reader to examine with me some detailed historical investigations into the development of Japanese cultures of aesthetic socialization.

Section Two

The Transformation of Associational Politics and the Rise of Aesthetic Publics

Prelude to Section Two

Humankind's search for the possibility of social orders built on horizontal associations of free individuals rather than on structures of vertical integration imposed from the top down is considered the central issue of contemporary political theory. In the real world, of course, an unequal distribution of power among people always governs social relations. Although it may seem utopian, humans have continuously attempted throughout history to theorize about and experiment with various forms of associations that allow participants to connect with one another voluntarily within horizontal structures. In the West, such heavily freighted terms as freedom, democracy, citizenship, and civility reflect centuries of philosophical contemplation and political struggle toward these ends. In particular, the emergence of voluntary horizontally structured associations for civic activities has been often regarded as an organizational prerequisite for the development of a stable democratic polity.

On the other hand, sociological realism also tells us that the rise of a democratic polity in history was not simply the result of the presence of the more horizontal and egalitarian associational life. Power politics always plays a role. Remember that the earlier form of parliamentary institutions in the medieval period was the product of an alliance of the landed aristocracy and the privileged urban elites. These institutions had, needless to say, an aspect of protecting their privileges and excluding others. Yet, the presence of these institutions of elite horizontal alliances became the source of counter-sovereign power that checked the overtly arbitrary use of power by the sovereign. In other words, horizontal associations were also striving to gain the authority and power necessary to develop into dominant forces. In the process of such power struggles, horizontal organizations often adopted exclusionary politics against "others." Regardless of the actual inequality and exclusionary politics that may prevail in these supposed horizontal communities and alliances, however, human beings appear to aspire to a form of community life based upon a horizontal fellowship.

The transformation of the word "public" in various societies often reflects the history of struggles between a horizontal association among members of a society and a hierarchical order imposed by the source of power and authority. The Japanese language is no exception. The native Japanese word for "public," *ōyake*, is an ancient word that originally meant either "great building" or its spatial location. The consensus of Japanese scholars is that *ōyake* referred to the storehouse of an ancient community that was used for keeping harvest surplus or tributary offerings.[1] Before the rise of the imperial *ritsuryō* government (a government with its own legal code) in the late seventh century, ancient Japanese agricultural communities were usually understood as lineage-based communities that solidified their cohesiveness through the ritual worship of common ancestors. Members of these communities appear to have made ritual offerings of the first fruits of harvest to their community chiefs. The large common storehouse, *ōyake*, became at once an image of the commonality of the group, as well as signifying the ritual sacredness of the great house. Thus, from the beginning, the Japanese term for "public" embraced a tension between horizontal and vertical images of human associations.

As ancient Japanese society became increasingly politically stratified, *ōyake* came to signify the political or religious authorities that controlled the storehouse. After the ancient imperial state formed a government with its own legal code (*ritsuryō*) in imitation of the Chinese legal system around the eighth century, the Chinese ideogram for *kō* (public) came to represent the indigenous term *ōyake*. (The same ideogram has been understood as having two distinct pronunciations, *kō* and *ōyake*.) At this point, both terms were predominantly used in reference to the political authority of the emperor's court. This development paralleled the centuries of preceding social processes in which the ritual authority of the emperor subordinated that of lesser chiefdoms and communities. Under this system of law, ordinary people were called *kōmin* (public persons) and owed services and taxes to the emperor's government. Thus, the ancient Japanese history of publics reflects a process of stratification in which a type of public originally formed around the imperial court came to reorganize and subordinate other lesser publics.

In the centuries that followed, Japanese terms for publicness in various official and non-official documents usually appeared in the context of the sovereignty and ritual sacredness of the emperor. This etymological transition meant that one of the root meanings of *ōyake*, "commonness," dropped out of Japanese usage.[2] In contrast to the authoritarian conception of the ancient public, the word for "private," *watakushi*, represented the arbitrary whims of individuals and as such was considered an object of devotion inferior to the public.[3] Mizoguchi Yūzō, a Japanese scholar, observed that this lack of moral universality, reflected in the distinction between public and private, characterized the uniquely Japanese ancient conception of public and private as compared with the Chinese notion. The conceptual and terminological transformation of public and private in a given society often reflects underlying social struggles in which a certain type of communicative sphere gains in authority and legitimacy at the expense of various other publics. By labeling a specific sphere as "the public," while considering others as minor publics or as private, those in power were often able to legitimate their rule. The etymological history of the term *public* in Japanese also reflects this political dynamic of stratifying publics.

Is it possible that the other root meaning of *ōyake*, namely the horizontal structure of commonality, completely disappeared from Japanese culture? The stereotypical view of the traditional Japanese value system depicts it as incurably hierarchical, with weak countervailing horizontal social associations. In fact, by the beginning of the medieval period – the epoch that I discuss in the following chapter – the formal intellectual understanding of the native term *kō* or *ōyake* (public) clearly associated it with the state – more specifically with the emperor's domain. An ancient nuance of the term *ōyake*, the large storehouse, the horizontal commonality of people, had become clearly watered down by then. Yet, this dilution of significance does not mean that the people of medieval Japan did not try to cultivate horizontal associations outside the realm of the state. To answer this question, we must step outside the boundaries of intellectual history. Regardless of intellectual formulations, the picture is very different if it includes actual practices and institutions that protected the private sphere against willful interference from political authorities. Hence, it is crucial not merely to investigate literary evidence for intellectuals' practiced terminology for public and private domains – a proper domain of intellectual history that usually examines the ideas and usages of distinguished writers – but also to examine social practice by people in concrete network contexts. Did people in fact value and strengthen their horizontal voluntary associations? What were the organizational conditions and cultural practices that enabled the development of such horizontal associations?

From this perspective, medieval Japanese society clearly strengthened the private domain and encouraged various forms of horizontal coalitions against the political authorities. It was during this period that there emerged new forms of alliance among people of different standings. Under the weak and unstable political framework of central polities, medieval Japan saw the fragmentation of power and continuous infighting among such various local powers as samurai warlords and militarized temples. This violent situation was a source of misery for ordinary people; at the same time, the medieval period in Japan was a time of flexibility and social mobility for those who managed to play their own game by taking advantage of the social fluidity that resulted from competing political units. Without a reliable source of protection, people experimented with various forms of alliances in order to defend their own political and economic interests. For example, villagers sometimes formed corporate entities and collectively negotiated security and tax payments with warring samurai lords. Minor samurai lords also often formed so-called *ikki* alliances that had a horizontal character. *Ikki* literally means "of one intention or in agreement." In the fourteenth century, the term implied the voluntary formation of a party associated for a special purpose. Although the medieval Japanese were not forceful advocates of a political ideology of horizontal associations, the organizational history of medieval Japan indicates that, in practice, the Japanese people had their own ways of tackling questions of social order and individual freedom and experimented with various forms of socio-political associations. In these innovative forms of association, the ancient root meaning of the term *ōyake* (public) discussed earlier – namely horizontal commonality – found new places to thrive.

In tracing the history of Japanese organizational experiments, one finds that the Japanese search for horizontal and voluntary social associations overlapped with the activities of aesthetic circles at a number of points. In fact, the realm of aesthetic practices sheds more light on the development of medieval theories of free associational life than any form of written work. Although medieval Japanese poets and performing artists did not develop theories of freedom, they nonetheless practiced the generation of alternative modes of socialization outside the hierarchical feudal order. To be sure, the existence of alternatives does not mean that these aesthetic communities did not reflect certain aspects of hierarchical exclusionary politics. Apart from the distinction between a teacher and students of an art, the supposed fraternity has its own limitations within the overall structure of coercive political hierarchies. But once individuals entered the sphere of aesthetic pursuits, however, various aesthetic ritual technologies made worldly social hierarchies temporarily void or at least less prominent; together the members "performed" a fictional fraternity mediated by aesthetic sharing. Thus, these loci of aesthetic socialization provided individuals with occasions of identity-switching, or moments of enjoying free association with others by temporarily detaching themselves from their feudal identities and obligations. The strength of the Japanese aesthetic publics lies not simply in their tendency to be egalitarian in spirit – although they were indeed egalitarian, at least to some degree, compared with the formal hierarchical order of feudal society. These spheres of

communication that centered on the pursuits of arts and poetry represented an important organizational innovation. The presence of these
aesthetic publics strengthened the free spirit of Japanese people because of
their organizational fluidity; they brought an openness and flexibility into
the social circuits of pre-modern associational life. With the emergence of
private centers of aesthetic socialization, medieval Japanese people had
begun to gain the potential to open up their network connections.

This close relationship between the performing arts and experimentation with social forms derives from the fact that the distinctive clusters of Japanese aesthetic forms did not emerge from solitary individuals
closeted in workrooms but from groups that were deeply involved in associational and communicative activities. This mode of art production
is very different from the modern way in which art is appreciated only
through an engagement with the final product – namely, the final version
of a work that hangs on the museum wall or issues from the printing
press.

During the medieval period, the so-called *za* (seated) forms of art and
literature came into being. The spirit of the *za* arts and literature was most
typically exemplified by the seated (*za*) communal creation and reception
of performing arts and literature, such as linked poetry (*renga*) and the tea
ceremony (*chanoyu*). The pleasure of these art forms lies in the sharing of
intense experiences of collaborative aesthetic processes in the *za* meeting
places. The *renga* is a collective form of poetry-making; several poets sit
together in a meeting place and produce short verses one by one to form
chains of poetry. An unexpected poetic development through collaboration is an essential component of the pleasure derived from this form of
poetry. On the other hand, the tea ceremony is a highly structured method
for preparing tea in the company of guests. The participants of the tea
ceremony enjoy the aesthetics of the setting, including the architecture of
the tearoom, the surrounding gardens, the utensils, the flower arrangements, and the calligraphy, as well as the ritual performance of brewing
and serving the tea.

Compared with the modern Western notion of artistic and literary creativity as an individualistic process of innovation in isolation, the world
of pre-modern Japanese poets and performing artists looks refreshingly
friendly and interactive. The people who participated in these artistic circles found intense personal satisfaction in the process of sharing the work
of aesthetic production, which was often regarded by medieval theorists as
having inherent spiritual qualities. Many distinctive Japanese art forms
and literary genres, including the tea ceremony, *Nō* theater, and linked
verse, originated in the medieval period and conveyed to later generations the conviction that artistic creativity entails a spiritual as well as
an aesthetic dimension. These medieval forms of art and poetry served

as prototypes of Japanese aesthetic philosophies and networks; they were transformed and popularized during the subsequent Tokugawa period.

Comparative Considerations

The collective production and consumption of literature and arts representing a shared universe of discourse was not limited to Japan but is a common phenomenon in the popular culture of many societies. For example, Clifford Geertz discusses the intensely political nature of Arabic communal poetry in Morocco in which performative verbal exchanges of poetic phrases are often representations of fights among individuals, rival families and factions, or even among political parties.[4] In Geertz's words, "the purest expressions of this tone are the direct combats between poets trying to outdo each other with their verses. Some subject – it may be just an object like a glass or tree – is chosen to get things going, and then the poets sing alternatively, sometimes the whole night long, as the crowd shouts its judgment, until one retires, bested by the other."[5]

Steven C. Caton's ethnography of oral poetry in North Yemen vividly reports that "the ideal is that every tribesman should be a poet or at least that every tribesman compose some poetry some of the time."[6] The production of oral poetry in this culture is related to two categories of events: such tribal ceremonial occasions as weddings and important historical situations tied to the lives of individual poets or to the affairs of the community.[7] Poetic exchanges are deeply implicated in the context of manifestoes, challenges, and accumulating points of honor for individuals and communities. The tradition of honorific interactive singing in the tradition of Arabic poetry has been widely influential. This form of poetry is said to have influenced the verses of the European troubadours and their metrical scheme.[8] According to Peter Fryer, even Brazilian challenge singing, semi-improvised songs by multiple singers known as *desafio*, is rooted in the customs of the Arabs of the Iberian peninsula, which was their home for about 500 years.[9]

The collective consumption of poetry is not a monopoly of the Arab world. To give a Western example, Peter Burke has reported on the collective dimension of popular literature in early modern Europe:

> Poems as well as plays were composed and recited by craftsmen in the chambers of rhetoric in the Netherlands and in the French puys. There were regular poetry competitions and prizes, like the jocs florals in Toulouse. Sixteenth-century German Meistergesang was largely an art-form of craftsmen, notably tailors, weavers and shoemakers; the complicated metres must have made the craft as difficult to master as the elaborate goldsmith's work cultivated

at the time in the same German cities. These organizations were at once expressions of civic patriotism, the cultural equivalent of the citizen-militia, with its feasts and shooting competitions, and an indication of how seriously the performing arts were taken in those days.[10]

In these instances from early modern Europe, however, poetry is created and received as a central manifestation of ritual solidarity or the contentious dynamics of pre-existing communities and social organizations. Burke's description of the popular culture of early modern Europe bears a family resemblance to the *za* mentality of medieval Japan, the ritualistic space of communication. Closely examined, however, the communal crafting of poetry and other arts in Japan reveals some distinctive characteristics and sensibilities.

One distinctive aspect of the Japanese *za* arts was their ability to produce voluntary networks of people outside the established social organizations. The spaces for the performance of *za* arts and poetry were able to gather individuals from different social backgrounds who could not sit together from the viewpoint of the feudal social order. In medieval Japan as in North Yemen or pre-industrial Europe, one could practice the collective arts in the context of a pre-existing community or group – a point that will be developed in detail later. Nonetheless, the distinctive quality of Japanese communal production and consumption of arts and poetry included a strong need to set spaces for performance apart from the existing order of society. By participating in the activities of such aesthetic communicative spheres, individuals attained feelings of emotional resonance with others. Thus, Ogata Tsutomu, a Japanese literary scholar, pointed out that "the origin of a [popular Japanese] conception that the presupposition and essence of literary activities lie in the function of creating collaborative harmony originated in performing arts during the medieval period."[11] Furthermore, there is something of a subtly liberating quality to the Japanese performing arts. They had a powerful ability to create an alternate reality for Japanese people even in the face of intensified feudal hierarchical social constraints.

Secondly, the practitioners of the Japanese *za* arts shared a clear artistic consciousness that valued the aesthetic and spiritual quality of the interactive collective process of creating art within the *za* space. The artists and poets in the *za* genres were acutely conscious of their artistic intentions and aesthetic standards; their highly refined artistic sensibilities cannot be reduced to a matter of group solidarity and social order. Furthermore, the performers of these arts left philosophical writings about their own craft. The philosophy that informed the arts and literature of medieval Japan is sometimes called *gei-dō ron*, or "the philosophy of the artistic way."

Gei-dō ron illustrates not only the presence of a remarkable degree of insight and self-consciousness on the part of the artists and writers of the period, who articulated the theories behind their practices, but also the existence of a distinctive set of ideas regarding the relationship between artistic individuality and the artistic publics.[12]

Consequently, unlike popular Arabic poetry, in which poetry is often a form of political rhetoric in dispute mediations,[13] on the surface, Japanese medieval arts and poetry were intensely aesthetic; there were few politically aggressive poems whose expressions directly touched upon the social and political dynamics of the time. All in all, the main tradition of Japanese poetry preferred to use words related to such natural symbols as snow, moon, and flowers and to interweave them with such human emotions as regret for the uncertainty of life and love. Not all Arabic poetry traditions can be limited to contentious usages, and not all Japanese poetry was intensely aesthetic. Yet, in Japan even samurai warriors, whose aggressive honorific culture is world-famous, could be vulnerable and aesthetically subtle in their poetry. Paradoxically, however, as the chapters that follow will explain, this strikingly aesthetic and personal nature of Japanese poetry and arts allowed the samurai to create alternative realities and to carve alternative spaces of public socialization.

The social dynamics of communal practices of poetry and arts, in conjunction with socio-political developments, intersected with the Japanese people's desire to associate with each other without being constrained by the formal feudal hierarchical order and norms. The aesthetic publics often served as a means of expanding the new voluntary horizontal social networks as a counterforce against the increasingly hierarchical reorganization of Japanese society. Moreover, since the traditional arts were usually performed in a communal space, they reflected the ideal of genteel social interaction – civility – in these publics. By prescribing certain ideals of socialization within these circles, the aesthetic theories of late medieval Japan inevitably entailed deep implications on Japanese cultures of sociability and communication. I will return to the analysis of the intrinsic mode of communication embedded in this poetry form later in this section. At this point, however, it is important to point out that the ritual program of linked-verse composition represents the ideal schema of public discourse, one of the ancient double root meanings of *ōyake* (public), commonness, which was wiped out in the process of the development of a hegemonic state by the late medieval period in Japan.

During the late medieval period, when the genuine inherent attraction of these arts and their ability to create an alternative reality outside the feudal order were combined with a political context in which people experimented with various forms of horizontal associations, the aesthetic networks sometimes served as a catalyst for social change. On the other hand, as the Japanese state system deepened its hierarchical control, it inevitably reorganized the structure of Japanese associational life in general – which in turn affected ways of aesthetic networking. In particular, with the rise of the Tokugawa state at the beginning of the seventeenth century, the medieval organizational dynamics in which horizontal alliances of local associations played an important role were inevitably obliged to change. Under these circumstances, the Tokugawa aesthetic publics continued to supply rich spheres of communication in civic life, but their social role shifted significantly. In the chapters that follow, I examine the rise and transformation of the horizontal aesthetic networks and their relationships with associational politics in the wider Japanese society from the medieval to the early modern period.

3

The Medieval Origin of Aesthetic Publics

Linked Poetry and the Ritual Logic of Freedom

The performing arts, including the interactive composition of poetry, have played an important role as spaces for socialization over several centuries of Japanese history. But just as the polished blade of a Japanese sword is the product of numerous sophisticated hardening and quenching techniques, it took Japanese culture several centuries to develop a repertoire of attractive methods of socialization and a refined aesthetic. How did such a distinctive style of aesthetic socialization come into being? In order to articulate the political origin of Japan's distinctive aesthetic cultures, I would like to invite the reader into the medieval Japanese world.

The *Za* Arts and Civility: An Overview

The so-called *za* arts and literature of Japan emerged during the medieval period. A form of linked poetry known as *renga* and the tea ceremony are typical examples of medieval aesthetic developments. These forms of arts and literature are sometimes called *za no bungei* (*za* literature and art) by Japanese scholars. The *za* arts took their names from the fact that they were performed collectively within a group of seated (*za*) participants.[1] *Za* usually referred to exclusive associations (e.g., guilds) during the medieval period, but the term literally meant "seats." *Za* indicates the space in which the group gathered for the meeting or performance.[2] Space for performing and appreciating the *za* arts was the most salient example of a site for private and horizontal socialization in medieval Japan. These sites of aesthetic appreciation constituted enclaves of free socialization in which people could temporarily suspend the application of feudal norms.

Unlike most contemporary conceptions of art and literature, the *za* aesthetic emphasizes the importance of immediate presence and group participation in a process of collaborative artistic creation. The true essence of the *za* art forms is grasped only on the occasion and within the space of the actual performance. The notion that true art does not reside in the performative act itself but in an interactive experience of *za* characterizes the understanding of the *za* arts.

The study of the medieval *za* arts is the key to understanding the distinctive characteristics of sociability in Japan. The rise of the *za* arts and literature had a very important effect on the development of Japanese culture because they produced both extremely attractive art forms and the institutionalization of concrete systems of social networks in which these arts could be practiced. While the development of art and literary forms themselves had an enduring impact on Japanese culture through sets of ideas and aesthetic symbols, the organizational and institutional aspects of creating public spaces had significant social and political implications for the communicative life of the Japanese people.

The procedure of linked-verse composition, or *renga*, best epitomizes the spirit of the *za* arts. A chain of linked verse in the *renga* tradition was made by a group of poets in a *za* space, with each poet contributing stanzas in turn. The poets who met for a *renga* session were producers and consumers simultaneously. The art of making linked poetry required the participants to adhere to structured rules for making appropriate verse sequences. Simply following these rules to the letter, however, did not necessarily make for good linked verse. The poets were required to have the sensitivity to appreciate the poetic atmosphere created by the others in the meeting. By itself, however, this spirit of collaboration and synchronic harmony was not enough. Each participating poet in the *za* had to create an unexpected development in the poetic sequence by adding a refreshing and often surprising stanza to the chain. Although each contribution was a response to the one that preceded it, there was no overarching plot or theme that governed the hundred or so verses in any given sequence. Each verse followed only its immediate predecessor; it was not linked directly to the others. This comparative freedom meant that unexpected poetic sequences could develop at every turn in the chain of verse. *Renga* meetings resembled a jam session for jazz musicians in that skilled participants could improvise and add to the others' spontaneous creativity without having to follow a fixed score.

Given the power of aesthetic ritualism, once people learned the formal rules of artistic procedures, they were able to socialize with strangers with reasonable confidence. Persons from very different social background and rank – elegant courtiers from the imperial household, fierce samurai warriors, Buddhist priests, or even members of marginal status groups – could sit together in a ritual space set apart for the enjoyment of these collaborative arts. The reader should recall that civility flourishes best in an intermediate zone of social relationships that lies between the intimate and the hostile. Civility tends to govern social relations across differences in rank and status because it provides a common ground for transactions between persons from different backgrounds. Socialization through the composition of linked poetry was an ideal vehicle for creating an atmosphere of civilized fellowship. Sōgi (1421–1502), one of the most distinguished poets of late medieval Japan, describes the virtue of participating in the sessions of linked verse as follows:

> We can say that most of our companions in linked verse sessions are just as close as cousins. Even when we are meeting them for the first time, once we get into the *za* world of linked poetry together, we feel an intimacy with one another. It is only in this way *(michi)* of linked poetry that older people do not feel uncomfortable socializing with their juniors, and that those of noble birth do not shun their social inferiors (*Yodo no watari*).[3]

In fact, the whole procedure of linked-verse composition and the tea ceremony resembles an educational program for developing civility in public space. Those who participated in this form of linked poetry (*renga*) had to compose short, connected verses one after the other within a circle of many poets. Note the fact that while social relations in this feudal society were primarily governed either by birth or coercive obligations, each poet entered the field of poetic socialization by his or her own free will. The *renga* poets gathered in the *za* spaces not as representatives of their group's interest but as individuals. These *renga* enthusiasts made themselves temporary outsiders to the feudal status hierarchy. Being free from feudal constraints, however, was not enough. In the procedure of making linked verse, each poet contributed his or her piece of poetry one after the other. In linked poetry, a verse that was directly connected to the image of the previous piece of poetry was considered an uninteresting link. A synergistic mentality by itself will not yield impressive pieces of poetry. An individual poet had to show his or her own original voice. Yet, to be effective, the participants had to accept the rules (*shikimoku*) that governed the linked-poetry sessions in order to enjoy the game. These rules resembled the structure of arrangements that free members of corporate entities voluntarily accept – the rules of the public that bind them in order to achieve a greater common good. Japanese poets were eager to learn the complex rules of linked-verse composition in order to participate in a sophisticated game of poetic socialization. Furthermore, in order to make a good poetic sequence, the participants had to develop a willingness to listen attentively to others and to appreciate their poetic creativity.

Without an ability to appreciate another's poetry, an individual poet could not contribute a good succeeding line to the sequences of verses. These characteristics of linked-poetry sessions were structurally similar to the civilized rules of public discourse.

Only a poet with an independent spirit who was also endowed with the grace of collaboration could compose an unexpected, refreshing, and yet subtle piece of verse. The excitement arose from the delicate balance and tension between collaboration and competition within a group of poets under the control of the "rules of the game" (*shikimoku*). The contrast between collaboration and competition was a dynamic source of the energy generated by this poetic genre. In this way, the genuine pleasure of poetic accomplishment was related to an important unspoken assumption of the sensibility of civic virtue.

The *za* aesthetic was animated by a common spirit that appeared in such other forms of medieval art as Nō drama[4] in terms of the valuation of emotional synergy associated with the sharing of direct experience in the artistic world. For example, Zeami (1363?–1443?), an exceptionally talented Nō performer and playwright who also wrote theoretical commentaries on the performing arts, used the term *za* in his treatise *Fūshi Kaden, (Transmission of the Flower of Acting Style)* as follows: "[True] art emerges in creating a moment of *za* (ichiza konryū), the blessing of shared happiness when the audience loves and admires the performance."[5]

Zeami frequently used the term *ichiza*, which can be translated as "one *za*," to signify either the organizational structure of a Nō troupe or a moment of *za* in which feelings of emotional delight and exultation were shared between the performers and the audience.[6] For Zeami, *za* signified not merely a physical entity but an occasion of spiritual rapture born of the emotional resonance and sympathy between performer and audience. The performer's body on the stage was not one's private property; the interaction between the consciousness of acting and the awareness of being seen by the audience meant that the performer's body itself became the link between the performer's self and the audience. In this sense, the human body in the sphere of the *za* arts acquired a new identity in the moment of performance.[7] On the other hand, we must note that this striking concept of human interaction emerged at a time when various organizations called *za*, which were intended to protect the mutual interests of their members, became a new political force in Japanese society. Zeami was the leader of a Nō company (*za*); he was understandably concerned about his troupe's popularity and financial prosperity. This ambiguous passage, however, clearly points to the complex origin of the *za* art tradition; *za* was an aesthetic notion that could not be neatly detached from the organizational realities of the time.

The Rise of *Za* Organizations

Several social-institutional and cultural-cognitive factors interactively contributed to the rise of this unique form of aesthetic socialization. One of the critical factors was the distinctive political and organizational development that encouraged horizontal forms of alliance. Medieval Japan witnessed the development of a variety of new associational networks for mutual protection through relatively horizontal forms of alliance, some of which were called *za* at the beginning of the Kamakura era. *Za* as an organizational category ranged from guilds of merchants and artisans to village religious organizations *(miyaza)* and troupes of such performing artists as Nō players. The formation of corporate associational ties outside the boundaries of formal political structures produced a social field in which the distinctive *za* art forms flourished. The *za* groups formed by merchants and craftspeople were essentially occupational guilds. The *za* associations in the outlying villages and towns, however, were usually territorial organizations that provided services for the ceremonies of local Shintō shrines (hence, called *miyaza* or shrine *za*). Marginalized people also formed *za* groups as a special kind of occupational guild, since most marginal subpopulations were assigned to clean or purify buildings or other areas that had been ritually polluted *(kegare)*. On the whole, performing artists were considered to have a marginal status, but they were also thought to have the magical ability of communicating with the other world. *Za* associations were one of the most distinctive forms of organization in medieval Japan because they enabled people to join together in a horizontal fashion in order to protect their interests.

The relationship between the rise of the *za* arts and the emergence of new types of corporate organization and social alliance has rarely been discussed in the scholarly literature.[8] Although the aesthetic interests of the *za* art gatherings and the *za* groups as socio-economic associations obviously represented different organizational purposes and functions, there is a clear resonance in both spirit and form between the two social entities. This gap in the scholarship has two drawbacks. First, without understanding the general organizational transformation of medieval Japanese society, we cannot make sense of the rise and popularity of the *za* literature that flourished in that society. Second, by not comparing studies of linked poetry to scholarship on the medieval social and political organizations, we fail to appreciate the spirit of medieval Japanese social organizations. Not only linked poetry but other forms of *za* art also grew out of the rich soil of associational life in which medieval Japanese people experimented with various horizontal ways of networking with one another.

The *za* occupational groups, including the performing artists' guilds, were usually under the patronage of Buddhist temples or other powerful

authorities and provided various services to their patrons. In return for
these services, they received exclusive privileges for their occupational
operations. Consequently, these organizations attempted to protect their
interests against outsiders. Once people became members of a particular *za* organization, however, they usually upheld the relative equality of
the members. In order to provide some internal structure for themselves,
the *za* organizations typically instituted a rule of seniority based either
on age or on date of membership. For example, two *za* troupes of *Sarugaku* (popular theaters that gave rise to Nō drama) actors in Yamato,
Yūzaki-za and Emai-za,[9] were under the patronage of the Kōfukuji, a
great Buddhist temple that controlled the entire province. These troupes
of performers organized their seating (*za*) order according to seniority just
like the practice of many village-based *miyaza* organizations. The actors'
manner of distributing their revenue was relatively egalitarian according
to their written rules of *za* organizations.[10]

   These corporate *za* associations signified the emergence of new forms of
social power in local communities. Yet these various types of association
were neither structured nor integrated into a coherent and stable national
hierarchy of power. In fact, it was the very nature of the decentralized
structures of the medieval Japanese state that allowed various kinds of
corporate entities to secure their safety and interests through organizing
themselves into a *za* group of some kind.

   At the same time, noting the relationship between the *za* organizations and the spirit of the *za* art forms is an insufficient explanation of
the symbolic force that these arts obtained – a force that was powerful
enough to create alternative realities in socialization. The ambiance that
attracted people to the aesthetic *za* gatherings cannot be understood only
as a reflection of the socio-economic *za* organizations. The ritual logic
of creating aesthetic publics was rooted in the wider culture, mentality,
and social networks of medieval Japanese people. Thus, our investigation into the origins of aesthetic publics requires us to recognize at least
three additional dimensions that contributed to the rise of unique artistic
and literary traditions: (1) the sophisticated cultural heritage of the imperial court, (2) the symbolic and ritual connections between the sacred
and performing arts, and (3) the contribution of marginal people to the
development of Japanese performing arts.

Beauty and Imperial Power

The *za* arts did not emerge out of a cultural vacuum. Their emergence was
preceded and anticipated by a noteworthy cultural and political development that placed the aesthetic realm at the center of Japanese society. It

was the emperor's court that refined the theory and practice of arts and literature and made them central to Japanese power relations.

Beauty and power have always been closely related in Japanese history. This observation, unfortunately, sounds like a cliché from contemporary academic discourse regarding the arts and literature. Nevertheless, it is particularly relevant to Japanese cultural developments because the realm of the beautiful was a distinctive source of power in the ancient Japanese imperial system. This source of power resided not only in socio-political authority but also in cosmic ritual power. It was deeply rooted in the ontology of human erotic forces and animistic views of nature.[11] The public authority of the ancient imperial system was predicated on the supremacy of this cosmic ritualism over those belonging to local clans and tribes. Poetry and the performing arts were understood to be infused by erotic and animistic energies (i.e., by the same sources as the emperor's cosmic authority). In this context, performing artists were considered servants of the *kuji*[12] (public affairs) because they enhanced the sovereign's authority within the ritual framework of his court.[13] The ideogram *ku* in *kuji* is the same as *kō* (public), expressing a hierarchical connection with the state and the emperor.[14]

Arts as Technologies of Transformation

Ancient and medieval Japanese understood the arts in general as technologies for the control and transformation of nature. This understanding of art (*gei, geinō*) bears some resemblance to one nuance of English usage, in which "art" may refer not only to aesthetic practice but also to such areas of skill as medicine ("the healing arts") or politics ("the art of the possible"). To the Japanese of centuries past, the performing arts and poetry were magical technologies to move or influence nature and to connect this present world with the unseen world beyond. In this sense, Japanese artists, craftspeople, and merchants were all considered artisans (*shokunin*) who possessed the ability to transform. Stonecutters or carpenters could transform a raw material into a finished object for use or decoration, while a trader could transform one material item into another through exchange in the marketplace. The arts and poetry were also rooted in this magical power of transformation; they were in their respective ways world-shaping technologies.

If the essence of an artisan's function is the alteration of nature and to link this world with the world to come, then the act of transformation is an expression of power. The Japanese emperor's ritual source of power was derived from this notion of transforming nature. The concept of power in ancient Japanese society was far more closely linked to the art of transformation than to any notion of logical persuasion. Thus, it is not surprising that the imperial court in this early period incorporated the power of performing artists and poets insofar as they represented technologies for changing the world.

The evolution of the court society in Kyoto (known as the Heian period, 794–1192), however, carried Japanese aesthetics to a new level beyond imperial ritualism. In Heian court society, all courtiers, men and women alike, were poets and performing artists (including musicians) of some sort; without these skills, they could hardly have functioned as courtiers. Readers familiar with "The Tale of Genji," written around 1000 by Lady Murasaki, would readily recognize that beauty played a more than purely aesthetic role in the ancient imperial court. For example, the rivalry between Prince Genji and his ambitious rival, Tō no Chūjō, was described in terms of a highly competitive dance performance, after which the audience judged Genji's performance aesthetically superior. In this way, political infighting among the emperor's courtiers was sometimes symbolically represented as intense ambition for recognition as a connoisseur of more sophisticated aesthetic tastes.

The Court as the Gatekeeper

A number of institutions developed within the imperial court for the purposes of judging the aesthetic quality of artistic productions and performances. Among the various cultural activities of the court, the compilation of the *chokusen-shū*, or official anthologies of *waka* verse, was considered one of the emperor's most important undertakings. Beginning with the *Kokinwaka-shū* at the beginning of the tenth century, there were ultimately twenty-one anthologies commissioned by a succession of emperors. The *chokusen-shū* set the standard for the quality of *waka* verse. The greatest honor that a poet could receive was to have his or her work included in an imperial anthology. The poets who were appointed as the editors of an anthology would inevitably exercise the greatest authority over the entire field of poetry.

In this way, the formation of a court society that was aesthetically cultivated led to an intense concern for aesthetic quality and authority. The cultivated grace of *waka* poetry extended the aesthetic capacities of the native Japanese language to their fullest extent. An excellent artistic performance, including the composition of poetry, was simultaneously perceived as an act of moving "heaven and earth"(*Kokinwaka-shū kanajō* or "Preface in *Kana* letters")[15] because it gave the gods pleasure.

This observation by itself, however, does not fully explain the important and complex position of Japanese poetry in the ancient court society. *Waka*, which literally means "Japanese songs," was regarded as personal and private poetry compared with the official Chinese styles of writing. As the term indicates, *waka* was composed primarily with native Japanese terms and expressed in indigenous *kana* phonetic letters, and it was contrasted specifically with Chinese poetry written in Chinese ideograms. In the Heian court, official legal and administrative documents were written in Chinese ideograms. Since Japanese was a completely different linguistic system from Chinese, the Chinese characters as ideograms were limited in their ability to express the natural flow of emotion in the Japanese language. The phonetic *kana* characters, which were called *on-nade* or "women's hand," allowed for a much fuller expression of indigenous Japanese terms, concepts, and personal emotion than the Chinese ideograms. Thus, *waka* poetry in a form of writing as well as in its contents was also understood as representing the culture of "Japaneseness." Only with the maturation and sophistication of *waka* poetry written in *kana* letters, Japanese language developed into a sophisticated language fully capable of expressing literary consciousness and delicate sensitivity. In this sense, the importance of *waka* poetry in the court lay not simply in poetry's symbolic and ritual function as a technology of transformation; the poetry was formative to articulate the collective identity of Japan compared with that of China. It was in such a context that men and women of the imperial court regarded the making of *waka* poetry as their essential means of social communications.

In a court society of this type, the organization of the court and aesthetic practice inevitably overlapped. For instance, the tradition of poetry competition (*uta awase)* in the Heian period (794–1192) was practiced within the court itself. It represented an integral and important dimension of life within the imperial circle.[16] Thus, although this form of poetry was used as a means of socialization, the social usages of courtly poetry should be distinguished from the private circles of aesthetic socialization that characterized the later period. The aesthetic form of socialization in the Heian period was a court-centered "courtesy" (in the sense of Norbert Elias's distinction, in contrast to "civility," which is defined as good behavior expected of everyone) in which even intimate relations between a man and woman could have serious political implications.

Linked Poetry: The Prototype of Japanese Aesthetic Publics

The development of forms of aesthetic socialization outside the court society signified the arrival of a social reality in which the imperial court's political and cultural grip over the rest of Japanese society was in decline. At the same time, various social forces and networks outside the court began to accumulate artistic and cultural capital. The increasing decentralization of political power in the late medieval period encouraged local economic initiatives that facilitated the development of cultural circles outside the elegant but formal imperial court. In contrast to the refined formality of the courtly *waka* poetry tradition, the *za* arts that matured during the late medieval period developed as ritual technologies for the consecration of a space of discourse that nullified the rules of sociability derived from formal political relationships. In other words, the spaces for *za* arts began to be regarded as separate from the rest of formal political society.

Among the various *za* art forms, it was clearly linked poetry (*renga*) that shaped the image of the *za* arts.[17] It articulated the essence of *za* earlier than the emergence of theories in the other *za* arts, such as the tea ceremony or flower arranging. Since the composition of linked verse is no longer widely practiced in modern Japan, however, it is hard for contemporary Japanese even to imagine the social and cultural significance of linked poetry in traditional Japanese culture.[18] The delights and satisfactions of participation in aesthetic publics were summarized by one enthusiast's claim that "nothing is more fun than doing *renga* (linked verse)" – a line that was given to the husband in a *kyōgen* comedy of the medieval period. In this play, the feisty wife threatens to leave her husband because he attends too many linked verse sessions and spends too much of their money doing so. After a major quarrel, the wife declares her intention to move out. To win her back, the husband recites a line of poetry – to which the wife wisely replies with a witty poem of her own. The couple is reconciled when the husband proposes to enjoy *renga* with his wife at home.[19]

Linked poetry was in essence performative literature. Nijō Yoshimoto (1320–1388)[20] noted the similarity between *renga* sessions and theatrical performances. "[Linked poetry is] just like dengaku or sarugaku [theatrical performances with dance music]. Since the essence of linked poetry lies in the enjoyment of a moment of *za*, the person who can make the *za* meeting exciting may be called a skillful poet."[21] The genuine pleasure that participants derived from *renga* sessions was an excitement born of unexpected encounters with other poets' contributions. Even poets who were not unusually gifted might produce lines of great insight from time to time. Each participant entered and explored an unmapped territory of cognitive associations through exchanges with the others in the session. As the chain of linked verse was built up line by line, the session participants would be caught up in a mood of rapturous enchantment.

Cherry Blossom Linked Verse

The origins of this form of poetry can be traced to a popular communal practice in the ancient world in which men and women in agrarian communities exchanged ritual poems on festival occasions. The imperial court embraced this poetic tradition in a more refined form during the Heian period. In the late Heian imperial anthologies of *waka* poetry, there appeared linked poems that were understood as miscellaneous *waka* styles. But although these linked forms of poetry were part of the literary tradition of the Heian court, linked verse had not yet developed the distinctive style, consciousness, and popularity that would blossom in the *za* literature of the later period. Around the beginning of the Kamakura period (1192–1333), however, the cultural climate underwent a marked change. Although the emperor's courtiers continued to enjoy their version of linked poetry, private circles of linked poetry enthusiasts (*jige renga*) grew up outside the court.

Around 1245–1250, during the reign of Emperor Gosaga, a curious literary fad began to attract the interest of the people of Kyoto. Every spring, as the cherry blossoms appeared in the courtyards of temples and shrines on the outskirts of the capital city, people came out of their homes to sit under the flowering trees and make linked poetry. The Cherry Blossom sessions were open to people of all status levels. There were courtly poets and vagabond poets, old and young, sitting side by side. The rise of the Cherry Blossom linked-poetry sessions in the mid-thirteenth century was one of the earliest representations of the spirit of the *za* arts that generated the enclaves of free aesthetic publics.

"The cherry blossoms in full bloom at Washio were so interesting, we played until the moon had set," one lady-in-waiting wrote in her diary.[22] During this period, linked-poetry sessions were sometimes held at night. Washio in Higashiyama is located in a suburb of Kyoto that is also known for its graveyards. On another occasion, a monk-poet started a session of linked poetry as the master of the ceremony by saluting the landscape of the session as follows:

> Under the cherry blossoms of Jishu,
>
>> Look, Spring!
>> White waterfall threads
>> of cherry blossoms
>
> – Zeshō
>
> (*Haru zo miru, shiroki wa taki no itozakura*)[23]

This opening stanza of a linked-verse sequence describes a setting in which the spring moonlight was illuminating the petals of the drooping cherry blossoms as if they were the white streams of a waterfall. Thus, the dreamy white petals of the cherry blossoms, as seen in a dim moonlit temple garden, helped to create a ritual space of otherworldliness.[24]

There were frequent records of open gatherings for the composition of linked verse at certain temples in Kyoto, including such temples and shrines as Bishamondō, Hōshouji, and Jishu-Gongen, which were known for hosting poetry sessions. This style of collective verse-making was therefore called *hana no moto renga*, or the Cherry Blossom Session of Linked Verse, and was widely practiced between the mid-thirteenth and mid-fourteenth centuries in open-air poetry meetings. The organizers of these Cherry Blossom linked-poetry sessions were usually Buddhist monks from lowly or modest social backgrounds. Many of these monks were known as *nenbutsu hijiri*, which means "*nenbutsu*-chanting monks." *Nenbutsu* refers to the chanting of the name of Amida Buddha, the Buddha of the Western Paradise. These monks often took care of funerals and graveyard work that touched upon the danger of pollution (*kegare*) associated with the dead.[25] The *nenbutsu*-chanting monks usually did not have a formal affiliation with an established sect or temple and simply wandered about.

The atmosphere of a Cherry Blossom session was intensely moving for its participants. The typical number of seated poets in a *za* session was not fixed but usually stood at around 10. Unlike the more formal linked-verse meetings of later periods, however, members of the audience that surrounded a circle of poets in a Cherry Blossom session were free to contribute their own poems to the circle. After one sequence of chain poems was made by seated members in the circle, the floor was open to the public. All the participants in the meeting would avidly search for the best follow-up verse, one after the other. Sometimes, dozens of poems were thrown in from the audience to provide the next stanza in a particularly difficult chain. When an unexpectedly interesting succeeding stanza was presented, the perceptive participants would be captivated by feelings of surprised exhilaration.

Mu'en and the Ritual Logic of Cherry Blossom Linked Poetry

The image of creating linked verse under the cherry blossoms in temple gardens challenges us to decode the ritual mechanisms that allowed the participants to suspend for a time the ordinary status boundaries. Closer observation of the operation of the Cherry Blossom sessions reveals the presence of multiple devices for creating spheres of *mu'en*, or "no relation." The word *mu'en* (*mu* means "absence" in literal English translation; *en* means "relationship"), originally a Buddhist term, implied the absence of a relationship to worldly constraints.

The symbolism of cherry blossoms, deeply embedded in the Japanese ethnomentality, offered an important ritual technology for making linked-verse sessions into *mu'en* spaces. This ritual dancing and singing in the spring under the full bloom of cherry blossoms may recall the cherry blossom viewing picnics so beloved by the modern Japanese. The medieval counterpart of the contemporary celebration, however, was more than a pleasant outdoor entertainment.

During cherry blossom season, medieval Japanese people performed a festival dance called *yasurai hana*, or "quieting blossoms," a ritual still carried out around many shrines in modern Japan. Men and women wearing festive costumes adorned with the pink flowers would dance and sing a song with the repeated refrain of *yasurai hana ya*, expressing their wish for a long cherry blossom season. This ritual was understood as a prayer for an abundant rice harvest – blossoms being a symbol of agricultural production – but also as an exorcism of the evils that caused epidemics. The earliest records of *yasurai hana* dancing pre-date the emergence of the cherry blossom linked-poetry sessions. In the fourth year of Ninnpei (1154), for example, *Ryōjinhishō kudenshū*, a famous compendium of *Imayō* folk songs compiled by retired emperor Goshirakawa-in (1127–1192), records that during that spring, "Men and women from Kyoto and its surroundings gathered at the Murasakino (Imamiya) shrine and enjoyed themselves by performing elegant dances (*fūryū*). They sang songs accompanied by flutes, drums and gongs, claiming that they were entertaining the gods."[26] This style of singing and dancing was quite distinctive and unlike any other popular music and dance styles of the time. Decorating their parasols with paper flowers, the people danced in their fashionable costumes to the clapping of hands. People from all class backgrounds and from every part of Kyoto came to see this springtime dancing.[27] The creation of festive ritual spaces during cherry blossom season had become a well-established custom by this time (Figure 3.1).

In Japanese folklore, cherry trees in blossom – especially the *shidare zakura*, or drooping cherry trees whose branches trail to the ground – symbolize the intersection of the land of the dead with the land of the living. The base of a cherry tree was also perceived in folklore as an entrance to the underworld. The ethnomentality of pre-modern Japan associated cherry blossom petals blown by the wind with storms caused by the spirits of the angry dead, or *goryō*.[28] The enraged spirits of the *goryō* were perceived to be the source of misfortune and disaster; a number of rituals existed for pacifying the *goryō*. The cheerful celebration of cherry blossom season with music, dance, and poetry, the antecedent of the modern cherry blossom viewing parties, originated in a ritual for pacifying the spirits of the underworld.[29] Thus, cherry trees were cosmic trees that connected this world with the other world.

The cherry trees blooming in the courtyards of temples and shrines signified that these places were *mu'en* in a sense of Amino Yoshihiko that they had no relation to the present world order because they were associated with the other world. In Amino's now classic work, *Mu'en,*

Figure 3.1. Dancing for the Cherry Blossoms. *Hanami Takagari Byōbuzu* by Unkoku Tōgan. Momoyama period, late sixteenth century. The medieval custom of *yasurai hana* (quieting the blossoms) is a ritual that is still observed at many shrines in modern Japan. Tōgan has depicted the elegant *fūryū* dance under the cherry blossoms.

Kugai, Raku (literally, "No Relationships, Public Area, Free Trade"), he used these indigenous medieval terms as key words in the presentation of a fresh and subversive image of medieval Japan.[30] In addition to the notion of *mu'en* (no relation) that I mentioned earlier, medieval Japanese people frequently used these words to describe the function of sanctuaries or other kinds of free space that were not under the direct control of higher political and economic authorities. For example, the term *kugai* (*ku* means "public" and *gai* means "realm") first originated in Zen temples and implied that a specific area and building were set aside for public use. Later, some temples that had socially recognized rights of immunity were also spoken of as *kugai*. From this usage, the term started to acquire a more general sense, according to Amino, "to refer to the domain of *kō* [public] that had nothing to do with the power of the state, but was related to *seken* [imagined community, society]; *kugai* is society's public."[31] The concept of *kugai* (public realm) or *mu'en* was associated with such places as markets, burial grounds, and riverbanks, as well as with such persons as traders and journeymen.[32]

In this sense, it was fitting that the Cherry Blossom linked-verse sessions were organized by such *nenbutsu hijiri* as Zenna because these monks not only renounced the world but also frequented funerals and grave-yards, the realm of the dead. They were persons who typified *mu'en* in that their bodies and very existence were sites of no-relation. *Mu'en* re-ferred to sacred places but also to such spaces as markets, trading posts, bridges, riverbanks, and graveyards. Bridges represented physical con-nections and geographical boundaries. Graveyards were the realm of the dead, in which the living communicated with their ancestors during fu-nerary rituals. Thus, *mu'en* spaces offered a kind of asylum at places of boundary intersection as spheres for transformation.

Because of the public, open, and *mu'en* nature of these poetry meetings, one record indicates that even "In,"[33] a retired emperor, visited a Cherry Blossom session as an individual participant. *Tsukuba shū* (1356), the first anthology of *renga*, includes a line of poetry with the explanation: "A poem composed on the occasion of the secret visit of the In's carriage under the cherry blossoms at Washio."[34] Predictably, the observation of hierarchical codes of courtesy appropriate to the formal order of feudal society was not required at the *hana no moto renga* meeting. The atmo-sphere of a Cherry Blossom linked-verse session was cheerful, playful, and easygoing. The master of ceremonies that day was a poet named Zenna, a *nenbutsu hijiri* and a leader of popular *renga* circles. A legend tells us that Zenna was drunk on that particular occasion and attempted to open the bamboo blinds on His Majesty's carriage, an incredible impertinence for a lowly monk on the fringes of polite society. The emperor generously tolerated Zenna's misbehavior.

The cherry blossoms were symbols of transformation, nodal points of this world and the other world, thus offering a perfect site for the creation of *mu'en* publics. The ritual of composing poetry under cherry blossoms not only shaped the later development of linked poetry but also most clearly articulated the essence of medieval aesthetic publics as creations of voluntary and horizontal association through the mechanism of *mu'en* symbolism.

The various usages of *kugai* and *mu'en* seem to indicate that *kugai* (public realm) emerged in medieval Japan at the intersection of multiple networks that permitted participants to uncouple from existing dominant ties. At one end of this intersection was the realm of the sacred, the world of the dead. *Kugai* thus represented the location of a public that allowed participants to shift their connections to the sacred. In so doing, the participants in *kugai* publics could uncouple from their secular feudal ties (*mu'en*) and form more horizontal ties with other participants. The terms *kugai* and *mu'en* were thus functionally connected.

In a similar way, the markets (usually held on particular days at this point in history) of medieval Japan were originally located at the intersection of this world and the other world in that they were held in front of temples during festivals. Furthermore, markets were spheres of transformation in that a commodity could be transformed into something different through exchange. Bridges represented physical connections and geographical boundaries. A poetic description of this concept is reflected in a legendary saying that "a market should be established at the rainbow's end."[35] People built shrines to the god of the marketplace. Katsumata Shizuo has described how the exchanges in these markets were regarded: "[B]oth sellers and buyers came to the marketplace and dedicated their goods to the deities. The gods then gave the exchanged goods to them."[36] In sum, *mu'en* spaces offered a kind of publicness at places of boundary intersection as spheres for transformation.

Earlier in this book, I sociologically redefined *publics* as sites of communicative spheres that emerge at the intersection of multiple network systems. It follows from this definition that there can be no more effective site to create alternative realities than connecting this world with the otherworldly. To claim that a space set apart for aesthetic socialization is a sphere for communication with the world of the sacred was the most effective reason why the participants in artistic performances could set aside the rules of socialization that apply to encounters in this world. At the ultimate junction of two domains of cognitive networks, the sacred and profane, there emerged a communicative sphere in which the norms of worldly constraints no longer mattered. This association of art and the sacred in the popular mentality may help to clarify the ritual procedures and symbolism of Cherry Blossom linked poetry. The drooping cherry blossom trees in the temple yard symbolized the entrance to the beyond. The oral performances of reciting poems one after another celebrated the moment of transformation from the profane to the sacred. It was in their connection with the realm of the sacred that the medieval performing arts derived their power to suspend the norms of the secular social order.

The Performing Arts and the Realm of the Sacred

The ritual symbolism of cherry blossoms as a bridge between this world and the next was deeply rooted in the popular mindset in which the performing arts and the realm of the gods were closely conjoined. We must note the fact that the Buddhist temples as well as the Shintō shrines were powerful socio-political forces throughout this period. The true vitality of medieval Japanese people's religiosity, however, was expressed in their ardent longing to touch and feel the presence of a world that they could not see. During an artistic performance, the audience felt that they shared the performance space with the sacred, that they were in the presence of the unseen and spiritual. For example, a medieval folk story gives us a vivid image of medieval people who regarded an artistic performance as a holy act. The story goes roughly as follows.

Shōkū, a famous priest who was deeply involved in the training at the Shosha mountain, wished to see the Fugen bodhisattva, or holy existence, who had postponed entering Nirvana in order to help other people reach enlightenment. Shōkū was shown in a dream that the leader of the courtesans in Eguchi, a port on the Yodo River, was the Fugen bodhisattva. Shōkū rushed to the courtesan's house in Eguchi. The leader of the courtesans was playing a *tsuzumi* drum and singing a popular *imayō* (literally, "Contemporary style") song with a group of party guests. Her song, in slightly free translation, runs as follows:

> In Subo there is a triple mansion
> Where without windy intervention
> The inner washbowl knows no tension
> Yet sports these little waves that ripple

Taken by her performance, as Shōkū closed his eyes, he saw the courtesan turned into Fugen bodhisattva, riding on a white elephant and uttering Buddhist truths in a beautiful voice:

> In the ocean of unimpeded true reality
> Where no winds of desire ever blow
> Waves of true suchness never cease to arise spontaneously[37]

(See note 37 for original Japanese.)

The image of wavelets in the popular song was transposed into a sacred phrase, *zuien shinnyo*, which means "ever-flowing enlightenment in every moment of existence." When Shōkū opened his eyes, he saw only the performing courtesan again. When he closed his eyes once more, she became the image of the bodhisattva.[38]

The image of wavelets in this story reflects the way that courtesans did business in the medieval period. These women often lived in towns that had grown into sea and river ports. Eguchi was a river port between Osaka and Kyoto. The courtesans of Eguchi solicited customers from their boats on the rippling water of the river. The poetic image of the transformation of a courtesan into Fugen bodhisattva, in particular the transposition of an image of wavelets into a Buddhist sacred phrase, symbolized "the existence of courtesans who mediate the sacred and profane through their performances, and of the role of performing arts in medieval society," in the words of the Japanese historian Abe Yasurō.[39]

Performing artists in the medieval period were assigned the task of entertaining, celebrating, and placating the gods. Although medieval performing artists were usually considered marginal people, they were also thought to have a special ability as go-betweens, joining this world and the world to come. Through the act of performing, or even being present as a spectator as in Shōkū's case, one could lift oneself above the plane of profane reality to the realm of the sacred. The notion of identity transformation in the act of performing and the function of connecting different worlds became important cultural resources in the formulation of the ritual logic of aesthetic socialization in later periods of Japanese history.

Fresh Wind from the Margins

Nonetheless, if the Japanese performing arts had become too closely attached to the realm of the sacred, the arts and literature would have been subordinated to religious interests. There are numerous examples in world cultures of performing arts that were intended solely to glorify the religion that patronized them. In these instances, religious goals and values tended to control the artists and conceded less autonomy to purely aesthetic activities. The high level of development of the Japanese performing arts and their evolution into alternative modes of private socialization might not have taken place if aesthetic values and standards had subserved purely religious ends. In fact, the arts might well have taken this course of development in medieval Japan since many artists' organizations in the late ancient and early medieval world originated as troupes of performers under the patronage of certain great temples and shrines.

In a similar fashion, the central position of the emperor's court in setting aesthetic tastes and standards virtually guaranteed a tendency toward exclusivity. As I explained earlier, the imperial power and the realm of the beautiful were closely associated because the latter was considered a ritual source of the emperor's power. Since aesthetic socialization was central to the operation of the court society, even members of the rising samurai class initially had difficulty gaining admission to it. In other words, from a sociological and organizational viewpoint, both the religious authorities and the sovereign might well have developed an exclusivist mindset that would have favored a closed circuit of aesthetic networks rather than an open circuit.

In contrast, the atmosphere of the *za* arts, as epitomized by the social networks of the Cherry Blossom linked-poetry sessions, was relatively open, egalitarian, and temporary. It was reminiscent of the ancient etymological root of "public" (*ōyake*), which meant "common to all." Socializing with the other people in a *za* circle could be *a transitory open-circuit experience* rather than becoming a member of an exclusive club. For example, the linked-poetry sessions often drew unexpected guests whose identities were unknown. To be sure, there were many possible forms that a gathering might take in the different *za* arts; some of the meetings could be very exclusive. Even so, however, there was an inexplicable spirit of lightness and playfulness in performances in the *za* arts. How did this sense of ephemeral lightness come into being?

I maintain that the involvement of marginal people in the medieval performing arts was an important factor in creating the atmosphere of playfulness and openness. No branch of the performing arts in the medieval period can be fully understood without an appreciation of the social dynamics of these subpopulations. The aesthetic publics of medieval Japan gained a new locus and function through the activities of performing artists who were categorized as socially marginal. Medieval Japanese society was enriched by the robust activities of marginal social groups whose social functions differed greatly. They are sometimes simply called "outcasts" in English but were classified or called by a variety of names in Japanese. Such marginal people as the *hinin* (literally, "non-person"), *kiyome* (purifiers), *kawara-mono* (riverbank people), and *inujinin* (dog shrine attendants) – those whose occupations required them to deal with ritual pollution (*kegare*) during funerals, executing criminals, making leathers, and similar occasions – could be considered *mu'en* persons. These groups of marginal people also included craftspeople,[40] dancers, musicians and other performing artists, shamans, magicians, gamblers, courtesans, and beggars. They were also outside the order of agricultural communities. For example, the *kawara-mono* were originally people who performed funerals and various cleaning jobs on riverbanks. Japanese riverbeds were often used as graveyards and as sites for executing criminals, and therefore were considered *mu'en* spaces, but they were also used as spaces for theatrical performances.[41] Although people in these marginal subpopulations labored under increasing discrimination, in particular during the late medieval period, they were at the same time thought to have a supernatural ability to cleanse the environment.[42] In contrast, the *kugutsu* (puppeteers) were a group of marginal entertainers who traveled extensively. Female *kugutsu* were often the kept women of wealthy men, but they also made names for themselves as skilled dancers and singers of the popular music of the time. Even the Nō plays, which eventually became an aristocratic art, originated with the Sarugaku *za* troupes of marginal people from Yamato province. Such troupes as Yūzaki-za and Emai-za emerged in villages that were known as *shōmoji* (popular monk-like performers) communities.[43]

The study of these marginal subpopulations has taken center stage amidst the exciting developments in medieval scholarship in Japan over the last few decades. Consequently, the study of the medieval marginal people's groups, their origins, statuses, functions, and evolution has been one of the most debated areas in contemporary Japanese historical scholarship. It is not my intention to engage or to review the complexities of the discussion of this subject here. However, the finding that these various "outcasts" were empowered in their own ways as groups during the early medieval period, and that they played significant political and military roles, changed the image of the medieval polity. Rather than simply being marginalized, paradoxically it was their very marginality that was a source of their power.[44] For the purpose of my argument, however, it is important to note the paradoxical nature of the existence of these marginal populations; they were usually directly patronized and controlled by either the emperor's court or the great temples and shrines, but, at the same time, they were often considered as people in the public realm (*kugai*), outside the local feudal order of society. If they were connected with the emperor or religious institutions, were they simply subordinates of these great institutions? If that is the case, how could their involvements in the arts bring a fresh wind to medieval arts? First of all, not all marginal groups were tightly affiliated with religious or secular authorities; the degree of attachment and incorporation also differed greatly among the various groups. Furthermore, most marginal people were economically independent through their trading activities, but they valued the exclusive privileges they received from the authorities because these privileges gave them economic advantages over their competitors. More importantly, their trading often required extensive travel across various feudal boundaries. By forming *za*-like groups and seeking the patronage of temples and other powerful institutions, these people obtained privileges and sacred images that made it easier for them to travel while earning their living. Unlike the more settled agricultural population, their boundary-crossing lifestyle was not easily governed by the local political authorities. Since they were always "outsiders" to the local established order, both as travelers and as those who were connected with the sacred realm, they were often exempted from local taxations. Mythological conceptions of marginality empowered the groups that were allowed to trespass boundaries, such as outcasts, courtesans, entertainers, and shamans, and to establish domains of public realm (*kugai*). Thus, by introducing these sacred outsiders from the realm of marginality, the space for the *za* arts itself became the public realm. The ritual logic of freedom in aesthetic publics would not have been complete without the involvement of marginal people.

The presence of these marginal performers in aesthetic gatherings, or the use of symbols that invited associations with *mu'en*, served as a reminder that participants had to leave behind their worldly identities when joining *za* art practices. For example, the *kasagi renga*, the "linked-verse sessions with bamboo hats," were held continuously throughout the medieval period and even under the Tokugawa shogunate.[45] Costumes, hats, hairstyles, and other decorative items symbolized an array of status categories in this period.[46] Amino Yoshihiko has remarked on the distinctive symbolism of bamboo (or rush) hats in this specific context. Hats made from plant fibers were often worn by such marginal people as the *hinin* (literally, "no person") and the *yamabushi* (mountain monks).[47] By wearing an item of clothing associated with marginal persons, the participants in the linked-verse sessions could temporarily transform themselves into persons outside the feudal order. Wearing these hats symbolized the renunciation of their "official" names and status in the outside world.[48]

The reader should recall the fact that to complete the no-relation sphere, the marginal people were also the agents who organized the Cherry Blossom poetry meetings. In the early stages of these springtime sessions, the organizers and leading participants were often the so-called *nenbutsu hijiri*, or "*nenbutsu*-chanting monks." They were located on the outskirts of social respectability, but those who engaged in these occupations that touched upon the dead were also considered to be *mu'en* persons endowed with special power to handle the danger of pollution (*kegare*) from contact with the dead. After the rise of the Jishū sect (1274), whose main practices also included chanting and wandering from one town to the next, the same function was often undertaken by the *nenbutsu*-chanting monks of this sect. The Jishū sect of Buddhism was founded by Ippen (1239–1289), a monk known for his radical renunciation of the world. The Jishū monks made a significant contribution to many fields in the performing arts during the medieval period, most notably the composition of linked verse, but also *Nō* drama, the tea ceremony, and storytelling.[49]

Two of the elements that constituted Jishū practice are critical to understanding the sect's strong association with the performing arts. The first is its emphasis on the body and performance. Ippen and his followers were known for their fervent practice of energetic dance combined with chanting. The surviving drawings of Ippen's practice depict Jishū traveling missions, in which the monks and nuns are shown together dancing in ecstasy while jumping and kicking in a circular pattern expressing their religious feeling in bodily movement. One critic of the Jishū practice described their practice as follows:

> In chanting *nenbutsu*, they shake their heads and move their shoulders as if they were wild horses. They are as noisy as mountain monkeys. Neither the men nor the women hide their private parts. (*Tengu Zōshi*, "[the Illustration of Mountain Goblins]")[50]

The more socially respectable Buddhist sects considered the Jishū practice of dancing in religious ecstasy as reckless and immoral. Unlike the philosophically more sophisticated and austere Zen aesthetic, the Jishū sect's contribution to the arts, including linked poetry, was more closely related to the dynamics of bodily performance and to popular culture. In fact, the influences of Zen and Jishū on the medieval performing arts were complementary – two energetic sources of inspiration that existed in uneasy tension.[51] Since the Jishū monks traveled around Japan, performing their dances and chants in various places, they were also responsible in large measure for popularizing linked verse in the more remote provinces. To be sure, not all the organizers and major poets of the Cherry Blossom sessions were Jishū priests, yet the close association between the Jishū sect and the composition of linked verse is clear from the historical record. In addition, the documents indicate that almost all the medieval performing arts included professional artists whose monastic names were common in the Jishū sect.[52]

The marginal status of the Jishū sect was the second important point of connection with the performing arts. Large, established Buddhist temples of this period were components of the medieval feudal power structure. In contrast, the Jishū monks were marginal persons, not simply because they renounced the political order and social norms of their feudal culture but because this sect was open to members of the particularly marginal population, including the *hinin* outcasts.[53] Thus, the socially ambivalent position of the Jishū sect, as well as its affinity with performative dance and religious chanting, made its monks the ideal organizers of the aesthetic enclaves of linked-verse sessions.[54]

The sacred stigma of marginality to medieval performing arts served as a double-edged sword. These marginal subpopulations often suffered from social discrimination. On the other hand, their position as *mu'en* persons gave them access to people of high rank because they were exempt from the standard operating procedures of the medieval status hierarchy. For example, when Zeami, a famous Nō performer, was still a young boy, the shogun Ashikaga Yoshimitsu (1358–1408) fell in love with this beautiful, talented youth and always had Zeami with him on public occasions. The shogun's favoritism invited criticism from the court, as is evident from a contemporary source: "They sit together and share food. These entertainers are no better than beggars. It is considered socially improper for the shogun to admire this child to the point that he is always in his company."[55] Thus, many branches of performing arts subsequently attempted to increase their respectability by refining and gentrifying their aesthetic qualities while toning down an emphasis on their magical roots.

Nonetheless, if the arts of medieval Japan had lacked the influence and the boundary-crossing experiences of the marginal subpopulations, they might not have embodied the lightness and freedom that made them so appealing to a wide range of men and women. The *mu'en* people gave the *za* arts their popular roots and connected them to both the highest and lowest strata of society. In other words, the *mu'en* people were like a fresh breeze stirring the waters of established medieval Japanese society. Their involvements brought in the refreshing energy and unpredictability of these arts and literary forms.

Conclusion

I have attempted to analyze the origin of a unique tradition in Japanese culture that reshaped a number of indigenous art forms and simultaneously facilitated the process of socialization as well as the intensification of aesthetic expression. In essence, the dynamic development of the *za* arts as central to refined aesthetics in Japan originally emerged from the interaction of four domains of social and cognitive networks: (1) the performing arts' social and symbolic connection with the realm of the sacred; (2) the refined cultural tradition of the emperor's court society; (3) a new set of corporate and voluntary associations that were more horizontal in their structures, such as the *za* guilds; and (4) the contributions of marginal people who exemplified the concept of *mu'en*. In fact, the intersection of these four cultural and social networks made possible this unique form of poetry.

As we have seen, the connection with sacredness was clearly a force that made the spaces for *za* meetings into ritual enclaves of freedom. On the other hand, this dimension of popular religion by itself would have been insufficient to shape the influential art forms into refined versions suitable for civic socialization. Without the influence of the sophisticated cultural resources and prestige of the court society, however, the *za* arts might not have impacted Japanese aesthetics so profoundly. Conversely, the influence of the court culture alone would not have fostered the development of the *za* arts outside elite circles. The *za* arts and poetry emerged at the time when the emperor's court society was in decline, while social powers outside the court began to accumulate cultural capital. The spirit of the *za* arts and poetry resembled the organizational culture of *za* organizations characterized by relatively horizontal associations. Without the medieval social-organizational developments that valued the ritual technologies of horizontal networking, the *za* arts might not have spread so extensively at the popular level. At the same time, these *za* organizations as well as feudal social relations in general emphasized the ritual solidarities of corporate members, resulting in a tendency toward exclusivism. If the contributions of the marginalized subpopulations had played no role in shaping the traditions of the *za* arts, it is doubtful whether these arts could have incorporated the powerful ritual technologies associated with the concept of *mu'en*. By claiming a connection with the realm of the sacred, these marginal subpopulations could create openings within the feudal status order that allowed some fresh air into a categorical order of society. Thus, linked poetry as an aesthetic public strategically located itself at the intersection of four cognitive and social network systems to generate spheres of freedom.

Once they emerged as an aesthetic style, the *za* arts had an enduring effect on the subsequent development of Japanese culture. They not only represented and popularized distinctive aesthetic sensitivities but also offered the Japanese society an important organizational model for networking. Their logic of creating temporary "no-relation" spaces by ritualistically creating connections with the other world became a useful cultural resource for forming voluntary horizontal associations.

Aside from such intersections of several institutions, there are noteworthy personal and inner dimensions of those individuals who participated in the aesthetic gatherings. The rise of *za* arts cultivated the minds and bodies of Japanese people in a distinctive way; aesthetic practices were translated into self-cultivating experiences, but this focus on a self did not imply isolation, on the contrary, self-cultivation took place through socialization. A human being is a socializing being and cannot develop and enrich his or her selfhood in splendid isolation. A solitary mindset alone cannot easily break through one's received view and sense of identity to elevate itself to a new realm of consciousness. Even a devotee in a contemplative religion who trains his or her mind in isolation constantly seeks to hear the voices from holy human beings and deities in order to overcome his or her own perceived and felt limits in religious practice. The logic of linked poetry produced a distinctive method of transcending the limit of an individual mind by deeply interacting with other poets. The pleasure of linked poetry lies in producing unexpected chains of poetic developments from moment to moment in a process that intensely challenges the limit of each individual's cognitive associations at every turn in stanza connections. In concrete terms, it was the artistic stimulus and inspiration from other participants in a meeting that managed to effect a breakthrough with respect to the aesthetic limitations of an individual poet. Whenever the synergy of intense collaboration yielded beautiful, refreshing, and unpredicted chains of linked verses, medieval people actually felt the force of the invisible world allowing them to break through their limits. Thus, medieval aesthetic publics as sites of *mu'en* (no relation) were established not only socially; they were strongly felt, personally and internally, by participants as the place to open a circuit to communicate with the realm of the invisible.

With a sense of exhilaration, people sometimes felt the workings of otherworldly forces in their moments of aesthetic performing. It was in this sense that medieval people found their aesthetic self-cultivating experiences to be parallel to religious experiences. Later, during the Tokugawa period, some branches of Japanese arts became more and more distant from their medieval religious and mythological roots. Even so, the mentality to learn and to perform traditional arts and poetry for the purpose of self-cultivation remained strong throughout Japanese history.

For understanding the internal and social experiences, the voice of a practitioner and critic of poetry may be helpful. Ōoka Makoto, a well-known modern Japanese poet who promotes and practices the art of linked verse in contemporary settings, explains this dual dynamics:

> In the actual setting of synergistic collaboration, only those poets who were acutely aware of the necessity of returning to a solitary mindset [*koshin*] were able to create astonishing pieces of poetry. Yet, when the poet was confined to the isolation of his or her own mind, his or her poetry lost its luminous color. As long as a significant degree of tension and conflict exists between the poet's desire for synergistic participation and the desire to return to his or her isolated mind, the resulting poetry will shimmer with rare luminosity.[56]

True art does not exist without a group; at the same time, real poetry is forged in the poet's solitary self-discipline outside the group. Artistic communities do not flourish apart from each participant's struggle to develop his or her own poetic voice in solitude. Anchored in such a deepened sense of individuality, which was further polished through social interactions, the *za* arts conjoined the dimensions of the aesthetic, sociability, and self-cultivation on multiple levels.

The medieval origin of Japanese aesthetic publics highlights the ritual logic of freedom embedded in these art forms that emerged at the point of intersection of many levels of social and cognitive networks. As a courtier, warrior, merchant, or wandering marginal person, an individual temporarily joined those meetings while carrying many prior attachments in the form of social and cognitive network constraints. To create a community of poets out of these individuals, it was necessary to decouple them from their existing constraints.

Japanese aesthetic publics consciously encouraged people to decouple from their existing ties in order to enter new communicative spheres. Only by switching their normal social and cognitive networks to the horizontal structure of the *za* meeting could participants in an aesthetic public connect with others as equal individuals. The medieval aesthetic spaces characterized by the ritual logic of *mu'en* (no relation) spaces were in fact filled with a set of intersecting networks. These not only connected the self with other individuals but also conjoined this world and the other world. In this sense, the *mu'en* space was in fact a space of *u'en* (literally, "the presence of relations") itself. It is from this intersection of social and cognitive network relations on multiple levels that the prototypical features of a distinctive Japanese aesthetic emerged.

In the following chapter, we look more closely at the maturation of the *za* arts in the late medieval world within the context of the rise and consolidation of the samurai's political power and the transformation of Japanese associational life.

4

The Late Medieval Transformation of Za Arts in Struggles between Vertical and Horizontal Alliances

The late medieval period in Japan was characterized by the dissolution of central authorities and political hierarchies. By this time, the ancient authority – the imperial court in Kyoto – had been seriously eroded by the emerging power of the samurai, the warrior class. The regional military houses – the samurai lords – were strengthening their grip on their lands and increasing their power and wealth. The members of this warrior class, however, were also having difficulties consolidating their power. Unlike the Kamakura shogunate (1192–1333), which was still able to maintain control over loose but coherent networks of samurai vassals, the comparatively weak Muromachi shogunate (1336–1573) had no possibility of building a stable national hierarchy among the samurai. On the other hand, as the decline of the emperor's prestige and power became apparent, the political and legal framework of the *shōen* (estate) landholding system weakened considerably.

None of the authorities of the period was strong enough to guarantee the continuation of the feudal landholding system. Since there was no reliable framework for the protection of properties and security, there were constant attempts to reconstruct and revise the relationships between patrons and clients. It was not only the master–follower relationships among the samurai warriors that were in flux. From the corporate villages to the craft guilds, late medieval people experimented with organizing themselves in various ways, always with the intention of finding better sources of protection. A bird's-eye view of late medieval Japanese society reveals a pattern of numerous clusters of networks whose organizing principles were highly dissimilar to one another. In other words, the late medieval period was an era of uncertainty filled with conspiracies, betrayals, and open armed competition.

This uneasy era, characterized by continuous political quarrels and sword-rattling, was at the same time the golden age of the *za* arts and poetry. This period also marked a point of departure for some of the performing arts from their ancient connection with magical forces that were closely associated with various categories of marginal people. While medieval people continued to experience and express strong emotions through their participation in frenzied festive performances, a more controlled and sophisticated form of aesthetic life was also emerging. The late medieval era was a period in which many branches of what are now considered "traditional Japanese arts" established their mature artistic styles. From the tea ceremony and flower arranging to linked poetry and *Nō* drama, the most traditional art forms achieved their stylistic self-definition in this period. It was not only that these artistic and poetic genres achieved a higher level of aesthetic sophistication; in addition, the participants developed a clearer perception of the process of socialization itself as an aesthetic activity.

For example, the act of offering a guest a cup of tea, which might be regarded as a simple gesture of hospitality in other cultures, began to assume the proportions of a major art form. Late medieval tea artists not only selected their tea utensils with great care and decorated their tearooms with exquisite attention to detail but also designed teahouses and their surrounding gardens as expressions of their high aesthetic standards.

The modern dichotomy between performers and audience did not strictly apply to these participatory art forms. The relationship between patrons and artists was also modified by the fact that both were considered participants in aesthetic publics; they were not categorized into separate groups of financial supporters and creative spirits. Some patrons were also known for their expert knowledge of the performing arts and poetry. The space and resources that these connoisseurs provided for aesthetic socialization transformed the culture of the Japanese salons of this period. The *za* arts became firmly institutionalized under the Muromachi shoguns, establishing a sophisticated level of taste as well as specific artistic idioms and codes that influenced Japanese culture for centuries to come. After the prototypical formulation of the ritual logic of aesthetic freedom, the late medieval development of spheres of aesthetic socialization became an element in the transformation of the Japanese state and of interpersonal associational networks.

Two Organizational Principles

When the established forms of patron–client relationships and the legal framework of the Japanese landholding system began to crumble, the regional samurai as well as the common people experimented with new forms of hierarchical or horizontal alliances to protect their own interests and security. The development and proliferation of the *za* arts during this period were conditioned by two opposing principles of political organization: the vertical integration of people into a unified political system through the reconstruction of coherent national hierarchies; and the formation of horizontal associational networks intended to safeguard common interests. The expansion and elaboration of vertical social and political networks contributed to the process of state formation. The long-standing samurai tradition of master–follower relationships represented a hierarchical pattern of networking that usually offered a convenient way to consolidate local samurai power. Once the regional *daimyo*, or warlords, had succeeded in streamlining and merging various regional groups of samurai, they attempted to obtain exclusive control over their territories by reducing the autonomy of local corporate bodies.

On the other hand, the principle of horizontal forms of alliance also gained renewed vitality during the fifteenth and sixteenth centuries. As we have seen, various forms of *za* associations such as craft guilds, territorially defined groups (e.g., *miyaza*, or shrine *za* in villages), and occupational groups of marginal people had an important historical role in early medieval Japan. In addition to the *za* organizations, however, other significant forms of horizontal networks emerged in the following centuries. For example, some villages grouped together to form *sōson*, which were corporate hamlets governed by their residents. The horizontal associations for mutual military protection were known as *ikki* (leagues). Some regional samurai sought to form mutual protection alliances among their peers through sharing rather than fighting over common interests. Under a sacred oath, the samurai signed a contract and formed a horizontal alliance. Soon, *ikki* became a popular form of self-defense network among village people as well as samurai. Those who formed *ikki* were able to manipulate competing local powers while at the same time organizing themselves in order to gain a measure of autonomy. The history of political organizations in late medieval Japan can be interpreted from a sociological perspective as a large-scale struggle between vertical and horizontal networking principles.[1]

The reader should recall the transformation of the native Japanese term for the public, *ōyake*, which originally signified a large storehouse for harvest produce. Of the two meanings of *ōyake*, the one addresses the commonality of the community, while the other points to the authority of the chief – the latter predominating with the emergence of the Japanese emperor system. Yet, in the actual practices of Japanese people, the "bottom-up" notion of the public never really died out. In fact, through strengthening the autonomous power of such medieval horizontal associations as the guilds, villages, and cities, as well as through creating ritual technologies that suspended the feudal order, medieval Japanese people gained a measure of protest for asserting their version of the public.[2]

The *za* arts shined most as a mechanism of creating aesthetic publics when they were implicitly and explicitly linked with the growing power of horizontal associations and alliances. The ritual logic of *za* arts and poetry, which brought about momentary experiences of egalitarian fellowship, had a strong affinity with the spirit that animated the horizontal networks. Of course, it was difficult to keep horizontally structured alliances reliable, given the uncertainties of the political situation. In the groups that gathered for performances of these arts, however, the mundane reality of power politics was temporarily put away.

On the other hand, the *za* arts and poetry did not function only to solidify existing associational ties. Rather, the aesthetic gatherings played a crucial role in allowing individuals to communicate with others outside their own groups. Although a shared enthusiasm for a particular art form does not form an immediate strong bond among its participants, it does encourage the formation of relationships outside the members' usual networks. In the fluid society of late medieval Japan, a setting in which people could not depend on their political alliances and hierarchical ties, they took very seriously the social networks created through contacts made in artistic gatherings. Thus, the samurai could be deeply involved in their usual politics of conspiracies, alliances, and betrayals at the same time that they were enthusiastic participants in the *renga* poetry meetings and the tea ceremony.

On the other hand, aesthetic socialization was also a useful tool for the powerful. By temporarily suspending the formalities of status distinction, the ruler could show favor to subordinates who had artistic skills and participated in the performing arts. As a result, the rulers tried to bring the realm of the beautiful within the scope of their power in a number of different ways. Professional performers in the *za* arts also valued the patronage of the powerful because it enhanced their artistic standing. In sum, the evolution of the za arts and the organizational transformation of medieval Japanese society were interrelated in a complex fashion.

The Topographical Shift of Japanese Publics

Kyoto, the Capital City

The establishment of the Muromachi shogunate in 1336 changed the cultural climate of the city of Kyoto. Unlike the shoguns of the Kamakura period, the Ashikaga shoguns situated their capital at Muromachi in

Kyoto, almost next door to the imperial court. Kyoto was governed by a military ruler for the first time in its history. The city was filled with samurai warriors, high and low. Not only the Ashikaga shogun and his family but his higher-ranking vassals, who had their own estates in the provinces, kept secondary houses in the capital city. According to one estimate, there were at least ten thousand mounted warriors living in Kyoto in the fourteenth century; they also brought their own retainers to the city.[3] Although the wealthier samurai absorbed the traditional culture of the imperial court, they also participated eagerly in the newer forms of aesthetic activities. In the fluid political situation of the period, the samurai were engaged in constant attempts to expand their networks of alliances. They developed a pattern of making their political contacts at banquets. Many of the performing arts flourished in the context of these banquets and evolved into more refined modes.

In addition, fourteenth-century Kyoto was beginning to emerge as a center of commerce and crafts production. A money economy developed and spread extensively for the first time in Japanese history during the thirteenth and fourteenth centuries. The examination of surviving trade contracts has made it clear that the use of *zeni* coins became common. Between 1284 and 1392, 563 (88%) of 641 surviving sales contracts were paid in *zeni*. Between 1393 and 1473, however, 531 (91%) out of 553 contracts were paid in *zeni*. Only 22 trade contracts were paid in rice in the later period.[4] Taxes to feudal lords were also generally paid in *zeni*. In addition, the number of different crafts, trades, and services that were offered multiplied, indicating the increasingly specialized division of labor in this society. Although the development of market mechanisms in this period was not as systematic as it became during the Tokugawa period, the flow of commodities and currency started to change the lifestyle of Muromachi society. Craftspeople and merchants organized themselves into various *za* guilds, seeking the protection of local temples and shrines in order to protect their interests against other feudal powers. They maintained constant vigilance in order to maintain their privileges against newcomers who tried to make inroads on their trading monopolies during this period. The self-government organizations of the Kyoto townspeople eventually grew out of these trade *za* organizations.[5]

The accumulation of wealth in and around the capital, and the concentration of the samurai houses in the city, attracted a number of performing artists. Most of them were marginal people who had organized themselves into *za* troupes. Paid performances (*kanjin*) were often held on the outskirts of Kyoto in such places as temples and the bed of the Kamo River, which had traditionally been regarded as *mu'en*, or no-relation, locations. There was a critical mass of potential spectators in Kyoto who were willing to pay to see some exciting artistic performances.

Festive Madness and Marginality

One example of the kind of group hysteria that could be stimulated by these events is a famous incident that took place in 1349 on the bank of the Kamo River at Shijyō (the forth street) known as Shijō *kawara* or Shijō Riverbank. A performance of the popular *Dengaku* dance brought the audience to a pitch of collective ecstasy. *Dengaku* can be translated literally as "rice paddy pleasure"; it originated in ancient agricultural rituals intended to thank the local gods for a good harvest. There were some amateur performers of *Dengaku* music and dance in Kyoto. By the time of the Muromachi shogunate, however, there were also two professional *za* troupes of *Dengaku* performers, the older one located in Kyoto and a new troupe, located in the city of Nara. Both troupes were scheduled to perform on the day in question. Numerous people from all ranks in society gathered for the performance, including the shogun, Ashikaga Takauji, and *Kanpaku* Nijō Yoshimoto, the highest ranking nobleman and a famous literati. The performers came on stage wearing unusual but splendid costumes and exhibited their skills in dance, music, and feats of acrobatic skill. When a boy of no more than eight or nine performed an acrobatic monkey dance wearing a mask – the monkey was a typical trickster figure in medieval Japan – the members of the audience roared with laughter and their excitement reached its peak. Suddenly, all 60 stands, which were full of happy spectators, collapsed. The final death toll was over a hundred.[6] The *Taiheiki*'s (Tale of the Grand Pacification) comment about this well-known incident blamed the rulers' excessive fondness for *Dengaku* theatrics for the fatal outcome. The shogun's enthusiasm for the performance was "not a good act," and it invited punishment from *Tengu*, a mountain goblin.[7]

This disaster, which is often cited in sources of the period, had a perfect mythological structure. The performing arts were rooted in ancient sources of magical ritual power. The riverbank itself was a marginal place for *mu'en* people to carry out their activities. It was like a potter's field – associated with the execution of criminals and the abandonment of unidentified corpses. As a result, the riverbank was considered *kegare*, or polluted; it was *mu'en*, outside of the regular order of things. The riverbank was a link with the other world, which might manifest itself at any time as a magical but dangerous power. The performing arts brought the invisible magical power to the surface, made it visible, and embodied it. Thus, the riverbank also became an ideal location for entertainment. When the ritual power inherent in the performing arts manifested itself as a subversive force that shook the world order, its appearance was usually considered dangerous for the ruler from the viewpoint of the social and political establishment. The critic who wrote the *Taiheiki* saw a subversive meaning in the collapse of the stands underneath an audience that represented the most powerful members of the Japanese nobility. The world order had been inverted by laughter and a monkey trickster performance, all because the shogun was too captivated by an art form that had a touch of madness in it.[8]

When the involvement of marginal people in an artistic performance led to a conjunction of marginality with the excitement of the eccentric performance itself, medieval Japanese people tended to think of mountain goblins and their evil deeds. The image of these malevolent mountain spirits overlapped with stereotypes of marginal people, whose hairstyles, dress, and way of life looked disturbingly deviant to the average observer. Performing artists had a social status in this period that was overlapping with, or only a short step removed from, that of the outcasts, who were simultaneously excluded from mainstream society yet regarded as bearers of sacred magical powers. Mass frenzy at artistic performances was a frequent occurrence during the medieval period. Not only the professional performers but ordinary people often engaged in agitated dancing on various occasions. This collective dancing fad, which was usually called *furyū*, involved people of both high and low standing, either as dancers or spectators. Occasionally, when this festive collective dancing stirred up radical passions, the explosive display of collective physical and emotional force threatened the established order. As we have seen, the period under consideration was characterized by the empowerment of horizontal forms of alliances among people known as *za, sōson,* and, in particular, *ikki*. The power of performing arts to induce people into alternative realities fueled and emboldened the social networks outside the established order (Figure 4.1). The mindset associated with this dancing mania was often described as *kuruu*, or "losing one's mind." A popular song of the period captured the mood:

> Who cares
> Whether you are serious or dull?
> Life is only a dream
> So just let yourself go wild!

> *(Nanishōzo, kusunde, Ichigo wa yumeyo, Tada kurue.)*
> *Kanginshū* (1518), an anthology of popular songs

The word *kurue* (go mad) in this popular song is a key to the medieval Japanese mentality. *Kuruu* was applied to excessive interest in and enthusiasm for gorgeous artistic spectacles; thus, the word implied a state of high emotional arousal accompanied by rapturous delight. The performing arts in Japan certainly derived a store of inexhaustible energy from their various relationships to madness, laughter, and marginality. In fact,

Figure 4.1. Manic Dancing. *Toyokuni Saireizu* by Iwasa Matabei. The Unification Period at the beginning of the seventeenth century. Mass frenzy at artistic performances was a frequent occurrence during the medieval period and a threat to the authorities. This painting depicts an episode of manic dancing that occurred at a memorial festival for Toyotomi Hideyoshi.

the association between the performing arts in Japan, including the *za* arts, and the ancient connection between magic and marginality is much more significant than the Western secondary literature in this area appears to recognize. And it was with this conjunction of magic, marginality, and passionate mentality of *kuruu* that mass frenzy dancing could be subversive and dangerous for the establishment.

On the other hand, if the performing arts in the medieval period had been too closely associated with sacred madness, they would not have been able to transform themselves into techniques of civilized socialization. Civility requires a certain degree of order and control; it is a mechanism that facilitates social contact among people from different backgrounds. A fit of collective hysteria could also bring people together at an artistic performance but on a different plane – within the force field of a dangerous subversive magical power – as the writer of the *Taiheiki* observed. If the performing arts had remained enmeshed with madness and marginality, they would have played only a limited role in the pre-modern transformation of Japanese culture. Here we must note a critical topographical shift in the performing arts in the late medieval period that moved the *za* arts and literary genres in the direction of greater rigor and control. In the process, some of the *za* art forms acquired greater cultural prestige in spite of their roots in the subcultures of the marginalized.

The Culture of Kaisho, the Elite Meeting Place

This topographical shift was a by-product of the political and economic transformation of Kyoto. The city was well-supplied with indoor meeting places (*kaisho*) that became centers of artistic performances enjoyed as a means of socialization. The houses of the shogun's major vassals and those of the princes and high-ranking aristocrats of the emperor's court were located close to one another in the vicinity of the imperial palace and the shogun's official residence. The beautiful temples and shrines of Kyoto also had large rooms that were suitable for public meetings. The tea ceremony, the art of flower arrangement, and the perfume game have sometimes been called *kaisho no bungei*, or "meeting-place arts," because of their historic connection with these public rooms. Nō plays also became a common form of banquet entertainment.

Yet one can safely make the generalization that the emergence of a critical mass of spectators who had developed an appreciation of the arts through frequent participation in aesthetic circles elevated the standards of the performing arts in Japan. Zeami's style of Nō drama, which emphasized the quality of *yūgen*, or "subtle grace," might not have come to fruition if he had not benefited from the patronage of aesthetically sophisticated aristocrats. At the same time, Zeami was also a stellar attraction at paid performances in the city. In order to obtain *tenka no meibō*, or "countrywide fame," Zeami recommended that performers should try to get good reviews in Kyoto. "The capital city has audiences of experienced connoisseurs," Zeami recalled, "and seeing the audience's reactions and overhearing both favorable and negative comments" will diminish one's faults as an actor and "polish one's performance until it shines like jewels."[9]

Nonetheless, even in the *kaisho* salons, the ritual logic of *mu'en* (no relation) was transformed into a mechanism to create an alternative reality within the established system. The presence of men and women of marginal status at banquets signified the temporary status of *mu'en* in the space of *kaisho*. Performing artists were often called *kugai mono*, or "persons of the public realm." The court of the Ashikaga shoguns was also served by a group of servants called *dōhō shū*, who shaved their hair in the manner of monks. They all took monastic names ending in -ami or -a; scholars have speculated that most of them were Jishū monks. As was mentioned in the previous chapter, the Jishū sect was known for its renunciation of the world and its close relationships with marginal people. The *dōhō shū* were included in the shogun's inner circle and carried out miscellaneous odd jobs and errands around the court. They were, however, not simply servants. The *dōhō shū* sometimes directed and presented artistic performances at parties, including the tea ceremony, decorated rooms with flowers and other decorative objects, and organized linked-poetry sessions.[10] The presence of *mu'en* persons in a group of people sharing an artistic performance represented ritual logic – that the space for performance was set apart for communication with the other world and therefore enabled the *kugai* (public realm), a temporary suspension of the feudal order. In this sense, the ritual logic of *mu'en* and *kugai* that had emerged in earlier centuries continued to play a role in the elite public spaces of the Muromachi period in order to generate ritual spaces.

The various *za* arts reached higher levels of refinement at different rates during the late medieval period. During the fourteenth century, the *za* arts still reflected a boisterous atmosphere, as they were a form of banquet entertainment. Linked poetry, the tea ceremony, the art of flower arrangement, and the perfume game were all structured as party games. For example, Sasaki Dōyo, a vassal of the shogun Ashikaga Takauji (1305–1358), held a fabulous party in a hall hung with leopard and tiger skins. After serving a ten-course meal and fine *sake*, he held a tea competition that featured a hundred prizes. By the late fifteenth century, however, the tea ceremony had developed a style called *wabi-cha*, or the "tea of simplicity." This new style was characterized by a refined restraint and a more intense Zen-like atmosphere of spirituality and otherworldliness.

By this time, the tea ceremony had become a means of socialization for the wealthier townspeople and higher-ranking samurai.

On the other hand, such marginal locations as riverbanks continued to be used for various popular art forms. The high-energy performances that were given still conveyed ancient memories of magical powers that could overturn the world order. Moreover, the ritual logic of *mu'en* remained vital throughout the medieval period. Some of the *za* art forms, however, began to move away from their older associations with the margins of society through their incorporation into the leisure-time activities of the upper classes.

The Diffusion of the *Za* Arts and Poetry

If the elite culture of the Muromachi *kaisho* had been the sole expression of aesthetic socialization in this era, the refinement of aesthetic activities would have been confined to aristocratic circles. The elitist pattern of socialization in the salons could not avoid conformity to a hierarchical social order even in the large common meeting rooms. The late medieval era was characterized by the emergence of another important type of aesthetic public related to the rise of local horizontal associations and the popularization of *za* arts in their associational life.

While the elite *kaisho* culture of Kyoto favored the refined traditions of the *za* arts, the political atmosphere of the time was clouded by the dissolution of the central authorities. The center of political gravity shifted to such regional political forces as the local samurai lords. In particular, after the Ōnin War (1467–1477), in which the two major vassals of the Ashikaga shogun fought each other over the issue of succession of the shogun's house, the whole country was plunged into a long period of continuous civil wars. The Ōnin War filled the streets of Kyoto with 300,000 men at one point; not surprisingly, it had a devastating effect on the capital city. Frequent pitched battles and the fires that resulted from them consumed palaces and temples as well as thousands of smaller houses.[11] After the war, most of the shogun's major vassals left Kyoto because it became increasingly difficult for them to control the local samurai in their home provinces. Ironically, however, the destructive impact of the war on Kyoto itself brought about the diffusion of the capital's high level of aesthetic culture to the outlying provinces. The professional artists and poets who had enjoyed the patronage of the Kyoto elite sought new opportunities outside the capital. By that point, the refined styles of the *za* arts that had flourished in the elegant *kaisho* culture had attracted a new group of enthusiasts who were interested in learning these arts. The problem, however, was the need for teachers; the high level of sophistication that had been attained by the practitioners of these arts meant that new students required competent professional guidance.

During this same time period, the networking activities of the professional linked-verse poets helped to popularize *renga* in the provinces. Given the declining power of the Muromachi shogunate and the imperial court in Kyoto, the professional poets traveled extensively throughout Japan cultivating the regional warlords as their patrons. Among the famous poets of this period, Sōgi (1421–1502) frequently traveled to Echigo province to seek the patronage of the warlord Uesugi. Sōchō (1448–1532), on the other hand, commuted between Suruga province and Kyoto. He served Imagawa, a powerful warlord in Suruga, but he also received support from a few other warlords.[12] The professional poets coordinated linked-verse-making sessions, served as the masters of ceremonies at the meetings, and could elevate the quality of poetic experiences for the local *za* groups.

Poetry and *Ikki* Political Alliances

The relationship between the political changes in late medieval Japanese society on the one hand and the *za* arts on the other is exemplified in the transformation of linked poetry (*renga*). After the prototypical ritual logic of aesthetic freedom under the cherry blossoms had been established earlier in the medieval era, *renga* was widely popularized. The development of linked verse during the late medieval period indicates that this genre was clearly pulled in both vertical and horizontal directions by different patterns of networking. The Ashikaga shoguns' patronage of linked-poetry sessions encouraged a greater degree of sophistication in this form of poetry. At the same time, the horizontal associations that were emerging in the socio-political dimension also made good use of *renga* poetry.

By the time of the disturbances of 1331–1337, which brought about the collapse of the Kamakura shogunate, linked verse was already considered a contemporary fad. In the famous record of the *Nijō gawara rakusho* (Graffiti of the *Nijō* Riverbank) written around this time, we find a writer claiming, "Both in Kyoto and Kamakura, [the popular trends of the moment are] . . . local popular song-like linked poetry sessions in various places; everybody wants to be a judge of these linked-verse sessions." The popular versions of linked-poetry sessions sometimes generated a raucous atmosphere.[13] For example, the famous legal code of Kenmu (1336) stated that some participants gather in the name of a tea meeting or linked-verse session but instead gamble for high stakes. Whereas some free-spirited linked-verse meetings turned into wild parties, others were well organized and grew to a huge scale. Large-scale "happenings," called "Ten Thousand Verses in a Day," developed during this period of unrest and afterward. The first event of this kind in the historical record, the so-called Kamakura Cherry Blossom Ten Thousand Verses in a Day, took place in the spring of 1320 under the cherry trees of Kamakura. A similar performance that was held in the Kitano shrine in the second year of the Eikyō era (1433) led to the formation of twenty *za*, or groups, seated together. One *za* group created five hundred verses of linked poetry. Even small-scale provincial lords began to immerse themselves in the composition of linked poetry. The third Muromachi shogun, Ashikaga Yoshimitsu, sponsored a large-scale ten-thousand-verse *renga* session in 1391, as did the shogun Ashikaga Yoshinori in 1433. The ten-thousand-verse *renga* at the Kitano shrine became an important ritual institution of the Muromachi shogunate.[14] The Muromachi shoguns also generously supported the Kitano shrine's cultural activities. With the shogunate's official support of *renga*, this style of poetry became more formal and codified.

While linked poetry became progressively more institutionalized and formal due to its connection with the political authorities, it did not lose its popular base during the medieval period. In the context of medieval Japan, the closest approximation to this aesthetic spirit of *mu'en* was the spirit of *ikki*. *Ikki* can be literally translated as "of one intention." With the decline of the central authority and continuous competition among the warlords in the outlying provinces, the late medieval period saw a widespread proliferation of *ikki* horizontal alliances. From around the mid-fourteenth and fifteenth centuries onward, horizontal alliances (*ikki*) among autonomous local samurai were formed throughout Japan, and the *ikki* claimed a shared public interest among their participants.[15] In this horizontal pattern of alliance, medieval people produced a sphere of public commonness, asserting that they would not submit to control by overlords. In this way, various types of private horizontal associations began to acquire a certain degree of publicness.

In the context of the continuous armed warfare of the fifteenth century, in which no one could count on the trustworthiness of individuals, it is not surprising that the samurai valued linked poetry for its relationship to feelings of trust and collaboration, temporary though these might be. Ogata Tsutomu, a Japanese literary scholar, has underscored the sensibility reflected in such writings of the period as *renga juttoku* (Ten Virtues of Linked Verse). The admonitions included "Become friends (*chiin*) without being overly familiar with one another"; or "There is to be no malice among the members once they have entered the *za* group, even if some have a grudge against others or are angry with them" (bajōshū, *renga nijuttoku*).[16] The samurai could be deeply involved in their usual politics of conspiracies, alliances, and betrayals at the same time that they were enthusiastic participants in the *renga* poetry meetings.

On the other hand, the ritual technology of initiating an *ikki* alliance articulated the spirit of a new form of horizontal coalition. First, a group of like-minded people drew up a document that set forth their agreement and the rules that governed it with the members' signatures attached. These signatures were often inscribed in a circular pattern on the documents to signify the equal status of the participants. The members sealed the alliance with pledges of mutual allegiance in a ritual called "One taste of the gods' water," or *ichimi shinsui*. The cup of gods' water mixed with the ashes of a burned paper that had recorded the vow with the signatures of all the *ikki* members was passed from one member to another for a ritual sip. All who had tasted the gods' water were considered equal under this ritualistic conception of an *ikki* public, in contrast to the vertical hierarchies of the samurai vassalage system. Thus, in order to avoid creating a hierarchy within the *ikki* organization, some surviving contracts for *ikki* alliances (*ikki keijō*) arranged the signatures of the participants in a circle that signified the equality of all the members.

The procedure for forming an *ikki* alliance resembled the technologies of making a *mu'en* space for linked-verse meetings. The egalitarian ideal of *ikki* echoed the spirit of the Cherry Blossom linked-verse sessions. The commonality of the popular linked-verse sessions resided in the equality of their members, symbolized by the physical transformation of their identities through the wearing of bamboo hats. Instead of drinking a cup of the gods' water and placing signatures in a circle, however, the poetry circles created chains of poems. Their temporary alliance in a space of no-relation created a temporary poetic community within it. Although the *ikki* alliances had political and military purposes while the poetry groups intended the communal enjoyment of an aesthetic world, both were infused by a similar spirit in their organization of independent-minded individuals in a temporary space of *mu'en* solidarity.

The provincial samurai who refused to be incorporated into the vertical hierarchies tried to counteract the power of the higher warlords by joining together in *ikki*. Unlike hierarchical military alliances among the samurai vassalage, the decisions of the *ikki* were made through discussions and by majority vote. These *ikki* alliances even occasionally cut across the distinction between the samurai and farmers. Moreover, the networking technology of the linked-verse sessions was appropriate to the nature of *ikki* alliances. Tsurusaki Hiroo's study of networking among samurai lords in the late medieval period found that their political alliances were reinforced by frequent meetings for the purpose of making linked verse (*renga*).[17] The participants clearly derived considerable satisfaction from the intellectual, social, and spiritual communion that they experienced within their poetry sessions. The *za* poetry groups offered ideal opportunities for socialization among landed samurai interested in forming *ikki* military alliances, which required horizontal structures of solidarity.

It was not surprising that the *ikki* alliances and linked-poetry circles were often related not only in their spirit but sometimes socially as well. According to Yasuda Jirō's study, the Higashisanchū *ikki* in Yamato province had a membership that overlapped almost entirely with the membership of the local *renga* organization. The Higashisanchū *ikki* organization was a group of small-scale *kokujin* who joined forces against the domination of more powerful warlords. Within the Higashisanchū *ikki* alliance, the *renga* group called Tenjin *renga kō*, or the Tenjin linked-verse society (Tenjin, the name of a Shinto deity, and *kō*, a corporation usually based upon a religious base), was formed. Although medieval linked-verse sessions were ordinarily temporary organizations, the Tenjin *renga kō* was not a short-term association; it had been a stable local institution since the 1360s. The group held an annual meeting for the sole purpose of making "a thousand poems of linked verse." In 1434, the group drew up a written agreement consisting of 18 articles that defined its organizational structure and by-laws. The group was headed by executive members selected by majority vote. The ten executive members took turns offering their residences for the annual meeting; otherwise, it was held at a nearby temple.[18] The society had its own properties (rice paddies) to finance the activities. Yasuda found that the networks of the Tenjin *renga kō* and the *ikki* alliance appeared to converge. The composition of the poetry was not simply a cultural activity but had a religious dimension that was politically instrumental in binding the participants to the *ikki* alliance.[19] On occasion, the poetry sessions were devoted to praying for good fortune and victory in warfare. In analyzing the networks of this *renga* group and their written "rules," Yasuda concluded that the Tenjin group of linked verse in this region was the *ikki* group itself. The spirit that animated the *ikki* groups, which detached individuals from the web of their other feudal obligations and brought them together in an egalitarian fellowship, resembled the prevailing atmosphere of the *renga* groups.[20]

Matsuoka Shinpei, in his insightful study of medieval linked verse, analyzed the affinity of the *ikki* and linked verse as follows:

> The first point of affinity stemmed from the aspect of harmony in linked verse. In making linked verse, a person could not compose a good succeeding line unless he had understood the poet who had preceded him, and digested and appreciated the previous line of verse. This degree of understanding was precisely the kind of consideration required to organize an *ikki* alliance. The second

point was the aspect of excitement in linked verse. The making of chains of poems incorporated accidental unexpectedness in the making of every stanza in a sequence because alterations were injected into the process of composition. Surprising and unexpected combinations of words and images eventually produced a state of intellectual excitement that caught up the entire group. This excitement was linked to the physical and spiritual energy that was necessary to mobilize the *ikki*.[21]

The fifteenth and sixteenth centuries witnessed the emergence of larger *ikki* organizations that sometimes included provincial farmers as well as samurai. The most famous *ikki* of this kind was the *ikki* of Yamahiro province, which was founded in 1485. It was said that 36 local samurai and farmers from the entire province met together to resist the troops of two warlords in the province who were at war with each other. The management of this *ikki* was republican to a degree that tempted a Japanese scholar to call this *ikki* "the people's parliament of the Warring States (sengoku) period." Despite the prevailing reputation of Japanese society as based on a hierarchical organization of people, late medieval Japan was sometimes called "the era of *ikki*," of voluntary horizontal associations of individuals who stood up to decide their own political and social concerns.

Although there were not many medieval *ikki* that left detailed records of their organizational structure and management, we have sufficient data to see that they emphasized horizontal structure and equality of the members and that they adopted a majority vote system. Although we have only limited documentation for instances of linked-poetry sessions within the *ikki*, there is an unmistakable cultural affinity between this form of poetry making and the *ikki* associations. The practice of the *za* arts with the technologies of *mu'en* thus indicate that the composition of poetry could be a stimulus compelling individuals to shift their network connections and suspend existing social ties in order to collaboratively engage in "a project." Poetry making thus proved to be an important device for creating political publics in this society.

The Decline of the *Za* Organizations and the Independent *Za* Spirit

We may be allowed to speculate that if the late medieval *ikki* had developed further along the path toward greater concentration and early modern state formation, Japan might have worked out a more horizontal pattern of concentration of the power of the landlord class at the beginning of the seventeenth century. The medieval *ikki* alliances had the potential to generate a more democratic tradition of self-government in Japan.

This scenario was not totally unrealistic given the fact that in medieval Europe the tradition of contractual rule – the concept of a contract made with the sovereign, evident in such a precedent as Magna Carta (1215) – was formulated because of the existence of decentralized polities with considerable local autonomy and representative assemblies. The tradition of self-determination and sovereignty shared among a number of corporate entities with privileges in the medieval era included the cities, the universities, and the church, as well as the feudal autonomy of the aristocracy. This political situation characterized by checks and balances of power generated theories and practices that opposed the arbitrary and unilateral exercise of monarchical authority. Subsequently, with the formation of early modern states that created more territorially concentrated and organized polities – absolutist states, as some historians would call them – the sovereigns could not easily obliterate the earlier traditions of privileged corporate bodies. Under the French *ancien régime* during the early modern period, for example, a variety of intermediate-level social organizations with different internal organizing principles (e.g., guilds, religious orders, cities, and villages) served as important constituents of this heterogeneous control mechanism. The day-to-day governing of the country was made possible only by collaboration among the "privileged" heterogeneous corporate bodies.[22] In other words, early modern state formation in Europe was constructed on the basis of the privileges and autonomy of various corporate entities. In fact, the lexicon of the *ancien régime* associated *privilège* with *liberté* and *franchise*, as exemplified by Voltaire's usage in his *Encyclopédie*.[23]

In contrast to the European pattern, the unification of Japan after 1600 favored the hierarchical reorganization of the samurai warrior class through the established logic of vassalage, which pre-supposed vertical alliances between masters and followers. It was the samurai's reconstituted hierarchical vassalage system that provided the organizational basis for the country's unification. In this process, while the autonomous privileges of the Japanese *za* guild organizations diminished, Japanese cities and corporate villages were also losing ground. Thus, privileges that these mid-level social organizations had acquired through centuries of struggle during the medieval period did not evolve into an organizing principle capable of defining the early modern state. Here and there, toward the end of the sixteenth century, the *ikki* associations as well as the *za* guilds were brutally subordinated by *sengoku daimyo* (the warlords), who wanted complete control over their territories. After more than a hundred years of continuous warfare among the samurai lords, it was the reconstituted form of vassalage, and its hierarchical organizations, that became the central organizing principle of early modern Japanese state formation.

The development of a unified Japanese state also diminished the social significance of various kinds of sanctuaries associated with marginal subpopulations. Although the ritual logic of *mu'en* (no relation) and *kugai* (public realm) assisted performing artists in their interactions with members of the nobility, their association with marginal groups kept their social status on the lowest level. As the transformation and reconstitution of the state progressed in this period, the samurai rulers attempted to streamline various overlapping complex systems of rights and privileges and incorporate a variety of social groups and territories into a coherent hierarchical order. This process of unification and stratification generally reinforced existing.prejudices and discrimination against members of marginal groups.

After more than a century of continuous strife among its warlords, Japan began to move toward internal unification during the late sixteenth century. After the assassination of Oda Nobunaga (1534–1582), a talented military leader who began the process of unification, Nobunaga's major vassal, Toyotomi Hideyoshi (1537–1598), completed the task of unifying the country. The unification rulers took strict stance against *ikki* leagues. For example, Oda Nobunaga killed more than 20,000 men and women of the *Ikkō ikki* in one battle near Isenagashima in 1574. He also prohibited *za* trade guilds in his castle town. The unification rulers and other warlords who wanted to stimulate the economies of their own castle cities saw the solidarity and exclusivity of the *za* guilds as a threat to their economic ambitions. As a result, the *za* guilds lost their exclusive privileges in the provincial castle cities. The magical association of marketplaces with *mu'en* also faded away.

This loss of corporate privilege was a corollary of the demilitarization of the general non-samurai population, beginning with Toyotomi Hideyoshi's famous "Sword-Hunting Edict" of 1588.[24] The unification rulers restricted the autonomy of a variety of medieval corporate groups that had previously enjoyed a measure of freedom. Their activities were supervised and controlled within the framework of the newly emergent state. As a type of social organization, the *za* groups could not compete.[25] As the social-organizational basis of the *za* art forms underwent its early modern transformation, the arts themselves were inevitably affected. Without the supporting organizational basis that could allow *mu'en* spaces to flourish, the logic and technology of aesthetic publics that nullified the feudal order also had a difficult time.

The project of successful unification and the construction of a more integrated state in Japan was coupled with a social process that diminished the medieval types of *mu'en* spaces. Thus, although the aesthetic publics continued to flourish as enclaves, their potential to foment political protest was curtailed. Performing artists who were subsidized by the rulers, on the other hand, could pursue the refinement of their arts for their own ends by moving upward in the social order. When their art forms were not related to the social basis of their independence, however, their artistic autonomy was supported only by their own aesthetic competence and the favor of their powerful patrons.

The Politics of the Tea Ceremony

The decline of the independent anti-authoritarian spirit of the *za* arts was embodied in the tragedy of an artistic genius with a strong independent mind who came too close to the power of an absolutist ruler. The name of this genius was Sen no Rikyū, a tea master who established the tea ceremony as one of the most refined *za* art forms. He acquired considerable authority through his perceived artistic excellence. His position, however, had been obtained through his close personal connection with the ruler, not through leadership of an independent *za* organization. The account that follows aptly illustrates this particular development at the end of the civil war period.

Like linked verse, the Japanese tea ceremony illustrates the distinctive characteristics of the *za* art forms as publics. The origins of the tea ceremony can be traced to the rigidly prescribed religious ceremonies in the Zen temples of the thirteenth and fourteenth centuries.[26] Outside the temples, the tea ceremony was also associated with formal banquets among the upper classes during the late medieval period. Although many elements of the ceremony were already present at this earlier stage of development, the tea ritual as a part of day-long banqueting lacked the spiritual intensity evident in later eras. During the Warring States period in the sixteenth century, however, the tea ceremony evolved into an independent art form and became a favorite occasion for socialization among the warlords. With the interpretive creativity of Sen no Rikyū (1521–1591) and other tea masters, the tea ceremony developed into a highly refined aesthetic ritual. In the ritualized space of the teahouses, merchants, lords, and monks could meet together as equals. In Rikyū's type of teahouse, the guest had to enter the structure through an artificially small and narrow sliding door (*nijiri-guchi*), which called for bent knees and stooped posture. Once inside, the participant found a space characterized by quiet simplicity and purity. Drinking tea from the same bowl passed from one guest to another fosters and symbolizes a spirit of oneness. It is of course true that the meetings of the *za* art groups were transitory compared to the *za* social organizations. But it is also the case that gatherings for the enjoyment of *za* art formed ritual spaces set off from external social relations and conducive to the formation of congenial egalitarian relationships among the members.

During the period of political consolidation in the late sixteenth century, the tea ceremony appealed to some of the most powerful *daimyo* and rulers – in particular, Oda Nobunaga and Toyotomi Hideyoshi. Oda Nobunaga, in fact, introduced what was called "the way of tea ceremony politics." After establishing his political hegemony, Nobunaga frequently hosted tea parties in his magnificent Azuchi castle as well as in his Kyoto residence, inviting warlords and rich merchants from Kyoto and Sakai. He claimed that he had garnered "more than enough gold, silver, and rice" in order to justify collecting the most famous tea utensils of his day as symbols of his preeminence as a connoisseur as well as a ruler. He was generous with his collection and often gave some of his most prized pieces as gifts to his vassals.

The sixteenth-century tea ceremony, however, was also marked by the emergence of commoners who loved the tea ritual. Tea enthusiasts often kept tea diaries or mementoes of the tea gatherings that they attended. For example, a merchant in Nara wrote, "The eleventh year of Tenmon [1542], the fourth month. I went to the party of Tennōjiya Sōtatsu at Sakai."[27] Many people kept tea diaries out of a clear aesthetic consciousness that valued the artistic dimension of the sharing of tea and the social importance of remembering the names of those in attendance at these gatherings. The frequent cross-listings of tea enthusiasts' names in the many extant diaries kept by writers who lived in Sakai, Nara, and Kyoto reveal that even though there was no formal organizational structure, there was an aesthetic public that owed its existence to the shared love of tea.

It is interesting to note that the *wabi-cha* style of tea ceremony evolved and flourished in the city of Sakai. Sakai was one of the few major Japanese cities that had achieved a significant degree of autonomy and self-government for a brief period because of the wealth it had accumulated from international trading. The city was governed and policed by a board of 36 merchant councillors, called *egōshū*, and was protected by gates and moats resembling those of the European free cities. One Western observer, a Jesuit priest named Gaspar Villela, reported in 1562 that Sakai was apparently immune from struggles and infighting among the warlords. He praised Sakai as the safest city in Japan. Once people come to this city, as Villela saw it, losers and winners all lived peacefully together in love and harmony.[28] To be sure, Villela's remarks fall far short of insinuating that Sakai had a particularly strong armed force. The city's security was based in part on the delicate balance of power among the competing local warlords. One could say that the city of Sakai itself represented a free space of *mu'en* (no relation) and that the tea ceremony that flourished in this city also embodied the spirit of *za*. It can come as no surprise that the merchants of Sakai were socialized through participation in the refined *za* arts.[29] Within their social circles, the wealthy merchants of Sakai raised the tea ceremony to a new level of aesthetic refinement.

A famous Sakai tea master in the *wabi* style, named Takeno Jōō (1502–1555), was a successful trader in military materiel. Other famous tea masters, including Kamiya Sōtan, Tsuda Sōkyū, and Imai Sokyū, were also leading merchants of the city. Compared with earlier forms of medieval performing arts with stronger popular roots, such as the chants and dancing of the Jishū monks, the sixteenth-century tea ceremony was more rarefied. It became an important means of socialization among the rich and prominent merchants of Sakai. By providing essential resources for the warring lords, Sakai's merchants grew rich alongside their samurai customers. They were not, however, on an equal political footing with the warlords. If Sakai and other Japanese cities had increased their autonomy and participated in the process of national unification on a more equal basis with the samurai, the tea ceremony might have evolved into a form of bourgeois socialization closer to European modes of civility. History did not unfold in this direction; the autonomy of Sakai proved to be short-lived. As the unification of the country progressed, Oda Nobunaga targeted the city for takeover. Although its citizens put up some measure of resistance, Nobunaga eventually gained military control of Sakai in 1568.

In 1574, Nobunaga appointed Sen no Rikyū (1522–1591) and Tsuda Sōkyū (?–1591) as his chief tea officers. Both tea masters hailed from Sakai. The Sakai tea masters were not simply otherworldly artists out of touch with political reality. Sen no Rikyū, now considered a virtual saint of the tea cult, was in fact a practical and realistic urbanite who once sent a thousand bullets to Nobunaga as a gift. The appointment of two Sakai merchants as Nobunaga's tea officers, however, symbolized the fact that the tea ceremony – a *za* art that had developed within an autonomous urban *za* organization – was now incorporated within Nobunaga's tea ceremony politics. One political application of the ceremony was its use as a social reward symbolizing the overlord's favor. For Nobunaga's vassals, an invitation to join the tea ceremony represented the most honorable treatment. Toyotomi Hideyoshi, who started his career as Oda Nobunaga's vassal, wrote in a personal letter after his predecessor's death: "The tea ceremony was the lord's [Nobunaga's] way of doing politics. He gave me permission to perform the tea ceremony, and I was most honored. I will never forget it."[30]

In addition to honoring its social dimension, Nobunaga and Hideyoshi used the tea ceremony for political ends. Nobunaga's successor not only completed the unfinished business of unification but also continued the way of tea politics on an even grander scale. As in the case of linked-verse making, the collective dimension of the tea ceremony facilitated networking among individuals and thus made the art form useful as a political tool. Conducted in a special small room constructed to impart an atmosphere of warmth and intimacy, the tea ceremony provided an ideal space for participants to socialize and enjoy a sense of communal solidarity.

With the help of Sen no Rikyū, Hideyoshi hosted a number of spectacular tea parties and attempted to place himself at the very center of the tea culture. For example, he announced in July of 1587 that he was hosting the famous "Great Public Tea Party" in the Kitano forest outside Kyoto. His public announcement invited all lovers of the tea ceremony, including ordinary townspeople and farmers, to this spectacular open-air event. Hideyoshi's invitation stated, "Bring only your teakettle or well bucket or whatever you have. If you have no tea, you may bring kogashi."[31] He encouraged the tea masters to hold their own makeshift versions of tea ceremonies under the pine trees of the Kitano forest. Hideyoshi promised to display all his precious tea utensils and to serve tea himself for the participants. At the same time, his ordinance warned that tea practitioners who did not attend the party would be prohibited from conducting tea ceremonies after the event. This ordinance is thus uncommonly revealing of the nature of Hideyoshi's tea politics. On the one hand, Hideyoshi was faithful to the traditional open spirit of the *za* arts, in which participants socialize with one another without regard to formal status distinctions. On the other hand, as the authoritarian ruler of a newly unified Japan, he attempted to confine the *za* spirit within a hierarchical power structure under his control.[32]

The Death of Sen no Rikyū

Through Sen no Rikyū's collaboration with Toyotomi Hideyoshi, he became, as Paul Varely put it, "in fact as well as in name"[33] Japan's leading practitioner of the tea ceremony. In turn, Rikyū's talent and authority were indispensable for the success of Hideyoshi's tea politics. A number of popular stories about the relationship between Rikyū and Hideyoshi convey the mixture of tension and cooperation that existed between these two strong characters as they collaborated in bringing the tea culture to new heights of refinement and elegance. One well-known legend tells about the day that Hideyoshi heard that Rikyū's tea garden was filled with beautiful morning glories. Inspired by the prospect of looking at some beautiful flowers, Hideyoshi visited Rikyū for morning tea but found no flowers in the garden. Profoundly disappointed, the ruler entered the tea master's small tearoom. There, a bunch of fresh, bright morning glories awaited him in the alcove. Hideyoshi and his associates felt refreshed. Sen no Rikyū's "morning glory tea meeting" became a famous example of the tea master's creative spirit.[34] During Hideyoshi's rule, Rikyū also served as his personal advisor, thus exercising substantial political influence within Hideyoshi's domestic circle. Later on, however, Hideyoshi ordered the death of the master of the tea ceremony on the grounds that Rikyū was attempting to surpass Hideyoshi's authority. Rikyū committed suicide by *seppuku* (*hara-kiri*), leaving behind a farewell poem that read[35]:

> Seventy years of life:
> Swoosh – with my enlightened treasure sword
> Let me kill Buddha and my Ancestors together,
> It is time to throw my sword to the sky![36]

Although Sen no Rikyū's poem clearly reflects the style of Zen poetry, the mentality expressed in these lines reveals an unexpected affinity with the medieval popular mindset of *kuruu*, or going mad. The *kouta*, or popular song of this time that I cited earlier in this chapter, declared that "Life is only a dream, So just let yourself go wild!" The passionate spirit of *kuruu* was shared by this master of the tea ceremony – a man ordinarily associated with an aesthetic of stoicism and self-control.

It has been suggested that Rikyū's death was most likely the end result of the long-lived personality and artistic friction between two strong-willed persons. Yet the full story of this tragic end to the once-collaborative relationship between the ruler and the tea master is not altogether clear. The official reason appears to be related to an incident involving Rikyū's placement of a wooden statue of himself above the gate of a famous Zen temple, Daitokuji in Kyoto, on the occasion of his donating the gate to the temple. His gesture was considered tantamount to elevating his artistic authority above Hideyoshi's because Hideyoshi was likely to use the gate on his visits to the Daitokuji. Although an act of this sort was clearly offensive by the standards of the period, modern scholars are not completely convinced that Hideyoshi would have ordered the death of his trusted tea master for this reason alone.

Surviving letters that were exchanged among Hideyoshi's courtiers at the time of Rikyū's death sentence offer another clue to this mysterious episode. It was rumored that Rikyū was accused of being a *maisu* (literally, a "priest-salesman").[37] *Maisu* was a pejorative term for describing a profit-oriented Buddhist priest. The hearsay evidence concerning Rikyū's death sentence, however, was connected to the essence of his aesthetic authority and genius. Although the tea ceremony was sometimes described as a purely spiritual ritual, it was also entangled in material and monetary considerations related to the equipment used. Enthusiastic appreciation of the beauty of the tea utensils is a large part of the tea ceremony experience. The unification rulers and the wealthy merchants of Sakai were considered arbiters of the tea culture because of their impressive collections of the most refined and expensive teapots, ladles, and other utensils. One of the lasting influences of the tea ceremony on standards of beauty in the wider Japanese culture is related to this point. The rise of the so-called *wabi-cha*, or "poverty" tea ceremony, resulted in a distinctive aesthetic characterized by elegant simplicity. The *wabi* tea ceremony offered the Japanese a novel standard of beauty. Paradoxically, the simplest teacups together with such items as teaspoons made from bamboo might cost a fortune once they acquired the cachet of special tea articles, or *meibutsu*. Materialism was obviously antithetical to the spiritual purity of the *wabi* tea ceremony, but it was part of human reality at the time that the value of tea articles was calculated in monetary terms. The most celebrated tea utensils were priceless – sometimes described as worthy to be offered in exchange for a castle. The key to a successful tea ceremony thus resided not simply in abstract spirituality but in the skillful assembly of beautiful utensils. Viewed from this angle, the tea ceremony was heavily implicated in connoisseurship and material fetishism.

The important point here is that Sen no Rikyū's most distinctive talent was his ability to define the aesthetic value of the implements used in the tea ceremony. With his unconventional eye for new forms of beauty, together with his association with Toyotomi Hideyoshi, Rikyū was in a unique position to profit financially from current interest in the tea ceremony. Once the tea master gave his expert opinion on a new type or pattern of tea utensil, its price skyrocketed. Rikyū own favorite style of flower vase, made from simple pieces of bamboo, cost a fortune. A new, domestically produced tea bowl that was relatively inexpensive when it first appeared on the market became a costly item after it received Rikyū's stamp of approval. Rikyū's contemporaries naturally assumed that he, as a clever merchant from Sakai, must have grown rich from his influence on the marketplace. The description of Sen no Rikyū as a *maisu* was probably derived from this aspect of his position as Toyotomi Hideyoshi's tea master.

In essence, although Hideyoshi admired Rikyū's talent, he could not tolerate his tea master's innovative spirit and independence. Rikyū's ultimate fate stemmed from the fact that although he was dependent on Hideyoshi's political power, he began to expand his sphere of influence in the world of the beautiful, where he could define its standards. Those standards were not only spiritual and aesthetic but also connected to concrete economic measurements, namely the cost of specific items in the marketplace. Rikyū's authority as the supreme tea master appeared to be so complete within the realm of the tea ceremony that even the ruler of the rest of Japan had little influence there. Hideyoshi's turning against his former advisor indicates, however, that the project of Japan's political unification had no room for the free artistic *za* spirit when that spirit was merged with mercantile concerns. Sen no Rikyū's death spelled the end of the anti-authoritarian *za* aesthetic publics and the simultaneous decline of the independent *za* social organizations.

5

Tokugawa State Formation and the Transformation of Aesthetic Publics

The consolidation of the Tokugawa state (1603–1867) at the beginning of the seventeenth century meant that the colorful medieval forms of publics that had supplied people with a measure of freedom were subordinated under the supreme authority of the shogunate. After the pacification of Japan under the Tokugawa shoguns, the artistic circles that had begun to spread throughout the general population again became enclaves of free communicative spheres, but in a way different from that of their medieval predecessors. The autonomous power of the various horizontally organized associations (e.g., *za*, *ikki*) that had energized the independent spirit of the medieval *za* arts was no longer readily available in the political arena. The Tokugawa aesthetic publics were able to build on the remnants of the medieval *za* spirit only by confining themselves to the inferior realm of *watakushi* (the private) and accepting the official boundaries set for them by the state. Thus, Tokugawa state formation had a critical impact on participation in the world of the beautiful through reorganizing the associational life of Japanese people.

The organizational structure of the Tokugawa state created both limits and opportunities for the networks of people interested in art and poetry. I will examine the lively activities, associational structures, and transformations of the Tokugawa art and literary circles in the next four chapters. In this chapter, I will provide a general overview of the idiosyncratic nature of the Tokugawa state from three angles: the nature of Tokugawa state formation, the transitions among the associational networks in the context of the early modern network revolution, and the categorical redefinition of publicness. It was only within these larger social contexts that the activities of popular aesthetic associations had their distinctive roles to play.

127

State Formation, Political Hierarchies, and Institutional Segmentation

After more than a hundred years of continuous infighting among the samurai warlords, the Tokugawa clan won control of the country after a series of decisive victories in large-scale battles. The Tokugawa shoguns legitimated their rule on the basis of their pacification of Japan and took a despotic approach to the enforcement of peace in every corner of the country. The shogunate also demonstrated in a number of symbolic ways that it was the power center of Japanese society; the shoguns controlled the coinage and established the official standards of weights and measures, as well as constructing durable roads and sea lanes for the transportation of people and commodities. The Tokugawa rulers not only imposed their control on political processes but allowed and encouraged commodity exchanges within the institutional framework and values of the state. In fact, the shogunate witnessed the rise of a complex system of nationwide commodity exchanges on a remarkably large scale.

In the sphere of politics, the transition from the medieval to the Tokugawa period was marked by a decisive victory of vertical principles of organization over horizontal principles. From the viewpoint of class politics, Tokugawa state formation may be regarded as a reinforcement of the samurai class's domination over farmers and other commoners, as the latter were deprived of their ability to defend themselves through a program of demilitarization called "sword-hunting." The organizational force that succeeded in reorganizing Japanese society along hierarchical lines was best represented by the samurai's vassalage organizations. Vassalage in the medieval period had been constructed primarily on vertical relationships between a master and his followers. The Tokugawa state used this traditional form of alliance among the samurai as an organizing principle to define the relationship between the shogun and *daimyo* as well as the relationships between the *daimyo* lords and their vassal samurai. By streamlining the nationwide hierarchies of the warrior class in this way, the samurai collectively subordinated other patterns of organization. The medieval horizontal alliances that had formed networks among independent people through coalitions based on mutuality and relative equality could not compete with the reorganization of the samurai hierarchies on a national scale.

People's ability to form horizontal associational ties outside the state, such as the medieval *ikki* and *za* organizations, was more rigorously restricted by a number of policies instituted by such unification rulers as Toyotomi Hideyoshi and Tokugawa Ieyasu. The *za* trade guilds were also prohibited from expanding their monopolistic tendencies, while the productive farmlands were carefully surveyed for purposes of taxation.

The Buddhist temples and Shintō shrines that formerly had military capabilities were also subdued and demilitarized by the rulers. The medieval horizontally structured publics – in particular, the *ikki* form of sacred alliance sealed by the participants' act of sharing a cup of the "gods' water" (*shinsui*) – were outlawed under the Tokugawa as criminal organizations. While the *ikki* as sacred alliances could claim to be a "public realm" during the medieval period, under the Tokugawa shogunate they were regarded as political factions, or *totō*, which was tantamount to treason. To be sure, peasants' collective actions against the authorities in practice continued forcefully throughout the Tokugawa period.[1] The hierarchical reorganization of publics under the supreme authority of the great public, or the shogunate, thus transformed the structural preconditions of communicative spheres in Tokugawa Japan.

Meanwhile, the samurai vassals were ordered to relocate their living quarters in the castle cities of the *daimyo*. The samurai relinquished autonomous direct control of their feudal land holdings; as a result, they were in no position to organize horizontal associations as a buffer against the higher authorities. Prior to Tokugawa Ieyasu's pacification of the country, the boundary between the samurai and non-samurai classes was not very clear; for example, it was not uncommon for individuals born outside the samurai class to acquit themselves well in battle and win promotion to full samurai status. Under the Tokugawa system, however, such a "career track" became impossible. Only men who had been born into vassalage to a *daimyo* or to the shogun himself were considered samurai under the Tokugawa system. This form of inherited status meant that the samurai effectively became cogs within the machinery of the state; consequently unlike in the medieval period, alliances between the samurai and commoners to form *ikki* became almost impossible.

In spite of the fact that Tokugawa Japan was governed effectively for two and a half centuries, the shoguns did not develop complex logistical techniques for governing their subjects directly through the staff of a permanent national bureaucracy. In this sense, although the Tokugawa shoguns appeared to wield despotic power, in actual practice they did not have effective direct control over individual citizens. Instead, Tokugawa society was deliberately divided into layers of different types of control units cumulatively integrated into a complex state system.

The Tokugawa state subdivided the Japanese population into groups demarcated by regional, occupational, and status boundaries. The mature pattern of the Tokugawa polity consisted of multiple layers of decentralized power structures integrated into the shogunate system. Each subordinate unit of control was allowed to be semi-autonomous at the same time that it fulfilled certain obligations (*yaku*) to higher levels of authority. The members of each association were governed primarily by a head who was a member of that organization, not a bureaucrat employed by the government. These associations usually consisted of members of similar status (*mibun*).

As a result, Japanese society was carved into a number of distinct, structurally separate, and formally unrelated – though in practice connected – social components. The state's implementation of institutional segmentation of its population was coupled with the overall streamlining of Japanese social hierarchies. The shogun stood at the pinnacle of the political pyramid as the master of all the *daimyo*, while the *daimyo* with the aid of their loyal samurai vassals controlled their own territories and subjects in general independence of the shogun. Villages, town wards, and various occupational and status organizations had semi-autonomous control and disciplinary power over their own affairs even though they were technically subordinate to the samurai authorities.

By assigning each social organization specific obligations while allowing them to remain semi-autonomous, the shoguns were able to construct an idiosyncratic hierarchy consisting of associations that were internally highly dissimilar. The main disciplinary strategy for enforcing this politically prescribed hierarchy is known as the policy of rule by status, or *mibun seido* (status institution), in Japanese historical scholarship. In order to maintain the samurai's exclusive right to rule in the face of an emerging market economy that had begun to connect regions and people across artificial political boundaries, the shoguns as well as the regional *daimyo* continuously elaborated and enforced the status hierarchies and institutional subdivisions. The Tokugawa state upheld this policy of hierarchical institutional segmentation and segregation for two and a half centuries.

At the same time, Tokugawa political processes cannot simply be caricatured as despotic and unidirectional. The indirect system of government allowed individual units of social control a certain degree of autonomy. These units were thus empowered to host various sites of public discourse. The aesthetic publics also emerged in this context; their activities often cut across the formal political boundaries of the different status, occupational, and regional control units. In essence, the spread of discursive spheres within early modern Japan was in part a response to official action and organization. These spheres did not, however, form an autonomous united communicative sphere capable of sustaining public political discourse. As a result, the structures of Japanese discursive spheres were not conducive either to direct control from the top down or to resistance from the bottom up. Two very different images of Tokugawa Japan, one reflecting an intensely controlled and hierarchically ordered formal society and the other conveying the relaxed and sensual dimension of popular culture, were like twins emerging from the same matrix of social networks.

The strength of the Tokugawa status system provided the backdrop that made the aesthetic publics so attractive to Tokugawa people. The aesthetic spheres' established ritual logic that temporarily decoupled participants from their status constraints became even more precious under the hegemony of the Tokugawa shoguns. In the socialization of aesthetic publics, individuals were able to socialize outside their *mibun*-based territorial or occupational organizations. They were also temporarily freed from their formal proprietary rankings (*kakushiki*) in their socialization, even if this freedom meant that they had to master the complicated rules of proper socialization – such as the procedures of the tea ceremony and the rules for composing linked verse.

We must also take into account that socialization outside the limits of these territorial or occupational units could be regarded as dubious activities under the Tokugawa regime. One of the shogunate's persistent policies was to prevent the formation of free popular horizontal associations in the political arena. For example, the famous *Buke Shohatto* (the Rule of Military Houses, issued in 1615), which set forth the shogunate's basic regulations of the *daimyo* lords, clearly stated that the *daimyo* were expected to discipline anyone who attempted to form new parties (*totō*).[2] A similar ordinance was imposed on the shogunate's vassals. Edicts forbidding the formation of parties were repeatedly posted in villages and towns across Japan throughout the Tokugawa period. In effect, the prohibition of *totō* became one of the most famous laws of the shogunate.[3]

The condemnation of *totō* made private aesthetic associations even more important for civic social life in this period. Circles for sharing enjoyment of the arts and literature were well-accepted and safe ways to organize voluntary associations that could draw people from different social backgrounds. The Tokugawa state's hierarchical redefinition of publicness also gave new and unexpected life to the notion of a private sphere that was considered inferior to but relatively unsupervised by the political authorities. People of various standings joined poetry groups and other artistic circles in their leisure time. Furthermore, the rapid growth of nationwide commercial networks also stimulated the formation and spread of aesthetic circles and facilitated the diffusion of various messages that arose within the aesthetic publics.

The Tokugawa Network Revolution

If institutional segmentation and segregation had been the only organizational side effects of Tokugawa state formation, aesthetic socialization might have remained a minor adjunct to an otherwise structurally segmented society. The emergence and proliferation of the Tokugawa aesthetic publics, however, were situated within the context of what I have called the Tokugawa network revolution; that is, the simultaneous expansion of various communicative networks in terms of their scale, density, and complexity. To recapitulate, Tokugawa Japan arrived at a critical moment of cultural history with the simultaneous developments of four kinds of social networks: (1) a phase of territorial state-making; (2) the formation of nationwide trade routes and commodities markets together with the emergence of urban consumption centers; and (3) the rise of commercial publishing. In addition, (4) the rise of aesthetic associational activities as centers for private socialization was a part of this network revolution, which transformed political and economic as well as sociocultural relations. Aesthetic associations received benefits of expanding political, economic, and communicative networks that allowed them to operate in a truly proto-modern fashion.

In the context of the shogunate's political system, political networks expanded to a nationwide level with the establishment of the Tokugawa state, while the shoguns' policy of institutional segmentation encouraged the development of cohesive and dense communication patterns within local units of control. The Tokugawa imposition of the alternate residence system (*sankin kōtai*) on the *daimyo*, which required the *daimyo* lords to commute between their castles in their home provinces and their formal residences in Edo, was particularly instrumental in expanding communication networks between the outlying provinces and the capital since a number of samurai bureaucrats accompanied their lords on their journeys. The paper-shuffling mentality that afflicted the shogunate's bureaucracy eventually penetrated the *daimyo* domains, even down to the level of the villages and occupational guilds. Although the Tokugawa shoguns did not develop a national system of tax collection, they did take surveys of the productive capacities of the provincial villages. As a result, each productive segment was loosely but identifiably situated within the framework of national hierarchies even though it was not controlled directly by the center. At the same time, the information that was collected was transmitted on an unprecedented scale as a corollary of Japan's political integration.

The segmented units of production themselves began to develop more complicated webs of social relations. The provincial *daimyo* polities, in particular those of the larger domains, developed a more systematic hierarchical organizational structure among their vassal samurai. In the previous period, the relationship between a master and his samurai vassals had been defined as a set of personal rewards and obligations, but the relations among the vassal samurai themselves had not been as clearly marked. But with the development of what I have elsewhere called vassalic bureaucracy under the Tokugawa, the samurai vassals were organized into a well-defined hierarchy measured by three indices: honor ranking (*kaku*); government office (*shoku*); and basic income level (*hōroku*).[4] Various local units of control also developed complex webs of social relations during the early modern period. In this way, the local units added to the density and cohesiveness of Tokugawa webs of social relations.

The expansion of nationwide market networks that was stimulated and facilitated by Tokugawa state formation further complicated the landscape of Japanese political relations. The rule of the shogunate and *daimyo* houses was based on an agrarian economy in which taxes paid in rice required a nationwide market that allowed the *daimyo* to exchange the grain for cash. Furthermore, the *daimyo* needed a secure supply of commodities in order to maintain their urban lifestyle as well as support their peasants' requirements for agricultural production. Consequently, local territorial markets developed within each *daimyo* domain with connections to the nationwide market system. The emergence of these regional and national markets, together with the development of infrastructures of distribution and communication, brought about a remarkable increase in the flow of commodities during the second half of the seventeenth century. The new pattern of Japanese market networks thus resembled the structure of the Tokugawa political system itself – integrated but decentralized.[5] These economic networks linked the various units of politically segmented territorial and occupational organizations in unforeseen ways. The inhabitants of a village in a distant province that was geographically and politically isolated could acquire effective connections to consumers in an urban center through traders who represented a variety of commodity exchange networks. These connections further encouraged the production of cash crops and commercial products that allowed wealthy landholders and merchants to accumulate capital. By the eighteenth century, the expansion of market networks transformed the qualities and structure of local social relations. The horizon of connectivity for an ordinary person also expanded significantly. The new market economy provided Tokugawa people with many incentives to travel, migrate, or otherwise make connection with other localities through commodity exchange.

On the other hand, this period also witnessed the incorporation of previously politically more autonomous social entities within the framework of state control. The zones of relative freedom – the religious sanctuaries and the marginal subpopulations that had been identified as *mu'en* (no relation) or *kugai* (public realm) during the medieval period – were drawn into the shogunate's political and economic system following national unification. Such marginal groups, which had enjoyed the privilege of trespassing certain feudal boundaries, were reorganized into status-based associations that were essentially a part of the Tokugawa state's control system. One function of the medieval marginal population, that of breathing fresh vigor into a tired society by their function of connecting different types of networks through boundary trespassing, passed to the new economic system. The Tokugawa marketplace – though then a less magical place compared to its medieval predecessor – became the center of vitality through connectivity within the institutionally segmented society of post-unification Japan.

Given the simultaneous expansion of political, associational, and market networks under the first Tokugawa shoguns, this development would certainly deserve the title of "network revolution." I will discuss the remarkable growth of Tokugawa commercial publishing as an information revolution in Chapter 11. At this point, however, it is important to note that the vitality of the Tokugawa aesthetic publics cannot be understood without the active role of commercial publishing in the operation of their associational activities.

On the other hand, the rise of knowledge-based associations as centers for socialization also complicated the relational structures of Tokugawa social interactions. Aesthetic networks might cut across feudally defined territorial, occupational, and status boundaries, but they could also be formed on the basis of neighborhood associations. In the latter case, the network of aesthetic activities might largely overlap with pre-existing political or economic ties. The most important point, however, was not simply the structural pattern of these aesthetic networks. The Tokugawa networks made a qualitative difference in social relations in that they allowed participants to switch at will, if only temporarily, from their existing strong ties to the alternative realities of aesthetic publics. Although this identity switching was not without precedent in the medieval form of aesthetic publics, aesthetic activities in the Tokugawa period were regarded as pleasurable and private rather than as sacred and religious. Thus, the expansion of aesthetic networks as private voluntary associations distinct from the political, economic, and other social networks not only increased the density and complexity of Tokugawa relational structures but added a new qualitative dimension to them. It was a dimension of openness and lightness that allowed the members of this society to break out of the formal status system and its confining structures. The society that allowed its citizens to form associational activities in such a fashion may well deserve to be called proto-modern.

Reorganizing the Hierarchy of Publicness

Parallel to this organizational transformation of the state and private associations was the categorical redefinition of publics. In this process, the medieval popular "bottom-up" notions of publicness were downgraded while the state-centered definition of publicness was promoted. This transformation was important for the formulation of the Tokugawa style of aesthetic publics as enclaves for private socialization.

The shogunate formulated a state-centered ideology of publicness (*ōyake*, or *kō*) that roughly corresponded to the organizational pattern of the Tokugawa state reviewed above. This ideology involved the categorical stratification of many levels of publicness. The Tokugawa shogunate claimed it was the *ōkōgi*, the great public propriety, the supreme public of the country. By accepting this political framework from the Tokugawa shogunate, the provincial *daimyo* could style themselves as lesser public authorities (*kōgi*) as long as they kept within the boundaries of the Tokugawa ruler's superior public authority.

Although the notions of "public" and "private" in natural languages are reciprocally influential in both theory and practice, the assignment of certain actions to the "public" sphere, even when they represent private interests, typically confers social merit on those actions and thereby endows the actor with a claim to moral legitimacy. The Tokugawa shoguns had to define their regime within a new context of publicness precisely because the Tokugawa government was conceived in a non-public way: as the result of continuous private fighting on a grand scale. Furthermore, the publicness of these shogun and *daimyo* polities was dubious since the shogunate administrations as well as the local *daimyo* governments were simply extensions of the households of the shogun or *daimyo* lords. Vassal samurai were not bureaucrats in the modern sense of the term but were still considered personal vassals of the shogun or the *daimyo* lord. Furthermore, neither Buddhist nor Confucian thought could provide a concept of natural or divine law to legitimate the public character of the rulers' domination. Sheer military supremacy and cunning political maneuvers constituted the Tokugawa's governing power.

The Tokugawa state, however, did not (and could not) totally crush the medieval legacy of self-governance of various mid-range organizations. After an initial violent period of unification, the Tokugawa rulers intelligently attempted to transform these organizations into servants of the new order. The various mid-range organizations – villages, wards in cities, guilds, and other occupational or status organizations – that had attained a measure of autonomy and "publicness from the bottom" during the medieval period were deprived of critical social and military bases for independence after the establishment of the Tokugawa shogunate. It is symbolically significant that the terms that represented publicness and autonomy from the ground up in medieval Japan, such as *kugai* and *mu'en*, acquired negative overtones during the Tokugawa period. Freedom through defining oneself as "no relation" was no longer, at least officially, an option for people under the Tokugawa system. The devaluation of the existing multiple local publics, together with the establishment of the shogun as supreme authority, allowed the Tokugawa system to form a new state-defined hierarchy of multiple public spheres.

The people of this hierarchically ordered society could hardly be described as submissive, as evidenced by several thousand peasant rebellions, village internal disputes, and urban uprisings recorded by Japanese historians throughout this period. Nor were radical means the only way that people voiced their opinions. In contrast with the authoritarian tone of the shogunate's official position, the system had room to incorporate opinions from the ground floor, so to speak, into the operation of the polity. For example, since each unit of control was given a measure of autonomy, individual viewpoints could be reflected in the operation of these mid-range organizations, which then became the pivotal focus of communicative activities. In the villages, which no longer had their samurai masters living on-site, the commoners of the village had genuine power to settle their own affairs through discussion among themselves. Some villages selected their chiefs, who were usually wealthy commoners, by voting. The samurai vassals – then more or less bureaucrats – developed a renewed sense of responsibility for governing during this period. The vassal samurai also felt greater loyalty toward the house of their *daimyo* master – his *o-ie*, or "honorable house" – than toward the shogun and the central authority he represented. The vassal samurai often submitted their own policy opinions to their superiors or *daimyo* lords themselves. Thus, within these various groups and political units, an array of vital policy-related communicative actions flourished. In short, in spite of its authoritarian appearance, Tokugawa Japan had a lively undercurrent of communicative activities.

Aesthetic Enclave Publics and the Invention of Private Life

In addition to this general form of communicative life, there was another aspect of Tokugawa organization that allowed for relatively unsupervised communicative activities in the private realm. Because of their intentionally decentralized system of social control, the shogunate did not develop full-fledged regulatory institutions (i.e., a police force, a national taxation system, a national bureaucracy, a national army) sufficiently competent to discipline individuals directly through the arms of government. An elaborate system of national legal codes and jurisprudence also did not develop under the Tokugawa system since the primary responsibility of enforcing controls on individual behavior remained at the local level. Thus, despite the authoritarian shogunate, Tokugawa society contained many open spaces that were relatively unsupervised – spheres of autonomy in practice rather than in principle – from the viewpoint of state control. In fact, there were vast territories of relatively unregulated private communicative spheres – admittedly inferior in the official hierarchy of publicness – available in the Tokugawa system. One might even say that the rigid hierarchical reclassification of publicness under Tokugawa hegemony almost inevitably required the invention of the notion of "private." It was in this realm that aesthetic socialization flourished as self-admittedly inferior and private but irresistibly attractive "enclave publics."

The Tokugawa aesthetic gatherings appeared at first glance to resemble their medieval predecessors in perpetuating the spirit of the *za* arts and poetry. The aesthetic enclave publics of the Tokugawa period, however, were subtly but distinctively different from those of earlier aesthetic publics in a number of ways. First of all, they operated at a greater distance from the ancient world of magic, in which the arts served as technologies for transforming nature. The arts and poetry of the Tokugawa period were more closely associated with private entertainment and socialization. The reader should recall that some of the traditional art forms of late medieval Japan began to distance themselves from those that remained more closely bound to the ancient magical worldview. These relatively sophisticated art forms were "purified" and "refined" as they differentiated themselves from the popular performing arts. The *za* arts became more suitable for controlled forms of socialization during their evolution into mainstream aesthetic activities. This process had an element of secularization built into it because it was implicitly interwoven with the process of Tokugawa state formation. In the world of government, the political forces that were related to ancient magical forms of power were losing ground while the samurai class that was attempting to reorganize the state relied on sheer military might. The medieval social sanctuaries that had been formed in spaces often associated with marginal subpopulations were greatly diminished in the early Tokugawa period.

To be sure, the weakening of publics formed from the bottom up in Tokugawa society did not mean that people in this period were not involved in lively communicative activities. The Tokugawa system was in fact built upon the assumption that villages, town wards, and other local units of control became local centers of communicative activities while they exercised their self-disciplinary functions. Therefore, these units of control were in continual negotiation with higher authorities, in part to represent the interest of the communities they served.

The hierarchy of Japanese publics was further complicated by the fact that any political sphere could be considered either *ōyake* (public) or *watakushi* (literally, "the private," usually used in a pejorative sense), depending on the viewer's location in the hierarchy. For instance, a *daimyo*'s *o-ie* (honorable house) was "the" public domain for anyone who belonged to the lord's household; from the perspective of the shogunate (*ōkōgi*, the great public propriety), however, the *daimyo* house belonged to an inferior level of "public" life (lesser public propriety) and so could be regarded as semi-private. The lower levels of the "public" domain were frequently described as *watakushi*, in contrast to a supposedly higher, more purely "public" sphere. Hence, an issue of concern to a *daimyo*'s polity was generally spoken of as "private," in comparison to a "public" problem involving the shogunate.

This particular observation, however, has another aspect. In a multi-layered power structure like the Tokugawa regime, nothing is genuinely public because everything simultaneously participates in the private domain. Even the supreme public authority, or *ōkōgi*, of the Tokugawa shogunate was in fact just an extension of the Tokugawa family household; the samurai "bureaucrats" were regarded as the shogun's private vassals. Note the fact that the Japanese notion of *ōyake* was connected to territorial definitions (spheres) rather than universalistic norms of justice. The Tokugawa reclassification of publics was a system of territorial ranking of publicness in a hierarchical order.

At the same time, under this official political hierarchy, no sphere was really considered truly private, as each level of involvement had its own assigned role and responsibility within the Tokugawa system of social control. At least, the domestic sphere was no longer the same as the medieval feudal prerogatives in which matters related to the *ie* (house) were determined by the head of the *ie* independently of the feudal master. Under the Tokugawa, for example, such domestic matters of the samurai houses as marriage and inheritance could not be completely private affairs because they were related to the continuity and maintenance of the vassal samurai's *o-ie* (honorable house) and were conceived as virtually hereditary family services owed to their masters. In other words, domestic issues were connected to the structural foundation of the regional *daimyo* polity, which consisted of a local public domain.

Beneath this complex reclassification of public and private, a new proto-modern conception of the private sphere was emerging. Aesthetic activities became the focus of genuinely private spheres of socialization, of space and time that people could set aside for enjoyment of one another in their leisure hours. Activities of aesthetic socialization were regarded as separate from work and house (*ie*) matters, which were understood as *ōyake*, or public in nature. In this way, the Tokugawa aesthetic publics reemerged primarily as private spheres for genuine pleasure and entertainment. Although the political and religious aspects of the medieval aesthetic publics were not completely submerged during the Tokugawa period, the aspect of personal satisfaction became central to these aesthetic activities. In this sense, the Tokugawa shogunate's reclassification of publicness unintentionally shaped the proto-modern function of the private sphere, in which individuals can enjoy a relatively unsupervised personal life.

6

The Rise of Aesthetic Civility

By the late seventeenth and early eighteenth centuries, the organizational overhaul of Japanese society was complete, with an accompanying discipline that guaranteed greater categorical stratification of the population. Every station in life now had a standardized image of proper deportment covering every detail of language, gesture, manner, dress, and the degree and pattern of self-control. Whether most people in fact followed all these minute prescriptions to the letter is a different question, but that a standard model of propriety was entering the popular imagination is beyond dispute. By this point in time, Japanese society had elaborated an idiosyncratic, full-blown distinction between public and private spheres. In the reformulated hierarchy of publics under the shogunate, the realm of *ōkogi*, or the "great public," was coextensive with the shogun's authority and dominated the hierarchy of lesser publics. Within this framework of the hierarchy of publics, no sphere was considered truly private, as each level of involvement had its own assigned role and responsibility in the Tokugawa system of social control. Ironically, as we have seen, this distinctive characteristic of the Tokugawa state, which redefined the state-centered hierarchy of publicness, almost ended by creating the consciously defined private sphere in the area of aesthetic socialization, even though private life was regarded as inferior (*watakushi*) compared with the official hierarchy of publicness. Paradoxically, this idiosyncratic dichotomy between public and private allowed the samurai as well as commoners to cherish fleeting moments of personal freedom in the amateur artistic circles relegated to the private domain.

Aesthetic Knowledge as Civility

This period experienced a new groundswell of popular enthusiasm for cultural self-improvement. At the beginning of the Tokugawa period,

140

the highest level of cultural knowledge and scholarship was the virtual monopoly of such elites as the upper samurai, the imperial aristocracy of Kyoto, privileged townsmen, and the higher-ranking priests of the major temples and shrines. During the late seventeenth century, however, with the establishment of early modern local communities coupled with expanding markets, the newly successful commoners in the towns and villages began to amass social and cultural capital. Cultural activities outside the realm of the state assumed increasing importance, given the growing energy and sophistication of these commoners who were gradually accumulating social and cultural power.

The increasing popularity of the performing arts, the polite arts, and poetry composition became conspicuous in the late seventeenth century when the emergence of nationwide commercial markets, together with the rise of for-profit publishing, led to cultural productions driven by market forces. By this time, systematic networks linking producers, traders, brokers, wholesalers, retailers, and consumers appeared in various areas of the Japanese economy. The market networks had three major foci – the prosperous metropolitan cities of Osaka, Kyoto, and Edo. These three centers had manifold connections with the thriving castle towns of the *daimyo* lords, which were the provincial hubs of the early modern market economy. Information traveled as freely and extensively as people and commodities. The commercial publishing industry of the seventeenth and eighteenth centuries was just one of many profitable enterprises that flourished in this newly configured nationwide market. Books about poetry and the arts were among the best money-makers for early Tokugawa publishers. Information about the arts and poetry had never before been so readily accessible to such a large segment of the Japanese people. A number of new commercial as well as non-commercial cultural networks prospered outside the environs of courtly society. These networks carried aesthetic standards and information that had once been the exclusive preserve of the aristocracy to all levels of Japanese society.

The widespread enthusiasm for learning the arts was one of the most distinctive characteristics of the early modern civilizing process in Japan. Tokugawa people loved the world of the beautiful – they were not passive spectators of artistic performances but active participants. This attitude of engagement stands in contrast with the relationship between patrons and producers of the arts in eighteenth-century Europe in which sponsorship of the arts became a form of investment in status symbols. Tokugawa Japan was able to develop its distinctive pattern of interest and participation in the arts partly because of the sheer size of its population of amateur art and poetry students. Although aristocratic patronage continued to play an important role in the world of artists, many performing artists and poets were able to earn a decent living as teachers because people from all

territorial, status, or occupational groupings were eager to pay for instruction in these arts. The widened base of economic support provided
by popular teaching made Tokugawa artists and poets relatively independent of aristocratic patronage. Each artistic or poetic genre thus formed
a shared universe comprised of sizable like-minded groups of people set
apart from the outside world. The increasing autonomy of the artistic
world became the basis of aesthetic publics in which the status distinctions that were operative in the political world were nullified.

From the late seventeenth century onward, there is documentary evidence for growing popular interest in learning *yūgei,* or "arts for pleasure," outside the upper layers of Tokugawa society. The historian Moriya
Takeshi defines *yūgei* as "various kinds of arts that a mass of amateur
students enjoyed as hobbies."[1] The newly rich merchant class benefited
from the rising level of commercial prosperity; so did the samurai, who
turned themselves into civilized gentlemen through their participation in
this trend. A 1685 tourist guide to the city of Kyoto called *Kyōhabutae*
lists the names of 241 "various masters" who earned their keep by giving instruction in different fields of learning, arts, and literature. The list
includes the names of medical doctors and other scholars, but 130 of the
241 masters taught nothing but *yūgei.* A similar list found in the files
of the Kyoto magistrate's office names 440 "various masters" (*shoshi*).[2]
These "masters" received fees in exchange for instructing amateur students. When the students received their certificates of competence, it was
the custom to give the teachers additional fees. It is astonishing that so
many cultural professionals were able to earn a living in this city primarily
by teaching the traditional arts and literature to amateurs.

The amateurs who were interested in learning *yūgei* usually went to the
masters' homes. Upper-level samurai and urban commoners who could afford the expense would invite the masters to their own residences. In addition, the better-known masters organized so-called *tsukinami,* or monthly
meetings. Kyoto, as we have seen, was filled with beautiful temples surrounded by gardens that provided ideal meeting places for those who
loved beauty. For example, in the late seventeenth century, meetings for
renga linked poetry were held on the tenth of each month in the Rokujō
Dōjō, a Jishū temple, and on the twenty-fifth of the month in the meeting
place at the Kitano shrine. The monthly meetings for *utai* (also known
as *Yōkyoku,* vocal music for Nō dramas) were held in the Sōrinji temple on the twenty-third of each month and at the Kōdaiji temple on the
seventeenth of each month. Meetings for *rikka* flower arrangement were
held at the Rokkakudō on the seventeenth of each month.[3] The schedules
for these meetings were well-established routines to the citizens of Kyoto,
but they were also known to outsiders through commercial publications.
Networks of aesthetic enthusiasts quickly spread throughout Japan.

The people of the Tokugawa period began to take advantage of a seemingly lasting peace accompanied by economic prosperity in their private lives. The shogunate's policy of "rule by status," however, restricted people's personal lifestyles since one's status defined the rules of socialization, dress codes, forms of address, and the scales and styles for various life rituals. In these circumstances, aesthetic circles functioned as nodal points for social networks of people who appreciated civilized knowledge. This network formation created a situation in which persons of respectable social standing almost had to equip themselves with cultural socializing skills.

For example, the samurai gentlemen, whose social status was officially defined by their military function, were supposed to be versed not only in the arts of swordsmanship, archery, and riding but also in calligraphy; the basics of Confucian philosophy; the polite arts; various styles of poetry composition; *utai*, the tea ceremony; flower arrangement; and the games of *igo* and *shōgi*.[4] Of course, no samurai, however gifted, could master all these arts to their fullest extent, but they were nonetheless considered the basis of an upper-class education. In fact, as the Tokugawa shogunate remained at peace year after year, the samurai began to consider cultural skills to be more important in their social life than the arts of war. It was not only members of the samurai class who valued artistic talent and expertise. Tokugawa merchants also considered knowledge of these arts an important prerequisite for admission into "good society." *Shōbai ōrai*, a popular guide to morals for the merchant class published in 1693, illustrates the popularity of the performing arts among the urban merchants and their families:

> Those who are born into merchant households must learn writing and calculation. After this basic education, those who have leisure for things other than their own trades may take lessons in such arts as the composition of *waka* verse, writing linked verses in *renga* style, making *haikai*-style poetry, flower arrangement, *kemari* (an aristocratic ball game), the tea ceremony, *utai* singing, dancing, or playing the small and large drums, flutes, *biwa*, and *koto*.[5]

The amateur arts groups supplied the occasions in Tokugawa society in which respectable people from different social backgrounds could mingle freely.[6] In this sense, the communicative spheres that emerged through these various art forms constituted important publics that emerged within private spheres in Tokugawa society. Unlike the "official" society, in which one's political status was the fundamental definition of one's lifestyle, the art circles allowed samurai, merchants, and farmers to come together around their common aesthetic interests. Acquiring the requisite skills for participation was not done simply for personal pleasure but was also essential for membership in these new publics.

Enclave Identities in Private Space

What were the attractions that made Tokugawa adults such eager students of aesthetic pursuits? There were, of course, some utilitarian reasons for joining aesthetic circles; a person might do so in order to extend the perimeter of his or her social networks. On the other hand, practical economic considerations do not fully explain the attraction of learning the performing arts. The words of a contemporary critic of this private realm offer instructive insight into the operation and attraction of aesthetic enclave publics. An old samurai in the early eighteenth century who had lived long enough to reflect on more than seven decades of history wrote a memoir entitled *Mukashi Mukashi Monogatari* (Stories of Olden Days) around 1732. The elderly man made frequent references to the growing interest among the samurai in learning popular performing arts:

> When these men are able to sing *jōruri* songs well enough, they are given names with the suffix *tayū* [the customary ending of the artist names conferred on accomplished *jōruri* performers] by their teachers. The students feel honored by this treatment. Within the circle, they address each other only as "*–tayū.*" Their samurai names are deemed appropriate only for official public matters. In their private life [*naishō*, or "inner truth"], they use only their *tayū* names. How deplorable![7]

Jōruri songs came from the versified scripts of puppet plays.[8] Two star performers, Uji Kaganojō (1635–1711) and Takemoto Gidayū (1651–1714), made this genre extraordinarily popular. In addition, these performing artists worked with such talented scriptwriters as Chikamatsu Monzaemon (1653–1724), who poured his considerable literary gifts into the scripts of puppet plays. *Jōruri* became not only one of the most popular types of theatrical performance of the time but also one of the most sophisticated of literary genres. Performing *jōruri* was physically and emotionally demanding. Many *jōruri* lyrics described emotionally charged love affairs, sensational events of the time, or exciting renditions of historical events. Numerous amateurs, however, both samurai and commoners, were captivated by the demanding art of *jōruri* with its lyrics and intense emotional world. The professional performers who made their living by making this sort of music or putting on puppet shows were considered *kawara-mono* (riverbank people) of marginal social status.

Unlike the "gentrified" performing arts that had been refined in the late medieval period, such as Nō drama and the tea ceremony, *jōruri* was a truly popular Tokugawa art form. Kaganojō acknowledged the lowly status of this art form in his essay: "In general, there is nothing that has been more looked down upon as a low-prestige matter than *jōruri*" (*Takenoko shū*, 1678).[9] From the viewpoint of the traditional official belief system of the warrior class, *jōruri*-singing samurai were out of the question. Yet *jōruri* music made its way even into the honorable houses of the samurai.

The younger samurai relegated their stuffy formal names to dull official occasions. Their real enthusiasm was directed toward learning *jōruri*. Names with the *-tayū* suffix were reserved for *jōruri* singers, and the master teachers allowed only accomplished students to use *-tayū* names. The adoption of *-tayū* names signified that spaces set aside for *jōruri* music constituted enclaves of aesthetic publics in which the members participated in alternative realities through their own enclave identities.

What is interesting in the old samurai's testimony is its reference to the private domain, to *naishō* or one's true inner life. The term *naishō* originated in a religious context; it was a Buddhist word that implied an inner or secret truth. This type of private activity, which provided the disguise of an enclave identity through the use of *-tayū* names, became an inner truth for samurai who enjoyed expressing themselves in song. It was attractive enough to the younger samurai to induce them to discard their official names in favor of their *-tayū* enclave identities. Only in using *-tayū* names were they able to socialize with one another as individuals without being hampered by the forms of socialization prescribed by their state-defined stations in life.

Involvement in the performing arts gave students occasional opportunities to display their new skills to friends and neighbors (Figure 6.1). The old samurai also noted that in former times only professional entertainers enlivened domestic banquets. It was rare in those days for either the host or his guests to act as performers at a banquet. However, the writer continues, nowadays womenfolk of samurai households – the wives, daughters, and ladies-in-waiting – have all taken up popular music on social occasions. His observation certainly illustrates the extent to which learning *yūgei* had become so widespread by the early eighteenth century that it had evolved into an important currency for social skills. There was a widespread attitude among the samurai that their indulgence in private amusements was tolerable as long as they attended to their official duties. Even some Confucian scholars quietly supported this view. As long as a person could shift social gears appropriately, so to speak, he or she would not be criticized for seeking access to the private enclaves that allowed a measure of personal freedom and spontaneity.

Figure 6.1. Student Recital. A recital given by amateur music students, from *Ehon kotosugai* by Jichōsai, 1805. The audience is listening intently, apparently impressed by the performers' enthusiasm. Involvement in the performing arts gave students occasional opportunities to display their new skills to friends and neighbors.

The Technology of Naming

The *jōruri*-singing samurai, who, as mentioned earlier, relied only on -*tayū* names within their circles, exemplified the seductive social appeal of alternative realities. Conferring an artist name symbolized the strength of the bond between the master-teacher and the recipient of the name. Since naming is usually the act of a parent or godparent, it also served as an apt symbol of creating a pseudofamilial tie between the teacher and the student. The significance of the act of naming, as well as the meaning of proper names themselves, has been a frequent locus of philosophical discussion in the West since Plato. Judaism and Christianity both regard naming as an act of divine authority or creative power. In the East, Confucianism also held that naming has a godlike dimension. The circles of artistic amateurs in Tokugawa Japan retained this ancient respect for the power of names even though they did not associate it with any specific religious or philosophical doctrine. In fact, the act of naming was an important ritual technology in the Tokugawa aesthetic publics for creating alternative realities.

Although some art schools placed heavy emphasis on the teacher's conferral of an artist name as an official recognition of achievement, such other circles as the *haikai* poetry groups used artist names in a more casual fashion. A poet or artist ofen chose his or her own artist or pen name. Regardless of the level of formality attached to the artist name, however, the name allowed a student to socialize with artistic peers by becoming temporarily freed from the restrictive state-centered status hierarchy. Although official identities were widely known, students who referred to one another by their artist names underscored the fact that they inhabited a temporary organization of enclave identities. The use of special artists' names represented the establishment of ritual enclaves, self-contained artistic universes that admitted each participant to a new and different order of reality. Identity switching was possible because these artistic circles were consecrated by various ritual and organizational technologies that created enclaves in which the participants' formal categorical identities in the larger society were temporarily set aside.

Since each circle usually used different artist names, and many people joined more than one group of amateurs, it was not unusual for people with active cultural lives to acquire several artist names. People could not only temporarily suspend their formal identities but could also allow different facets of their personality to emerge through the use of different artist names in different circles. The realm of art forms as publics was thus defined by the bestowal of new names on its members.

The ritual technology used by *jōruri* enthusiasts for creating spaces for temporary freedom through the use of *-tayū* names for group members is reminiscent of the medieval *mu'en* (no-relation) technology. In terms of creating temporary spheres in which individuals were able to decouple from existing social constraints, the Tokugawa cultural circles inherited the medieval technologies of freedom. On the other hand, the overall social context in which these technologies were applied was very different from that of the previous period. The independence of the samurai as holders of feudal estates and their proud identity as warriors now existed in name only; their former glories had passed into history and legend. The *jōruri*-singing samurai was a phenomenon that is best understood as an example of a Tokugawa proto-modern style of private life in the context of centuries of redefining the categories of public and private under the pax Tokugawa.

The Three Dimensions of the Tokugawa Status System

The question inevitably arises as to why space for private life in this neo-feudal society was set apart primarily by aesthetic activities. The Tokugawa shoguns' strict prohibition of forming private alliances and political parties was certainly a major reason for preferring aesthetic activities as safe opportunities for socialization. There was a more complex structural factor, however, that made aesthetic circles a predictable focus of private social life. The reader may better understand the appeal of aesthetic publics from an articulation of the complex nature of the Tokugawa status (*mibun*) system.

Although the *mibun* status system is often misunderstood to be no more than a hierarchical categorization of status rankings intended to distinguish the ruling samurai class from the rest of the population, the implications of the system went far beyond legal categorization. The distinctive strength of the Tokugawa status system can be best understood sociologically on the basis of three aspects of its operation. The first point concerns what Takagi Shōsaku has called the "system of *yaku*," which means obligations or roles. Each status category was conceived as having a specific responsibility for fulfilling the group's designated duties (*yaku*) to the state. For example, the samurai owed military responsibilities to the authorities, while the farmers paid taxes in grain. The latter group was presumably protected by military service rendered by the former. Furthermore, the *yaku* system of obligation was also connected to the *ie* (house) system and individual members' responsibilities for the continuity and prosperity of the *ie*. The male head of the *ie* was usually obligated to participate in deciding matters that affected his local community as part of his *yaku*.

Second, the Tokugawa *mibun* system was linked to concrete territorial or occupational social groups. These mid-range organizations, such as villages, town wards, various trade associations, and outcast groups, had existed in the previous period, but they were reorganized under the Tokugawa system. Although the Tokugawa mid-range organizations continued to be semi-autonomous, they differed from their medieval predecessors in that they were not allowed to have self-defense capabilities. They were corporate entities that supposedly cooperated with the authorities. The members of these territorial or occupational groups shared the same status and were headed by chiefs who also belonged to the same status group. From this perspective, *mibun*-based organizations were conceived as mediators between the state and individual subjects. Regional units of control were able in most cases to incorporate, represent, or mediate people's opinions on local affairs. On the other hand, participation in these formal communicative spheres was obligatory rather than voluntary in nature.

Third, the order of status hierarchies was represented by differentiating formal rankings (*kakushiki*) defined by various status symbols and proprietary rules. There were numerous kinds of status symbols in Tokugawa society. For example, samurai rankings were meticulously differentiated by dress codes, forms of address, seatings in the castle, scales of expenditure and styles permitted for weddings, and so on. The non-samurai population were also expected to adjust all aspects of their lifestyles and patterns of socialization in ways considered appropriate to their status ranking. Conformity with the status system implied acceptance of strict official control over various aspects of one's life – which prevented free socialization among people of different rankings.

The attractiveness of the aesthetic publics was closely related to the per-
vasiveness of the Tokugawa *mibun* system along these three dimensions.
The traditions of the aesthetic publics safely overrode these three types of
restrictions. First of all, an individual's decision to take lessons in poetry
and the arts and to join networks of aesthetic enthusiasts was voluntary
in nature. Participants in aesthetic networks were not representing their
respective *ie* (house). Therefore, their membership in these groups did not
involve a sense of official obligation or *yaku*, in contrast to their participation in *mibun*-based associational life. Second, the networks of aesthetic
circles connected individuals outside the boundaries of territorial, occupational, and status groups that consisted primarily of people from the
same background. Without formally leaving the membership of *mibun*-
based societies, one could socialize legitimately with people from other
mibun groupings. Third, the rules of *kakushiki* propriety associated with
the *mibun* status system did not apply to the world of aesthetic publics.
The established ritual logic of creating a space for no-relation helped individuals to free themselves from feudal restrictions on their lifestyles.
In the hierarchically structured, status-oriented Tokugawa system, even
the most privileged members suffered from a sense of confinement; the
circumstances of noble birth circumscribed their opportunities for excitement and adventure as much as poverty or low status handicapped others.
The formal code of civility that defined social relations between persons
of different status alerted individuals to the need for continuous monitor-
ing of their relative position on the social map. In short, participation in
an aesthetic public was a precious opportunity for stepping outside the
bonds of the status system.

The *Nouveaux Riches* and the Aesthetic Publics

Tokugawa people valued the opportunities that were offered in the aesthetic circles to form bonds with kindred spirits they would not have otherwise encountered. This openness was an attractive compensation for
the rigid status system that confined individuals within fixed categories
defined at birth. In contrast to the official status system, merchants and
other commoners could aspire to the higher reaches of the aesthetic world
without risking punishment.

By the late seventeenth century, as Japan's economic expansion in this
period led to the emergence of a sizable mercantile class, a group of *nouveaux riches* rose to prominence alongside the declining older merchant
families of the unification period. The more prosperous they grew, however, the more they found themselves attracted to the traditional performing arts and the more they invested their leisure time in learning them.

During the late seventeenth century, Osaka became the new center of an economic boom led by these *nouveaux riches*. Ihara Saikaku (1642–1693), an astute observer and one of the most celebrated writers of the time, described the Osaka merchants of his day:

> In general, the Osaka rich were not descendants of old families that had prospered for many generations. Most of them were the type of person who was formerly called "Kichizō" or "Sansuke" [typical "redneck" names] but now they strive to enrich themselves. They have learned to socialize with people from "good" families while learning poetry-making, playing kemari [a ball game], archery, koto-harp, flute, or drum music, the perfume game, or the tea ceremony. By that time they have lost their countrified accents.[10]

Saikaku captured the essential features of an upwardly mobile subpopulation at the epicenter of a developing market economy. In this new economic climate, many young men from the more remote provinces of Japan were working hard to establish themselves. For those who were fortunate enough to attain a measure of success, the Tokugawa cultural circles served as finishing schools that turned entrepreneurs of humble origins into sophisticated urban businessmen. The writers of the period were aware of the attraction of new money to old conventions. Nishikawa Joken (1648–1724), a contemporary observer, described the relationship between Tokugawa economic prosperity, the human desire for status, and the popularization of aristocratic manners in his *Chōnin bukuro* (The Merchant's Wisdom Bag):

> Now that the townspeople have piled up a lot of money, they proudly attempt to raise their status by aping the manners of the aristocracy and the samurai. When the rest of the people, whether educated or not, look at these newly refined city folk, they are consumed with envy and push themselves to the limit in order to imitate [their polite arts]. In this way, the behaviors associated with the polite arts became the custom of the country as a whole.[11]

Joken's words convey the essential characteristic of the Tokugawa civilizing process. It was the more prosperous and reputable merchant families who attempted to emulate the cultural standards of the upper classes and pioneered the process of mass enculturation. The circles that usually accepted both samurai and non-samurai members resembled the British gentlemen's clubs of a bygone era in which socialization between members of the old aristocracy and the new business elite helped to create modern upper-class culture. In other words, the aesthetic means of socialization

in Tokugawa Japan became an important mode of civility during this period. As long as artistic pursuits did not interfere with business matters,
they were considered morally acceptable activities for members of the
merchant class.

The move toward higher standards of enculturation was not limited
to urban samurai and merchants. In fact, the world of the beautiful began to incorporate samurai and commoners as well as cities and villages.
In the outlying villages, the chiefs (*shōya*) and the better-off commoners were most affected by this trend. As mediators between the samurai
authorities and other village folk, they became very conscious of status
differentials, both between themselves and the samurai as well as between
themselves and their fellow villagers. Kawachiya Kashō, a village chief and
sake brewer in a village in the Osaka hinterland around the beginning of
the eighteenth century, wrote a long moral treatise for his family's benefit.
This document includes a noteworthy subsection entitled "The Need to
Learn the Performing Arts." In this section, Kawachiya noted, "Those
who know their responsibilities can learn the performing arts when they
have spare time for their own enjoyment."[12] Unlike the mindset of the
jōruri-singing samurai, whose economic basis was secure, Kashō's social
consciousness was that of a man whose primary concern was the ongoing
prosperity of his family business. Understandably, he regarded the arts as
pastimes for one's leisure hours, not pleasures that preoccupied one's time
to the degree of forgetting the requirements of business. He recommended
that his family members learn calligraphy and the ability to calculate as
the foundations of their education because these skills are the most useful. He then listed some "useful arts," such as the composition of *waka*
and *haikai* poetry, playing various music instruments, singing Nō songs,
flower arrangement, and traditional cooking (*hōchō*), citing their moral
and psychological benefits. On the other hand, Kashō considered learning
to play such games as *igo*, *shōgi*, and *sugoroku* (Japanese backgammon)
to be potentially addictive and therefore "useless." Even so, Kashō conceded that learning these "useless" games had some social benefit: "it may
be difficult to reject it because it is necessary to entertain interesting guests
or to attend meetings with various people."[13]

Generally, members of the *shōya* class, who were commoners who tried
to distinguish themselves from the ordinary villagers, had high cultural
aspirations. Kashō was good at *haikai* poetry, but once it became too popular, to the degree that, in his own words, "even women, children, and
lowlifes" write *haikai*, he showed off by reading *waka* poetry and performing in Nō plays in order to distinguish himself from the hoi polloi.[14]
Kashō's attitude toward cultural consumption reflected the presence of a
hegemonic hierarchy ordering the different branches of intellectual and
aesthetic knowledge in this period.

A village head, Yoda Sōzo, wrote the following in a set of precepts composed for his family in 1760: "For the sake of honorable socializing (*hitomae majiri*), one should acquire some knowledge of the rules for playing *go* and *shōgi*; for singing Nō drama songs (*yōkyoku*), and performing the polite arts (*shitsuke*)." It is interesting to see that Yoda used the term *hitomae* (literally, "person-front") to describe the necessity of learning the polite arts. *Hitomae*, or social appearance (*hito* means "person" in literal translation, and *mae* means "front"), denotes the honorable status that allows a person to face a peer. *Majiri* means "to socialize." The term *hitomae* concerns one's social reputation; for example, it is used in letters that were exchanged among the 47 samurai involved in the famous vendetta to describe an honorific feeling that they experienced as being unable to face fellow samurai as independent honorable persons if they allowed their dead master's enemy to survive.[15] *Hitomae* thus implied a sense of honor in a symbolic community in which members shared values that governed behavior and standards that determined rewards and punishment. In other words, *hitomae* assumed the existence of an imagined community. Yoda's use of the same word thus indicates that a deficiency of the skills required for artistic socializing would mar one's reputation as a decent member of good society. Acquiring aesthetic knowledge became a precondition for having a worthy reputation in polite society. One consequence of this development was the rapid formation of cultural as well as commercial networks. In spite of the fact that early modern Japan was deliberately divided into various territorial and categorical segments, the country was drawn together in the private realm through social and cognitive networks of poetry and the other arts.

It is important to note that enthusiastic participation in amateur artistic groups was not always met with universal approval. In spite of the obvious social utility for merchants in joining these circles, we also find many examples of contemporary admonitions against overindulgence in artistic activities.[16] These warnings, however, had nothing to do with puritanical disapproval of "art" as intrinsically "immoral" but rather with the risk of what we would now call addictive behavior. For the Tokugawa merchants, learning *yūgei* could be seductively attractive, sometimes to the point of interfering with business activities. Popular novels of the period often described merchants who lost their fortunes because of overinvolvement in *yūgei* and consequent neglect of their commercial responsibilities. *Chōnin kōken roku* (Observations of the City-Dweller's World), a moral treatise written in 1728 by the head of the Mitsui family, included a number of cautionary tales about careless merchants who lost money because of their excessive fondness for artistic and literary pursuits.[17] These and other morality stories indicate that Tokugawa people did not join amateur arts circles solely for commercial networking or similar utilitarian purposes. If the appeal of these groups had been largely confined to making business contacts, it is difficult to see why contemporary moralists would have thought it necessary to warn that they could be dangerously habit-forming. Warnings against the addictive potential of the amateur arts groups simply tell us that aesthetic studies were genuinely attractive to Tokugawa people.

The Arts and Boundary Trespass

During the eighteenth century, the vital center of Tokugawa cultural activities moved from the ruling samurai class to the populations of the larger and more sophisticated cities. By this time, the cultural heritage of the medieval period had been assimilated, popularized, and translated into more contemporary cultural idioms. For example, commoners in the Tokugawa period had some knowledge of courtly *waka* poetry, the famous passages of *Nō* drama, and such classics of ancient and medieval literature as "The Tale of Genji" and "The Tales of Heike." *Haikai*, popular styles of poetry-making, *Kabuki* theater, and such popular illustrated stories as *gesaku* fiction were all associated primarily with the culture of urban commoners, and all assumed a certain basic knowledge of medieval themes. On the other hand, the samurai were also attracted to the liveliness and spontaneity of popular culture. Some lesser samurai even began to participate in popular cultural productions.

Although the enclaves of aesthetic publics were not intended to threaten the authorities insofar as they were understood as private, or *watakushi*, loci for the temporary switching of fictional identities, the growing popularization of aesthetic networking practices began to blur the outlines of the *mibun*-based categories. As the samurai and the urban commoners began to share similar cultural idioms and enthusiasm, they were implicitly contributing to the collapse of some parts of the *mibun* system. This symbolic trespassing across official status boundaries was bidirectional. From the side of the upwardly mobile, some rich commoners who aspired to greater cultural prestige took lessons in such "traditional" arts with medieval origins as the tea ceremony, *Nō* singing (*utai*), *ikebana* flower arrangement, and the composition of *waka* poetry. From the other direction, the samurai who should have been mastering the finer points of *Nō* music were attracted to *jōruri* and other performing arts that originated in popular commoner culture.

This trespassing of boundaries, however, went beyond official status distinctions. In the first half of the Tokugawa period, most participants in the amateur arts groups were male. Although many Japanese performing arts convey an impression of what the Western world stereotypes as

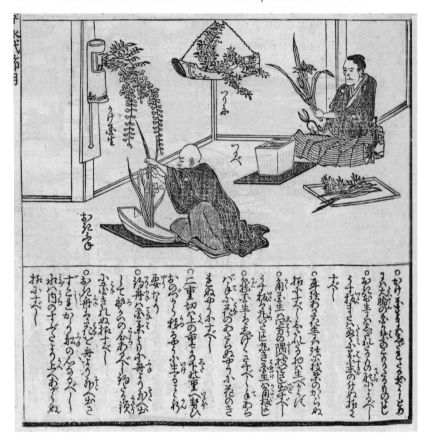

Figure 6.2. *Ikebana*, Gentlemen's Hobby. A page from *Dai Nihon eidai setsuyō mujinnzō*. Although many Japanese performing arts convey an impression of what the Western world stereotypes as "feminine," the early Tokugawa cultural circles were really more like "gentlemen's clubs." Male students in fact dominated even *ikebana*, the art of flower arrangement. It was only after the mid-eighteenth century or so that female students became conspicuous participants in these cultural groups.

"feminine," the early Tokugawa cultural circles were originally more like gentlemen's clubs, particularly in arts of the upper classes such as the tea ceremony. Male students in fact dominated even *ikebana*, the art of flower arrangement, which might appear to be a prototypically feminine activity, during this period (Figure 6.2). It was only after the mid-eighteenth century that female students became conspicuous participants in these cultural groups. The gender gap was in part a reflection of Japanese women's social segregation during this period. More to the point, however, the fact that socially respectable and economically powerful men were eager to join the art circles indicated that the polite and performing arts were not simply accessories to their lifestyle.

In the early development of the Tokugawa cultural circles, learning the arts of civilized society was roughly equivalent to becoming a member of an eighteenth-century English gentlemen's club. By joining a prestigious aesthetic circle, a male student could obtain entry into social networks and information that would not have been available to him otherwise.[18] Toward the end of the eighteenth and the beginning of the nineteenth centuries, however, the popularity of learning the performing arts extended well beyond this original function. Although some of the established art forms continued to reflect an aura of social privilege, learning the performing arts and poetry became so popular that the networks of aesthetic circles and associations were less comparable with privileged clubs for gentlemen. The love of beauty was clearly not exclusive to the male members of the upper classes. Although the degree of female participation in these cultural activities varied across the different genres, women generally increased their presence in these aesthetic networks in the later Tokugawa period.

In the early Tokugawa era, most female members of the cultural circles came from the higher samurai families and the *goten jochū*, or "castle maids," who were young women from urban commoner families serving in *daimyo* households as ladies-in-waiting. Female participation in artistic groups was a practice that was quickly transmitted to the households of urban commoners, who often sent their daughters to become castle maids in the families of higher-ranking samurai. To have one's daughter in service as a *goten jochū* was equivalent to placing her in an upper-class finishing school. The institution of the castle maids was a conspicuous practice in Edo since all the *daimyo* had to keep official residences in the shogun's city. By the mid-Tokugawa period, when the wealthier merchant houses in Edo had achieved an impressive level of prosperity and social respectability, their daughters were often sent to learn good manners in the households of the upper samurai. In sending off their daughters to be *goten jochū* in these elite households, the parents often assumed heavy expenses for the girls' pre-service education. It has been said that these urban commoner parents raised their attractive daughters "as one polishes a jewel on one's palm."[19] This early education was necessary if the girl was to be accepted for employment in a *daimyo* household; she had to have some cultural skills already under her belt, so to speak. Ujiie Mikito's study of the records of an upper samurai household indicates that girls from urban commoner families actually had to demonstrate their cultural competence at what amounted to job interviews.[20] Many of the girls claimed to have mastered a number of skills, including dancing, music, and calligraphy.[21]

As a result, sending daughters to tutors in the various performing arts became a virtual fad among the wealthy merchant families by the late eighteenth century. Shikitei Sanba's novel *Ukiyoburo* (Bath House in the Floating World) contains a humorous description of a girl named Okado, who complains that she has no "time off" for play. Every day, from morning through evening, her schedule is filled with different lessons; before breakfast, she has her *shamisen* (three-stringed instrument) lesson, followed by her dance lesson. Next comes a tutorial in reading and writing. After a trip to the public bathhouse in the late afternoon, Okado must go to a *koto* (Japanese harp) lesson. In the evening, she has to review the day's lessons at home. The following excerpt is taken from Okado's conversation with her chum in the bathhouse:

> Absolutely nothing is better than having a day without lessons. That's why I always long for the New Year holidays.... I don't have any time to play. I really hate these lessons.... My Dad said to Mom, "Let Okado move at her own pace. She will remember these arts somehow. The lessons are only to help her land a job [in the samurai household, not for accomplishment]." But Mom is so strict! She answered Dad, "If Okado is going to take these lessons, she should really get into them so that her body takes in the arts and remembers them in depth.... Because she finds you a pushover, she won't listen to me!" Do you know, my Mom in fact doesn't know how to read and write because she was born out in the back country, surrounded by the mountains and sea.... Mom also can't play the *shamisen*. She told me that that is all the more reason why she wants her daughter to learn these arts. She would never listen to anyone else's opinion about this stuff. Wohumm.... it's too much![22]

The attitude of Okado's mother reflects the extent of commoner participation in the performing arts by the late eighteenth and early nineteenth centuries. Taking lessons in the performing arts became so widespread that even the children of humble parents who themselves might not have acquired aesthetic and literary skills from their upbringing were pushed to improve themselves. Mothers and fathers in the middle strata of Japanese society were eager to have daughters as well as sons groomed for full participation in the Tokugawa version of the good life. From the evidence in Okado's description, her parents were apparently commoners. Playing the *shamisen*, a three-stringed instrument used for *Kabuki* and *jōruri* music, was also considered more appropriate for commoners than for the samurai elite. Okado's parents, however, clearly believed that an ability to play the *shamisen* would improve her chances of obtaining a position in the household of one of the higher-ranking samurai.

Although Okado is a fictional character, she was not intended to represent an exceptional girl of this era. Learning popular music and dance became prerequisites for commoners' daughters hoping to find positions in upper samurai households simply because the samurai shared the commoners' enthusiasm for popular culture. Many essays of this period mention the fact that many samurai enjoyed and learned arts and music originally associated with commoners. This type of aesthetic "slumming" was not uncommon, as the author of *Seji kenmonroku* (The Chronicle of the World Observed, 1822) observed. The writer lamented the behavior of contemporary samurai who "consider playing *shamisen* and other *yūgei* so interesting to bone marrow. Their appearance is also not in keeping with the samurai style."[23] By this time, the most attractive performing arts and poetic genres had absorbed a strong flavor of commoner culture. Innovations in the arts and aesthetic tastes did not come from the samurai class but from the urban townspeople in conjunction with popular entertainers. Although people clearly recognized that such popular forms of music as *shamisen, nagauta* (song for *Kabuki* theater) and *jōruri* were closely linked to theatrical performers and entertainers of lower status in the official hierarchy, in actual practice the samurai families of the late Tokugawa period were drawn to the lively popular culture of the large cities. When people came together to share their enjoyment of performing arts that reflected this culture, feudal status boundaries became practically meaningless.

One piece of evidence from a samurai's household of the late Tokugawa period regarding children's *keiko* (lessons) also indicates that it was common for the daughters of the lesser samurai to take *shamisen* lessons, although an upper samurai household would probably have their daughters take *koto* lessons as well. The *koto* was a harp-like instrument that was older than the *shamisen* and hence more prestigious. An oral testimony by a son of a former samurai described his upbringing and his sister's childhood in Edo as follows:

> It was in the old time, around the era of bunkyū (1861–1864). In our residential area, Hacchobori [an area for samurai officers who worked as a security force for the city of Edo], our town magistrate's senior officers' (*yoriki*) families, as well as junior officers' (*dōshin*) families – the girls usually took *shamisen* lessons. The daughters of the higher-ranking officers might also learn the *koto*. The boys might learn *yōkyoku* [songs from Nō drama].... Since my sister turned seven, she also started taking *nagauta*

[popular songs] lessons. A house servant always accompanied her every day when she went to her lessons.[24]

The only boundary that his sister was not allowed to cross was to make a uniform *kimono* for herself as a student of *nagauta* singing. The parents considered the fashionable style of the uniform *kimono* more suitable for entertainers than for a *katagi* (literally, straight) person, and certainly inappropriate for the daughter of a good family.

Learning the performing arts changed the lifestyle of Tokugawa people to the degree that Kinugawa Yasuki, a Japanese historian, rightfully compares it to the "changes brought about in our lifestyles and customs by the popularization of television."[25] The changes that art and literary networks brought into Tokugawa social life were not limited to the popularization of the art forms themselves. They created "publics," or spheres of socialization that represented intersections of various social and cognitive networks. These spheres of communication extended beyond occasional gatherings of people from different social backgrounds. Although samurai and commoners might socialize with one another in their pursuit of beauty, sharing the cognitive universe of such artistic genres as *jōruri* also represented boundary-crossing in terms of the *mibun* status distinctions. From people of humble background to the samurai and *daimyo*, this institutionally segregated society with feudal status boundaries was united by a love of and enthusiastic aspirations toward aesthetic enculturation. Although shared interests in music lessons and other artistic activities did not usually affect people's formal status rankings, common standards of aesthetic excellence made social boundaries less significant. In this sense, civility in Tokugawa Japan entered through the back door, as it were, using aesthetic pursuits as its entrance.

In the late Tokugawa period, during the seemingly everlasting peace under the Tokugawa, all kinds of hobbies flourished in this prosperous society, enlivening the lives of men and women. For example, there were gardening enthusiasts who were cultivating chrysanthemums, azaleas, and morning glories of incredible shapes and colors. These gardeners were not only skilled craftsmen but were also highly social individuals who were dynamically connected through loosely interlinked networks that were maintained through their ongoing participation in a number of competitive exhibitions.[26] These activities went far beyond what we nowadays consider as hobbies, and they also did not fit into the image of the performing arts as we use the term in modern English. Nonetheless, they were perceived as "*gei*" or "*geinō*," terms close to the broad usage of arts in English. Being equipped with *gei* was a way to socialize with each other in society. With the rise of these enthusiastic "hobbyists" who were freely transgressing various social boundaries, there also emerged various public spaces that facilitated proto-modern styles of aesthetic socialization.

For example, in this context ancient customs of cherry blossom viewing gained renewed enthusiasm.

Let us imagine ourselves as participants in a cherry blossom viewing party in the city of Edo during the late Tokugawa period. The city's best locations for viewing the flowering trees, such as the Ueno hill and the Sumida riverbank, are filled with Edo citizens of every station. From ladies-in-waiting at the *daimyo*'s households to provincial samurai touring the capital city, from groups of people from the poorer backstreet neighborhoods to families from the large and well-off merchant houses, old people and children, all crowd into the cherry blossom groves. Groups of community schoolteachers and children, as well as instructors in the performing arts and their students, also join the picnics. The women in particular but also the men have togged themselves out in their most fashionable *kimonos* to show off and have prepared some elaborate picnic food. The entertainment – music and dancing – is a common accompaniment of cherry blossom picnics. Although the medieval linked-verse sessions under the cherry blossoms in the spirit of *mu'en* have faded from popular memory, Tokugawa people from all levels of the class system have rediscovered cherry blossom viewing (*hanami*) and have made it the most popular seasonal entertainment. The residential area of Edo is zoned into neighborhoods of similar status groups (for example, two-thirds of the area is reserved for the samurai), but all of them may enter the common space set aside for enjoying the cherry blossoms. The spirit of sharing in this festive atmosphere defines the Tokugawa style of cherry blossom parties.

In this temporary free zone, secular and entertainment-oriented though it is compared to the more ritualistic medieval *mu'en* (no-relation) places, various groups of people sit shoulder to shoulder, with spaces separated only by thin curtains. The light curtains only partially block the view of other groups, but the sounds of music and singing, the smell of good food, and the sight of attractive men and women pass easily through the thin fabric. It is sometimes possible to peek through the curtains or even join another group for a few moments. The music and dancing may help to form a connection between two people who have not met previously.

Cherry blossom viewing parties sometimes lead to love affairs between men and women or between two men. Women and men may tie pieces of paper with their poems to the branches of the cherry trees. They may hand out strips of fancy papers with their poems to attractive men and women in other parties. Poetry, especially *haikai* poems, was conceived as a means of communication among strangers at these parties (Plate 1). Ono Sawako, a specialist who has studied the cherry blossom viewing parties in Edo in this period, has noted that: "It is interesting that communication among unknown people at the cherry blossom viewing sites was carried out, not in ordinary language but in poetry – indicating that these sites were governed by norms outside those of everyday life."[27]

We can extend her observation by remarking that the cherry blossom picnic site partitioned by curtains resembles that of late Tokugawa society. The partitions of status boundaries were like flimsy curtains waving in the wind; they did require a modicum of acknowledgment. It was possible, however, for those who had aesthetic socializing skills as common cultural knowledge to slip across the partitions. Attractive cultural practices could easily carry persons across the status differentials like the festive sounds of music and dancing at the cherry blossom parties. The degree of "stranger-ship" may be an indication of the degree of civility in a given society. Having incorporated aesthetic knowledge as a way of socializing "strangers," the cherry blossom parties demonstrate that aesthetic civility had become an integral part of the grammar of sociability in Tokugawa society.

Cultural Authorities and the Autonomy of Aesthetic Fields

The remarkable popularization of aesthetic knowledge in this period did not come about only as the result of increased demand for instruction. Since we have already observed the "demand side" of the story, we should now turn our attention to the "supply side" of Tokugawa popular enculturation. It was the initiative of professional artists, poets, and other cultural entrepreneurs that made a uniquely aesthetic-driven haven in this society possible. Although Japanese artists and poets were generally inspired to achieve otherworldly beauty in their expressions (following the medieval origin of aesthetic traditions), they could not live in a world of Zen-like retreat; they strove hard to increase their economic standing and authority in various ways. In order to create alternative realities in aesthetic publics within the context of a hierarchical feudal authority structure, artists as well as the world of beauty itself needed to sustain some level of authority. The traditional teachings of many Japanese arts ideally and normatively supported aesthetic egalitarianism, as was discussed in the previous chapter. Ideals and normative arguments aside, however, aesthetic egalitarianism alone could not establish the autonomy of an aesthetic realm in this hierarchically restructured society. Although the Tokugawa artists and poets inherited the rich cultural resources of ritual technology that enabled the segregation of their world of aesthetic socialization from the feudal order, the ritual technologies alone were not enough to create and sustain artistic activities.

The reader should recall that the social status of performing artists was open to question in this society. Many professional artists and poets in the medieval period came from marginal subpopulations. For example, many dancers and musicians – even Nō players – had been originally perceived as marginal *kawara-mono*, riverbank people. Although some of the art forms, including *Nō* drama and the tea ceremony, had acquired a certain patina of refinement and "gentrification" from the late medieval period through the first half of the Tokugawa period, there were other popular performing arts whose status was still ambiguous. On the other hand, there were many amateur artists and poets whose feudal social status was much higher than that of the professional artists. Aesthetic group activities in which professional artists were treated as subordinate to amateur high-ranking students would not engender an ideal setting for enjoying alternative realities. In this circumstance, professional artists naturally sought ways to increase their authority in the world of beauty.[28]

I will make use of the concept of "cultural fields" as elaborated by Pierre Bourdieu in order to clarify the point I wish to make. Bourdieu observed that certain artistic and literary fields in nineteenth-century Europe began to be considered "a world apart, subject to its own laws."[29] In premodern Europe, artists were limited in their activities by such external constraints as those of the state, the church, and the tastes of aristocratic patrons. In contrast, the literary fields in Europe attained maximum autonomy by the second half of the nineteenth century in that writers could exercise their cultural authority largely independent of political and economic considerations. "The state of the power relations in this struggle," Bourdieu wrote, "depends on the overall degree of autonomy possessed by the field; that is, the extent to which it manages to impose its own norms and sanctions on the whole set of producers."[30] This degree of autonomy is always relative and varies considerably across periods, fields, and national traditions. Following the emergence of various internal institutions (e.g., journals, professional critics, or the granting of academic degrees to practitioners), some fields came to be regarded as having independent authority to judge the merits of artistic productions within their purviews.

The concept of aesthetic autonomy is important in understanding the mechanisms by which aesthetic spheres become central to civic communicative life. The belief that aesthetic pursuits have their own rules and standards, and are subject to judgment only by those who have proved themselves to be competent practitioners of the art in question, was important not only for the activities themselves but also for the establishment of communicative spheres free of such external constraints as a politically defined status system. In short, the possibility of creative enclaves depended on widespread acceptance of the notion of aesthetic autonomy.

One way that artists could increase their authority was to associate themselves with the highest-ranking patrons through patronage – the higher in status the patron (such as a *daimyo* lord or preferably the shogun), the more respect the artist would command among the lesser samurai and wealthy merchants. It was a quick route to increasing the social respectability and authority of professional artists; however, personal patronage carried with it the risk that artists might lose their autonomy, as they were reliant on the individual temperament of their patrons. The reader should recall the tragedy of Sen no Rikyū, whose collaboration with the ruler Toyotomi Hideyoshi eventually cost him his life. Linking one's livelihood and artistic authority to the personal favor of the powerful left little room for autonomy.

One route for artists to increase their autonomy was to obtain financial support directly from mass audiences via the market as a way to diffuse the sources of their income. This method of liberating artists from private patronage, however, had its own pitfalls. As Pierre Bourdieu has observed, the individualization and atomization of contemporary artistic and literary fields through commercialization had "liberating" as well as "alienating" effects.[31] The process can be said to have "liberated" artists and writers in that they were no longer exclusively controlled by the arbitrary caprices of elite patrons. By directing their efforts toward an unspecified number of consumers in the marketplace, artists, composers, and writers began to acquire greater autonomy over the content of their creations. Instead of being governed by the arbitrary will of aristocratic patrons, however, artists had to follow the unpredictable moods of consumers as well as the whims of the dealers and publishers who controlled the market. Furthermore, working to satisfy a faceless mass of consumers often meant intellectual isolation for artists and writers. In the modern art world, the producers and consumers of art or literature are segregated by the market system. The lives of modern artists and writers thus tend to be restricted to their own study or studio. By contrast, the old style of private patronage, which revered the arts within the closed ranks of aristocratic salons, tended to bring professional artists together with those who appreciated their work.

At an intermediary stage between personal aristocratic patronage and the contemporary mass-market system, early modern European states instituted royal academies for artists and scholars. A select group of creative individuals acquired a measure of aesthetic or scientific authority under the auspices of the monarch. In contrast to personal patronage from aristocrats, artists accepted into academy membership collectively gained greater authority and freedom while exercising a gatekeeping power over "lesser" lights in their field. Although the Tokugawa shoguns continued to patronize small groups of artists and scholars, they did not develop a system of organizational patronage comparable to the royal academies of the West. Without organized public support for artists and scholars, or a functional gatekeeping institution, the writers and artists of Tokugawa Japan were dependent on the forces of the popular market.

During the eighteenth and nineteenth centuries, however, the arts and literature of Tokugawa Japan followed a distinctive path of development. Private patronage continued to play a role in this period, but the new market forces made themselves felt. For example, a commercial publishing industry (discussed at greater length in Chapter 11) prospered in this period and redefined the phenomenon of "best-sellers." Yet, in the field of performing arts and poetry, given the growing number of amateur students, professional artists and poets could make their living primarily through instruction. Teaching many students on a fee-per-lesson basis stabilized the lives of many performing artists and poets. This option also increased artists' autonomy by widening their economic basis in ways that exclusive aristocratic patronage did not allow. The situation encouraged some artists and poets to organize amateur students and form their own schools. The result was the creation of numerous communities of professional, semi-professional, and amateur cultural enthusiasts. It was also a good solution for avoiding the atomization of artists and poets. Professional artists and poets were surrounded by a sizable audience of the like-minded, who were themselves aspiring to be productive artists. Given this shared aesthetic universe, the alienating effects of modern markets on the producers of art and literature were not a significant problem in Tokugawa Japan. The task of Tokugawa artists and poets was to maintain this shared universe by forming various institutions to determine field-specific criteria for judging artistic productions while recruiting and instructing new students on an ongoing basis.

The artistic community attempted to respond to such challenges by experimenting with several different organizational structures. Two major types of aesthetic organizations emerged in this period and helped to energize the Tokugawa cultural fields. The first type of teaching method was the so-called *iemoto*, or grand master system. The *iemoto* system ideally aimed at enhancing the authority of the grand master by creating a hierarchical order of professional teachers, semi-professionals, and amateur students. By increasing the authority of the grand master, the art school attempted to support the status of enclave publics in which students temporarily suspended the hierarchical status order of feudal society. The grand master ranked high above the pyramidal structure of professional–intermediate teachers and amateurs. The authority of the *iemoto* was critical to prescribing and sustaining the alternative realities in enclave publics. Credentials were particularly important in the polite arts because, unlike painting or music, their criteria of excellence or originality are comparatively ambiguous. After all, how can one evaluate the relative artistic merits or authenticity of different ways to hold a teacup? The *iemoto* system can be seen as an intelligent adaptation of those arts to the newly expanding art instruction market by utilizing some idioms of feudalistic authority.

On the other hand, not all aesthetic associations developed a hierarchically structured *iemoto* system. There were more open, more fluid, and less structured circles that also successfully produced enclave publics. In such circles, the teachers' roles were important, but they did not develop the pyramidal authority structure of the *iemoto*. The *haikai* poetry circles that I will discuss in the next chapter were typical of the more flexible styles of aesthetic associations. These horizontally structured associations had several different names, including *ren* and *kumi*. A *ren* association could be organized for a short-term project; moreover, the organizer of the *ren* was not necessarily a professional teacher. For example, a neighborhood shopkeeper might gather a circle of amateur poets and invite a professional poet to critique their pieces. Being relatively loose, decentralized, and horizontal, the *haikai* networks had an advantage in spreading the popularity of this art form. These horizontally structured networks tended to be relatively ephemeral, but they could incorporate market trends more rapidly than the *iemoto*. The *ren* introduced several innovations, such as monthly poetry competitions with prizes, which helped to increase the autonomy of their aesthetic fields.

Although the *iemoto* and *ren* looked quite different from the outside, one hierarchical and formal in structure and the other more horizontal and ephemeral, both types of organizations emerged in response to two major socio-political conditions – the political structure segmented by status boundaries and the expanding market economy. The two different types of organizations took different paths toward securing aesthetic autonomy for their teachers and students. The following chapter will discuss the activities of the *haikai* poetry networks, which consisted of relatively loose, temporary, and weak social ties. In contrast to the relative informality of the poetry networks, the hierarchical and formal qualities of the *iemoto* system departed from the older ideal image of an aesthetic public characterized by the spirit of *mu'en*. Nonetheless, the *iemoto* system of art instruction merits our attention because it brought about a greater measure of aesthetic autonomy. By increasing the authority of the grand master, the *iemoto* system established a cultural field with aesthetic standards that effectively overrode formal status distinctions.

The *Iemoto* System, the Invention of New Art Organizations

Ie means "house," and *moto* literally means "original." The *iemoto* system was hierarchical in structure, with the *iemoto* themselves – the grand masters – holding positions of paternalistic authority over the lesser instructors and students. As the term itself indicates, the system made heavy use of Japanese paternalistic idioms usually associated with family and kinship. The *iemoto* system is still a vital institution in contemporary Japan for promoting the study and practice of the traditional arts. In a typical large-scale *iemoto*, the grand master issued different levels of certification to students, while most of the actual instruction was carried out by local teachers. While the local teachers earned their incomes from tutoring students, the grand master received certification fees every time that a student progressed to a higher degree. On the other hand, the system did provide a form of credentialing for the local teachers; their connection to the authority of the grand master served as proof of their competency and authenticity.[32] Although the term *iemoto* itself was a product of the mid-eighteenth century, it quickly became standard usage.

The most distinctive characteristics of the modern *iemoto* are the result of the organizational innovations of the eighteenth century. The strength of the Tokugawa *iemoto* system was that it was already adapted to capitalist business operations while it made use of some seemingly traditional idioms to increase its aesthetic authority. The system enabled the grand master to recruit a large number of amateur students into a well-organized franchise system while establishing the *iemoto* as the sole arbiter of the content of the tradition. This organizational pattern enhanced the autonomy of a cultural field to the extent that the authority of the *iemoto* was able to supersede the status hierarchy of the feudal system. The merger of feudal and capitalistic organizational characteristics allowed the *iemoto* art schools, whose historical origins dated back to the medieval period, to remain economically viable businesses in modern Japan. Still today, some modern *iemoto* for the tea ceremony and *ikebana* have enrolled as many as a million amateur students.

Since the *iemoto* system also made use of quasi-kinship language to describe the relationship between the grand master and his students, the system appears at first glance as little more than a transplantation of the paternalistic ideology of the *ie*. The association created under the authority of the *iemoto*, however, was a purely voluntary organization, as participation in its courses of instruction was a matter of individual initiative. In this sense, the art schools were typical Tokugawa protomodern organizations. Once a group of students from different regional, occupational, and class backgrounds had accepted the authority of the *iemoto*, they could socialize with one another as if they were members of a family.

Some specific figures from surviving student lists tell an interesting story. The Ikenobō School in Kyoto is said to be founded by Ikenobō Senkō during the unification era for instruction in *ikebana*. It is the oldest *iemoto* school for the study of flower arrangement still in existence in modern Japan. The school's records of student names between 1678 and 1750 listed about 1,200 students by year of registration. Most registrations of new students resulted from contacts with intermediate teachers living in other cities or provinces. These mid-level instructors recommended their local students to the *iemoto* in Kyoto. In some cases, the same agent, apparently indicative of some intermediate teachers having considerable local influence as well as entrepreneurial spirit, referred dozens of new students.[33] The *iemoto* system undoubtedly opened up some "secret" or hidden traditions of the arts to the wider population through standardized curricula. At the same time, it concentrated authority within the *iemoto* and decreased the possibility that the more accomplished students would become independent of the grand master. The *iemoto*'s monopoly of issuing certificates made the whole system resemble a kind of franchise.

The cumulative efforts of recruiting and networking allowed the Ikenobō School to move to a proto-modern form of art school by the beginning of the nineteenth century. In the fourteenth year of Bunka (1817), the school held a special event for its retiring *iemoto* grand master at a Jishū temple in Kyoto. From provinces all over the country, 1,251 students exhibited their flower arrangements to honor the master teacher. The exhibition was crowded by more than 2,400 vases filled with flowers, 450 vessels in the so-called *rikka* style, and 846 vases in the *ikebana* style.[34] The exhibition catalog listed exhibitors according to their hierarchical positions since a meticulously differentiated ranking system had developed in this school. The Ikenobō School is said to have had more than 20,000 students by 1817.[35] It is impressive that an art school based in Kyoto was able to attract such a large number of students from every part of Japan.

By the beginning of the nineteenth century, the *iemoto* system spread into other branches of the arts. A pamphlet printed during the early nineteenth century, called *Shoryū iemoto kagami*, or "The Mirror of the Many Iemoto," listed the names of *iemoto* establishments in 31 different fields in the arts, literature, and scholarship. The list included the art of making flower arrangements, dancing or singing songs of various genres, performing the tea ceremony, writing *haikai* poetry, and learning such board games as *go* or *shōgi*. Each field was represented by several *iemoto*. For example, the tea ceremony had three *iemoto* in this list, while the art of flower arrangement was represented by two *iemoto*. It would be inaccurate to assume that each art form was dominated by a single *iemoto*; in most cases, there was competition among several master teachers in the field. Although all the grand masters listed could freely refer to themselves as *iemoto*, or at least the list named them as such, some were relatively unconcerned with building pyramidal organizational structures. Moriya Takeshi, a Japanese historian, has noted that among the 31 grand masters listed in the *Shoryū iemoto kagami*, only those offering instruction in the tea ceremony, flower arranging, the perfume game, and *utai* singing actually represented the organizational structure of the *iemoto* system in its fullest form.[36]

Authority and Commercial Structure of the *Iemoto* System

The authority of the *iemoto* grand master was promoted as a power that exercised ultimate control over the quality and authenticity of the student's artistic production. To this end, it was necessary to emphasize the importance of the lineage of the true tradition of the art. This emphasis on continuity of tradition was especially true in the tea ceremony schools; the grand masters who could claim descent from Sen no Rikyū elevated the tea master's tragic death to the level of aesthetic martyrdom and emphasized his authority as the embodiment of the true spirit of the tea ceremony. The legend grew to become an important ingredient in protecting his descendents' position as charismatic leaders of the tea ceremony *iemoto*. The increased authority bestowed on the legend of the *iemoto* lineage helped students follow the order of the aesthetic world, while considering their fellow students as temporarily equal under the authority of the *iemoto*. Its authority also attracted students from different social classes to aesthetic associations, while the advanced certificate issued by the *iemoto* carried with it a somewhat legendary air of authority.[37] The authority vested in the *iemoto* can be thought of as a social as well as an aesthetic consecration of the artistic sphere. Unlike the status hierarchy that defined the external political world, the tea ceremony schools allowed even commoner students to aspire to upward mobility through promotion to higher positions whose prestige was guaranteed by the grand master's authority. In this way, the *iemoto* system both reflected the commoners' new cultural aspirations and partially satisfied their desires to rise in the world.

Certificates and Name-Takers

The elevation of the master teacher's authority was not by itself, however, an invention of the Tokugawa period. In the older traditional arts, the act of *sōden*, or the transmission of higher knowledge from a master to a student, had been a matter of importance since the medieval period. Masters who had the ability to transmit such knowledge were highly respected. Even so, the Tokugawa *iemoto* system represented a departure from older conceptions of artistic instruction as the private transmission of carefully guarded secret lore.

Following the pioneering work of Nishiyama Matsunosuke, Japanese scholars generally agree that the essence of the Tokugawa grand master system that distinguished it from its medieval predecessor had to do with the fact that the *iemoto*, or grand master, monopolized the right to grant *sōden*, or certification, to his students. Although this manner of granting credentials sounds trivial, turning the right to issue a certificate of competence into the private property of the *iemoto* carried with it a number of significant organizational implications.[38] In the medieval model, once a disciple obtained *sōden*, he could set up shop as a new master and produce his art in his own right, as well as recruit the next generation of disciples. As long as an art form is transmitted in this way, it may generate a lineage or succession of artists but not a large, cohesive structure and center of instruction.

Under the new *iemoto* system, even though an advanced student had obtained the highest certificate that the school could confer, he or she did not thereby gain the right to certify new students. The "graduates" remained as intermediate-level teachers in the art school; they were able only to recommend their students to the *iemoto* for the coveted certificates. On the other hand, when the grand master maintained an authoritative reputation, or "brand name," so to speak, the intermediate teachers also benefited from their association with the school because they had larger groups of amateur students to instruct. As a result, the invention of the *iemoto* system was the critical key to the construction of large-scale formal organizations in the various aesthetic fields.

Furthermore, the *iemoto* system opened up some secret or hidden traditions of their arts to the wider population through standardized curricula of teaching. Without standardizing instructional procedures, it was difficult to control the quality of instruction of a large number of amateur students taking lessons from intermediate teachers. The obvious drawback of this standardization was the loss of the spontaneity and flexibility that had animated many of the early grand masters in the various arts. For example, in the Sen tea ceremony schools, the so-called *shichiji shiki*, the staff came up with seven games of the tea ceremony as a pedagogical device. *Shichiji shiki* was introduced around the mid-eighteenth century, at the time that the Sen family adopted the *iemoto* structure.[39] The introduction of a playful game-like element to the intensity of the tea ceremony rituals helped to keep beginning students interested. Furthermore, the curriculum of the tea ceremony was divided into seven stages, and an amateur student was encouraged to progress step-by-step in order to receive the higher certificates.[40] Without this process of standardization under the *iemoto* system, it is doubtful whether most of the traditional art forms would have survived into the modern period. Because the *iemoto* system incorporated a step-by-step educational program, it made the arts accessible to anyone who could afford the lessons and was willing to follow instructions. In contrast to the more exclusive one-to-one pattern of instruction that characterized the medieval period, the *iemoto* system opened up the traditional arts to a larger segment of the population willing to pay fees in exchange for teaching.

Running parallel to this development was the new availability of commercially printed books on the arts. The boom in Tokugawa commercial publishing during the late seventeenth century meant that a large number of introductory guides to the tea ceremony, flower arranging, and other traditional arts were printed in this period.[41] A number of introductory books such as *Nō no kinmōzui* (*Illustrated Introduction to Nō*, 1687), became best-sellers of the period. I will discuss Tokugawa commercial publishing in further detail in Chapter 11. At this point, it is important to note that the publication of these guides to the different art forms reflected more than a growing popular demand for learning; it also subtly signified a new departure from the medieval mentality, namely a break from secrecy in connection with the arts. The straightforward explanations of art forms, which had been closely guarded secrets, sometimes accompanied by ample illustrations, were intended to open hidden knowledge to a wider audience.

The *iemoto* system created a web of social and symbiotic relationships between the grand master and the intermediate instructors. In particular, the technology of naming to create alternative identities was most effectively utilized in the *iemoto* system. In the *iemoto* system, the grand master conferred an artist name on an accomplished student in recognition of artistic merit or achievement. The person who was given an official artist name in the *iemoto* system was called a *natori*, or name-taker, and was entitled to teach artistic skills to others. Just as parents give names to their children, the grand master's act of naming the student symbolized the artist's acquisition of a new identity as a full member of an "in" group, as if he or she were a part of the *iemoto*'s family. In this way, those who had been recognized for their skills in this field could leave behind their formal categorical identities as merchants, heads of families, or caretakers of *kagyō* (family businesses) and temporarily become individual artists with social recognition – even if only within relatively small local circles of amateur artists.[42] The use of quasi-familial communitarian ideology in non-kinship-based organizations is a frequent feature of Japanese patterns of social organization. This ideology, familiar to us as the preferred management style of the large corporations of post-war Japan until very recently, serves as a ritual technology for enhancing cohesion and *esprit de corps* of a group. The invention of the *iemoto* system was one of the salient examples of proto-modern organizational invention in Japan.

Thus, the *iemoto* system in various performing arts had to invent the "tradition" of each art in the process of standardizing the content of the arts. Moreover, with the invention of the *iemoto* system, the Japanese aesthetic world completed the Tokugawa style of establishing its own alternative hierarchy. Although the authority of the *iemoto* could not undermine the state-centered definition of social hierarchy, the *iemoto* created its own criteria of hierarchy and developed distinctive ritual technologies to promote the alternative realities to the state-centered world. In other words, the *iemoto* system was one route to consecrating the sphere of communication set apart from the order of the dominant public and the hierarchical world of feudal authorities headed by the supreme public propriety (*ō-kōgi*) of the shogunate.

In sum, the *iemoto* system was one of several effective institutions that developed during the Tokugawa period and served to increase the autonomy of various cultural fields. On the other hand, the *iemoto* lacked the advantage of flexibility. Greater formalization of the educational structure effectively preserved artistic traditions; however, the *iemoto*'s demand for its students' loyalty inhibited the development of weak ties. Thus, it could not foster the lightness and expansiveness that characterized aesthetic networks that connected people in unexpected ways. In the next chapter, I will discuss another type of aesthetic tie, more horizontal and ephemeral, but one that encouraged an expansive and relaxed style of networking among people. This was the type of tie that characterized the *haikai* poetry networks – the most widely disseminated and dynamic aesthetic networks in Tokugawa Japan.

7

The Haikai, *Network Poetry*

The Politics of Border Crossing and Subversion

By the second half of the eighteenth century, Tokugawa Japan, from cities to villages, enjoyed a rich and varied endowment of cultural and artistic circles. Nonetheless, in terms of the popularity and extensiveness of the resulting social networks, no cultural circles were more influential than those that formed around the composition of *haikai* poetry. The *haikai* poetry networks were undoubtedly the most widespread form of cultural network and represented a typical example of voluntary associations in Tokugawa Japan.

The *haikai* was the poetry of networks.[1] Individuals who became a part of the *haikai* circles received cognitive associational as well as social networks. The *haikai* universe encouraged the participating poets to socialize with others by neglecting worldly categorical identities of individuals. The *haikai* poetry was originally a popular version of linked poetry that emerged in the late medieval period. During the Tokugawa period, poets experimented with various styles of *haikai*. In the course of this experimentation, the *hokku* (first stanza of linked poetry) came to be appreciated as an independent form of poetry, which later came to be known as *haiku*. Socialization in the *haikai* enclave publics encouraged people to suspend feudal categorical identities. Such experiences of crossing boundaries created dynamics of social relations distinct from feudal requirements. Once a person had gotten seriously involved in *haikai* activities, they had an automatic entrée to other poetry circles, including introductions to poets they had not previously met. *Haikai* in this sense was not simply a genre of poetry but a passport to the world of Tokugawa aesthetic publics.

For example, a woman poet, Igarashi Hamamo, had an extensive poetic journey for four years with her father, Baifu, who was also a *haikai* poet. Leaving her husband (who had married into his wife's family) behind, Hamamo joined numerous *haikai* linked-poetry–making sessions (*za*) in provinces that she and her father visited between 1806 and 1810.

171

There, both men and women of various social backgrounds and literary achievements joined the poetry-making sessions of *za* (seating) as equal participants. While the father and daughter traveled together attending local circles' linked-verse sessions, Hamamo also developed her independent projects. She attempted to identify local woman poets; she often succeeded in organizing them into women-only linked-verse sessions. Hamamo later edited and published anthologies of *haikai* linked poetry that consisted of linked-verse sequences, the products of woman poets' linked-verse sessions.[2] Hamamo was only one of a number of peripatetic poets who felt safe traveling around the provinces of Japan, trusting to the hospitality of local members of the *haikai* networks.

Once connected with the *haikai* literary world, whose members communicated with one another through letters and frequent publications, a poet could easily travel throughout Japan by requesting lodging and support from local *haikai* poets and groups of amateurs. Although the Tokugawa regime officially discouraged people from traveling freely – especially those who lacked proper documentation, which was part of the shoguns' policy of institutional division and segmentation – the state could not effectively control the movements of those who relied on the networks of cultural circles. Furthermore, during the second half of the Tokugawa period, the regime relaxed restrictions on women's travel. This development, coupled with the maturation of nationwide trade networks, meant that even women could safely travel about the country in order to participate in *haikai* activities. Since the Tokugawa state based its measures of social control on institutional segmentation of the population, the remarkable networking abilities of *haikai* groups, which connected people in ways that could not be contained within the traditional categorical and regional boundaries, functionally eroded the policy of institutional segmentation. *Haikai* networks became breathing spaces, in a manner of speaking, within Tokugawa society that kept people from feeling suffocated by the smothering artificiality of feudal social relations.

During the eighteenth and nineteenth centuries, the social and cognitive networks associated with *haikai* poetry became so intricately interwoven with the fabric of Tokugawa society that we cannot understand any literary or artistic productions in this period without some knowledge of the symbolic paradigms and actual social networks associated with the *haikai*. Furthermore, their open and fluid networking styles were highly adaptable to the operation of commercial market networks. With their remarkable ability to create private associational networks and adaptability to connect with commercial markets, the *haikai* poetry networks epitomized the Tokugawa style of aesthetic enclave publics. The *haikai* circles brought together persons from different regional, status, occupational, and gender categories within the temporary public worlds created by a common interest in this type of poetry. In fact, although the *mu'en* spirit of freedom that had animated the medieval linked-verse Cherry Blossom sessions had evaporated under the pressures of political unification and commercialization, the Tokugawa *haikai* circles recaptured something of this subversive free spirit.

From the time of its emergence during the late medieval period, *haikai* poetry was subversive literature. It was a popular form of linked verse (*haikai no renga*) at a time when *renga* linked verse was becoming more and more formalized and rule-bound. The word *haikai* is a compound of two Chinese ideograms – *hai* means "performing" and *kai* means "joke or folly." *Haikai*, therefore, originally meant "foolish performance," and it began as an intentionally non-aristocratic (*zoku*) genre, as compared with the elegant and courtly (*ga*) genres. In this sense, *haikai* originated as a movement to bring an increasingly refined form of poetry back to a more popular sensibility.

As a genre of literature, the *haikai* bloomed during the late seventeenth century with the inspiring work of Matsuo Bashō (1644–1694) and his collaborating disciples. Bashō practiced primarily the *haikai* linked verse. In its structure, *haikai* linked poetry opened with a 17-syllable *hokku* (initiating verse) divided into three lines of 5, 7, and 5 syllables, respectively. The *hokku* was followed by a 14-syllable (7–7) second stanza, a 17-syllable (5–7–5) third verse, a 14-syllable fourth verse, and so on, alternating in sequence.

A formal session for making *haikai*-style linked verse might begin in a room with the painted figure of a "patron saint" of poetry, such as Tenjin[3] or Kakinomoto Hitomaro,[4] hanging in an alcove. While burning incense, the master of ceremonies would recite each line and copy every verse on a sheet of paper.[5] The next author would repeat the first unit and was required to add the next unit on the spot, with little time for reflection. In this way, the format of the linked-verse poetry meeting compelled each participant to be both a contributor and recipient. The number of stanzas varied. Although in *renga* linked verse the number could reach 100 stanzas or more, *haikai* linked verse of the Bashō style during the Tokugawa period usually employed the 36-stanza form. However, various ways of linking sequences of poems existed. For example, Bashō left an impressively lyrical piece, "*kari ganemo*," in a style of *ryōgin* (two-person poetry) sequences exchanged between Bashō and his beloved disciple Etsujin that carried a subtle and intimate resonance of two poets' emotion.

The temporal dynamic of collaboration in a *za* group was the element that Bashō cherished most – as is reflected in his dictum that poetry is "only garbage once it is taken away from the linked-verse table."[6] As Bashō's remark suggests, linked verse was perceived as having its true existence only in the moment of collaboration and within the space of a *za* public.

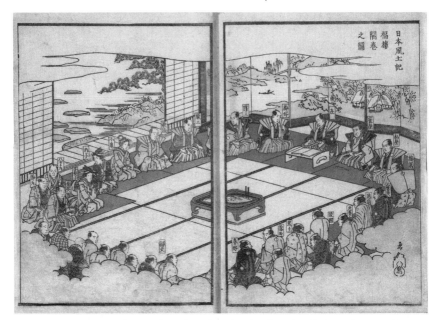

Figure 7.1. Poetry Meeting. A gathering for a *kyōka* (comic poetry) contest, from *Kyōka nihon fūdoki* by Yoshima Gakutei, 1831. The artist has shown himself presiding at center right. This is a record of an actual poetry meeting; each poet in the seating has a name label in this picture. The participants include three woman poets: Kogame, Uchiko, and Chieko.

The creation of a collaborative poetic world was made possible within a basic framework of prescribed *shikimoku*, or codes – the grammar of linked poetry, so to speak.

This unusual form of poetry was not simply a word game but rather a system that encouraged participating individuals to be equal partners in the spaces of *za* (seating)(Figure 7.1). Although the site of the *haikai* could produce only a temporary sphere of alternative realities, *za* allowed participants to deviate from the framework of formal society, such as title, status, gender, and age. Such an experience of private socialization would quietly influence social relations outside the *za*, creating more flexible and fluid situations.

The Horizontal Structure of *Haikai* Organizations

The Tokugawa *haikai* circles merit further investigation based on my inquiry into early modern aesthetic publics and associational life. To begin with, the circles that met to write *haikai* were the most popular of the many knowledge-based associational ties, including amateur artistic and scholarly groups, that formed during this period. Furthermore, unlike the more pseudoaristocratic styles of performing arts organized under the hierarchical authority structure of the *iemoto* (grand master) system that I discussed in the previous chapter, the *haikai* circles tended to be more horizontal in structure.

The term *iemoto* was never used in *haikai* groups; the teacher was usually called a *sōshō*. Although we can trace the lineage of some schools of the *haikai*, it was unusual for *sōshō* to inherit their positions through their family lines. In Edo, the groups and lineages of the *sōshō* were often called *za* (seating).[7] A circle of amateur poets was variously called a *kumi* (group), *ren* (link), or *kumi-ren* and was formed in most cases on a neighborhood basis. In the *za* meeting place of *haikai* linked verse, the role of a *sōshō* was that of critic and moderator of communal poetry-making. The *sōshō*'s relationship to the *haikai* circle was not necessarily exclusive in that a given circle might have several *sōshō* as instructors. Some circles that were associated with a particular style of *haikai* writing sometimes gave rise to a line or succession of *sōshō*, but the succession was closer to the modern style of artistic or literary lineage in which the most capable student assumes the leadership of the school or group when the master dies.

The lack of a formal hierarchical organizational structure meant that *haikai* groups were relatively ephemeral. A number of different types of *haikai* circles emerged, declined, and disappeared from time to time.[8] Even regional networks of poetry circles tended to flourish for a time and then fade. There were a few centers that extended their associational networks across several provinces, but these centers rarely approached the structural definition or longevity of the *iemoto* schools. On the other hand, the relatively loose, decentralized, and horizontal organization of the *haikai* networks was an advantage in popularizing the art form. It made the craft of poetry accessible to a large number of amateur students across regional, status, and gender boundaries. Although the *haikai* networks included some professional poetry instructors who charged fees for their services and could be considered nodal points of the networks, most of the participants in the *kumi* were simply amateurs with other "official" occupational and social identities.

Although a variety of the *haikai* style – independent short verse rather than linked verse – became very popular during the Tokugawa period, it was nonetheless the spirit of linked *haikai* verse that carried the original spirit of medieval linked verse. The place of *haikai* poetry-making was called *za*, following the medieval origin of tradition. The spirit of *za* was to make the framework of control in formal society temporarily void.

Feudal status hierarchy, as well as gender and age categories, did not affect poets in the *za*. At least within the ritual procedure of the linked verse, such an earthly difference was neglected by calling each other by simple first names or given pen names (*haimei*). Although various genres of performing arts also developed the similar social effect of transformation, the *haikai* poetry exhibited the most salient example of this identity-switching effect.

Naming was an important technology in generating an alternative reality for *haikai* enclaves. Participants in *haikai* circles never used the formal names that would reflect their status identities; the members went by their *haikai* poet-names. Unlike the *iemoto* system in which receiving an artist name from the grand master was considered a sign of formal recognition of the student's accomplishment and his or her formal inclusion into the quasi-family of the *iemoto* school, the *haikai* names did not yield such a formal procedure. The *haikai* poet-names were not closely kept secrets, as if they were aliases used by members of a criminal underground, but simply functioned as the most commonly used names in the context of private activities. Using the *haikai* names did not hide the poets' formal identities. Participants in the *haikai* circle socialized with each other, knowing their formal identities as the samurai, rich merchants, or humble commoners. The use of the *haikai* name simply signaled a message that they were participating in circle activities as private individuals.

Many Japanese cities and villages in this period were endowed with *haikai* circles that were interconnected in an almost unimaginable variety of ways, from famous master poets to semi-professional *haikai* enthusiasts, in all parts of the country. The *haikai* networks frequently overlapped with local business or political organizations because the patterns of recruitment were similar. The networks of *haikai* poets were important assets for Japanese society because they represented precious resources of horizontal and voluntary forms of popular alliance built in private spheres. Therefore, the pattern of socialization seen in these circles also represented a form of Tokugawa civility not through their official formal identities but through their enclave identities as private, cultured persons.

Furthermore, learning how to compose *haikai* poetry was equivalent to receiving an inheritance – in this case, the vast cultural capital accumulated over centuries of Japanese classical literary tradition. This cultural capital had become the personal endowment of a growing number of Tokugawa individuals. The social impact of the poetry circles was even more striking because they were always coupled with participants' incorporation into actual social networks, the endowment of so-called social capital. A *haikai* poet in Tokugawa society never practiced his or her craft in isolation. Because the creation and appreciation of *haikai* required the presence of fellow citizens of the same symbolic universe, most amateur poets participated in local *haikai* circles that were usually connected to *haikai* masters with wider regional or national reputations. Through the learning of *haikai* poetry, men and women of humble backgrounds acquired their own expressions and extended their social networks. Thus, with this simultaneous endowment of cultural and social capital in the supposedly inferior *watakushi* (private) realm, the *haikai* networks were quietly transforming the undercurrent of Tokugawa society.

Peter Burke has described the relationship between elite and popular culture in early modern Europe as follows:

> The professional tradition-bearers ... are only the tip of the iceberg, but the others are barely visible. They were the amateurs and there were the semi-professionals, part-time specialists who had another occupation but might derive a supplementary income from their singing, playing or healing. We know about them only when they were organized into societies, or attracted the attention of the upper classes or the authorities for some reason because they were outstanding performers, or suspect of sedition, heresy or witchcraft.[9]

The situation in Tokugawa Japan was different from its European counterpart. The primary difference was the greater visibility of the Japanese amateur poets as compared with the "pros." The Tokugawa amateur and semi-professional poets enjoyed the advantages of their well-developed networks, which included media for recording and publishing their works. Amateur as well as professional poets during this period could have their *haikai* printed on simple pamphlets or handouts similar to the *Flugschriften* of sixteenth-century Europe. The Japanese pamphlets were printed with the flexible and inexpensive woodblock technique; enough copies of *haikai* anthologies – often self-financed by participating groups of poets – have survived to be the subject of the scholarly curiosity of modern historians.

The commercial publishing houses that came into being during the economic boom of the seventeenth century found it profitable to publish *haikai* anthologies that included poems by semi-professional and amateur poets. Beginners' guidebooks on the art of *haikai* composition flooded the popular book market. These entrepreneurial activities in turn contributed to the increased popularity of *haikai* writing and *haikai* circles. The commercial operations of the Tokugawa *haikai* circles would not have existed without an economically profitable publishing trade, capitalistic "literary agent" systems, and other infrastructures of a market economy.

Early *Haikai* Networks

The introduction of an element of wordplay or entertainment in *haikai* instruction made this form of poetry even more attractive to groups of amateurs. One popular technique of *haikai* composition that had a game-like quality was called *maeku-zuke*, literally "responding to the front line" or "verse-capping." Although there were varieties of *maeku-zuke*, in a typical form, the master poet would present the first line of a poem and a student would respond with a second line. *Maeku-zuke* began as a simplified version of linked-verse *haikai* and was considered a useful propaedeutic for familiarizing students with the rules of *haikai* composition. However, verse-capping later became an independent, popular literary category. Verse-capping was characterized by clever plays on words and touches of popular humor. Verse-capping made its first appearance during the Manji era (1658–1660) when a master poet living in Sakai, a city in Senshū province, met with a group of amateur poets in Kawachi province who enjoyed responding to the master poet's first lines.[10] As this technique of playful collaborative composition spread to other *haikai* circles, it generated a number of inventive variations, including *kanmuri-zuke*, *rokku-zuke*, *kasa-zuke*, and *kutsu-zuke*. *Maeku-zuke* and its variants were not considered highbrow literature; rather, their success depended on the writers' wit and facility with words.

The introduction of verse-capping increased the popularity of *haikai* groups even further when it was coupled with the *ten-tori* (point-generating), or competitive scoring system. The *ten-tori* is an ancient Japanese method of literary criticism that originated in the aristocratic settings of *waka* poetry. The ancient and medieval courtier-poets would come together for *uta awase*, or "poetry-making meetings," social occasions that carried an element of competition. A master poet who served as the judge of the gathering would award points to each poem that was submitted during the course of the meeting. The popular *haikai* circles then borrowed the *ten-tori* scoring system from the *waka* tradition and turned it into a more accessible format that lent itself to commercialization.

Commercialization of the *Haikai* Practice

The chief respect in which the Tokugawa *haikai* circles differed from the collective *za* artists of medieval Japan was the infiltration of early modern commercialism. This does not imply that the extension of the *haikai* poetry networks was driven only by a profit motive. Rather, the dynamic expansion of the *haikai* networks was connected in a number of ways to the overarching development of the Tokugawa market economy that was then blossoming. In particular, the *haikai* circles benefited from two important organizational innovations: (1) the use of *kaisho* (agents) to mobilize amateur poets and connect them to professional poets; and (2) the use of commercial presses to promote and facilitate the operations of the poetry groups.

By the mid-seventeenth century, the combination of *maeku-zuke* and the *ten-tori* scoring system had produced a class of literary agents who served as couriers between established master poets and local groups of amateurs. These agents would receive the first line of a poem from the master poet and transmit it to the amateur groups. The local poets then composed their responding lines and paid a fee to the agent for every entry they submitted for evaluation. The agent consolidated the entries, made a fair copy of the list, and submitted it to the master. These agents were called *kaisho* (literally "meeting places"), *seisho moto* (transcribers, literally "copyists"), or *toritsugi* (literally "mediators"). The master awarded points according to his judgment of each entry's quality; in return, he received fees from the agents. The master usually offered not only points but also prizes for the best entries, a system guaranteed to stimulate competition among the amateur poets. The contest cycle closed with the distribution of a printed pamphlet listing the winning poems, the authors' pen names, and the names of their circles (*kumi-ren*). For many of these would-be writers, the possibility of their work appearing in print injected a measure of excitement into their ordinary daily routines. The genuine pleasure that Tokugawa people derived from reading other people's poetry, together with learning the "tricks of the trade" from commercial publications, also enhanced the popularity of *haikai*. By 1681–1687, *maeku-zuke* competitions had become institutionalized commercial operations centered in Kyoto and Osaka.[11]

To be sure, since *haikai* groups were an important means of social networking for amateur poets, the dimension of personal encounter at *haikai* poetry-making sessions (*kukai*) was considered the most important aspect of *haikai* socialization throughout the Tokugawa period. In these private meetings, each aspiring poet presented his or her own spontaneous contributions and enjoyed the emotional resonance, cognitive associations, and unrehearsed surges of aesthetic feeling that were stimulated by the presentations of the other members. On many occasions, a professional *sōshō* would be invited to the *kukai* to critique the contributions by awarding points. We can assume that the relative informality and interpersonal dimension of these meetings were among their most attractive features. If, however, the *haikai* circles had relied upon face-to-face meetings or word of mouth as their sole means of enlarging their networks, in all likelihood their development would have been limited.

The concomitant development and prosperity of Tokugawa commercial publishing was a major factor in increasing popular interest in *haikai* writing. The publishers found that many of their best-sellers were instruction manuals that coached readers on raising their scores in *maeku-zuke* competitions. For example, a book entitled *Sake ya ko no hana* (Make This Flower Bloom) was published in 1692. It contained examples of winning entries together with critiques and "pointers" from famous master poets.[12] Like contemporary Japanese college preparatory guidebooks, the *haikai* manuals sometimes analyzed the literary preferences of specific *sōshō* and advised readers seeking high scores to tailor their writing accordingly. A flood of these publications hit the market after the late seventeenth century, partly because improvements in printing technology allowed for rapid turnaround. It was possible to publish the results of a poetry competition shortly after the winners were announced because the woodblock carvers were quick and efficient workers.

During this era, given Kyoto's prestige as a center of traditional culture, its townspeople frequently socialized through a number of activities in the polite arts, including *haikai* circles. Although Kyoto was a rich cultural medium for the initial development of new poets, its dense concentration of professional poets and associated high level of competition meant that most *haikai* masters had to form networks of contacts in the provinces for their economic survival. *Haikai* enthusiasts in the provinces – in particular those who lived in the rapidly growing castle cities that served the regional *daimyo* as political and commercial centers – were delighted to welcome master poets associated with the *haikai* circles of Kyoto. As the Tokugawa shoguns improved the infrastructure of Japan's long-distance transportation and market networks, it was predictable that the Kyoto master poets would extend their entrepreneurial activities to the distant provinces of Japan.

On the initiative of local agents, the connection between amateur poetry and the growth of the commercial publishing industry brought into the circles of *haikai* enthusiasts sectors of the population that had never been touched by high culture. One *haikai* poet, Nakajima Zuiryū, described the extent of this transformation:

> Nowadays, the popularity of the *maeku-zuke* has disseminated *haikai*-making to the rural areas and outlying provinces.... Even a fisherman might carry four or five copies of printed *maeku-zuke* collections on his boat [and study them during] his spare moments in handling his fishing nets. (*Teitoku Eidaiki*, 1692)[13]

At this point, it was equally predictable that the Kyoto poets could not remain in the "cultural export" business indefinitely. By the beginning of the eighteenth century, the outlying provinces had accumulated their own cultural capital and had their own groups of professional *haikai* poets who were prospering from the commercial operation of *ten-tori* games.[14] The provincial agents no longer functioned solely as couriers between their home areas and the Kyoto *haikai* networks but also distributed poetry and published contest results in their own provinces. From the regional centers, the *haikai* circles then spread out into the more remote communities, including the rural villages. The rise of the provincial *ten-tori* operations, however, did not mean that the *haikai* circles in the smaller towns and farming communities were out of touch with the traditional centers of poetry. The local operations paid keen attention to literary trends in Kyoto and Edo and remained in contact with poets of national reputation.

By the late Tokugawa period, Japan had three layers of popular *haikai* networks: circles at the neighborhood level; professional poets with circles in the major cities of the provinces; and professional poets of national reputation with circles in Kyoto, Osaka, and Edo. Although the *haikai* circles at any level were largely autonomous in their regular functioning, all three sets of networks were flexibly interconnected and overlapped with one another.[15]

If we look at a ten-page publication sponsored by *kaisho* agents that was printed in Kyoto in the sixth year of Genroku, we find that the agents were in a profitable line of work. This booklet, entitled *Haikai Arukanaka*, announced the results of a recent poetry competition that had attracted more than 10,600 entries. The booklet's appendices included lists of agents and the number of entries that each had collected. Forty-one agents covering 15 provinces had collected the entries. The agents were listed by shop name, their own name, or the name of their *kumi-ren* (local circle). In any case, the evidence indicates that the agents did not work in isolation but were connected to local *haikai* circles in their communities. Of the 41 agents listed in the booklet, two mentioned shop names that were most likely their places of business. One agent ran an indigo store in Echizen province, and the other's business is simply called "the fabric store" in Sakai, a city in Senshū province.[16] The agent at the indigo shop collected over 1,300 contest entries, whereas the one who ran the fabric store collected 200.

A contemporary novel, *Chūgi taiheiki* (Tale of Loyal Grand Pacification), describes the owner of a noodle shop who decides to become a *haikai* agent because his noodle business is not doing very well.[17] Sometimes, the owners of establishments associated with some form of entertainment, such as teahouses or Yoshiwara brothels, became *haikai* agents because they could easily collect contest entries from their customers. For owners of local businessess with heavy customer traffic (e.g., retail clothing stores and restaurants), "moonlighting" as *haikai* agents was a safe and profitable addition to their core business; organizing their customers as *haikai* circles not only guaranteed a steady flow of entry fees but created goodwill. In other words, members of their amateur poets' circle were likely to become loyal customers of their core business.

Bashō's Criticism of Commercialization

Some *haikai* contests offered large prizes in order to attract a large pool of entries. The situation began to resemble modern lotteries; in some cases, the grand prize was roughly 400 times the size of the entry fee, certainly enough to whet the popular appetite for this kind of competition. On one occasion, the city of Edo issued a stern warning to the promoters of "verse-capping" *haikai* contests:

> The city announced on an earlier occasion that it is concerned about the *Haikai* instructors who award points in poetry contests. The practices called *maeku-zuke* or *kanmuri-zuke* that offer prizes are easily confused with [illegal] gambling; therefore, the city has previously prohibited them.... From now on people who violate this rule shall be questioned by the city wardens, and [if they are found to be gambling operators] remanded to the authorities. (Edo Town Ordinance, the ninth year of Kyōhō, 1724)[18]

It was not only the governing authorities that deplored the popularity of the *ten-tori* (point-generating) system and its de facto commercialization of the *haikai* subculture. Those who considered the *haikai* as serious a literary genre as communal poetry criticized this commercialized system. A letter written by master *haikai* poet Matsuo Bashō is outspoken in its criticism of the commercial aspect of poetry competitions:

> There are people who spend all their time day and night preparing entries for the scored poetry contests. They are constantly running around not knowing the true way. Although they are simply strayed confused persons of the poetry world, they are only filling bellies of the point-giving judges, and filling the agents' cash boxes. Consequently, they are probably better than those who commit crimes.[19]

His vehement hostility against *ten-tori* almost betrayed our modern image of Bashō as a saintly spiritual seeker in the world of poetry. Bashō did not want his accomplished disciples to prostitute their talents as contest judges and advised them to distance themselves from the popular craze. In this respect, Bashō remained within the tradition of medieval *za* linked poetry; he believed that his art should touch the participants in a *za* circle directly, not through such intermediaries as agents and printers.[20]

Some of Bashō's poetry was written in the course of travel to the un-
derdeveloped regions of Japan.[21] His following piece expresses his determination to persevere in his journey even if death should befall him on
the road:

> My bones may breach on this wasteland
> I know it in my heart
> while the wind pierces my body

> (*Nozarashi o kokoro ni kazeno shimu mi kana*)[22]

Bashō's travels were motivated by a desire to emulate Saigyō (1118–
1190), a medieval otherworldly poet of the road, but they also embodied
the spirit of early medieval popular linked-poetry circles that arose outside
the court (*jige renga*). These circles had developed in close association
with the free-spirited members of marginal subpopulations who traveled
extensively.

From a practical standpoint, however, Bashō's extensive tours were
made possible because there were enough amateur *haikai* poets in these
economically backward areas, even in the late seventeenth century, to extend hospitality to him and to other famous poets. The amateurs, whose
incomes were drawn from a variety of sources, welcomed and hosted
the sophisticated poets from the prosperous cities. Bashō did not practice
point-generating *haikai*, but he was supported by the donation of cash and
other goods and free lodging offered by his rich supporters. The very foundation of the popular *haikai* networks that made Bashō's travel possible,
however, also represented a force that separated the course of early modern Japanese poetry from the medieval cultural tradition. The popularity
of word games like *maeku-zuke*, *ten-tori* competitions, the incentives of
prizes, agents, and commercial publication all helped to disseminate this
form of poetry far more widely than the forms of any previous period.

Kikaku, one of Bashō's high disciples, who was said to be the only
person Bashō permitted to act as a point-giving teacher, thus glorified his
spirit with a self-reflection:

> Poetry is what I sell
> Short life not my debts concerns me
> So I drink the year out[23]

> – Kikaku

> (*Shi akindo toshi o musaboru sakate kana*)

Here, we see Kikaku's acclaim of his almost bohemian spirit of pride and
self-pity, alluringly projecting the ideal image of an otherworldly drinking
poet from the Chinese classics, even though in reality he was admitting

that his livelihood depended on selling poetry. Thus, even Bashō's followers could not get away from the reality of the time, in which such private circle activities were enmeshed and supported by the rising commercial networks.

In spite of Bashō's criticism, it is fair to say that the injection of commercialism, such as the use of agents and commercial competition, was the basis for empowering the *haikai* literary world. Had the involvement of commercialism not occurred, it is doubtful whether the *haikai* could have mobilized the enthusiastic aspiration of people to the degree that the authorities had to issue ordinances against the *haikai* competition.

Popular "Monthly" *Haikai* in Edo

In the course of the eighteenth century, Edo, the capital of the Tokugawa shoguns, began to overtake Kyoto and Osaka as a cultural center, developing dense networks of teachers and amateur students competing for prizes in the *haikai* contests. Edo in this period had a large number of *haikai* publications, anthologies, and handbooks, together with frequent one-page reports of contest winners from the city that featured the addresses and agents of various professional poetry teachers. Most neighborhoods sponsored a *haikai* circle, and there was enough demand in the city to support several dozen professional poets specializing in different styles of popular *haikai*. The Edo master poets were also able to run thriving commercial poetry competitions. These poets sometimes called their own style of poetry *Edo-ku*, or "Edo verse," and took considerable pride in their urban wittiness and sophistication.[24] *Edo-ku* was not, however, a homogeneous "school" of poetry but rather included a range of styles and tastes. Many *sōshō* wrote in the tradition of Bashō, whereas others favored the more popular humorous styles.

The Edo *haikai* circles had two distinctive features. First, they introduced regular monthly *ten-tori* competitions called *tsukinami*, which literally means "monthly," although the *tsukinami* sometimes took place two or three times a month. The members of the Edo circles fixed the contest date every month, and everything from the collection of entries to the distribution of the printed winners list was well-programmed for rapid turnaround by the commercial publishers.[25] After the competition cycle was closed for the month, the circles usually distributed copies of simple *ichimai zuri*, or "one-page notices." In spite of their name, the "one-page notices" often ran several pages.

The second innovation was the Edo circles' cultivation of authorial anonymity. From the early seventeenth century onward, the names of individual writers were omitted from the printed versions of their poems.

These names, of course, were not the poets' given names but rather their pen names, or *haimai*. But in an abrupt change instituted around the turn of the eighteenth century, publications of winning poems mentioned only the name of the author's *haikai* circle. This "no author name" system constitutes a curious phenomenon. According to Miyata Masanobu's study, one of the earliest examples of the no-author-name system occurs in *Nakōdo guchi* (1709) in the records of the monthly sessions of a master poet named Baika. Baika's agents sent more than 10,000 entries to his well-attended *tsukinami*. The winning poems were then published in *Nakōdo guchi* (The Mouth of Go-Between). All the prize-winning pieces were listed under the names of the circles (*kumi-ren*) in which their authors held membership. For the year 1709, *Nakōdo guchi* lists 132 *kumi-ren* as the host circles of the winners in the pamphlet. It appears that the no-author-name system was better established among the Edo *haikai* circles than in other regions.

This peculiar preference for anonymity may have originated in Edo because of the high percentage of samurai participants in the city's *haikai* circles. Since the circles often took their names from the neighborhoods in which they met, an examination of the 132 circles mentioned in *Nakōdo guchi* indicates that many of them were located in neighborhoods that were officially designated as samurai residential areas. Edo was divided into residential sectors for urban commoners and samurai, respectively. In the early part of the eighteenth century, about half of Edo's one million residents were samurai and their associates, while the remainder was made up of urban commoners. Given that some of the neighborhoods whose names appeared in *Nakōdo guchi* were restricted to samurai, and that *haikai* circles usually met within walking distance of their members, we may reasonably conclude that the membership of these circles was predominantly samurai. A surviving copy of a one-page competition report has a handwritten marginal note to the effect that the line was composed by Lord Tayasu Munetake (1715–1771), a younger son of the eighth shogun, Tokugawa Yoshimune, and a famous patron of literature.[26] Although the *haikai* circles were generally associated with "middlebrow" commoners' culture rather than the high culture of the governing elite, the samurai around this era took advantage of their freedom from official bureaucratic duty to enjoy participating in various leisure-time activities across status lines.

Just as commoners' lives were dominated by the samurai authorities, the samurai's lives were also full of restriction and frustration. Although there was a good reason that the samurai found an outlet for their frustration in the world of the *haikai*, the samurai poets preferred an extra measure of privacy when they participated in *maeku-zuke*. This was partly because of the possibility of appearing in print with a winning entry and partly because the "lowbrow" idioms and humorous tone of *haikai* poetry would ordinarily have been considered beneath their dignity. Tokugawa cultured people often had several artist names, one for each group, but *haikai* names were most frequently used as names for private activities. In this sense, revealing a *haikai* name in print might have proved akin to revealing one's identity.

The Rise of Senryū: Comical Verse and Critical Spirits

As Bashō has lamented, the commercial operation of *haikai* poetry competitions certainly diluted the communal and intense aesthetic spirit of the *za* art. Yet, the commercial success of the *haikai* had its own merit in increasing popular participation in this genre, while encouraging the development of a critical spirit among Tokugawa people.

Among the many Edo *haikai* masters in the second half of the eighteenth century, Karai Senryū (1718–1790) was the most commercially successful.[27] Senryū's manner of awarding points in poetry competitions was enlivened by wit and good humor and clearly reflected the sensibility and lifestyle of the urban commoner class.[28] In Senryū's operation, the hopeful contestant submitted his or her poem to an agent along with an entry fee of 12 mon (about 75% of the cost of a bowl of noodles).[29] Once the deadline had passed, the agent made a fair copy of all the entries and delivered it to the *kairin* (an exclusive agent for the master poet/judge), who collected lists from all the agents. The *kairin* then took the entire collection to Karai Senryū. After Senryū selected the winning pieces, they were printed in simple pamphlets and distributed to all the Edo agents. Senryū's own poetry production is not well-known. He was successful not because of his talent as a poet but primarily because of his fairness and competence as a judge of poetry and because of his well-organized commercial operations. During Senryū's 33 years as a master poet/judge, 71 of his poetry competitions drew over 10,000 entries each; some exceeded 20,000. Senryū preferred poems that could be understood independently – a format with wide popular appeal. In addition to Senryū's monthly report on his poetry competitions, he published a yearly anthology of winning pieces under the title of *Yanagi daru* (The Willow Cask). In the course of his career as a master poet, 25 volumes of *Yanagi daru* were published and functioned as his school's unofficial poetry journal. Senryū retained the no-author-name policy in his *ten-tori* contests.

Some famous entries that incorporated shrewd insights into popular opinion were on everyone's lips:

> "A government official's baby quickly learns how to clench its hand."
> (*yakunin no kowa nigi nigi o yoku oboe*)

[Tokugawa government functionaries often took bribes,
    described as "grasping money in one's fist."]
"Oh, please, dear Koban, stay with me for only one night."
(*Kore Koban, Tatta hitoban, Itekurero*)
[A Koban is an oval-shaped gold coin.]

We must note here that although Senryū was apparently the most commercially successful poet/judge during this period, his was not the only
haikai operation in Edo. Some circles in Edo were associated with *sōshō*
poet/judges who favored the more literary style of Bashō. Aspiring amateurs could thus submit their attempts to *sōshō* whose preferences were
more in line with their own. Most of the professional *haikai* poets' incomes were just good enough to support their humble lifestyles; however,
poetry could occasionally produce economically advantaged poets who
could afford rich lifestyles. For example, Ōshima Ryōta (1718–1787) in
Edo boasted more than three thousand students; forty of them were practicing professional poets. Several *daimyo* houses were also his clients.
From Edo, Ryōta's networks were geographically as well as socially extensive. He had several houses in provinces as branch schools. He could
afford to travel by palanquin accompanied by a few assistants.[30] It would
be difficult to estimate either the number of *haikai* circles that were active in the city or the number of *haikai* poems that flowed through the
commercial channels every month. Even the incomplete data supplied
by the better-known operations such as Senryū's indicate that the Tokugawa *haikai* circles kept the judges, the agents, and the printers very busy.
From the *daimyo* down to the artisans and day-laborers, people from every social level moved within the same poetic universe. They also shared
the anticipation and excitement of submitting their work to the monthly
competitions.

Woman Poets and Their Entrepreneurial Activities

The *haikai* also empowered women by giving them words for expressions
and social networks. Although the majority of amateur poets were male,
the *haikai* records indicate that women's participation in the *haikai* circles
was also significant. There are many surviving records of woman poets
in the provinces as well as in the larger cities, and the number of woman
writers appears to have increased during the course of the eighteenth
century. In fact, the degree of women's participation in the literary universe
of the *haikai* was unusually impressive in the standard of the eighteenth
and early nineteenth centuries in the world.

Bessho Makiko, who extensively surveyed women's participation in the
haikai world, counted 130 instances of what she called "women *haikai*

literature," which included *haikai* publications and anthologies written or edited by woman poets or anthologies that collected only woman poets' works. For example, as early as 1702, Ōta Shirayuki in Mikawa Province edited an anthology entitled *Haikai Mikawa Komoachi*, which collected the works of 66 woman poets from various provinces. All these female poets were contemporary persons who belonged to the school of Bashō, reflecting Bashō's open attitude toward women's participation. Another anthology of work by female *haikai* poets called *Ayanishiki*, which comprised 40 poems, was published in 1758. This "women-only" book – its preface and illustrations were also done by women – was widely circulated.[31] The Edo no-author-name system complicates identification of the gender of participants in the capital's *ten-tori* contests, but there is documentary evidence that some women submitted entries to the juried competitions that awarded prize money. The *haikai* circles had an egalitarian tendency that disregarded the official categorical identifiers of gender as well as status. By 1774, when *Tamamo-shū*, another anthology of female *haikai* poets, was published, it included 449 poems by 117 woman poets of the past and present. Women's participation in the world of *haikai* poetry was no longer an exceptional phenomenon.

Although such famous female poets as Kaga no Chiyojo (1703–1775) did not live on the income they made from writing *haikai*, some Tokugawa women actually gained their economic independence by teaching the art of writing *haikai*. For example, Shiba Sonome (1664–1718), a daughter of a Shintō priest in Iseyamada, and her husband became disciples of Bashō. She is one of the earliest examples of a woman who was a *sōshō*, a master teaching poet. After her husband's death, she moved from Osaka to Edo by herself and established her business teaching the *haikai* point-giving so that she could support herself by fees from her students. Sonome's name was well-known through her active publishing activities. Like today's writers, Tokugawa poets' reputations hinged on their publication activities. The more they published their own and their students' work, the more their pieces were selected to be in the influential anthologies and the more they were able to enhance their status in the *haikai* networks.

As the commercial operation of the popular *haikai* became popular in Edo, a woman poet/judge whose name is recorded as either Keijo or Tōjo was running the business of poetry competitions. She ran a commercial poetry contest operation between 1744 and 1760. Keijo rejected poems that were explicitly coarse or licentious and usually chose pieces that blended witty humor with sympathetic insights into commoners' daily lives.[32] During the An'ei era (1772–1781), Tanigawa Denjo, a woman point-giving master poet, was also well-known in Edo's mainstream *haikai* literary circles. She lived in a humble house in downtown Edo and made poetry from the intricate observation of her small world. Another famous example of a woman *sōshō* was Enomōto Seifu (1732–1814) of Hachiōji, a village in the Edo hinterland. She was well-known for her organizational skills and established her own *haikai* association, Matsubara-an, which had connections with a number of semi-professional and amateur poets not only in the region around Hachiōji and Edo but also as far away as Kōshū and Sōshū. Seifu's *haikai* lineage was a nodal point for rural poetry meetings that attracted semi-professional and amateur poets from a wide radius around her village.[33]

Still another dramatic example of a professional woman poet is Nagamatsu Shokyūni (1714–1781). She was the daughter of a *shōya*, the head of a village in Chikugo province, and wife to another wealthy village headman. When Shokyūni was 29 years old, she fell in love with the traveling professional *haikai* poet Kohaku, who was visiting her village. She became his lover and ran away with him. After Kohaku's death, Shokyūni became a *sōshō* in Kyoto. Her independence as a professional master teaching poet was supported by her active publishing activities. After her husband's death, she first traveled through various southern provinces in order to collect commemorative pieces of her late husband from friends and students. For a professional poet, traveling was a means of earning from local students as well as the best way of getting name recognition in the literary world. The resulting anthology, entitled *Sono Angya* (That Travel on Foot, 1766), became her first edited book that was published with her own name. Her rising reputation was proven by the fact that her own poems were selected for various contemporary *haikai* anthologies published locally around this time. She also started to regularly publish her students' poems as simple pamphlets. Shokyūni hardly had any source of income other than from *haikai*, but her reputation allowed her to travel extensively. As a professional teacher of the art of poetry composition, Shokyūni also corresponded with her students and critiqued their poems through the mail. She traveled widely to network with her students in the southern provinces and made trips to Edo and the northeastern provinces in order to retrace the route of Bashō's famous journey to northeast Japan. Shokyūni's career illustrates the fact that once a person acquired a reputation as a competent *haikai* poet, the population of *haikai* enthusiasts was so large that even women could earn their own livings as professional teachers of *haikai* composition.[34]

On the other hand, Igarashi Hamamo, a woman master poet that I cited earlier, was unique in her devotion to the linked-verse style of the *haikai*. Although the linked-verse style was the main road of the *haikai*, the difficulty in making a formal 36 sequences of stanzas in the Bashō style, and the difficulty of publishing them, made its practice less popular compared to more independent pieces. Igarashi was not only joining numerous linked-verse sessions with other famous poets but organized many sessions as a leader. Her publication of a women-only linked-verse anthology was the result of her organizing abilities. The composition of linked verse required participants to develop considerable agility in shifting among a number of different cognitive associational "maps" because their poetry had a reactive or responsorial quality. In other words, the linked-verse poet was not creating a poem *de novo* out of her private wellspring of inspiration but was carefully crafting a response to another poet's line.[35]

These catalogs of female poets clearly indicate that women's participation in *haikai* poetry was far from taboo. Of course, we must take into account that female poets had been a part of the ancient and medieval court tradition of *waka* poetry. However, these older examples of female poets occurred in the court and were protected physically and economically by the institution of the court. Considering this difference, the vitality and entrepreneurial spirit of the female master poets in Tokugawa Japan are impressive as pioneers, even in a global context.

We must also keep in mind the fact that professional woman writers were rare in the comparable period in Europe. Women continuously wrote down their own thoughts and poetic inspirations throughout Japanese history, but this was usually limited to the women of the elite families. It was still difficult to make a living from writing and teaching. These examples of female professional poets symbolize the fact that the demand of amateur poets who sought master teaching and participation in *haikai* circles became so broad that it allowed even women to enter into and profit from the business of poetry teaching.

Vigorous activities of Tokugawa female master poets symbolically indicate the ongoing transformation of Tokugawa society. Although this society was officially governed by the samurai elite and integrated rigidly by hierarchical organizations and norms, in fact, in a practical sense, this samurai's system of domination was eroded by the empowerment of those people like Shokyūni. This woman, with her own will, cut herself from her feudal social relationships that would economically protect her for the rest of her life. With all agony over her sense of guilt for her parents and home village, she was able to support her own life and secure her freedom of movement throughout the country. It is ironic, to be sure, that it was the Tokugawa state that laid the infrastructure of her free movement. The shogunate constructed major roads throughout the country and made travel less hazardous. In 1802, when a comic travel novel entitled *Tōkaidōchū Hizakurige* (Travel on Foot, the Tokai Road) became the best-seller of the time, it was said that a blind person's independent trip, women's groups, and even children's trips were not uncommon during this period.[36]

With the help of this development, we are fortunate to know, for example, from an anthology published in 1702, that even a voice of an eight-year-old girl named Haru has made such a sweet piece.

> How many nights should I sleep
> Before the New Year Day
> When father plays battledore and shuttlecock[37]

> – Haru, an 8-year-old girl from Osaka

> (*Imaikutsu Netaraba Tōsama hane tsuku zo*)[38]

The joyous anticipation of a little girl three hundred years ago, whose identity is known only by her first name, Haru, can reach the modern reader only because of the survival of this published anthology, which was a collection of the works of woman poets and was edited by a woman. In fact, there is nothing known about most female poets in these various anthologies other than their pieces of poetry.

"Haikai-nization": Allusion and Subversion

Haikai networks brought a fresh wind to a Tokugawa society that was officially segregated by feudal categorical boundaries of region, status, and gender. In addition to those organizational characteristics, however, the *haikai* poetry had a particular strength to break through feudal categorical restrictions due to its literary substance and styles. Remember the fact that I have emphasized the importance of cognitive functions of switching network connections when we enter communicative actions. This function of intersecting and switching cognitive network connections was literally built into the work of the *haikai* poetry.[39]

To excel in writing this form of verse, the amateur poet had to obey two exacting but contradictory rules. One was strict adherence to form; in this case the characteristics of the verse itself coupled with an extensive command of literary conventions and allusions to classical literature. The relevant literary conventions included symbolic references and associations, such as using a bush warbler to represent the season of spring. At the same time, the *haikai* poet had to transcend the boundaries of strict form with a fresh or creative combination of words in order to bring the reader to a new and profound insight or experience – and all within the space of 17 (or in some cases more or fewer) syllables. The popularization of the poetic form or genre thus entailed the popularization of its concomitant universe of reference.

An important component in the cognitive complexity of *haikai* poetry was its incorporation of two different sources of subject matter as well as its literary technique. One source was derived from the classical standards of the imperial court; the other was drawn from the contemporary interests, tastes, and opinions of the commoners. What we may call the "haikai-nization" of the poetic tradition involved the transfer of classical images to the settings, contexts, and sensibility of urban commoner life. Ishikawa Jun, a perceptive critic and fiction writer, once articulated the inherently deconstructive nature of *haikai* poetry in that it breaks down the identity of words as signifiers by transferring them into different contexts that alter their meanings. Ishikawa offered a useful insight when he noted in his essay first published in 1943, long before deconstruction and post-modernism became fashionable in Western literary criticism, that this method of haikai-nization is "generally the fundamental literary method at work in any type of literature that arose from the sensibility of Edo commoners.... This spirit of Edo literature ... would mislead and elude the grasp of any modernistic approach to literary analysis."[40] The superimposition of an originally aristocratic image on popular non-aristocratic texts was sometimes called *yatsushi* (disguising). A successful transfer of a classical image to an appropriate popular context would result in multivocality, laughter, and a sense of exhilaration.[41]

The *haikai* did not simply use the established imagery of nature, landscapes, and historical events but subverted them. As a result of the haikainization of the classical Japanese corpus, the *haikai*-making itself began to function as a "cognitive public" in which different cognitive associational networks coexisted in a state of paradox and tension that required the poets to constantly toggle between associational connections. The spirit of *haikai* poetry not only rejected the conventional notion of fixed categorical identities for people or objects; it also opposed the notion of stable networks of cognitive and conceptual associations.[42]

Haikai thus provided two seemingly contradictory cultural resources within its universe of discourse. For one thing, the spread of *haikai* itself represented a kind of "civilizing" process, to use Norbert Elias's words, in which people from various social classes could gain access to stored cultural resources. Second, *haikai* represented subversion and laughter, the upending of the everyday world, and a reflection of the color and sensuality of the Tokugawa lifestyle. In other words, *haikai* brought together two modes of discourse, one refined and elegant, the other subversive and popular; the participants learned to shuttle rapidly back and forth between the two spheres of discourse.

The Rise of Commonality and Fun-Loving Spirits

Once the horizontal structures of the *kumi-ren*, which focused on the sharing and exchange of knowledge, had become familiar features within the city neighborhoods and smaller rural communities of Tokugawa Japan, they provided an organizational model for other associational activities. The formula of gathering neighborhood groups, setting up a system of agents and couriers, charging entrance fees, and making use of the commercial publishing industry was easily applied to other cultural activities. Popular competitions and exhibitions of a wide range of visual and literary arts flourished as variations on the model derived from the *haikai* circles. We can consider *shogakai* (calligraphy and painting meeting) as an illustrative example. *Shogakai* were performing exhibitions open to the public in which famous professional painters, calligraphers, and similar artists demonstrated their skills on the spot. After the organizer and his team of assistants chose the date and invited the professionals, they distributed one-page announcements in nearby cities. Those who attended the exhibition paid an admission fee at the gate. In similar fashion, gardening enthusiasts, including people who specialized in *bonsai* trees or potted flowers, arranged and publicized competitive exhibitions. Other types of literary gatherings, such as *kyōka*, or humorous *waka* poetry, formed networks of circles that extended from the metropolitan areas into the provinces and often overlapped with the *haikai* networks. All of these literary circles and hobby groups formed dense spheres of enclave publics characterized by a spirit of lively curiosity and playfulness.

From the late eighteenth to early nineteenth centuries in Edo, when its urban culture was at its zenith, its citizens enjoyed an unparalleled variety of groups that catered to hobby enthusiasts. Many of the popular circles followed organizational patterns that resembled those of the *haikai* circles; they were open, egalitarian, flexible, and supplied close connections to commercial networks through competitions for prize money. In this era filled with the spirit of Huizinga's *homo ludens*, almost any enjoyable activity could stimulate the formation of a network of interested amateurs in a society animated by a spirit of playfulness as well as a desire for self-improvement. For example, there were many circles for bird lovers, such as groups for bush warbler and quail enthusiasts. The members held competitions for breeding the best singing birds. Gardening groups competed to grow perfect forms of *bonsai* or the rarest specimens of chrysanthemums. Tanaka Yūko has pointed out that many of these cultural circles borrowed their organizational models from that of the *haikai* circles.[43] As we have seen, the *haikai* circles almost from the outset paid agents to organize members, held competitions with prizes and entrance fees to stimulate popular interest, and used woodblock printings to promote and facilitate networking. These commercial methods of organization were readily applicable to a wide variety of other hobby groups.

One of the most conspicuous heroes of this networking society was Ōta Nanpo (1749–1823), an important writer and intermediary in the literary activities of the "Tennmei salons" (1781–1789). Ōta, who was born into the family of a lower vassal (*gokenin*) of the shogun, made his reputation in comic poetry (*kyōka*) under the pen name Ōta Shokusanjin. Talented, sociable, and always interested in forming new networks of people, he became a hero in the Tokugawa literary world. He used many other literary names that reflected not only his wide range of interests but also his skillful capacity for switching personas. In fact, Ōta's career under multiple names characterizes the Tokugawa civilizing process, in which the development of cross-status civilized knowledge was carried by enclave rather than formal identities.

Ōta began his literary career when he was 19 years old, winning acclaim for his comic poem "Yomo no Akara" (*Yomo* was the name of a famous store, *akara* was baby talk for *sake* – Ōta liked to drink). When he wrote orthodox poetry in the Chinese manner, however, he used the name of Nanpo, which was considered appropriate for a man of letters. When Ōta turned to Chinese-style poetic parody, he used the name Neboke sensei (Mr. Half-Asleep). Ōta's comic novels were published under such pen names as Yamanote Bakahito (Uptown Idiot). He used several other *noms de plume* along with his formal samurai name, Ōta Naojirō. As the samurai Naojirō, Ōta was able to present himself as a modestly successful man of a lower-status samurai family; in addition, he was known as a brilliant scholar by the standards of the period's formal scholarship, which somewhat enhanced his position among his samurai contemporaries. On the other hand, Ōta's upward mobility in his formal identity as a samurai did not jibe with the colorful activities of his enclave identities. Born to the lower status family as the shogun's vassal (*gokenin*, a category of the lower samurai who could not have an official audience with the shogun), although his literary ability was well-known in samurai private circles, he was never admitted to the shogun's inner circle. As a private person, however, Ōta was a star in the Edo literary world, making connections with other cultured people whose official standings were vastly different from his own. His success was due to his brilliant subversion of classical texts and critical observations of life hidden beneath a comical style of writing. The networks of various literary groups overlapped with one another in complicated ways and formed close relationships with commercial publishers. Although Ōta was not known as a *haikai* poet per se, his subversive spirit and his very existence were in the spirit of *haikai* performative comedy.[44]

In this world of subversive humor, people tried to enjoy themselves by rejecting all sober forms of discourse, including rational argument. In a spirit of the *haikai*, they joyfully carved the space of enclave publics in which feudal norms of sociability were temporarily suspended. People planned a variety of unusual events while announcing and promoting

Figure 7.2. Drinking Contest. Senju's *sake* drinking contest, from *Tōin Zukan*. Pictorial scroll, ca. 1815. Two men are drinking *sake* from large cups while other competitors wait their turn. Cultured people in the Tokugawa period made use of existing aesthetic networks to organize fun events as well as serious literary and artistic activities.

them through the already existing cultural and commercial networks. The spirit that animated these "happenings" is well-exemplified by the pictorial record of one such event, now part of the Spencer Collection of the New York Public Library. The event was known as "The Sake Drinking Battle" and was held in 1815 in Senju, a suburb of Edo (Figure 7.2).This drinking contest was coordinated by a local *haikai* poet, Koi Inkyo (Retired Carp, an obvious pseudonym), who was also a station shopkeeper, on the sixtieth birthday of Nakaya Rokuuemon, a local well-to-do owner of a profitable messenger service. The idea behind the "happening" was simply to provide an ample supply of free *sake* to anyone who wanted to show off an ability to hold his liquor. On the day itself, a prominent sign was hung on the gate of Nakaya's mansion that read, "No Admission for Bad Guests – Teetotalers [*geko*] and Logical Minds [*rikutsu*]."[45] Several huge, beautifully lacquered *sake* cups were prepared for the "good" guests. Famous literati – including Sakai Hoitsū and Tani Bunchō – were invited from Edo to serve as judges of the drinking competition.

Sakai Hoitsū (1761–1828) was a famous painter and *haikai* poet of the time, but his presence was particularly symbolic for an enclave public because his feudal identity was that of a younger brother of the lord Sakai Tadasawa, the lord of the Himeji Castle. The judges sat on red carpets and enjoyed the drinking as well, with local courtesans as attendants. One by one, the guests happily emptied the huge *sake* cups, while some collapsed on the spot.

This event took place in Senju, which was at the time located on the periphery of Edo. The town was also the first station along the Nikko road and boasted a number of scenic spots nearby. Many Edo residents who enjoyed cultural gatherings, such as the *haikai*-making events held at various attractive locations along the Sumida River, often came to visit the Senju station. Extensive networks of *haikai* circles also characterized this area, thus connecting the local literati. That was why one of the local *haikai* poets in this network, Koi Inkyo, was suitable as the organizer of the drinking competition. As a courier, Nakaya was well-connected with the local cultured people and the stylish sophisticates of Edo itself. After the contest, the ranking of the drinkers was printed with a woodblock in the manner of a ranking sheet for *sumō* wrestlers and was widely distributed. The event was recorded on a pictorial scroll, and the painting was displayed at the local *shogakai* (calligraphy and painting exhibition). It was no coincidence that Ōta Nanbo wrote an essay commemorating the event. It was precisely the ability to be foolish by temporarily suspending one's rational faculties (*rikutsu*) that animated the stylish Edo literati. It was through their enclave identities in private publics that the cultured people of Tokugawa Japan found relaxation through free association with one another. The whole procedure of this event conveyed the sensibility of the *haikai* world (performative joking, disguising, and subversion) and how its extensiveness and efficacy of associational networks added to their enjoyment.

The state of anarchy that resulted from such group activities was appealing to both samurai and commoner poets. For the samurai, imprisoned as they were within a maze of obligations and conventions attached to a set of hierarchical rankings, the challenge of learning the new "language" of the commoners' lifestyle and mentality was a large part of the attraction of those circles. The reader should recall that the samurai's formal categorical identities in the public realm (*ōyake*) were defined at birth by the position of their house (*ie*) on the vertical status ladder of the Tokugawa hierarchy. Since the shogunate's pacification of the country had removed the possibility of military adventures, the samurai's chances of having unexpected and exciting life experiences were minimal. As a result, they found their excursions into the speech patterns and mindset of the "lower orders" to be a liberating revelation. The composition of humorous and satirical poetry allowed them to view their social position from a different angle – to appreciate it as relative rather than absolute.

For the commoners, on the other hand, the cultural circles, in particular such competitive poetry as the *ten-tori* competition, offered a vacation from the frustration of living at the bottom of the Tokugawa status pyramid as well as an opportunity to participate in a form of poetry that did not demand a high level of classical scholarship. The less rigorous rules of composition, the use of vernacular Japanese, and the freedom to write about everyday subject matter made poetry accessible to anyone with a reasonable level of literacy. Once a person entered a network of poetry circles, his or her membership was like a ticket that admitted its bearer to extensive networks of many other kinds.

Thus, for members of any status category, the *kumi-ren* functioned as publics in which the participants enjoyed shifting verbal gears and switching among their different cognitive networks. There could be nothing in this playful pastime to make the authorities uneasy. If anything, the authorities themselves were happily participating in poetry-making sessions in their after-hours literary personas. *Haikai* was only a civilized word game played in the inferior realm of *watakushi*, the private. Consequently, although officers of the shogunate periodically cracked down on these activities when the authorities considered them to have gone too far, they revived as soon as official control was relaxed.

The Artist as Public Person

The networks of art and literature enthusiasts were not fully contained within the sphere of private life, however. Once the aesthetic publics of Tokugawa Japan were accepted as self-acknowledged components of the "inferior" private domain of social life and were allowed to function as spheres of cross-status social interactions for members using enclave identities, the possibility of turning these networks to unexpected uses emerged. During the early nineteenth century, various kinds of networks related to the arts and literature overlapped with one another, providing their participants with rich social and cultural resources. I will reserve discussion of several explicit projects that involved the use of *haikai* networks as vehicles of protest for the next chapter. At this point, however, I wish to point out that there were some notable attempts to integrate individual identity through evading certain types of political restrictions during the late Tokugawa period. The aesthetic dimension of personal identity sometimes provided individuals with a foundation for the construction of selfhood outside the formal control of a feudal state.

On the other hand, however, such attempts at identity formation and integration often ended in tragedy. We find an instructive example of this conflict in the case of Watanabe Kazan (1793–1841), a painter from a samurai family. Kazan is an interesting example of an artist's identity construction as a "public man"; while he cultivated his artistic gifts, he kept a sense of public responsibility derived from the internalized honorific consciousness typical of a man of the samurai class.[46]

Watanabe Kazan was born into a samurai family in Tawara. He later became an Elder (*karō*) for Tawara-han, a very small *daimyo* domain ruled by Lord Miyake, and acquired a reputation as a first-class painter of the period. Always eager to acquire new knowledge while delighting in the companionship of others regardless of their status, Kazan epitomized the spirit of the early nineteenth-century Japanese literati. He was a respectable samurai with a strong sense of duty to his government. Nonetheless, the very foundation of the samurai's political economy, the shogun's regime, was beginning to crumble. The weaknesses of the shogunate became particularly evident when the black ships from the West threatened the self-imposed isolation of Tokugawa Japan. Kazan was for a time able to shape a dual social identity in the politically precarious situation of the late Tokugawa era, supporting himself as a successful painter while carrying out his public duties as a samurai worthy of high regard.

The world in which Kazan lived offered him the satisfactions of membership in a number of interconnected aesthetic and literary publics while he served his lord as a "public" man in the eyes of Tokugawa officialdom. He spent his off-duty time mingling with all kinds of art and poetry lovers that he encountered through the aesthetic networks of the period. Although Kazan was personally more interested in painting than in any other art or literary form, he did not discriminate against any other aesthetic enthusiasts, treating them all as his equals. Within this interdisciplinary approach, which was not uncommon among cultivated Tokugawa people, Kazan regularly attended a number of *shogakai*, which were meetings for calligraphy and painting open to the public. He was also well-known to commercial publishers as an author and illustrator. Through these and other social connections, he interacted with many literati whose status backgrounds were quite different from his own.

Watanabe Kazan recorded his encounters in a succession of travel journals and diaries that allow us to study his social networks and the process of his identity construction. The recent publication of a new multivolume edition of the collected works of Watanabe Kazan has greatly simplified access to his journals, diaries, and personal correspondence.[47] For example, in the second year of Tenpō (1831), he visited Atsugi in Sagami province, which adjoins the city of Edo. The primary purpose of this short trip was to meet and socialize with the local cultural enthusiasts.

Kazan's travel notes often feature his own illustrations with *haikai* poems written by new acquaintances and old friends. Even though Kazan had made his reputation in artistic circles as a painter, the *haikai* poetry networks were very helpful during this trip. The first entry in this travel journal records Kazan's visit to a *haikai* master (*sōshō*) named Hasegawa, who was known as Eguchi Kogetsu in the *haikai* world. Hasegawa lived in Aoyama, which was on the outskirts of Edo at that time. After leaving Hasegawa's house, Kazan spent his first night at an inn in Masuya. The owner of this humble village inn happened to be an amateur *haikai* poet. During his overnight stay, Kazan also encountered a few guests with whom he enjoyed some pleasant casual conversation. *Sake* was brought in, and the group began to enjoy an informal drinking party. One of the guests was a tough-looking man named Magobei, who made his living as a hunter and blacksmith but also composed *haikai* poetry. The innkeeper and the other guests asked Kazan to demonstrate his skill in calligraphy and painting; he obliged them by improvising dozens of examples of his work on the spot. The members of the party also composed a number of *haikai* poems. The gathering, however, was not confined to politically inoffensive aesthetic activities. As the excitement continued to build amid a general atmosphere of congeniality, Magobei launched into outspoken criticism of the local *daimyo*'s harsh policies, recounting the tragic history of a recent uprising in the vicinity that ended with the execution of its leader. Kazan jotted down several *haikai* poems produced in this gathering in his journal as well as Magobei's political opinion.[48] This example illustrates Kazan's pattern of socializing with local people wherever he went without regard to their social position through the media of poetry and painting. In fact, the composition of *haikai* poetry served new acquaintances as a gesture of simultaneous introduction and welcome. From this perspective, Kazan was a full participant in the world of *haikai* aesthetic civility, in which the craft of poetry composition served as an entrée to pleasant interactions with congenial strangers.

Kazan was not always well-received, however. On one occasion, he was traveling through an area where he had no personal contacts from previous visits. He tried to contact a well-to-do person in the neighborhood on the basis of a letter of introduction from a friend. Kazan was rebuffed by the gentleman, who mistook him for a vagabond artist who was down on his luck and panhandling. Displeased by this lack of courtesy, Kazan decided to stay at a nearby inn in Mannenya. He then said to the owner of this inn, in a proud and straightforward manner:

> I am a vassal of the Lord Miyake Tosanokami, and also a painter in a manner of speaking – a strange man, you might think. If this town has anyone who is my peer (*ware ni hitoshiki hito*),

I would like to have a night's conversation with them. To any book readers, calligraphers, *waka* and *haikai* poets, or anyone who writes poetry in the Chinese style, enjoys a good discussion, or likes to listen to stories, please convey my invitation to them. I will buy *sake* and some food. I like poetry and painting, but I am not a beggar. I am a gentleman with a good living from my lord's stipend.[49]

Note the reference to "my peer," which could also be translated as "human being equal to me." Kazan was immediately rewarded with a delightful evening in the company of several local literati, not all from the samurai class, who enjoyed a night of talking, drinking, dancing, and singing with him. As usual, Kazan wrote down the *haikai* poems produced by the group in his journal together with his own illustrations of this memorable impromptu gathering.

   Kazan's invitation led to more than a simple drinking party, however; local political issues surfaced once again. In the course of the evening, a village chief (commoner) named Surugaya Hikohachi openly criticized the local *daimyo* and even went so far as to say: "It would be better to re-place this lord! (*"tonosama o torikaetaran koso yokarubeshi to omou"*)[50] As an honorable samurai with a deeply ingrained sense of loyalty to his own master, Kazan could not accept this radical opinion and stated his opposition to Hikohachi's argument. At the same time, Kazan admired Hikohachi's strong sense of justice as well as his frank, open, and honor-able character. Ransai, another guest who had been listening to this dis-cussion, made the persuasive point that, indeed, different types of rulers do make a major difference in the lives of their subjects. Ransai analyzed the local political situation as follows:

> In my opinion, it would be best if the Atsugi region were to come under the direct rule of the shogun or at least become the estate of one of the shogun's immediate vassals, rather than re-maining a small daimyo domain. . . . The shogun's territories are usually governed more generously and fairly. The shogun's lo-cal agent in his territories is usually a lesser samurai and easy to deal with. . . . Therefore, people tend to be more tractable. . . . In contrast, a daimyo who governs a small domain [like the present lord who rules Atsugi] has more power over the smallest details of our lives, and uses that power harshly.[51]

Since Atsugi was close to Edo, the shogun's castle city, Ransai's opinion was not completely unrealistic. He said that he intended to persuade some powerful vassal of the shogun by networking with his medical clients. Ransai was a medical doctor. "I am sure that if I emphasize how rich a territory Atsugi is, one of the shogun's powerful banner men will try to take it away [from the present lord]."[52] Kazan was left speechless by the clever realism of this political analysis because it was so different from the conventional narrow worldview of the samurai class, whose ethical system emphasized the virtue of loyalty to one's immediate master.

From this perspective, Kazan's trip to Atsugi was more than an aesthetic pilgrimage for a cultivated samurai; it provided several occasions for learning the political realities of a changing society. It was only through meetings with fellow aesthetes, however, that Kazan could engage in serious criticism of contemporary politics. He wrote down people's observations and critiques in his private notes. There is no doubt that his apparently casual socializing with people that he met through the local aesthetic networks became an education in political awareness. The pattern of socialization described in the writings of Kazan challenges the prevailing notion that pre-modern non-Western societies such as Tokugawa Japan did not develop spheres of critical discourse regarding political matters. These cultured commoners in the Atsugi region expressed the clear conviction that the regional government could be changed in order to improve the quality of people's lives. Although the people who gathered to share Kazan's hospitality had no conscious intention of replacing the shogunate itself – at that point in time, two centuries of stability made the Tokugawa regime look relatively impervious to change – their political realism found possibilities for change at the local level. They regarded the regional authority as an organizational functionary rather than a focus of personal loyalty. The critical spirit that animated these people had clearly escaped the confines of feudal norms and social relations. Although Kazan's meetings with articulate provincials such as these were made possible through networks with an aesthetic orientation, late Tokugawa Japan began to produce larger numbers of people with a critical political consciousness. This consciousness in turn was supported by numerous spheres of voluntary socialization that made use of the established logic of aesthetic enclave publics. The realms of beauty and politics were gradually but seamlessly connected in the context of Kazan's personal networks. If we summarize Tokugawa society dismissively as a feudal pre-modern society because it lacked civil society, while ignoring the widespread networks of voluntary associations and the freedom they offered to those who were disenchanted with the political status quo, we are making a serious mistake.

This observation, however, does not mean that Tokugawa aesthetic civility did not have its limitations. Kazan's sense of public duty, which was typical for a man of the samurai class, began to conflict with his growing sense of personal responsibility as a politically conscious individual. He recognized that his primary responsibilities as a political man were officially limited to loyal service to the lord of a very small territory. In addition, Kazan had also acquired a sense of self-confidence as an accomplished painter. Given his aesthetic identity, Kazan came to regard himself as a public man in a larger world outside the limits of his small feudal territory. He wrote in his personal correspondence to a trusted friend, "...that I am an Elder in a tiny provincial domain.... My hands, however, are 'public hands' that belong to the world and to history (*tenka hyakuse no kōshu*). With a brush in my hand, I could travel openly and publicly (*kōgyō*) as a painter, even as far as China or India."[53] Kazan later became involved in the Dutch Learning network and began to produce critical political writings based upon new information from the West. He was arrested by the shogunate in 1839 and later placed under house arrest in his home castle town of Tawara. In 1841, he committed suicide out of fear that his way of life would politically damage his master, Lord Miyake of the Tawara domain. Under the Tokugawa system, the lives of people who tried to integrate their private enclave identities with their public personae often ended as tragically as that of Watanabe Kazan, even as late as the 1840s.

Although the members of the Tokugawa aesthetic publics were tolerated by the authorities as long as their private activities were conducted under their enclave identities, it was difficult to confine the relationships that were formed within these private enclaves. One may reasonably assume that the repeated experience of switching network connections in the course of meeting a range of other people in the aesthetic circles was an increasingly influential factor in the process of identity formation and revision. As Watanabe Kazan's example indicates, there were many poets and artists who quietly began to regard their enclave identities as more profound expressions of their inner selves than their formal feudal titles. Furthermore, the realm of the beautiful generated so many networks with an exponentially large number of possible intersections that it was impossible to prevent their eventual encroachment on political matters. I will explore this complex question – the political influence of the private aesthetic networks – more fully in the next chapter from the perspective of popular contentious movements and their relationship to the *haikai* networks.

Here we must return to Kazan's impressive claim that a painter's hands belong to the public domain. His identification of his work as an artist with his public persona was not an intellectual abstraction; it came to explicit awareness and formulation through his actual experiences of aesthetic networking. The domain of aesthetics formed connections among Tokugawa people separated by feudal categories with the world of commonality, in the ancient sense of the word *ōyake*, a large common house. Acquiring the skills of aesthetic civility allowed Tokugawa individuals who wanted to move beyond feudal boundaries to do so within the spacious framework of a larger community. If it was the aesthetic networks that allowed their members to exchange their political identities for citizenship in a common world, then it is hardly remarkable that aesthetic identities were so influential in shaping the minds of Tokugawa people.

8

Poetry and Protest: The Rise of Social Power

During the late Tokugawa period, economically advanced regions of Japan saw the phenomenon of proto-industrialization: the vigorous rise of cottage industries that produced commercial goods such as textiles, *sake* brewing, potteries, and fertilizers. Commercial agriculture flourished in many regions, which increased the flow of cash to some rural people. As Tokugawa Japan entered the nineteenth century, the signs of the national-scale market activities and commercialization were observed everywhere. Such socio-economic transformation was accompanied by the rise of popular literacy and the spread of elementary education through private community schools called *terakoya*. It was under these conditions that the network of cultural associations became deeply enmeshed with the social and economic networks of Japanese society. Aesthetic publics' ability to generate alternative realities sometimes provided a jumping board for mobilizing people's contentious actions in local communities.

The experience of people switching their identities to those of poets or artists was coupled with a temporary suspension of their formal feudal identities. People experienced a periodic alteration of their personal identities because they enjoyed a different quality of social relations in these circles. Since the state's disciplinary strategy demanded the categorical segregation of people, the trespassing of feudal categorical boundaries in the aesthetic circles constituted a form of latent protest to the Tokugawa order.

However, the linkage of poetry and protest did not end only with the categorical reformulation and mentality transformation. When the rise of aesthetic networks coincided with the socio-political transformation of Tokugawa society and the changing nature of local communities, the rise of aesthetic publics and their networks of voluntary associations began to have a different meaning. Although Tokugawa Japan at this stage can still be described with a label of "civility without civil society," given the fact that civil liberty was not codified and protected by the neo-feudal

204

Tokugawa regime, this society was curiously well-equipped with networks of various types of people that had developed an ability to decide and assert their own social and political matters. When networks of artists and poets came to enmesh with socio-political and economic networks in communities, qualities of social relations in communities were also in transition.

Among all sundry collections of regional, occupational, and status groups that were incorporated into the decentralized yet integrated Tokugawa national hierarchies, village communities had been historically the most powerful base for political protest. The revenue of grain taxes was the main source of income for the shogunate and the local *daimyo* polities; villages collectively had the responsibility of paying grain taxes, and in doing so they kept some negotiating power with the samurai authorities. Villager-organized contentious actions of *ikki* also peaked in the nineteenth century. Unlike the medieval *ikki* leagues that I discussed in Chapter 4, Tokugawa *ikki* did not include the samurai. Tokugawa *ikki* were usually based on village organizations (remember the fact that the samurai were no longer living in villages during this period). Villagers sometimes formed networks of contentious actions that crossed the boundaries of political domains. This phenomenon can be called the rise of social power. The remarkable developments of networks of aesthetic circles and traveling art professionals further expanded spheres of social interactions that were invisible and uncontrollable from the viewpoint of the state authorities. Thus, from the late eighteenth to the nineteenth centuries, with the development of proto-industrialization, the rise of social power and aesthetic publics often overlapped in a new way. The strong presence of aesthetic networks in local communities was a cause as well as a consequence of the transformation of communities.

The Rise of Cultured Rural People

Toward the nineteenth century, Tokugawa local communities were endowed with intersecting networks of production, commerce, and aesthetic circles. Although these different kinds of networks never conflated each other, together they made social relations of communities much more flexible and open-ended.

In particular, the authorities were disturbed by the fact that these activities were enjoyed not only by the elite villagers but by the common people as well. Although the activities themselves were generally tolerated, the idea of peasants partaking of too many cultural activities was disgusting to the authorities, who feared their consumptive lifestyle might decrease their tax-paying abilities. One of those officials wrote a report to the authorities in the early nineteenth century that stated, "The most recent findings are that people's lifestyles have deteriorated." This officer was the magistrate in charge of supervising provinces in the Kantō (the *Kantō torishimari deyaku*) responsible for the order and security of towns and villages of the eight provinces comprising the area surrounding Edo. Provinces were under the shogun's direct rule. He noted in his report in 1826:

> Performing artists of various types go out from Edo to visit different areas in the Kantō and generally wander around. These people include masterless samurai, Confucian scholars, painters and calligraphers, *haikai* masters, *ikebana* teachers, and masters of *igo* or *shōgi* games. They organize meetings, get permits from the local village officials, and earn good money from wealthy people in the area, and encourage luxurious spending. As a result, the peasants get lazy and neglect farming because of their bad influence.... I recommend the prohibition of those wandering people visiting villages. Luxurious consumption is not good for the good people.[1]

The report continued to criticize rural cultural activities. The villagers were not only enjoying those activities, but they were also engaging in swordsmanship, and "fencing masters were also wandering around villages.... Even with previous prohibition, it has not stopped." The provinces of the Kantō were dominated by commercial agriculture in this period and were also developing flourishing cottage industries such as cotton and silk weaving. The hosts of the visiting performing and martial artists from Edo were village executives and gamblers (*bakuto*) who were local bosses. They helped artists and poets schedule meetings in towns and villages and facilitated the mobilization of villagers. The presence of commercial capital in villages clearly helped them to support many traveling cultural professionals.

The official's report is one of many indications that the economically advanced regions of rural Japan had developed networks of amateur enthusiasts by the end of the eighteenth century that were capable of hosting traveling intellectuals and artists across an array of fields. Of the many amateur associations in the rural areas, the *haikai* circles were again the most typical, and they constituted the space of publics able to host visitors from the outside. The spheres of publics that were created by provincial amateur associations were usually organized by the more affluent and influential members, but they remained open to outsiders as well as to the less successful members of the community. The remarkable rise of the rural cultured people could not be fully understood from a viewpoint of increasing economic capital accumulated in local towns and villages.

Without the presence of the local amateur networks, it is doubtful whether rural communities would have had the structures or mechanisms to welcome such varieties of professionals, intellectuals, poets, painters, dancers, *Kabuki* actors, musicians, and *igo* and *shōgi* players.[2]

The sociological notion of social capital – readily available social resources in the form of social networks – helps us to understand the dynamics of a new situation facing rural Japan during the late eighteenth and early nineteenth centuries. The rural society of Tokugawa Japan was not simply accumulating economic capital that in turn attracted a variety of hobby teachers. In fact, rural Japan became endowed with networks of people that for the first time reached beyond traditional kinship ties or communal neighborhood ties. Hobbyist circles were organizing people within villages and extending into the outside world. In other words, these rural villages entailed "network-rich" communities that encouraged people to act on their own behalf by taking advantage of those networks. Therefore, it appears that once social capital is invested in society, the network relations begin to function in unexpected ways that may in fact depart dramatically from the original context of the relationship. For example, friendships formed among a group of college classmates may become an effective business or political network if one of the members of the circle invites the others to invest in a new business or help out in a campaign for public office. Structures embodied within relationships can function as resources for individual actors and can be combined with other forms of capital to produce different social outcomes. Individuals can use social networks as resources for their own ends and can combine them with other forms of capital – economic, political, and cultural – to produce different social outcomes. The policing official of the shogunate was frustrated because he observed the rise of uncontrollable "social power," power derived from networked people who effectively functioned outside state control.

People often overlapped their participation in these various circles. Simultaneous membership in a number of different groups was not confined to purely aesthetic interests and activities. In fact, as will be discussed later, the *haikai* networks in the agricultural provinces from the late Tokugawa to the early Meiji periods often overlapped with the political networks of the contentious movements.[3] The regions of Japan with a high level of grassroots participation in political mobilization before and after the Meiji restoration correspondingly had a high density of *haikai* networks. This combination of poetry and politics was not without its irony, considering the fact that the Tokugawa civilizing process entered through the back door, so to speak, as a private arena deemed inferior to the public (*ōyake, kō*) forum. The question then arises: How could the development of networks of amateur poets signify, as well as catalyze, the emergence of social power – in other words, a network capacity for political mobilization outside the state?

The *Haikai* Network in Japan's Snow Country

Since the wide proliferation of the Tokugawa poetry groups even into rural areas is unusual in the history of any country, a closer look at a specific example of these amateur circles may convey the flavor of their activities. I have chosen to focus on Echigo province, a rural area of Japan, rather than on Edo or another large city, precisely because the existence of poetry groups in outlying areas or farming villages would be unusual from a comparative viewpoint.

Echigo province was economically backward and has been called the "snow country" of Japan because in winter the houses are often covered by ten or more feet of snow. In 1800, a young tradesman named Suzuki Bokushi (1770–1842), living in Shiozawa-mura, a village in Uoniwa County, made a promise to himself to organize a literary project in his province on an unprecedented scale. He decided to set up an "Open *Haikai* Poetry Competition with Ten Judges" in Echigo. Poetry contests of this sort were very popular at the time. Suzuki himself was a small-scale trader in *chijimifu*, a kind of cloth made of hemp. *Chijimifu* was the basis of a regional cottage industry – it was produced primarily by farm women in their homes, particularly during the long winters. The local traders in this commodity were middlemen who purchased the *chijimifu* from the farm families and carried the cloth on their own backs for trading. The expansion of the Japanese commercial market economy during the seventeenth and eighteenth centuries increased the numbers of these local traders, whose networks connected the snow country to the national consumption centers. He was known as a hard worker, a successful trader who made his living honestly. Throughout his life, he was devoted to his family business as well as to art and literature.[4] He later described his commitments as follows: "Although I enjoyed the world of refined elegance, I was also exceptionally diligent in keeping up with my business concerns. . . . Even in snow storms I often ate my lunch on my feet, while I was carrying my goods on my shoulders."

Suzuki Bokushi organized his literary project with his characteristic energy, carefulness, and perseverance. He began by circulating a one-page announcement of the competition through various local networks. Contestants were asked to submit the customary application fee of 16 mon per entry – about the cost of a bowl of noodles. Suzuki and his associates probably distributed the announcements during their trading trips. Within eight months, 4,022 *haikai* entries had been submitted by men and women from different status groups. Most of the submissions came from *haikai* circles in the villages closest to Bokushi's home, but others were sent from circles in the provinces of Jōshū and Bushū, which formed part of the *chijimifu* trading route to Edo.

Bokushi's hard work did not end with the distribution of his handbills. He made ten meticulous copies of each entry – over 40,000 copies in all – and sent them to ten famous *haikai* poet-instructors who had agreed to serve as judges. These judges were scattered all over Japan, from such large cities as Edo and Osaka to towns in Sanuki province on the island of Shikoku; all were far removed from Echigo. The ten judges then gave points to each entry on a 1-to-9 scale. After the organizer computed the total points for each entry, 299 poems were chosen as winners. The winners' poems were printed, and a special *haikai*-making party was organized in celebration. The winners' *haikai* were inscribed on two wooden panels that were dedicated at the local Shintō shrine.

The extensiveness of the network resources that this young trader was able to mobilize is remarkable. The surprisingly large number of entrants from these largely agricultural provinces is clear evidence of a rich endowment of communicative networks. "Ten-Judge Competitions" were an established popular style of *haikai* competition during this period, which Bokushi simply emulated. The practices of such competitions were made possible only by the dense and extended networks of the *haikai* circles. The intricate and efficient *haikai* network that was involved in Bokushi's contest was by no means unusual. There were many *haikai* circles and other types of amateur artistic groups in both the cities and rural areas of Tokugawa Japan that included samurai, priests, merchants, artisans, and farmers. The reader can imagine that if the agricultural provinces supported literary activities with such enthusiasm, the larger cities must have been extremely lively centers for artistic and literary circles. Careful examination of the evolution of the large-scale popular *haikai* networks around Kyoto, Osaka, and Edo proves, as a matter of fact, that the *haikai* network in the snow country was not only usual but was built on a century of previous institutional development that had stimulated the growth of *haikai* networks throughout Japan.

Complex Overlapping Networks

The local communities of Japan in this period had networks based on three major organizing principles. The first was network relationships based on kinship, probably the fundamental type of network in many societies. The second type included networks based on political structures. The Tokugawa villages were connected to the upper reaches of the political system by basic units of administration. The rural villages were governed semi-autonomously by the villagers themselves because the samurai lords were obliged to live in castle cities during this period. This pattern, of course, meant that the villagers had to form political networks among themselves in order to handle their day-to-day internal affairs. The third type of network included economic and commercial relationships. The economic system of the Tokugawa farming communities had originally been contained within the framework of local grain production. This relatively undeveloped agricultural economy produced barely enough surplus to pay the grain taxes due the samurai authorities. As the commercialization of the Tokugawa economy moved outward from the cities, however, the agrarian villages were incorporated within the dense networks of the national market economy. In particular, the commercialization of textile production and related agricultural products markedly altered the face of the agrarian communities, especially in advanced regions like the Kinai (near Kyoto and Osaka) and the Kantō provinces.

The amateur artistic and literary associations, including the *haikai* circles, clearly added a significant new principle of network organization to the agrarian communities, namely group formation based on shared knowledge rather than ascriptive principles or political reasons. Furthermore, in the Japanese experience, the *haikai* circles were the earliest and most extensive examples of knowledge-based networks in which the individuals who chose to participate constituted the basic units of membership rather than their *ie* or families. This focus on the individual formed a sharp contrast with other principles of network organization during this period. In political networks, for example, the basic unit of administrative jurisdiction was the *ie*, or house. Each person's formal status was defined on the basis of his or her *ie* (house). Moreover, it was the *ie*, and not the individuals within it, that was responsible for tax payments. In economic matters also, the prosperity of a farmer or trader was understood as fulfillment of responsibility for the well-being of the family business rather than an individual success story. But in the *haikai* circles, membership was purely a personal matter. This regard for the individual added a new dimension to the network structure of the Tokugawa village communities.

We have already noted that the *haikai* groups had formed three loosely organized tiers by the late eighteenth century: the circles of urban sophisticates in Edo, Osaka, and Kyoto; circles at the provincial level, centered in the *daimyo* castle towns; and circles at the level of the smaller communities. Even in the outlying villages, there were *haikai* circles within walking distance of almost any member of the community. The important point in this context is that the *haikai* circles in rural communities often overlapped with the pre-existing networks based on kinship, local self-government, or commercial interests. In the case of the *haikai* groups, the nature of this poetry simultaneously satisfied people's desire for individualistic self-expression and their desire to retain the spirit of horizontal solidarity within their local communities. Many trading relationships among the rural merchants also acquired a social dimension through the *haikai* circles. In fact, in several instances, the commercial trading networks that crisscrossed the agrarian communities – such as Suzuki Bokushi's *chijimifu* trade route – overlapped with the *haikai* circles' patterns of recruitment. But even though the amateur poetry networks were considered private and personal, they allowed and encouraged free development beyond the boundaries of existing social relationships. Through the socialization that took place in the *haikai* circles, the political and economic networks sometimes intersected and strengthened. For example, parents found brides for their sons through the amateur literary networks. By adding a new organizational principle to the older bases of network formation, the *haikai* circles raised the density, scale, and dynamics of rural networks to a qualitatively different level.

To be more precise, the circles' ability to link the population of rural Japan and other knowledge-based networks in the outside world qualitatively changed the cultural capital of the village communities. On the one hand, it is certainly true that even before the Tokugawa economy underwent its rapid expansion in the seventeenth century, the Japanese agrarian communities were never completely isolated. They had always retained certain connections to the rest of Japan via overland trading routes. On the other hand, in terms of knowledge-based networks, the Tokugawa *haikai* circles and similar artistic networks created more institutionalized and systematic ways of connecting villagers to the outside cultural milieu.

The *Haikai* Circles and Kokugaku in the Edo Hinterland

Let me offer the reader a few more specific examples of how villagers became connected to the outside world. A Japanese historian, Sugi Hitoshi, has published a study of the *haikai* network in Bushū province between Ōme station and Ōgimachiya, an area that consisted of seven villages strung along a trading route. The published results of a *haikai* competition that was held in 1846 listed 50 winners in a field of 9,300 entries. The 1846 booklet, which was unusually detailed for a *haikai* publication, included the names of the winning poets, their official status, their occupations, and their other hobbies. The 50 winners included three women and 43 persons officially classified as belonging to the *hyakushō* (conventionally understood as farmers), although 15 of these "*hyakushō*" were in fact local merchants and owners of cottage industries. The other competition winners included several lesser samurai, Buddhist and Shintō priests, and a medical doctor. With respect to their other cultural pursuits, 18 poets were described as especially ardent devotees of *haikai*. Apart from *haikai* poetry, nine winners listed *ikebana*, another nine mentioned *kyōka* (humorous *waka* poetry), three listed fencing, and two were interested in *waka* poetry. Kokugaku (native learning), *gesaku* (humorous fiction), the tea ceremony, and *ukiyo-e* prints were each listed by only one person.

Sugi speculated on the basis of his findings in the Kantō provinces that the culture enthusiasts in these largely rural areas of Japan included only a minuscule percentage of persons schooled in the Japanese classics or classic *waka* poetry – the foundation for learning the Kokugaku. At most, these highly educated persons would have entailed no more than 1–2% of the provincial *haikai* poets. In Haijima, a town in the Tama region, only one of approximately one hundred known *haikai* poets in the mid-nineteenth century had some background in Kokugaku and *waka* poetry. Students of classical learning tended to come from the wealthier families in the region, but these members of the rural cultural elite were connected to the less-educated cultural enthusiasts through the *haikai* circles.[5]

Although Sugi's findings and conclusion may seem minor, they have significant implications in understanding the Japanese political revival of the nineteenth century. It is generally accepted by Japanese historians that Kokugaku, or the "School of Native Learning," was a major influence on the grassroots political movements that preceded the collapse of the Tokugawa shogunate and Meiji Restoration in 1868. Kokugaku began as an intellectual movement that claimed to find "true" Japanese sensibility in the national classics rather than in Buddhism or Confucianism. The adherents of this school thus insisted on the necessity of in-depth study of the literary productions of the imperial court. This combination of romantic nostalgia and scholarly research into the sources of the Japanese collective identity evolved into an effective political ideology in the mid-nineteenth century when the shogunate became threatened by the forces of Western imperialism.

The Kokugaku's Strategic Position in Networks

The School of Native Learning is usually regarded as an intellectual antecedent of the Meiji Restoration in that it contributed to the reformulated nationalist version of a cultural and political system centered on the emperor. The Meiji Restoration is typically described as a "revolution from above," in which a segment of the samurai-elite rebelled against the shogun and finally ushered in the downfall of the long-lasting Tokugawa *bakuhan* state. During the process of the Meiji restoration, however, a significant number of the grassroots revolutionaries who claimed to be samurai in fact were not "official" members of the samurai class. They were the members of wealthy upper-class farmer families who apparently were often mobilized through their local Kokugaku networks.[6]

These data present the historian with a question of interpretation. It is known that none of the branches of the Kokugaku movement ever enlisted a sizable number of disciples. The skills required to read and comprehend the original texts of the Japanese classics demanded perseverance and commitment, as well as intelligence. The various Kokugaku schools therefore organized a relatively small fraction of the educated population in the various provinces[7]; the extensiveness of their networking was not as large as the pervasive popularity of the *haikai* networks.

On the other hand, if a Kokugaku student were a key person in his local community and well-connected via the *haikai* circles to a wider range of the rural cultured population – as well as to national networks of the Kokugaku and other cultural activities – the Kokugaku movement itself could mobilize a much larger group of political sympathizers in the agricultural provinces than the actual number of its enrollees would suggest. One of the famous literary models of the process that carried some young men from *haikai* circles to Kokugaku classrooms and thence to political mobilization is Aoyama Hanzō, the protagonist of Shimazaki Tōson's famous autobiographical novel, *Yoakemae* (Before the Dawn). The novel's primary setting is Shimazaki's hometown in the Kiso Valley in Nagano prefecture. The area's cultural infrastructure was known to have been first established through the *haikai* circles that arose there during the late Tokugawa period. Following this development, the Hirata school of Kokugaku was established in the area. It supplied the inspiration that motivated Aoyama Hanzō, a local well-to-do farmer (*gōnō*), to join other activists in supporting the Meiji Restoration. Hanzō's idealistic dreams for social renewal were betrayed by the hasty modernization/Westernization policies of the Meiji government. Once the new ruling oligarchy had supplanted the shogunate, it turned away from inclusive policies, which excluded many grassroots activists (from wealthy farming families) from the political process. These disillusioned local leaders often redirected their energies toward regional renovation movements; some of them eventually joined the "freedom and people's rights" (*Jiyū Minken*) groups. These indigenous democratic movements that emerged in the agricultural regions of late nineteenth-century Japan made a remarkable contribution to the history of Japanese democracy. They could only thrive because of the social and cultural capital accumulated by the rural *haikai* circles of the Tokugawa period.

Western scholarship on the intellectual developments leading to the Meiji Restoration thus tends to focus on the study of the School of Native Learning as an intellectual prelude to the Meiji Restoration. That is understandable given the fact that the Kokugaku activists played a role in rallying the restoration. Yet, the development of social networks through the popularity of the *haikai* poetry and other arts was rarely discussed in relation to the rise of social power. However, unlike the School of Native Learning, which was started originally for the study of *waka* poetry and other Japanese classics, the *haikai* was much more popular and suitable for busy people with their own occupations who could not devote much time to in-depth scholarship of classics. A contemporary *haikai* leader also perceived this situation and claimed that the *haikai* was the means of expressing aesthetic tastes for people with real works. "*Waka* may be good for courtiers, wealthy merchants and farmers, Shinto priests, and retired persons" who had a lot of spare time, but the *haikai* was for everybody who wanted to express "the way of aesthetics and elegance inherent in Japan" ("*nihon ni sonaeshi fūga no michi*")[8] by using colloquial and common vocabulary.

Through this process of cultural popularization and dissemination by the *haikai* networks, the image of an ideal Japan, defined by the cultural idioms of an imperial dynasty, captured the popular imagination because the emperor's court symbolized the venerable antiquity, historical continuity, and aesthetic refinement associated with elite culture. A number of different courtly cultural idioms were popularized through relatively inexpensive for-profit publications, as well as the activities of amateur literary and artistic circles. This situation was not without its irony in that the process of Tokugawa dissemination of elite culture was carried out through largely commercial networks within a political framework shaped by a ruling class of former warriors – not by the imperial aristocracy that had originally defined these cultural standards. At the same time, the dominant samurai class promoted the cultural imagery of the emperor's household, which became a part of the constitutive vocabulary of Japanese collective cultural identities. This cultural development was a prelude to the Meiji restoration of 1868, which united the Japanese people under the revitalized image of the ancient imperial house.

Rural Literacy and *Haikai* Circles

To be sure, the activities of the agrarian *haikai* circles were made possible by a relatively high rate of literacy among the Japanese peasantry. As was mentioned earlier in this book, there is no reliable way of calculating the average rate of literacy in Tokugawa Japan. But it is known that, even in rural areas, it was not unusual for farming families with modest incomes to send their children to school. One interesting source of relevant data is a survey that was made of the participants in the Chichibu Rebellion (also known as the Konmin-tō, the "Poor People's Party" Rebellion) of 1884. A number of poor peasants joined the rebels. After this large-scale jacquerie was suppressed, the police tested the participants for literacy and found that about 40% of the 581 questioned were literate.[9] Although this incident took place 16 years after the Meiji Restoration, the relatively high rate of literacy reflects the scope of the Tokugawa community education system. When one considers the fact that adult males involved in the 1884 rebellion had been educated in a communal private school system developed during the Tokugawa period, rather than in a modernized system of public education,[10] a 40% literacy rate is quite impressive.[11]

Other illustrative data regarding rural literacy are derived from the commemorative records of small rural community schools (*terakoya*). We may consider as a typical example of a cultured farmer Aizawa Muan, who was active from the late eighteenth to the first half of the nineteenth century in Kamikoide, a small village in the foothills of the Akagi Mountains in Joshū province. Muan owned an average or slightly larger than average farm, which was cultivated primarily by his family workforce. But he also ran a small private community school in Kamikoide. In this village of 78 farming families, about 60% left records of sending their children to Muan's school, although only 10 of the 135 students were female. The students came from families whose holdings varied in size, but the majority of families had only average- or small-sized farms. Muan used a textbook of his own composition for teaching the students to read; the text derived much of its content from legal and tax-related documents.[12] Although the data on rural literacy are unsystematic at best, some demographers estimate that by the early nineteenth century many farming families saw to it that male offspring received at least some kind of education. In particular, farmers in the more advanced areas of commercial agriculture were concerned about educating their sons so that they would be able to calculate commodity prices and make similar computations. The rising rate of literacy in the rural communities of Tokugawa Japan was certainly conducive to the proliferation of *haikai* circles and other cultural activities.

In fact, nineteenth-century Japan must have been one of the most literate societies in the world – even before the introduction of modern educational systems. On the other hand, we should not overestimate the level of literacy as a measure of popular cultural power. Among the rural peasantry, literacy by itself would have been insufficient to constitute a social force. Analysis of popular collective uprisings indicates that peasants who were barely literate could organize effective political actions. In my opinion, the level of the combination of cultural capital and social capital is a more interesting and telling index of social force than the rate of literacy alone. Those villages that had accumulated a significant amount of cultural capital simultaneously developed extensive sets of culture-based networks extending to the outside world. Muan's case again presents an interesting picture. He was a leader of the local *haikai* circle as well as a schoolmaster. His circle, which had about 60 members, was a cultural network that drew members from as many as 17 neighboring villages at the foot of Mount Akagi.[13] Muan kept abreast of contemporary intellectual trends while contributing his own firm viewpoints to large-scale cultural networks. In short, he played a key role in at least three different village networks. His position as the local schoolmaster made him influential in the transmission of knowledge inside and around the village. He was also a central figure in the regional *haikai* networks. Because of the respect that Muan commanded within the *haikai* circuit, his reputation and connections with others extended far beyond the range of his immediate surroundings. The presence of a cultured person like Muan in a rural area reflects the expanding cultural and social power of the Tokugawa villages.

Put somewhat differently, the local *haikai* circles and other groups of amateur cultural enthusiasts mediated the accumulation of cultural and social capital in the rural areas of Tokugawa Japan. Furthermore, the reader should note that the activities of rural culture enthusiasts like Muan had no official connection with the samurai authorities. His contributions were all voluntary, and he did not receive any government funding or recognition. In other words, Muan's cultural and educational networks were social spheres that operated outside the state's control and beneath its notice. These autonomous spheres of publics created a space filled with the potential of increased social power for the rural population.

Poetry Circles and Freedom and People's Rights Movements

The links between the agrarian *haikai* circles and the *Jiyū Minken*, or "freedom and people's rights" movements, in the Tama region illustrate the explicit connection between popular literary networks and the rise of social power. The Tama region lies in the Edo hinterland and had grown prosperous from the introduction of commercial agriculture during the late Tokugawa period. The area has had a reputation for silk and textile production and trading since the late eighteenth century. Complex and extensive networks of village *haikai* groups developed in this area along the routes of the silk traders. The Tama region is also known to Japanese historians as the center of the *Jiyū Minken Undō* (the freedom and people's rights movements) after the Meiji Restoration in 1868.[14] The vigorous democratic movements in this region were supported by grassroots activities and have become an icon of Japanese popular democracy through the definitive studies of Irokawa Daikichi, a Japanese historian. The symbol of Tama's politicized cultural energy was the composition of the so-called Itsukaichi Constitution (1881), a draft version of a national constitution written by the people of Itsukaichi. This private draft of a modern constitution, which included progressive provisions for human rights and civic freedom, was planned and sponsored by local cultural circles called "The Itsukaichi Lecture Group."[15]

Areas like Tama that were known as centers of popular agitation for democracy and people's rights also had reputations, in most cases, as regions with a high concentration of *haikai* circles in the late Tokugawa era. Recent excavation of primary sources has shed further light on the contributions of local cultural networks to political mobilization in the Tama region. For example, in the small city of Fukuu, the Matsubara-an school had a succession of *haikai* circles with extensive networks in the area since the late Tokugawa period. The amateur poetry networks overlapped with the silk and textile trading networks that supported the region's economy and extended both cultural and economic connections as far as Edo and Yokohama. In the immediate vicinity of Fukuu, the *haikai* circles not only included the well-to-do farmers and merchants but also the less prosperous farmers, as well as the Shintō priests and other local intellectuals.[16] Some names of famous political and intellectual leaders of the democratic movements of the 1880s, such as Ishizaka Masataka, appear in the regional *haikai* publications of the 1870s. The *haikai* circles in part also overlapped with amateur groups interested in Chinese-style poetry and several different upper-class literary genres. Taken together, these groups comprised a kind of local cultural public by the mid-nineteenth century.

The strength of the amateur *haikai* circles lay in their ability to recruit the politically influential residents of the area across national party lines.[17] The circle participants also organized lecture groups and *shogakai*, which were open exhibitions of painting and calligraphy in which famous professionals demonstrated their skills on the spot.[18] The participants in the *haikai* circles and *shogakai* included the most distinguished local activists for the freedom and people's rights movements. The leaders of these grassroots political action groups had enjoyed long-standing social ties with one another through their various cultural activities prior to the wave of political enthusiasm that swept over the region in the 1880s. These cultural and social networks had laid the groundwork for such remarkable activities as the draft of the "Itsukaichi Constitution," as well as other local initiatives for political change.

The *Haikai* Networks and the Poor People's Party Rebellion

The connection between the culture of the *haikai* groups and political mobilization is even more apparent in the case of the so-called Chichibu Rebellion, or *Konmin-tō* (Poor People's Party) Rebellion, a large-scale peasant uprising against the Meiji government in 1884. Chichibu is a mountainous region that was also known for silk production in the nineteenth century. By the time of the Meiji Restoration, silk had become the main Japanese export, a driving force behind the modern nation-building that had begun less than two decades earlier. A sudden sharp drop in the price of silk, however, had hurt the Chichibu region's economy around this time. The Poor People's Party clamored for government reform and drew several thousand armed peasants into violent demonstrations. The region had supported a flourishing network of *haikai* circles since the Tokugawa period. Inoue Denzō, one of the leaders of the rebellion, was sentenced to death but escaped to Hokkaido, the northernmost island of Japan. Denzō, who was known as a peasant *haikai* poet, continued to write poetry for local *haikai* circles from his hideout in Ishikari, Hokkaido. The historian Moriyama Gunjirō was inspired by Denzō's case to research local shrines in the Chichibu for *haikai* dedication panels. *Haikai* circles had developed the custom that after a particularly intense *haikai* linked-verse meeting or any other noteworthy cultural achievement, the participants would inscribe a record of the event on wooden panels and dedicate them to the local Shintō shrine.

Moriyama's survey reveals a high degree of correlation between the number of panels in community shrines and the extent of the area's involvement in the rebellion. The high density of the cultural networks in the mountain villages of Chichibu appeared to be effective in mobilizing the population for political activities. Moriyama found 120 examples of dedication panels in this region; 91 were dedicated by *haikai* groups, and the remainder commemorated such other cultural activities as martial arts. Although most of the pieces found in the shrine were conventional love poems and comical pieces, some poems clearly whiffed of rebellion.

One striking panel, dedicated a few months before the rebellion, was found in the local shrine to Sakura Sōgo in Nagaru village. This popular type of Shintō shrine was associated with the cult of Sakura Sōgo, a legendary leader of a peasant uprising in the Sakura region during the early Tokugawa period. He was supposed to have been executed in the mid-seventeenth century in the course of an attempt to rescue the villagers from the tyranny of a particularly brutal overlord. He is, as Anne Walthall noted, "the archetype of the peasant martyr, a man who deliberately sacrificed himself on behalf of his community."[19] Identifying the presence of a Sakura Sōgo shrine in a community of the uprising was telling. Moriyama was surprised to find two poetry panels dedicated in this shrine in the very same year of the Poor People's Party Uprising. Apparently, just as the medieval *ikki* horizontal alliances often had linked-verse sessions before their military actions, peasants in this community had two poetry-making sessions to solidify their dedication to their project of protest.

Furthermore, Sakura was the family name of this legendary leader of the rebellion, but it is also a homonym of cherry blossom. The prayer to the god of Sakura was also a prayer to cherry blossoms. As we have seen in Chapter 3, medieval Japan had various kinds of spheres of *mu'en* (no relation) that provided people with opportunities to uncouple themselves from their feudal network constraints. The aesthetic publics formulated around the *za* arts, such as Cherry Blossom linked-verse sessions, utilized technologies of producing "mu'en no-relation" to the feudal categorical order by linking to the depth of ethnomentality in Japanese folklore. The symbolism of cherry trees that connected this world to the dead and the involvement of marginal people of *mu'en* were such examples. The rise of the Tokugawa state, which laid a more integrated system of control over the country, diminished uncontrolled spaces in which freedom created by *mu'en* technologies could thrive. In an unexpected way, however, the older memory of the symbolism of cherry blossoms as the connection of the world of the living and the dead came to play a role in this late nineteenth-century commemorative session of poetry before the rebellion.

In the panel dated April 1884, there are many suggestive pieces of verse such as:

> Cherry blossoms bloom
> And you and I bloom
> To bear fruits and seeds in the future
>
> (*saita sakura to omai to watashi, sue niya mito naru tane to naru*)

This poem is taking a convention of a popular love song, but it appears to imply that collective action will do good for the future. The ethnomentality of poetry and protest evident in the medieval link between the *ikki* league and linked verse was also thriving in the prayer to the god of Sakura in these poems. There is also such a direct voice of anger:

> The abolition of the samurai
> Only brought the misery of conscription;
> The suffering of parents never ends.[20]
>
> – Kōzō
>
> (*Buke o haishite chōhei sawagi, Oyano kurō ga taewasenu*)

> Shall we pray to the God of Sakura?
> I will be joined to you forever, dear Sōgo![21]
>
> – Baigetsu
>
> (*ogan kakeyoka sakura no kami e sue wa omai to sōgasan*)

The active presence of *haikai* networks thus represented the simultaneous accumulation of significant cultural and social capital in the smaller communities of the late nineteenth century. Although Moriyama did not find the contemporary *haikai* panels from every village that participated in the Chichibu Rebellion, he sometimes found older *haikai* panels in these communities. The periods in which these older panels of the *haikai* were dedicated corresponded to the times of peasant uprisings such as the Tenmei (1781–1789), Tenpo (1830–1844), and Keiō (1865–1868) eras.

These grassroots cultural activities were primarily carried out through artistic and literary networks that drew upon intuitive and indirect methods of communication. However, once the Tokugawa people had acquired their cultural and social capital, the cultural developments of the late Tokugawa period indicated that they could mobilize their resources in unexpected ways.

9

Tacit Modes of Communication
and Japanese National Identity

In the preceding six chapters, I illustrated the close relationship between the world of beauty and the world of politics by focusing on the transformation of aesthetic associational activities. Since the summit view of aesthetics such as the tea ceremony and *haiku* has been so often described as "mysterious aesthetic spirituality" by the Western media, I intend to show more "lived" aspects of their practices in society in relation to the culture and organization of sociability in Japan. It does not imply, however, that their aesthetic practice did not have spiritual components or that the intellectual ideas embedded in these arts and poetry did not have an impact on Japanese culture.

In this chapter, therefore, I will temporarily leave the organizational context of this art form and will explore the communicative culture and ideas embedded in these arts.

Framing the Tacit Knowledge as the Meta-Canon

Pre-modern Japanese people's motivations for participation in the art and poetry circles varied from person to person. The types, styles, and structures of these aesthetic networks also represented a range of possibilities that generated diverse cultural frameworks for sociability. As a consequence of this decentralized multiplicity of aesthetic publics, Tokugawa Japan enjoyed considerable cultural diversity. Within this diversity, however, some distinctive types of "cultural framing" emerged that bracketed local activities.

This chapter focuses on one such meta-theory that comprehended poetry and the various performing arts – namely, a high valuation on tacit modes of knowing and communicating. The emphasis on tacit modes of knowledge and communication is a distinctive feature of the Japanese performing arts that attained virtually meta-canonical status. The fact that

221

learning the performing arts and poetry became central to the culture of sociability left a distinct imprint on Japanese culture at large. Even though a student might be motivated to learn an art only as a hobby, immersing oneself in the rules, aesthetic standards, and spiritual disposition required by the art through actual performance or production represented a much deeper level of enculturation than simply being a passive spectator of "real" artists. As aesthetic practices became more and more popularized among the Japanese people, the tacit modes of communication embedded in these arts and poetry also became increasingly influential.

Tacit modes of knowledge and communication are built on the understanding that the most precious and valuable knowledge is hidden beyond reasoned logical investigation or linguistic articulation. A corollary to this implicit assumption is a distinctive view of the relationship between mind and body in which the physical deployment of a performer's body becomes the conduit for realizing the ultimate reality. When these two assumptions were applied to the dynamics of group activities within the performing arts, they helped establish a mindset within the *za* (seating) groups that valued experiencing reality in its fullness through tacit forms of interpersonal communication.

Tacit modes of communication pre-suppose that human cognitive potentials can unfold through a variety of communicative means. Gestures, sign language, or other means of communication can be used to elicit latent cognitive associations. To be sure, tacit modes of communication can assume either a verbal or non-verbal form, or a combination of both. In fact, they can involve a broad array of forms and means of communication. In so doing, they acknowledge the limitations of knowledge acquired through concepts alone.

Non-Duality and Aesthetic Practice

The roots of the tacit modes of communication in the *za* arts were multidimensional and included the influence of the indigenous Japanese religion, Shintō. In particular, as we have observed in Chapter 3, the animistic worldview of the ancient Japanese people as reflected in Shintō set the basic tone of Japanese aesthetics, which permeated the various artistic and poetic genres from *waka* poetry to the performing arts. Nonetheless, these tacit modes, as seen in the *za* aesthetic, acquired an articulated philosophical voice in the medieval period through the influence of Buddhist ontological philosophy. The distinctive characteristic of the *za* genre was its production by active performers and poets who discussed and analyzed their own artistic or literary practices. Just as the Zen masters described their own experiences in meditation, practitioners of the *za* arts attempted to explain their own practices in order to pass them on to the next generation of performers and poets. Since the medieval period entailed the heyday of Buddhist influence in Japan, these art forms absorbed Buddhist epistemology and idioms; they claimed their artistic regimens also constituted the "way" *(michi or dō)* to ultimate reality and formulated theories about their artistic approaches to ineffable knowledge.[1]

It was the emphasis on direct experience that connected aesthetic experience with Buddhist philosophy. The religious groups of medieval Japan, including Zen and Jishū monks as well as the Pure Land and Tendai sects of Buddhism, cultivated the theory and practice of approaching truth through meditation and other direct forms of experience. For example, Dōgen (1200–1253) offered a brilliant summation of medieval Buddhist philosophy in the opening chapter of *Shōbō genzō* (Treasury of the True Dharma Eye), which looked at the limitations of human conceptual ability to experience reality. "Do not base your practice on the assumption that reality must become the object of one's knowledge and be grasped conceptually. Although the ultimate nature of reality is immediately and manifestly experienced, the self does not necessarily always grasp that intimate knowledge. [Because it is beyond superficial understanding,] observation and understanding may not always accompany it."[2] Here, Dōgen acknowledges the limitations of rational conceptual approaches to the quest for enlightenment. The ultimate is knowable, but the path to that knowledge must be tacitly and directly experienced rather than conceptually grasped. To be sure, Dōgen's work is also proof that medieval Japanese produced literature that reflected rigorous analysis and highly developed logic; his writing includes penetrating insights into the relationship among language, experience, and enlightenment. He invented his own idiosyncratic prose style and idioms to describe realities beyond conceptual definition – the realm that he grasped primarily through direct experience – to the extent that he could articulate his experiences in words. For the most part, however, Dōgen, as well as other Japanese Buddhist thinkers, used reason and language to articulate the path toward enlightenment and to help others who were seeking insight through direct experience.[3]

Through the embodied knowledge of a performing art, the student may acquire a universal method for cultivating the depth of human experience through "learning without awareness." Michael Polanyi once remarked, "If there is learning without awareness, there must be also discovery without awareness, since discovery is but learning from nature."[4] Here, Polanyi refers primarily to the process of scientific discovery, but his insight resonates with the comments of Dōgen on approaching reality through tacit knowing.

Dōgen, along with many other medieval religious and/or aesthetic thinkers, observed that knowing the subject and the object of knowing include each other in the direct experience of reality. In meditation, in which the self is both the subject and object of observation, the true way of knowing is not dualistic. Rather, it is a tacit knowledge derived through direct experience. The aim of meditation, as in chanting, dancing, and other ritual practices, is to experience this "dropping away" of mind and body in the quest for the freedom that lies beyond conceptualization. Human attachment to concepts and logical reasoning inevitably entails the duality of subject and object. This non-dualistic approach in turn supported and legitimated the rigorous honing of artistic skills (called *keiko*, or training, particularly training via repetitive exercises) as a route to the state of empty mind, or *mushin*.

The Buddhist theory of non-duality was difficult for ordinary people to grasp, insofar as the popular practices of Buddhism centered on human longings for well-being in this life and after death, not on highbrow philosophical formulas. In contrast, the practice of one's favorite art brought enjoyment as well as spiritual refinement through a process of learning. The traditional arts in Japan thus became a reservoir of the spiritual worldview and conveyed it to segments of the population that could not otherwise be reached through the philosophical dimension of Buddhism. To be sure, it should be pointed out, however, that the Japanese medieval arts were not subordinate in any way to institutional Buddhism or Shintōism. Although many medieval performing arts originated as companies associated with temples and shrines, medieval arts began to develop their own spheres of influence and the artists did not consider their activities to be missionary expressions (see Chapter 4).

Zeami (1363–1442) articulated his theory of true Nō drama thus:

> [T]he performance of the ultimate true player is ... as Tendai Myoshaku [a famous commentary of the Tendai Sect of Buddhism] noted, 'beyond linguistic descriptions, mystic in emerging at the point beyond the understanding of mind, that is to say, in wonder beyond conception (*myō*). That is the way the performance should be. ... [In such a true performance] there is no single artificial effort, no attempt as to how to perform; there is only a feeling of empty mind (*mukan no kan*). It emerges with the consciousness that detaches from one's narrow self-centered consciousness (*riken no ken*, or distanced viewing).[5]

Zeami's aesthetic theory originated from his own experience of performing and expressed his ultimate ideal of performance. It aimed at realization beyond linguistic conception. Zeami's expressions of aesthetic theories are always difficult to decipher since he is trying to express tacitly ways of knowing the depth of experience through his years of artistic practices.

Buddhist philosophical idioms helped him to describe his years of experience in this performing art.

Zeami's prescription of ideal performance with an empty mind was not exceptional. Various performing arts, including martial arts, developed a similar ideal. Although some arts, such as the tea ceremony and Nō drama, had developed more articulated ideologies with a clear connection to Buddhist ontology, others transmitted a similar understanding of physical discipline and spirituality as "taken for granted naturalness" through their practices. In particular, performing arts such as *jōruri* narrative singing and *shamisen* (a banjo-like three-stringed instrument) music were among the "popular culture" of the Tokugawa era that developed from the "floating world (*ukiyo*)," such as seen in the sentiments of the Tokugawa townspeople. Although this population did not articulate overblown aesthetic theories embodying the idioms of Buddhist philosophies, it did anticipate extracorporeal realization by cultivating the self through physical training. In fact, by this time, a similar attitude toward personal cultivation arose as a non-sectarian doctrine permeating most practicing "arts" in Japan, including craft arts and martial arts. The valuation of tacit modes of communication became so ubiquitous that, even lacking any sectarian affiliation, it attained a status of taken for granted naturalness in the minds of the Japanese people.

Consequently, Yuasa Yasuo, a contemporary Japanese scholar, describes the common assumption that dominated aesthetic philosophies:

> [In training in an art,] initially, the body's movements do not follow the dictates of the mind. The body is heavy, resistant to the mind's movement; in this sense, the body is an object opposing the living subject's mode of being. That is, the mind (or consciousness) and the body exhibit an ambiguous subjective–objective dichotomy within the self's mode of being. To harmonize the mind and body through training is to eliminate this ambiguity in practice; it amounts to subjectivizing the body, making it the lived subject. This is a practical, not a conceptual, understanding.[6]

The experience of training in a performing art cultivates the relationships between the subjective self and body in which the body is perceived as "the other." The body is in fact the self, even though the performer may feel otherwise. The experience of knowing oneself through cultivating and deploying body movements was in fact a discovery of the self that cannot be understood through mere consciousness. This means that the body serves as the sphere of interaction between two systems of cognitive networks: the subjective self and embodied knowledge. In this communicative training process, the body became the sphere of realization in which a new identity of the self emerged through overcoming the duality of subject and object. Furthermore, since a performing art usually has an audience (either imagined or actual others), one's body thus becomes a bridge between the performer's subjectivity and others. Yuasa eloquently articulates this linking dynamics, where the body plays the role of what I would term a "public" according to the way I defined it earlier, as a communicative sphere emerging at the intersection of two or more separate network domains, thus allowing a new identity to emerge.

When tacit ways of knowing and self-cultivation were coupled with the group dynamics of the collective *za* (seating) arts, theories of unspoken communication as a means of socialization began to emerge. Because performing arts involved expression through body movements before the audience, the body not only constituted a link between the subjective self and physical self but also hosted the intimate conversation between the self and the other in the audience. The art of the tea ceremony best exemplifies this development. This distinctive art form has its epistemological foundation in the theory of tacit knowing of Buddhist philosophy, but it extended the theory to an interpersonal exchange in civilized secular life.

The unique contribution of the Japanese tea ceremony to human rituals of hospitality lies in its combination of sociability and aesthetics. The tea ceremony was also "a performing art that is mediated by the movement of the body."[7] The host's care and consideration is expressed through artistry of motion and gesture. Students of the tea ceremony were enjoined to master each step singly until they could perform the entire sequence without apparent effort. The movements and gestures of the tea ceremony should be as smooth and unforced as the flow of water.

A famous theoretical discussion of the "way of tea" from *Nanbōroku* includes the following explanation of the elusive "one mind":

> To a question, "How do guests and host put themselves in the proper frame of mind for tea?" Eki (Rikyū) answered, "Connecting with one another's feelings is considered the best way. However, do not try too hard to take account of the others' feelings. An enlightened host and guests can be comfortable with each other without striving to do so. It often happens that beginners attempt to tune into one another's feelings and so turn aside from the right path. Thus, it is good to be sensitive to the others' feelings, but it is bad to make forced adjustments."[8]

Here, Rikyū refers to the ideal of human beings' knowing one another as an effortless sensing through tacit communication. The guests were expected to reciprocate through their unspoken appreciation of the host's hospitality and concern for their comfort. Nonetheless, once students of the tea ceremony "tried" too much to tune into one another, the entire atmosphere became too artificial and dualistic. The fact that this particular art form was widely popularized during the Tokugawa period and achieved a kind of aesthetic authority had a significant impact on the Japanese ideal of sociability; namely, there emerged a popular notion that the deepest human communication took place through silent aesthetic communion. The idealization of tacit modes of communication was most fully expanded in the development of the tea ceremony ideology.

The Tacit Mode of Communication in Linked Poetry

The tacit mode of communication in *renga* and *haikai* linked poetry developed differently from that of the performing arts since it relies exclusively on words for its communication. Linked poetry was governed by strict lexical rules, or a grammar of poetry. Knowing and adhering to the grammar of linked-verse composition is, however, only the beginning. Unlike the tea ceremony, in which a student at the introductory level could be present as a guest at a tea meeting as long as he or she could reproduce the basic pattern of physical movements, even the beginner poet was required to contribute a verse of his or her own on short notice in a linked-poetry session. The genre thus required a greater degree of creative spontaneity on the student's part.

The emphasis on tacit communication in linked poetry developed out of the specific technique employed by this genre, namely forming a continuous poetic chain out of verses contributed in sequence by different individuals. A logically coherent but predictable succession of linking verses would hardly contribute to the creation of an exciting poetic universe. The poets were usually required to insert refreshing transitions or breaks from the preceding chain of thought.

Japanese linked verse usually sees direct connections of stanzas as evidence of a lack of skill on the grounds that they exclude subtlety and the element of surprise. Direct linkages do not contribute to unexpected, fresh, or interesting developments in the chain. The art of linked poetry thus required participating poets to continually deconstruct, uncouple, and reconstruct the poetic images and cognitive associations presented in the meeting. At the same time, a new poetic element in a chain of verse should sense and recognize the mood of the previous verse and connect with it. Thus, the *haikai* poets had to maintain a delicate balance between two contradictory requirements. In other words, forging the connection itself was regarded as a form of silent communication between a given poet and his or her immediate predecessor.

To assist new poets in acquiring a "feel" for tacit communication by cultivating their intuition and openness to the contributions of other members of a *haikai* circle, some *haikai* masters did leave behind written guidance on the cultivation of nuanced associational sensitivity that relied on metaphors related to sense perception. Morikawa Kyoriku (1656–1715), a disciple of Bashō, enumerated several different methods for constructing a good associational line: (1) Sensing the *nioi*, or fragrance, of the previous stanza. In this technique of apperception, a poet sought to intuit the residual traces of human emotion, appearance, or seasonal atmosphere created by the preceding line, not its precise words or explicit meaning. (2) Sensing the *omokage*, or shadow, of the preceding stanza. Here the poet focused on the sense of sight to reimage the world portrayed in the preceding stanza. (3) Sensing the *hibiki*, or lingering sound, of the previous stanza.[9] Here one attended to the sense of hearing to catch the echoes of the sounds or indications of movement described in the previous stanza. Altogether, Kyoriku offered eight methods for composing the next stanza in a chain of linked verse by explaining how one might gain access to the world evoked by the previous poet and then develop and enrich that world with one's own contribution.[10] Notice his use of metaphor derived from sense perception to grasp or absorb the mood of the preceding stanza and accentuate its rich suggestiveness. There was no such thing as a "right" or "correct" interpretation of the text.

We will now examine a specific example of linked verse in order to illustrate the rules of composition that structured this form of tacit communication. Each stanza had to conform to requirements attached to its position in the numerical sequence as well as maintain a poetic association with the preceding stanza. Our example is taken from *Sarumino* (The Monkey's Straw Raincoat):

1   Even the kite's feathers
    Have been combed sleek:
    First flash of winter rain.

                            – Kyorai

2   A gust of wind –
    The shaken leaves grow still.

                            – Bashō

3   From morning onward
    His trousers have been dampened
    By crossing streams

                            – Bonchō

4 The bamboo bow set
   To frighten the badger away

   – Fumikuni

5 Leaves of ivy hang over the door
   In the light of the early evening moon

   – Bashō

The first stanza of the linked-verse poem is intended to establish the basic mood of the piece. In this example, the first poet, Kyorai, wants to convey a sense of the gloom of early winter. A kite's feather is usually puffy, but a light rainfall has naturally smoothed it down. This poetic scene reflects an appreciation of quiet loneliness. As a rule, the second stanza is a follow-up piece; it must have some associative continuity with the world depicted in the first unit. Thus, Bashō, the second poet, speaks of a gust of wind and leaves, which fits with the earlier references to winter and calm. The third poet in the sequence is required to break with the mood established in the first two stanzas in order to make a fresh development. Bonchō, the third writer, turns to the river and the time of day, but instead of describing nature in further detail, he brings a human figure into the center of the action. The third stanza describes the humdrum activity of a peasant wading through the river. Also, the water element is carried over from the first line but is switched from rain to river. This stanza breaks with the first two by adding a shade of humor with its mention of the man's clumsy wet trousers. At the same time, Bonchō's stanza is associated with the imagery of the second stanza; it implies a sequence of action. After the gust of wind dies down, the peasant crosses the river. The fourth line is another follow-up piece, and is not supposed to introduce a striking new image but continue the associative pattern of the third stanza. As the peasant wades through the water, the fourth poet imagines him finding a bow made from bamboo in the low bushes near the edge of the water. The bow is analogous to the Western scarecrow – it is a device to frighten away small animals that might eat the crops. The fifth line, as a rule, must be related to the moon. The moon is a common theme of elegance in the courtly *waka* tradition, but it is also used in Zen Buddhism as a symbol of the enlightened mind. Here Bashō understands the fourth stanza's setting as a remote rural area and so draws a picture of a lonely, secluded cottage, visible in the moonlight but undisturbed by visitors – an isolation suggested by the reference to the ivy hanging over the door. The circle of collaborative verse continued until the poets reached the thirty-sixth stanga.[11]

Tacit communication in *haikai* verse relies on the opaqueness and ambiguity inherent in the elliptical nature of the Japanese language. For example, in Japanese it is possible to construct a sentence without a subject, which allows the second poet in a linked-verse meeting to transfer a part of the description in the previous verse to a different context. The third verse in the example brings in the image of a peasant crossing the river. However, since the poet was not required to specify the subject, the lines are open to various interpretations. The fourth poet sensed this ambiguity and contributed a verse that did not require such explanatory phrases as "he saw the bamboo bow." This open-endedness in turn allowed the next poet, Bashō, to describe a simple rural hut without connecting it with the human subject of the third verse. Thus, each successive verse in the poem altered the picture by shifting the angle of the poetic images presented by the preceding verses as well as by adding new details.

The creative use of "the unspecifiability of particulars," to borrow Michael Polanyi's phrase, was often used in this form of poetry.[12] To make a fresh but contextually appropriate line of verse, the *haikai* poet might look at the preceding line and isolate a particular word or a phrase in order to elaborate on an implicit multivocal meaning, image, or atmosphere. This specification then serves as a bridge to the next line. Sometimes, a poet might specify one of the many images or moods conveyed by the previous line and then superimpose it on a different context. When a given word or image is removed from its immediate context, however, its meaning is inherently modified by its isolation, just as a patch of color may appear to change its hue when placed against different background colors.

At each occasion of linking verses, the poet carefully attended to the invisible and ambiguous atmosphere created by the previous poet. This wordless comprehension was the basic pre-condition of linked verse. The poet creates his or her own world by adding his or her own contribution to the chain. This presentation–sensing–response nexus was completed by the unspoken communication in which participants offered their appreciation of the new verse as well as the poet's interpretation of the previous line. Consequently, Tokugawa *haikai* poetry circles popularized such ambiguous notions as sensing the implicit meaning of the text. They encouraged development of a popular view that not only embraced ambiguity but viewed it as a deeper way of knowing and communicating.

The Ambiguous and Japan

An awareness of the presence of multiple methods of knowing in any culture alerts us to the danger of making any simplistic summaries of its representative communicative style. Yet, the prevalence of and authority ascribed to tacit modes of communication in early modern Japan stand in stark contrast to post-Enlightenment Europe's idealized preference for explicitly reasoned communicative styles – in particular in spheres of public discourse that require rational critical articulation. The theorists of the European Enlightenment placed a high value on critical rational exchanges at a time when the Tokugawa Japanese were attracted to artistic and literary circles that prized tacit modes of communication.

When the *za* arts became popularized on an unprecedented scale, the distinctive messages of social discipline encoded within performances of and instruction in these arts were legitimized and made widely available to the broader population. In this sense, this communicative development was also an expression of Tokugawa proto-modernity. It was this process of popularizing the practices of tacit modes of communication that made possible the next step of intellectual formulation that assumed the tacit modes of communication as being central to the Japanese cultural tradition. Donald Levine, an American sociologist, called the modern preferred mode of communication that began around 1600 "the flight from ambiguity."[13] In contrast, the Tokugawa idealization of tacit modes of communication might be called "the flight to ambiguity."

On the basis of this unprecedented cultural popularization, an intellectual reformulation of "Japaneseness" began to spread. This effort to essentialize led to an ideological convergence between "Japaneseness" and ambiguity, thus creating a most disputed legacy of communicative cultures for modern Japan. The tacit modes of communication embedded in aesthetic and literary practices have been rich cultural resources for the Japanese people because they value and promote the human cognitive potential for alternative ways of knowing. Why then could the very notion of ambiguity in Japanese communicative culture become such a controversial issue, all the way to a dispute at the podium of Nobel Prize lectures? Remember how Oe Kenzaburo countered Kawabata Yasunari in the skirmish between Japan's two Nobel laureates in literature that I cited in the book's Introduction. Kawabata opened his Nobel lecture with a discussion of poems about the moon by a medieval Buddhist contemplative named Myōe, not a likely topic for serious criticism. However, Oe Kenzaburo, Japan's second Nobel laureate in literature, delivered a provocative critique of Kawabata's Nobel Prize lecture from the same podium where Kawabata stood a few decades earlier. Oe proclaimed: "I cannot utter in unison with Kawabata the phrase, 'Japan, the Beautiful and Myself'.... [O]ne can never understand or feel sympathetic towards these Zen poems except by giving up one's self and willingly penetrating into the closed shells of these words." Oe concluded his prize lecture entitled "Japan, the Ambiguous and Myself" by stating that "[T]his ambiguous orientation of Japan drove the country into the position of invader in Asia."[14]

What are we to make of such a shocking accusation? Neither the activity of writing Zen poems nor any of the other aesthetic practices among the pre-modern Japanese were the source of the political ambiguity problem that Oe signaled. As we have seen, Tokugawa aesthetic circle activities were largely popular hobbyist activities that had nothing to do with an ideological formulation of "Japaneseness." Rather, they represented the people's effort to carve out a sphere of horizontal socialization in spite of the Tokugawas' feudal divide-and-rule policies. The first potential problem arose much later.

With the rise of general interest in artistic and literary activities, scholars of the School of Native Learning (Kokugaku) played a major role in the ideological formulation that combined tacit modes with "Japaneseness."[15] The major concern of the School was to determine the "purest" form of the Japanese tradition, "uncontaminated" by such outside influences as Confucianism and Buddhism. The School of Native Learning originated among philological scholars of the Japanese classics. In their competitive stance against Neo-Confucian scholars and Buddhist traditions, they questioned what was really "the tradition" of the Japanese uncontaminated by foreign influences. The core of the Japanese tradition as they perceived it was the culture of the ancient imperial court. Curiously enough, however, in their effort to construct a national cultural identity, these scholars gave ambiguity and opaqueness a new ideological formulation at the same time that they placed a high value on emotional expressiveness conveyed through aesthetic tacit communication.

The Kokugaku scholars were skillful cultural "framers" who were obsessed with defining the essential elements of Japanese cultural identity. A forerunner of the school was Kamo no Mabuchi (1697–1769), best known as a scholar of *waka* poetry. Mabuchi sought to explicate the uncorrupted "Ancient Way" (*inishie no michi*) of Japan and "Our Country's Way" (*kuni no tefuri*) through the study of the Japanese classics. According to Mabuchi, the investigation is difficult because "the human mind is hard to comprehend through words."[16] Compared to the "Chinese Way" (*kara no tefuri*), the "Japanese Way" can be described metaphorically as an emphasis on subtle "in-between" colors (e.g., purple rather than red or blue) and "transitional natures." For example, Mabuchi stated that "the existence of four seasons does not mean that there are sharp boundaries and distinctions between four categories."[17] In essence, the four seasons as we experience them are a series of continuous transitions. Mabuchi saw the Japanese Ancient Way as the ambiguous and transitional nature of being free from artificial or argumentative boundaries.[18] In contrast, he saw the Chinese Way as emphasizing sharp distinctions through linguistic articulation and moral argumentation. He regarded the Chinese neo-Confucian universalization of the human mind as a rationalistic (*kotowari*) prejudice.

Interestingly enough, from the Heian period onward, the Japanese often associated China symbolically with the central, the universal, and the masculine, whereas Japan represented the peripheral, particular, and feminine. For example, Chinese-style calligraphy, which uses Chinese characters, is often called *otokode*, or "male hand," whereas the flowing cursive style of calligraphy that uses Japanese phonemes is called *onnade*, or "female hand." The aristocratic elite was obliged to use *otokode* for documents concerning matters of state; however, male writers customarily used *onnade* in order to express the unforced flow of emotion that characterized *waka* poetry. *Onnade* was considered more suitable for literary expression, which was understandable because the "female hand" was suited to the Japanese language. In sum, although the Japanese respected and admired the high culture of imperial China, they often experienced its universal scope and comprehensiveness as distant from and alien to their own. Although these feelings had always been part of the Japanese mental landscape, they were neither clearly articulated nor ideologically linked to essentializing the "pure" and "supreme" identity of Japanese culture prior to the emergence of the Kokugaku, or School of Native Learning, in the eighteenth century. Rather, the cultural idioms of Chinese civilization had always been admired and incorporated – with significant modifications, to be sure – into Japanese culture without hostility.

The nineteenth-century Kokugaku scholars wanted to remake this history. To this end, they painted an idealized picture of ancient Japan as untainted by foreign influences, inaccurate though that presentation was. Nonetheless, its classical literature enshrined the perfect image of the ideal Japan. The subtle and tacit expressions of human emotion found in the classics thus represented the purest form of native consciousness, in contrast with the rationalized moralism of Chinese Confucianism. Of all the Kokugaku proponents, Motoori Norinaga (1730–1801) was the most articulate and influential in terms of turning the school into the voice of Japanese collective cultural identity. Throughout his career, he sought the pure essence of *yamato gokoro*, or authentic Japanese sensibility,[19] as contrasted with *kara gokoro*, or Chinese sensibility.

Motoori Norinaga regarded rational critical argumentation as central to the Chinese establishment of moral distinction. In comparison with the importance of logic in Chinese moral philosophy, he identified the core of Japanese sensibility as the "natural" flow of human feeling as expressed in the classical court literature of the ancient period. He had a profound admiration for the sensitive, fluid, textured, and poetic descriptions of the phenomenological realities of life and the world *mono no aware* (the pity of things, or sorrow of being) in the ancient court literature and poetry. The phrase *mono no aware*, taken from "The Tale of Genji," is difficult to translate into English. But, for Motoori, the value of attaining a level not mediated by moralistic judgment or articulated language would be a profound identification with the impermanent and transitional nature of being. Ironically, therefore, he formulated unique and effective logical arguments capable of analyzing classical texts and promoting the depth of flowing emotion and devaluing the moralistic logic of the *kara gokoro*.

By elevating the private sentiments and expressions of *mono no aware* in "The Tale of Genji" to canonical status, Motoori assigned the highest value to the feminine personal discourse of the court literature, called *taoyame buri*, or "feminine style." The dichotomy between reason and emotion was identified with the distinction between public and private, and Motoori consequently defined the emotional and the private as the central components of Japanese sensibility.[20]

So far, so good. Motoori Norinaga supplied an overdue reassessment of the value of the private realm in Japan during a period when the private sphere, or *watakushi*, was usually devalued in favor of the *ōyake*, or public, which was often equated with matters of state. Where Motoori's scholarship remained within the boundaries of aesthetic redefinition and philosophical inquiries into the significance of private emotional life, his penetrating insights into the classical texts formed a significant contribution to later studies of Japanese culture.

Motoori Norinaga, however, was not content with a reclamation project – that is, of adding a classical dimension to a pluralistic culture. Rather, he elevated his position to the status of aesthetic imperialism, declaring the absolute supremacy of a Japanese collective identity as defined by *yamato gokoro* (Japanese mind). In order to reclaim the value of the Japanese classical literary tradition, the School of Native Learning had to redefine its Chinese counterpart as a culture of affectation. In order to establish the value of the local and personal (i.e., Japan) over that of the central and universal (i.e., China), Norinaga had to go one step further and pronounce a sweeping judgment of the inferiority of supposed Chinese rational logical discourse as compared with the Japanese flow of natural human feeling.

Norinaga, as well as other scholars of Native Learning, arrived at a method of inquiry into Japanese identity by eliminating supposed historical foreign influences on Japanese culture in order to essentialize the pure Japanese tradition. However, the ancient and medieval Japanese had imported rich cultural institutions – from writing systems to philosophical traditions – from China. By eliminating foreign influences as much as possible, Motoori and his disciples and colleagues entered the business of unproductive essentializing as if peeling an onion down to nothingness.

The philosophy of Motoori and his intellectual heirs became the driving ideology behind some collective uprisings leading to the Meiji Restoration within the global context of nineteenth-century imperialism. The search for the Japanese identity entered its next stage when Japan was threatened by the visit of Commodore Perry's black ships (1853), which demanded opening up the country after two centuries of isolationist policy. The Kokubaku school's reinterpretation of the purest Japanese identity appealed to the concerned Japanese who, through their self-encouraging drive to assert the supremacy of the Japanese cultural tradition, were finally appreciating their vulnerable position in world politics. In an ironic reversal, however, the subsequent development of Meiji nationalism employed the masculine image of the Japanese nation crowned by the paternal image of a Meiji emperor and devalued the supposed feminine flow of human emotion that Norinaga admired so much.[21] When intuitive modes of expression and understanding were placed at the core of Japanese identity and considered superior to the linguistic articulation and exchange equated with foreign influence, Motoori opened a Pandora's box that led to the development and inspiration of popular chauvinistic discourse.

Section Three

Market, State, and Categorical Politics

Prelude to Section Three

Our investigation has so far covered centuries of Japanese cultural history, from medieval poetry gatherings under cherry trees in bloom to circles that brought together Tokugawa people who were seeking sociability through aesthetic activities. Although the activities of voluntary aesthetic associations provided stable sites for social interaction within this feudally segmented society, they did not constitute the only sphere of civic sociability that was available outside politically defined clusters of social relations. Since I have provided the main structure of my cases and arguments regarding associational politics and the realm of the beautiful in Section Two, I now wish to turn to another line of argumentation that complements the materials already presented. It concerns the cultural ramifications of the expansion of a large-scale commercial market economy within a society that was deliberately partitioned along territorial and status lines by the Tokugawa rulers.

Japan at the time of its unification around 1600 was a largely agrarian society with few cities of impressive size. However, by the beginning of the eighteenth century, Japan had well-developed nationwide networks of commodity exchange as well as a system of central and regional markets that conveyed a wide variety of goods to urban consumers with expensive and sophisticated tastes. Networks of commercial transactions became an increasingly important force in Tokugawa society with regard to connecting people and channeling information. Furthermore, as we have already seen, the operation of the Tokugawa aesthetic networks was greatly facilitated by the vitality of contemporary commerce. For example, the profitable operation of the *haikai* poetry competitions would not have been possible without the existence of rapid and efficient commercial printing presses and the involvement of a new class of literary agents. But one must add that the effects of commercialization on cultural activities within the widening context of urban life were more extensive and pervasive than simply facilitating the growth of aesthetic associations. The influence of economic factors on the Tokugawa civilizing process helped to define the formation of Japanese civility and cultural identities in aesthetic categories.

Imagine yourself living in the city of Edo under the commanding view of the shogun's castle during the late eighteenth century. The city was carefully zoned by the authorities in order to distinguish and separate residential areas reserved for samurai from those open to commoners. Although the grounds immediately surrounding the castle and the areas designated for the official residences of the *daimyo* and other upper samurai were dignified and sufficiently imposing to remind the viewer of the power hierarchy in this society, the most vibrant areas in Edo were the downtown commercial districts. There were a number of "up-market" shops and thriving markets for such commodities as fish and vegetables. The streets were thronged with crowds of passersby, customers, and browsers, as well as people bringing goods to shops and markets. The voices of peddlers and vendors calling out from their stalls, along with the quieter tones inside the established shops lining the streets, gave the city an air of cheerful industriousness. Nearly two centuries of peace under the Tokugawa shoguns had transformed this city of a million people into a truly proto-modern metropolis of consumption.

It was within this urban context that people from all social classes formed new attachments to beautiful objects and the aesthetic traditions that produced them. Tokugawa commerce changed people's material life at home in significant ways. The economic prosperity of the period meant that beauty entered the daily life of all Tokugawa people, lowly and high alike, in the form of goods and commodities. A length of cotton fabric for *kimono*, striped in subtle shades of blue and brown, or a sturdy white ceramic rice bowl decorated with a simple blue pattern – such unpretentious commercially produced goods became part of the everyday life of ordinary working people for the first time in Japanese history. The cloth and the bowl are examples of the kinds of items from Tokugawa cottage industries that were made more widely available by the development of extensive commercial networks. Prior to the Tokugawa era, only the privileged few could enjoy beautifully colored *kimono* and cherish the creamy surface of ceramic ware. Of course, the more fortunate of the shogun's subjects could afford more luxurious fabrics and costlier tableware than those on the lower levels of the economic order. For the well-to-do, there were printed catalogs of *kimono* patterns and various lifestyle guides – commercially produced manuals of civilized knowledge – that helped them in their aspirations to gracious living. Without invoking any high-flown aesthetic theory comparable to the medieval aesthetic theories of the performing arts that we have examined in the previous chapter, the makers and sellers of well-crafted, reasonably priced articles for the home began to revolutionize the aesthetic life of the Japanese people.

Not only was the everyday life of the people enriched by the availability of attractive commercially produced goods, but their communicative life as well was framed and deeply colored by commercial enterprises and activities. Working men and women might enjoy sharing the latest gossip with their neighbors at one of the hundreds of commercial bathhouses in their residential areas in the city after a hard day's work. They might appreciate the latest fashion in *kimono* worn by a passerby while having their hair done at a neighborhood salon where the hairdressers would try out the most intricate new styles on them. At home, a person might enjoy the delivery of a best-seller from one of hundreds of book rental shops. Such sensational events as love suicides and revenge killings would quickly appear on the commercial stage in a puppet play, *Kabuki* performance, or professional storytelling, and these modes of popularization might yield new books in their turn. A fashion trend might emerge through the imitation of a popular actor's personal style in clothing. The rumor mill ground incessantly in this densely populated city, while the remarkably efficient production of woodblock prints amplified each item of gossip. Taken together, the bathhouses, book rental shops, *kimono* shops, commercial theaters, hair salons, and other commercial establishments facilitated interactions among people, forming different types of social and cognitive networks. As a result, they encouraged and supported the development of new communicative publics.

The new Japanese economy posed a particularly difficult challenge for the Tokugawa state. The shogunate's organizational structure depended on the deliberate segmentation of the population under indirect control, while the constant traffic in goods and services that was essential to economic growth could not be confined within the political boundaries defined by the government. In sum, a bird's-eye view of Tokugawa society in the middle of the period would perceive two realms, one a rigid hierarchical political structure characterized by segmentation and demands for lifelong commitment to assigned duties and the other a looser and more flexible set of categories of social relations that cut across the official definitions and divisions. In spite of the fast-paced expansion of its commercial networks, however, the Tokugawa state did not change the basic nature of the samurai regime. It also made no significant alterations in its integrated but intentionally decentralized state structure, which was combined with a policy of institutional segmentation of the population. In fact, the formal political structures of hierarchical segmentation would have looked like icebergs floating on the surface of a sea of relatively fluid human networks.

Although the world of commerce was increasingly tangible and attractive to ordinary people, the categorical order based upon the official political hierarchies often looked comparatively unrealistic. For example, the so-called samurai were understood to be a ruling class based on military ability and service, but their relative economic position declined considerably compared with that of the merchant class. The samurai's supposed martial prowess – the source of their political legitimacy – was increasingly difficult to display and prove in a society blessed with perpetual peace. Consequently, the shoguns and allied *daimyo* fought an ongoing rearguard action against the potential of the forces of the marketplace to overthrow the categories, organizations, and authorities defined by the political order. On the other hand, the shoguns and the members of the samurai class were also urban-based consumers in need of commercial services. The primary base of their income was a grain tax that was usually paid in rice; these tax payments in turn required a large-scale market system for cashing them in. Economic necessity meant that the Tokugawa shoguns could not adopt a rigid anti-business policy. Instead, their attempts to regulate the market took the form of such cultural–political policies as the enforcement of status distinctions in dress and lifestyle and the censorship of undesirable publications.

The rulers' ambivalence toward the business world leads us to recognize that much of the power of the Tokugawa regime was predicated on categorical classifications manifested by lifestyles. This fact also made the realm of the beautiful central to Tokugawa communicative life. The reader should recall that a system of status distinctions was the principal strategy that governed the Tokugawa order. This status system (*mibun*) was closely connected to codes of propriety and external lifestyle regulation. For the state to maintain its institutional hierarchies and divisions, it had to define and maintain the categorical identities of various status groups according to their respective social obligations. For example, the symbolic transgression of categorical protest through the display of "inappropriate" lifestyles, coupled with the glamorous images of such transgressions that circulated in printed matter, endangered the stability of the Tokugawa order. It is at this point that the political and economic history of Tokugawa Japan intersects most significantly with the history of its aesthetic and cultural standards because the growing availability of affordable goods and services allowed individuals greater freedom to cultivate and express their own aesthetic tastes and lifestyles.

The three essays that comprise Section Three are concerned with cultural developments associated with the idiosyncratic relationships between the state and the economy of Tokugawa Japan. This section contains three case studies whose thematic foci are somewhat different from one another, but all reflect the cultural trends that developed within the framework of the shogunate's distinctive state–market relationships. The three topics are the relationship between *kimono* fashions and categorical politics, the rise of Tokugawa commercial publishing, and the elaboration of hierarchical etiquette and manners. Unlike the chapters in Section Two, in which I traced the chronological evolution of Japanese aesthetic associational life, each of the chapters in this section can be read independently as an articulation of subject matter important in its own right for understanding Tokugawa cultural developments. Although these three topics do not represent by any means an exhaustive list of subject matter for understanding the relationships among the state, the economy, and patterns of Tokugawa civility, they are nonetheless historically and theoretically key institutional developments. I will analyze the distinctive ways in which the emergence of a nationwide market for goods and services was involved in the process of cultural development by providing detailed descriptions of the effects of market–state interactions on the communicative life of Tokugawa people.

The state's tireless attempts to avoid the political damage resulting from the influence of commercial enterprise on communicative spheres impacted Tokugawa cultural developments because the shoguns sought to regulate people's communicative activities. At the same time, in a society that was already highly aesthetically conscious, rebellion against the official hierarchies often surfaced in the form of challenges to status distinctions based on aesthetic tastes and lifestyles. Fashion was one of the most popular media for contentious activity in this sense because of its codifying function; that is, it helped to create social images of personal identity. After discussing the politics of fashion in Chapter 10, I will turn my attention to the study of the fledgling commercial publishing industry. Chapter 11 will examine the development of Japanese commercial publishing and the ways in which it transformed people's acquisition of information. Printed books, pamphlets, and illustrations became an integral part of Tokugawa social and cultural life at the same time that they helped to form new connections among people and subcultures that had formerly had little contact with one another. Just as fashion encourages communicative actions, books have a corresponding ability to form "publics" by themselves. After analyzing the complex web of relationships that commercially printed books helped to form within Tokugawa society, I will turn my attention to the codes of etiquette and manners that were popularized by the Tokugawa printed manuals. In Chapter 12, I will analyze the ideal of sociability that was disseminated by these manuals.

The three essays that follow will focus on the transformation of political and cultural categories that unfolded in the course of the changing relationship between the state and the marketplace. The reader will note that beauty played a distinctive role in the reformulation of categorical identities in this dynamic from the definition of status categories and good taste in fashion to the spread of a formal ideal of sociability.

10

Categorical Protest from the Floating World: Fashion, State, and Gender

The fluid and dynamic interactions among the formation of categorical identities, the development of categorical stratification, and the political and economic developments of the Tokugawa state are vividly exemplified by the development of "fashion politics." External appearance, as signified by a person's choice of costume, hairstyle, cosmetics, and other decorative accessories, can function as a critical means of expressing as well as classifying a person's categorical identity; in other words, it becomes a powerful human "identity kit." Because of fashion's close connection with the formation of identities and publics, control or influence over an individual's or group's dress code acquires political overtones. In the course of Tokugawa proto-modernization, the underlying processes of boundary redefinition involving a range of categorical identities were often expressively negotiated through the politics of fashion. Fashion is a lens through which the modern observer can trace the outlines of categorical reshuffling, in which new definitions of status, gender, and aesthetic taste entered the cultural mix of Tokugawa society.

A series of developments in the Japanese economy and urban culture during the seventeenth century led to a remarkable and unexpected phenomenon: the rise of popular fashion. Tokugawa people, men and women alike, became fashion-conscious to an unprecedented degree; discussions of trends in *kimono* fabrics and colors, tasteful accessories, and other possessions connected with the "good life" played an increasingly larger role in social communication. The word "fashion" in this context entails more than simple changes in clothing styles, as these transitions had existed long before the Tokugawa era. Tokugawa trend-setting differed from that of previous eras because it was linked in an evident manner to the operations of a large-scale market economy. Fashion as a popular phenomenon was made possible only through the increase of productive forces to a certain level and the concomitant development

245

of elaborate commercial networks and transportation infrastructures.[1] The presence of complex and extended networks of communication brought about by the expansion of commercial printing and nation-wide trading networks also distinguished Tokugawa fashion from that of earlier historical periods in Japan in that these communication networks delivered fashion information over wide areas rapidly and efficiently.

As with many socio-cultural changes, the relationship between Tokugawa fashions and the Tokugawa economy was reciprocal; that is, fashion crazes were not only the consequence of economic and commu-nicative developments but also a critical cause of further development. Some of these changes reflected both an overall increase in the popula-tion of Japan and an increase in population density in large cities like Edo. The shoguns of this period ruled a country that supported large population concentrations in urban centers for the first time in its his-tory. By 1700, Japan had become one of the most urbanized societies in the world. For example, in the early eighteenth century, Edo had about a million inhabitants who had to purchase *kimono, obi* (sash), under-wear, footwear, and various accessories for their everyday lives. Osaka had well over 400,000 inhabitants. Kanazawa and Nagoya each had populations of around 100,000. In addition to the townspeople's high level of fashion consciousness, their sheer level of demand for daily cloth-ing was enormous. This demand stimulated technological innovations in agriculture; upgrades in the technical skills and equipment of weavers, dyers, and tailors; and improvements in sea and overland transport for traders. The production and consumption of cotton, silk, and linen fabrics was the driving force that transformed Japan's economy from the largely self-sufficient agricultural economy of 1600 to a large-scale commercial economy during the course of the eighteenth century.

The introduction of fashionable costumes into one's life is not confined to material enhancement. Displaying one's personal style to onlookers or appreciating and critiquing the fashion statements of others in turn cre-ates emotional bonds or friction among individuals and builds a potential for social and symbolic exchanges. In this sense, fashion generates a site of communication; it is a type of aesthetic public. Georg Simmel correctly expressed this subtle point in stating that fashion satisfies the demand for social adaptation through imitation: "[Fashion] leads the individual upon the road which all travel." At the same time, Simmel argued that fashion satisfies the need for differentiation and individuality, the "tendency to-wards dissimilarity, the desire for change and contrast."[2] One's choice in dress is a bridge to the larger social order as well as a point of conflict and compromise between individual aspirations and social judgments. Fash-ion as a communicative process hinges upon this intrinsic dual nature, being simultaneously a social and individual phenomenon. Because fashion has such a strong codifying function, power holders in any society have been frequently tempted to engineer its ideal image by regulating their subordinates' appearance.

A state's attempt to control fashion thus means the regulation of this communicative process. By defining a certain type of fashion discourse that visually represented the Tokugawa social order (namely, a dress code correlated with status levels within an official social hierarchy and "proper" gender distinctions) as the formal accepted discourse while devaluing popular inventive fashion as legally and morally unacceptable, the state attempted to construct an ideal image of society on its own terms. This process represented a technology of power engineered by creating a categorical stratification of publics as interactional–discursive spheres. Thus, the process of fashion politics in Tokugawa Japan reflects political struggles that defined and negotiated the hierarchies and interrelationships among communicative sites of publics where fashion discourse was produced.

The State, the Rise of a New Aesthetic, and Categorical Stratification

The following analysis will articulate the social processes that led to the emergence of an important new aesthetic in early modern Japan. The aesthetic in question was often given the name *iki*, which is Japanese for "stylish," "chic," or "dandified," and dominated the world of fashion during the late Tokugawa period. Kuki Shūzō, a Japanese philosopher, once attempted to explain the nuances of *iki* by comparing it with the French term *esprit*[3] because *iki* is a representative expression of Japanese aesthetic sensitivity. The term originated within Japanese courtesan culture to describe a refined eroticism with a sense of restraint as well as pride. *Iki* then came to be applied more generally to the prevailing standards of taste in urban popular culture. In Tokugawa popular culture, referring to a man or woman as *"iki"* meant not only appreciating the person's refined taste but also praising the style of living and inner quality. Though the term itself has broader ramifications that emerged from the subtle tensions in social relations, I will focus on *iki*'s manifestations in the styles and color schemes of dress and personal adornment. The urban sensibility of the late Tokugawa period favored color schemes with subtle hues and subdued shades of brown, gray, and navy, with an occasional dash of more brilliant color. It was one of the first major aesthetic trends in Japan to have close connections with a thriving commercial market economy.[4]

Figure 10.1. Bath Women. *Yuna* (bath women), from *Yunazu*, early seventeenth century. Unlike the more elegant but stereotyped depictions of courtesans during the later Tokugawa period, these women clearly show defiance. Their high spirits were expressed by bold, colorful patterns and a relaxed style of wearing their *kimono*.

This aesthetic was not the product of some powerful genius or any fashionable individual regarded as an icon of style. Rather, the emergence of *iki* during the late Tokugawa period can best be understood as a situational phenomenon involving an incremental agglomeration of largely unplanned social interactions that entailed many regional innovations and modifications. At the same time, this process of aesthetic category formation was intimately connected to the political dynamics of creating and enforcing more coercive social categories, the "status politics" that served the shogunate as a means of social control.

In early seventeenth-century Japan, around the time of the country's unification, high-fashion costumes for either sex were anything but subdued. Trendy fashions for both men and women involved flamboyant color schemes, including the frequent use of red and gold to highlight bold designs. Dress styles displayed the wearer's power and wealth with unconcealed exuberance, making liberal use of obviously expensive materials and colorful designs. As the Tokugawa shoguns succeeded the unification rulers, Oda Nobunaga and Toyotomi Hideyoshi, they set themselves the task of regulating their subjects' increasing appetite for fashion as part of their effort to enforce social hierarchies. In spite of their initial attempts, Tokugawa society was still characterized by chaotic deviations from categorical order during the early seventeenth century. With the new political rule not yet firmly installed, stabilization into a new order took place rather hesitantly. In the early Tokugawa period, definitions, styles, and expressions of status categories through fashion stayed in flux. Expressions of gender categories through fashion did not have time to congeal into stereotypes (Figures 10.1 and 10.2; Plate 2). Such deviant fashion

Figure 10.2. *Kabuki* Performers. A female *Kabuki* performance at the Shijō riverbank. *Shijō kawara yūrakuzu*, early seventeenth century. A group of 13 women, beautifully dressed in the male *kabuki-mono* style, dance to the accompaniment of several *shamisen* players. The leading actress, Kyūsuke, is wearing a male costume, sitting in the middle of the circle on a chair covered with tiger skin.

statements were all marked by surprisingly bold designs and colors, in stark contrast to the later periods in the Tokugawa era.

In contrast to the vibrant display of color and opulence that marked the early Tokugawa period, however, the later period favored more sophisticated, controlled, and subdued styles in *kimono* fashion. People's status, age, gender, and occupation were demarcated by minute differentiations in style, color, and type of fabric used to make their *kimono*. For example, adult males tended to wear dark colors as their workday "uniform," while young women were allowed a palette of lighter and more cheerful colors. These differentiations were not confined to the *kimono* of the upper classes. Even the working population of Tokugawa Japan could enjoy quietly modulated colors woven into the fabric of their *kimono*. Wearing a subtly tasteful *kimono* appropriate to one's social position became an additional element of civility in Tokugawa life. The refinement of the Tokugawa *kimono* culture, represented by, but not limited to, the emergence of *iki*, was carried out in an institutional field shaped by the state's constant regulation of fashion. The evolution of the elegant urban *kimono* culture of the later Tokugawa period is intrinsically linked, albeit in an unplanned manner, to the dynamics of the cultural dimensions of state development.

The complex and dynamic relationships characterizing the regulation of Tokugawa fashion and the emergence of a new aesthetic category calls for renewed investigation on two fronts. First, the regulation of fashion in Tokugawa Japan was not merely a consequence of state development; conversely, it also represented a critical source of that development. The Tokugawa state has been recognized by historians as a government that ruled by segmenting its subjects into strict status hierarchies. But, as we closely examine the historical development of the shogunate, we do not find a clear legal statement of "rule by status" at the outset of the Tokugawa period. The boundaries between the various status groups were sometimes blurred, and the rankings within a status group – in particular among the samurai – were often neither settled nor clearly articulated. In order to trace the development of Tokugawa status categories, historians have depended heavily on chronological analysis of various fashion ordinances and dress codes promulgated by the authorities from time to time.[5] The politics of fashion represented the state's *learning process*. The most creative and robust cultural innovations in Tokugawa fashion came largely from the "rule-breakers" (i.e., the politically disadvantaged). In the course of responding to the challenges of a number of small-scale category violators, the authorities had to articulate their design of categorical inequality and develop a strategy to sustain it. Fashion regulation was therefore not an epiphenomenon of state development but rather a component of its central process. In essence, the state's enactment of social discipline and the people's cultural productions in the area of fashion were interactive and dialectical processes.

Second, on the level of epistemology, Tokugawa fashion provides a case study in the necessity of developing a non-essentialist view of the formation of categorical identities. The Japanese experience suggests that the distribution of aesthetic tastes in fashion was closely related but not confined to the hierarchy of organizationally well-bounded social categories (i.e., "hard" social categories). In real life, the boundaries of hard social categories are often not as unyielding as we expect. Furthermore, the multiple criteria of categorical identities are in constant competition – a situation that requires us to take a non-deterministic approach to the relationship between cultural tastes and class membership, status distinctions, and gender categories. The transgression of a boundary through local creation and the acquisition of a supposedly "soft" aesthetic taste often exposes the ambiguity and vulnerability of that boundary and thereby threatens the firmness of the existing hard social categories.

The Material and Technological Basis of Tokugawa Fashion

A passage from an unusually straightforward memoir written by a samurai's daughter known as Oan illuminates the critical period of transition for the emergence of popular Japanese fashion. Oan wrote down her experiences before dying in her eighties sometime during the Kanmon era (1661–1672). She represents an eyewitness whose life spanned two distinct periods of Japanese history. As a young girl, she was exposed to the violence and bloodshed of the last phase of the civil war. As she matured into womanhood, Oan's life was changed by the comparative peacefulness of life under the Tokugawa regime and the commercial expansion and material comforts that went with it.

> [When I was young] I did not have many clothes. When I was thirteen years old, I had only a single light-blue *katabira* [summer] outfit, and it was home-made. I wore it until I was seventeen. [Since the dress became too short] It was difficult for me [as I grew taller] because my shins were exposed. I badly wanted a new *katabira* that could hide my legs. . . . Nowadays young people crave stylish clothing; they spend a lot of money on it, and they eat a wide variety of delicacies.[6]

Oan's experience marks the early seventeenth century as an important turning point in Japanese material culture. Although silk had been known to the Japanese since ancient times, during the medieval period ordinary people made clothes out of fabric woven from various rough grass-based fibers called *asa* (hemp, ramie, or "china-grass").[7] *Asa* was usually spun, woven, and made into clothing within self-sufficient local economies.

The Coming of Cotton

In contrast to these other natural fibers, the Japanese did not begin to grow cotton until the late fifteenth century. Cotton itself is indigenous to India, where it was in production as early as 1800 B.C. Although ancient China also appears to have learned the techniques of cotton production, its Korean neighbor began domestic cultivation relatively late – around A.D. 1360 – because of its cooler climate. There are scattered records of unsuccessful attempts to cultivate cotton in ancient Japan.[8] Although surviving records do not provide many details about the sustained production of cotton in Japan, it was only during the Warring States period (1467–1568) that cotton cultivation was extended to the relatively warm regions of the country. During the second half of the sixteenth century, Japanese farmers further expanded the acreage under cultivation. Because of its functional advantages, cotton came to be used extensively by vassal samurai for everyday clothing in the late sixteenth century. It was only by the early seventeenth century that cotton fields had appeared in many regions of Japan; they even occupied about half of the total agricultural area near Osaka.[9] This explosive expansion of cotton production was the driving force behind the commercialization of the Japanese economy during the early Tokugawa period.

Asa was a labor-intensive product. In particular, the raw materials of *asa* production did not travel well; they had to be processed and spun within a short time after harvest. Weaving *asa* was also time-consuming. Nagahara Keiji has estimated that a medieval farm woman who wove *asa* at home on a daily basis during fall and winter could produce fabric sufficient for only three or four *kimono* before the spring season of intensive agriculture required her attention elsewhere. This amount of production yielded little surplus beyond family consumption.[10] In contrast, cotton enabled higher levels of productivity in both spinning and weaving. Furthermore, compared to *asa*, because of the structure of its fibers, raw cotton was much easier to transport than grassy materials, which allowed a more efficient division of labor in the process of textile manufacture. Since cotton was suitable for production through division of labor, it made room for middlemen at every step of processing. The manufacture of cotton was several times more productive than weaving *asa*. Increased productivity in turn made commercial weaving establishments in rural areas economically feasible. Since cotton fabric provided better insulation than *asa*, the demand for cotton in northern Japan was predictably high. But because cotton grew better in the warmer climates of the southern islands, the geographical difference stimulated long-distance trading. Consequently, dynamic networks for cotton trading came into being that linked producers and traders throughout Japan. Even the northern regions of Japan, which did not produce raw cotton, nevertheless developed their own weaving industries. The spread of the weaving of cotton textiles in different regions of Japan further elaborated the commercial networks.[11] In this sense, cotton was a driving force behind the expansion of Tokugawa commerce.

Cotton was also more receptive to dyes and printed designs.[12] The rise in cotton production thus allowed ordinary Japanese to enjoy wearing attractively colored *kimono* for the first time in the country's history. Before this period, the luxury of aesthetically pleasing designs was confined to those who could afford to wear silk. The resultant increase in the supply of inexpensive but warm cotton fabric revolutionized the daily clothing of ordinary people and laid the social foundation of Tokugawa fashion.[13] Around the time of the Kan'ei and Kanmon eras (1624–1672), cotton became the material of everyday clothing among ordinary people.[14] The material and economic basis of popular *kimono* fashions as such was made possible only by the increase in domestic cotton production.

As mentioned earlier, fashion is both a stimulus and a result of economic development. It is well-known that the cotton industry was a major factor in the proto-industrialization of Europe and was the springboard for the early stages of industrialization. When a significant segment of the Japanese population began to purchase clothing rather than producing, weaving, and dyeing it at home, the resultant volume of commodities exchange was so large that it precipitated changes in the basic organizing principles of society. The route of cotton transportation extended from southern to northern Japan by means of an impressive array of networks, sometimes called the "Cotton Road of Japan."[15] Cotton textiles passed through the hands of several sets of traders and middlemen in order to reach metropolitan consumers. Thus, the extensive networks of the cotton trade incorporated a large population into the web of Japan's expanding commercial economy.

Silk: The Passion for Beauty

The increased availability of silk textiles also enriched the fashion culture of the early Tokugawa period for the upper classes. The late sixteenth century immediately prior to the unification period was a time of rapid growth in international trade. Even though the Tokugawa shoguns imposed strict controls on international trade after unification, we must note that they did not prohibit international trade as such. The shogunate's policy was aimed at keeping the provincial *daimyo* out of direct involvement in profitable trading. Thus, Chinese silk, always a sought-after item among the upper classes, continued to enter the Japanese market under the shoguns' direct surveillance. The households of the *daimyo* and the upper samurai were always sources of heavy demand for high-quality silk garments, as these luxuries advertised the samurai's prestige and power.

For over a millennium, Asians had prized good silk fabric as highly as gold. In particular, the upper classes of Japan had always regarded the delicacy of Chinese silk textiles as an external badge of wealth, status, and power. At the beginning of the Tokugawa period, the quality of Japanese indigenous silk could not match the high standards of its Chinese counterpart; the available techniques of weaving did not produce fabric of sufficient fineness of texture. This initial difference, however, was not an obstacle to the development of the Japanese silk industry. In the first place, the upper classes of Japan proved to be an unlimited market for silk garments. The increased availability of Chinese silk after unification only whetted their appetites for more high-quality fabric. In addition, the pacification of Japan under Tokugawa dominance meant that the *daimyo* were forbidden to invest their incomes in fortifications and other military materiel. They even had to be careful that repairs to existing castles were not mistaken for military preparations against the shogun. The shoguns did not, however, object to the *daimyo* and upper samurai spending lavishly on their wardrobes. Thus, after the establishment of the Tokugawa regime, the members of the upper classes stepped up their consumption of luxurious and fashionable silk garments.

As a consequence of these changes in spending patterns, enormous amounts of raw silk and silk textiles were imported from China to gratify the tastes of the Japanese elite. The development of mining during the Warring States period had increased Japanese reserves of gold and silver. Since early modern Japan had little export trade, the reserves of precious metals dwindled to a degree that alarmed the shogunate. Eventually, however, the exhaustion of gold and silver by the mid-Tokugawa period discouraged the further importation of Chinese silk. In 1641, 110,000 *kin* (about 66,000 kilograms, or 145,200 pounds) of Chinese silk were brought into Japan. That amount had decreased by 1711 to 40,000 *kin*, and to 10,000 *kin* by 1716.

The decrease in imported Chinese silk, however, was related to the expansion of the domestic silk industry and also the exhaustion of precious metal reserves. The increased availability of imported raw silk from China allowed for the expansion of domestic silk-weaving industries during the seventeenth century.[16] Nishijin in Kyoto emerged as a center of high-quality woven silk whose technique and designs were comparable to the quality of Chinese products. Meanwhile, domestic sericulture was also on the rise, both in terms of output and technological improvement. Japan's domestic production of raw silk replaced Chinese imports by the eighteenth century. The history of the Japanese silk industry is an illustrative example of the *import-substitute* pattern of industrial development. The silk production and associated textile industries thus spread throughout Japan and were the driving forces of rural industrialization. In fact, this prosperous domestic silk industry became an export industry during the Meiji period and financed Japan's effort to modernize and industrialize in the late nineteenth and early twentieth centuries. The desire for quality dress fabrics thus facilitated the commercialization of the Japanese economy. Once the material basis of production was established, the appetite for quality *kimono* being already firmly rooted in Japanese culture, led to the next stage: mass consumption of quality fashion. The development of domestic cotton and silk production gave Tokugawa popular fashion its material basis.

Sumptuary Regulations and Fashion Politics

Sumptuary regulations were a fact of life for Tokugawa people for over two centuries. Prior to this period, some *sengoku daimyo*, or warlords, had regulated their vassals' daily attire as part of maintaining military discipline; however, the *sengoku daimyo* did not attempt to control commoners' dress.[17] Only with the establishment of the shogunate did political regulation of external appearance affect ordinary people and everyday "working gear" – as distinct from military dress codes or the requirements of religious ritual. Even in the nineteenth century, the Tokugawa rulers were still embroiled in sumptuary regulation. The surviving records of town ordinances (*machibure*)[18] reveal the authorities' intense interest in matters of dress. One of the earlier examples of this legislation dates from February 22, 1648:

> Townspeople's servants [non-*samurai*] are forbidden to wear silk clothing. This order has been issued previously; be sure to observe it. Only silk *tsumugi* [silk of lower quality] may be worn. This order must be published not only to property holders but also to their tenants.[19]

A week after this decree, the magistrate set forth 23 detailed articles regulating the citizens' lifestyle, including such minor matters as: "*sumō* wrestlers' loincloths should not be made of silk." With the gradual increase of wealth in urban sectors, regulations pertaining to the lifestyles of urban commoners became more nit-picky and intrusive. The next year, the town magistrate issued a similar ordinance that prohibited townspeople from wearing imported woolen coats along with other rules prohibiting the use of intricate gold lacquer designs on their furniture or saddles.[20]

The minutiae of dress and decoration that the shoguns attempted to control led to some obvious questions. Why were the Tokugawa rulers so insistent on regulating people's appearance – from formal dress for samurai to loincloths for *sumō* wrestlers – for over two centuries? Why were ordinary people so interested in fashion in the face of the authorities' constant interference?

Fashion regulations provided opportunities not only for domination but also for resistance. Since the maintenance of hierarchical categorical identities through myths, rituals, and visual codification played a critical role in the Tokugawa order, breaking the spell of that categorical order by ridiculing it – through the wearing of experimental styles – could rupture the pretensions of the official system, even when the wearers remained unconscious of the contentious overtones of their clothing. As we will see later, the ritual activities of the "floating world" that valued amorous sensuality over the norms of the formal political hierarchy thus had the potential to undermine the Tokugawa order.

A *sumō* wrestler of humble origin patronized by a powerful *daimyo* might want to dress as if he were the lord's personal vassal. Wearing a silk loincloth in his wrestling matches might seem appropriate to him as a sign of his new identity. Similarly, the son of a peasant family hired as a manservant in a samurai household might want to pass himself off as a part of the masculine warrior elite. A rich merchant might display his wealth by dressing his housemaids in silk, as if his household was akin to that of a noble samurai family. Popular *Kabuki* actors, who were often traditionally considered semi-outcasts,[21] might advertise their celebrity status through unusually gorgeous or outlandish costumes. All of these examples point to ways in which people could alter their appearance in order to obscure or transgress formal categorical identification.

With the expansion of Japan's commercial market economy, there was a general increase in opportunities for economic upward mobility. Under the Tokugawa system, however, wealth and status did not necessarily correspond, and this discrepancy was a frequent cause of tension in people's categorical identities. Since the samurai were not allowed to engage in business activities for profit, the vassal samurai lost their initial financial advantage over the merchant class toward the late Tokugawa period. In other words, under the Tokugawa system, the politically entrenched samurai class was economically disenfranchised and could not enjoy the fruits of commercial prosperity, while the economically advantaged merchant class could not gain access to either the society of honor or the formal political process.

The value of fashion regulation for the purpose of domination does not mean that sumptuary laws were effectively enforced. From the beginning, such regulations proved extremely difficult to enforce; therefore, they had to be repeatedly issued. As the commercial market economy expanded, it brought about a significant increase in the flow of people and information as well as commodities. Increased internal migration created various opportunities to escape from the schematic division of status groups. The Tokugawa authorities were thus kept busy responding to and regulating various fashion transgressions. In so doing, they articulated their own view of the desirable social hierarchy in an ever-changing society.

Sumptuary Regulations in Comparative Perspective

The significance of Japan's distinctive experience of commercialization within the political framework of a neo-feudal state can be better articulated when we compare the Tokugawa decrees with the fashion regulations of early modern Europe. The Tokugawa shogunate, however, was not the only early modern culture with an intense concern over sumptuary regulations. Many late medieval and early modern European countries attempted to control their citizens' expenditures on dress and personal adornment. The first sumptuary legislation regarding new styles appeared in France in 1294 and spread throughout Europe as states and cities attempted to regulate people's appearance for the next five centuries. These Western societies had previously both ancient and medieval dress codes, but the sumptuary regulations that developed during the late medieval and early modern periods were clearly associated with the decline of the older feudal aristocratic order and the rise of a money-centered capitalist society. N. B. Harte analyzes the case of pre-industrial England in the following manner: "Two developments in late medieval and early modern society made sumptuary legislation necessary. The first was the expansion in the number of different stations in life and the increasing mobility between them; the second was the rise of fashion."[22]

In England, sumptuary legislation reached its peak during the sixteenth century; the acts of this period contained the most complex and hierarchically ordered differentiations in dress. In France, 18 royal decrees were passed between 1485 and 1660 restricting clothes and ornamentation. Daniel Roche cites a decree of 1514 that explicitly identifies social ranking and clothes, "prohibiting absolutely categorically all persons, commoners, non-nobles ... from assuming the title of nobility either in their style or in their clothes."[23] For two centuries, the French monarchs attempted to restrict the wearing of silk to the nobility because the non-nobles' affectation of this luxury undermined a visual marker of social distinction.

The phenomenon of sumptuary regulation emerges when a society dominated by an aristocratic hierarchical system is in the process of transition toward a new system that allows for greater upward mobility. Such legislation indicates the beginning of a period in which money rather than inheritance becomes the primary determinant of one's lifestyle and status. From this perspective, sumptuary laws can be understood as a form of hegemonic resistance from an aristocratic order attempting to freeze the structural changes taking place in the society. In 1776, Poland became the last holdout from dress regulation in Europe. In the same year, Adam Smith, in *The Wealth of Nations*, castigated dress regulations imposed by a state as "the highest impertinence and presumption . . . in kings and ministers."[24] English sumptuary regulation had ended in 1604, much earlier than in France or Germany.

Once a society underwent major capitalist development, and the *bourgeoisie*'s social and political power became firmly established, sumptuary regulations – which are difficult to enforce under any circumstances – became obsolete. The fact that Britain abandoned sumptuary regulations much earlier than the continental European countries illustrates its advanced position with regard to the capitalist economic developments taking place in Europe. This does not mean, however, that the British state did not interfere with the consumption of textiles after 1604. Fashion regulations – as economic policies intended to protect British industries – continued. It is well-known, for example, that the flood of Indian cotton into the British market triggered the prohibition of Indian calico in 1720, which helped the growth of domestic cotton industries. This type of law, however, was essentially a manifestation of mercantilist policies and distinct from earlier sumptuary regulations intended to maintain status hierarchies.[25]

In contrast, Japanese sumptuary regulations began with the rise of the Tokugawa state, lasted much longer, and were much more detailed than their European counterparts. Since there was no alliance between the mercantile class and the samurai regime, there were no instances of regulating consumption to protect domestic textile industries. The similarities and differences between sumptuary regulations in Europe and Japan were closely linked to the distinctive patterns of the relationships between the state and capital.

In France, for example, sumptuary legislation supported the crown's effort to sell titles of nobility and their privileges to rich commoners; if commoners were allowed to wear silk without paying for the privilege, the crown's coffers would suffer. In contrast, the Tokugawa shoguns did not institutionalize the sale of offices or samurai status; therefore, the state

Plate 1. *Hanami* and Poetry. A scene from an Edo cherry blossom viewing party, from *Ōka eika no zu* by Katsukawa Haruyuki. The young women behind the curtain are keeping close watch on a good-looking youth who is about to write a few lines of poetry, probably in reply to a poem sent by a woman. Exchanging poems was a form of courtship at public cherry blossom viewing parties.

Plate 2. Female *Kabuki* Performer. Uneme onstage, from *Kabuki-zukan*, ca. 1605. Uneme's striking attire is part of her impersonation of a stylish *kabuki-mono* playboy living it up at a teahouse. She is not only wearing swords but also a cross as a sign of social deviance.

Plate 3. An Example of an *Iki* Color Scheme. *Woman Reading a Letter* by Utagawa Kunisada (1786–1864), nineteenth century. This woman embodies *iki*, or stylish chic, with her outer *kimono* in dark shades layered over a red undergarment.

Plate 4. Relaxed Lifestyle of Tokugawa Commoners. Kimonos. *Fugaku Sanjūrokkei Gohyaku rakanji sazidō*, by Katsushika Hokusai, nineteenth century. People are leisurely enjoying the view of Mt. Fuji. Indigo-dyed cotton became the fabric of choice for daily wear for working people during the Tokugawa period. Cotton threads dyed in two or three different shades of indigo could easily be woven into stripes or other subtle patterns, allowing weavers to create a wide range of attractive textiles.

lacked the motivation of protecting a source of income through fashion regulation. The shoguns and *daimyo* also did not consider the merchant class or textile industries as major sources of revenue; rather, they continued to rely on grain tax revenues from the agricultural sector. Not until the nineteenth century did the provincial *daimyo* governments start to expand their sources of income by levying taxes on commercial agriculture and cottage industries. Consequently, we should not erroneously assume that Tokugawa fashion regulations were related to the regime's desire to maximize its revenue. The strict and repetitious regulation of the urban population's fashion consumption was driven primarily by political motives. The shogunate was unconcerned with imposing new taxes on the expanding trade in commercial textiles and also never enunciated a formal mercantile policy. As a result, fashion regulations per se did not extend the administrative arms of the government, as they would have if the shoguns had instituted a new system of tax collection.

These differences do not imply, however, that the shoguns were hostile to commercial enterprise. In fact, the Tokugawa rulers were generally more permissive toward urban commoners' consumption patterns. The townspeople were mostly merchants and artisans and were not regarded as major sources of tax revenue; instead, they were expected to produce and distribute the commodities that the samurai class needed for the upkeep of their urban lifestyle. The authorities recognized, for the most part, that suppressing urban consumption would lower the vitality of the cities. Consequently, the shoguns allowed the townspeople relative freedom in their lifestyles, as long as they did not violate the principles of status hierarchy to any great extent. Unlike the peasantry, men with full citizen status and their wives were allowed to wear silk, although their garments were to be modest and in keeping with their non-samurai standing. Their servants and maids were forbidden to use silk, however. The relative lack of restrictions on the urban commoners was the basis for the expansion of their urban culture and interest in fashion.

In contrast, the shoguns and *daimyo* were concerned that greater consumption in farmers' households would result in less agricultural surplus for the samurai's revenue. Hence, in addition to the concern for status distinctions, fashion regulations for farmers were motivated to secure their tax revenues.[26] The earliest Tokugawa dress code for the farmer class was promulgated in 1628 (the fifth year of Kan'ei) and stated: "Regarding farmers' clothing, it should be made of grass fiber (*asa*) and cotton." The village chiefs were, however, allowed to wear *tsumugi*, or silk of lower quality, in order to bolster their prestige within the village communities. Throughout the Tokugawa period, the prohibition of peasants wearing silk was a basic policy of the shogunate, and it was applied to *obi* as well as other garments and accessories. The edict of 1643 also prohibited the use of certain dyes, including *murasaki*, a purple dye produced by gromwell, and *kōbai*, a pink-red dye obtained from safflower.[27] In the medieval system of color symbolism, purple was reserved for the nobility, whereas reddish pink could only be worn by samurai. More to the point, however, these pigments were usually available only through commerce; as a result, their use served to introduce the peasantry to a higher standard of consumption. The shogunate's sumptuary regulations were not limited to dress but extended to other aspects of the farmers' lives. In the same 1643 edict, the shogun declared that "farmers should eat miscellaneous grains for their ordinary fare; they should eat less rice."[28]

The rapid upgrading of popular tastes in clothing posed a problem for the new Tokugawa state, as the increased availability of commercial materials to a broad range of the population obscured visual status differentials. With this development of a material basis, the foundations for the emergence of fashion politics, as well as the development of a Tokugawa fashion aesthetic, were simultaneously laid.

Kabuki: Categorical Resistance from the Floating World

By the middle of the Tokugawa period, when the mature state system had been consolidated, status distinctions were woven so deeply into the fabric of Japanese society that it must have appeared as if they had been planned and implemented from the beginning. In the early years of the shogunate, the boundaries of status categories had not yet been fixed, and the collective identity of each status was still ambiguous. The politics of Tokugawa fashion resulted from this systemic ambiguity. On the one hand, the samurai who had been successfully incorporated into state hierarchies as vassals of the shogun or *daimyo* were still relatively easily domesticated. But the fringe members of the samurai class, and those who were unhappy about their lowly assigned ranking within the new order, proved to be a source of problems.

During the early Tokugawa period, the discontent caused by rigidly enforced status demarcations was most vividly expressed through the deviant fashions of the *kabuki-mono*. *Kabuki* literally means "not straight," and *mono* means "a person"; hence, "crooked person." From the late sixteenth century to the early seventeenth century, the time of the shogunate's consolidation, groups of young men appeared on the scene who were characterized by showy, offbeat styles of clothing. Most of these young men appear to have come from the fringes of the samurai communities; they were menservants in samurai households, masterless samurai, and low-ranking samurai. During the Warring States period, these marginal members of the samurai class could often achieve promotion to full samurai status through participation in battle. After the pacification of the country, however, this possibility for promotion was closed off. These fringe samurai sometimes formed a kind of horizontal self-defense alliance that cut across feudal master–servant relations. They sometimes shared homosexual tastes. Their deviant fashions hence symbolized both their solidarity among themselves and their frustration with the system.

In legal terms, the *kabuki-mono* were defined solely by their outlandish dress. The shogunate's earliest decree against them appeared in 1615 and specified seven deviations from the male dress code as marks of *kabuki-mono* membership. First, their hairstyle was hard to ignore; they favored a "skinhead" look above the forehead and temples, with long hair hanging from the back of the head rather than tied in a topknot. Long swords, showy red scabbards, and distinctive large sword guards were also considered evidence of being *kabuki-mono*.[29] The law decreed imprisonment as the penalty for this style of dress along with imposing a fine on the person's master. According to the ordinance of 1615, the *kabuki-mono* also smoked forbidden tobacco and loitered in public places, to the annoyance of passersby. Since many of them were servants of samurai, they often went out with their masters, dressed in their wild costumes and acting rowdy. While waiting for their masters on the stools outside the samurai residences, they often had loud conversations or amused themselves by dancing and singing in the open street. They were proud of their trendy outfits, which sometimes included imported velvet collars, short *kimono* with lead weights sewn into the hem, wide belts, and so forth.[30]

The following episode involving a *kabuki-mono* conveys a clear picture of their irrepressible rebellious spirit. In 1612, nine years after Tokugawa Ieyasu became the first shogun, a group of *kabuki-mono* led by one Ōtori Ichibei caused a public disturbance in Edo. Miura Jōshin's (ca. 1565– 1644) *Keichō kenmonshū* (The Chronicle of the Observation during the Keichō Era)[31] describes the incident:

> Recently, there was a young man called Ōtori Ichibei. He had no proper association with any household belonging to samurai, farmer, craftsman, or merchant. He was always accompanied by young people who favored deviant fashions. They ascribed manly honor to one another, were always chattering about heroic deeds, and always getting involved in dangerous situations. Ichibei was not a townsman, not a samurai, but an unusual man.[32]

The fact that Ōtori cannot be classified under any of the official status categories touches on the most dangerous aspect of the *kabuki-mono* from the authorities' point of view. Ōtori's group was arrested because one of its members murdered the *shogun*'s banner man, an officer who had killed a servant who was a member of Ōtori's group. The killing of the banner man was an act of retaliation. According to *Tokugawa Jikki* (The Official Record of the Tokugawa Clan), the group "had collected several hundred juvenile delinquents and hoods around the city; they injured people and upset them." Ōtori was apparently not just a violent gangster, however. He was regarded as a "man of honor" and had a charismatic character. He carried a long sword with the inscribed phrase, "Twenty-five is too long to live! Ichibei." The members remained deeply loyal to him and promised to defend one another. When Ōtori was arrested, according to Miura Jōshin, the authorities tortured him by hanging him from the ceiling, forcing him to reveal all the names of the "same kind of people." Ōtori agreed to confess but asked for a thick notebook for writing out the names of members. When the magistrate gave him the notebook, Ōtori began to write the names of all the *daimyo* lords; in his opinion, the *daimyo* were the "same kind of people."[33] Ōtori's group failed to take over the country only because he was born too late.

We do not have any reliable documentation of the organizational structure of the early *kabuki-mono*. Apparently, the Tokugawa authorities did not understand the loose structure of these groups of marginal people that popped up simultaneously in different regions. A record of the Kaga domain from 1612 notes that the authorities had arrested 63 violent *kabuki-mono* in the cities of Kanazawa and Takaoka.[34] The authorities executed all of them in order to intimidate the remainder.[35] In 1619, more than 70 malicious "mischievous persons" (*itazura-mono*) were arrested in Kyoto. They belonged to groups with names like *Ibara gumi* (Thorny Group) and *Kawara bakama gumi* (Leather Trousers Group).[36] Although the *kabuki-mono* sporadically formed local groups or gangs, they never organized a large-scale protest movement or articulated a platform for revolt. Instead, they spread their message of discontent and non-conformity primarily by affecting specific fashions in dress and behavior. In sum, it was because *kabuki-mono* by itself was a fashion statement that the groups were able to infiltrate different regions of Japan without any formal structural connections.

The *shogun*'s key strategy of social control was to eradicate the taste for *kabuki* fashions from the ruling class and prevent them from patronizing lower-class *kabuki-mono*. The *daimyo* were still practicing warlords at that time, and many of them enjoyed having retinues of soldiers and servants in showy, decorative clothing. The 1615 edict against the *kabuki-mono*, as we have seen, established penalties for masters as well as underlings who were involved with the deviants. As a reflection of this political situation, the Rule of Military Houses (*Buke Shohatto*) was promulgated in 1615, right after the shogun's definitive victory at the Summer Battle of

Osaka. The Rule clearly outlined the general principles of the samurai's dress code:

> Clothing should not be confusing. Differences between masters and vassals, between superiors and inferiors should be distinct.... The costumes of soldiers and servants have been recently getting too luxurious and decorative, using such materials as twill and brocade. Be sure to control these tendencies, as they are not the old way.[37]

In 1606, Tokugawa Ieyasu, the founder of the Tokugawa regime, ordered the punishment of ten *kabuki-mono*, including some of Tokugawa's vassals who favored their fashions.[38] Although the *daimyo*'s open adaptations of *kabuki* culture seem to have declined after this incident, they still occasionally hired menservants who dressed like *kabuki-mono*. Consequently, the ordinances of 1617[39] and 1632[40] ordered higher-ranking samurai not to allow themselves to be seen with *kabuki-mono* in public. In the Kaga *han*, Lord Maeda also prescribed detailed fines for the employers of *kabuki-mono*; the fine was prorated according to the samurai's income and was levied at up to 30 pieces of silver. Further legal enactments against the *kabuki-mono*, including an ordinance from 1645, the second year of *Shōhō*, repeatedly complained that previous ordinances were being ignored.

Kabuki Theaters: Gender and the Floating World

The categorical resistance of the *kabuki-mono* clearly had a gender dimension. The culture of male–male love was part of the culture of the *kabuki-mono*. Although homosexuality itself was not condemned as a vice in Tokugawa society, for the *kabuki-mono* it could easily lead to transgressions because the romanticized ethic of male–male love placed a higher loyalty on personal bonds than the official feudal norms of loyalty would permit. For example, the murder of a shogunate's high official by a servant, a famous case in 1612, was an act of retaliation for the killing of the servant's friend, who was also a *kabuki-mono*.[41] Under the romanticized ethic of male–male love, intimate committed relationships between two individuals were sometimes considered more important than loyalty to the master. Behind this subversion of the feudal ethic by homosexual ethics, however, there was a broader range of expressions of gender categories in the early Tokugawa period. In this era of social uncertainty, the description of women's beauty was not characterized by stereotypes.

264
 Market, State, and Categorical Politics

The *Kabuki* theater, a world-famous Japanese theatrical tradition, began as a dramatization of the extraordinary clothing and conduct of the *kabuki-mono*. This style of theater is usually dated from around 1603, when a woman named Okuni and her associates settled near the Gojō Bridge in Kyoto and started to perform *kabuki* dancing. Okuni is said to have worn "deviant fashions imitating male costume, with swords, daggers and unusual outfits. She [Okuni] conducted herself like a man, playing with women from the tea houses."[42] Thereafter, "others copied her and opened *kabuki* theaters in various areas."[43] The reader should note that Okuni dressed and acted like a stereotypical *kabuki-mono*. The *Kabuki* theater was thus not far removed from its origins in the "street theater" provided by groups of *kabuki-mono* in the outside world. By the creation of the commercial *Kabuki* theaters as aesthetic publics, *kabuki* lifestyles were popularized as the iconography of the period.

The *Kabuki* theater was remarkable for its timing as well as its content. It emerged in the same year that Tokugawa Ieyasu received the title of shogun from the imperial court (1603) and formally established the shogunate government. It is unusual for a new art form to emerge at the same time as the establishment of a new political regime, except in situations of intentional state patronage of artistic development. The consolidation of the Tokugawa state and the rise of the *Kabuki* theater can be rightly regarded as twin progeny of the preceding civil war period. A century of social upheaval during the sixteenth century had released popular artistic and economic energies. The establishment of the shogunate, however, meant the end of an era of relative social fluidity, as the new regime began to reinforce the barriers between classes and define different ranks within the social order. From the viewpoint of the early seventeenth century, however, the process of state-making was still under way, and nobody anticipated the lengthy period of domestic tranquility that lay ahead. The explosive energies that could not be channeled into the service of the new order found their outlet in the *Kabuki* culture. These theaters gave artistic form and expression to popular trends and thus became a commercial success.

The early seventeenth-century writer, Miura Jōshin, who chronicled the rise and fall of Ōtori's *kabuki-mono* group, also described the appearance of the first *Kabuki* theater in Edo. He wrote: "[T]he trendiest recent development in Edo city is the kabuki women's performances in the Yoshiwara quarter," since the courtesans of the Yoshiwara district commonly directed the *Kabuki* companies in early seventeenth-century Edo. Jōshin continues:

> When a large placard was posted at Nakabashi, announcing that there would be a kabuki performance by Ikushima Tango-no-kami, a crowd gathered, and high and low alike thronged to it.

After they had waited impatiently for the leading dancer's appearance, the curtain rose, she came out, and walked down the runway. She was gaily dressed, wore a long and a short sword worked in gold, and had a flint-bag and gourd hanging from her waist. Appearing with a clown, her bearing, as she sauntered by in high spirits, did not appear to be that of a woman but of a handsome attractive man.... The people in the pit and the boxes craned their necks and, nodding their heads, rocked themselves into an absent-minded daze.... The outer corners of her eyes were like hibiscus blossoms, her lips like red flowers.... Anyone who would not fall in love with such a beautiful body is more to be feared than a ghost.[44]

In addition to the leading dancer, there were 50 or 60 other beautifully dressed young women dancing in a graceful yet striking way to the accompaniment of *shamisen*, drums, and flutes. The music appealed to people's emotions, with such lyrics as "Let yourself go wild in this dreamy floating world" (*ukiyo*), and completely intoxicated the audience[45] (Figure 10.2).

Jōshin's eyewitness account of the Yoshiwara *Kabuki* theater appears to be an accurate description of early *Kabuki* performances, in which most of the actors were women. The subversion of gender roles was a part of the social deviance that made *Kabuki* so attractive to urban audiences. The symbolic dimension of the phenomenon was reflected in the fact that the leading female performers in the *Kabuki* troupes often used such male identifiers as a feudal title of nobility as their stage names. In this example, Tangonokami means "the lord of Tango." According to Jōshin, Okuni, the founder of *Kabuki* theater, also claimed a lordly title, Kitano Tsushima no kami, or "the lord of Tsushima province." Other famous actresses in this period included Sadojima Shōkichi, Murayama Sakon (male names), and Dekijima Nagato no kami (a lordly title). Many all-female *Kabuki* troupes adopted the titles of male nobles for their leading actresses. One of the most popular performances was one in which a well-known actress impersonated a stylish playboy with a fashion of *kabuki-mono*, living it up at a teahouse. The actresses and their performances were popular subjects of genre painting during this period. One such painting by an unknown painter, known as *Kabuki-zukan*, is a splendid depiction of a teahouse performance by an actress called Uneme (Plate 2). The main figure of this painting is dressed like a man of fashion, just like the dancer in Jōshin's account who was pretending to be a playboy out to seduce a woman. The *Kabuki* performance that Jōshin saw was apparently not an isolated case. The leading actress even dared to wear a cross hanging around her neck. This symbol, which the actress was wearing before the shogunate's strict prohibition of Christianity, did not

266 Market, State, and Categorical Politics

mean that she was a Christian. It was simply a deviant affectation on the part of a stylish *kabuki-mono*. The audience in this picture was clearly taken with the glamorous stage performance. The contemporary viewer can see men, women, and children, aristocratic and lowly, entering into an alternative reality. There are even two Westerners in the audience in this picture. Mediated by Uneme's subversive performance, the *Kabuki* theater became the temporary setting for an aesthetic public that left worldly status differences outside its doors (Figure 10.3).

The fundamental transgression of *Kabuki* theater was its exploitation of the power of human eroticism infused with an aesthetic element. When spectators gathered to watch a performance on the *Kabuki* stage, their erotic feelings were fused into a collective experience through the sharing of an aesthetic. Similarly, the *kabuki-mono* groups in the street were supposedly formed around homosexual relationships.[46] The *kabuki* subculture, both on the stage and on the street, violated status as well as gender boundaries; it encouraged people to discard their inhibitions and escape from the confines of the official order. *Kabuki* fashions helped to produce a ritual space that introduced individuals to the "floating world," or *ukiyo*, which was disconnected from the formal structures of Tokugawa society.

Ukiyo is an important term in Tokugawa cultural history. In its original medieval Buddhist context, *ukiyo* referred to the "world of sorrows," from *uki* meaning "suffering" and *yo* meaning "world." In the Tokugawa period, however, the same word came to signify the "floating world" – in this instance *uki* is a homophone that means "floating."[47] The secularized usage of *ukiyo* preserved its original connotation derived from the Buddhist theory of impermanence but reflected changes in attitude toward the transitory nature of being. *Ukiyo* as the floating world no longer implied a pessimistic outlook but rather echoed the sentiment of *carpe diem*: if everything is transitory, why not enjoy this moment of life? Given its association with a hedonistic perspective, *ukiyo* also usually conveyed a suggestion of amorous activity. The "floating world" thus symbolized the urban commoners' receptiveness to a sensuous lifestyle that was diametrically opposed to the strict hierarchical discipline imposed by the Tokugawa state.

By presenting the world of *ukiyo* as subversive to the categorical order of the Tokugawa state, *Kabuki* theatrical performances were intrinsically threatening to the shogunate system. Apart from the intrinsic deviance of a subculture tinged with eroticism, entertainers as a general social category had adopted the tradition of *mu'en* (no relation) in the medieval period. Theatrical performers were sometimes labeled pejoratively as *kawara-mono*, or "riverbank people," because medieval entertainment was often performed on the banks of a river. The choice of site

Figure 10.3. A *Kabuki* Audience. The audience enjoys a performance by Uneme's female troupe, from *Kabuki-zukan* ca. 1605. The group includes men, women, and children from a range of social classes. There are even two Westerners in the picture.

was not without significance. In medieval Japan, riverbanks were the preferred location for funerals and executions; they were spaces that connected death and life and were therefore suitable for the dedication of performances for the dead spirits to placate them.[48] Like the medieval composition of linked verse under cherry blossoms that was discussed in Chapter 3, the sites of theatrical performances became temporary loci of "no-relation" (*mu'en*) outside the categories of the feudal social order. Erotic suggestiveness, dance, and fashion provided the ritual technology to create a communicative sphere filled with color and passion.

Following the appearance of the *kabuki* subculture, the shogunate conducted a symbolic crusade against it on two fronts. One target was the *kabuki-mono* groups who flaunted their deviant attire on the streets; the other was the theatrical *Kabuki* stage that gave aesthetic form to the counter-cultural spirit of the *kabuki-mono*. The state took a hard line against the *kabuki-mono*. The shoguns and regional *daimyo* often arrested and publicly executed them. The shogunate imposed much stricter regulations on livery; the clothing of the lowest-ranking samurai and the servants in samurai houses was regulated with particular care since these marginal men were considered potential *kabuki-mono*.[49] In 1631, the shogunate officially closed off the possibility of a samurai's servant being promoted to full samurai status. These regulations can be understood as efforts to define the social identities of persons on the fringes of the samurai class by drawing clear lines between the samurai and commoners. Higher-ranking samurai who imitated the style of the *kabuki-mono* were also strictly punished. An important part of the shogunate's disciplinary strategy resulted from its learning process in dealing with these deviant groups.

The shogunate's policy toward the *Kabuki* theater and the courtesan quarter took a different turn; namely, the demarcation of a *cordon sanitaire*. The shoguns segregated the theaters and the ladies of the *demimonde* and thus created a kind of official "adult entertainment district." Prior to 1617, the shogunate granted Shōji Jin'uemnon permission to establish a courtesan quarter by concentrating the houses of prostitution that had been dispersed throughout Edo into one area, the Yoshiwara quarter. Brothels outside this ward were considered illegal.[50] The style of *Kabuki* performance mentioned earlier was permitted during this early period in order to attract a clientele to the newly defined courtesan quarter. However, once the entertainment proved to be a little too popular, the courtesans' *Kabuki* theaters were closed down.[51] At that time, the city of Edo was expanding rapidly as the political capital of Japan and had a predominantly male population. In 1656, the original Yoshiwara, located near the center of the city, was relocated to a new site (New Yoshiwara) near Asakusa. The move was completed in 1657 and was facilitated by the Great Fire of Meireki in the same year. As a result, New Yoshiwara was constructed with a set of walls surrounded by moats and was accessible only through the "Great Gate."[52] The segregation of prostitution was thus completed. Within this restricted sphere, high-ranking courtesans and their wealthy customers created the glittering "court society" of the floating world.

The *Kabuki* theaters underwent a similar evolution. In 1627, the shogunate prohibited women from appearing on the *Kabuki* stage. In 1640, the shogun issued another ordinance against the "mixing of men and women on the stage," indicating that the earlier regulation was being violated.[53] Because of these regulations, *Kabuki* became a male-only dramatic form, in which some actors played female roles.[54] This change, however, did not "correct" the problem of erotic disorder as the shogunate had hoped. Instead of being entranced by female beauty, male spectators now fell in love with the beautiful boys (*wakashū*) who played the women's parts in the dramas. Tokugawa Japanese were generally tolerant of cross-dressing and homosexual affairs. Beautiful young men clad in sensual feminine costumes were considered seductively attractive in this context, and their eagerness to create a convincingly feminine appearance was combined with a homosexual lifestyle. These *wakashū*, with their long, flowing sleeves and exaggerated hairstyles, were not only attractive to men but also appealed to women as fashion models and trendsetters.[55] Indeed, women and *wakashū* often appear to be interchangeable in the paintings and prints of this period, except for a few small gender cues related to hairstyles and clothing.[56] These ambiguous gender boundaries extended beyond matters of external dress.

During this period, the Japanese had a generally relaxed attitude regarding variations in sexual orientation. Although there were words in the Japanese vocabulary for expressing personal preferences or dislikes in styles of sexual behavior, such categories as "homosexual" for denoting inherent lifelong characteristics of a group of persons did not exist. In contrast to the restrictive legislation of European countries, in which homosexual acts were often classed as felonies, the Tokugawa Japanese considered such acts or preferences as matters of taste that could change across time or vary from person to person. In addition, members of the samurai class often idealized love between two males – particularly relationships between protective older men and young *wakashū*. Male bonding of this type among the samurai had originated in a medieval warrior society; by the Tokugawa period, it was perceived simply as another ancient Japanese custom. Although some Tokugawa Confucian scholars considered sexual relationships between men as immoral on the grounds that they violated human nature, they also tended to consider these relationships a minor

vice. The other religious traditions of Japan were also relatively tolerant of male–male relationships. In the medieval Buddhist temples and
Shintō shrines, there were many young boys, called *chigo*, who dressed in
beautiful *kimono*. These *chigo* were often involved in love relationships
with older monks. Besides the sexual dimension of such relationships, the
physical beauty of the youths was appreciated as an embodiment of divine
spirit, an otherworldly connection between human and divine.

When these long-standing attitudes and customs combined with the fluidity of gender categories in the *Kabuki* performances, it was predictable
that the prohibition of female dancers did not decrease the erotic intensity
of the Tokugawa stage. Men's external appearance in this period was no
less important than women's, and fads in women's and men's costumes
were mutually influential. The mixing of female and male trends and fashions characterized the unsettled categories of erotic aestheticism during
this period. In 1661, the shogun finally moved the large *Kabuki* theaters
to segregated quarters of the city and compelled the actors to live within
those districts. Throughout the Tokugawa period, only four large theaters
and several smaller ones had legal permission to hold performances. This
development meant that the female *kabuki* spirit was confined within the
great wall of the Yoshiwara courtesan quarter, while the *Kabuki* theater
became a male-only institution in a restricted theater district. Because
the theaters and brothels were officially licensed, they enjoyed a certain
prestige and were increasingly separated from the street culture of the
kabuki-mono.

The shogunate's segregation policies had an ironic side effect, however:
the isolation of both sets of entertainers enabled them to create alternative realities – spheres of existence with social rituals different from
those of the outside world. Star actors became magnets of popular attention. They were expected to be different from the rest of society; as
a result, their professional styles and personal tastes set fashion trends.
With this geographical separation, official licensure, and gender special-
ization, these two forms of entertainment became even more institutionalized, thus intensifying and concentrating the spirit of the "floating world."
The marginalization and segregation of performers and courtesans meant
on the one hand that the medieval *za* spirit and the tradition of "no relation" (*mu'en*) could find a social niche for survival. On the other hand,
however, the floating world was a kind of performative space different
from the informality of the riverbank. The performers of the floating
world were no longer the independent traveling actors of the medieval
period. The public licensing of a limited degree of freedom and autonomy within entertainment areas was associated with their incorporation
into the hierarchy of the Tokugawa state. Their place in the hierarchy of
publics under the Tokugawa system was clearly defined geographically

and socially. The *Kabuki* theaters and courtesan district were regarded as socially useful outlets within the government's system of control – as "places for vice" (*akusho*). The structural transformation of the entertainment sector thus ran parallel to the general pattern of the transformation of the structures and hierarchies of publics from medieval to early modern Japanese society.

The Rise of Urban Mass Fashion

With the maturity of the Japanese commercial market in the late seventeenth century, the main actors in fashion politics were no longer the *kabuki-mono*. Instead, the urban commoners now filled this role. Between the government's detailed dress regulations and their own increasing financial problems, the samurai largely lost their creative energy as social trendsetters. Although the *daimyo* (and, to a lesser degree, their higher-ranking vassals) continued to patronize the makers of luxurious custom-made *kimono*, since their ceremonial obligations required expensive garments appropriate to their rank, these robes were not the products of an innovative fashion culture. By the late seventeenth century, the majority of the samurai population had been "domesticated," having exchanged their previous military duties for hereditary standing in a class of quasi-bureaucrats. At the same time, the adult males of the samurai class adopted a more sober style of everyday clothing that symbolized self-discipline and established status. Commoners, especially the merchant class, took the place of the samurai as the main arbiters of taste, a position corresponding to their increased economic power.

One sign of the expansion of commercial fashion around the Kanmon era (1661–1672) was the appearance of pattern books for dyed cloth, called *hiinagata*. The *hiinagata* were used to place orders for *kimono*. Customers selected their favorite patterns from the design books and then ordered custom-made garments. Producers and purveyors of textiles also studied these books in order to meet the demand for designs that were currently in fashion.[57] The first example of this innovation, *On Hiinagata* (1666), contained two hundred patterns for *kosode kimono*.[58] A typical page in this sample book showed a line drawing of the back view of a *kimono* with bold patterns. Color specifications and various decorative techniques were also indicated. After this pioneering example, hundreds of *hiinagata* were published in rapid succession. These books informed readers of bold new designs and various dyeing techniques, patterns for embroidery, intricate dappled materials, and gold and silver leaf appliqués. The publication of sample books marked the birth of popular interest in fashion and the rise of a lucrative fashion industry. The resulting production of mass fashions and the increased level of taste consciousness further encouraged the expansion of production, trade, and information networks associated with the fashion industry.

The taste of the era – sometimes called "Kanmon patterns" – that can be documented from the *hiinagata* pattern books reflected Japan's new economic vitality. The Kanmon era corresponded with the rapid expansion of long-distance trade and the establishment of a national market economy. The typical successful Kanmon merchant was a risk-taking entrepreneur who took advantage of fast-paced economic changes. The designs for luxurious silk *kosode* (a form of *kimono*) of this era were typically splendid and striking, yet fresh. In *On Hiinagata*, the favorite background color was red or variations of red; it appeared in 27 of the 180 patterns depicted for young women. Yellow was next on the list. Pattern placement was bold and expansive; the designers used the entire back of the *kimono*, including long sleeves, as if it were a rectangular canvas. One common pattern placement began the design from the upper right corner or right side of the corner and carried it diagonally to the hem. Unlike earlier designs that favored smaller patterns placed symmetrically or distributed evenly throughout the material, Kanmon design preferred large, bold patterns extending diagonally or asymmetrically across the garment. This produced an elegant, carefully crafted, yet assertive *kosode*.

The popularization of high-quality *kimono* in the late seventeenth century was epitomized by the phenomenal success of a famous Edo retail establishment, Echigoya, founded in 1673. Before Echigoya, salesmen from *kimono* retailers customarily visited customers such as *daimyo* and upper *samurai* at home. In contrast, Echigoya focused on the mass market and sold its merchandise on a cash-only basis within the store itself for fixed, low prices.[59] Subsequently, the number of retail shops increased. The names and addresses of 17 major stores appeared in a list of Edo *kimono* retailers published in 1697. A similar directory published in 1735 (*Edo Gofuku Ten Nayose*, or The List of Kimono Shops in Edo) counted 63 major clothiers, reflecting the maturation of the popular commercial clothing market.[60] Although Echigoya remained on the list of the top *kimono* retailers, other major *kimono* stores, such as Shirokiya and Daimaru, also prospered by adapting Echigoya's mass-market strategy. The coming of the retail stores meant that fashion trends became increasingly commercialized as retailers competed with one another to push the latest patterns. Since Kyoto remained the center of high-quality silk textile production, most Edo retail shops had bases in Kyoto, where the textiles were purchased for their Edo consumers. In essence, the retail establishments were nodes for market networks as well as aesthetic fashion networks. Consequently, the textile production centers obtained better consumer feedback, which in turn further enhanced the social phenomenon of fashion.

With the rise of the *kimono* retail shops, the density of the economic and aesthetic networks focused on the *kimono* trade incorporated even more people into the marketing networks.

Fashion Contests and Sumptuary Regulations

From the late seventeenth century to the early eighteenth century, legendary stories of fashion contests, or *date kurabe* (literally, "stylishness competitions"), circulated among the Tokugawa public. The wife of a famous Edo merchant, Ishikawa Rokubei, was said to have gone all the way to Kyoto, a center of costume design, to attend a private fashion contest with a well-known Kyoto clotheshorse, the wife of Naniwaya Jūuemon. Ishikawa's wife won the contest by wearing a surprise – a black costume with an intricate nandin pattern; all the nandin seeds were made of coral. Another famous anecdote concerned the wife of Nakamura Kuranosuke, a citizen of Kyoto who patronized the famous artist Ogata Kōrin. On Kōrin's advice, Nakamura's wife wore a simple white satin *kimono* with a black robe. She won out over other participants who wore gorgeously colored *kimono*.[61] Although these stories received wide circulation, we cannot corroborate their historical accuracy. Their symbolic meaning suggests that fashion had become a matter of serious competition and that innovative designs were favored over traditional tastes in these circumstances.

The late seventeenth century saw the peak of innovative, elaborate, and costly designs. The most time-consuming techniques, such as gold embroidery and *sō kanoko* (an intricately dappled cloth that takes about a year to complete), were very popular during this period as displays of wealth. The costumes of the merchants' womenfolk were especially gorgeous in order to advertise the household's wealth. Since the merchants' aspirations toward upward mobility were blocked by status boundaries, they substituted expensive clothing – which became an index of economic rank and privilege – for social promotion. Luxurious garments were effective demonstrations of their wealth, which triggered an endless stream of sumptuary regulations. The popular *Ōnna Chōhōki* (The Lady's Treasury), published in 1692, noted this trend: "Fashionable dyed patterns change every five to eight years."[62]

The best-known anecdote about Ishikawa's wife had to do with her encounter with the fifth shogun. One day in 1681, she set up a room facing the street overlooking the shogun's procession, which was passing by. Elaborately dressed, and surrounded by clouds of burning incense, this woman, accompanied by her maids, was sitting in the room against a golden folding screen watching the procession as if she were showing off her tasteful dress to the shogun. The shogun noticed her and ordered an investigation. When the officers identified her as a commoner's wife, the authorities imposed strict sanctions on the entire family. The Ishikawas were banished from Edo on the grounds of conspicuous consumption inappropriate to their status, and their property was confiscated for the crimes of pride and extravagance.[63] The shogun's confiscation of the Ishikawas' property actually took place; the seizure can be verified from a number of contemporary official and private records. While we cannot corroborate the precise details of this episode, the interpretation must be considered as the "right" contemporary explanation of a punishment meted out to a powerful family.

In reviewing the Edo town magistrate's record of ordinances (*machibure*) from the seventeenth century, we find that restrictions on commoners' appearance and lifestyle came in waves. Each of the years 1649, 1656, and 1668 saw more than five ordinances concerning such issues. The enforcement of these laws was irregular at best, however, and often lapsed altogether after a brief period of time. In terms of both content and number, the ordinances of 1683 were the most precise and meticulous in restricting the consumption of urban commoners. The sumptuary law of 1683, two years after the incident of the Ishikawa family, prohibited the use of golden foil, golden embroidery, and *sō kanoko* (dappled cloth), all very expensive but popular techniques for making upscale costumes for women's *kimono*. "In general," the ordinance continues, "it is forbidden to make novelty woven or dyed textiles."[64] The statute limited the price of women's *kosode* clothing to a maximum of 200 *moku*.[65] In the same year, the shogun also commanded that "servants and housemaids may wear only cotton or linen. Servants and maids who work in townspeople's households may not use silk in any article of clothing, including collars, belts and sashes, caps, gloves, handkerchief pockets, and wallets."[66] Women of the urban commoner class who already owned dresses with gold embroidery or golden brocade were forbidden to wear them.[67]

Although the law certainly sounds very restrictive in forbidding servants to use silk, it left their masters alone. The shoguns realized that too many restrictions on the consumption of urban residents decreased the vitality of the cities. The shogunate's policy is better understood as intending to prevent visual status reversals in which the merchants appeared to be living better than the samurai.

Official rulings could not, of course, change the merchants' craving for fashionably expensive attire, and the Tokugawa fashion regulations had to be repeatedly enacted after the 1683 ordinances. Frequent proclamations of sumptuary laws, together with an occasional official display of coercive power, as exemplified by the confiscation of the Ishikawas' property, did have an impact on fashion. Sometimes, in fact, the laws redirected contemporary trends. According to *Tose Hayaru Hinagata* (Contemporary Fashionable Patterns), published just after the strict rules of 1683 and illustrated by a famous *ukiyo-e* painter, Hishikawa Moronobu, the prohibition on expensive techniques swept away the use of *sō kanoko* and showy golden and silver embroidery; instead, the pattern book recommended elegant and clever dyed designs.[68] After 1683, artistic techniques for dying *kimono*, such as *yuzen* dyeing (hand-painting on silk fabric with starch resist), grew more sophisticated and refined.

This quick response in the form of a new design trend during the Genroku era (1688–1704) was not simply evidence of submission to the shogunate's policy; rather, it was the cumulative result of the activities of fashion entrepreneurs within a politically circumscribed environment. Although the state could define boundaries through prohibitions, the authorities could not create new fashions within those boundaries. These innovations resulted from the dynamics of the marketplace, in which entrepreneurs and designers produced several new trends in rapid succession in order to satisfy the increasingly refined taste of their customers. The short stories collected in Ihara Saikaku's *Saikaku Oritome*, first published in 1694, include tales about two merchants who started from nothing and later became successful by inventing new methods of dyeing *kimono*.[69] People with nimble minds and inventive responses to the demands of the market could make money in this society.

These trends became particularly marked after the institution of stricter policies by the eighth shogun, Yoshimune (reigning between 1716 and 1744), who emphasized the virtue of frugality. Yoshimune, whose political ideal was a return to the era of the first shogun, Ieyasu, was sober and restrained in his personal tastes. The shogun limited his daily consumption of food and clothing, avoiding expensive materials. He preferred to wear dull-colored clothing, usually black or brown.[70] He strongly disapproved of high living, whether among samurai or commoner families.[71] Yoshimune's campaign against conspicuous consumption was revived whenever the shogunate's policy makers attempted to tighten social controls or reform the government. In the years that followed, the famous Kansei reform by *rōjū*, or Chief of Senior Councillors, Matsudaira Sadanobu (1787–1793), and the Tenpō reform by *rōjū* Mizuno Tadakuni, Counselor of State (1841–1843), were accompanied by strict controls on luxurious fashions and lifestyles.

The government's repeated sumptuary regulations certainly prepared the way for the rise of a subdued urban taste in fashion. In this more mature and sophisticated fashion aesthetic, one could express one's individuality without violating the law of the state. Good taste was expressed by subtle stylistic differences and intelligence in design.

Fashion Civility and Categorical Order

By the early eighteenth century, the state had made clothing a clear marker of the boundaries between the classes. In the late Tokugawa period, after centuries of sumptuary regulations and the status distinction system, the growing sophistication of taste and material cultures meant that the selection of clothing colors and materials developed in a complex manner along two dimensions: the individual's status on the one hand, and the differentiation between formal ceremonial occasions and daily life on the other. For example, the shop owners of Edo would wear shiny black silk (*kuro habutae*) formal dress on ceremonial occasions, but for semiformal parties, they might choose a fine-striped silk *kimono* material with a matte finish. For women of urban commoner status, fine-patterned silk crepe (*chirimen*) *kimono* called *komon* were considered dressier, whereas fine-striped *kimono* were considered less formal, even though they were also made of silk. In the houses of high-ranking samurai, ladies-in-waiting might wear striped silk patterns for everyday or informal occasions. On formal occasions, however, they would wear elegant shiny silk *kimono* with delicate dyed patterns, such as flowers or themes taken from classic literature. Lower maids in the same house would usually wear woven stripes, but on formal occasions they might wear matte woven silk with patterns. For the most part, people wore somber colors and avoided shiny-surfaced materials for daily wear. Bright colors and bold patterns were reserved mainly for upper-class women's ceremonial dress. Mix-ups about the formality of a given occasion were considered as grave as transgressions of class distinctions.

In the unification era, in contrast, the samurai often wore unusual brilliantly colored clothing to show off their power and wealth. Men were important players in the fashion game. Male participation in fashion, however, declined during the eighteenth century. The late Tokugawa period made women the arbiters of fashion, while men in respectable occupations tended to retreat from that aesthetic arena. The subtle expression of eroticism through fashion was reserved mostly for women. Men's dress, in contrast, consisted of functional working gear. This was especially true for the samurai class, whose clothing was regarded as a symbol of their public duties and internal virtues of self-control. This increasing gender differentiation in fashion is, curiously enough, close to what we usually consider the primary gender distinction in modern Western fashion culture. During the same historical period, European and American upper-class men began to wear dark colors and clothes of undistinguished cut. In this cultural context, it is understandable that Western visitors to Japan in the nineteenth century were impressed by the "Quaker-like" gentlemanliness of male Japanese dress. The British visitors, in particular, were reminded of their own puritan dress standards and regarded the dark colors and dull fabrics of Japanese men's *kimono* as signs of good taste and advanced civilization.[72]

Although the shoguns' sumptuary regulations obviously had some effect on changes in taste, the state's ability to exert effective control over fashion trends was limited. The other factors that require consideration in this context concern the transformation of the nature of work and alterations of gender categories and relations.

The transformation of work was most clearly evident in the case of the samurai, who transformed themselves from self-equipped mounted warriors in the medieval period to sober quasi-bureaucrats living on hereditary stipends. During the Warring States period, the samurai favored resplendent and colorful dress as an outward and visible sign of their pride and their two fonts of power – military strength and landownership. Their sense of masculinity was also intimately connected to those two authoritarian aspects. The extraordinary designs of samurai costumes during this period, including the use of bright colors and gold trim, reflected this martial machismo.

The vassal samurai now lived in the castle cities of their *daimyo* lords and no longer had direct control over their ancestral property. Many samurai received only hereditary stipends. Although physical prowess – including skill in martial arts – was still respected among the samurai, it no longer guaranteed a glorious career. Their workplaces were now offices filled with paper-shuffling duties and tedious demands. In addition, their income was derived from grain tax revenues and remained relatively fixed; they lacked the economic mobility of the merchants. As the income of the samurai began to decline relative to that of the merchant class, the authorities as well as the lower samurai began to idealize a more restrained lifestyle.

Since high status and wealth were no longer correlated in Tokugawa society, the straightforward flaunting of wealth through wardrobe display declined in social approval. To be sure, samurai at all levels were obliged to have some fine apparel appropriate to their status for wear on ritual occasions. The same principle applied to women in upper samurai households. Moreover, it was common for brides from good families to purchase several *kimono* of high quality as part of the wedding preparations. As a result, upper samurai families continued to be reliable customers of the traders in *kimono* fabric. The samurai, however, were no longer fashion trendsetters. The dress of male samurai thus became dull, dark, and sober, as befitted bureaucrats, and increasingly came to resemble the styles considered appropriate for European gentlemen.

The urban commoners had a more complicated relationship to fashion trends. Although they were subject to sumptuary regulations, their tastes were granted relatively free reign once they accepted the official boundaries. Their lives were less restricted by the minutiae of official rankings that complicated the lives of the samurai. Yet, as we have seen, by the late eighteenth century, the phase of "fashion competition" had run its course. With the maturation of the Tokugawa market economy and the institutionalization of the large merchant houses, the commoners' work culture also became more conservative and status-conscious. The wealthier merchants had more occasions to socialize with the samurai, which also required the adoption of more conservative attire. In this way, the use of dark, dull colors for everyday business wear became a norm for the merchants in this context.

The institutionalization of a sober, male-dominated workplace culture, both among the samurai and in the large merchant houses, also meant that women were more tightly confined within the domestic sphere. Although many large merchant houses had been founded on the joint efforts of a married couple, as the business grew, the distinction between the management and the household became identified with the contrast between the public and the private spheres. Predictably, the women were relegated to the domestic sphere. Although the merchants' wives and daughters could enjoy the luxury of high-quality *kimono* with bright colors and interesting designs, this aesthetic advantage was in part a reflection of the fact that their daily life was separated from the merchants' places of business.

After more than a century of repeated sumptuary legislation, the Tokugawa Japanese elaborated categories of appropriate costumes that were closely correlated with their formal collective identities. Highly differentiated codes of dressing according to the individual's formal social identities – by status, age, and gender – emerged. Sober, subdued colors were favored, in striking contrast to the earlier Tokugawa fashion, in which people often admired showy colors and bold designs. Restrained tastes and highly hierarchical categories were, at least in part, the result of the social discipline that the Tokugawa state implemented for the two and a half centuries of its dominance.

In this sense, the shogunate's sumptuary regulations were partially successful in leaving a clear imprint on Japanese fashion culture. Since the rules defined only the outer boundaries of permissibility, however, the more finely tuned classifications of propriety were not necessarily established by law. Thus, a sense of modesty in fashion, fashion civility so to speak, emerged largely autonomously within the politically circumscribed environment. Yet violations of the canons of propriety would disturb the Japanese citizen's sense of order as much as an infraction of the legal code.

This order, which visually codified individuals into social categories, was an external representation of pre-modern Japanese "civic society" that allowed individuals of various backgrounds to interact extensively but only within a hierarchically structured environment. It was within this sense of categorical order that new themes and variations on *kimono* styles were introduced in Tokugawa Japan.

The Rise of Urban Chic: *Iki*

The intricacies of the shogunate's classification system did not deprive Tokugawa fashion of its creative zest. If anything, urban culture used these categories as resources as a novel aesthetic took shape within the townspeople's culture. A distinctive fashion aesthetic emerged in the context of the communicative activities of the publics formed among urban commoners as a by-product of the expansion of commercial interests and networks. The "Waga koromo," a contemporary essay, commented on the directional reversal of trends in style in the late Tokugawa period: "Recent fashions in costumes and hair styles have moved from the lower to the upper classes. Even the upper samurai women sometimes copy urban commoners' styles."[73]

By the second half of the eighteenth century, Japanese interest in fashion had generated a sensitive and subtle aesthetic that is still considered an important cultural component. According to the new standards, expensive costumes still signified wealth, but they did not have to be showy. The most costly materials were often dark and quiet-looking, the products of incredible skill and laborious work. The use of expensive materials in hidden parts of the *kimono* such as the lining, or in undergarments, was also popular. Individuals could display their personal taste and wealth in an understated manner due to the development of highly sophisticated techniques for fashioning textiles and other decorative products.

Although there exist abundant historical records of Tokugawa fashions, a passage from a contemporary work of fiction, Shikitei Sanba's *Ukiyo buro* (Bath House in the Floating World), contains a vivid example of casual conversation generated by the fashions of the moment. The following passage is a dialogue between two young women gossiping about a fashionable woman who has just passed by wearing a *rokō-cha* (greenish-brown) *kimono*.

> [Looking out from the public bathhouse]
> Oie: "Okabe, did you notice the lady who just passed by on the street?"
> Okabe: "No."

Oie: "Wow! She looked simply gorgeous! She was wearing a *rokō-cha kimono* made of chirimen silk crepe, with a lining of black dappled cloth. Underneath, she wore two layers of petticoats in the same black dappled cloth. Under that, she wore a red silk juban slip. The collar was made of white satin. Her stylishly shaped *obi* was gray, made of thick, stiff *atsuita* brocade nine sun wide.[74] She was slender in build, and resembled the late Yonezō[75] playing a mature woman. Even a woman would fall for her, how much more a man!

But hey, to my surprise, when I walked by the hairdresser's place earlier, there was a bunch of young guys hanging around there, looking at the same lady, and commenting to each other, "Look at that woman, women nowadays all wear that greenish color. Too bad that a good-looking dame has to wear an outfit the color of horseshit." Isn't it disgusting, the way men talk?[76]

The "modernity" of the two young women's conversation about fashion in this passage is striking to the modern reader. The stylish lady was wearing a sober *rokō-cha*, a greenish-brown *kimono*. This subdued color was named after a star *Kabuki* actor, Segawa Kikunojō the Second (1741–1773), who played female roles. Rōkō was the actor's pen name as a *haikai* poet, and *cha* means brown. The color was believed to be the actor's favorite. In this conversation, the greenish-brown *kimono* was set off by black and gray linings and highlighted by a glimpse of red undergarment. The flowing layers of the *kimono* surrounded a slender body framed by a white satin neckline. The taste to perceive this sophisticated and subtle style as "gorgeous" certainly reflected a mature urban aestheticism. Oie and Okabe's shared knowledge of the *Kabuki* theater also shaped their discourse. Neighborhood chitchat about fashion is a typical example of a temporary public: fluid and small in scale but well-connected to a number of other cognitive networks. The power of popular fashion lies in its ability to generate many such fluid small-scale publics linked to larger information networks. We can see in this moment of "focused gathering," to borrow Goffman's term, how the women's emotional energy was stirred up by their excitement about the subject matter. Furthermore, by sharing an evaluation of a stranger's style, Oie and Okabe's small neighborhood was connected to the larger world of high fashion culture and to an even wider cultural frame of reference centering around the *Kabuki* theater aesthetic. Local celebrities became typical nodal points of communicative networks in popular culture who could generate enormous amounts of emotional energy and attention. Fashion in Tokugawa Japan was a social phenomenon closely tied to the popularity of well-known entertainers and other "stars." Even apparently casual conversations about the latest styles made economic waves, so to speak. By this time, the fashion industry either comprised or influenced a major portion of the Tokugawa commercial economy. In spite of frequent sumptuary regulations, the Tokugawa people created lively and vivacious discursive spheres focused on fashion.

Sophistication by itself, however, is not an adequate explanation of the ongoing vitality of Tokugawa fashion under the pressure of successive sumptuary regulations. Innovation and experimentation in fashion were side effects of the shogunate's original disciplinary strategy, which did not completely eradicate the culture of the floating world. The shoguns had permitted the two centers of the floating world – the *Kabuki* theaters and the courtesans' quarter, or *akusho* ("space of vice") – to exist as long as they kept within the limits of official policy. Paradoxically, the containment of the theaters and the "red light district" actually stimulated the ritualistic intensity and development of information networks connected with these areas. Although the shoguns made periodic attempts to control excessive luxury in the theaters and courtesans' quarter, they did not forbid people from exploring the imagery of the floating world as a temporary release from the formal constraints of the Tokugawa state. New fashions continuously arose from these special spheres.

In the urban culture of the second half of the Tokugawa period, the "court society" (in the sense of Norbert Elias's use of the term) that disseminated high fashion no longer resided in the shogun's castle. The crowds that attended these performances created the perfect situation for fashion-watching, as *Onna chōhōki* (The Lady's Treasury) duly noted. "Almost all the new trends in dyed patterns come from the kabuki theaters."[77] Housemaids, servants, and nurses had occasion to attend kabuki performances as companions or chaperones since their mistresses usually would not attend the theater unaccompanied.[78] Moreover, the less expensive seats were well within the reach of ordinary people. Popular *Kabuki* actors became trendsetters for both styles and colors. People often imitated a small detail of their favorite actor's personal style, such as a color, the shape of a cap, a hairstyle, the manner of tying the *obi*, or an intricate pattern, in their own daily costumes. During the late eighteenth century, market forces speeded up and intensified the dissemination of *kabuki* fashions. By this time, popular actors were consciously designing their own dyed patterns as a form of advertisement, wearing their distinctive patterns not only on stage but on other occasions as well.[79] The actors' fans then wore these patterns as a sign of their loyal patronage. Merchants of *kimono* shops and of various fancy goods put the actors' logos and patterns on their commodities. As a result, the combination of the fans' enthusiasm, the actors' self-promotion, and the merchants' commercial interest made *Kabuki* theaters the centers of high fashion.

Toward the end of the eighteenth century, a major trend in Japanese urban taste was a kind of dandyism resembling modern urban chic. The fashionable color schemes of the late Tokugawa period tended toward subtle hues and subdued colors such as brown, gray, or navy, with occasional touches of brighter colors for contrast. Popular shades included reddish gray (*beni kake nezumi*), lavender gray (*fuji nezumi*), and silver gray (*gin nezumi*). These hues were quiet and restrained, but also distinctive in their inclusion of an intriguing afterthought of a brighter color. A small amount of brilliant color might also be used to accent an overall restrained color scheme. A delicate fine-patterned dyed silk *kimono* called *komon* often featured these subdued hues and became a popular choice among urban women.

This aesthetic was often called *iki* during the late eighteenth and early nineteenth centuries. *Iki*, as we have seen, referred to a restrained eroticism derived from the courtesan culture. It was not simply a trend in fashion; it also reflected an underlying desire to be alluring in a polished and graceful manner. These two elements were held in static tension. The mental component of *iki* was also connected to the homonym *iki*, which means "spirit" or "pride." This mentality developed within the floating world, whose inhabitants exemplified an attitude of acceptance regarding their assignment to an inferior place in the formal social pecking order combined with spirited confidence in their inner self-worth. From this perspective, *iki* was the chosen response of urban commoners who were condemned to live in a world in which only the samurai officially commanded respect. The townspeople rarely organized violent protests against the samurai elite, but their covert resistance was often expressed in aesthetic terms. *Iki* was the central aesthetic category of the Edo townspeople. Rich merchants would proudly wear cotton *kimono* with silk linings. Wealthy financiers (*fuda sashi*) affected expensive imported *sarasa* clothing under cover of a coarse cotton *kimono*. The *iki* aesthetic regarded excessive displays of wealth as vulgar and unsophisticated, or *yabo*. In sum, the combination of restraint and dandyism that characterized *iki* resulted from the economic prosperity of the fashion industries, the rising concentration of wealth in urban centers, and legal pressures from the political authorities[80] (Plate 3).

By the late eighteenth and the early nineteenth centuries, not only had the phenomenon of mass fashion become prevalent, but also the quality of sensitivity displayed in urban fashion taste revealed a degree of subtle sophistication that characterized it as a sign of proto-modernity. This refined taste in fashion was not the monopoly of the wealthiest townspeople. Rather, it characterized the urban commoner class as a whole. Fashion discourse played an important role in the communicative life of Tokugawa citizens in that it crossed status lines. Given this general passion for fashion and the rise of commercial culture, it is no wonder that even maids began to acquire fashionable items such as silver hair pins in the late Tokugawa period. Behind the masters and ladies of the samurai and wealthy merchant households who could indulge themselves in elegant silk *kimono*, there were many maids and servants who meticulously cleaned the floors so that their masters' fine garments would not get dirty. They were the people who wore cotton to work.

For the working population, striped cotton became the fabric of choice for daily wear. Indigo-dyed threads in two or three different hues could easily be woven into stripes in cotton cloth, creating a wide range of subtly patterned textiles.[81] Thus, even those who could afford only cotton had the opportunity to express their personal preferences in patterns. From the time of the Kyōho era, when stringent orders of frugality were imposed, striped patterns became very popular as everyday wear for all classes.[82] Solid yarn-dyed stripes were more durable, as well as looking colorful and sensible, and could even be *iki* if chicly selected. Thus, even the maids who worked in merchant houses could enjoy a range of new delicate hues in their humble cotton striped *kimono* and could also choose their preferred hairpin styles.

Yosano Buson's well-known narrative poem called "*Shunpū batei no kyoku*," or "Variation on Spring Wind and Riverbank," published in 1777, is a good illustration of the spread of popular interest in fashion. This piece describes a maidservant's enjoyment of a holiday trip home in urban fashion style. The young coquette wanders along the riverbank to her home in the country, proudly displaying her newest fashions along the way while looking down on the lifestyle of the country folk. Buson wrote in a personal letter to a friend that the famous poem was based on his own childhood observations and memories. "When I was a child, I always played with my chums along the riverbank. People and boats were always coming and going along the river."[83] The poet was born in 1716 in the country around Osaka. The river was an opening to the world for the rural villages because it connected them with the larger city of Osaka. Buson continued: "Among the passersby on the river, I used to see country girls who worked as housemaids in Osaka. They would adopt the urban fashions of the day. Their hairstyles imitated those of courtesans. . . . But the young flirts still missed their families and used to come home on holiday to visit their parents."[84] The cultural aspirations of working-class migrants who imitated urban styles, a conspicuous feature of modern Japanese culture until quite recently, had been already noted by the eighteenth-century poet.

Fashion as an Agent of Change

Once people from the lower orders could afford to be fashionable, the volume of demand for clothing became enormous. Under the eighth shogun, Yoshimune, the population of the country reached some thirty million. In the city of Edo alone, a million men and women had to get dressed each morning, which gives some idea of the number of *kimono, obi* belts, collars, underwear, and sandals that had to be produced, transported, and sold to meet the demand. In 1736, statistics for goods shipped to the Osaka market from various regions of Japan indicate that the total amount of textiles was valued at 12,000 *kan* (a unit of silver). Cotton textiles (white and striped) came to 44.6%, Kyoto silk textiles[85] 14.2%, silk 12.1%, imported Chinese cloth 9.5%, and *asa* 9.4%. The lion's share of the fabric market then was clearly supported by the working classes, who wore cotton as their daily working attire. The goods passed through the hands of several sets of traders in order to reach metropolitan consumers, which means that the extensive networks of the cotton trade incorporated a large population into the web of the expanding commercial economy. In the second half of the Tokugawa period, the expansion of cotton and silk production incorporated Japanese agricultural communities into the dense networks of a large-scale market economy. This development further impacted on the various regional "putting-out" textile industries, producing a situation resembling the so-called proto-industrialization of Europe.[86] The increased cotton production spurred related areas of commercial production, the increased cultivation of indigo plants being the most conspicuous example.

Indigo was used not only for making shades of blue but also for creating subtle shades of blue-brown such as *onando cha*[87] (Plate 4). In the early eighteenth century, Awa, Awaji, Yamashiro, and Settsu provinces were famous for their commercial production of indigo. The market for fish-based fertilizer (*hoshika*) expanded in turn because the cultivation of lucrative plants such as cotton and indigo required this type of soil nutrient.[88]

During the late Tokugawa period, the regional *daimyo* governments started to encourage their peasants to undertake commercial agricultural production and handicraft manufacturing. Some local governments also attempted to monopolize trading in these commodities in order to export them to other provinces. Taxes on commodities became important sources of revenue for samurai governments in serious financial difficulty. This diversification of revenue sources, however, was a fundamental departure from the rice-dependent Tokugawa feudal fiscal system. During the late eighteenth and early nineteenth centuries, there were frequent collective uprisings in the rural areas that had experienced proto-industrialization in opposition to government interference with their commodity production and trade. In 1781, for example, the silk producers in Jōshū province successfully opposed the shogun's establishment of official centers for the silk trade. In the Osaka region in 1823, local non-privileged merchants and producers of cotton and vegetable oils initiated a large-scale petition. They mobilized men from 1,307 villages and appealed directly to the shogunate to abolish the monopoly of a few privileged Osaka merchants.[89] So-called village internal conflicts, or *mura sōdō*, also erupted frequently in these regions as ordinary peasants filed numerous lawsuits citing the conduct of village officials. The increase in village internal conflicts undermined the Tokugawa indirect system of social control because the shogun and *daimyo* expected village officials to act as their agents in keeping the villagers under control. The latent contradiction between the feudal political system and ongoing capitalist economic development finally and fitfully surfaced at this point. Throughout the country, conflicts and struggles among the peasantry, owners of rural cottage industries, and the samurai authorities became commonplace. The earliest intimations of political revolution, which would lead to the overturning of the shogunate in 1868, were first noticeable in the economic sphere. Popular cravings for fashion were thus at least partly responsible for eroding the foundation of the Tokugawa state.

At the same time, fashion as an agent of change was not confined to the socio-political dimension of Tokugawa life. Beauty entered the lives of ordinary Japanese people as a wearable aesthetic in the form of *kimono* fashion trends and carried men as well as women into a new realm of aesthetic consciousness. Centuries of political struggle centering on *kimono* fashions significantly altered the Japanese people's level of aesthetic sensitivity. Although people's external appearances looked as if they were in compliance with feudal categories, in reality the bridging functions of the new commercial enterprises and the shogunate's policy of "divide and rule" collided in the marketplace. Tokugawa Japan harbored a growing population of aesthetic individualists who assumed the importance of beauty in their personal attire as a necessity of life.

11

The Information Revolution

Japanese Commercial Publishing and Styles of Proto-modernity

Introduction

Tokugawa proto-modernity coincided with the vigorous development of the commercial publishing industry. The oldest Japanese publishing houses were established in Kyoto at the beginning of the seventeenth century, around the time that Tokugawa Ieyasu, the first shogun, was completing the country's pacification.[1] Many of the Tokugawa publishers were also involved in the retail trade, and their stores were simply called *honya*, or "book establishments." The following two centuries of development transformed the Japanese book trade into one of the most vital publishing cultures in the world at that time.

The first Japanese trade catalog, called *Wakan shoseki mokuroku* (The List of Japanese and Chinese Books in Print), was published in 1666 and listed 2,589 titles. By the time the 1670 catalog went to print, this number had jumped to 3,866 titles, whereas the 1685 list contained 5,934 titles and that of 1692 contained 7,181 titles.[2] Following the remarkable growth in commercial publishing in the second half of the seventeenth century, the eighteenth century saw the popular audience for books grow exponentially as publishers and traders cultivated a new readership by introducing popular subjects presented in an appealing way. According to the city of Edo's official record for 1808, the capital alone had 656 commercial book-lending shops – more than the number of public baths; in the same year, there were 523 commercial bathhouses in the city of Edo.[3] Considering the Japanese fondness for bathing (a custom that had by this time become a part of their lifestyle, even of Edo's working population), it is reasonable to assume that renting books from such shops was also a commonplace activity.

By the early nineteenth century, Japan had become crisscrossed by networks of printed information. An essay published in Osaka in 1807 contains a vivid description of the social phenomenon known as a best-seller.

286

In that year, the Kabuki Theater in Osaka had a new stage hit based on a previously published novel. The citizens of Osaka were excited about the theatrical production, and the novel became more and more popular. Osaka had about three hundred book rental shops at this time. The *kashihon ya*, or commercial book rental shops, found that their business boomed when such a best-seller hit the market:

> The men from the commercial book rental shops put "Three Days Only" labels on the book copies. The delivery men dash into the street. The enthusiastic reception of this book in Osaka is unbelievable beyond description.[4]

The emergence of best-sellers – which were already prominent in the early eighteenth century – indicates that commercial printing, in tandem with the formation of market networks, had changed the nature of information diffusion in Japanese society. Furthermore, the combination of two clusters of cultural networks, publishing and theatrical performance, is remarkable. The expansion of commercial publishing did not simply imply the increased availability of printed books for reading but also introduced the potential of printed media to publicize other forms of cultural activities and human networking. For example, as we have seen, the numerous quick-reference books on *haikai* poetry's lexicon and associations invited novices to jump-start their poetry composition. The amateur poets' enthusiasm was satisfied by the availability of accessible, efficient, and relatively inexpensive commercial publishing that published their pieces. Handy reference books became readily available in almost all branches of aesthetic pursuits and hobbies, including the tea ceremony, flower arrangements, various kinds of singing, *shamisen* music, horticulture, *igo*, and *shōgi* games. Interest in new dress styles would not have been as intense if there had been no *kimono* pattern books or illustrations of high fashion as modeled by courtesans and *Kabuki* actors. In this way, printed matter served as a cognitive bridge in this officially segmented society that connected people outside their local network clusters. The entry of affordable printed material in people's lives represented as well as enabled proto-modern styles of cultural life.

In the Introduction, I defined a network revolution as the simultaneous expansion of various types of social and communicative networks in terms of density, scale, and complexity. Along with the extension of existing political, economic, and associational networks, the rise of commercial publishing was one of the constituent elements of the Tokugawa network revolution. At the time that this network revolution occurred, the availability of cultural resources for diffusion directed the course of developments emanating from the information explosion. For example, literary and artistic classics, as well as introductory information about aesthetic interests and gracious living, were readily available and politically safe forms of knowledge that were also in high demand. Konta Yōzō has rightly described this aspect of the rise of commercial publishing as "the process through which the classics of the aristocracy became the classics of all who were Japanese by birth."[5] Thus, Tokugawa commercial publishing served to disseminate images of Japan in aesthetic terms to the widest possible audience.

Nonetheless, we should not focus too narrowly on the content of the information diffused through commercially produced books. The diffusion, multiplication, and standardization of knowledge are important, but they are only one part of the story of the Tokugawa publishing industry. Books do more than convey knowledge through text and images; they also bring together various groups of people and fields of knowledge in a dynamic manner. In other words, books produce "publics" as I defined the term sociologically – communicative spheres that emerge at the intersections of social and cognitive networks. Books influence the emerging patterns of publics on three distinct network levels. First, the experience of reading a book may provide a temporal shifting of cognitive network connections, and this experience is likely to leave an imprint on a person's patterns of cognitive associational networks, or mental disposition. Second, a book or print may stimulate conversation among its readers, thus facilitating associational activities and communication. It may foster political or ideological movements or simply generate gossip and rumor. In any case, reading a book is not a purely personal activity – it always carries a certain potential for social activities through intersecting social networks. Third, commercial publishing forms and sustains network connections that go well beyond the reader level. In Tokugawa Japan, books were physical entities that were produced and distributed commercially. Changes in cognition and socialization are nested within a complex infrastructure of production, trading, and consumption of books as cultural commodities.

Just as in the case of fashion regulations, the distinctive Tokugawa state–market relationship had a significant influence on the activities of the early modern publishing industry. The shoguns continuously attempted to shut off unauthorized leakages of information through commercial publications, although the publishers often found ways to evade the regulations. At the same time, the trajectory of Tokugawa publishing was also shaped by the industry's internal organizational structure. There were numerous highly competitive small-scale printing shops in the major cities that relied on the flexible and relatively low-cost techniques of woodblock printing. The result was a particular organizational culture that allowed reader-friendly business operations to flourish. The following pages will identify and discuss the internal and external organizational dynamics of

Tokugawa publishing and book distribution that characterized Tokugawa proto-modernity.

History of Tokugawa Commercial Publishing: A Comparative Overview

The vitality of the Japanese publishing industry during the Tokugawa period raises questions about its comparatively distinctive features. Since about 1450 in Europe, when manuscripts were "impressed" on paper by a mechanical printing press and movable type, the commercialization of printing empowered the development of a prototypical form of capitalist production involving printing machines and workers. According to Lucien Febvre and Henri-Jean Martin, as many as two hundred million volumes had been printed in Europe by 1600. The sheer volume of printed matter well deserves to be called an information explosion. The cultural significance of the emergence of commercial presses, however, extended far beyond the large number of printed volumes.

The emergence of commercial publishing as a profitable industry has distinct sociological implications. In many pre-modern societies, printing was primarily patronized by the wealthy and powerful – usually the nobility and religious institutions. Such monumental projects as printing sacred texts or canons would be the most appropriate products of this particular social configuration. In contrast, publishing under the logic of commercial capitalism depends on the demands of a large-scale readership rather than the patronage of elites. If we take commercial printing as a specific example of the network effects of market expansion, we find that scholars have long considered the emergence of commercial printing houses as *sui generis*, unique to the early capitalistic phase of European history. Entrepreneurial publishers in close contact with the dynamics of the popular market can bring unorthodox information into their society by taking risks for the sake of larger profits or by attempting to cultivate a broader readership than presently exists. In comparison to printing projects sponsored by political or religious authorities, commercial publication has long been considered a pre-condition of European modernity. Scholars have propounded a variety of theories regarding the emergence of major cultural and intellectual phenomena in early modern Europe by analyzing their connection with the rise of commercial publishing. For example, as Robert Darnton has shown, the spread of Enlightenment ideas would have been impossible without the existence of commercial publishers. The diffusion of post-Cartesian medical and scientific information was also inseparable from the established credibility of publishers who were willing to print material that challenged older views. In addition, commercial publishing also helped to change the political climate of Europe insofar as the civic discourse that flourished in eighteenth-century cafes and reading circles fed on journals and newspapers, as well as other political and philosophical publications of the period.[6] Furthermore, "print capitalism" – in particular, publishing in vernacular languages rather than in Latin – facilitated the development of what Benedict Anderson has termed "imagined communities,"[7] the forerunners of nationalism. Finally, Norbert Elias's theory regarding the origins of Western European civility was also based on the availability of printing, which enabled such influential manuals as Erasmus's *De civilitate morum puerilium* (On Civility and Good Manners in Youth) to be translated into and published in many European languages. All these and other institutional developments that contributed to the emergence of modern Europe were related in one way or another to commercial publishing.

Clearly, Japanese publishing in the proto-modern period did not mediate or diffuse the equivalent of Enlightenment philosophy, scientific knowledge, or democratic civic discourse. On the other hand, however, the vitality of the Japanese industry is evident from the types of publications that it produced as well as from the variety and popularity of the communicative activities that it fostered. But to measure the comparative vitality of the Tokugawa publishing industry is not an easy task. The growth of the publishing industry in France, however, offers a suggestive comparison. According to Roger Chartier, although the significant development of printed books began much earlier in this part of Europe, French printed titles numbered between five hundred and one thousand annually in the sixteenth and seventeenth centuries, rising to two thousand per year at the end of the *ancien régime*.[8] Japan, though clearly a late developer, was probably producing around 1,500 titles annually toward the end of the Tokugawa regime, according to Henry Smith.[9] In Britain, Germany, and France, the commercial lending libraries, institutions functionally similar to Japanese book rental shops, were considered an important stimulus of the popularization of reading in the late eighteenth century – a phenomenon that was also visible in Tokugawa Japan. Because of the limited primary sources in European countries and Japan, as well as sharp differences in the nature of available primary materials combined with very different social, economic, and political contexts, we cannot simply take the numerical data at face value. We can, however, acknowledge that the commercial success of the Tokugawa book industry stands up very well in comparison with any contemporaneous European example.

In addition, the sheer speed of expansion of commercial publishing under the shogunate is remarkable given the fact that the publishing industry in Japan was virtually non-existent before 1600. By the late seventeenth century, in the space of a few decades following the introduction of commercial printing, a large number of printed books were circulating throughout Tokugawa Japan. The rapidity of this development made it a genuine "information revolution."

The vitality of Tokugawa commercial publishing is even more startling in view of the relatively primitive equipment used to produce the books. Japanese books were produced by a laborious process of carving wooden blocks by hand for direct impression on rice paper. Whereas French printers worked with a technological innovation, namely movable type, which brought about what Elizabeth Eisenstein has termed a "media revolution,"[10] their counterparts in Japan had to carve entire sentences with mirror-image letters on a single wooden block. Although this wood-block process may appear inefficient, the sophisticated craftsmanship of the carvers was both well-adapted to the Japanese writing system, surprisingly speedy, and economically cost-effective. That the Japanese "information revolution" was made possible with technology known in principle since the ancient period is striking in view of the strong emphasis in Western scholarship – though not unchallenged in more recent works – on the invention of printing as a *technological-material* agent of social transformation[11]; the Japanese case suggests that the invention of printing machinery is not the universal Book of Genesis for the narrative concerning the history of printed books.[12]

Early Development and Revival of Japanese Woodblock Printing

Japan's return to woodblock printing following a brief phase of experimentation with movable type poses an intriguing theoretical question because it challenges the earlier thesis of the history of printing, namely that technology determines the speed and direction of social change. It is a remarkable development in view of the fact that Tokugawa Japan had already encountered the technology of movable fonts.

Prior to the Tokugawa period, printed materials had been produced under the auspices of the larger temples and shrines, the imperial court, or other powerful aristocratic patrons.[13] In particular, the Buddhist temples of pre-Tokugawa Japan had contributed a great deal to the development of printing from the eighth century onward. The monks, understandably, were primarily concerned with the publication of Buddhist classics and other religious writings, although the Muromachi period (1336–1573) saw an increased interest in the printing of such Chinese classics as Confucian literature and Chinese poetry. For example, the Gozan (literally "Five Mountains") editions appeared during the Muromachi period.

These were editions of Chinese classics produced by five famous Zen temples then the centers of the study of Chinese classic literature and Confucianism as well as Buddhism.[14] It would be incorrect, however, to think of printed books as enjoying a wide circulation in this period; the primary method of book reproduction was still meticulous hand-copying of original manuscripts. This was particularly true for Japanese literature because it included genres that rarely appeared in print before the Tokugawa period.

One important technological stimulus for the development of Japanese book production came from the West in the late sixteenth century. The Western form of movable type was brought to Japan by Jesuit missionaries in the 1590s. These missionaries produced a variety of books written in Japanese on Japanese language and culture as well as Christian doctrine. The new method of printing, however, was largely confined to the small circle of missionaries. After the shoguns officially prohibited Christianity in 1611, Jesuit printing understandably disappeared. By historical coincidence, however, another form of movable-type printing was imported from Korea as part of the spoils of war during the same period. When the unification ruler Toyotomi Hideyoshi invaded Korea in 1593, his generals brought back a variety of Korean printing presses, metal type fonts, and printed books as booty. The unification rulers, imperial courtiers, and provincial *daimyo*, as well as Buddhist monks, made many attempts to sponsor the Korean method of movable-type printing insofar as publishing projects were still considered a cultural symbol of a ruler's power and prestige.[15] Subsequently, the first generation of Japanese publishing firms began to produce books by using movable-font techniques. Taken together, both Western and Korean influences laid the foundation for the Japanese publishing industry in the early seventeenth century. The immediate result of these innovations was the emergence in Kyoto of the first generation of commercial publishers and booksellers. The early Kyoto publishers used the movable-type technique. As they were still under the patronage of Buddhist temples and political rulers, most of their output was printed editions of Buddhist texts and classics. The new method of printing, imported from a neighboring East Asian culture, was not the immediate catalyst of the dramatic growth in commercial publication. Scholars in the field of Japanese publishing history generally regard the Kanei era (1624–1643) as the beginning of full-scale commercial publishing operations. The pioneering firms, however, did not adopt the Korean version of movable type but instead favored a return to the earlier method of woodblock printing. By the end of the Kanei era, the revival of the woodblock technique and the consequent decline of movable-type printing had established an irreversible trend.[16] Thus, when commercial publishing boomed during the second half of the seventeenth century, the printers used the traditional woodblock method for popular literary productions.

The reasons behind the Japanese preference for the older method of woodblock printing appear somewhat mysterious. One theory advanced by several scholars credits the technological weakness of the East Asian method of typography; its movable fonts could produce only a hundred copies or so at one time.[17] In contrast, a woodblock printer can obtain a considerably larger number of copies from one block. Thus, woodblock printing was an economical method at a time of growing market demand. The limitations of reproduction in Tokugawa movable typesetting, however, are still discussed in Japanese scholarly circles. In my opinion, the decision to revert to woodblock printing was driven by market forces – in essence, the commercialization of publishing during this period. First of all, the complexity of the Japanese writing system made movable type an initially costly investment for the publisher. Unlike the Western vernaculars, whose printing fonts needed only the 26 letters of the Roman alphabet, supplemented by Arabic numerals and punctuation marks, written Japanese required multiple sets of several thousand Chinese ideograms before a printer could set up shop. Most independent publishers lacked the capital necessary for such a large investment. As a result, movable typography in East Asian societies was better suited to monumental projects sponsored by the imperial court or wealthy shrines.

No less important was the fact that woodblock printing conferred the significant advantage of simplifying the process of printing second or third editions. If the publishers wanted to maximize returns on their investment, they had to print as many copies as possible. This consideration did not necessarily favor movable type. It is of course true that if the Japanese had invented a method of preserving typesetting, such as stereotyped lead plates made from impressions of type blocks in clay or soft metal, the situation could have been different. Even in Europe, however, methods of stereotyping did not find broad use until the late eighteenth century. Even if we assume that producing more than a hundred copies from a font of movable type was technically possible during this period, it is doubtful whether this method of reproduction was economically sound. In the mid-seventeenth century, Tokugawa publishers were still unlikely to print a large number of copies.[18] For the operation of a steady business, several hundred copies would have been considered risky for an initial press run. Thus, woodblocks were preferred to movable type not only because they produced more copies but because they accommodated publishers' needs for flexibility in production. Woodblocks allowed publishers to run off additional printings fairly quickly whenever the first printing sold out.

Furthermore, in the initial phases of the Tokugawa publishing industry, there was no procedure for establishing copyright except the physical presence of the woodblocks themselves.[19] Once inscribed, the cut blocks became the "property" of the publisher's family and thereby became tradable entities.[20] When a publisher sold his woodblocks, the sale was regarded as a transfer of publishing rights to the purchaser. Although copyrights acquired better protection after the development of publishing guilds, they were developed primarily to protect the rights of those who carved the woodblocks and received the guild's permission to print the book. The function of inscribed woodblocks as a surrogate definition of publication rights was evident in instances of self-financed printing. An author could underwrite the publication of his or her own manuscript by paying a fee to a commercial publisher; the author then ordinarily kept the woodblocks.[21] In contrast, movable-type printing did not allow comparable proof of ownership rights after completion of the press run.[22]

An additional dimension of the Tokugawa preference for woodblock printing was the block's aesthetic–functional qualities. The aesthetic of this period favored flowing cursive handwriting, which was very difficult to reproduce in movable typography that required all copies of a given character or letter to be identical and interchangeable. As the popularization of reading progressed alongside the expansion of commercial publishing, the functional advantages of woodblock prints also became obvious. In woodblock printing, witty illustrations or even colorful pictures could be easily incorporated into the page layout together with the text. Many of the most popular genres in commercial publishing were illustrated works during the late Tokugawa period. Since the new Tokugawa readership lacked a traditional educational background, the fact that woodblock printing could easily accommodate *furigana* (transliterations of Chinese characters consisting of *kana* phonemes written beside the character in much smaller fonts) was also an attractive feature. Indeed, since Chinese ideograms functioned within the Japanese language system in a manner similar to the persistence of Latin roots in English, reading might have been a less popular activity in Tokugawa society without the development of *furigana* printing. But given the widespread appeal of attractive pictures and *furigana* annotations, Tokugawa publishers produced books suitable for popular consumption, especially among readers who stood outside the established social and literary elites.

To sum up, although the return to woodblock printing by Tokugawa commercial publishers may look like cultural conservatism, the businessmen had good economic incentives to favor this method. It was the very impetus of the publishers' move toward commercialization that encouraged Japanese entrepreneurs to return to woodblock printing. The significance of the Japanese experience is the evidence it supplies that a flourishing publishing industry does not require the introduction of mechanical printing as a necessary pre-condition.

Competition, Production Methods, and
Reader-Friendly Books

As the main location of publishing moved from the studios of Buddhist temples to commercial publishing houses, publication became less subject to control by established religious institutions. Of course, this statement requires some qualification. The demands for Buddhist sacred texts, Chinese classics, and Confucian texts remained strong throughout the period; some Buddhist temples continued to support the publication of their own religious texts. Yet, compared to their prominence in the medieval period, it is fair to say that religious organizations played increasingly smaller roles in the world of Tokugawa publishing.[23]

In the Tokugawa book world, publishing was above all else a commercial activity. This characteristic meant that the supply-and-demand dynamic of a capitalist economy controlled the distribution and expansion of publishing. In addition, the decision to return to woodblock printing helped the commercial publishing industry to develop some interesting characteristics. First of all, this method of printing kept demand for capital relatively low. The fairly modest amount of capital required for start-up was a constant inducement to small entrepreneurs to enter the publishing business. Throughout the Tokugawa period, 3,757 new publisher-booksellers emerged, while 1,530 were known to have closed down (Figure 11.1). Because the businesses that ceased operation were not always clearly identified, we cannot use these data as the basis for calculating the number of publishers active in any certain period.[24] Rather, we must note the energetic rhythm of the publishing business. There were always new entries in the field – as well as failures – throughout the period.

The patterns of establishment of new publishing firms in Kyoto, Osaka, Edo, and other provinces throughout the Tokugawa period are summarized in Figure 11.2. Although those in the trade at the time often deplored the presence of "excessive competition," the frequent emergence of new publishers invigorated the industry. Publishers vied with one another to come up with new genres of printed matter that would be both useful and attractive. If movable type had been the only available method of printing, given its requirement of a large initial investment in machinery and huge sets of fonts, coupled with its lack of flexibility for later printings, small merchants would have been excluded from commercial publishing for financial reasons. This limitation would have inhibited the development of the industry as a whole, as one source of its vitality was the continuous influx of newcomers, who often brought with them fresh ideas.[25]

A second characteristic that contributed to the formation of the distinctive Tokugawa book culture was the reader-friendly appearance of the books themselves – in particular, the use of *furigana* and attractive

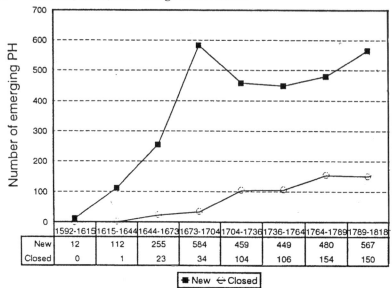

Figure 11.1. Number of New and Closed Publishing Houses in Japan, 1592–1818. *Source*: Constructed based on data culled from Morita Seigo "Edoki Shoten no hassei keikō"; see note 24.

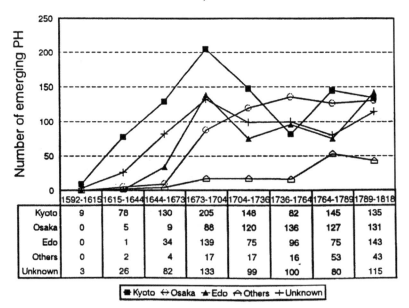

Figure 11.2. Number of Emerging Publishing Houses in Japan, 1592–1818. *Source*: Constructed based on data culled from Morita Seigo, "Edoki Shoten no hassei keikō"; see note 24.

illustrations. These features encouraged the habit of reading in a large segment of the population outside the traditional elite circles of readership.[26] The Japanese return to woodblock printing thus made an important contribution to the spread of civilizing influences among ordinary people. Tokugawa publishers were able to adapt rapidly and efficiently to changing tastes and market trends by bringing out large numbers of titles in the newer popular genres. This flexibility might have been lacking if Japanese publishing had been dominated by wealthy capitalists or aristocratic sources of patronage.

Third, unlike the European counterpart, in which commercial *printers* – with a substantial investment in machinery, equipment, and technological skills, coupled with the difficulties surrounding second and third printings – played a much larger role, woodblock printing enabled Tokugawa *publishers* to take more independent initiatives regarding the production of culture. Had the development of Tokugawa printing centered on the same machinery, the substantial investment involved and the difficulties in printing small runs of successive editions with movable fonts might have resulted in the dominance of large printing houses reliant on contract jobs from such patrons as religious organizations. Instead, the return to woodblock printing allowed Tokugawa publishing houses to function as primary centers of planning and initiating publishing projects. During the Tokugawa period, wood-carvers were independent craftsmen who worked on publishers' orders. Although the carvers were functionally similar to Western printers, they had no investment in any machinery except their own skilled hands. As a result, publishers with a profit motive were central to the production of books in Tokugawa Japan. This characteristic further accelerated a preference for books that were closely connected to the demands of the market.

The Popularization of Literature and the Spread of Civilized Knowledge

The period from the late seventeenth to the beginning of the eighteenth century also saw the maturation of a national market economy that made publishing for a mass market commercially profitable. The core of the Japanese publishing industry gradually shifted from Kyoto to Osaka, which had become the commercial capital of the country. By 1697, Osaka had a population of approximately 370,000 that supported 37 publisher-booksellers, according to a city guidebook. This is certainly a respectable number even by modern standards.[27] The Osaka book traders, however, had a different business orientation from that of their counterparts in Kyoto. Unlike Kyoto publishers, who grew up in the center of

Table 11.1. *Japanese book titles, 1666–1692*

	Total number of titles	Scholarly/religious books	Other
1666	2,693	1,514 (56%)	1,179 (44%)
1692	7,163	3,031 (42%)	4,132 (58%)

Sources: *Wakan Shoseki Mokuroku* (List of Japanese and Chinese Books in Print, 1666); *Koueki Shoseki Mokuroku* (List of Books in Print, 1692).

traditional medieval high culture, Osaka publishers had to consider the tastes and interests of a new popular market. Consequently, they brought out such innovative publications as Ihara Sukiyaki's famous stories of the "floating world," as well as many kinds of "how-to" books and other manuals.

In Kyoto, various lists of books in print, or *shoseki mokuroku*, appeared at regular intervals from the late seventeenth century onward.[28] An examination of these catalogs indicates not only the extent of the growth and commercialization of Japanese publishing but also an increasing tendency toward literary popularization and secularization in the course of the seventeenth century.[29] As Table 11.1 indicates, the total number of titles in print increased by more than 250% over a period of 26 years. This remarkable increase reflects the booming expansion of the publishing market following the establishment of the shogunate. The Kyoto book lists were categorized under subject headings. As Table 11.1 illustrates, traditional scholarly books on Buddhism and Confucianism – the original subject matter of temple publishing – still comprised a major fraction of titles on both lists. On the other hand, titles of a less academic nature – fiction, practical books, and "how-to" literature – multiplied significantly during the period in question. Close observation of the categories indicates that the 1685 catalog has titles listed under "music," "flower arrangement," "travel writing," "fashion books and illustrated books," "fiction," and "romance and entertainment," whereas the earlier catalogs lack such classifications. The number of manuals for writing *haikai* poetry also showed a dramatic upsurge. In the 1670 list, *haikai* poetry included only 133 titles, whereas the 1685 list contained 358 and the 1692 list had 676.[30] The popularity of how-to books and introductory guides to the various arts indicates that the new Tokugawa readership was no mere collection of passive consumers but included active participants in cultural production. The publishers' efforts to market their wares to a mass audience are also evident in the expansion of the genre of "Amorous Books." The 1670 catalog has no subcategory for this type of literature. By 1685, however, 55 titles were listed, and by 1692 the number had grown to 119. The 1692 catalog even added a subcategory of "pillow pictures and entertainments."

An excerpt from a conversation between two Tokugawa publishers illustrates the vitality of Tokugawa book production:

> [A publisher from Kyoto said,] "These days we have to put the heavy [academic] works on the back burner to keep the business in good shape. The stuff like *kōshoku-bon* ["Amorous Books"] and *chōhōki* is much more popular." A publisher from Osaka replied, "Oh, I couldn't agree with you more. Since *Kanai Chōhōki* [The Handbook for Domestic Life] hit the stands this kind of book has taken over the Osaka market."[31]

One can easily imagine this exchange occurring between two contemporary Japanese publishers since romantic fiction and how-to books are still best-selling genres in Japan as elsewhere. But in fact this snatch of conversation appeared in an essay called *Genroku Taiheiki* (Peaceful Chronicle of Genroku), published in 1702, when the political tranquility of the Tokugawa period had brought prosperity to a number of commercial ventures.[32] Among the various practical books, the *chōhōki* were especially popular during the Genroku period (1688–1702). *Chōhō* has several different meanings, including "great treasure," "convenience," and "methods."[33] More than 20 different *chōhōki* came off the presses during the Genroku era, a period that witnessed the emergence of the lifestyle of urbanized commoners as a distinctive subculture in Tokugawa Japan. Although no book with *chōhōki* in its title appeared on the publishers' list of 1670, there were 12 such titles on the list of 1692.

By the mid- to late eighteenth century, the proportion of religious titles had shrunk considerably. In the lists of 1754 and 1772, only about 15% of the titles were related to Buddhism.[34] This small percentage presents a striking contrast to the seventeenth-century catalogs, in which Buddhist literature typically comprised roughly 40% of all titles. To be sure, Buddhist publications continued to be strong sellers during the Tokugawa period. In the later Tokugawa period, however, the center of gravity and innovation in commercial publishing had clearly shifted away from Buddhist texts in the direction of secular materials. The secularization of the readership, in terms of its increasing interest in non-religious topics, established a clear trend in Japanese commercial publishing.

The popularization of literary subject matter in the Tokugawa period should not be interpreted, however, as a break with the traditions of medieval Japanese culture. By the time Tokugawa commercial publishing came into full operation, a number of different literary genres had already circulated in handwritten manuscripts. These included classical tales, *waka* poetry, essays, and the lyrics of Nō drama. Although these manuscripts did not circulate widely outside courtly circles, they preserved and consolidated a rich and impressive canon of aristocratic literature that had attained classic stature. These classics had come to embody all the polish and refinement that the ordinary reader associated with the upper classes. Predictably, the commercial publishers first turned to the classics in their appraisal of the popular market and brought out printed editions of these works that were within the reach of culture-hungry readers outside the aristocracy. Japan's civilizing process helped to disseminate the major concepts and images of the medieval period among a larger population.

The Spread of Literacy

The expansion of book distribution networks reflected as well as promoted the popularization of reading under the shogunate. Ronald Dore has attempted to measure this phenomenon in terms of the percentage of school-age children in actual school attendance. Dore estimates that 43% of boys and 10% of girls received some kind of schooling by the end of the Tokugawa period. Although this figure is quite high for a pre-modern society, some scholars believe that Dore's estimate is too conservative.[35] In any case, however, measurements of the literacy rate in the general population for this period are inevitably speculative because reliable data are scarce. It is likely, however, that the number of adults with some reading ability was considerably higher than the figures for school attendance suggest, in view of the fact that formal schooling was usually called *tenarai*, literally "hand-learning," because it included learning to copy characters with a brush. Without attendance at *tenarai*, the average Japanese would find it very difficult to write correctly or read the complicated Chinese characters. On the other hand, many people were able to read some types of simple material provided they had somehow learned to read the *kana* phonemes. The samurai class certainly boasted a higher rate of literacy than the commoners, since most samurai men occupied government administrative posts that required a working knowledge of writing. During this early period, it is a reasonable assumption that most Japanese with good reading ability – including the ability to read Chinese characters – were either upper-class townspeople or farmers who did not have to perform manual labor.

From the beginning of Tokugawa state formation, the shogunate's system of social control required leading commoners to have a good command of reading and writing. As the Tokugawa bureaucracy settled into its permanent structure, a paper-shuffling mentality characterized the procedures of the samurai's vassalic bureaucracy. Subordinates were forced to adhere to an elaborate set of rules when filing petitions and preparing formal documents for their administrative superiors. Since the Tokugawa state lacked direct methods of social control, the task of routine social discipline fell to such mid-range organizations as villages, city wards, and trade guilds. This delegation of responsibility in turn meant that executive members of village governing boards or trade guilds – who were not members of the samurai class – were also required to write numerous reports and petitions to the samurai authorities in addition to keeping adequate records of local affairs.

Numerous ordinances and orders were also handed down from the samurai government to the villages and city wards, and they had to be read aloud by some responsible literate individual to those who could not read. In this way, people with higher degrees of literacy usually became the key members of communities because they were better equipped to function as the nodes of communication networks. As a result, a high degree of literacy could give some persons a hegemonic edge over fellow villagers who did not have such skills. Thus, besides their political function of relaying official decrees to the villagers, the village chiefs tended to serve as information centers through their purchases of commercially produced books and prints. We find some interesting examples of a *shōya*'s (village head, commoner status) literary interests in diaries and records from the Osaka hinterland. For example, a wealthy eighteenth-century farmer named Mori Chōemon, in Kusaka village, which was connected to Osaka by water transport on the Yamato River, faithfully recorded the visits of traveling book traders in his diary.[36] Once a month or so, he was visited by a book trader from one of the Osaka shops who rented as well as sold books.[37] Mori was a good customer who made frequent purchases; in August 1727, he noted the purchase of three books: one on old calendars, one a guide to the city of Edo, and one on letter writing. A month later, he bought two more books. In October, he acquired a well-known large, illustrated encyclopedia in 80 volumes, the *Wakan sansai zue* (Japanese and Chinese Things Illustrated). He also borrowed a number of works of fiction, including ghost stories and war tales.[38] Interestingly, Mori's diary also contains many entries in which he notes that he had loaned some of his books to other villagers, as well as reminders to himself to borrow books from other villagers. These included books on highly cultured subjects, which indicates that the owners of books were not limited to the *shōya*'s household, according to Yokota Fuyuhiko.[39] At the same time, there clearly were more readers in the village than book owners, and "there was a network of book lending among the villagers.... [T]he diary tells us that such social relationships were not limited to book lending, but also included a variety of such cultural associational activities as Chinese poetry, *igo* games, flower arranging, and *jōruri* songs."[40] The Mori family's cultural life was situated within the context of the Tokugawa network of aesthetic circles that has been described in earlier chapters.

Literacy among the commoner population spread rapidly outside the wealthier commoner families by the turn of the eighteenth century. A story published in 1725 indicates that access to elementary education had markedly expanded within one generation. The father of a family who runs a rice-cleaning shop is talking to his children:

> [Father]: "When your dad was young, kids weren't given a tutor for writing and reading (*tenarai*) unless the family was really well-off. In any town ward, there were at most only three to five people who could write. Your dad, of course, didn't have a tutor. I can't even form the character "i" [the first character of the Japanese syllabary] correctly. Somehow, though, I managed to learn to read from experience. Nowadays the world has changed, and even the daughter of a humble household like ours can have lessons in writing and reading."[41]

It is clear that the smooth functioning of the Tokugawa market economy depended on written communicative exchanges, a requirement that encouraged more people to learn to write in order to participate. Capitalist operations required the keeping of account books and sales records as well as writing contracts and various other documents. The high demand for literacy in commercial enterprises is evident from even a cursory review of the dozens of manuals and guidebooks during this period. Many writing handbooks featured model examples of contract letters. For example, a model letter for hiring a nurse for a baby was included in a Tokugawa encyclopedic dictionary, or *setsuyō-shū*. Even the smaller merchants regarded some reading ability as a business necessity – as exemplified by the owner of the rice-cleaning shop who acquired the rudiments of literacy "from experience" in the absence of childhood schooling (Figure 11.3).

Peddlers and Book Rental Shops: Networks of Book Distribution

Changes in readership, book ownership, and the actual production of books comprise only part of the story of the popular information revolution. Just as continuous small investments of capital invigorated and expanded the publishing industry, the development of book distribution networks put printed books within the reach of ordinary people. From the beginnings of Japanese commercial publishing, book peddlers played an important role in the distribution of popular books.[42] Some of these vendors advertised their books in a "town crier" fashion by calling out their wares from the street.[43] In addition to the itinerant peddlers, many retail bookstores, sometimes combined with publishing houses, could be found in the major cities by the Genroku era (1688–1704). To promote their publications, such book establishments also sold their products door-to-door.

Figure 11.3. Education for Girls. Girls learning to read and write, from *Ehon Sakaegusa* (Picture Book of Prosperity) by Katsukawa Harushio. Illustrated book, 1790. Education for girls became more widespread in the late Tokugawa period.

Many book peddlers were employed by large booksellers in major cities and visited their good customers in outlying towns and villages on a regular basis. These peddlers sold as well as rented books. In addition, mail-order service was available for readers in outlying districts. Peddlers carrying piles of books on their shoulders became a familiar part of the Tokugawa landscape by the late seventeenth century in rural areas as well as in the cities. The book peddler became such a familiar figure that he even appeared in various *ukiyo-e* prints. A physician named Phillipp Franz von Siebold, who arrived at Nagasaki in 1823 as the medical professional for the Dutch trade mission, was deeply impressed by the itinerant peddlers carrying full loads of books in their backpacks. When von Siebold asked Japanese craftsmen to make some dolls that he thought representative of Japanese life for his ethnographical collection, they never failed to make the figure of a hard-working book peddler (Figure 11.4).

One symbolic measure of the popularization of reading was the proliferation of *kashihon ya*, or commercial book rental shops. Nagatomo Chiyoji, who has done extensive research into the history of the *kashihon ya* during the Tokugawa period, maintains that these book rental shops were in existence by the late seventeenth century, if not sooner.[44] By the eighteenth century, the book rental shops increased the circulation of

Figure 11.4. Peddler Doll. The figure, most likely, of a book peddler. Phillipp Franz von Siebold, who arrived at Nagasaki in 1823 as the medical professional for the Dutch trade mission, asked Japanese crafts-men to make some dolls that he thought representative of Japanese life for his ethnographical collection.

books among readers who could not easily afford to buy them outright. In the *kashihon ya*, a reader could borrow a copy of a new book for about one-sixth of the purchase price – although the cost varied considerably from store to store.[45] The *kashihon ya* began to flourish even more vigorously toward the end of the eighteenth century. Records indicate that when the book rental shops were ordered by the shogunate to form self-governing groups, Edo alone had over 656 such shops by 1808. Another Edo record from the 1830s listed 800 book renting shops.[46] The owners and employees of these stores charged out books not only in the shops themselves but also carried them personally to the houses of regular customers. If anything, the house-to-house visits appear to have been more common than customers' trips to the stores since we have so many descriptions in Tokugawa literature of book dealers with copies to rent visiting their customers' houses.[47]

For customers with limited reading skills, the Tokugawa bookstores offered plenty of illustrated humorous works that could be enjoyed even without a high level of literacy. Included among these illustrated books were works that verged on the pornographic. Thus, a collection of *senryū* (comical short verses) called *Yanagidaru* (the Willow Cask) included the following suggestive verses about book renting shops:

Kashihon ya	A book rental shop
Muhitsu ni kasumo	Carrying copies for
Moteitaru	Those who cannot write
Kashihon ya	A book rental merchant
Nanio misetaka	Was slapped by the customer
Dō tsukare	What did he show her?[48]

The first comical verse indicates that the shops served not only "readers" but also patrons who were barely literate. Illustrated works of light fiction could be enjoyed by readers of modest attainment because the pictures were the center of interest in this genre. Some illustrations were quite explicit, as the second poem suggests. Taken together, these verses reflect the everyday familiarity of books in the lives of Tokugawa people, even those with marginal reading abilities.

Book rental shops were major forces in the creation and promotion of the new phenomenon of best-sellers. At the beginning of the nineteenth century, Santō Kyōden (1761–1816), a writer of popular fiction, emphasized the importance of the book dealer's recommendations for a publication's sale:

> [A book is] like a prospective bride looking for a husband. . . . The publisher is the parent, and the reader is the groom . . . [with] the

bookshop owner as the go-between. . . . A go-between might say, "Here is such-and-such a girl. She looks like a perfect match! . . . If a go-between promotes and praises the prospective bride to minimize weak points and to interpret bad qualities as signs of good character, even a not-so-popular girl can find a desirable husband! Everything about a book's success depends on good promotion by the honorable book rental shops.[49]

Because Tokugawa booksellers usually visited their customers' houses, they became quite knowledgeable about readers' tastes and preferences. The book merchants could describe the current trendsetters in each reader's favorite category and keep him or her abreast of new titles. During the late Tokugawa period, it became possible for publishers to print a thousand copies of an average *gesaku* (popular comical fiction), safe in the knowledge that they could expect solid sales to the network of lending libraries, which amounted to about a thousand shops nationwide. *Gesaku* became the most popular genre in Edo in the late Tokugawa period; among them, copiously illustrated books for light reading sometimes called *kibyōshi*, or "books with yellow covers," dominated the popular book market. The publishers kept the price of *kibyōshi* very low. A thin volume with illustrations might cost 8 to 12 *mon* at the beginning of the nineteenth century. This sum was slightly higher than the cost of a visit to a public bathhouse but probably less than a simple bowl of *soba* noodles, which usually cost 16 *mon*.[50]

State Regulation of Publishing

The combination of a high rate of literacy, efficient printing technology, and extensive distribution networks meant that printed materials had a major impact on the daily communicative life of Tokugawa people. In contrast with the formal political order, which subdivided the population according to a complicated hierarchy of feudal categories, books carried information to their readers without regard to social status. Given the small scale and large number of publishing companies, as well as the flexibility of woodblock technology, one might have expected the emergence of critical discourse against the feudal order expressed in printed media. In actual fact, however, the Tokugawa regime made the organization of intellectual political opposition quite difficult, even though subversive expressions were abundant in Tokugawa commercial publishing.

The shogunate, still a military regime at heart, had no compunction about the prohibition of antigovernmental actions and discourse. The shoguns also borrowed a system of book censorship from the Chinese at Nagasaki in order to block Christian books written in Chinese from entering Japan. The Tokugawa policy of strict regulation of international trade and limited diplomatic relations with other countries simplified the process of book censorship. Japan's geographical isolation and the distinctiveness of the Japanese language made it easier for the shoguns to control underground publishing produced outside Japan as long as they kept close tabs on the port of Nagasaki, which was the only official location for international trade.[51]

On the other hand, the Tokugawa shoguns lacked strong direct methods of social control on their domestic terrain. The shogunate did not institute a nationwide office of state censorship for publishing. Furthermore, Edo and other large Japanese cities during this period did not have an effective police force directly supervised by the shogunate. The magistrate offices of South and North Edo, which took turns overseeing city administration, from fire prevention and publishing activities to the adjudication of civil suits, operated with a staff of about 500 samurai officers. Of this number, only 24 were assigned to "patrol duties" resembling the functions of a modern police officer.

The shoguns' efforts to control domestic publishing were intensified around the time when the Tokugawa economy was prospering and the commercial publishing industry had begun full-scale operations during the late seventeenth century.[52] The regime frequently issued warnings against the publication of anything "new." For example, one ordinance (Edo Town Ordinance of 1673) said: "Do not mention matters related to the kōgi [the public authority, i.e., the shogunate]. When you plan to publish anything that might annoy others, or that deals with new and curious matters, you must file a petition with the magistrate's office and receive guidance."[53] Obviously, these admonitions cannot have had much effect since similar ordinances were constantly being issued. The shoguns' enforcement of censorship edicts continued to be arbitrary at best, reflecting the differing attitudes of rulers and policy makers in different eras.

Around that time, the versatility of woodblock printing allowed the Japanese commercial publishers to produce popular books of a kind that the authorities had never seen before. For example, the "Yaoya Oshichi Great Fire" of 1682, in which an adolescent named Oshichi allegedly started a fire so that she could see her lover again and instead succeeded in burning down the major part of downtown Edo, was an event made to order for yellow journalism and public interest in tales of private passion and public catastrophe. Oshichi's public execution at the tender age of 17 added a further touch of drama to the story. Subsequently, Oshichi became the heroine of popular Japanese songs and stories. Street musicians openly played songs that retold Oshichi's dramatic story. The popular writer Saikaku adapted her biography for his novel *Yaoya Monogatari*

(The Story of Yaoya Oshichi, 1686), while a *Kabuki* production called *Oshichi Utasaibun* (Ritual Songs for Oshichi) was performed in Osaka.[54] These are just a few examples of the steamy atmosphere generated by the overlapping communicative networks of the theater, the printed media, and gossip about sensational current events. The circulation of spicy rumors and songs was especially damaging to the image of ideal order that the shogun's castle town of Edo was supposed to represent. An ordinance of 1686 subsequently attempted to lay down the law:

> These days, there are city dwellers who publish such outrageous materials as reckless songs and rumors about recent events. House owners in urban areas should look into these matters carefully and try to prevent [their tenants] from publishing such things. Those who sell these items on street corners should be apprehended by the town warden and reported to the authorities.[55]

The ethnomentality shared by samurai authorities and commoners alike often placed rumor and reckless songs in the same category as natural disasters – as omens or oracular revelations of wrongdoing on the ruler's part. In an urban society with as many interconnections as Edo in the Tokugawa period, any item of oral gossip was quickly translated into more credible printed forms of expression and carried throughout the country in the book peddlers' backpacks. Printed materials amplified the impact of unofficial information by linking and combining different types of communicative activity.

The inauguration of the eighth Tokugawa shogun, Yoshimune, who was known for his militant opposition to conspicuous spending and moral laxity, was marked by an attempt to construct a more effective system of surveillance of the publishing industry. In 1721, the shogunate prohibited the publication of *yomiuri*, a collection of loose news sheets about current events, which were characterized by popular forms of yellow journalism that often focused on such sensational topics as love suicides.[56] Even then, the shogunate did not institute a direct system of censorship, choosing instead to rely on the publishers' guilds' self-regulation. The Publishing Regulations of 1722 can be summarized as follows:

1. From now on, any new or confusing interpretations of Confucianism, Buddhism, Shintō, medicine, or poetry are prohibited.
2. Amorous stories are not to be published.
3. It is forbidden to discuss other families' genealogies.
4. The author's and publisher's real names must be printed at the end of the book.

5. It is not permissible to mention the name of the Honorable Gongen [the first shogun, Tokugawa Ieyasu] or anything regarding the Tokugawa clan under any circumstances.

These rules must be carefully observed. . . . Any new publication is to be meticulously examined by the guild.[57]

Following these regulations, all publishers were required to submit manuscripts to the guild for permission to publish before the woodblocks were carved. Predictably, the "amorous books" disappeared from the trade book catalogs published by the guild, although these items continued to be available on the open market. The Tokugawa publishers became particularly careful to avoid irritating the shoguns through references to current events, especially those of a scandalous nature.

Under this new regulation, when a Tokugawa publisher wanted to publish new books or to carve new woodblocks to reprint previously published books, he had to submit a formal petition and a manuscript to the guild's coordinators (*gyōji*). If the *gyōji* judged a manuscript to be in violation of the shogunate's regulations, they turned down the application. If they had difficulty evaluating the manuscript, they sent it to the shogunate's magistrate for a final judgment. If the *gyōji* thought the manuscript resembled a book on another publisher's list, they circulated it among the members of the guild. If the book passed muster as a completely new project, with the guild's seal of approval, the publisher applied to the shogunate for permission to carve a new woodblock in addition to submitting the manuscript (*kaihan negai*). Only after these steps had been completed was permission granted for publication. After the carving was complete, the publisher then sent the woodblock to the guild in order to register the copyright. Once registered, the copyright was protected even if the woodblock was destroyed by fire.

Following the liberal mercantile policies of Tanuma Okitsugu, who controlled the shogun's government between 1767 and 1786, the so-called Kansei reforms were instituted by the more conservative Matsudaira Sadanobu. Starting in 1787, Sadanobu, as *rōjū* (Chief of Senior Councillors), attempted to implement strict social policies to control the increasingly commercialized Tokugawa culture, and book publishing became an important target for political reform.[58] Around this time, a number of humorous stories parodied Sadanobu's political rigidity. This time, the shogunate extended its disciplinary horizon not only to the *mono no hon,* or "highbrow" book guild, but also to the popular *sōshi* book guilds and even the rental bookstore guilds. According to Takizawa Bakin, a contemporary popular writer, 42 titles of popular fiction that had not received proper permission from the guild in 1796–1797 were banned.[59] In addition, Sadanobu cracked down on the so-called "literati in the Tenmei salon," a loose assemblage of writers and poets who gathered to enjoy comic poetry (*kyōka*) and illustrated humorous stories (*kibyōshi*). For example, Hōseidō Kisanji, who was in fact a vassal samurai of the Akita *han* named Hirazawa Heikaku, was reprimanded by his master and stopped writing fiction. Koikawa Harumachi, also a vassal samurai, received a summons to appear before Matsudaira Sadanobu. He was reported to have died from an illness, but some believed that he had committed suicide. On the side of serious publications, Hayashi Shihei (1738–1793), who published books on the danger of foreign invasion, was placed under house arrest (*chikkyo*), and his books and woodblocks were confiscated. It was not for private citizens to discuss the shogun's policies. Sadanobu's heavy-handed penalties discouraged writers from pursuing their activities.

Therefore, politically conscious scholars tended to submit their manuscripts on political subjects directly to powerful individual samurai, hoping that their opinions would be appreciated and adopted by the authorities. Under such circumstances, particularly after the introduction of guild censorship, the bulk of intellectual production during this period was never published but was instead circulated and preserved in the form of handwritten copies.[60]

However, the shogunate's policies on cultural and lifestyle matters changed frequently, depending on the policy makers in charge at the time. Furthermore, there were numerous instances of entrepreneurs who were willing to test the boundaries of the shogunate's rigidity and the established guilds' power to enforce the shogunate's rules. Because the capital needed for a publishing venture in the Tokugawa period was a relatively small amount and directly connected to the marketplace, the publishers' guilds never acquired a complete monopoly on publication. Throughout the Tokugawa period, new publishers were constantly emerging and declining. Underground publishing outside the control of the guilds was also easily carried out because woodblock printing did not require visibly conspicuous machinery and space. The Tokugawa publishing industry never lost its adventurous spirit.

Organizational Structures of the Tokugawa Intellectual World

We have reviewed several major structural factors that contributed to the success of or otherwise influenced the Tokugawa publishing industry, namely the flexible and competitive publishing market; the patterns of book distribution; a high rate of literacy among the general population; and the shoguns' attempts to regulate the content of publications. In addition, we should briefly review other factors that affected the social position of publishing under the shogunate. These include: (1) the attitude of the state toward the intellectual world; (2) organizations of intellectuals; and (3) the composition of the ruling elite. Although these factors may seem to be tangential to the history of books narrowly defined, they are nonetheless critical to an adequate understanding of the social position of publishing in Tokugawa Japan. The French experience will serve to clarify the sociological point I wish to make. For example, we find that the *ancien régime* in France not only implemented direct censorship of printed matter but also supported scholars and men of letters through state subsidies of royal academies. Large sums of money were lavished on favored poets, dramatists, and other writers. Although the French state's largesse to literature and the fine arts may seem to reflect a deep interest in culture, its generous funding was channeled only to individuals and journals of honorable standing in the world of letters. Robert Darnton describes the situation in French publishing under the *ancien régime*:

> ...during the late eighteenth century; and that word is the term one meets everywhere in the Old Regime: privilege. Books themselves bore privileges granted by the grace of the king.... Privileged journals exploited royally granted monopolies. The privileged Comédie Française, Académie Royale de Musique and Académie Royale de Peinture et de Sculpture legally monopolized the stage, opera and the plastic arts. The Académie Française restricted literary immortality to forty privileged individuals, while privileged bodies like the Académie des Sciences and the Société Royale de Médecine dominated the world of science. And above all these corps rose the supremely privileged cultural elite who kept *le monde* all to themselves.[61]

One immediate effect of state patronage in the French model was an increase in state control of printed discourse. Perhaps, however, a more serious effect was the literary establishment's intensified control over nonestablished discourse. In the French model of well-organized literary establishments with direct censorship, a monopolistic printing guild, and a centralized police force, literary "outsiders" were obliged to go, according to Darnton, to underworld printers.

In contrast to the French pattern, the military nature of the Tokugawa regime was not conducive to the state's organized effort to control the world of scholarship. The Tokugawa shogunate did not establish a public guild of intellectuals, scholars, or artists. The Tokugawa shoguns, whose family itself was descended from a provincial military lord, differed from the aristocrats of the imperial court, whose elitism and sense of class identity were based on their ability to compose *waka* poetry and participate in similar ritualized cultural activities. As military rulers, most shoguns and their immediate subordinates did not attempt to promote aggressively certain literary tastes or standards of scholarship over others. Apart from the shoguns' official patronage of the Hayashi Confucian School, the Tokugawa rulers did not develop publicly recognized institutions that monopolized artistic or intellectual prestige or privilege.[62] Although the shogunate's regulation of publishing appears heavy-handed by modern standards, it did not have a systematic cultural policy that would have justified the foundation of a gatekeeper institution. Thus, with some notable exceptions, such as Matsudaira Sadanobu, the state authorities did not ordinarily intervene in ideological controversies among the literati.

Tokugawa intellectuals were institutionally less officially organized to the degree that they could exercise the function of gatekeeping over the content of publication. Tokugawa Japan never adopted the Chinese system of Confucian civil service examinations, which organized the literati into a hierarchy of scholar-bureaucrats. The Chinese examination system provided a direct route to joining the ruling elite while maintaining high standards of Confucian scholarship, ideological rigor, and writing style. Kai-wing Chow has noted that "... [s]tudents preparing for all levels of the civil service examination constituted one of the largest reading publics in the sixteenth and seventeenth centuries."[63] Consequently, the publication of Confucian texts and study guides was the most important part of commercial publishing in late imperial China. Commentaries on the *Four Books* (the most important Confucian classics for examinations) were published to help students pass the examinations. Since the examinations required not only in-depth knowledge of the Confucian canon but also a high level of literary skill and stylistic sophistication, the publication of examination aids became a full-blown industry. The rise of commercial publishing in China provided scholars with new opportunities for income and fame as editors and writers of examination guides. As a result, the civil service examination system became the central focus of the Chinese scholar's intellectual life in one way or another.

In contrast, commercial publishing in Tokugawa Japan did not have an institutional and intellectual focus comparable to the Chinese examination system. The ruling class of Tokugawa Japan was the samurai, whose collective identity stemmed from the warrior culture of the medieval period. Although, with the pacification of the Tokugawa, the samurai formed what I refer to as "vassalic bureaucracy," they were a breed very different from the Chinese mandarins, scholar-gentlemen who had passed the most competitive examinations in the Confucian system. The samurai's status was primarily hereditary; they were not required to meet any kind of academic standard. To be sure, the cultivated samurai's reading list usually included such Confucian classics as the *Four Books* and assorted commentaries on them. Considered as an educational tool for the training of a samurai's moral character, Neo-Confucianism's influence increased over the course of the Tokugawa period. Yet, for the samurai elite, there also existed a countervailing tendency based on the medieval legacy of the warrior culture to prize actions above words. Between the hereditary status system and military tradition, the position of Confucian scholars under the shogunate was relatively marginal. Scholars in Tokugawa Japan were typically regarded as experts on a par with artists, poets, medical doctors, and other specialists who served as private tutors in the circle of the *daimyo* and shogun houses. The lack of institutionally privileged authority in the Tokugawa intellectual world also meant that it was difficult to formulate an authoritative discourse that commanded the political ruler's respect.

The relatively weak organization and lack of strong institutional support of Japanese intellectuals had one significant advantage: it created an environment favorable to cultural–entrepreneurial initiatives coming from commercial publishers. To begin with, Japanese commercial publishers were not hampered by the constraints frequently imposed by privileged intellectual or religious gatekeeping institutions regarding the content of publications. Scholars and amateur poets also had an option of relatively inexpensive self-financed publishing. The most attractive contribution of Tokugawa publishing to proto-modern communicative activities was not its promotion of highbrow intellectual discourse, however, but rather its encouragement of non-authoritative but creative activities that brought together many different areas of cultural production. I shall continue with an exploration of this genuinely proto-modern form of relationship between printed materials and people.

Print Media as Bridges: Proto-Modern Styles of Publishing and Reading

The commercially produced books of the Tokugawa period did more than convey information that had not been previously available to ordinary consumers. A century of cultural developments associated with books and other printed materials deeply changed the cultural landscape of Tokugawa Japan. Although such writers as Saikaku (1642–1693) still assumed that their readers were relatively cultivated, fiction written in the late eighteenth century, with its colloquial expressions and illustrations, was clearly intended for a much broader audience. As we have already seen, inexpensive handbooks and dictionaries of various kinds became indispensable items during this period, even in households of moderate income. The economic success of commercial printing led not only to the wide dissemination of printed materials but also to the growing interdependence of the various art forms and literary genres.

The mentality of the floating world also spilled over the cultural walls intended to confine it when popular prints began to idealize the residents of the "bad quarters" (*akusho*), the courtesans, and *Kabuki* actors. The new cultural reality of the period made it clear that beauty was no longer the monopoly of the privileged classes. All of these factors and developments confronted the shogunate with an unprecedented flood of printed materials that were questionable by traditional standards. These publications did not directly attack the Tokugawa regime; however, by presenting a seductively attractive world outside the shogunate's categorical order and hierarchies, they pointed to the existence of alternative possibilities.

Oral Reading

One of the characteristics of the proto-modern style of Tokugawa print culture was its particularly close relationship with oral culture. People during this period often read books aloud. Printed materials bridged written and oral culture through the inclusion of legends, rumor, and gossip as well as such performative arts as storytelling and theatrical performance. The rise of commercial publishing in Japan cannot be understood simply as the colonization of oral culture by written culture; rather, Tokugawa commercial publishing formed a new bridge between the two worlds, invigorating and transforming both of them. These enriched forms of communication then posed an ongoing threat to the stability of the Tokugawa state, concerned as it was with preserving the categorical status quo.

Scholars of Tokugawa literature have pointed to the existence of an unusually close relationship between the published literature of the period and the transmission of information by voice.[64] Popular fiction in the late Tokugawa period consisted almost entirely of conversations with very little descriptive narrative between scenes. This conversational style resembles the scripts of theatrical performances. Readers of these stories most likely read the conversational parts aloud, sometimes semi-performing to an audience. Illustrations frequently supplemented the abbreviated situational descriptions.[65]

Maeda Ai offers a glimpse into the subjective experience of reading Tokugawa popular fiction: "The cursive style of characters in woodblock printing was hard to read... therefore, the reader read slowly. Even when he or she was not reading aloud, the impression of a voice emerged in the mind of the reader at this slow pace. Modern readers who are accustomed to silent reading read fiction much more rapidly than premodern people."[66]

To be sure, these features do not imply that there were no instances of silent reading or of individuals reading by themselves. Yokota Fuyuhiko has analyzed the diary of a *sake* brewer who left an account of his reading habits. He was clearly used to reading alone at night in his futon bed under a mosquito net or at his reading desk; it is likely he read silently, Yokota noted.[67] Nonetheless, even when the Tokugawa reader was silently occupied with a work of fiction, he or she felt a kind of intimacy with the book's author through an imagined voice conveyed by the prose rhythms, the many colloquial conversations, a calligraphic style that reflected the author's or copyist's handwriting, and punctuation that conveyed latent intonations. In this type of reading experience, the reader's subjective self was primed for interaction with others through the book itself as well as through communal reading. The custom of reading aloud thus brought Tokugawa readers into lively conversations with their favorite works of fiction. In this sense, Tokugawa reading was a mental as well as a physical experience mediated by the voice; hence, it resembled participation in the performing arts. This connection with oral culture as such, however, should not be mistaken to imply that Japanese print culture was connected to an "unspoiled" popular culture. In fact, oral performances were heavily influenced by the commercial networks and print culture of the time.

Just as Tokugawa amateur poets switched their identities when they attended the *haikai* circle gatherings, intense and engaged reading of theatrical fiction would carry the reader's mind to the floating world, temporarily decoupling the reader from the feudal political order. It was the rise of the proto-modern reader in a distinctively Tokugawa style. Some European historians regarded private, silent, and individualistic reading habits as a departure from the traditional custom of communal reading. Guglielmo Cavallo and Roger Chartier, who are highly skeptical regarding any simplistic contrast between two contrasting reading styles – communal and individualistic, or new and old – also agree that, "Insatiable reading undoubtedly played an essential role [throughout Europe, but especially in France] in detaching subjects from their rulers and Christians from their churches."[68]

Clearly, the case of Tokugawa Japan rejects the simple dichotomy of silent-individualistic and communal–pre-modern reading styles. However, Cavallo and Chartier's view that reading created the moment of detachment from the formal order of society is suggestive because it was exactly the point that Tokugawa books presented an unintended threat to the shogunate. Just as Tokugawa amateur poets switched their identities when they attended the *haikai* circle gatherings, intense and engaged reading of a theatrical fiction would carry the reader's mind to the floating world, temporarily decoupling the reader from the feudal political order.

Theater, Fiction, and Rumor: Overlapping Networks

In addition to bookshops and book peddlers, the major Japanese cities in the Tokugawa period were richly endowed with commercial theaters of various types, which supplied copious material for popular publications. In Edo alone, there were always three or four commercial *Kabuki* theaters in operation at any given time with regular performance schedules. Osaka also had a flourishing group of *Kabuki* and *Jōruri* puppet theaters. These were all purely commercial ventures supported by entrance fees paid by the audience. In addition, many other kinds of popular performance, including singing, dancing, and storytelling, were very well attended. The styles of storytelling ranged from traditional retellings of such classic historical tales as the "Tale of Heike" and the *Taiheiki* to narration of other historical events, the singing of *jōruri* songs, entertaining popular Buddhist moral preaching (*dangi*), and the discussion of current or historical topics (*kōshaku*).

It was no exaggeration to speak of Edo as a city of theaters. In addition to the four large *Kabuki* theaters, small neighborhood theaters called *yose* came into being toward the end of the eighteenth century. The *yose*, which resembled vaudeville theaters, staged various kinds of performances from storytelling and *jōruri* singing to sleight-of-hand magic and shadow pictures (*kage e*). The *yose* also helped to popularize *rakugo*, a form of comic monologue. The earliest known *yose* was established in 1745, but within 50 years this type of theater had become so commonplace that there was a *yose* in virtually every town ward in Edo. The audiences were a mix of men and women from a variety of social backgrounds. When Mizuno Tadakuni, the shogun's *rōjū*, or Chief of Senior Councillors, instituted the Tenpō reform (1842–1844) in order to impose firmer controls on the theaters, there were said to be 211 *yose* in the city of Edo.[69] Soon after Mizuno fell from power, the *yose* quickly reemerged. The colloquial speech used in *rakugo* reflected the mindset and conversational style of the ordinary Edo commoners and provided material for the fiction writers of the period. In contrast, French or British theaters during roughly the same period usually operated under royal or aristocratic patronage.[70]

The magnitude of Tokugawa theater culture is startling given the fact that the Japanese theaters were fee-based commercial establishments. None of them were the equivalent of the royal theaters of early modern Europe. The new popularity of fiction in Tokugawa Japan was closely connected to the dynamic world of theaters, dramatic performance, and storytelling. The interpersonal networks that drew together writers, performing artists, and publishers across formal status lines during this period led to creative experimentation with what might be called mixed media.

For example, Chikamatsu Monzaemon (1653–1724) adapted his plot from an actual love suicide that had taken place in Osaka just a month before the first performance of his play. A famous phrase taken from a *jōruri* puppet drama script by Chikamatsu crystallizes the image of two lovers who take their last journey together in pre-dawn darkness in search of a place to spend their final moments:

> The last of life, the end of night. The metaphor for dying lovers is roadside frost by the withered grasses of the field. The frost fades even as they walk along the path. Oh, sorrow, it is just a dream within a dream. (*Sonezaki Shinjū*, The Love Suicide of Sonezaki, jōruri lyrics for a puppet play first performed in 1703)

Chikamatsu's powerful verses turned these journalistic incidents into a heart-rending conception of emotional passion in which feudal norms, social boundaries, and the emerging feudal–capitalist obligations of merchant life under the Tokugawa order were all defied. The beautiful *jōruri* lyrics not only appeared in print but were also performed independently as storytelling music. The lyrics included both the dialogue and the narratives recited by a single actor. A *jōruri* storyteller put himself or herself completely into the moods and emotions of different characters in the play, thus creating an alternative reality. Learning to sing *jōruri* songs was a popular pastime for Tokugawa people. As a result, *jōruri* lyrics became one of the most popular and consistently profitable genres of Tokugawa commercial publishing.

Once a theatrical production became a big hit, spinoffs could also become profitable, or vice versa. The glamorization of love suicide found in drama as well as fiction led to a number of actual suicides during this period. It is said that between 1703 and 1704 there were nine hundred cases of love suicide in Kyoto and Osaka,[71] and these tragedies did not even mark the peak of the love suicide craze. The drama and published fiction of this period clearly reflected a journalistic attitude in terms of their fascination with current sensational incidents and their critical stance toward established hierarchical categories. *Dangi* storytelling, which was moral sermonizing that drew on current gossip and recent events to attract an audience, helped to shape *gesaku* (popular comic fiction, often with many illustrations) fiction. Tokugawa publishers never missed an opportunity to cash in on the popularity of *dangi* storytelling and made collections of these moral narratives into popular books. *Dangi* anthologies became instantly popular when they emerged in the mid-eighteenth century.[72] The content and style of *dangi* stories inspired a number of *gesaku* novelists, such as Hiraga Gennai (1728–1779), who produced best-sellers in late eighteenth-century Edo.[73]

Konta Yōzō reported the interesting case of a provocative writer who was executed in 1758 because of his effective critical discourse using the power of mixed media. The writer, Baba Bunkō, was a typical Tokugawa popular critic in that his power resided in powerful oral performance as a well-known storyteller, or *kōdan*, and his use of the increasingly popular rental bookshops to circulate his books. Bunkō regaled his listeners with stories of journalistic and political interest. One day, Bunkō was arrested while boldly lecturing about a recent large-scale peasant rebellion in front of a packed audience of two hundred listeners. According to the sentence, not only did he lecture on forbidden topics related to the shogunate's politics but also produced numerous handwritten books and gave them to the rental bookstores for circulation among interested readers. The books covered such delicate topics as the urinary incontinence of the shogun Ieshige. According to gossip, this particular shogun was an unintelligent, lascivious alcoholic. It was reported that three new toilets for the shogun's exclusive use had been constructed on the route between his castle and his ancestral temple in Ueno because he could not travel even a short distance without relieving himself. Several book merchants were arrested along with Bunkō. Apparently, it was the rental merchants who had encouraged Bunkō to write these irreverent books and copy them by hand for circulation. Bunkō was sentenced to death with *gokumon*, a public display of his head after execution to serve as a visual intimidation to others.[74]

Bunkō's fate illuminates a number of aspects of Tokugawa communicative life. It is clear that by the mid-eighteenth century there was no lack of popular interest in current political matters, as evidenced by the large audiences turning out to hear Bunkō. Moreover, the book merchants obviously considered the circulation of such books to be sufficiently profitable to be worth the risk. Gossip about news items from the shogun's court became the subject of conversation in the shogun's castle city. On the other hand, when the subject matter directly touched on current shogunal politics, the rulers often responded with harsh penalties.

Parodic Literature in the Tokugawa Civilizing Process

It was under this circumstance that artists and writers of Tokugawa Japan found laughter an effective tool of cultural subversion and took advantage of the growing commercial market for popular books to spread their messages. Parodies became a popular genre of publishing because at that point the Tokugawa civilizing process had effectively disseminated common idioms and images throughout Japan. The widespread images derived from pre-Tokugawa Japanese literature helped in making parodies of period pieces. Furthermore, the booming popularity of *haikai* poetry, which required writers to subvert classical images, had accustomed Tokugawa people to humorous or satirical imitations of other works. The superimposition of classical images onto contemporary scenes, sometimes called *mitate*, was a literary device that appeared in many artistic and literary genres. The frequent use of *mitate* is an index of the high degree of cultivation of the Tokugawa readership. The popularity of parodic literature in this period reveals not only the existence of a critical attitude on the part of Tokugawa people but also their knowledge of the classical Japanese tradition.

For example, Santō Kyōden's comical novel, *Tama Migaku Aoto ga Zeni* (1790), illustrated by the famous *ukiyo-e* painter Kitagawa Utamaro, was an obvious satire of Matsudaira Sadanobu's policies. Sadanobu is best described as a cultivated but authoritarian lord who attempted to clean up Japanese society by putting commercialism in its place. Sadanobu's austerity policy quickly became unpopular among Edo citizens. Kyōden took advantage of the popular mood of the moment and moved the contemporary situation to the medieval period, choosing as his protagonist Hojō Tokiyori (1227–1263), the regent of the Kamakura shogun. During the era of the moralistic, penny-pinching Tokiyori, according to Kyōden's story, the people of Japan all grew very serious and stopped wasting time on frivolity. The image of the stylish man-about-town was transformed into that of an uptight workaholic who tried to maximize his work time by minimizing his visits to the latrine. It should go without saying that this caricature was the polar opposite of the dandies who frequented the fashionable haunts of the Tokugawa "floating world." Kyōden's novel humorously describes a fictional work-obsessed society in which nothing is wasted. Theater people and courtesans are transformed into working folk. The only waste and malfunction in this society, Kyōden says, are belly buttons and the holes in the center of coins. Kyōden's comical critique was transparently directed at the straitlaced domestic policies of Matsudaira Sadanobu.[75] Kyōden was sentenced to be "handcuffed for fifty days," while half of the property of Tsutaya Jūsaburō, the publisher, was confiscated.

Fiction writers of this period often transferred topics of current interest to "period" settings in order to convey political criticism between the lines of the story, so to speak. The popular readership applauded the writers' implicit challenges to authority; then as now, they derived considerable pleasure from decoding the true identities of the persons being parodied. In this case, Hojō Tokiyori's reputation in history for Zen-inspired self-control and economizing was already familiar to the Tokugawa population through a famous Nō play called *Hachinoki* as well as through other popular publications.

One of the most conspicuous examples of Tokugawa parody was a take-off on Lady Murasaki's great literary achievement, "The Tale of Genji," a product of the ancient Heian imperial court. "The Tale of Genji" became known to the wider Tokugawa reading public through popularization even though most readers might not have read the full text of the story

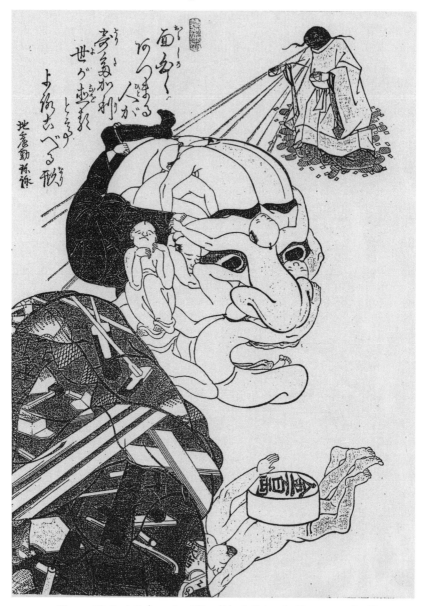

Figure 11.5. A Subversive Woodblock Print 1. *Namazu-e*, by Utagawa Kuniyoshi (ca. nineteenth century). The *namazu* (catfish), the legendary symbol of the power of earthquakes, is standing at the upper right dressed in a Shintō costume and sending supernatural beams to the ground. The man's face is composed of many human figures, and he is receiving 100 ryō (a unit of money) in his hand from the catfish. The

itself. A famous best-seller of the late Tokugawa period, *Nise Murasaki Inaka Genji* (The Fake Purple Rural Genji), narrated by Tanehiko Ryūtei and illustrated by Utagawa Kunisada, parodied "The Tale of Genji" by transferring the older story to the court of the Muromachi shogun. The "purple" in the title is a reference to Lady Murasaki Shikibu, the author of the original story. One volume of *Nise Murasaki* sold fifteen thousand copies, an impressive figure for the period. The Tokugawa version was rumored to be a *roman à clef* about the present shogun's harem, which may have accounted in part for its large sales. Between 1829 and 1849, a series based on *Nise Murasaki* ran to 38 stories and 52 volumes. At that point, the shogunate finally prohibited this popular series.

Political parodies with a strong anti-establishment tone in the guise of popular fiction often made the best-seller lists of Tokugawa Japan. Given the potential for large profits with this type of fiction, the commercial publishers were often willing to risk offending the shogun or other high officials. Printed illustrations alone proved to be an equally effective form of aesthetic subversion, however. The prints of the Tokugawa period were usually either one-page pictures with brief captions or thin booklets. An interesting category of such subversive one-page prints was *namazu-e* (catfish prints), which reached its highest popularity right after the great earthquake of Asei (1855) that occurred at the time of political turbulences shaking the shogunate's order after the visit of Commodore Perry to Japan in 1853. For example, in one such print, the *namazu* (catfish), the legendary symbol of the power of earthquakes, is standing at the upper right dressed in a Shintō costume and sending supernatural beams to the ground. The man's face is composed of many human figures, and he is receiving 100 ryō (a unit of money) in his hand from the catfish. The man is wearing a *kimono* with patterns that describe many carpentry tools. The caption includes the anticipation of *yonaoshi* (world reform) caused by the earthquake. The implication of this picture is the situation after an earthquake where, due to the high demand for rebuilding houses, many people earn money by engaging in construction jobs (see Figure 11.5). In another example (Figure 11.6), the *namazu* is depicted as a strong man helping poor people by squeezing the wealthy until gold bursts from their bodies.[76] These prints not only represent the upheaval and subsequent redistribution of money caused by the earthquake but also the desire in

Figure 11.5 *(cont.)* man is wearing a *kimono* with patterns that describe many carpentry tools. The caption includes the anticipation of *yonaoshi* (world reform) caused by the earthquake. The implication of the picture is the situation after an earthquake where, due to the high demand for rebuilding houses, many people earn money by engaging in construction jobs.

Figure 11.6. A Subversive Woodblock Print 2. *Namazu-e*, an illustrated one-page woodblock print, nineteenth century. This illustration made use of the legendary *namazu*, or catfish, that supposedly caused the earthquake. The *namazu* is depicted here as a strong man helping poor people by squeezing the wealthy until gold bursts from their bodies. The development of efficient commercial printing methods facilitated the spread of popular subversive opinions.

people's minds for a radical transformation of the social order – a transformation that would occur a decade later with the Meiji Restoration. In fact, the publishers were often gambling for high stakes. If it were rumored that a specific item of printed matter might have difficulty with the shogunate authorities or be withdrawn from circulation, the print would often sell out. News of the confiscation got out, however, and worked as excellent word-of-mouth advertising. The publishers who had made press runs before the confiscation made a fortune from what amounted to free publicity.[77]

In short, the introduction of books into the daily life of a large readership had two sides. First, it had the effect of keeping Tokugawa culture relatively conservative because the most readily available cultural resources at the time of the Japanese information revolution were the texts and images of the classical Japanese tradition. The development of a nationwide market for printed books in Tokugawa Japan strengthened and popularized the conservative aspects of the civilizing process through its popularization of the supposed behavioral standards of the ancient imperial court. Although the shogunate's attempts to regulate the publishing industry were far from effective, their ongoing authoritarian stance against critical discourse prevented instances of political criticism from growing into integrated spheres of civic discourse linked by print media. Secondly, however, the most vital part of the Tokugawa publishing industry was deeply connected to the demand of the popular audience. The spread of a subversive spirit in popular publications was possible because of the ongoing popularization of the classics; idioms and images that had once been confined to an exclusive group of aristocrats had been transmitted to a much larger segment of the Japanese population through the mechanisms of the marketplace. Over the long term, however, the profit-driven publication of subversive materials with a counter-cultural "feel" helped to undermine both the tradition itself and the society that treasured it. In this sense, both conservative and subversive expressions were twin growths of the distinctive style of Tokugawa civilizing processes.

12

Hierarchical Civility and Beauty

Etiquette and Manners in Tokugawa Manuals

Introduction

Etiquette and manners, physical as well as verbal, comprise a powerful means of communication. The force of these cultural rules of conduct lies in their ability to discipline and regulate people's behavior without causing them to feel compelled or controlled. Those who accept the dictates of their culture are often voluntarily emulating and accepting what they perceive to be the norms of cultivated behavior. Thus, the process of enculturation can effectively embody a new kind of social discipline. The conventional view relegates etiquette to the superficial role of containing communicative content. However, in an interactive ritual, more important than "what" one says, "how" he or she says it demonstrates one's relative categorical position to the other along the dimensions of power relations, social distance, and affection. The true relationship of interactive parties is often revealed not by the content of conversations but by the physical or verbal manner of interactions.

The Tokugawa codes of etiquette that dominated formal or distanced social interactions were characterized by an emphasis on the status differentials between the interacting parties – an element that might be called hierarchical civility. In contrast to the comparatively horizontally structured grammar of sociability that prevailed in the aesthetic enclaves, hierarchical civility appeared to be compatible with the operative ideology of the Tokugawa state, namely rule by status. On the street, an observer would see people bowing to each other, each degree of inclination a precise reflection of the status differential between the interacting parties. Well-trained house servants standing in an entryway would instantly appraise the status differential between a guest and the master of the house and receive the guest in a manner appropriate to his or her rank. People walking along the street could be classified according to their dress, hairstyle, and mannerisms, which signaled their official status, gender, occupation, and age group. The shogun's subjects made use of these external differences as visual cues that allowed them to address strangers with reasonable assurance that they would not commit a social gaffe. Interactional rituals among strangers flowed smoothly in Tokugawa society as long as people were accurate in their perceptions of their relative status in different contexts.

On the surface, civility in Tokugawa Japan therefore reflected a feudal hierarchical society's concern with observing and preserving distinctions in status. The status (*mibun*) system was accompanied by the differentiation of formal propriety rankings (*kakushiki*) that stratified people into increasingly segmented hierarchies within each major *mibun* classification.[1] Although the state-imposed status stratification was pervasive in this society, its actual practice of categorization was fluid and filled with ambiguity. In actual social interactions, the power relations of two persons were not necessarily determined by the mere measurement of officially defined status definitions. "Actual" power relations of two persons engaged in interactions would be determined by an array of factors – including money, knowledge, age, and political skills – and actors' strategic uses of these resources. Furthermore, when the speaker's and addressee's relative positionality of official status scales was unknown, such as in the case of street encounters, the actual practice of social hierarchy was determined by the actor's strategic judgment and use of cultural idioms. Civility was relied on as the grammar of socialization on such occasions.

Thus, in a highly stratified society such as Tokugawa Japan, the rich physical and verbal vocabulary of expressing differences was the mechanism for facilitating smooth communication among individuals with different social backgrounds. Because Tokugawa people emotionally were heavily invested in status rankings, transgressing the obvious boundaries of propriety stood to increase the enormous emotional cost of the transaction.[2] As a result, the purpose of interaction itself could fail when the interacting parties' sense of categorical boundaries was threatened. Tokugawa Japan thus developed an incredibly rich and refined physical and verbal vocabulary of manners in acknowledging and appreciating hierarchical boundaries as norms of polite social interaction.

Although the smooth enactment of Tokugawa interactional rituals might have appeared to outside observers to be "second nature" to the actors involved, the print-mediated aspect of civility was also a distinctive feature of Tokugawa cultures of sociability. In Chapter 11, on the commercial publishing industry, I argued that the Tokugawa information revolution had led in two contradictory cultural directions, the promotion of conservative cultural trends on the one hand and the simultaneous dissemination of popular counter-cultural developments on the other. The former direction was linked to the formation and popularization of canonical cultural knowledge in every branch of art and literature. This process of canonization meant that the classics that had formerly found their readers among the elites of the medieval period became the aesthetic standards of a broader population in Tokugawa Japan. Nor was this process confined to the fields of literature and the performing arts. Etiquette and manners also underwent the same evolution, namely the establishment of a body of authoritative knowledge and the popularization of that corpus. The abbreviated and simplified version of the conventional grammar of sociability that had developed during the late medieval period became a frequent feature of handbooks popularizing civilized knowledge.

To be sure, because of the Tokugawa policy of institutional segmentation, the wide variations in customs and manners between small regional areas during this period require modifications in the conventional Western image of Japan as culturally homogenous. For example, each village customarily had detailed rules for seating arrangements, dress codes, and gift exchanges on ceremonial occasions among its members. The distinctive characteristic of Tokugawa cultural development was the simultaneous popular recognition of more culturally prestigious and general rules of sociability to be applied outside social relations in one's local networks. In addition, local rules were often inadequate for handling new relations in this increasingly interconnected society. Some persons also came to believe that learning the "better" rules of conduct would enhance their standing within the local community. Just as people were motivated to join poetry and artistic circles in order to enhance their prestige, they often understood good manners as an important step on the path of cultural upward mobility.

From this perspective, it is not surprising that the better-heeled members of these local communities became particularly conscious of the importance of acquiring civilized knowledge. For example, Yoda Nagayasu (1674–1758), a wealthy farmer and village chief (*shōya*) in Kai province, was a faithful diary-keeper whose journal allows us a glimpse into his cultural development. Yoda acquired some 66 books over the course of his life, including some "how-to" books for learning the polite arts – several *chōhōki*, guidebooks for gracious living, an Ogasawara-style etiquette book, and a *setsuyō-shū*, an encyclopedic dictionary. We know that he not only owned these books but thoroughly internalized their disciplinary message; he composed a "Family Rule," or set of precepts for his household members, which includes the following injunctions: "Follow the rules for good manners precisely; this rule is nothing more than distinguishing clearly between persons of higher and lower status. Always make a clear distinction between senior and junior within each status."[3] Such an internalization of formal manners was not uncommon among the Tokugawa people.

The evolution of the rules of sociability that governed Tokugawa civility offers an illustrative case study of the impact of state–market relationships and the critical timing of the expansion of communicative networks on the formation of Japanese polite culture. As Tokugawa Japan developed a nationwide market economy in the late seventeenth century, the social relations mediated by capitalist exchanges of goods and money acquired a new quality of impersonality within a polity that was still feudal in structure. At the same time, the social relations mediated by a capitalist economy lacked the organizational power necessary to establish new rules of sociability. Meanwhile, the ongoing proliferation of political, economic, and cognitive network connections generated an unprecedented variety of communicative spheres. As a result of continued samurai domination, the Tokugawa Japanese adapted and popularized vertically structured codes of civility to govern formal social interactions as a tentative common norm of sociability for people living in an age of complex communicative requirements.

The world of hierarchical civility deserves in-depth investigation in its own light not simply because of its pervasive influence on the culture of sociability in general but also because it provided the background that made aesthetic associational activities more attractive. As we have seen in Section Two, the world of beauty had a socio-political dimension throughout Japanese history and often generated strong messages of protest. The Tokugawa aesthetic publics were attractive to large numbers of people because once they joined an art or poetry circle, the ritual technologies of these arts temporarily nullified the rigid hierarchical norms of socialization. Moreover, the conventional code of hierarchical civility became widely accepted as a paradigm of the culture of socialization; thus breaking categorical boundaries through aesthetic circle activities became increasingly attractive to people who were frustrated with the restrictions imposed by the Tokugawa system. Furthermore, ironical as it may seem, the codes of hierarchical civility themselves were heavily influenced by the traditions of performing arts and were thereby aesthetically defined. For these reasons, hierarchical patterns of civility and aesthetic standards of civility were in many ways twin outgrowths of Tokugawa social developments that cannot be understood separately.

Tokugawa Books of Civilized Knowledge

Commercially published books of civilized knowledge were practical reference books and manuals during the Tokugawa period – books of the sort often cataloged simply as *zassho*, or "miscellaneous books," in modern Japanese archives. Yokoyama Toshio, who pioneered the study of the *setsuyō-shū* manuals as civilized knowledge, noted the power of the *setsuyō-shū* to create a commonsense definition of standard knowledge. Since the *setsuyō-shū* became a standard item in literate households, Yokoyama noted that if people did not deviate from the standards set forth in the *setsuyō-shū* when formality was required in either manners or writing, others would accept their behavior as appropriate even though the *setsuyō-shū* was not explicitly cited.[4]

In fact, the whole range of various practical handbooks for civilized knowledge contributed their distinctive patterns to a rich tapestry of propriety. For the most part, these manuals have been given a variety of labels; to name a few, there were *chōhōki* (treasure books, manuals); *setsuyō-shū* (dictionaries, often encyclopedic); *kinmō zui* (illustrated encyclopedias written at the introductory level); *shorei-shū* (guidebooks for formal manners); *shosatsu-shū* (correspondence guidebooks); and *ōrai mono* (collections of model correspondence used as elementary school textbooks). In addition, almost all genres of performing arts and poetry composition produced handbooks for amateur students that were very popular. These manuals were brimming with useful information, often accompanied by many illustrations, in response to ordinary people's desire for self-improvement and the acquisition of "upscale" knowledge.

Among these manuals, the *chōhōki* and *setsuyō-shū* are genres whose selling point was their intelligent summaries of various civilized knowledge. *Chōhō* had a number of different meanings, including "great treasure," "convenience," and "methods."[5] The *chōhōki* summarized a wide range of essential information ranging from medical advice (such as information for women on childbirth and child rearing) to the titles of government officials and literary idioms from medieval court culture. Summaries of the polite arts and the correct forms for formal letter writing were standard entries in this genre of books. *Chōhōki* were very popular from the late seventeenth to the early eighteenth centuries. The *setsuyō-shū*, in contrast, evolved from their original form as dictionaries in the sixteenth century into copiously illustrated tomes by the middle of the eighteenth century. By then, no family that conducted written correspondence would have been without at least one copy of this type of *setsuyō-shū*. The *setsuyō-shū* were considered essential household items because they explained the meaning and pronunciation of Chinese ideograms – information widely considered the most difficult element of proper written Japanese. Although formal correspondence required the use of many Chinese characters, they were easily forgotten, especially those not frequently used. In addition, the combination of standard dictionary functions with convenient references to other branches of the polite arts, maps, and historical information made the *setsuyō-shū* the most popular genre of Tokugawa handbooks of civilized knowledge.

Although the practical how-to books and manuals rarely impress us with their authors' intellectual force, given that they were intended to be little more than summary presentations of standard information, their tone of repetitive conventionalism proves my point precisely; it suggests the emergence of standardized accounts that represented the common cultural "database" of the literate population of Tokugawa Japan.

On occasion, writers with encyclopedia knowledge tried their hand at writing for a popular audience. Among these, the best-known included Kaibara Ekken (1630–1714), a famous Confucian scholar and physician trained in Chinese medicine. Ekken published *Yōjōkun* (The Precept for Health), a best-selling home health guide that combined Confucian ethics with medical information, and *Onna Daigaku* (College for Women), a book of moral advice and family ethics for women that blended Confucian precepts with Japanese feudal ethical standards. Ekken combined his own ethical observations with a wide range of practical knowledge. Although Ekken did not write *chōhōki*, he published an etiquette book called *Sanrei Guketsu* (Oral Transmission of the Three Proprieties).

For the most part, however, writers of Ekken's caliber were unusual in this genre, and most of the handbooks were clearly detached from any sort of moralizing. Most of the writers of Tokugawa books of civilized knowledge were not well-known. The commercial publishers enlisted an army of cultured mediocrities who were skilled collectors of assorted bits of information and capable of trimming and translating them to fit the demands of the new mass market.

The writers who produced the Tokugawa books of civilized knowledge were on occasion condescending toward their audience. Their attitude is exemplified in a shamelessly straightforward statement by the author of *Shonin Chōhōki*[6] (Everybody's Treasury), who noted in his preface that the book was "intended for gusha [stupid people] who nod off and cannot understand difficult books." For such dummies, the preface continues, he has collected "essential information for survival in this world." Although these books of civilized knowledge frequently included large amounts of material on the manners and culture of the upper classes, we should not assume on the basis of this subject matter that these books were intended strictly for an elite readership. It is more than likely that these books were found particularly useful by commoners who were striving to move upward in the social order rather than by those born into established families; the latter acquired the cultural conventions of established society through their upbringing. In the subsequent period, during the mid- to late eighteenth century, the *setsuyō-shū* turned in even more practical directions; they simply presented lists of essential facts to their readers without any moral gloss. The disjunction between ethics and civilized knowledge became even more conspicuous in the later manuals.

The role of entrepreneurial publishers in the production of these manuals is described in a preface to another guidebook, entitled *Nan Chōhōki* (The Gentlemen's Treasury), written in 1693 by Inamura Jōhaku. Inamura was already well-known as the author of the successful handbook *Onna Chōhōki* (The Lady's Treasury, 1692), a compendium of everything that a cultivated "lady of the house" ought to know – ranging from table etiquette to child rearing. Inamura recounts a visit from his publisher: "One day, the publisher came to see me and spoke very highly of my previous work, the five-volume *Onna Chōhōki*, which has been published with many printings because it is a truly universal treasure."[7] The publisher in question, who appears to have had a good nose for best-sellers, asked Jōhaku to write a second manual, this time one for men. From this point, Jōhaku went on to become the happy author of at least 11 books of polite manners and civilized knowledge, including *Nenju Chōhōki* (The Everyday Treasury, 1693) and *Buke Chōhōki* (The Samurai's Treasury, 1694).

These books in this sense symbolized the market-driven nature of the Tokugawa civilizing process. Yet, the gist of the etiquette and manners detailed in these books was suitable for maintaining the hierarchical values of the Tokugawa state. This fact reflects the ambiguous status of the Tokugawa books of civilized knowledge, which had to be politically correct as well as commercially successful.

Tokugawa Manners: Power and Beauty

A closer look at some common topics related to formal manners and etiquette in the Tokugawa period will reveal two distinctive characteristics of Tokugawa codes of manners. One is meticulously differentiated idioms for expressing differences; the second is a distinctive method of deploying the body for social communicative purposes. The first point is perhaps best illustrated by the elaborate rules governing letter writing.

Formal Correspondence

During this period, spoken Japanese had so many distinctive regional dialects that people from remote provinces had difficulty communicating with one another. Although the regional dialects belonged to the same linguistic family, the wide variations in vocabulary and pronunciation sometimes made them virtually different languages. In contrast to its spoken forms, however, written Japanese was much more standardized. This situation was exaggerated by the fact that the Tokugawa shogunate introduced a paper-shuffling mentality into the political process. As the shogunate's vassalic bureaucracy matured, the samurai were constantly required to write reports, formal letters, answers to requests from superior authorities, and a host of other official papers. In terms of the calligraphy required, the style was standardized to the so-called *oie ryū* for official papers. Furthermore, in an integrated but decentralized polity, various mid-range organizations of semi-autonomous status – villages, city wards, and occupational groups – had to write frequent official reports and petitions to the authorities.

With the increased importance of written communication, Tokugawa men and women frequently consulted letter-writing manuals because correspondence was the form of social interaction with the worst potential booby traps. If a writer wanted to compose a letter in the appropriate form, he or she had to be exquisitely attuned to all the implications of his or her social position relative to the recipient; age, nature and degree of relationship, gender, and other social factors all had to be taken into account. The *Shosatsu Chōhōki* (1740), a guidebook for correspondence, took a very practical approach to this complex issue. Its table of contents begins with a neat tabulation of the possible status combinations:

> Letters for the New Year celebration
> A model letter to a social superior
> A model letter to a peer
> A model letter to a social inferior
> Letters to those who have not been seen for a long time
> A letter to a social superior
> A letter to a peer
> A letter to a social inferior[8]

Each model letter is followed by a glossary of a hundred synonyms for some key words used in the letter so that the reader can easily construct his or her own variation on the letter. These synonyms are also classified according to the three degrees of politeness. For example, for a letter of condolence to a man whose father had passed away, the glossary suggests a dozen different ways of describing "your late father," such as "your most respectable father," and so forth. The abundant stock of vocabulary and exquisitely subtle shades of polite nuance is simply beyond translation. These classifications were applied to the composition of an actual letter as follows: if the deceased person had been the father of one's superior, one would choose the most respectful idiom to describe "your father" from the glossary. In other words, the evaluation of the relative power relation between the two parties was left to the person who consulted the book; the manual, however, gave a range of choices in phrasing for each level of relative status.

The letter's outward appearance was just as important as its contents. Many books of etiquette listed detailed rules concerning the exterior of the letter. For example, there were rules for letter wrapping that varied according to the letter's formality, the occasion, and the status of the addressee. Moreover, the calligraphic forms for the address itself were governed by elaborate rules. These calligraphic forms included both the terms of address and their further differentiation by writing style. In a letter to a samurai, a commoner had to use the most polite level of address written in the most formal and precise calligraphic style. On the other hand, a samurai could address a commoner with the same *sama* or *dono* if the commoner were a very respectable person. The samurai, however, could use a more informal calligraphic style in a letter to a commoner than the style considered appropriate for use with his social equals. Mistakes in forms of address or idiomatic expressions often resulted in serious social consequences.[9]

Embodied Stratification and Embodied Beauty

The deployment of the body in acknowledging and expressing status differences was the most basic principle in Tokugawa manners. *Ogasawara shorei daizen* (The Complete Book of Ogasawara School Manners),[10] an introductory guide to formal etiquette, sets forth three distinct levels of politeness for almost every gesture – *shin*, the most formal; *gyō*, moderately formal; and *so*, informal – with each of these three levels subdivided, in turn, into three degrees, resulting in nine distinct forms of politeness. The situational context and status differences between the persons involved determined which degree of formality one should employ. Unlike letter writing, however, a person would find it difficult to grasp the correct postures and gestures from words alone. With the advent of Tokugawa woodblock printing, which could easily incorporate illustrations into texts, the manuals of formal manners were supplemented with copious illustrations.

Bowing

The rules for bowing provide the most instructive example for illustrating bodily expressions of status stratification in Tokugawa Japan. The following description covers the basic principles of bowing in a *zashiki* (a reception room) room (that is, while kneeling on a *tatami* mat). Formal (*shin*) bowing: "Place both hands flat on the floor and bow until your nose almost touches your hands. This is the way you should bow to honorable persons." Moderate (*gyō*) bowing to one's social peers, to whom one must still demonstrate modesty: "Place both hands close together on the floor, and bow your head a little less than in formal bowing." Informal (*sō*) bowing, to one's inferiors: "Put both hands on the floor some distance apart, and incline your head only slightly" (Figure 12.1, part 1). Of course, the appropriate form of bowing was also determined by the occasion. If one meets a respectable senior on the street, one should bow deeply, bending at the knees until the hands touch the feet (Figure 12.1, part 2). The person of higher rank in this case would respond by bowing only slightly, a gesture that would embody and reflect the status differential.

The description above, exquisitely detailed and explicitly hierarchical, was from the teaching of the Ogasawara School that laid out the basic foundation of Tokugawa formal manners. The Ogasawara School was the most influential school of formal manners that originated during the preceding Muromachi period. During this period, two vassal families of the Ashikaga shogun, Ogasawara and Ise, claimed hereditary status as arbiters of good manners and proper ritual conduct at the Ashikaga shogunate's court society. During the Tokugawa period, the Ogasawara School grew more influential than that of the Ise family in part because the main lineage of the Ogasawara family attained *daimyo* status during the Tokugawa shogunate. Furthermore, a number of instructors in the Ogasawara tradition tutored students from both samurai and commoner families. In actual practice, the style of etiquette that was popularized during the Tokugawa period under the Ogasawara label (so to speak) had been finely modified at many points to meet contemporary needs.[11] There were tutors in Edo and many other cities who advertised themselves as teachers of Ogasawara School manners. Although some vassal samurai who were required to participate in various ceremonial rituals studied with such tutors, most commoners did not take lessons from etiquette teachers. The printed instructions contained in the etiquette handbooks provided only glimpses of the world of formal manners. There were many commercially printed introductions to Ogasawara School manners during this period – information that had been previously transmitted in secret from teachers to dedicated students.

Although the Ogasawara School's teaching was often considered too rigid even by Tokugawa standards, the basic concern for differentiating body positions and movement according to the relative social standings of the interacting parties was generally accepted. When Wada Nobusada wrote a famous guide to etiquette, *Rinji Kyaku ashirai* (Flexible Rules for Welcoming Guests), in 1830,[12] he was well aware of criticisms of the Ogasawara School. He thus claimed that he had softened the rigid dictates of the Ogasawara School and simplified them for ease of comprehension and accessibility. If one applies this principle of simplification to the

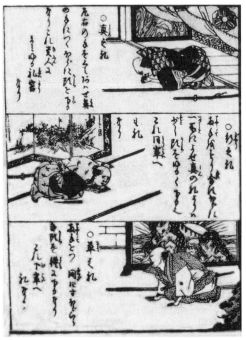

(1)

(2)

Figure 12.1. Variety of Bowing. (1) Three ways of bowing. The upper column: formal bowing to a senior; the middle column: ordinary bowing to a peer; the lower column: casual bowing to an inferior. From *Ogasawara shorei daizen* (The Complete Book of Ogasawara School of Manners). (2) Bowing on the street to a senior: Bend the body until the fingers are touching one's insteps. From *Shorei daigaku* (The College of Manners).

different degrees of bowing, what are the practical results? For example, let us consider a servant's greeting on behalf of his master (the host) to a guest arriving in the entryway of the house. The host's servant is sitting on the floor to receive the guest, who is standing at the entrance. According to Wada Nobusada, "If the guest seems to be the host's superior or his peer, receive him by bowing and touching one's hands to the floor. If the guest appears obviously inferior to the host in status, one should bow only by touching one hand to the floor; then listen to the guest's greeting." Although Wada certainly attempted to formulate more flexible rules for everyday etiquette, his basic principle was not so different from that of the Ogasawara School, which also upheld the importance of the embodiment of status differentiation.

Fan Etiquette

A younger person might understandably want to fan himself when he meets with an honorable elder on a hot summer day. What should he do in this circumstance? *Shorei daigaku*[13] (The College of Manners), depicts a modest boy who opens a fan only halfway, inclining his upper body slightly. The accompanying caption reads, "One of your hands should touch the floor while you are fanning yourself." The boy is almost bowing as he waves his fan. The covert message of the injunction is that one should not express desires for bodily relief straightforwardly in front of older persons. If one's needs are urgent (which could be understandable), one should express suitable modesty through elegant body language. The function of body movement in this school of etiquette (i.e., partial closure of the fan combined with a slight bow) allows the actor to meet his or her physical need while simultaneously maintaining an attitude of deference toward the person of higher status (Figure 12.2, part 1).

Clearing the Nasal Passages

Western researchers in the field of medieval and early modern etiquette often focus on instructions regarding nose-blowing because they impress modern readers with the wide difference between late medieval and contemporary attitudes toward bodily functions. Norbert Elias noted that medieval people usually blew their noses into their fingers; therefore, etiquette manuals recommended blowing one's nose into the fingers of the left hand if one ate and took meat from the common dish with the right. In contrast, medieval Japanese courtiers already served food with individualized dishes and utensils, and they did not have to be advised against blowing their noses into their fingers or onto their sleeves.

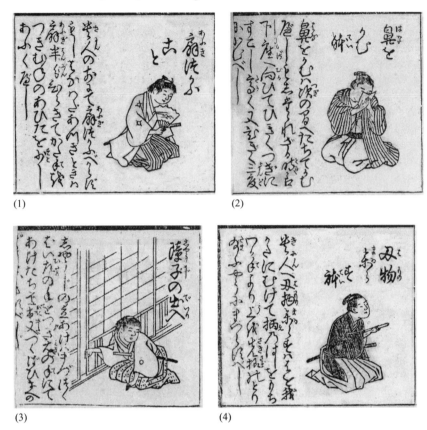

(1)   (2)

(3)   (4)

Figure 12.2. Embodied Modesty. (1) The use of a fan. (2) Blowing one's nose. (3) Opening a sliding *shōji* door. (4) Passing a sword to another person. From *Shorei daigaku* (The College of Manners).

The standard Ogasawara teaching during the Tokugawa period for a person who needed to clear his nose courteously was so painstakingly prescribed as to appear almost comical to the modern Western reader. From *Shorei daigaku*: "Go into the next room; face one of its interior corners, and blow two or three times." The accompanying illustration shows a boy using *hana gami*, the Tokugawa ancestor of paper tissues. The underlying message is that well-bred persons do not discharge their bodily fluids – even nasal secretions – in front of respectable people (see Figure 12.2, part 2).

Sliding Doors

The important common characteristic of these instructions is their very well-programmed method of expressing modesty by bodily expressions.

They not only enjoin impressionable young students of manners to be self-effacing and polite, or refrain from doing something untoward, they also clearly prescribe specific sequences of movements and gestures to demonstrate the proper expressions of modesty and politeness. "When you open a sliding door to enter a room," the same textbook says, "you must first kneel down on the floor, touching your left hand on the floor, and open the sliding door with your right hand. Then you may enter the room on your knees." This series of gestures is an expression of respect to those who are already in the room (Figure 12.2, part 3). This entire sequence of movements must be performed elegantly and beautifully, with as much physical grace as possible.

If these highly prescribed rules of manners only enforced and reaffirmed the existing hierarchical order of society, however, the influence of these manners might have been more limited. They retained the aesthetically pleasing flavor of the elegant court culture that gave the students of manners a sense of self-improvement. Furthermore, although these codes of manners may appear rigid and tedious to modern eyes, they were more than ceremonial procedures that reinforced hierarchical values. These standards of proper behavior also taught the young consideration for others through concrete gestures and meaningful sequences of movement.

For example, the modesty embodied in the proper manner for using a fan or for clearing one's nose was not only useful for expressing respect for a senior but also served as a general expression of consideration for the feelings of others. In both cases, the public display of bodily needs or desires was considered ugly and unpleasant to behold. Another clear example concerns the proper method for passing a sword from one samurai to another. Samurai in the Tokugawa period always carried a set of two swords. There were extensive and detailed discussions in the etiquette books regarding the handling of these weapons, but one basic principle always appeared in introductions to sword etiquette books. That was the injunction never to pass a sword by holding it by the handle with the sharp tip pointing toward the receiver, even when the blade is covered by a sheath (Figure 12.2, part 4). This prohibition reflected care for the receiver's safety, but it also made sense within the samurai community because it minimized the fear that the person passing the sword might turn it against the recipient.

Table Manners

The act of eating together has strong symbolic meaning in almost all human societies. The English word "company," like the French *compagnie*, is derived from the Latin *cum panis*, "with bread," which conveys the

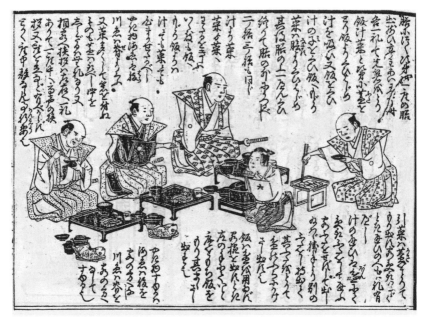

(1)

(2)

idea of shared nourishment.[14] Sharing a meal or giving food to someone conveys a double-edged symbolic meaning, however: equality and oneness on the one hand, and subordination to a master on the other. Because of this twofold meaning, sharing meals can be an effective ritual tool for confirming a hierarchical order, as well as a mechanism for creating horizontal solidarity. In Japan, the ritual of eating food together had symbolic associations with sharing food with the Shintō gods through whom human bonds were renewed and recreated. Eating a meal together sometimes helps to form horizontal alliances among members of a group. In any case, occasions to eat together are inevitable and at the same time one of the most delicate moments of human interaction.

Consequently, table manners were considered one of the most important areas of etiquette for Tokugawa people. *Edo daisetsuyō kainaizō*, an encyclopedic *setsuyō-shū*, explains the reasons for the book's emphasis on table manners:

> Unless you learn the basic information regarding table manners and proper food service for guests, you will appear vulgar and coarse in the eyes of others. In order to give you a sense of what a [well-bred] person should know, the following article [on etiquette] will list several introductory essentials.[15]

The method of serving was individualized, the food being portioned into small dishes (see Figure 12.3, part 1). Dishes, bowls, and chopsticks were rarely shared. Similar instructions, though less elaborate, were reproduced in various places in the Tokugawa versions of etiquette books. For example, *Shogaku bunshō narabini Yorozu shitsukekata mokuroku* (Introduction to Good Writing and Manners for Various Occasions),[16] from the early seventeenth century, explained the technique of peeling a Japanese melon as follows: "When you peel a melon, first wash your hands as well as the knife," and then "peel from the top down . . . cut six and a half pieces of skin," and finally, "cut a small piece and eat it." Similar instructions were offered for other dishes: "When you eat rice, pick up your chopsticks and take two mouthfuls. Then hold up your soup bowl

---

Figure 12.3. Elegant Manners. (1) Instruction on table manners and the method of serving food. The food was typically served on small and low individual tables with several small dishes. From *Yamato setsuyō-shū shikkai nō* (Japan's Dictionary for All Matters). (2) The way of serving *sake*. Holding the handle of the pot with your right hand, your four fingers should rest together on the underside of the handle with your thumb gently placed on the top. Your left thumb should lightly touch the cover, while the left-hand fingers hold the side. From *Onna shorei ayanishiki* (The Brocade of Women's Manners).

by the left hand." Needless to say, these movements as a whole were to be executed precisely and smoothly.

An example of consideration for others can be observed in *Onna shorei ayanishiki* (The Brocade of Women's Manners), a women's etiquette book, in which we find an article on how to feed a child a dumpling in public. It reads as follows: "To give a dumpling (*manjū*) to a small child, first place the dumpling on a piece of paper and cut it into three pieces as illustrated. Then, give one piece of it to the little one; after he finishes eating, offer him another piece." The manner expressed caring for the small child's safety by avoiding offering him too large a mouthful while maintaining the elegant appearance of the nurse or mother who was feeding the child.

The observation of Tokugawa manners brings us to a point of comparative interest. In his pioneering work on the Western history of manners, Norbert Elias emphasized that the medieval European literature of manners had a very different attitude toward human boundaries than that characterizing contemporary Western societies. He summarized the standard of medieval court manners as follows:

> People help themselves from communal dishes. Solids (above all, meat) are taken by hand, liquids with ladles or spoons. However, soups and sauces are still very frequently drunk. For a long period, too, there are no special implements for different foods. The same knife or spoon is used. The same glasses are drunk from. At the end of the Middle Ages, the fork appears as an instrument for taking food from the common dish. A courtier thought nothing of blowing his nose on his sleeve.[17]

But with the coming of "civility" in the early modern period, as Elias traces the process, failure to confine certain bodily functions to one's private room gradually became unthinkably bad manners. Furthermore, the new etiquette's emphasis on stricter control of bodily urges and spatial segmentation (such as greater respect for interpersonal physical boundaries, segmenting spaces inside houses to separate private rooms from semi-public areas, and segmenting the body into zones of greater or lesser intimacy) heralded the modern West's conception of personal selfhood. The rise of spatial differentiation and more individualized table manners are considered markers of the changing sensibility of post-medieval Europe.

Clearly, medieval Japanese courtiers were instructed in much more detailed and procedurally defined physical movements. Even tables had become individualized by the medieval period; in fact, guests at formal banquets were often given several small low tables with a few small dishes on each. In the sixteenth century, a late medieval manual from the Ogasawara School described good table manners as follows:

> To eat a bowl of rice: Hold the bowl and pick up a small portion of rice with your chopsticks two or three times. Then, proceed to the soup. Eat rice again twice or so. After that, you may eat from other dishes. Begin with a portion of *shōjin* [a vegetarian dish] or *aemaze* [fish meats marinated in vinegar or *sake*].[18]

All these dishes were served on low personal tables set with a few small plates and bowls. Japanese formal manners in the early modern period did not show a clear departure from those of the late medieval era in terms of the degree of bodily restriction. In fact, it was long after the period of Westernization that Japanese middle-class families began using a low common table called a *chabudai* in order to eat a meal in their living rooms. This finding clearly indicates that the conventional dichotomy of segmentation and individualization of space as reflected in contemporary, holistic, or communal European examples is not readily applicable to the Japanese case. Communal table manners cannot be described simply as pre-modern since formal Chinese banquets continued to be communal, while pre-modern Japanese table manners were already predominantly individualized. As with publishing and reading patterns, Tokugawa table manners of the proto-modern style were clearly taking their own direction distinct from Western examples.

By reviewing the intricate and complex rules of formal table manners, one may wonder to what degree the kind of formal etiquette detailed in these manuals reflected the actual practice of politeness in socialization among the Tokugawa people. The answer is simple: There should be some discrepancy between the ideal presented in books and the reality in practice. The formal etiquette and manners set down in those books were ideal models that were originally intended for more aristocratic usage in the medieval era. The articles on manners were written with formal occasions in mind. Furthermore, Tokugawa etiquette was something of a performing art. We must note here that highly prescriptive body movements cannot be fully conveyed by the short summary of etiquette presented in these books. These deficiencies were obvious to people at the time the Tokugawa books of civilized knowledge were published.

Even with these limitations, however, the frequent appearance of these articles in the most highly referenced handbooks and manuals predictably popularized the image that there was a formal way of elegant socialization. The Tokugawa Japanese who were functionally literate were exposed to new images of a privileged social world through these books of civilized knowledge. Although ordinary people may not feel obliged to practice, for example, nine degrees of differentiating bowing and eating only one side of a fish, they nonetheless came to realize the existence of a prestigious cultural standard beyond their daily life by the aid of these handbooks.

Beauty as a Mechanism of Control

Tokugawa people themselves considered the Ogasawara School as a kind of school for the performing arts along the lines of the tea ceremony schools. Performing artists in Japan generally attempt to shape a body capable of the graceful execution of stylized movement through practiced repetition of motions and gestures. The simple serving of a cup of tea in the tea ceremony makes it obvious at a glance whether the server is a novice or an accomplished student. Ideally, all social interactions should be performed with the same manner of confident elegance.

Tokugawa manners and etiquette were characterized by an emphasis on aesthetic qualities as well as by their prescriptive nature. To be sure, a graceful and confident physical carriage was certainly appreciated in the court traditions of Europe and elsewhere. But the strong influence of the performing arts in Japan meant that Japanese formal manners regarded beauty as a major implement of socialization.

This aesthetic emphasis was also true for serving food and drinks to guests, a standard entry in most etiquette books. *Onna shorei ayanishiki* (The Brocade of Women's Manners) explains the proper way to hold a *sake* pot. The instructions are minutely detailed with respect to the "elegant" placement of the hands. Hold the handle of the pot with your right hand; your four fingers should rest together on the underside of the handle, with your thumb gently placed on the top. Your left thumb should lightly touch the cover, while the rest of the left-hand fingers hold the side (Figure 12.3, part 2). The illustration of the gesture conveys the prescribed sense of exquisite refinement.

The pervasive interest in beauty at mealtimes was not limited to physical movements. To give an example of formal table manners, Kaibara Ekken (1630–1714) recommended that well-bred people eating fish should eat only one side of their portion; the fish was then to be turned over in order not to display the eaten – and therefore messy – side to others at the table. Dishes and bowls with food stains and other signs of mealtime use were considered dirty and ugly. "Dirty" in this context refers to aesthetic unpleasantness rather than contamination in the medical sense.[19] Of course, we can speculate that only the rich who could afford this level of formality – such as the *daimyo* – would have practiced such a wasteful method of consumption. In eating round sweet dumplings, Ekken advised biting the same corner of the dumpling twice – because if one took only one bite, most likely the soft surface of the dough would retain the imprint of the teeth, which would "look ugly." His recommendations in such matters are noteworthy because they illustrate the importance of the criterion of beauty in governing Japanese formal manners.[20]

Table manners also called for careful use of chopsticks. "Ugly-looking ways of eating," wrote Ise Sadatake, "include *madoi hashi* [strayed chopsticks] – partaking of dishes here and there as if one is confused and lost" – and "*yoko bashi* [side chopsticks] – licking rice or other bits of food from the side of the chopsticks." He also warned that "the tip of the chopsticks can be moistened for about 1 *sun* [3.03 cm] – but should not be too long."[21] Chopsticks soiled by food particles were considered an affront to aesthetic standards.

The Japanese system of propriety clearly entailed a different method of creating the social body through a set of strictly prescribed movements.[22] In contrast, Steven Ozment's study of family life in Reformation Europe provides some illuminating comparative insights. He reports that etiquette books for children in Reformation Europe stressed the importance of "always maintaining an equable temperament" (Erasmus) and "moderation" (Brunfels).[23] These books for children tend to focus on the "no-nos": "Eat only small pieces, not too great in quantity"; "Don't pick your teeth with a knife"; and "Don't blow on your soup or drink, for, although your whole body may not be smelly, your breath may stink."[24] Otto Brunfels, whose books were published in the early sixteenth century, teaches table manners accordingly: "Make sure your nails are cut and your hands washed. Sit up straight, comply with the requests of those around you . . . Do not cut your bread on your chest or in your hands. . . . Do not fall upon your plate like a pig upon a trough. Do not mix your foods together. Do not eat with your fingers."[25] The sequence of "do nots" continues. Although there is certainly some instruction regarding physical deportment in Western etiquette books, such as the injunction not to slouch or slump at the table, the basic tone of these books of manners implied that the body is a potential source of sin and corruption to be monitored and disciplined by strict piety.[26] It is easy to find the influence of religious tradition because of Christianity's high valuation of piety, modesty, and humility regarding the body; and the religious basis of good conduct was widely popularized throughout Europe by the practice of Christianity itself. Even before the Reformation era, vowed religious in monastic orders were expected to practice physical modesty, including the custody of the eyes, to avoid the appearance of gluttony at mealtimes, to curb expressions of anger, and so forth. Because monks and nuns lived in communities rather than as isolated anchorites or hermits, their rules typically included points of etiquette intended to ease the strains of communal life as well as regulations governing worship, work, and private possessions. Although these monastic rules had some influence on pious laypeople who made periodic religious retreats, the books in which they were recorded did not have a wide circulation outside the cloister, in part because they were written in ecclesiastical Latin.

As in medieval Europe, where monasteries produced the rules of conduct for monks and nuns, Zen monasteries produced written rules of table manners for monks. Zen Buddhism was closely tied to cooking and eating because food preparation and eating were considered a part of spiritual cultivation. The simple and straightforward style of serving meals in the Zen monasteries must have influenced the tea ceremony's approach to serving and consuming a simple meal. In addition, the Zen monasteries' eating styles exercised some influence on formal table manners in the outside world. The influence of Zen on the history of Japanese manners, however, was comparatively and functionally different from that of Christianity on European manners. Japanese Buddhism had a different view of the body, considering it not as a source of temptations to sin but as a potential intermediary in deepening a person's spirituality.[27]

In contrast, the distinctively secular conception of Japanese aesthetic propriety was represented by the term *shitsuke*, which means "social discipline" in modern Japanese. During the late medieval and Tokugawa periods, however, the term was also used to describe the Ogasawara style of formal manners. Most of the articles on etiquette in the *chōhōki* or *setsuyō-shū* are entitled "*yorozu shitsuke-kata*," which can be translated roughly as "methods of various manners."

The indigenous *kanji* ideogram for *shitsuke*, which was invented in Japan during the medieval era rather than being imported from China, symbolically represented the indigenous ideal of the social body. Most of the *kanji* ideograms in the Japanese writing system were imported from China; the Japanese have added few ideograms of their own. The ideogram for *shitsuke* consists of two elements, the left part designating "body" and the right signifying "beauty." Obviously, the Japanese recognized that there was no Chinese ideogram that was adequate to describe a native conception of propriety in which physical beauty played an important role. The character implies physical grace allied with habitual discipline of body. Nonetheless, the native word *shitsuke* itself is older than the *kanji* ideogram *shitsuke*. It probably originated in agriculture, and it describes the plucking of rice seedlings from nursery beds with skillful replanting in a straight line at regular intervals. The rice seedlings lined up with mathematical precision in the paddy, well-prepared for future growth, suggested good preparation and discipline. *Shitsuke* also describes a technique for basting cloth inside a garment to help the finished product retain its shape. The thread used in the basting is called *shitsuke* thread to convey its role in shaping the garment. Thus, *shitsuke* was an appropriate term for describing discipline of the body in accordance with the rules of good manners.[28]

Japanese formal etiquette and manners clearly shared a tradition of bodily discipline with the distinctive aesthetic theories of the medieval performing arts that were discussed in Chapter 9. The distinctive characteristic of medieval performing arts was their emphasis on the relationship between a careful aesthetic training of the corporeal body and personal and internal cultivation. It was through the repeated training of body movements in the performing arts that unity of body and mind might be actualized. Such a view is more conducive to the development of *procedures* of propriety as models for emulation. Achieving beauty in physical movements as the result of observing and performing the requisite gestures was a major physical mechanism of control in Japanese codes of manners. In this way, beauty became a mechanism of control not only for bodily desires and functions but, through its creation of a social body, it also functioned as a mechanism of control for sociability.

Whether or not the Japanese ideal of prescriptive bodily discipline is less repressive than Western traditions of "negative" discipline is a problematic issue. Beauty in Japanese manners functioned as a strong controlling mechanism. From another angle, one can legitimately argue that the prescriptive formulation of gracious manners presented in Japanese books of civilized knowledge is in fact a more invasive mode of behavioral regulation. This line of argumentation assumes that prohibitive formulations of etiquette and manners do no more than circumscribe the lower limits of acceptable behavior. On the other hand, the prescriptive formulas of Japanese codes of conduct force the agent to strive for an aesthetic maximum rather than a moral minimum.

The point I would like to make here is that repression as a category of "representative" modes does not yield meaningful comparisons between Japanese and European modes of social discipline. It is best simply to acknowledge that Japan in the Tokugawa period was developing its own style of disciplinary culture that embraced a specific understanding of the relationship between body and mind and that this development is a part of Japan's distinctive style of proto-modernity. At the same time, if the Tokugawa ideal of civility had not been related to aesthetic ideals but only attached to a hierarchical political order, it would not have been as influential in the wider population. Its association with the culture of the performing arts and their distinctive aesthetic consciousness meant that the influence of Tokugawa civility was more enduring as well as more pervasive.

Confucian Propriety and Beauty

The casual observer of Tokugawa standards of propriety may come to the conclusion that the codes of Tokugawa civility were nothing more than a Japanese version of Confucian notions of propriety. The words of the village chief Yoda Nagayasu that were cited in the introduction to this chapter state that the rule of propriety is "nothing more than distinguishing clearly between persons of higher and lower status." His statement may appear to do little more than echo Confucian principles of conduct. But what this village chief read for the sake of learning hierarchical standards of propriety was the etiquette book of the Ogasawara School, which had nothing to do with Confucian *codes* of propriety. Although the Japanese manuals used some Confucian idioms, their recipe for proper conduct was different from the Chinese Confucian version; it stood much closer to the traditions of Japanese court rituals and the performing arts.[29]

The Confucian concept of propriety is usually romanized as *li* in Chinese and *rei* in Japanese. *Li* is often translated into English as "rituals," "ceremonies," or more abstractly as "propriety." The Confucian concept of *li* included such various kinds of concrete ceremonial rules as funerary rites, weddings, and the rituals and ceremonies of ancestor worship. It also related to the rules of inheritance and marriage. Although the Japanese appreciated the basic notion of *li* as a method of civilizing and improving human nature through the proper observation of ceremonies and rituals, they did not import the Chinese patrilineal kinship system along with the writings of Confucius and consequently found it impossible to transfer the observance of the ceremonial injunctions of Chinese *li*. The absence of these ceremonies did not mean that the ancient Chinese system of *li* had no influence on Japanese culture. The Confucian classics, including those works devoted to *li*, were read and absorbed by the Japanese people. From models of letter writing to *li* as a system of moral reflection, Confucianism influenced Japanese cultural practices in many ways. Furthermore, there have been repeated efforts by Japanese Confucian scholars since ancient times to bring Japanese rituals (e.g., mourning rituals) closer to Chinese Confucian standards. These attempts, however, had very limited success and were characterized by simplification of the original Confucian formulas rather than the reworking of Japanese customs in Confucian terms. Since the ritual procedures of Chinese *li* included criteria for deciding hierarchical ranking and kinship distances among clan members, the Japanese could not transplant the Chinese system in its fullness without importing the Chinese rules of kinship. In contrast to the Koreans, who reorganized their system of inheritance and marriage according to Confucian standards, the Japanese were quite selective in what they borrowed from the Chinese Confucian system.

For example, the *Chu Tzu chia-li* (House Rituals of Chu Hsi) was the most influential book of propriety in medieval and early modern East Asia. It was written in the twelfth century, but it had little influence on Tokugawa codes of etiquette and manners in these manuals. The Ogasawara-inspired point of etiquette regarding blowing one's nose – three times quietly, facing the interior corner of a room – would be laughable from the viewpoint of Confucian propriety. The lack of influence of Confucianism on Japanese standards of etiquette is remarkable given the fact that Chu Hsi's moral philosophy was the basis of Neo-Confucian thought in Tokugawa Japan. On the other hand – and here is a rather confusing point of argument – although the indigenous Japanese system of ritual propriety claimed little influence from the actual ritual codes of Confucian propriety, the term *rei* and an ideology of respecting hierarchy through the rules of propriety was firmly encoded in Tokugawa culture. An unexpected consequence of this twisted path of naturalizing the notion of *li* was that *rei* was regarded as the observance of propriety based upon the indigenous social hierarchy at the time in Japan.

In contrast, the Ogasawara School referred to its own manners as *shitsuke-kata*, or the *shitsuke* method. The aim of *shitsuke-kata* was the embodiment of elegance and polish through repetitious physical training, a process that eventually led students to an integrated harmony of body and mind. Aspirants to the performing arts could attain the requisite high level of precision and seeming effortlessness only through long and arduous practice and disciplined commitment.[30]

The early modern how-to books use *shitsuke* and *rei* interchangeably in their texts as names for the same kind of codified social interactions. Sometimes they even bore two titles on the front page, such as *Shorei-shū* (collection of various *rei*) and *Yorozu Shitsuke-kata* (various types of *shitsuke*). During the Tokugawa period, books of etiquette and manners were either called *shitsuke-kata sho* (literally, "books on the way of *shitsuke*") or *shorei-shū* (literally, "books about various *rei*"). However, in spite of the titular differentiation, they are essentially the same type of etiquette book.[31] This convergence of the two terms suggests the nature of the emerging standard of good behavior for all classes during this period – an ideal of physical elegance expressive of politeness and simultaneously sensitive to the recognition of status differentials. The Japanese ideal of sociability was built on the foundation of Japanese aesthetic culture and reinforced by certain aspects of Confucian morality that were compatible with the shogunate's political principle of rule by status.

The Rise of Polite Capitalism

As conservative standards of etiquette began to percolate throughout Tokugawa commercial society, merchants whose business depended upon the favor of samurai officers were obviously receptive to the requirements of hierarchical civility. They were also concerned about their reputation among their peers regarding their own level of knowledge of the polite arts as well as their reputation among their employees.

The reader should recall my earlier observation that civility has a social function of reducing "emotional transaction cost."[32] Furthermore, civility does not simply constitute the codes of politeness but rather is anchored to categorical structures and social relations in general. When both parties in social interactions behave with an implicit understanding of the categorical structures behind civility, an unnecessary increase in emotional transaction cost can be avoided. Since one of the functions of civility, however, is to lower the emotional cost of human transactions through defining politeness without disturbing the transacting parties' self-respect and sense of propriety, it requires serious consideration of the categorical relations between or among the parties.

The emergence of Japanese capitalism from its early phase into maturity during the Tokugawa period took place under a samurai regime. Although the samurai were not allowed to engage in business for themselves, they still occupied a strategic position in the Japanese market economy, both as consumers and as market gatekeepers. Businessmen in this period could not hope to be financially successful unless they had some dealings with the samurai – who were the most status-conscious and propriety-minded inhabitants of this society. Consequently, the better-established merchant houses tended to become ever more conscious of matters of propriety. In addition, the expansion of business operations meant that the merchant houses had to concern themselves with regulating larger numbers of employees. The most immediate example of a complex organization at the time of the expansion of the larger Tokugawa merchant houses was the samurai bureaucracy that had developed within the *daimyo* houses. The vertical structures of the samurai organizations were held in place by strict codes of propriety. This hierarchical model appeared to be useful for maintaining order among the employees of the larger merchant houses. Furthermore, since the categorical structures of the entire society were essentially feudal in nature, merchant houses that instituted a hierarchical code of propriety could acquire an image of establishment and increase their credibility. Preserving the trust of their colleagues and customers became a central concern of the more successful Tokugawa merchants.

Merchants' business associations with the upper-class customers, especially with the samurai officers, were another incentive for enculturation in a feudal normative mode of socialization. Merchants had a number of possibilities for interaction with higher-level samurai, who were generally more status-conscious. A close examination of a hundred years (1753–1859) of records from the family business of a wealthy Osaka merchant, Sukematsuya, paints a vivid picture of how a successful businessman could be encultured through his business associations. In the Tokugawa system, many Osaka merchants struck exclusive contracts with certain feudal domains (*han*) to serve as their sales agents in the rice market. Sukematsuya had four such contracts with the feudal *daimyo* domains. The records from 1771 indicate that Shinjirō, the head of this merchant house, paid frequent visits to the high samurai households and even to the lords themselves; on each occasion, he wore formal dress and brought a gift for the privilege of a formal greeting. He might have been offered a cup of *sake* on these occasions. This act of hospitality was also a bonding ritual that had to be handled with the appropriate manners. Shinjirō also frequently exchanged gifts with samurai officers who were vassals of these *daimyo* lords and invited them at least once a year to banquets at his house or took them to *sumō* wrestling matches.[33] All this socializing and business entertainment suggests that he was quite knowledgeable about the rules for socializing with samurai.

Some merchant houses found the observation of hierarchical codes of sociability useful for maintaining discipline among their own employees. By the eighteenth century, the larger Japanese merchant houses had developed a system of long-term employment based on the successive promotion of employees who began their careers as young apprentices living on the premises. This pattern of hiring and promotion developed alongside forms of strict internal discipline for employees that resembled the methods of control used by the samurai houses with their vassals. The merchant houses used various rules of propriety to differentiate their employees. This organizational development was supported by the shogunate's policy of rule by status, which tried to strengthen the authority of the masters of merchant houses over their employees. The employers in turn were legally responsible for their employees' behavior.

Many merchant houses established their own internal standards of discipline. In the early Tokugawa period, internal codes of proper behavior for employees of commercial establishments were relatively concise. As the larger merchant houses grew in scale over the course of the eighteenth century, however, more and more merchants adopted elaborate rules of conduct in order to strengthen their control over their employees. This process of elaboration is exemplified by the successive editions of the rules of conduct for the employees of Shirokiya, a successful clothing retailer. In 1671, the rules of the house were short and simple: (1) obey the shogun's laws; (2) report wrongdoing on the part of colleagues; (3) be humble, honest, and do not consort with prostitutes. By the mid-eighteenth century, however, Shirokiya's rules had become considerably more complicated in order to maintain a strict hierarchical order and discipline within the company. The company's rulebooks from 1725 and 1741 spelled out the details of company policy, including rules governing socialization with customers, trade partners, and family members. A junior employee had to use the polite forms of address even with colleagues who were even just one year senior.[34] This strategy of controlling workers through differentiation of manners and language was apparently copied from the methods of social control used by organizations in the samurai government. Employee dress and hairstyles were also carefully controlled.

Understandably, the larger merchant houses with rigid internal codes of propriety were also concerned about the manners that their employees displayed toward customers. Since the aim of such a code was to please customers, and formal manners in society were hierarchical, business establishments predictably tried to treat customers as if they were all feudal lords. For example, the large merchant house of Kobayashi Chōjiya spelled out rules for employees in the late Tokugawa period that stressed the importance of etiquette and good manners toward clients. The rules prescribed the proper way to offer tea, stating for example that the employee must serve the customer by sitting "one *tatami* mat below the customer's seat." All employees had to bow to customers in the most formal manner, touching both hands on the floor. Mizuguchiya, a clothing shop in the city of Nagoya, included the following in its instructions to employees: "When a customer enters the shop, you must bow first [before the customer's greeting], and offer tea and tobacco immediately.... Be polite and never treat the customer rudely." This emphasis on good manners recurs throughout the written rules of the Tokugawa merchant houses.[35]

In sum, the more successful the business, the more involved was the merchant house in social as well as economic transactions with the politically powerful. Tokugawa Japan developed and popularized highly differentiated idioms of expressing politeness, verbally and physically, within the framework of the neo-feudal state. Tokugawa merchant houses emerged within the cultural and political context of this status conscious society. Consequently, rather than inventing new modes of etiquette appropriate for a new emerging proto-modern market economy, Tokugawa Japan created a breed of merchants who were eager to learn and to adapt to the hierarchical convention of Tokugawa polite society. A thorough knowledge of polite words and manners and the ability to differentiate between them properly and strategically were prerequisites for the successful operation of business.

Although hierarchical civility could be effectively used to express Tokugawa feudal hierarchy such as among senior samurai and junior samurai, or samurai and a commoner, it was also applied to new emerging settings of social encounters such as business transactions. In particular, the fact that this hierarchical civility influenced the social relations of nascent early capitalism in Tokugawa Japan made a significant impact on the rise of what might be called "polite capitalism" in Japan.

It is important to note the fact that elaborate prescriptive codes of civility were not tied to fixed systems of political order because it opened a possibility to use this elaborate system of politeness in various new social settings – business transactions as well as the post-Tokugawa social relations. To understand this mechanism of transfer from feudal hierarchical codes of politeness to commercial settings, some findings in theories of politeness give us some insight. Studies on the cognitive psychology of politeness, such as Penelope Brown and Stephen Levinson's important contributions to politeness theory, provide crucial insight. Their theory of politeness assumed that polite exchanges, through physical or verbal manners, are universally characterized by simultaneous development along two dimensions – power and distance.[36] In other words, polite physical or verbal expressions could be used to address those who are hierarchically seniors but also those who are not familiar. This in turn meant that these idioms of politeness that expressed the vertical relationship between interacting parties could be easily transferred to express relative distance or intimacy of the interacting parties. For example, one may use a very polite expression with someone just met, but as intimacy develops, he or she would loosen their usage of polite wording. On the other hand, someone who always employs polite manners and forms of address even with persons who appear to be his or her inferiors may acquire a reputation for politeness and moral decency. At the same time, if a person uses only polite forms in casual conversation, he or she runs the risk of being thought "too distant" or incapable of relating openly or intimately with others. One can express such a subtle management of social distance by employing idioms originally intended to express hierarchical social relations.

We have already seen ample examples of the existence of rich shades of physical and verbal vocabulary in expressing hierarchy in Tokugawa Japan. When a society with a rich polite vocabulary originally meant to express the shades of feudal hierarchical differences encountered the rise of capitalistic social relations, polite expressions could be transferred to the social relations in newly emerging social contexts. For example, a seller often assumes a demeanor of deferential politeness to a customer. In return, the typical Japanese customer tends to regard such courtesy as his or her due, as if he or she were a feudal lord. In such a case of market transaction, the seller can intentionally exploit the idiom of politeness in order to please the customer. A similar situation pertains to employees in modern Japanese corporations: juniors are always required to use humble and respectful verbal and physical manners toward seniors. Of course, although modern Japanese business culture has become increasingly less deferential these days, it still strikes us as a distinctive way to transact business.

Nonetheless, if the behavior differentials of Tokugawa etiquette had been no more than the results of political enforcement from the top down, the abolition of the shogunate's political structures should have led to the quick evaporation of customs associated with hierarchical values. However, when these customs of hierarchical politeness were simultaneously associated with voluntary enculturation of aesthetically pleasing politeness popularized by the products of a commercial publishing industry, the situation became much more complicated. In fact, the codes of politeness in Tokugawa Japan had by then become a refined culture of socialization among individuals who were in contact with each other through this increasingly complex commercial society. The heavy doses of politeness in the business world, which might be called polite capitalism, originated during the period of Tokugawa neo-feudal development as formal ways of sociability.

Hierarchical Civility and the Image of Japan

In this way, hierarchical standards of civility spread to larger segments of the general population, not simply as the result of political enforcement but primarily through a combination of various actors' strategic behaviors and the institutional forces of a market economy. The fact that people regarded vertically structured codes of civility as more prestigious and sophisticated was an important contribution to the formation of Japanese culture.

Nonetheless, the popularization of standards of etiquette and manners inspired by medieval court tradition was only a part of the evolution of print-mediated civility. With the development of a market economy on a national scale, beauty as such became not only affordable to most members of Tokugawa society but neatly categorized and packaged as well with the emergence of the commercial publishing industry. The popularization of a hierarchical ideal of formal manners was only a part of this process of cultural dissemination. The process included the popularization of all kinds of conventional knowledge, ranging from summaries of performing arts and poetry to geographical and social information about the space called Japan. Although the compilers of the handbooks and manuals did not draw explicit connections between each piece of information that they supplied and a larger vision of Japanese tradition, taken together, their work redrafted people's cognitive associational maps of their country. The process of collating and popularizing this stock of basic information emerged during the Tokugawa period. Increasingly people came to accept an ideal picture of Japan as politically divided and compartmentalized but culturally united by a glorious aesthetic tradition.

I must also emphasize that hierarchical structured civility was only one of several major modes of civility in Tokugawa Japan. In Section Two, I examined the history of Japanese aesthetic life, in which voluntary associations centered on arts and poetry played a critical role in patterns of socialization. Socialization emerging from shared enjoyment of the performing arts and poetry reconfigured the interactional spheres that became a central focus of pre-modern voluntary associational life. This culture of sociability allowed its participants to decouple temporarily from the political constraints of feudal norms. The result was a feeling of fellowship rather than hierarchical order that characterized the culture of sociability in the Japanese aesthetic publics. Tokugawa society was thus enriched by the presence of multiple modes of civility.

The publication of popular handbooks of civilized knowledge clearly demonstrated the convergence of this accumulated information with a loosely constructed image of Japanese tradition. To be sure, the entries in these handbooks and dictionaries varied from one to another. Yet we can still identify two major recurrent topics in these books of civilized knowledge. The first concerns self-identification of position and orientation in time and space. The Tokugawa manuals are crammed full of introductory historical, geographical, and socio-political information. It is not an exaggeration to say that almost all the *setsuyō-shū* manuals open with either an eye-catching map or pictorial illustrations of famous cities and geographical landmarks. The earlier published manuals sometimes included a rudimentary world map with illustrations of various actual and imagined countries (Figure 12.4). The geographical information that was presented also tended to emphasize places and locations made famous by the *waka* poetry of the imperial court. *Waka* poetry made frequent references to *uta makura*, or famous place names, that became associated in readers' minds with the strong emotional and aesthetic impact of the poetry itself. By looking at pages of these manuals, not only poetry lovers but other people could gain a clearer sense of what the celebrated locations actually looked like as a part of their civilized knowledge (Figure 12.5).

If the articles on geography reflected Tokugawa readers' need to orient themselves spatially, the historical articles helped them locate themselves in the dimension of time (Figure 12.6). For example, *Dai Nihon eidai setsuyō mujinzō*, a typical voluminous encyclopedic *setsuyō-shū* first published in the mid-nineteenth century, featured an article comparing famous

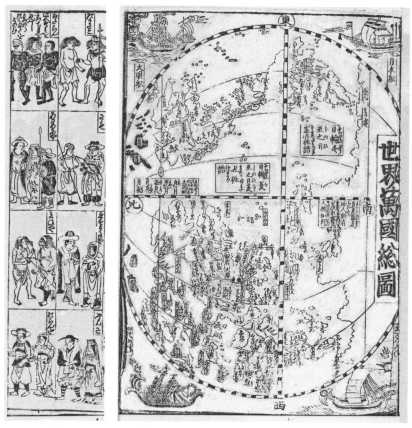

Figure 12.4. World Map and People of Foreign Countries. Almost all the *setsuyō-shū* (encyclopedic dictionary) open with eye-catching maps. This late seventeenth-century version of the manual features only a rudimentary world map (sample page shown on right) and illustrations of people in actual and imagined countries outside Japan (section of a page shown on left). It includes people of China, the Philippines, India, and Holland dressed in their own costumes as the Japanese imagined them. In addition, it features illustrations of imaginary lands such as a country of small people and a country of tall people. In later periods, maps in such publications became more and more accurate. From *Daii setsuyō-shū* (The Dictionary of Great Authority).

東海道
富士川

Figure 12.5. Mt. Fuji. A page from a *setsuyō-shū* handbook. Colored original. Pictorial illustrations of geographical landmarks were common features of Tokugawa manuals. The same book also contained pictures of the famous Nikkō shrine, the Tsukuba mountain, Nihonbashi (bridge) of Edo, and many famous festivals that were distinctive for the beautiful space called Japan. From *Edo dai setsuyō kainaizō* (Edo Great Dictionary).

Figure 12.6. History of Civilized Knowledge. A scene of the commanding ruler Hideyoshi – the man who united Japan – and his two generals. Names and images of historical figures are popular features of
Tokugawa manuals. On this page, the upper column and the lower column feature famous landmarks in *waka* poetry. It is typical of pages in
Tokugawa manuals that different kinds of knowledge are packed into
one page without logical connection. From *Yamato setsuyō-shū shikkai
nō* (Japan's Dictionary for All Matters).

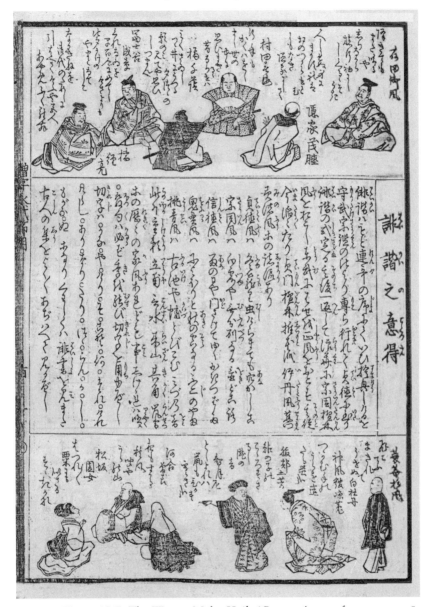

Figure 12.7. The Way to Make *Haikai* Poetry. A page from a *setsuyō-shū*. Common entries in such manuals were summaries of various branches of the arts and poetry. Here, the upper and lower columns of the introductory pages include a number of portraits of well-known poets in *haikai* poetry. The middle column summarizes the rules of making *haikai* poetry. From *Dai Nihon eidai setsuyō-shū*.

historical figures of Japan and China, with well-drawn illustrations for each figure, in proper chronological order. This particular *setsuyō-shū* also contains a long list of major historical events beginning with the legendary founding of Japan. Curiosity concerning one's position on the social and political ladders was directed to the articles on political offices or the names of provinces and their ruling *daimyo*. Offices and titles of the imperial court were regular features of these handbooks. This type of entry, which was included for the sake of Tokugawa "social studies," so to speak, was usually drawn from such well-known publications as *Bukan* (Military Mirror), which featured regularly updated information about the major samurai houses. Similarly, many of the social and political maps included in these manuals were derived from more specialized sources. The handbooks contained very little commentary on these entries; they were simply catalogs of such information as the names of nobles, the location of castles, the amount of rice production, distances from Edo, illustrations of family crests, and drawings of the spears and military symbols that were carried at the head of *daimyo* processions.

The second category of information in these books may be called essential knowledge for gracious living. The introductory articles on various polite arts fit into this category. For example, *Nan Chōhōki* (The Gentleman's Treasury) features a summary explanation of Chinese (*kanshi*) and Japanese (*waka*) styles of poetry. Some manuals of this type included lists of the most famous *waka* and *haikai* poets together with their portraits. For example, the *Dai Nihon eidai setsuyō* opened its account of poetry with the origin of *waka* poetry. The next page featured a summary of rules for linked-poetry composition followed by a page describing *haikai*. The upper and lower columns of these introductory pages included a number of portraits of well-known poets in various genres, older courtly figures as well as more recent *haikai* writers (Figure 12.7). After these portraits, the lower columns on the pages that followed listed some examples of seasonal banquet menus. The volume also includes an article on *utai* vocal music for *Nō* plays. The tea ceremony and the art of flower arrangement are topics that always appear in such works – including books intended for a male readership, as the title *The Gentleman's Treasury* indicates. Articles on formal etiquette and manners also belong in this category.

These collections of summary knowledge in various fields indicate that every branch of expertise had become standardized. At the same time, there was no specific editorial principle that organized or integrated these entries; the handbooks were simply put together in response to the demands of popular readership. For example, an account of techniques for wrapping gifts for ceremonial occasions in one *setsuyō-shū* adjoins the entry on the kinds of masks used in *Nō* dramas. The most important criterion for selecting these items appears to have been their usefulness in gracious living in that not knowing the conventions of polite behavior would shame an uncultivated person seeking to participate in Tokugawa social life. At the same time, the reader should note that civilized standards of gracious living were closely intertwined in the handbooks with the readers' demand for reliable information about physical, social, and historical realities in a society of ever-growing network connections. The image of a rich historical and artistic heritage thus emerged from these seemingly unrelated bits and pieces of civilized knowledge. Hierarchical standards of civility were attached to this image of Japan since they were considered to be part of a noble tradition of beauty.

Section Four

Concluding Reflections

13

The Rise of Aesthetic Japan

The news of the Opium War between Great Britain and China (1840–1842) and of the humiliating concessions in the treaty that China had to accept after the war alerted the Japanese elite to the political realities of the world outside their country. The opinions of some intellectuals outside the shogun's inner circle began to circulate among the literati, while less formal networking quietly began among concerned political activists. A critical event occurred in 1853 with the entry of Commodore Matthew Perry and his four "black ships" into the Bay of Edo to demand the opening of Japan to the West. The spell of the pax Tokugawa was finally broken by the apparent military superiority of the American naval vessels. The visual impact of four foreign ships lying at anchor in the bay in front of the shogun's own castle affected ordinary people as well as their rulers. The rumor mill began to grind, and unofficial publications swiftly carried the unsettling news of the black ships from the West to the most remote provinces of Japan. The presence and activity of dense and complex webs of communicative networks made it impossible to hide the shogunate's inability to respond to this crisis.

In spite of the sharp internal political rupture caused by Perry's mission, Japan reentered the world of global politics in the mid-nineteenth century with a relatively coherent view of its own cultural tradition. Throughout the Tokugawa period, the shogunate's policy of segmentation had increased the cohesiveness and awareness of regional *daimyo* polities.[1] By then, many *daimyo* polities had governed their own territories and subjects for centuries by relying on loyal vassal samurai. Many larger domains also developed various economic and financial policies to increase their revenues. While establishing cohesive organizations, they developed pride in their own ways of life. Following the collapse of the shogun's dynasty and the ruling samurai class in the late nineteenth century, it would have been possible in theory for the structurally separate *daimyo* domains to become independent states. In reality, however, Japan avoided political disunity. Furthermore, there was no strong interest in or commitment to ideologies of cultural separatism. Although the building of the various institutions of a modern nation-state was a daunting task, Meiji Japan was not burdened by the additional necessity of having to construct a cultural ideology of national coherence from scratch. Rather, the new government and its collaborating intellectuals were able to build this new cultural ideology of Japan as the nation-state on the foundation of the proto-modern images of the space called Japan. Within only 30 years after the so-called Meiji Restoration of 1868, Japan had already brought itself into the modern world as an up-to-date nation-state equipped with a constitution and a parliamentary system under the venerable authority of the emperor as its new national symbol.

Historians and social scientists have often probed the reasons for the swiftness of Japan's emergence as a modern nation during the Meiji period through the use of imperial symbolism when the emperor had been virtually deprived of actual political power for centuries. Behind the political accomplishments of the Meiji government, however, there had been a less visible but nonetheless distinguished cultural achievement that allowed Meiji Japanese to regard their cultural coherence as a given. Bonds of civility had connected Tokugawa people, loosely but definitely, in a symbolic plane of commonality in spite of the meticulously segmented nature of the Tokugawa polity. To be sure, this image of commonality was not rooted in a sharply focused ideology because it did not result from the confluence of national political narratives. The emergence of a loosely constructed image of Japan during the Tokugawa period was not a clearly defined process. People enjoyed participating in various cultural circles and learned cultural skills for their own purposes. Through this process, unintentionally, large segments of the Japanese population began to partake in and assimilate aesthetic cultures that were rooted in Japan's past. The process of ideological articulation that transformed these sensibilities into a more reified image of Japan came considerably later. An ideological formulation of Japan's cultural identity became conspicuous only with the rise of nationalistic sentiment, the expansion of the influence of the Kokugaku (the School of Native Learning), and the eventual construction of the Meiji nation-state, which served as a lens that brought the various images of Japan into sharper focus. The tradition of an aesthetic Japan inherited from the Tokugawa period, although certainly important, was not the sole dimension in creating an image of Japan that connected the people to their own past in a distinctive way.

The formation of a nation-state is usually understood as a process of internal equalization of status among individual citizens. From this point of view, a territorial state becomes a nation-state only when it breaks down such older categories as birth, regional origin, or ethnicity and binds individuals directly to the state. Although Tokugawa Japan had become a politically integrated entity, its *daimyo* system and strict hierarchy of status distinctions meant that it hardly deserved the name of a nation-state. Furthermore, the long-lasting Tokugawa shogunate upheld a policy of institutional segmentation that emphasized the observance of *internal differences* rather than the *unity* of the population. The case of Tokugawa Japan offers us an interesting instance of loose but tenacious cognitive networks involving a collective identity that emerged before the rise of a nation-state in the modern sense.

In this book, I have used the historical sociology of complexity and networks as a vantage point from which to analyze Japan's distinctive route toward modernity. In this chapter, I will sociologically reexamine several complex social processes during the early modern period in Japan. My aim is to articulate the mechanisms that allowed the multidimensional results of the Tokugawa network revolution to converge to the construction of Japan's cultural identity as a dwelling place of beauty.

The Positionality of Aesthetic Publics in Tokugawa Social Topology

I began my inquiry with the assumption that what I have called the Tokugawa network revolution is central to understanding the development of Japan's cultural identities in aesthetic terms. The simultaneous expansion of political, economic, associational, and communicative networks laid the organizational foundations for Tokugawa cultural developments. The resulting network reconfigurations within the framework of the neo-feudal state influenced the ways in which people encountered one another.

In the course of this analysis, I identified the structural advantages that unintentionally drew the popular aesthetic circles into the center of Tokugawa social life. The structural advantages were driven by political dynamics. First, I have focused on the influence of the nature and developmental trajectory of the Tokugawa state in this regard. The Tokugawa shoguns shrewdly divided the society under their rule into distinct semi-autonomous components while at the same time reorganizing these components as formal and multilayered hierarchies. As a result, Japanese society was politically carved into a number of structurally separate and formally unrelated – though in practice connected – social components. While the shoguns were careful to maintain the boundaries that separated various social groups with their respective assigned duties, they also restructured and streamlined the multilayered social hierarchies within each structurally distinct unit of control. The shogunate subordinated and incorporated groups that had been more or less independent in the previous era while making hierarchies stronger than ever. In this context, the term "hierarchies" refers to clusters of networks that were stratified by power and status differentials.

One of the strategies that the shoguns employed in streamlining these hierarchies was manipulation of the indigenous terms for publicness, such as *kōgi, kō*, and *ōyake*. By claiming itself to be the supreme source of public propriety, the shogunate constructed idiosyncratic hierarchies of publicness in which local *daimyo* states represented regional sources of public propriety. The Tokugawa state reconstructed the hierarchies of publicness while prohibiting or subordinating various horizontal associations that had been active in forming local publics or society's publics, so to speak, during the previous era.

It was within this social topology that the various hobby circles – the aesthetic publics – became *positionally* very important in the private social life of Tokugawa people. Having been culturally established before the Tokugawa era, aesthetic associational activities were considered respectable and safe ways of socializing privately with other people even across the official regional, occupational, and status boundaries set by the state. Unlike official definitions of hierarchies of publicness that represent hierarchies of power and authority, voluntary participation in these circles in fact came closer to signifying one of the ancient root meanings of publicness, that of common spheres constructed by the association of private individuals.

Participation in the activities of the aesthetic circles did not mean that the members disowned their official identities as samurai or commoners. They were still closely hemmed in by social obligations and norms predicated by the Tokugawa political system. The popularity of these circles across all divisions of geography and status, however, did create loose linkages on a plane of commonality among amateur artists and poets who were stratified and segmented by political definitions.

Weak Ties and Multiple Identities

Compared with feudal political ties or primordial territorial and kinship ties that enforced heavy obligations and lifelong commitment – that is to say strong ties – aesthetic circles represented more or less weak ties in the sense of Mark Granovetter's usage. Compared with strong ties, which tend to form among small clusters of people, weak ties often carry information much more widely and extensively. Therefore, contrast with those highly localized cohesive networks, the operation of these collective arts and poetry circles brought some openness to Japanese society since the aesthetic publics served as bridges among individuals from very different backgrounds. Even in a relatively small community in which the aesthetic circles largely overlapped with existing village networks, however, the ritual logic of an aesthetic public encouraged people to consider its space as temporarily distinct from existing ties. Thus, the Tokugawa network revolution was characterized not only by an increase in the scale and density of network intersections but also represented a qualitative difference in terms of an increase in the number of weaker ties that drew together clusters of people in unexpected ways.

The aesthetic enclave publics had the ability to create alternative realities by periodically allowing Tokugawa people to slip outside the boundaries of convention. By sitting together with people from different regional or occupational networks, or even other participants from the same neighborhood, members of the aesthetic publics temporarily decoupled from their existing ties and switched their identities from those of loyal samurai or humble farmers to those of skilled artists or poets. Such frequent experiences of attending aesthetic circles quietly transformed personal identities as well as the quality of social relationships. By connecting individuals to larger worlds of network, imagery, and meaning, the aesthetic publics enabled at least some of them to begin to consider their true identity in wider terms than the formal identities bestowed on them by the state.

The reader should recall my earlier reference to samurai who loved popular *jōruri* songs so much that they drew the fire of a contemporary critic.[2] Frequent experiences of shifting identity from formal feudal status to aesthetic enclave identities made the individual citizens of this society recognize that the feudal boundaries set by the Tokugawa order determined just one of many possible modes of sociability. Unlike a feudal identity that put the self into a neatly categorized set of boxes, the self as a poet or an artist linked the individual to a larger universe of commonality. The official ideology of the Tokugawa shogunate required the samurai to concentrate attention on their public duties as assigned by the shogun. Merchants, farmers, and others were to focus similarly on their own respective occupational duties. Yet, the presence of aesthetic circles, even though they were officially considered private and therefore inferior enclaves of socialization, enabled structurally separate individuals to connect with others who belonged to different clusters of networks. It is not surprising that in such a situation some Tokugawa people began to consider their identities within the enclaves of aesthetic publics to be more accurate reflections of their true selves. This new self-assessment is reflected in the words of a samurai painter, Watanabe Kazan: "I am the Elder of a tiny provincial domain. . . . [M]y hands, however, are "public hands" that belong to the world and to history."[3] Participation in the activities of aesthetic groups helped to form individuals who felt themselves to be part of a universal fellowship rather than prisoners of a hierarchically segmented political structure.

The distinctive vitality of these pre-modern associations lies in the fact that group activities led participants to a conscious awareness of the multiplicity of their identities. These sites of aesthetic sociability developed a number of ritual technologies over the course of history that made it easier for participants to decouple themselves for brief intervals of time from feudal network constraints. As a result, the ritual technologies of the aesthetic publics not only allowed individual members temporary release from feudal social realities but also encouraged them to switch their identities intentionally in different communicative settings.

We must also note the point that participation in these cultural circles was purely voluntary; it was a matter of decisions made by individuals. Although it is difficult to define the distinctive quality of modern social life in any precise way, the possibility of multiple affiliational identities made on the basis of individual choice seems to be an important index of modernity. Any society that does not allow individuals associational ties other than those they are born with – whether territorial or religious affiliations or kinship ties – cannot be called modern. Although Tokugawa Japan was deliberately organized as a segmented society in which individuals were destined to live within structurally separate components, its aesthetic networks nevertheless facilitated individual choices regarding associational ties. Yet, having developed a domain of voluntary associational ties on the plane of private aesthetic socializing, this society truly deserves the name of proto-modern as far as its civic culture is concerned.

Although the government officially relegated communicative spheres devoted to aesthetic pursuits to the inferior domain of the private, or *watakushi*, they were nonetheless more active, open, and attractive loci for socialization. The popular images of Japan as a land dedicated to beauty were cultural emergent properties that were manifested in these spheres of communication.[4] Since aesthetic socialization brought together people who were otherwise divided and confined by the Tokugawa policy of institutional status divisions, it also connected people with the common culture – as so perceived – of Japan. Although Tokugawa people were separated from one another in terms of their social roles, lifestyles, and fashions, they nonetheless began to share the same cultural idioms, aesthetic activities, and images of Japanese tradition.

The Strength of Overlapping Networks

As we have seen in Chapter 9, the Kokugaku (School of Native Learning) scholars of the eighteenth and nineteenth centuries, most notably

Motoori Norinaga (1730–1801), painted an idealized picture of the ancient Japanese aesthetic as expressed in the classical literature. Consequently, the work of Norinaga and his colleagues in looking for "true" Japaneseness in the Japanese classics gave additional publicity to the image of Japan as a country with a proud aesthetic heritage. As a result, a number of intellectual historians have been attracted to the Kokugaku movement because the group clearly had the potential to lay the symbolic foundations of a national identity before the rise of the nation-state. It is not my intention to devalue the significance of such efforts.

However, my research indicates that the Kokugaku scholars did not single-handedly invent the image of an aesthetic Japan. The growing social influence of the Kokugaku movement during the late Tokugawa period cannot be understood only in terms of intellectual history through an analysis of texts and ideas produced by the Kokugaku writers themselves; we must situate this movement within the context of the larger social and cultural history of the time. Widespread enthusiasm for poetry composition and the other arts, as well as the popularization of aesthetic knowledge through the commercial book trade, had already emerged during the first half of the Tokugawa period, much earlier than the peak of the Kokugaku movement. For example, the *chōhōki* and other manuals of civilized knowledge had compiled standardized lists of literary idioms and outlines of basic information about the performing arts as early as the late seventeenth century. Introductory guides to *haikai* poetry and other traditional arts were already "best-sellers" at the same time that the aesthetic circles began to attract large numbers of participants. Furthermore, as was mentioned earlier, even during the nineteenth century, the number of *haikai* poets at the provincial level was estimated to be fifty to a hundred times higher than the number of Kokugaku participants.[5] As I discussed in Chapter 8, in terms of social connections, the *haikai* poetry networks were far more dense and complex than those of the Native Learning intellectuals. By acquainting themselves with the classics and the courtly traditions of Japanese arts and literature in the course of their participation in these groups, however, they opened themselves to a view of Japan as a land of distinguished aesthetic traditions. Although the enthusiastic consumers of popular commercial publications also did not involve themselves in intellectual arguments about the precise definition and nature of Japan's aesthetic identity, they nonetheless popularized and naturalized the assumption that their country had an ancient and honorable tradition of devotion to beauty.

What started as spontaneous associations developed in an unplanned way into a conglomeration of networks. These fully contingent Tokugawa network experiments gave rise to yet a higher level of emergence: an interesting network effect appeared that might be called "the strength of overlapping networks." The most prevalent were the *haikai* poetry networks, but, in addition, even in agricultural provinces there were many other knowledge-based networks such as flower arrangements, *jōruri* singing, *kyōka* (comic poetry), *igo* games, *waka* poetry, and *shogakai* (open exhibitions of arts and calligraphy). All these networks formed overlapping patterns of patchworks that crisscrossed with other organizational networks based on kinship, political-territorial, and commercial links. Although these various types of networks were never systematically connected in any particular way, they nonetheless began to affect each other. In the world of aesthetic publics, it was common for a cultured individual to join several artistic networks.

As a result, these networks began to generate loosely overlapping circles of individuals. A duality relation began to take shape, with people linking networks and networks linking people. Since the formal order of Tokugawa society was still characterized by hierarchical modes of civility, this world of loose but tangible social connections that allowed individuals to socialize within the shared interests in arts and knowledge were in fact the spheres of public communication and were vital and tremendously attractive for those who participated. These loosely coupled individuals positioned at the intersections of overlapping networks had access to open circuits through which new knowledge could flow. Whenever a member of those well-established aesthetic publics entered into a new network of knowledge such as the Dutch Learning (*rangaku*) or Kokugaku, friends and acquaintances in aesthetic hobby associations also would gain some knowledge about those new directions. Tokugawa society thus carved out ever more detailed spheres of civic socialization in and through these overlapping networks.

Due to the two phenomena of the strength of overlapping networks and the strength of weak ties, Japanese civic society had developed a seemingly ephemeral yet surprisingly robust multilayered network infrastructure that was informal yet more resilient than the formal Tokugawa structures that crumbled when the country was opened to the West. The emergence of the image of Japan as an aesthetic treasure-house was an unintended consequence of the cultural developments that grew out of this network revolution.

The Market-Driven Formation of the Japanese Tradition

The expanding scale of the national economy and the rapid growth of urban centers within the institutional framework set by the prior development of a neo-feudal state left distinctive marks on the emerging aesthetic images of Japan. The most obvious connection in this respect was the popularization of aesthetic idioms through the rise of a popular commercial publishing industry. The Tokugawa publishing houses were small in scale by contemporary standards, based as they were on a highly sophisticated and efficient but essentially old-fashioned woodblock technology. The majority of the early modern publishers were not linked to or subsidized by any political or religious authority. The high ranking of introductory books on poetry composition and manuals for civilized life on the publishing lists reflected the fact that the acquisition of these arts was central to the civic life of Tokugawa people. Through such publications as well as through the process of learning the traditional arts and the craft of poetry, Tokugawa people began to develop a cognitive associational map regarding the geographical entity called Japan.

Moreover, the process of literary popularization paved the way for further developments within the literary tradition itself. Once Tokugawa writers could assume widespread knowledge of the major characters or episodes in the classical tradition, they could allude to this information in order to increase their readers' pleasure at being "in the know." Even the "lowbrow" novels and picture books of the late Tokugawa period often borrowed familiar plot lines or idioms from the classics as the basis for parodies. We may grant the improbability that the majority of new readers could master a large body of classical literature; reading the ancient texts cannot have been easy for them. But it is important to recognize that, in addition to the classical texts themselves, their characters, story lines, and imagery were widely disseminated in forms that were more accessible to readers lacking the benefit of an elite education.

I have referred to the cognitive associational map that did not originally have a fixed ideological structure or coherent political narrative as "the Japanese tradition." To give a quick impression of this powerful yet loosely constructed image of Japan, let me turn once more to the pages of the Tokugawa popular commercial guidebooks for civilized knowledge. The expression "Nihon" or "Nippon" for Japan, as in such expressions as "the three best landscapes in Nihon" (*Nihon sankei*), often appeared in these manuals. On the other hand, Nihonbashi (the "Japan Bridge") in Edo was a frequently featured scene in these manuals as the famous starting point of the major national roads. We should also note that the term Nihon (or Nippon) began to be used frequently in commercial publications during the Tokugawa period.[6] Although Nihon or Nippon had been used as the official name of the country for many centuries, the appearance of this term in commercial publishing, coupled with the popularization of the geographical image of the space called Japan, distinguished the cultural development of the Tokugawa period.

On page after page, a surprising variety of information was condensed into small multiple columns with lively illustrations. These entries would have induced their readers to think of their homeland as unsurpassed in beauty, filled with populous and prosperous cities, picturesque landscapes, sacred shrines and temples, and sites immortalized in literature or history. Furthermore, the guidebooks depicted the people of this land as cultured and gracious persons who had mastered the arts of politeness as well as aesthetic appreciation. The reader should, however, note the fact that these manuals rarely defined or reflected a formal aesthetic or philosophy of beauty. The manuals' standard method of describing basic civilized knowledge was the enumeration of summary items one after another. This "card catalog" approach to information constituted a loosely arranged but not well-structured cognitive map. Through these lists of "must-knows," however, there emerged an indistinct but powerful image of the society that the readers lived in – a space called Japan and filled with cherished and beautiful traditions. Compared with an ideologically more structured or moralistic presentation of a collective identity, the eclectic assortments of idioms and images in the manuals were perceived by their first readers as less intimidating and more "natural." These relatively informal cognitive associational maps were nonetheless ready to receive new interpretations in changed historical contexts.

The Emperor's Position in the Tokugawa State System and Its Unexpected Consequences

The massive popular enculturation that took place through the country's economic expansion under the shogunate had unexpected political consequences that became apparent only when Tokugawa Japan was threatened by the Western powers in the mid-nineteenth century. At the beginning of the Tokugawa period, the shogunate distinguished between the emperor's court as a realm of beauty and scholarship and the shogunate as the realm of political and military power. In order to establish the shogunate as *ōkōgi*, the supreme public authority, the emperor's position had to be completely depoliticized. In order to achieve this end, the Tokugawa shogunate adopted the unusual tactic of compiling a comprehensive set of rules for the Kyoto court. The *Kuge shohatto* (Regulations for the Imperial Court and Aristocracy) of 1615 stipulated that the emperor and his court should devote themselves to various arts (*shogeinō*) – in particular, the art of learning (*gogakumon*). Learning, in this context, meant education in traditional court rituals and ceremonies. The emperor was expected to be the master of ceremonial tradition, which included the polite arts of the ancient court. This devotion was to be the imperial household's special service to the state, comparable with the samurai's provision of military service to the shoguns. This policy had significant implications for the Tokugawa cultivation of beauty.

The depoliticization of the emperor's court through restricting it to the pursuit of the courtly ceremonial and aesthetic traditions, however, had an unexpected side effect that became apparent only later on. The emperor held an exceptional position within the framework of the Tokugawa feudal status system. The status hierarchy in Tokugawa Japan had a twofold structure. The first and more obvious hierarchy placed the shogun at the top of the status pyramid, while the second, less evident hierarchy was headed by the emperor. The second status hierarchy headed by the emperor carried only symbolic values and did not yield actual political power. Although the shoguns were not opposed to artistic pursuits and were in fact eager to enhance their own cultural standards as the military rulers, they had no interest in supplanting the emperor as the *arbiter elegantiarum*. Even when the emperor was all but powerless politically, he never lost his high position in the esteem of the people because of his implicit dominion over the virtual realm. In fact, in the middle of the Tokugawa period, when the pax Tokugawa looked as if it would last forever, the shogun's authority seemed to require no legitimation by the emperor. Yet, in the popular mind, the emperor never completely lost his symbolic power precisely because his court and the image of traditional courtly aesthetic traditions came to be more closely intertwined. Anyone in Tokugawa society who claimed to be aesthetically refined would recognize the courtly aesthetic, poetry, and polite arts as the ultimate standards of high culture. Thus, the more widely the civilizing process of Tokugawa Japan was disseminated, the more entrenched the cultural position of the imperial court became in the imagination of the Japanese people.

Thus, as more individuals eagerly sought higher levels of cultural refinement through enjoyment of the arts and poetry, the central role of the imperial court in maintaining Japanese aesthetic traditions became self-evident. This situation facilitated, at least in part, the sudden revival of imperial symbolism in the late nineteenth century as the center of national unity when the Tokugawa shogunate's inability to respond to the forces of Western imperialism became clear.

Tokugawa Proto-Modernity and the Modern Japanese Nation-State

The rise of a new model of civility and the proliferation of social interactional spheres centering on poetry and performing arts during the Tokugawa period lead us to conclude that prior to Japan's intensive period of Westernization following the Meiji Restoration in 1868, Tokugawa

Japan was moving toward its own version of "proto-modernity," or "modernity before modernization," in the dimension of cultures of sociability. The experience of a sense of commonality formed through shared aesthetic experiences paved the way for the next phase of Japanese cultural developments in the process of constructing a modern nation-state. The appearance of images of Japan as a country defined by aesthetic excellence was not the result of political initiatives on the part of rulers but was rather the product of people's networking and market forces. Although the Tokugawa state's idiosyncratic structure and policies did leave their mark on the course of cultural developments, it was primarily the cultural entrepreneurs of this period who created a variety of new channels of communication and cultural diffusion. The Tokugawa popularization of aesthetic knowledge was driven primarily by market forces rather than by top-down enforcement of an ideology.

In addition, the participatory nature of popular artistic activities was a distinctive feature of the Tokugawa civilizing process. People voluntarily networked with one another through the polite and performing arts. In these networks, they actively participated in sharing, performing, and creating artistic objects or events. Tokugawa people enjoyed their culture's traditional arts as active performers and participants in their own right; they did not attend cultural events as admirers or patrons of professional artists and musicians. Even though a student might be motivated to learn an art only for purposes of socialization, the process of immersing oneself in the rules, the aesthetic standards, and the spiritual disposition required by the art through actual performance or production represented a much deeper level of enculturation than simply being a passive spectator of "real" artists. In this context, learning the skills of poetry composition or any other of the performing arts represented a process of embodiment of aesthetic knowledge.

The emergence of the aesthetic image of Japan was the accumulative result of largely unplanned social actions in historical contingencies. As a consequence of these two distinctive features of the Tokugawa aesthetic popularizing process – its market-driven and participatory characteristics – the notion of a Japanese aesthetic tradition came to feel much more "natural" to the people living under the Tokugawa regime. Its encounter with the hegemonic power of the Western nations required Japan to reconstruct its ethnic cultural identity in the global political theater as well as fashion a notion of citizenship and national cultural identity within the framework of its new political constitution. Pre-existing images of Japan as an aesthetic nation were quickly exploited in order to shape Japanese cultural identities for the global context as well as domestic needs.

Japan underwent rapid changes following the Meiji Restoration of 1868. In particular, the fact that the process of nation-building under the

Meiji regime was based on the Western model of modern nation-states with strong armies and centralized bureaucracies increased the penetration of central government control into local communities and regional cultural practices. The process of modernization that Natsume Sōseki (1867–1916) called "internally motivated" in his 1911 lecture on "The Civilization of Modern-Day Japan," namely the civilization that developed "naturally from within, as a flower opens"[7] during the Tokugawa period, "was sidetracked." Sōseki observed that Japan had been "painfully" compelled by the external forces of Westernization to take a different and less congenial route to modernity. Having been born into an urban Edo family, Sōseki was acutely aware of his cultural roots among the Tokugawa townspeople. Their heritage of aesthetic interests coupled with enjoyment of various forms of entertainment was intensely private, whereas the mainstream of the new culture was based on Western science and technology coupled with a nationalistic goal. To consider the ongoing process of Westernization as externally compelled was a common response, even for members of the Meiji elite who successfully adapted themselves to the new cultural requirements of a modern nation-state.

Let us not, however, overlook a critical point. Westernization and modernization cannot be described simply as a transition from the "naturalness" of *Gemeinschaft* to the "artificiality" of *Gesellschaft* as such. The Japanese themselves became highly self-conscious about externally coercive forms of civilization because they had already developed a cultural identity predicated on their perceived "traditional" and "natural" civilization and their ways of life. In fact, the culture of Tokugawa Japan was the product of what the historian Ōishi Shinzaburō has called "the most deliberately and politically created society in Japanese history."[8] It was precisely because Tokugawa Japan had already drawn a clear cognitive map of its own culture – not simply as a "natural" given but as a construct articulated through such "artificial" means of communication as commercial publications – that such Meiji Japanese as Sōseki could become remarkably self-critical and reflective regarding their "externally forced" pattern of "civilizing." The construction of Japan as a modern nation-state and the development of industrialization within this new political framework were thus facilitated by the presence of a cognitive framework among post-Tokugawa Japanese people that pre-supposed the existence of a natural sense of *Gemeinschaft* in Tokugawa Japan. The aesthetic socialization of Tokugawa people generated an image of aesthetic Japan as if it had been a natural description of the geographical entity called Japan. This image was resilient and useful; it allowed the Meiji Japanese to regard their cultural identity as a given, and it gave the Meiji leaders more options for mobilizing the loyalty of their fellow citizens. Thus, I regard the aesthetic image of modern Japan as an emergent property that evolved out of the hobbies of amateur enthusiasts into a cultural reality of an image of Japan as an aesthetic homeland. This cultural reality in turn prepared the country in an implicit and subtle fashion for its reconstitution as a modern nation-state.

Aesthetic Japan: Continuous Reformulations

Japan has continuously reformulated its past and present cultural identities in various historical contexts. A detailed exploration of the refocusing of these aesthetic images in the post-Tokugawa period is beyond the scope of this book. A cursory look at this development, however, reveals the presence of different usages of these aesthetic images, some of them contradictory, reflecting the resilience as well as the durability of this icon. Since the image of aesthetic Japan was multidimensional, allowing for various interpretations, it was used and refurbished to suit a variety of different actors' purposes. I proposed earlier that the relationship between social or cognitive network dynamics and the cultural and identity practices that issue from them should be understood as a form of emergent property. The paradoxical aspect of emergent properties lies precisely in the fact that they are at the same time "nothing more" than what is already given at a lower level of description, yet simultaneously "completely different" once emerged, and in that qualitative sense "far more" compared to the lower level. Culture as an emergent property is thus continually open to refocusing and renegotiation. Once consolidated as a set of relatively stable cognitive associational maps, however, a culture and identity that have emerged through actions in publics may have more reified or "thing-like" effects in the social world. Since the image of Japan as the repository of a great aesthetic tradition was firmly ingrained in the imagination of the Japanese people, it became a useful cultural resource that allowed a number of political and economic actors in the modern period to exploit it for a range of different purposes.

For example, when Japan reentered the world of global politics in the late nineteenth century, the government highlighted the refined craftsmanship of Japanese artisans by sending a number of beautiful examples of Japanese crafts and arts to be showcased at world expositions. These elaborate examples of artistic talent symbolized Japan's pride as a nation among nations after more than two centuries of isolation. Furthermore, the revenue gained from exporting the exquisitely crafted products of the Tokugawa cottage industries, from silk to ceramics, enabled the Meiji government to cover the costs of the early phase of Japanese industrialization.

On the other hand, remember the fact that various manuals of civilized knowledge, from tourist guidebooks to *chōhōki* and *setsuyō-shū*, featured a list of historical famous places such as old temples and famous poetic landscapes. The Meiji government made it a high priority to define and to preserve these famous temples and landscapes as national aesthetic treasures in order to enhance the image of Japan. This enhanced image, in turn, was understood to facilitate the integration of the population under the cultural authority of the emperor. It also would help to elevate the status of Japan as a civilized country in the world. It was in this context that in 1897 the Old Temples and Shrines Preservation Law was enacted. In addition, the Law of the Preservation for Historical Sites and Distinguished Landscapes was enacted in 1919 as a consequence of wide-spread movements for promoting preservation.[9] On the other hand, with the expansion of Japan's military capability and imperialistic ambitions, the aesthetic image of Japan was used to reinforce the top-down ideologies of nation-building and patriotism by infusing them with emotional warmth and feelings of love for the homeland. New texts for the popular songs taught in music classes in the public schools romanticized the poetic images of the land called Japan using the major and minor scales of Western music. The so-called *Monbushō shōka* (songs selected by the Ministry of Education) included a number of such popular songs as *Hana* ("Cherry Blossoms"), *Kojo no tsuki* ("The Moon Shines on an Old Castle"), and *Oborozukiyo* ("Misty Moon Night") that reflected the themes of the Japanese poetic tradition but also used Western musical notation and harmonies. The beloved song *Furusato* ("My Old Place") was another favorite that expressed and encouraged nostalgic affection for the beautiful scenery of rural Japan.

In contrast to this sentimental romanticism, the emperor was redrafted as a paternalistic symbol of Japan's military strength – a radical change in imperial symbolism compared with the Tokugawa distinction between the shogun as military commander-in-chief and the emperor as the traditional elegant representative of the courtly arts and scholarship. This was a radical political change, since the pre-modern imperial court was characterized by a traditional and rather feminine court culture. Ladies-in-waiting had always surrounded the emperor; he was normally wearing a long elegant robe, appearing with white make-up and painted eyebrows. Although this kind of feminine image was transformed drastically into the new masculine figure of the Meiji emperor, with beard and military costume, this process did not replace or reject the older aesthetic image of Japan. The image of the emperor as a militaristic father figure coexisted with the symbol of a homeland that embraced people with maternal acceptance, however sublimated this second theme might have been.[10] And it was the latter image that was deeply rooted in the world of poetry and beauty associated with the imperial courtly tradition of Japan. When the army mentality joined hands with an aesthetic tradition, as Emiko Ohnuki-Tierney's work on the militarization of Japanese aesthetics indicates, such traditional symbols of Japan as cherry blossoms were often used to mobilize people's patriotic sacrifices for their glorious homeland. Not all mobilized soldiers were persuaded by the militarized interpretation of Japanese aesthetics. However, even those who did not accept the official ideology of state militarism were affected by the connection; Japanese soldiers perceived their self-sacrifice for the sake of their country as analogous to the fragile and transitory beauty of cherry blossoms.[11]

One should not assume that the Japanese aesthetic tradition was simply redirected toward the project of nationalism. The reader should recall that the pre-modern private enclaves of aesthetic publics kept the realm of beauty distinct from the realm of public policy. The spirit of fun-loving Tokugawa aesthetic socialization had little concern for efficiency; it even admitted a certain aimlessness, so to speak, as an official good because off-hours socializing was understood as a strictly private matter. The pleasures of a social life were themselves sufficient to motivate networking activities. In this, the Tokugawa mindset was far removed from the spirit of nation-building and industrialization, which required a sense of purpose and dedication to efficiency. This aspect of the Tokugawa cultural legacy was preserved by those who were either personally unwilling or politically unable to collaborate with the nationalistic goals of the Meiji regime; they were the people whom Yamaguchi Masao has called *haisha*, or "losers." In the history of Japan's modern nation-building, Yamaguchi has portrayed a number of Japanese citizens who avoided involvement in state-centered hierarchies and organizations of Meiji Japan while constructing "another, less visible modern Japan" through voluntary initiatives involving networking in various fields.[12] From scholarship and journalism to the educational, cultural, and commercial establishments, however, private initiatives and networks of these "losers" have left their imprint everywhere on modern Japanese cultural history. The presence of these civic counters to the ideologies of state-led modernization, which were inherited from the private networking efforts of the cultured people of the Tokugawa period, have in fact greatly enriched modern Japanese history.

On the other hand, the realm of beauty became useful for political reconstitution of Japan's image on occasion precisely because of its presumed distance from politics. For example, soon after the defeat of 1945, Japan quickly reconfigured its self-image around its aesthetic and cultural traditions. It was claimed that the country should be a *bunka kokka*, or cultivated nation, one that stood on its reputation for cultural excellence. While the Japanese people eventually found that economic growth provided their real recovery of confidence, the utopian image of a peaceful *bunka kokka* became an implicit goal, a therapeutic symbol that could be shared by conflicting political camps during the post-war period. The aesthetic images of Japan have proved to be remarkably resilient and flexible, precisely because they appear to be apolitical when they are in fact being used for political purposes.

History is filled with unpredictable developments and unintended consequences. The process through which images of aesthetic Japan were originated and refocused in several steps provides an example. At each step, the various actors acted purposely and deliberately, yet the accumulated result went beyond what was ever intended; what is more, it went beyond what was ever even imagined as a possible outcome. This type of inherent contingency is something I had found already while researching the material that led to my earlier book, *The Taming of the Samurai*. Continuing my research for the current book only strengthened my conclusions by providing me with completely different examples. Having said this, I have to confess something altogether different, a personal reaction that I did not anticipate. After completing the research that underlies the detailed case studies of pre-modern cultural practices, what impresses me most is not the sophisticated achievements of the Japanese cultivation of beauty; nor is it the unexpected role of this appreciation of the beautiful in creating an image of Japan as an aesthetic homeland. It is the fervent desire of ordinary people to bring a greater measure of beauty into their life, conjoined as it is with their equally sincere desire to enjoy greater freedom in their social exchanges. When we take time to consider the elegance of Japanese arts and poetry, let us not forget the existence of the equally beautiful and valuable experiments in social networking among the Japanese people.

Epilogue

Toward a Pluralistic View of Communication Styles

The popularization of the performing arts during the Tokugawa period left its legacy to Japanese culture not only in the areas of civility and cultural identity but also in its preferred modes of communication. The fact that the aesthetic circles became central to Tokugawa civic associational life inevitably raised the status of the tacit styles of communication embedded within these art forms. To be sure, there are always multiple modes of communication in any society; the emergence of a mode of communication as a favored style does not entail the automatic disappearance of other styles. But as I have observed in Chapter 9, the theoretical writings that emanated from the schools of the performing arts deepened the appreciation of amateur students for knowledge acquired only through physical self-discipline or the creation of poetry.

My investigation into the practices and categories of the Japanese people led me to focus on aesthetic associational life in Japan, a rather unusual subject in political sociology. This focus, however, allowed me to enter into a number of theoretical reconsiderations that question not only the interpretation of social change in Japan but also that of such well-studied phenomena as early modern European social developments.

My research has explored the mechanisms by which the changing structure of the relationships of multiple publics affects the process of forming collective cultural identities. In contrast with Habermas's historically specific but essentially normative approach to public spheres, I intend to reconstitute the notion of publics from a sociological and ontological perspective. Habermas provided an idealized picture of the eighteenth-century bourgeois public sphere, in such loci as cafes, salons, and reading circles, as the single comprehensive arena for the formation of public opinion based on rational-critical debates. My argument in Chapter 2 begins not only by assuming a multiplicity of kinds and natures of publics but also by investigating their hierarchies and interrelationships. In addition, I emphasize that in order to properly analyze the interrelationships among publics, we must reconnect the theory of publics with theories regarding such macrosocial networks as states and economic markets. This last point is the final step in the long journey taken within the pages of this book – an examination of the history of Japanese aesthetic publics in relation to the history of the Japanese state, associational networks, and economic development.

The case of Tokugawa Japan demonstrates that robust communicative activities can exist as the domain of private citizens under a feudal regime. Furthermore, my investigation into the history of Japanese associational organizations has shown that popular artistic and poetry networks stimulated the formation of horizontal associational networks that counteracted the dominant power. These networks also reinforced the solidarity of associations for collective actions from time to time. The close relationship between the medieval *ikki* organizations and poetry circles discussed in Chapter 4, and the complex overlapping of village contentious movements with poetry composition discussed in Chapter 8, are two examples of this reinforcement.

The modes of communication that dominated the Tokugawa aesthetic publics were artistic and poetic rather than the rational–critical methods of public debates. Publics of this nature – popular, decentralized, and intuitive – constitute the diametrical opposite of Habermas's model of the unitary, bourgeois, and rational public sphere of late eighteenth-century Europe. Nonetheless, the history of the Tokugawa aesthetic publics should not be understood only as an example of a sharp contrast between East and West. Rather, we should reexamine the interrelationships and hierarchical structures of various kinds of publics in early modern Europe, too, including those that employed tacit and artistic modes of communication. If we assume that Habermas's idealized model is the normative condition of possibility for the emergence of social power in the service of democratization, we would be surprised to find any straightforward connection between the *haikai* circles of Tokugawa Japan and the popular democratic movements of the Meiji period.

While I certainly appreciate the strong points of the Tokugawa contribution to the Japanese cultural tradition, I must also acknowledge certain disquieting features of this proto-modern heritage. As I see it, the Tokugawa period left a major problem for posterity to solve in the areas of communication for political discourse even though these areas are simultaneously connected to some attractive aspects of Japanese culture. The problem becomes manifest when the traditional Japanese non-discursive modes of communication are used outside their proper domains. These modes are particularly problematic when they are used in political publics associated with a hierarchical power structure because they may serve as a pretext to discourage the linguistic articulation of critical discourse. Even now, when Japanese people attempt to improve their level of interpersonal communication, they usually seek to foster a sense of community among the interacting parties. This feeling, however, cannot be achieved if the speaker relies too exclusively on rational discursive modes of communication, as he or she may be considered argumentative and egocentric in the pejorative sense – a response that decreases the intensity of the emotional bond. Although there is nothing inherently wrong with the tacit modes of communication embodied in the Japanese performing arts and poetry, the resulting ambiguity can be problematic when these modes pervade political and civic discourse. In political publics, it is often the case that the starting point of communication is the articulation of differences in order to negotiate a compromise. Tacit modes of communication cannot function effectively in such a context. Communication styles of this type create problems in terms of transparency because "inside" cultural knowledge and emotional communion cannot be readily shared among the interacting parties.

Clearly, the problem is not tacit modes of communication per se, representing as they do rich cognitive potentials for various ways of knowing and communicating. The real world, however, is complicated by the unequal distribution of power among publics as well as within a public. We often observe people attempting to import systems, rules, or stories from their prior networks into the interactional space of another public. For example, a successful business entrepreneur may carry his delusions of grandeur into his informal social groups. The Tokugawa Japanese had the perfect word for people who confuse their publics in this way – namely *yabo* (crude, coarse, or vulgar), as opposed to *iki* (stylish), with its connotations of fashionable refinement. *Yabo* as a pejorative originated in the "floating world" of Edo to describe the samurai bullies and *nouveau riche* merchants who attempted to impose their own rules of the game on the counter-culture of the floating world.

In this era of globalization, we hear more and more voices reminding us of the need to respect differences. And indeed, we should not forget that the style of communication appropriate to a particular public is not always fitting in other contexts. Stories and communicative styles produced within a given public that are cultivated and shared by participants in that public should not be forced upon others in different publics. Given this perspective, I do not subscribe to the modernist view that the ambiguities of Japanese modes of communication are singularly problematic. On the contrary, within the setting of appropriate publics, tacit modes of communication underscore human cognitive potentials that cannot be manifested by the use of concepts alone. The problem arises when such modes are allowed to spill over into civic and political publics. This problem can become truly pernicious since the people who make this kind of mistake often do not realize that their communication is ineffective given that the mode they employ worked so well in the other contexts in which it had evolved naturally over the centuries.

It is also a fact of life in the modern world that we participate in multiple publics in society and are constantly switching connections from one to another. I have based my argument on the assumption of a plurality of publics because multiplicity is inherent in human cognitive functioning and sociability. One important function of a public lies in its role of decoupling participants from pre-existing network domains. People participating in either discursive or nondiscursive communication within the interactional space of a public will experience a temporal suspension of the social and cognitive networks that existed prior to their participation. Although I consider that publics as sites for switching identities are universal features of human cognitive functioning, the tradition of the Japanese aesthetic publics underscores the importance of identity switching through ritual mechanisms of sociability. At this point, it is important to note that suspending such an old identity in order to switch to a new identity is a normative requirement of discourse in a democratic civic setting. In order to listen well to others and come to understand them, one should temporarily suspend one's own position. As I discussed in Chapter 3, a uniquely collective form of Japanese arts and poetry that emphasized horizontal fellowship emerged in the conflict-ridden medieval society through the clever use of the ritual logic of *mu'en* (no relation) that underscores the importance of decoupling temporarily from one's existing identities. *Mu'en* applied to people and sites that trespassed borders and intersected multiple worlds and thereby could form connections between this world and the worlds of the sacred and the dead. By choosing for meetings a site and style that invited associations with the symbolism of *mu'en*, such as meeting under cherry blossoms or letting outcasts participate, participants were strongly reminded that they had to leave behind their feudal identities while joining aesthetic publics. The ritual logic of Tokugawa aesthetic publics was informed by a modified use of this old ritual *mu'en* logic, transforming it for the purpose of civilized sociability in an age of proto-modern commercial society.

The contemporary situation may look quite different from the outwardly peaceful Tokugawa era. One of the major themes of my book, however, is to offer a contrasting picture of the complexity of early modern Japanese society. Tokugawa people, divided and segregated as they were by a feudal state, confronted serious challenges in sociability because of the sudden expansion of their political, economic, and cognitive horizons. The Tokugawa Japanese coped with the fixed political restrictions imposed by their authoritarian rulers by building interpersonal networks through aesthetic modes of socialization. In the collaborative spaces created by aesthetic activities, people willingly created temporary communities by sharing their stories with others without imposing their own, even while they acknowledged the social fragility of their aesthetic publics. Thus, although the dominant mode of communication in these aesthetic associations appeared to emphasize sameness and naturalness, it was precisely the acceptance of differences and the unfolding of each member's individuality that were in fact the starting points for the formation of the aesthetic publics. It is interesting to observe the development of ritual technologies in the Japanese aesthetic publics for creating and maintaining these publics in the face of challenges to sociability posed by political and economic pressures. The current world situation with its communicative demands and challenges is in many ways structurally similar to the situation in the Tokugawa era. The normative implication of the Japanese aesthetic publics thus resides, paradoxically, in underscoring the human ability to create connectivity by means of decoupling into a "no relation" mode within relational networks.

We frequently observe polities in the contemporary world whose democratic systems have been paralyzed because their members speak only for the narrow interests of their respective constituencies. It is also a common difficulty for the process of democratization in multiethnic and multireligious societies to generate open circuits among clusters of strong networks. The need for such suspensions has become increasingly acute in modern society, with its global demands for rapid shifting among different cognitive networks. At one point in time we may be sending an e-mail to someone in one country; the next moment we may receive a fax from someone else in another country; then we may get a phone call from a relative or an unrelated stranger – all in the space of just a few minutes. In general, the exchange and circulation of tremendous amounts of information and capital at cyberspeed in virtual space have transformed people's perceptions of time and space. Successive waves of international migration and the ease with which we can travel to faraway countries have dramatically increased our direct contacts with others whose communication styles differ dramatically from our own.

It may be that the modern world requires a new form of global civility for effective communication. Although much of the Tokugawa period's organizational experimentation with aesthetic publics was a product of historical contingencies and culturally specific to Japan as well, the experience of this society may incorporate an aspect of human communicative action that holds meaning for our age of worldwide cybercommunication. To achieve this goal of a new civility, we must begin with a pluralistic view of publics on a global scale without seeking to impose one mode out of many on others less privileged. Such a pluralism of communicative styles, however, will not work unless it stands on a functional common ground of human intercommunication. However, the creation of a common ground is tricky because even if it is for the purpose of communication, it is only one step removed from imposing the standard of the most dominant force for communication. That was why the medieval Japanese people used a ritual mechanism of creating a public that emphasized the nature of *mu'en* (no relation) to satisfy human desire to trespass politically laid out borders and boundaries. This type of commonality, based upon switching of identities, will not usher in a reduction of diversity; rather, it will be predicated on the conscious ability to shift among different identities through suspending a pre-constituted definition of one's personhood.

Notes

Introduction

1. For their lectures, see Kawabata Yasunari, *Japan, the Beautiful and My-self: The 1968 Nobel Prize Acceptance Speech*, Translated by Edward G. Seidensticker (Tokyo: Kodansha International, 1969), and Oe Kenzaburo, *Japan, the Ambiguous and Myself: The Nobel Prize Speech and other Lectures* (New York: Kōdansha International, 1995).
2. I am not in complete agreement with Oe's apparently modernist view, nor am I fully comfortable with Kawabata's praise of an idealized aesthetic Japan. I hope that the historical survey and analysis in this book will clarify my response to their positions.
3. This book will address a disquieting issue in Japanese history; namely, the rise of "Japan" as a cultural entity. Whenever we carefully consider the entity called Japan, geographical or otherwise, we find something that by its very nature is complex, multidimensional, and fluid. Regarding the ontological examination of identity, see Chapter 2 for more detail.

    The terms *beauty* and the *aesthetic* are used throughout this book not in the familiar German idealists' sense but simply to describe the human feelings that appreciate sensually, visually and emotionally pleasing phenomena or objects, often associated with arts and literature but not limited to them.
4. Ōoka Makoto, *Kotonoha gusa* (Tokyo: Sekai bunka sha, 1996), p. 10. There were 643 *haiku* journals published in 1987 according to Inui Hiroyuki, *Haiku no genzai to koten* (Tokyo: Heibonsha, 1988), p. 8.
5. My sociological usage of the term publics differs from that in natural languages loaded with their own political histories. The transformation of the word "public" in various societies often reflects the history of political struggles because by defining certain actions or entities as public, "the realm of the public" can often demand normative precedence over that of the private. The historical survey that follows in this book includes an analysis of the transformation of such Japanese terms as *ōyake* and *kō*. In such cases, I will use the native Japanese terms. My approach may be contrasted with Jürgen Habermas's normative concept of "the public sphere" defined as an

institutionalized realm of discursive interactions in which citizens deliberate about their common affairs through rational–critical debates. See Jürgen Habermas, *The Structural Transformation of the Public Sphere: An Inquiry into a Category of Bourgeois Society*, translated by Thomas Burger (Cambridge, MA: MIT Press, 1989). The ontological and sociological foundation for my historical analysis of identities, publics, and social structures will be more fully discussed in Chapter 2.

6. Alexis de Tocqueville, *Democracy in America*, edited by J. P. Mayer, translated by George Lawrence (Garden City, NY: Anchor Books, 1969), pp. 513–514. From this perspective, an analysis of the long tradition of voluntary horizontal associations in Japanese society is essential to a fuller understanding of the political history of Japan.

7. See Chapter 7 for a more accurate description of this point.

8. He distinguishes between organizationally less bounded or emotionally less committed relationships, which he calls "weak ties," and more durable and obligated network relationships, or "strong ties." See Mark Granovetter, "The Strength of Weak Ties," *American Journal of Sociology* 78 (1985): 1360–1380.

9. See, for example, Robert Putnam, *Making Democracy Work: Civic Traditions in Modern Italy* (Princeton, NJ: Princeton University Press, 1992). I will discuss this subject more in Chapter 1.

10. The Western form of modernity – linked to the emergence of the image of a "modern" person as an isolated, autonomous self – is a unique historical constellation that happened to become the most influential model because of the cumulative advantages conferred by scientific and technological knowledge and the West's domination of global politics. In my work, however, I propose to suspend the exclusive use of the Occidental model of modernity in that it tends to distort the understanding of the phase of pre-Westernization in non-Western societies.

11. Franklin F. Mendels, "Proto-Industrialization: The First Phase of the Industrialization Process," *Journal of Economic History* 12, no. 1 (1972): 241; Peter Kriedte, Hans Medick, and Jürgen Schlumbohm, *Industrialization before Industrialization*, translated by Beate Schempp (Cambridge: Cambridge University Press, 1981).

12. Richard Tilly and Charles Tilly, "Agenda for European Economic History in the 1970's," *Journal of Economic History* 31 (1970): 185.

13. Saitō Osamu, *Proto kōgyōka no jidai* (Tokyo: Nihon hyōronsha, 1985); Saitō Osamu, "The Rural Economy: Commercial Agriculture, By-Employment, and Wage Work," in Marius Jansen and Gilbert Rozman, editors, *Japan in Transition* (Princeton, NJ: Princeton University Press, 1986); Saitō Osamu, *Shōke no sekai, Uradana no sekai* (Tokyo: Riburo pōto, 1987).

Chapter 1

1. His letter, quoted by Tsukasa Kōdera, "Van Gogh's Utopian Japonisme," in Willem van Gulik, Charlotte van Rappard-Boon, and Keiko van Bremen-Ito,

editors, *Catalogue of the Van Gogh Museum's Collection of Japanese Prints* (Zwolle: Waanders, 1991), p. 35.

2. The shogunate's policy of isolation does not mean that Tokugawa Japan was in fact isolated from international politics. Rather, the shogunate's policy can be seen as the government's response to the global politics in this era. Regarding Tokugawa Japan's relationships with the outside world, see Ronald P. Toby, *State and Diplomacy in Early Modern Japan* (Tokyo: Stanford University Press, 1984).

3. Regarding Kaempher's observations, in addition to works listed in note 7, see Yokoyama Toshio, "Setsuyō-shū to nihon bunmei," Haga Tōru, editor, in *Edo towa nanika*, vol. 1, *Tokugawa no heiwa* (Tokyo: Shibundō, 1985).

4. Engelbert Kaempfer, *The History of Japan: Together with a Description of the Kingdom of Siam, 1690–92*, vol. 2, translated by J. G. Scheuchzer (Glasgow: James MacLehose and Sons, 1906 edition), pp. 194–195.

5. Engelbert Kaempfer, *History of Japan*, vol. 1, p. xxxi.

6. Engelbert Kaempfer, *History of Japan*, vol. 2, p. 357.

7. Beatrice M. Bodart-Bailey, *Kenperu to tokugawa tsunayoshi* (Tokyo: Chūō kōronsha, 1994); Beatrice M. Bodart-Bailey, "Kaempfer Restored," *Monumenta Nipponica* 43 (1988): 1; Beatrice M. Bodart-Bailey and Derek Massarella, editors, *The Furthest Goal: Engelbert Kaempfer's Encounter with Tokugawa Japan* (Kent: Japan Library, 1995); Engelbert Kaempfer, *Kaempfer's Japan-Tokugawa Culture Observed*, edited, translated, and annotated by Beatrice M. Bodart-Bailey (Honolulu: University of Hawaii Press, 1999). In Japanese, see Kobori Keiichirō, "Kenperu no tabi to sakokuron," in *Edo towa nanika vol 1: Tokugawa no heiwa* (Tokyo: Shibundō, 1985).

8. Uchikawa Yoshimi and Miyachi Masato, editors, *Gaikoku ni miru nihon*, vol. 1, *genbunhen* (Tokyo: Mainichi kominikēshonzu, 1990), p. 150.

9. Yokoyama Toshio, "Bunbeijin no shikaku," in Yokoyama Toshio, editor, *Shikaku no 19 seiki* (Kyoto: Shibunkaku, 1992). In addition, British emissaries met the hostility of the Chinese people at this time because of their government's involvement in the Opium War.

10. Yokoyama Toshio, *Japan in the Victorian Mind* (London: Macmillan, 1987).

11. Watanabe Kyōji, *Yukishi yo no omokage* (Fukuoka: Ashi shobō: 1998).

12. Roger Chartier, "From Texts to Manners, A Concept and Its Books: Civilité Between Aristocratic Distinction and Popular Appropriation," in Roger Chartier, editor, *The Cultural Uses of Print in Early Modern France* (Princeton, NJ: Princeton University Press), p. 78.

13. Norbert Elias, *The Civilizing Process*, translated by Edmund Jephcott (Oxford: Blackwell, 1982); Marvin B. Becker, *Civility and Society in Western Europe, 1300–1600* (Bloomington: Indiana University Press, 1988).

14. Roger Chartier, "From Texts to Manners," p. 71.

15. Eiko Ikegami, "Citizenship and National Identity in Early Meiji Japan, 1868–1889: Comparative Assessment," *International Review of Social History* 40, Supplement 3 (1995): 185–221.

16. On the issue of civility and citizenship, see Michael Walzer, "Civility and Civic Virtue in Contemporary America," in Michael Walzer, editor, *Radical Principles* (New York: Basic Books, 1980); Adam B. Seligman, "Agency, Civility, and the Paradox of Solidarity," in *The Problem of Trust*, edited by Adam B. Seligman (Princeton, NJ: Princeton University Press, 1997); Rogers Brubaker, *Citizenship and Nationhood in France and Germany* (Cambridge, MA: Harvard University Press, 1992).

17. Jürgen Habermas, *The Structural Transformation of the Public Sphere* (Cambridge: MIT Press, 1989), p. 12.

18. Peter Gay, *Pleasure Wars: The Bourgeois Experience – Victoria to Freud* (New York: Norton, 1998), p. 3.

19. Peter Gay, *Pleasure Wars*, p. 87.

20. Kaempfer personally preferred the model of the enlightened monarch. Kaempfer saw the fear of a zealous witch-hunt craze in his youth in which a relative lost his life. The fact that this irrational, zealous action was supported by the city council government might have convinced him that the enlightened monarchy was superior to republicanism, which could turn to irrational mobocracy.

21. Albert Hirschman, *The Passions and the Interests* (Princeton, NJ: Princeton University Press, 1977).

22. J. G. A. Pocock, *Virtue, Commerce, and History* (Cambridge: Cambridge University Press, 1985), p. 15. See also J. G. A. Pocock, *The Machiavellian Moment: Florentine Political Thought and the Atlantic Republican Tradition* (Princeton, NJ: Princeton University Press, 1975); Joyce Oldham Appleby, *Economic Thought and Ideology in Seventeenth-Century England* (Princeton, NJ: Princeton University Press, 1978).

23. J. G. A. Pocock, *Virtue, Commerce, and History*, p. 115.

24. Allan Silver, "'Two Different Sorts of Commerce' – Friendship and Strangership in Civil Society," in *Public and Private in Thought and Practice: Perspectives on a Grand Dichotomy*, Jeff Weintraub and Krishan Kumar, editors (Chicago: University of Chicago Press, 1997).

25. Allan Silver, "Two Different Sorts of Commerce," p. 232.

26. Allan Silver, "Two Different Sorts of Commerce," p. 233.

27. On the other hand, more recent developments of sociological studies of comparative state formation have articulated different paths of political developments due to the divergent patterns of early modern state formation.

28. Oliver E. Williamson, "The Economics of Organization: The Transaction Cost Approach," *American Journal of Sociology* 87 (1981): 548–577; Oliver E. Williamson, *Economic Institutions of Capitalism* (New York: Free Press, 1985).

29. Douglass C. North and Robert Paul Thomas, *The Rise of the Western World: A New Economic History* (Cambridge: Cambridge University Press, 1973).

30. Douglass C. North, *Structure and Change in Economic History* (New York: Norton, 1981), p. 17.

31. See Avner Greif, "Contract Enforceability and Economic Institutions in Early Trade: The Maghiribi Traders' Coalition," *American Economic Review* (June

1993): 525–543; Avner Greif, "Reputation and Coalitions in Early Trade: Evidence on Maghiribi Traders," *Journal of Economic Review* (December 1989): 857–882; Avner Greif, "The Organization of Long-Distance Trade: Reputation and Coalitions in the Geniza Documents and Genoa during the Eleventh and Twelfth Centuries," *The Journal of Economic History* 51, Issue 2 (June 1991): 459–462. Okazaki Tetsuji has emphasized the role of *kabunakama* guilds in Tokugawa Japan to construct trust in economic transactions. See Okazaki Tetsuji, *Edo no Shijōkeizai* (Tokyo: Kōdannsha, 1999).

32. In medieval Japan, it was always a very difficult task for the master to control the centrifugal tendencies of independent-minded samurai vassals. The fact that vassalage pre-supposed the uncertainty of the parties actually encouraged the sophistication of social institutions for constructing trust. The reputation of honor for the samurai was not only the achievement of creditability but also an emotional drive for warriors to fight bravely. See Eiko Ikegami, *The Taming of the Samurai* (Cambridge, MA: Harvard University Press, 1995).

33. Charles Tilly, *Coercion, Capital, and European States, A.D. 990–1990* (Oxford: Basil Blackwell, 1990).

34. Specialists in medieval Japanese history have accumulated a rich literature of historical evidence that robust commercial activities and long-distance trade existed during the medieval era. It is not my intention to downplay the significance of this literature.

35. Ōishi Shinzaburō, *Edo Jidai* (Tokyo: Chuō kōronsha, 1977); Kozo Yamamura, "Returns on Reunification: Economic Growth in Japan 1550–1650," in *Japan before Tokugawa: Political Consolidation and Economic Growth, 1500–1650*, Keiji Nagahara, John W. Hall, and Kozo Yamamura, editors (Princeton, NJ: Princeton University Press, 1981).

36. Thereafter, the population generally remained around that level until the late nineteenth century. See, for example, Umemura Mataji, "Tokugawa jidai no jinkō to keizai," in Umemura Mataji et al., *Nihon keizai no hatten: suryō keizaishi ronshū* (Tokyo: Nihon keizai shinbunsha, 1976); Hayami Tōru, *Suryō Keizaishi Nyūmon* (Tokyo: Nihon hyōronsha, 1975).

37. Gilbert Rozman, *Urban Networks in Ch'ing China and Tokugawa Japan* (Princeton, NJ: Princeton University Press, 1973), p. 6; John W. Hall, "Castle Town and Modern Urbanization," in John W. Hall, Marius B. Jansen, Susan Hanley, and Kozo Yamamura, editors, *Economic and Demographic Change in Preindustrial Japan 1600–1868* (Princeton, NJ: Princeton University Press, 1977).

38. I emphasized this point in Ikegami, "Citizenship and National Identity in Early Meiji Japan." S. N. Eisenstadt also discussed this point at length in *Japanese Civilization: A Comparative View* (Chicago: University of Chicago, 1996).

39. Ise Sadatake, *Teijō zakkii* (Tokyo: Heibonsha, 1985, originally published in 1843).

40. J. V. Beckett, *The Aristocracy in England: 1660–1914* (Oxford: Blackwell, 1986), p. 100. I realize that there are many scholarly reservations about the

British open-elite theory. However, I am using quick overviews of British and French examples to make the point that cultural mobility per se should be distinguished from cultural mobility coupled with social mobility.

Chapter 2

1. Hayden White, *The Content of the Form: Narrative Discourse and Historical Representation* (Baltimore: Johns Hopkins University Press, 1987), p. 1.
2. For some recent work on network analysis that emphasizes the symbolic and phenomenological dimensions of netwoks, see Andrew Abbott, *The System of Professions* (Chicago: University of Chicago Press, 1988); Christopher K. Ansell, "Symbolic Networks: The Realignment of the French Working Class, 1887–1894," *American Journal of Sociology* 103 (1997): 359–390; Stephen Brint, "Hidden Meanings: Cultural Content and Context in Harrison White's Structural Sociology," *Sociological Theory* 10 (1992): 194–208; Randall Collins, *The Sociology of Philosophers* (Cambridge, MA: Harvard University Press, 1998); John Mohr and Vincent Duqenne, "The Duality of Culture and Practice: Poverty Relief in New York City, 1888–1917," *Theory and Society* 26 (1997): 305–356; Mustafa Emirbayer, "Manifesto for a Relational Sociology," *American Journal of Sociology* 103 (1997): 281–317; Margaret R. Somers, "Citizenship and the Place of the Public Sphere: Law, Community, and Political Culture in the Transition to Democracy," *American Review of Sociology* 58 (October 1993): 587–620; Harrison C. White, *Identity and Control* (Princeton, NJ: Princeton University Press, 1992).
3. Harrison C. White, "Where Do Languages Come From?" Unpublished manuscript, 1996.
4. In focusing on switching, Harrison White presented a bold thesis in which he stated: "Sociocultural reality was constructed only when there was switching back and forth between at least two domains, everyday and ceremonial, with their continuing networks." Harrison C. White, "Network Switchings and Bayesian Forks: Reconstructing the Social and Behavioral Sciences," *Social Research* 62 (1995): 1035–1063; Ann Miche and Harrison White, "Between Conversation and Situation: Public Switching Dynamics Across Network Domains," *Social Research* (Fall 1988): 695–724.
5. Piet Hut, "There Are No Things," in *The Great Inventions of the Past 2000 Years*, John Brockman, editor (New York: Simon and Schuster, 2000).
6. P. W. Anderson, "More is Different," *Science* 177 (1972): 393.
7. For an overview regarding developments and applications of complexity theories in various disciplines, see Y. Bar-Yam, editor, *Dynamics of Complex Systems* (Reading, MA: Addison-Wesley, 1997). See also Y. Bar-Yam, editor, *Proceedings of the International Conference on Complex Systems* (Cambridge: Perseus Books, 2000); Mitchell Waldrop, *Complexity: The Emerging Science at the Edge of Order and Chaos* (New York: Simon and Schuster, 1992); Nicholas Rescher, *Complexity: A Philosophical Overview* (New Brunswick, NJ: Transaction Publishers, 1988); Stuart Kauffman, *At Home in the Universe* (New York: Oxford University Press, 1995).

8. Norbert Elias, *What Is Sociology?* translated by Stephen Mennell and Grace Morrissey (New York: Columbia University Press, 1978), p. 112.
9. Charles Tilly, *Durable Inequality* (Chicago: University of Chicago Press, 1997).
10. Ann Swidler, "Culture in Action: Symbols and Strategies," *American Sociological Review* 51 (April 1986): 273–286.
11. Hilary Putnam, "A Half Century of Philosophy, Viewed from Within," *Daedalus* 126, no. 1 (1997): 175–208.
12. Hilary Putnam, "A Half Century of Philosophy," p. 196.
13. The epistemological interpretation of this phenomenon has been a subject of lively debates among researchers in the cognitive study of consciousness. See, for example, D. J. Chalmers, "Facing up to the Problem of Consciousness," *Journal of Consciousness Studies* 2, no. 3 (1995): 200–219; D. J. Chalmers, *The Conscious Mind* (New York: Oxford University Press, 1996); Piet Hut and Roger Shepard, "Turning 'the Hard Problem' Upside Down," *Journal of Consciousness Studies* 3, no. 4 (1996): 313–329.
14. Jürgen Habermas, *The Structural Transformation of the Public Sphere: An Inquiry into a Category of Bourgeois Society*, translated by Thomas Burger (Cambridge, MA: MIT Press, 1989).
15. For example, see the following feminist works: Nancy Fraser, "Rethinking the Public Sphere: A Contribution to the Critique of Actually Existing Democracy," in Craig Calhoun, editor, *Habermas and the Public Sphere* (Cambridge, MA: MIT Press, 1992); Mary P. Ryan, *Women in Public: Between Banners and Ballots, 1825–1880* (Baltimore: Johns Hopkins University Press, 1990); Mary P. Ryan, "Gender and Public Access: Women's Politics in Nineteenth-Century America," in Craig Calhoun, editor, *Habermas and the Public Sphere* (Cambridge, MA: MIT Press, 1992).
16. Mark Granovetter, "The Strength of Weak Ties," *American Journal of Sociology* 78 (1985): 1360–1380.
17. A similar focus on the space, sphere, and frame of reference for discursive activities is presently shared by political theorists who are concerned with such topics as the historical emergence of national identity, citizenship, and democracy. For example, Benedict Anderson's now-classical definition of nationalism as an *imagined community* suggests that national identity as such cannot be separated from discussions of common cognitive frames of reference. The recent resurgence of neo-Tocquevillian approaches to civic democracy assumes that associational life provides one of the most important loci for private participation in public politics. See also Robert Putnam, *Making Democracy Work*. While Anderson regarded the emergence of nationalism as a by-product of the rise of cognitive associational networks, the imagined frame of reference, Putnam looks at concrete social associational networks as a possible ground for the operative efficiency of a democracy. Although their approaches and topics differ, both scholars demonstrate an awareness of the underlying network dynamics in the creation of certain types of communicative activities. Furthermore, rather than considering nationalism or democracy as pre-existing entities, they focus on the imagined–cognitive or actual–organizational *sites* in which interactional and discursive practices are

actually carried out. Culture and politics are most intricately conjoined at this point.

Prelude to Section Two

1. Mizoguchi Yūzō, "Chūgoku ni okeru kō to shi," *Shisō* 669 (1980): 19; Mizoguchi Yūzō, *Chugoku no Kō to shi* (Tokyo: Kenbun shuppan, 1995); Yoshida Takashi, "Kōchi kōmin ni tsuite," edited by Sakamoto Tarō sensei koki kinen kan, *Zoku nihon kodai shi ronshū chūkan* (Tokyo: Yoshikawa kōbunkan, 1972), p. 405; see also Mizoguchi Yūzō, *Kō shi*, Series *Ichibo no jiten* (Tokyo: Sanseidō, 1996); Yoshida Takashi, "Yake ni tsuite no kiso teki kōsatsu," in Inoue Mitsusada, hakushi kanreki kinenkai edition, *Kodaishi Ronsō, chūkan* (Tokyo: Yoshikawa kōbunkan, 1978); Tawara Shirō, "Nihon no kō to shi," in *Chūgoku no kō to shi* (Tokyo: Kenbun shuppan, 1995). The dual meaning of *ōyake*, sovereignty and commonness, appears to have strong support from scholars. Yet, as Mizoguchi's survey *Kō shi* (pp. 19–22) indicated, this understanding has not reached to the definitions of the term in various Japanese dictionaries such as *Nihon kokugo dai jiten*.
2. Mizoguchi Yūzō, *Kō shi*, pp. 20–21.
3. Yasunaga Toshinobu, *Nihon ni okeru "kō" to "shi"* (Tokyo: Nihon keizai shinbunsha, 1976), pp. 35–38.
4. Clifford Geertz, "Art as a cultural system," in *Local Knowledge* (New York: Basic Books, 1983), 2000 edition, pp. 109–120.
5. Clifford Geertz, *Local Knowledge*, p. 116.
6. Steven Caton, *Peaks of Yemen I Summon: Poetry as Cultural Practice in a North Yemeni Tribe* (Berkeley: University of California Press, 1990), p. 56.
7. Steven Caton's cases of poetry in male tribesmen found the use of poetry an act of constructing the selfhood of the poet as a man "capable of containing violence in the symbolic game of honor" (Caton, *Peaks of Yemen I Summon*, p. 109). See, in contrast, Lila Abu-Lughod's ethnography of Bedouin women's poetry practices, *Veiled Sentiments: Honor and Poetry in a Bedouin Society*, second edition (Berkeley: University of California Press, 1999, originally published in 1986). Abu-Lughod reports about "the tension between the honor code's ideals and emotional entailments in their poetry" (pp. 186–207). Japanese poetry tradition, on the other hand, at least on the surface, did not manifest such a sharp gender difference in the usage of poetry. The main themes of Japanese ancient and medieval poets, men as well as women, centered on the aesthetic appreciation of nature and life as well as on the expressions of innermost vulnerability and love. After all, one strong strand of Japanese poetry traditions stemmed from an exchange of poems between a man and woman. Thus, in the courtly origin of Japanese poetry traditions, men and women shared the same universe of poetic aesthetics and practices.
8. Daniel Norman, *The Arabs and Medieval Europe*, 2nd edition (London and New York: Longman, 1979), p. 103.

9. In Portugal, such a tradition is called "duel singing." According to Peter Fryer, the root of Brazilian challenge songs stemmed from the mixture of three cultures – African, Portuguese, and Arabic – in "the Atlantic cultural triangles" already merged in Portugal. See Peter Fryer, *Rhythms of Resistance: African Musical Heritage in Brazil* (Hanover, NH: Wesleyan University Press, 2000).
10. Peter Burke, *Popular Culture in Early Modern Europe* (New York: Harper & Row, 1978), pp. 103–104.
11. Ogata Tsutomu, *Za no bungaku* (Tokyo: Kadokawa shoten, 1973), p. 33.
12. See, for example, various texts of aesthetic philosophies reprinted in *Nihon shisō taikei*, vol. 23: Hayashi Tasusaburo et al. *Kodai chūsei geijutsu ron* (Tokyo: Iwanami shoten, 1973); Nishiyama Matsunosuke, Watanabe Ichiro, and Gunji Masakatsu, editors, *Nihon shisō taikei*, vol. 61: *Kinsei geidō ron* (Tokyo: Iwanami shoten, 1972). The richness of the field of *geidō ron* (the artistic way) is simply amazing.
13. See, on this point, Clifford Geertz, "Art as a cultural system," and Steven Caton, *Peaks of Yemen I Summon*.

Chapter 3

1. Ogata Tsutomu, *Za no bungaku* (Tokyo: Kadokawa shoten, 1973); Yakame Noridatsu, *Shōfū haikai ni okeru za no ishiki* (Tokyo: Ōfūsha, 1974); Yamaori Tetsuo, *"za" no bunkaron* (Tokyo: Kosei shppansha, 1981). In this book, I refer to the *za* arts as including both performing arts and poetry. The medieval forms of the collective performing arts and linked verse are also called *yoriai* (meetings) or *kaisho* (meeting places) literature in Japanese historical scholarship. They were primarily late medieval institutions. Regardless of the different labels applied to them, however, a common characteristic of the *za* arts was that they were "performed" in their respective meeting places.
2. On the meaning of *za*, see also Miura Hiroyuki, "Za no igi ni tsukite," in his book *Hōseishi no kenkyū ge* (Tokyo: Iwanami shoten, 1944); Hayashiya Tatsusaburō, "Chūsei geinō za no kenkyū," in his book *Chūsei geinōshi no kenkyū* (Tokyo: Iwanami shoten, 1960). The reader is also referred to the pioneering work of Hayashiya Tatsusaburō, which discussed the connection between the growth of social networks in villages and medieval aesthetics, "Gōmin no soshiki to bunka," in his book *Chūsei bunka no kichō* (Tokyo: Tokyo daigaku shuppan kai, 1953).
3. Ogata Tsutomu, *Za no bungaku*, p. 34.
4. *Nō* is a highly symbolic form of drama that includes dancing and music.
5. Zeami, *Fūshi Kaden*, reprinted in Omote Akira, Kato Shuichi, editors, *Nihon shisō taikei*, vol. 24: *Zeami, Zenchiku* (Tokyo: Iwanami shoten, 1974), p. 45. For Zeami's usage of *ichiza*, see Omote Akira's commentary in *Nihon shisō taikei, vol. 24*, pp. 488–489.
6. One can therefore interpret the phrase *ichiza konryu*, or the construction of one (*ichi*) *za*, in the preceding citation as referring to the organization

of a *za* troupe among *Nō* performers rather than solely a spiritual space characterized by *za*. However, in Zeami's *Shūgyoku tokuka*, the phrase *ichiza jyōjyū no kannō* clearly refers to the attainment of a *za* moment in which performers and audience share an experience of emotional synergy. See Zeami, *Iwanami nihon shisō taikei*, vol. I *Zeami*, p. 185.

7. Ishiguro Kichijirō, *Chūsei geidō ron no shisō* (Tokyo: Kokusho kankōkai, 1993).

8. The available English-language literature on medieval Japanese linked poetry is limited in terms of the historical context of this distinctive genre. In particular, the relationship between the *za* poetry groups and the organizational transformation of medieval Japanese society has never been systematically discussed.

9. On the Yūzaki-za rule, see Omote Akira, Kato Shuichi, editors, "Seshi rokujū igo sarugaku dangi," in *Nihon shisō taikei Zeami, Zenchiku* (Tokyo: Iwanami shoten, 1974). For Emai-za, see Omote Akira and Itō Masayoshi, editors, *Konparu Kodensho shūsei* (Tokyo: Wanya shoten, 1969).

10. Wakita Haruko, "Chūsei sarugakuza no soshiki kōsei," *Zeami*, vol. 1, pp. 78–93.

11. See Oowa Iwao, *Yūjo to tennō* (Tokyo: Hakusuisha, 1993), and Tanahashi Mitsuo, *Goshirakawa hōō* (Tokyo: Kōdansha, 1995), for an introduction to this issue. See also Suzuki Hideo, *Ō no uta: Kodai kayōron* (Tokyo: Chikuma shobō, 1999), for the relationship between the sovereign and poetry in Japan.

12. Kuroda Toshio, "Chūsei no mibun sei to hisen kannen," in *Chūsei no kokka to shūkyō* (Tokyo: Iwanami shoten, 1975), pp. 365–368.

13. Sakurai Yoshirō, "Geinōshi eno shiza," in his book *Chūsei nihon no ōken, shūkyō, geinō* (Tokyo: Jinbun shoin, 1988), p. 203; Kuroda Toshio, "Chūsei no mibun sei to hisen kannen," in *Chūsei no kokka to shukyō* (Tokyo: Iwanami shoten, 1975).

14. Although the performing arts as part of ancient imperial rituals certainly functioned as "public affairs" during state ceremonies, there were popular performing arts that could not be systematically incorporated into the state-sanctioned hierarchies. Even so, such popular performing artists as courtesans and traveling female shamans, who were on the margins of the status hierarchy, were not excluded from the realm of the sovereign. Many historical documents and stories featured the connection between the sovereign realm and popular performing artists.

15. "Kanajō" (preface in *kana* letters of *Kokin wakashū*), edited and annotated by Kyūsojin Hitaku, *Kokin wakashū* (Tokyo: Kōdansha, 1979), vol. 1, pp. 14–15.

16. For the ancient root of Japanese identity, see Eiko Ikegami, "The Emergence of Aesthetic Japan." In Joshua Fogel, editor, *Japan and China* (Philadelphia: University of Pennsylvania Press, 2005).

17. The styles, directives, and other codes involved in *renga* varied over several centuries of development. Some *renga* were more serious and formal, others more popular and humorous. Readers who are seeking literary analysis in English and translations of texts are referred to: Earl Roy Miner, *Japanese*

Linked Poetry: An Account with Translations of Renga and Haikai Sequences (Princeton, NJ: Princeton University Press, 1979); Steven D. Carter, *The Road to Komatsubara: A Classical Reading of the Renga hyakuin* (Cambridge, MA: Harvard University Press, East Asian Monographs, 1987); Steven D. Carter, *Three Poets at Yuyama* (Berkeley: Institute of East Asian Studies, University of California at Berkeley, 1983); Esperanza Ramirez-Christensen, *Heart's Flower: The Life and Poetry of Shinkei* (Stanford, CA: Stanford University Press, 1994). The reader is also referred to the English translation of Konishi Jin'ichi's monumental work, *A History of Japanese Literature*. Volume 3 contains an extensive introduction to linked poetry. See Konishi Jin'ichi, *A History of Japanese Literature*, translated by Aileen Gatten and Mark Harbison, edited by Earl Miner (Princeton, NJ: Princeton University Press, 1991).

18. The practice of linked verse in a traditional form requires a shared poetic universe that no longer exists in the general Japanese population. Regarding the general history of linked verse in Japanese, see Shimazu Tadao, *Rengashi no kenkyū* (Tokyo: Kadokawa shoten, 1969); Fukui Kyūzō, *Renga no shiteki kenkyū zen* (Tokyo: Yūseidō, 1969); Kidō Saizō, *Rengashi Ronkō, Zōhoban* (Tokyo: Meiji shoin, 1993). In addition, the reader may wish to consult Kaneko Kinjirō, *Tsukuba shū no kenkyū* (Tokyo: Fūma shobō, 1965); Kaneko Kinjirō, *Shinsen Tsukubashū no kenkyū* (Tokyo: Fūma shobō, 1969); and Ijichi Tetsuo, *Renga no sekai* (Tokyo: Yoshikawa kōbunkan, 1967). Studies written in Japanese provide a more detailed account of the social background of linked poetry. I have greatly benefited from these detailed studies, as is indicated by the analysis that follows.

19. See the kyōgen "Mikazuki," cited by Hiroo Tsurusaki, *Sengoku no kenryoku to yoriai no bungei* (Osaka: Izumi shoin, 1988), pp. 1–2.

20. Nijō Yoshimoto was a medieval aristocrat and writer who produced seminal books on the theory of linked-verse composition and a famous anthology of renga, *Tsukuba shū*. He also held the office of a *Sesshō kanpaku*, the highest office in the emperor's court.

21. Nijō Yoshimoto, "Jyūmon saihishō," reprinted in *Nihon koten bungaku taikei, vol. 66: Rengaron shū Hairon shū* (Tokyo: Iwanami shoten, 1961). Nijō's theory of poetry influenced a number of medieval artists, including Zeami, who was under Nijō's patronage as a boy. Regarding the close relationship between *Nō* drama and linked poetry, see Shimazu Tadao, *Nō to Renga* (Osaka: Izumi shoin, 1990).

22. *Benno Naishi Nikki*, "The Third Year of Kennchō (1251), Third Month 11th," cited by Suzuki Yasumasa, "Hana no moto renga shoki no shosō," *Geibun Kenkyū* 36 (1977), p. 197.

23. *Tsukuba shū*, no. 2060, edited and annotated by Kaneko Kintarō (Tokyo: Benseisha, 1978).

24. According to Suzuki Yasumasa, "Hana no moto renga shoki no shosō," pp. 196–207.

25. The reader is referred to the ethnographic insights of now classic works by Yanagida Kunio, "Kebōzu kō" and "Zokusei enkaku shi," in *Yanagida*

Kunio Zenshū, vol. 11 (Tokyo: Chikuma shobō, 1990). More recently, Miyata Noboru has also discussed the *hijiri* from the perspective of folklore. "Hijiri no matsuei," *Rettō no bunka*, vol. 4 (Tokyo: Nihon Editor School Press, 1987).

26. Goshirakawa Hōō, in *Ryōjinhishō*, vol. 14, edited by Sasaki Nobutsuna (Tokyo: Iwanami shoten, 1931), pp. 170–171.

27. Goshirakawa Hōō, *Ryōjinhishō*, pp. 170–171. See Geinōshi Kenkyūkai, editor, *Yasuraihana chosa hōkokusho* (Kyoto: Yasuraiodori hozonkai, 1977).

28. Yanagida Kunio, "Shidare zakura no mondai," *Shinshū zuihitsu*, in *Yanagita Kunio zenshu*, vol. 24 (Tokyo: Chikuma shobō, 1990). See also Matsuoka Shinpei, *Utage no shintai – basara kara zeami e* (Tokyo: Iwanami shoten, 1991), pp. 52–53. Regarding the symbolism of cherry blossoms, see: Takagi Kiyoko, *Sakura: sono sei to zoku* (Tokyo: Chuo Koronsha, 1996); Saito Shoji, *Nihonjin to sakura: Hana no shisoshi* (Tokyo: Yasaka shobo, 2002); Makino Kazuharu, *Shin sakura no seishinshi* (Tokyo: Chūō kōron shinsha, 2002). In English, see Emiko Ohnuki-Tierney, *Kamikaze, Cherry Blossoms, and Nationalism* (Chicago: University of Chicago Press, 2002).

29. Matsuoka Shinpei, *Utage no shintai*, p. 51.

30. Amino Yoshihiko, *Mu'en kugai raku* (Tokyo: Heibonsha, 1978). See also Amino Yoshihiko, *Nihon chūsei no hinōgyōmin* (Tokyo: Iwanami shoten, 1984). Amino's work influenced various branches of Japanese scholarship. For an interesting application of the term *mu'en* to the interpretation of the theory of justice, see Tsuchiya Keiichirō, *Seigiron/Jiyūron: Mu'en shakai nihon no seigi* (Tokyo: Iwanamo shoten, 1996).

31. Amino Yoshihiko, *Nihon chūsei toshi no sekai* (Tokyo: Chikuma shoō, 1996), p. 47.

32. See Kuroda Hideo's analysis of marginal places in *Kyōkai no chūsei shōchō no chūsei* (Tokyo: Tōkyō daigaku shuppankai, 1986). The analysis was carried out with the extensive use of pictorial materials.

33. *In* is the honorary title of a retired emperor who was usually the father of a young emperor. In most cases, the *In* was the actual ruler of the imperial court.

34. A poem composed by Zenna, *Tsukuba shū*, no. 2053. See Matsuoka Shinpei's insightful argument in *Utage no shintai*, p. 53.

35. Fujiwara no Munetada, *Chūyūki*. From an entry for the sixth year of Kanji (1092), seventh day of the sixth month.

36. Katsumata Shizuo, "Baibai, Shichiire to shoyū kannen," *Nihon no shakaishi*: vol. 4, *Futan to zōyo* (Tokyo: Iwanami shoten, 1986). See also Sasamoto Shōji, *Ikyō o musubu shōnin to shokunin. Nihon no chusei*, vol. 3 (Tokyo: Chūōkōronshinsha, 2002).

37. The original Japanese text consists of these two phrases:

> *Subō murozumi no, nakanaru mitarai ni, kaze wa fukanedo sasara namitasu/*
> *Jissō muro no taikai ni, gojin rokuyoku no kaze wa fukane domo, zuien shinnyo no nami tatanu tokinashi/*

38. *Kojidan: vol. 3*, reprinted in *Kokushi taikei (shintei zōho): vol. 18, Uji shūi monogatari* (Tokyo: Yoshikawa kobunkan, 2000). Variations of this story appeared in several collections of stories in the medieval period. They include *Senjyūshō* and *Sangoku denki.*

39. Abe Yasurō, *Yuya no kōgō* (Nagoya: Nagoya daigaku shuppankai, 1998), p. 152. See also Abe Yasurō, *Seija no suisan* (Nagoya: Nagoya daigaku shuppankai, 2001); and Wakita Haruko, *Josei geinō no genryū* (Tokyo: Kadokawa shoten, 2001).

40. During the early medieval period, the larger temples and shrines were centers of consumption that required enormous amounts of many different kinds of goods and services to maintain their rituals, buildings, decorative objects, clergy, and other supporting members. In order to secure steady supplies of various goods and services, the great temples encouraged various craftspeople and merchants to form organizations by offering them political protection and economic privileges. These benefits led to the development of the *za* trade guilds around the great temples and shrines.

41. Later, the word became a pejorative term for actors since the *Kabuki* theaters originated along the bed of the Kamo River in Kyoto.

42. For Japanese historiography regarding the concept of *kegare* and the outcast groups, see Yamamoto Kōji, "Kizoku shakai ni okeru kegare to chitsujo," *Nihon shi kenkyū* no. 289 (1986); and see Yamamoto Kōji, *Kegare to ōharae* (Tokyo: Heibonsha, 1992), for the discussion of social practices of *kegare* avoidance. Niunoya Tetsuichi, *Kebiichi–Chūsei no kegare to kenryoku* (Tokyo: Heibonsha, 1986), reveals the fact that outcasts embodied policing and execution force for the capital under the *kebiishi*. See also Kuroda Toshio, *Nihon chūsei no kokka to shūkyō* (Tokyo: Iwanami shoten, 1975), and Amino Yoshihiko, *Chūsei no Hinin to Yūjo* (Tokyo: Akashi shoten, 1994). I have also discussed the relationship between the concept of *kegare*, the outcast groups, and the emergence of the samurai in my book *The Taming of the Samurai*, pp. 96–97, 113–117.

43. Wakita Haruko, "Chūsei sarugaku za no soshiki kōsei," *Zeami. Chūsei no geijyutsu to bunka*, vol. 1, no. 1(2002), p. 79. See also Wakita Haruko, "*Chūsei geinōza no kōzō to sabetsu*," in Martin Collcutt and Wakita Haruko, editors, *Shūen bunka to mibun sabetsu* (Kyoto: Shibunkaku shuppan, 2001). Sunakawa Hiroshi, *Heike monogatari shinkō* (Tokyo: Tokyo Bijyutsu, 1982), discusses the relationship between marginal people and literature.

44. It is in this sense that I use the term "marginal people" to denote those various kinds and names of subpopulations in this book.

45. Geinōshi Kenkyūkai, editor, *Nihon geinōshi: vol. 4, chūsei-kinsei* (Tokyo: Hōsei daigaku shuppan kai, 1985), p. 83.

46. According to Kuroda Hideo, one of the pioneers in the use of pictorial materials in medieval Japanese history. See for example, Kuroda Hideo, *Sugata to shigusa no chūsei shi* (Tokyo: Heibonsha, 1986).

47. Amino Yoshihiko, *Igyō no ōken* (Tokyo: Heibonsha, 1993), pp. 120–144.

48. Matsuoka Shinpei, *Utage no shintai*, p. 52; Geinōshi Kenkyūkai, editor, *Nihon geinōshi: vol. 3, chūsei* (Tokyo: Hōsei University Press, 1983),

pp. 83–85; Ijichi Tetsuo, *Renga no sekai*; Shimazu Tadao, *Renga no kenkyū* (Tokyo: Kadokawa shoten, 1973).

49. In *Tsukuba-shū*, the first anthology of linked poetry, there are six poets whose names end with the suffix -*shōnin* (meaning "Reverend" or "Father") including *ippen shōnin*, who most likely belonged to the *Jishū* order. In addition to the famous poet Zenna, there are 26 poets whose names end with -ami or -a. They were not necessarily all *Jishū* monks but are likely to have been, according to Kaneko Kinjirō, *Rengashi to kikō* (Tokyo: Ōfūsha, 1992), p. 59. See also Kadokawa Genyoshi, "Jishū bungei no seiritsu," in his book *Katarimono bungei no hassei* (Tokyo: Tokyodō shuppan, 1975).

50. The *Tengu Zōshi*, section 4. This is a pictorial scroll that can be seen in Jinatsu Shigeki and Ueno Kenji, editors, *Zoku Nihon emaki taisei*, vol. 19 (Tokyo: Chūō kōron, 1984). Kuroda Hideo, in *Sugata to Shigusa no Chūseishi*, pp. 15–29, has an interesting account on this pictorial scroll. See also Kuroda Hideo's analysis on the other scroll in Ippen, "Futatsu no ippen seie nit it suite," *Rekishi no yomikata: vol. 1, Kaiga shiryō no yomikata* (Tokyo: Asahi shinbunsha, 1988). Amino Yoshihiko, *Chūsei no hinin to yūjo* (Tokyo: Akaishi shoten, 1994), pp. 95–108, also discusses this issue.

51. In fact, although these two sects of Buddhism differed significantly in their doctrinal emphases, the actual practices and culture of the rank-and-file monks – the Zen *unsui* (itinerant monks; *unsui* means literally "clouds and water") and the Jishū traveling monks – had much in common.

52. Names that have "-a" or "-ami" as suffixes are often the religious names of *nenbutsu hijiri*, and monks of the Jishū sect.

53. Amino Yoshihiko, *Chūsei no hinin to yūjyo*, pp. 94–107.

54. As of 2000, Yugyō-ji in Fujisawa City in Kanagawa, the head temple of the Jishū sect, still conducts an annual ceremony that begins with a ritual of *renga* composition. Regarding the role of the Jishū monks and the popularization of medieval popular art and literature, see Kiyomitsu Kanai, "Jishū no yūgyō to bungei no chihō denpa," *Bungaku* 54, no. 12 (1986): 181–204; and Kanai Kiyomitsu, *Jishū bungei kenkyū* (Tokyo: Kamaza shobo, 1967).

55. Gumaiki in an entry of the fourth year of Eiwa, June 7th. Cited by Hayashi Tatsusaburo, *Chūsei Geinōshi no kenkyu*.

56. Ōoka Makoto, *Utage to koshin* (Tokyo: Shūeisha, 1978), p. 153.

Chapter 4

1. I am not making the claim that the *za* and *ikki* organizations were democratic in the modern sense of the term. Although they were horizontal in structure, they were exclusive associations formed by members of the privileged people.

2. On medieval *ikki*, see Eiko Ikegami, *The Taming of the Samurai* (Cambridge, MA: Harvard University Press, 1995), pp. 121–134; Katsumata Shizuo, *Ikki* (Tokyo: Tokyo University Press, 1983); David L. Davis, "Ikki in Late

Medieval Japan," in John Hall and Jeffrey Mass, ed., *Medieval Japan: Essays in Institutional History* (Stanford, CA: Stanford University Press, 1974); Aoki Michio et al., *Ikki* (Tokyo: Tokyo University Press, 1981).

3. *Kyoto no rekishi*, vol. 3 (Kyoto: Gakugei shorin, 1968), p. 35.

4. *Kyoto no rekishi*, vol. 3, pp. 3–4. For a more recent, detailed work on the medieval use of money in commercial transactions, see Uranagase Takashi, *Chūsei nihon kahei ryūtsūshi: torihiki shudan no henka to yōin* (Tokyo: Keisō shobō, 2001). On the Japanese history of money in general, see Obata Jun, *Nihon kehei ryūtsūshi* (Tokyo: Toeshoin, 1969, originally published in 1930); Takizawa Takeo, *Nihon no kahei no rekishi* (Tokyo: Yoshikawa kōbunkan, 1996).

5. Wakita Haruko, *Nihon chūsei toshiron* (Tokyo: Tokyo daigaku shuppankai, 1981), p. 97. On Kyoto and *za* organizations, see also *Kyoto no rekishi*, vol. 2, Takahashi Yasuo, *Kyoto chūsei toshishi kenkyū* (Kyoto: Shibunkaku shuppan, 1983); Akamatsu Toshihide, "Machi za no seiritsu ni tsuite," in his book *Kodai chūsei shakai keizaishi* (Kyoto: Heirakuji shoten, 1972). On the overview of the studies of medieval cities, see Gomi Fumihiko, editor, *Toshi no chūsei* (Tokyo: Yoshikawa kōbunkan, 1992); Amino Yoshihiko, *Nihon chūsei toshi no sekai* (Tokyo: Chikuma shōbō, 1996).

6. Nakahara Moromori, *Moromori ki, Shiryō sanshū, Zoku gunsho ruijyū* (Tokyo: Zoku gunsho ruijyū kankōkai, 1968–1982), vol. 11, pp. 44–45.

7. *Taiheiki*, vol. 27, said that it was *"yokaranu koto nari tozo."* Gotō Tanji, Okami Masao, and Kamada Kisaburo, editors, *Nihon koten bungaku taikei* (Tokyo: Iwanami shoten, 1960), pp. 34–36. *Taiheiki* is a fictional account of the historical events. In this case, however, the event is also recorded in other sources.

8. Sakurai Yoshirō, "Geinōshi eno shiza," in his book *Chūsei nihon no ōken shūkyō, geinō* (Kyoto: Jinbun shoin, 1988).

9. Zeami, "Kakyō," reprinted in *Nihon shisōtaikei Zeami, Zenchiku* (Tokyo: Iwanami shoten, 1974), p. 99.

10. The function of the *dōhō shū* and the extent of their association with the Jishū has been much debated among the Japanese scholars. For a balanced review of this subject, the reader is referred to Shimazu Tadao, *Nō to renga* (Tokyo: Izumi shoin, 1990), pp. 56–77.

11. For an excellent account of the aftereffects of the Ōnin War, see Mary Elizabeth Berry, *The Culture of Civil War in Kyoto* (Berkeley: University of California Press, 1994).

12. Tsurusaki Hiroo, *Sengoku o iku rengashi Sōchō* (Tokyo: Kadokawa shoten, 1999).

13. According to Yoshida Kenkō (1283?–1352?) in his book *Tsurezuregusa*, Cherry Blossom linked-poetry sessions in the countryside were characterized by "drinking and composing linked poetry, and even breaking off large branches of the tree in a thoughtless manner . . ." (Tokyo: Nihon Koten Bugakukai, 1972).

14. The deity of the Kitano shrine, Tenjin, came to be considered the patron god of linked verse. The Ashikaga shoguns appointed an official poet

laureate or master poet (*renga sōshō*) who was also usually in charge of the shrine's *kaisho*. See Geinōshi Kenkyūkai, editor, *Nihon geinōshi*, vol. 3, p. 88.

15. The term *ikki* is usually associated with rebellions that occurred during the Tokugawa period. In medieval Japanese usage, however, *ikki* implied an organization, alliance, or project, usually military in nature, with overtones of opposition to higher authorities rather than to specific events. Regarding the usage of *ikki* in the medieval period, see David L. Davis, "*Ikki* in Late Medieval Japan," in John W. Hall and Jeffrey P. Mass, editors, *Medieval Japan: Essays in Institutional History* (Stanford, CA: Stanford University Press, 1974). See also Katsumata Shizuo, *Ikki* (Tokyo: Iwanami shoten, 1983); Minegishi Sumio, "Chuseishakai to ikki," in Aoki Michio et al., editors, *Ikki*, vol. 1 (Tokyo: University of Tokyo Press, 1981). For an overview of *ikki* studies in Japan, see the five volumes of Aoki Michio et al., editors, *Ikki* (Tokyo: Tokyo University Press, 1981).

16. Ogata Tsutomu, *Za no bungaku* (Tokyo: Kadokawa shoten, 1973), p. 34.

17. Tsurusaki Hiroo, *Sengoku no kenryoku to yoriai no bungei* (Osaka: Izumi shoin, 1988); Tsurusaki Hiroo, "Sengoku shoki no settsu kokujin sō no dōkō – akutagawa jō noseshi to sono bungei, toku ni renga o chūshin toshite," in Murata Shōzō, editor, *Sengoku daimyo ronshū kinki daimyo no kenkyū*, vol. 5 (Tokyo: Yoshikawa kōbunkan, 1986).

18. Ten was the maximum number of executives according to the code.

19. Yasuda Jirō, "Yamato koku Higashiyamauchi ikki," in Murata Shūzō, editor, *Kinki daimyo no kenkyū*. Donald Keen discusses the famous incident of Akechi Mitsuhide's *renga* session, which was held only a few days before Mitsuhide killed Oda Nobunaga in 1582. See "Jōba, a Sixteenth-Century Poet of Linked Verse," in George Elison and Bardwell L. Smith, editors, *Warlords, Artists, and Commoners: Japan in the Sixteenth Century* (Honolulu: University of Hawaii Press, 1981).

20. To be sure, linked poetry was popular not only among local samurai who would gather together in *ikki* but also among the ambitious warlords and rulers.

21. Matsuoka Shinpei, *Utage no shintai*, pp. 69–70.

22. This statement requires immediate qualification since an absolutist monarch is understood to govern the country with the aid of a permanent professional dependent bureaucracy and army – unlike the decentralized Tokugawa polity. On the other hand, Bourbon France was not as centralized as idealized descriptions may suggest; recent revisionist scholarship on the *ancien régime* reveals the inaccuracy of a picture of absolute central control. For examples, see Roland Mousnier, *The Institutions of France Under the Absolute Monarchy, 1598–1789*, two vols., translated by Brian Pearce (Chicago: University of Chicago Press, 1979–1984).

23. Voltaire, *Encyclopédie* (Paris: Briasson, 1757), t. VII, article on *franchise*.

24. For an account of Toyotomi Hideyoshi's life and an evaluation of his achievement, see the detailed biography by Mary Elizabeth Berry, *Hideyoshi* (Cambridge, MA: Harvard University Press, 1989). See also George Ellison,

"Hideyoshi, the Bountiful Minister," in Bardwell L. Smith and George Ellison, editors, *Warlords, Artists, and Commoners*.

25. Although commercial guild organizations called *kabunakama* were revived in the later Tokugawa period, they were formed with the shogun's permission.

26. Kumakura Isao, "Girei to shite no chanoyu," *Girei bunka* 1 (1981). For an overview of the history of the tea ceremony in English, see Paul Valery and Isao Kumakura, editors, *Tea in Japan: Essays on the History of Chanoyu* (Honolulu: University of Hawaii Press, 1989). This work is a reliable collection of essays by Western and Japanese specialists on the tea ceremony. See also H. Paul Valery, "The Culture of Tea: From Its Origins to Sen no Rikyū," in Bardwell L. Smith and George Ellison, editors, *Warlords, Artists, and Commoners*; Jennifer L. Anderson, *An Introduction to Japanese Tea Ritual* (Albany: State University of New York Press, 1991); Herbert E. Plutschow, *Historical Chanoyu* (Tokyo: The Japan Times, 1986). The reader is also referred to an interesting anthropological analysis of the tea ritual by Dorinne Kondo, "The Way of Tea: Symbolic Analysis," *Man* 20 (1985): 289–306. There is an enormous amount of secondary literature on the tea ceremony in Japan; I have only scratched the surface of its history in these pages.

27. Matsuya Hisamasa, Hisayashi, and Hisashige, "Matsuiya Kaiki," in Sen Sōshitsu, editor, *Chadō koten zenshū* (Kyoto: Tankō sha, 1957): vol. 9:1. The reader is also referred to Kumakura Isao et al., *Shiryō ni yoru cha no yu no rekishi jō* (Tokyo: Shufu no tomosha, 1994), pp. 303–305. For further analysis of the tea diarists, see Mary Elizabeth Berry, *The Culture of Civil War* (Berkeley: University of California Press, 1994), pp. 259–284.

28. Murakami Naojirō, "1562 nen sakai hatsu padore Gaspar Villela yori yasokai no padre oyobi iruman ni kokurishi shokan," Murakami Naojiro, translator, *Yasokaishi nihon tsūshin* (Tokyo: Yukakudō, [1927] 1966), pp. 55–56; Asao Naohiro et al., *Sakai no Rekishi – toshi jichi no genryū* (Tokyo: Kadokawa shoten, 1999); Toyoda Takeshi, *Sakai – shōnin no shinshutsu to toshi no jiyū*, Second edition (Tokyo: Shibundō, 1966). For a history of the city of Sakai in English, see V. Dixon Morris, "The City of Sakai and Urban Autonomy," in Bardwell L. Smith and George Ellison, editors, *Warlords, Artists, and Commoners*.

29. Sakaishi hakubutsukan, editors, *Sakaishū: chanoyu o tsukutta hito tachi, 100 shūnen kinen tokubetsuten*, Catalogue of an exhibition on the Sakai tea circles (Sakai: Sakai city, 1989). Predictably, Sakai also had active *renga* linked-poetry circles. See Tsurusaki Hirō, "The Poet Shōkō and the salons of Sakai," translated by Steven D. Carter, in Steven D. Carter, editor, *Literary Patronage in Late Medieval Japan* (Ann Arbor: University of Michigan Press, 1993), pp. 45–62.

30. From a letter written soon after Oda Nobunaga's death in 1582, reprinted in Kumakura Isao et al., editors, *Shiryō ni yoru chanoyu no rekiji, jō* (Tokyo: Shufu no tomo, 1994), pp. 329–333.

31. *Kogashi* is an inexpensive substitute for tea made from rice or barley.

32. Toyotomi Hideyoshi's ordinance and related materials are included in Isao Kumakura et al., editors, *Shiryō ni yoru jō*, pp. 404–414.

33. "Sen no Rikyū," in Paul Valery and Isao Kumakura, editors, *Tea in Japan*, p. 37.

34. According to Kuzumi Soan (1613–1699), this impressive story was already well-known in his time. See *Chawa Shigetsushu*, reprinted in Hayashiya Tatsusaburō, Yokoki Kiyoshi, and Narabayashi Tadao, editors, *Nihon no chasho* (Tokyo: Heibonsha, 1972), pp. 25–26.

35. For Sen no Rikyū's farewell poem and related primary materials, see Kumakura et al., *Shiryō ni yoru*, pp. 415–434.

36. A metaphor for the enlightened mind that sees beyond duality.

37. Togami Hajime, *Sen no Rikyū: hito mono kane* (Tokyo: Tōsui shobō, 1998, p. 132. Togami cites four contemporary letters that refer to Sen no Rikyū as a *maisu*.

Chapter 5

1. However, the structure, strategy, and legitimacy of peasant collective actions as well as the legal framework that controlled these activities changed significantly. In addition, Tokugawa documents do not often use the term *ikki* to refer to these collective actions. The literature of Tokugawa peasant collective actions is abundant, but few seriously examine conceptual definitions of the term *ikki*. Hosaka Satoru's work *Hyakushō ikki to sono sahō* (Tokyo: Yoshikawa kōbunkan, 2002) is insightful on this topic.

2. *Gotōke reijō*, no. 3, reprinted in Ishii Ryōsuke, editor, *Kinsei hōsei shiryō*, vol. 3 (Tokyo: Sōbunsha, 1959).

3. In one of the shogunate's most famous legal cases, the episode of the 47 ronin, one of the critical reasons that the avengers were sentenced to die by *seppuku* was that they committed the crime of forming a party (*totō*).

4. My book *The Taming of the Samurai*, pp. 267–277, explains this system in more detail.

5. I call it "a complex integrated yet decentralized state structure." For my view of Tokugawa state formation, see *The Taming of the Samurai*, pp. 151–194. Recent historiographies of Tokugawa Japan in English also underscore the complex duality of the Tokugawa state. See Marc Ravina, *Land and Lordships in Early Modern Japan* (Stanford, CA: Stanford University Press, 1999); Luke S. Roberts, *Mercantilism in a Japanese Domain: The Merchant Origins of Economic Nationalism in 18th Century Tosa* (Cambridge: Cambridge University Press, 1999).

Chapter 6

1. Moriya Takeshi, *Kinsei geinōshi no kenkyū* (Tokyo: Kōbundō, 1985), p. 119.

2. Moriya Takeshi, *Kinsei geinōshi no kenkyū*, pp. 65–67; Moriya Takeshi, "Yūgei and Chōnin society in Edo period," *Acta Asiatica* (November 1977): 32–54.

3. In "Kyō habutae oritome," published in the second year of the Genroku, 1689, cited by Moriya Takeshi, "Asobi no kankyō," in *Kyoto shomin seikatsushi*, edited by CDI (Kyoto: Kyoto Shinyō kinko, 1973), p. 259.

4. *Shōgi* is a Japanese game similar to chess.

5. Reprinted in *Nihon Kyōkasho Taikei*, vol. 12, 1968. The *biwa* and *koto* are stringed instruments. The *koto* most closely resembles a Western harp.

6. To be sure, we should note that the hobby circle networks were usually organized on a regional basis. Due to the policy of institutional segregation, such territorial groups as villages and urban wards usually consisted of people from the same status category. Therefore, in a relatively small village circle without significant connections to networks at the provincial or national level, the members were likely to belong primarily to one feudal status group. Even in such small circles as a village-based *igo* game group, however, the location for the players' meetings would bring together different types of villagers, in terms of economic standing and occupational background, who might not mingle with one another without a shared hobby. On the other hand, aesthetic associations that developed extensive networks at local, provincial, and national levels, such as *haiku* poetry-making, *ikebana* flower arrangement, and the tea ceremony, had the ability to bring together people from very different status groups or social/regional backgrounds. For a detailed network study regarding the circles of *igo* and *shōgi* players of the villages in the Edo hinterland, see Kobayashi Fumio, "Bunka network to chiiki shakai," in Watanabe Nobuo, editor, *Kinsei nihon no seikatsu bunka to chiiki shakai* (Tokyo: Kawade shobō shinsha, 1995).

7. *Mukashi Mukashi Monogatari*, attributed to Niimi Masaasa. He was said to be 81 years old in 1732. Reprinted in *Nihon shomin shiryō shūsei*, vol. 8 (Tokyo: Sanichi shobō, 1969), p. 397.

8. *Jōruri* started out as a form of storytelling in the medieval period, but it became associated with *kugutsu* puppet plays at the beginning of the seventeenth century and was performed at locations along the Shijō bank of the Komo River in Kyoto. The puppet theater is now known as *bunraku*.

9. Uji Kaganojō, *Nihon shisō taikei: Kinsei geidō ron* (Tokyo: Iwanami shoten, 1972), p. 405.

10. Ihara Saikaku, *Nihon Eidaigura*, reprinted in Asō Isoji and Fuji Akio, editors, *Taiyaku saikaku zenshū*, vol. 12 (Tokyo: Meiji shoin, 1975), p. 19. Kichizō and Sansuke were names with lowly associations; they were common given names among peasants, servants, or less prosperous merchants.

11. Nishikawa Joken, *Chōnin bukuro*, reprinted in *Kinsei chōnin shisō: Nihon shisō taikei*, vol. 59, edited by Nakamura Yukihiko (Tokyo: Iwanami shoten, 1975), p. 98.

12. *Kawachiya Kashō kyūki*, in Nomura Yutaka and Yui Kitarō, editors, (Tokyo: Seibyndō, 1955), p. 123. The book was originally written around the Genrou (1688–1704) and Hōei (1704–1711) eras.

13. *Kawachiya Kashō kyūki*, p. 125.

14. *Kawachiya Kashō kyūki*, "Geinō o shinarau beki koto," p. 103, p. 124.

15. "*Hitomae*" was the serious concern among the famous 47 ronin avengers. See Ikegami, *Taming of the Samurai*, pp. 230–233.

16. For the moral standards of the merchant class in this respect, see Miyamoto Mataji, *Kinsei shōgyō keiei no kenkyū* (Kyoto: Oyasu shuppan, 1948); Miyamoto Mataji, *Kinsei shōnin ishiki no kenkyu* (Tokyo: Kōdansha, 1977, original edition published in 1941).

17. Mitsui Takafusa, the fourth family head of the Mitsui, "Chōnin kōken roku," reprinted in *Nihon shiso taikei, Vol. 59: Kinsei chōnin shisō*, Nakamura Yukihiko, editor (Tokyo: Iwanami shoten, 1975).

18. Women were not particularly excluded from *haikai* poetry composition. In addition, dancing and music in the style of commoners tended to have a higher level of female participation. On the other hand, such *za* performing arts as the tea ceremony and *ikebana*, which originated during the medieval period and developed along with the acculturation of the samurai class, attracted a predominance of male students during the Tokugawa period. These performing arts were considered upper-class genres suitable for serious socialization among gentlemen. In fact, female predominance in schools for the tea ceremony and *ikebana* is a phenomenon of the twentieth century.

19. In *Fuzoku Shichiyudan*, cited in Ujiie Mikito, "Nichijō sei no naka no bushi bunka," *Nihon Minzoku taikei 11: Toshi to inaka* (Tokyo: Shogakukan, 1985), p. 359. The phrase itself comes from an essay published in 1756.

20. Ujiie Mikito, "Nichijō sei no naka no bushi bunka," pp. 355–360. One reason for the careful selection of *goten jochū* was that girls who received training in prestigious samurai households were considered more desirable as brides. As wives, they would have the skills required to supervise a number of employees or servants and to entertain other prestigious merchants.

21. Ujiie Mikito, ibid.

22. Shikitei Sanba, *Ukiyoburo, Nihon koten bungaku taikei*, vol. 63 (Tokyo: Iwanami shoten, 1957), pp. 184–185.

23. Buyōinshi, *Seji kenmonroku* (1822), reprinted in *Nihon shomin seikatsu shiryō shūsei*, vol. 8 (Tokyo: Sannichi shobō, 1969).

24. Hara Taneaki, "Okeiko to tenarai," *Edo jidai bunka* 1, no. 5 (June 1922): 223. On the issue of Tokugawa literacy, see Chapter 11.

25. Kinugawa Yasuki, "Iemoto Seido no Shakai teki haikei," *Rekishi Kōron* 4, no. 4 (1978), p. 46.

26. Tanahashi Masahiro, *Edo no dōraku* (Tokyo: Kōdansha, 1995), pp. 22–86; Aoki Kōichirō, *Edo no Engei* (Tokyo: Chikuma shobō, 1998).

27. Ono Sawako, *Edo no hanami* (Tokyo: Tsukiji shokan, 1992), p. 139. Edo was truly a garden city. See Shirahata Yōzaburō, "Hanami to toshi Edo," in Nakamura Kenjirō, editor, *Rekishi no naka no toshi* (Tokyo: Mineruba shobō, 1983); Toyoshima Hiroaki, *Sumidagawa to sono ryogan: Jo, chū, ge* (Tokyo: Hōshūshoin, 1962). Shirahata Yōzaburō, *Daimyō teien* (Tokyo: Kōdansha, 1974), clarified the political use of the *daimyo*'s private gardens for sociability.

28. The status of Tokugawa professional artists is a complex issue that I cannot discuss further in this book. The reader is referred to Yokoyama Fuyuhiko, editor, *Geinō bunka no sekai* (Tokyo: Yoshikawa kōbunkan, 2000).

29. Pierre Bourdieu, *The Rules of Art*, translated by Susan Emanuel (London: Polity Press, 1996), p. 48.

30. Pierre Bourdieu, *The Field of Cultural Production* (Cambridge: Polity Press, 1993), p. 27.

31. Pierre Bourdieu, *The Rules of Art*, p. 55. Regarding the *haikai* tradition and its communal and ethnographical roots, see Toshirō Kiyosaki, *Haikai to Minzoku-gaku* (Tokyo: Iwasaki bijutsusha, 1967).

32. In the typical modern *iemoto* structure, the grand master and the intermediate teachers shared the revenue from certifying the students. The commercial aspect of this system of art instruction derived from the *iemoto*'s monopoly of certification. The content of instruction by intermediate teachers was perceived to be the same as that of the grand master. From an organizational perspective, the *iemoto* system operated like a modern restaurant franchise in which the company logo, menu, and manner of food preparation are usually common to every establishment in the chain. A paternalistic conception of authority has always been an important component of *iemoto* art schools because it unifies the franchise system.

33. Itō Toshiko, "Rikka kara ikebana e," *Rekishi Kōron* 4, no. 4 (1978): 28–49. The text of Ikenobō's student list is reprinted with an introduction by Moriya Takeshi, "Ikenobō eidai monteichō – sono ichi," *Geinōshi kenkyū* 63 (1980): 45–67.

34. The *rikka* was an older, more formal style of arrangement, while the *ikebana* style was made for decorating the alcoves of ordinary houses of the Tokugawa era.

35. Moriya Katsuhisa, "Iemoto seido to sono soshiki," in *Tokushū, iemoto seido to nihon no shakai* of *Rekishi Kōron* 4, no. 4 (1978): 93.

36. Moriya Takeshi, *Kinsei geinō bunkashi no kenkyū* (Tokyo: Kōbundō, 1992), p. 86.

37. In practice, as long as the *iemoto* system incorporated certain aspects of commercial capitalism, the power of money certainly played a role in social stratification within the artistic communities. The richer merchants, for example, could afford private lessons from famous tea masters and hosted impressive tea ceremony sessions at which they displayed their collections of exquisitely expensive tea utensils. In this way, the power of money asserted itself in the art schools.

38. The historical study of the *iemoto* system was pioneered in the post-war period by the massive works of Nishiyama Matsunosuke. See his book *Iemoto no kenkyū* (Tokyo: Yoshikawa kōbunkan, 1982, originally published in 1959), p. 9, for further details regarding the origins of the *iemoto* system. Hayashiya Tatsusaburō's works were also important early contributions to the field. See in particular Hayashiya Tatsusaburō, "Iemoto in seido no kakuritsu," in *Shisō no kagaku* (1953). The works of Moriya Takeshi synthesize the more recent developments in the field. See his *Kinsei geinōshi no kenkyū* (Tokyo: Kōbundō, 1985). The reader is referred in particular to the special issue *Tokushū, iemoto seido to nihon no shakai* of *Rekishi Kōron* 4, no. 4 (1978), for bibliographical surveys and other overviews of the field.

39. Nishiyama Matsunosuke, *Zusetsu Sadō taikei Chano bunkashi* (Tokyo: Kadokawa shoten, 1962), p. 221.

40. Hisada Muneya, "Keiko yori ōgi made," in *Zusetsu Sadō taikei: Chakai to temae*, edited by Hayashiya Tatsusaburō and Nagashima Fukutarō (Tokyo: Kadokawa shoten, 1964), pp. 156–208.

41. Moriya Takeshi, "Iemoto seido: So no keisei o megutte," *Kokuritsu minzokugaku hakubutsukan kenkyū hōkoku* 4, no. 4 (1979); Hayashiya Tatsusaburō, "Sadōzensho no seiritsu," in *Koten bunka no sōzō* (Tokyo: University of

Tokyo Press, 1964); Kinugawa Yasuki, "*Iemoto* seido no shakai teki haikei," *Rekishi kōron* 4, no. 4 (1978): 41–49.

42. One of the distinctive characteristics of the Japanese *ie* system was its organizational incorporation of people who were not blood relatives of the house through fictional kinship ties so that the *ie* could strengthen its organizational efficacy and ensure its generational continuity. It is in this connection that the American anthropologist Francis Hsu once described the *iemoto* school as a symbolic institution of Japanese social organization that can be compared to "clan" in China, "caste" in India, and "club" in the United States. See Francis Hsu, *Iemoto: The Heart of Japan* (Cambridge, MA: Schenckman, 1975).

Chapter 7

1. Tanaka Yūko first used the term "network" in relation to the *haikai* poetry of the Tokugawa period in her pioneering work *Edo no sōzōryoku* (Tokyo: Chikuma shobō, 1990), p. 69. She approaches the subject from the perspective of literary analysis, however. My intentions in the present volume include a discussion of the group dynamics of the *haikai* circles together with an analysis of the sociological implications of their network structures. The positionality of the *haikai* networks should also be understood as an outcome of the long-term development of network structures in Japanese society since the medieval period, as I have already discussed in the previous chapters.

2. Bessho Makiko, "Kasenhyakunijyukkan no tabi: Igarashi Hamamo," in her book *Kotoba o tenishita onnatachi: Haikai ni miru joseishi* (Tokyo: Origin shuppan sentā, 1993), pp. 84–135.

3. Tenjin is the Shintō name for Sugawara no Michizane (845–903), who was a famous ancient scholar revered as the god of scholarship and literature.

4. An ancient poet whose poems are included in *Manyoshū*, the oldest Japanese poetry anthology (ca. eighth century).

5. For the ritual dimension of the *haikai* meeting, see Hama Rintarō, "Wazaogi no seishin," *Nihon bungaku* 36, no. 8 (1987): 1–10.

6. This saying was cited by Bashō's disciple Dohō's "Sanzōshi," Minami Shinichi, editor, *Sanzōshi: sōshaku* (Tokyo: Kazama shobō, 1964). For Bashō and *za*, see Noridatsu Yakame, *Shōfū haikai ni okeru za no ishiki* (Tokyo: Ōfūsha, 1974); Ogata Tsutomu, *Za no bungaku* (Tokyo: Kadokawa shoten, 1973).

7. Iwata Hideyuki, "Kaisetsu, edo za no meishō to kōten tsukekushū no kufū," in Katsutada Suzuki, editor, *Edoza tentori haikaishū* (Tokyo: Iwanami shoten, 1993), pp. 499–507.

8. We can, however, trace some succession lines of *haikai* teachers (*soshō*), although their succession was usually less formalized than those in the *iemoto* organizations. See, for example, the following study of the *haikai* schools in Edo: Iwata Hideyuki, "Edo-za no meishō to kōtentsukekushū no kufū," in Suzuki Katsutada et al., editors, *Shin nihon koten bungaku taikei, vol. 72: Edoza tentori haikaishū* (Tokyo: Iwanami shoten, 1993). The *kumi-ren* circles were even more unstable. See Ōno Atsuyuki, "Shūgetsu-hyū manku awase ni okeru kumiren no shōchō," *Bungaku* 54 (December 1986): 205–218.

9. Peter Burke, *Popular Culture in Early Modern Europe* (New York: Harper Torchbooks, 1978), p. 102.

10. A game of *maeku-zuke* is described in *Haikai Takama no Uguisu*, published in 1696. Hirano Yoshihiro, the editor of this book, recalled the game as an experience of his youth. The text is quoted in Miyata Masanobu, *Zappai shi no kenkyū* (Tokyo: Akao shōbundō, 1972), pp. 31–32.

11. Watanabe Shinichirō, *Edo no sui tanshikei bungaku: Maeku-zuke* (Tokyo: Miki shobō, 1994), p. 24.

12. Some examples of these "how to succeed" manuals are reprinted in Suzuki Katsutada, editor, *Edoza tentori haikaishū*.

13. Cited in Miyata Masanobu, *Zappai shi no kenkyū* (Tokyo: Akao shōbundō, 1972), p. 116.

14. Miyata Masanobu, *Zappai shi*, pp. 298–309.

15. Miyata's work gives a clear overview of the *haikai* networks at the provincial level. For primary materials other than those reprinted in studies of Tokugawa literature, the so-called *kenshi* and *sonshi*, which are histories of prefectures and villages edited by the local communities, often include a significant amount of information about local *haikai* networks. For Kyūshū area, the reader is referred to: Ōuchi Hatsuo, *Kinsei kyūshū haidan shi no kenkyū* (Fukuoka: Kyūshū daigaku shuppankai, 1983); Ōuchi Hatsuo, *Kinsei no haikai to haidan* (Tokyo: Izumi shoin, 1994). See also Wada Tokuichi, *Ecchū haikaishi* (Tokyo: Ofūsha, 1981), for Hokuriku area; Okamoto Masaru, *Kinsei haidanshi shinkō* (Tokyo: Ofūsha, 1988), for Sendai and Ise provinces; and Kira Sueo, *Genroku kyoto haidan kenkyū* (Tokyo: Benseisha, 1985), for Kyoto.

16. Miyata Masanobu, *Zappai shi*, pp. 107–111.

17. This novel was published around the Genroku era. Cited in Watanabe Shinichirō, *Edo no sui*, p. 186.

18. Reprinted in Kinsei Shiryō Kenkyūkai, editor, *Shōhō jiroku* no. 1935, p. 272 (Tokyo: Gakujutsu Shinkōkai, 1965). See also *Shōhō jiroku* no. 1931, pp. 269–270.

19. In his letter in 1692. See Matsuo Bashō in *Bunshū Shin nihon koten bungaku zenshu*, Toyama Susumu, editor (Tokyo: Shincho sha, 1978), pp. 208–211. Also on his attitude on *ten-tori* (point-generating), see Suzuki Katsutada, "Kaisetsu: sōron," in his book *Edoza tentori haikaishū*, pp. 474–475; Shirahase Haruo, *Traces of Dreams* (Stanford, CA: Stanford University Press, 1998), pp. 154–159.

20. Bashō himself did not reject the witty lighthearted aspect of *haikai* poetry. Rather, he placed lightness at the heart of his later work.

21. Other *haikai* poets also published their travel poems. An early famous example is Ōyodo Michikaze's *Nihon angya bunshū*, originally published in the second year of Genroku, which collected his prose while he traveled throughout Japan for seven years.

22. This is my translation.

23. The first line of linked verse, "Shi Akindo no Maki" ("Poetry is what I sell"). I adapted here the translation of Miner and Odagiri. This is a rather free translation from the original but captured the spirit of mixed pride and self-pity.

See Bashō, *The Monkey's Straw Raincoat*, Earl Miner and Hiroko Odagiri, translators (Princeton, NJ: Princeton University Press, 1981), p. 48.

24. For example, the 1702 publication of a poetry collection entitled *Akaeboshi* used the phrase *edo-ku*, "the collection of *edo-ku*," at the end of the volume. Similarly, *Takara bune* (1703) claimed to record "the winners of an *edo-ku maekuzuke* competition." In light of this usage, the identity of Edo-style popular *haikai* emerged around the beginning of the eighteenth century. See Watanabe Shinichirō, "Edo-ku," in his book *Edo no sui, tanshikei bungaku, maekuzuke*, pp. 84–96.

25. Suzuki Katsutada, *Kinsei haikaishi no kisō* (Nagoya: Nagoya daigaku shuppankai, 1992), pp. 329–342; Masanobu Miyata, *Zappai shi*, p. 292.

26. Hamada Giichirō, *Senryū, Kyōka: Rekishi shinsho 82* (Tokyo: Kyōikusha, 1979), p. 23.

27. There are a number of scholarly studies of Karai Senryū as well as reprinted texts of selected pieces by this poet. For an overview, see Hamada Giichirō, "Senryū," Miyata Masanobu, editor, *Haifū yanagidaru: Shinchō Nihon koten shūsei* (Tokyo: Shinchōsha, 1984). Karai Senryū did not publish his own poetry. See Suzuki Katsudata, *Musaku no shidōsha – Karai Senryū* (Tokyo: Shintensha, 1982).

28. The term *senryū* became a generic term for a type of comical and witty *haikai* in modern Japanese.

29. Ono Takeo, *Edo Bukka jiten* (Tokyo: Tenbōsha, 1993), p. 348.

30. Takagi Sōgo, *Haikai Jinmei Jiten* (Tokyo: Gennandō shoten, 1970).

31. Bessho Makiko, *Kotoba o tenishita onnatachi* (Tokyo: Origin shuppan, 1993).

32. Watanabe Shinichirō, "Edo-ku," in *Edo no sui*, pp. 139–151.

33. Tada Jinichi, "Tama chiiki no haikai kōryū ni miru zaison bunka no hirogari," *Chihōshi kenkyū* 40, no. 4 (1990): p. 69.

34. Ōuchi Hatsuo et al., *Kohaku an Shokyūni zenshū* (Tokyo: Izumi shoin, 1986); Atsuko Kanamori, *Edo no onna haikaishi Okuno hosomichi oiku-Shōkyu ni no shōgai* (Tokyo: Shōbunsha, 1998); Yokoyama Seiga, *Jyoryū haikashi* (Tokyo: Tōeishobō, 1972).

35. Bessho Makiko, "Kasen hyakujijyukkan no tabi," in *Kotoba o tenishita*, pp. 95–135.

36. Kanamori Atsuko, *Edo no onna haikai shi: Oku no hosomichi o iku: Shokyūni no shōgai* (Tokyo: Shōbunsha, 1998). See also Shiba Keiko, *Kinsei onna tabi nikki* (Tokyo: Yoshikawa kōbunkan, 1997).

37. Playing the Japanese style of battledore and shuttlecock is the favorite pastime, especially for girls, in the days of the New Year celebration, the most joyous holiday season of the year.

38. Ōta Shirayuki, editor, *Haikai Mikawa Komachi* (1702). Reprinted in Yasui Shosa, editor, *Shōmon chinsho hyakushufukkoku ban* (Kyoto: Shibunkaku, 1971). Regarding the list of female *haikai* anthologies and other books, see Bessho Makiko, *Kotoba o tenishita*.

39. See Chapter 2 for my argument on switching and publics.

40. Ishikawa Jun, "Edo jin no hassōhō ni tsuite," *Ishikawa Jun senshū*, vol. 14 (Tokyo: Iwanami shoten, 1980, originally published in 1943), p. 175. More

recently, Haruo Shirane explained this duality: "*Haikai* was the poetry of
perpetual recontextualization in which the ownership of a text was playfully
seized and passed from one individual or subculture to another." See Haruo
Shirane, *Traces of Dreams*, p. 11.

41. Regarding the role of humor in the history of Japanese poetry, see Suzuki
    Tōzō, *Haikai no keifu: Sono warai* (Tokyo: Chūō kōronsha, 1989).
42. The resulting multivocality means that modern Japanese cannot understand
    the majority of Tokugawa *haikai* without the help of detailed commentaries.
43. Tanaka Yūko, *Edo no sōzōryoku* (Tokyo: Chikuma shobō, 1990).
44. Iijima Kōichi and Katō Ikuya, "Anei Tenmei ki no bunjin tachi to *haikai*," in
    their book *Edo haikai nishi higashi* (Tokyo: Misuzu shobō, 2002), pp. 76–
    106; Ikezawa Ichirō, *Edo bunjin ron* (Tokyo: Kyūko shobō, 2000); Hamada
    Giichirō, *Ōta Nanbo* (Tokyo: Yoshikawa Kōbunkan, 1986).
45. Based upon the description of the pictorial scroll, *Tōin Zukan* in the New
    York Public Library, Spencer Collection.
46. For the transformation of the samurai's culture of honor as an internal
    virtue, see my book *The Taming of the Samurai*. Regarding Watanabe
    Kazan, see Sugimoto Fumiko, "Eshi: Watanabe Kazan, Gakō to Bushi
    no aida," in Yokoyama Fuyuhiko, editor, *Geino Bunka no sekai* (Tokyo:
    Yoshikawa kōbunkan, 2000), pp. 227–274; Saitō Masasuke, *Jinbutsu sōsho:
    Watanabe Kazan* (Tokyo: Yoshikawa kōbunkan, 1986); Saitō Masasuke,
    "Watanabe Kazan no shōgai to shisō," in Suganuma Teizō, editor,
    Teihon Watanabe Kazan shū, vol. 3 (Tokyo: Kyodoshuppansha, 1991);
    Suganuma Teizō, *Watanabe Kazan, hitoto geijyutsu* (Tokyo: Nigensha,
    1982).
47. For example, see Ozawa Kōichi and Haga Noboru, editors, *Watanabe Kazan
    shū*, vol. 1 (Tokyo: Nihon Tosho Center, 1999), pp. 316–349, with regard to
    his visit to Atsugi.
48. Ibid., pp. 321–323.
49. Ibid., p. 337.
50. Ibid., p. 337.
51. Ibid., p. 337.
52. Ibid., p. 337.
53. Ozawa Kōichi and Haga Noboru, editors, *Watanabe Kazan shū*, vol. 3
    (Tokyo: Nihon Tosho Center, 1999), p. 254.

Chapter 8

1. A report of Kōno Keisuke, a *Kantō torishimari deyaku*. The document
   was reprinted in an article by Kobayashi Fumio, "Bunka netwāku to chiiki
   shakai," in Nobuo Watanabe, editor, *Kinsei nihon seikatsu bunka to chiiki
   shakai* (Tokyo: Kawade shobō shinsha, 1995), pp. 78–79.
2. See the study of village cultural pastimes such as *igo*, *shōgi*, and dance in
   Kobayashi Fumio, "Bunka netwāku to chiiki shakai."
3. Moriyama Gunjirō, *Minshū hoki to matsuri* (Tokyo: Chikuma shobō, 1981);
   Sugi Hitoshi, "Kaseiki no shakai to bunka," in Aoki Michio and Yamada
   Tadao, editors, *Koza nihon kinseishi 6: Tenpōki no shakai to seiji* (Tokyo:

Yūhikaku, 1981); Sugi Hitoshi, "Zaison bunka no kōryūken to kaisō kozō," *Minshūshi kenkyū* 45 (1993): 43–62; Tada Jinichi, "Tama chiiki no haikai kōryū ni miru zaison bunka no hirogari," *Chihōshi kenkyū* 40, no. 4 (1990): 62–75.

4. "Niigataken Kyōiku Iinkai," in Miya Eiji, editor, *Suzuki Bokushi shiryōshū* (Niigataken Shiozawamachi: Niigata-ken Kyōikuiinkai, 1961). Suzuki Bokushi later published a well-known essay, *Hokuetsu seppu*, in 1836. He was 67 years old. See Suzuki Bokushi kenshōkai, editors, *Hokuetsu seppu to Suzuki Bokushi* (Shiozawa machi, Niigata: Suzuki Bokushi kenshōkai, 1963).

5. Sugi Hitoshi, "Zaison bunka no kōryūken to kaisō kozō," *Minshūshi kenkyū* 45 (1993): 43–62; see also Sugi Hitoshi, "Kinsei zaison bunka ni okeru gijyutsu to shōhin to bunka no kōryū," *Waseda jitsugyō gattsukō kenkyū kiyō* 25 (1991); "Kaseiki no shakai to bunka," in Aoki Michio and Yamada Tadao, editors, *Kōza nihon kinseishi 6: Tenpōki no shakai to seiji.* For views on Tokugawa rural culture and social protest in English, see: Anne Walthall, *Social Protest and Popular Culture in Eighteenth Century Japan* (Tucson: University of Arizona Press, 1986); Herman Ooms, *Tokugawa Village Practice: Class, Status, Power, Law* (Berkeley: University of California Press, 1996); William Kelly, *Deference and Defiance in Nineteenth-Century Japan* (Princeton, NJ: Princeton University Press, 1985).

6. Haga Noboru, *Bakumatsu kokugaku no kenkyū* (Tokyo: Kyōiku shuppan sentā, 1978); Numata Tetsu, "Shisei sōmō no kokugaku," in Furukawa Tetsushi and Ishida Ichiro, editors, *Nihon shisōshi kōza* (Tokyo: Yūzankaku, 1976).

7. Haga Noboru, "Kinsei kokugaku kenkyū suishin no tame ni," in Haga Noboru, editor, *Bakumatsu Kokugaku no kenkyū* (Tokyo: Kyōiku shuppan sentā, 1978).

8. "Bakuisha zuihitsu," in *Haikai bunko* 18. Cited by Aoki Michio, "Chiiki bunka no seisei," in Asao Naohiro et al. *Iwanami kōza nihon tsūshi*, vol. 15 (Tokyo: Iwanami shoten, 1995).

9. Moriyama Gunjirō, *Minshū hoki to matsuri*, p. 175. It is also possible that these figures are somewhat lower than the actual rate. Some of the prisoners may have feigned illiteracy in the belief that the authorities would interpret the ability to read and write as evidence that they were leaders of the rebellion.

10. In fact, the rebels' agenda included opposition to mandatory public schooling.

11. See also Chapter 11 for the question of literacy.

12. Takahashi Satoshi, "Kinsei kōki jōshū akagi seinanroku chiiki ni okeru minshū no kyōiku bunka undō to so no kiban," *Gunma daigaku kyōiku gakubu kiyō: jin bun shakai hen* 36 (1987): 172–200.

13. Ibid.

14. For an overview of Tokugawa and post-Tokugawa collective actions in English, see James White, *Ikki: Social Conflict and Political Protest in Early Modern Japan* (Ithaca, NY: Cornell University Press, 1995); William W. Kelly, *Deference and Defiance in Nineteenth-Century Japan* (Princeton, NJ: Princeton University Press, 1985); Eiko Ikegami and Charles Tilly, "State Formation and Contention in Japan and France," in John M. Merriman, James

L. McClain, and Ugata Kaoru, editors, *Edo and Paris* (Ithaca, NY: Cornell University Press, 1995); Eiko Ikegami, "Citizenship and National Identity in Early Meiji Japan, 1868–1889: A Comparative Assessment," *International Review of Social History* 40, Supplement 3 (1995): 185–221; Roger Bowen, *Rebellion and Democracy in Meiji Japan: A Study of Commoners in the Popular Right Movement* (Berkeley: University of California Press, 1980); Anne Walthall, editor and translator, *Peasant Uprisings in Japan: A Critical Anthology of Peasant Histories* (Chicago: University of Chicago Press, 1991).

15. Irokawa Daikichi, Ei Hideo, and Arai Katsuhiro, *Minshū kenpō no sōzō* (Tokyo: Hyoronsha, 1970); Irokawa Daikichi, *Meiji Seishinshi* (Tokyo: Koga shobō, 1964).

16. Tada Jinichi, "Tama chiiki no haikai kōryū ni miru zaison bunka no hirogari," *Chihōshi kenkyū* 40, no. 4 (1990): 62–75.

17. Ibid., pp. 70–72.

18. *Shogakai* (open exhibitions) were a very interesting popular form of aesthetic public in the late Tokugawa period that directly connected cultural professionals with a popular audience. Unfortunately, I do not have the space to elaborate on this topic, but see: Kobayashi Tadashi, "Edo no shogakai," in *Edo towa nanika 1: Tokugawa no heiwa*, edited by Haga Tōru (Tokyo: Shibundō, 1985); Robert Chambel, "Tenpōki zengo no shogakai," *Kinsei bungei* 47 (1987): 47–72.

19. "The Sakura Sōgo Story," in Anne Walthall, editor and translator, *Peasant Uprisings in Japan*, p. 35.

20. This and the preceding piece were in a form of *dodoitsu*, a popular song style. The abolition of the samurai's privileged status resulted in the formation of a national standing army mustered through universal conscription.

21. Moriyama Gunjirō, *Minshū hōki to matsuri*, pp. 132–133. Written in the form of a love song, the verse expresses the author's determination to be another Sōgo.

Chapter 9

1. Ishiguro Kichijirō, *Chūsei geidōron no shisō* (Tokyo: Kokusho kankōkai, 1993); Terada Tōru, *Michi no shisō* (Tokyo: Sōbunsha, 1978).

2. Dōgen, "Shōbōgenzō, daiichi, genjyōkōan," in *Nihon shisō taikei: Dōgen, jō* (Tokyo: Iwanami shoten, 1970), p. 38. Dōgen used highly symbolic language in his attempts to articulate the inexpressible dimension of reality. Therefore, his writings can be translated in several different ways. My translation here is indebted to Sōichi Nakamura's translation of the text into modern Japanese as well as to other attempts to translate the texts into English. See Nakamura Sōichi, *Zenyaku Shōbōgenzō* (Tokyo: Seishin shobō, 1970), pp. 6–7. The reader should note, however, that Dōgen is expressing in this passage an assumption of Buddhist philosophy that was common to different sects of Buddhism, not a notion specific to Zen.

3. People in ancient Japan also believed that words had a power of their own, or *kotodama*, that could move or shape the external world. But, in spite

of this belief, no Japanese religion developed a strong interest in linguistic articulation and truth claims comparable to those of late medieval Judaism and Christianity. Generally, the Japanese intellectuals tended to regard words as means rather than ends in themselves.

4. Michael Polanyi, *Knowing and Being* (Chicago: University of Chicago Press, 1969), p. 143.

5. Zeami, "Yūgaku shūdō fūken," *Zeami Zenchiku: Nihon shisō taikei* (Tokyo: Iwanamishoten, 1974), p. 166.

6. Yuasa Yasuo, *The Body: Toward an Eastern Mind-Body Theory*, edited by T. P. Kasulis, translated by Nagatomo Shigenori and T. P. Kasulis (Albany: State University of New York Press, 1987), p. 105; Yuasa Yasuo, *Shintai: Tōyōteki shinshinron no kokoromi* (Tokyo: Sōbunsha, 1977); Yuasa Yauo: *Shintai no Uchūsei* (Tokyo: Iwanami Shoten, 1994). To be sure, this way of thinking is not limited to art forms that involve physical activity. In fact, it was *waka* poetry that first developed an elaborate theory of aesthetics. In the field of linked poetry, Shinkei (1406–1475) is famous for advocating the theory of "the oneness of the way of poetry and the way of Buddhism."

7. Tanigawa Tatsuzō, *Cha no bigaku* (Kyoto: Tanōsha, 1977), p. 19.

8. *Nanbōroku*, reprinted in Kumakura Isao, *Nanbōroku o yomu* (Kyoto: Tankōsha, 1983), p. 21; Yokoi Kiyoshi, "Nanbōroku oboegaki kaisetsu," in *Nihon no chasho*, edited by Hayashiya Tatsusaburō et al. (Tokyo: Heibonsha, 1971); Nishiyama Matsunosuke, "Kinsei no yūgeiron," in Nishiyama Matsunosuke, Watanabe Ichirō, and Gunji Masakatsu, editors, *Nihon shisō taikei vol. 61: Kinsei geidōron* (Tokyo: Iwanami shoten, 1972). *Nanbōroku* is supposedly a transcription of Sen no Rikyū's sayings and discourses. The text of this book itself was "discovered" in 1686, a hundred years after the tragic death of Sen no Rikyū. Although the book was immediately recognized in Tokugawa tea circles as a masterpiece of tea theory, there has been considerable discussion in the scholarly literature as to the accuracy of the book's attribution to Sen no Rikyū. It is possible that the discovery of the book itself was related to an effort of a student of the tea ceremony at the time, who attempted to elevate Sen no Rikyū as a saint-like figure in order to promote the position of the art itself. However, since I am discussing here an ideological aspect of the tea ceremony, the point is not whether the book was the direct product of Sen no Rikyū. The book is, at any rate, a reliable guide to how Tokugawa people regarded Sen no Rikyū's teaching.

9. Readers trained in Western patterns of poetic analysis should note that *hibiki* does not imply sounds within the words or syllables themselves (e.g., assonance or alliteration) but sounds connected with the setting or situation described in the poem.

10. Morikawa Kyoriku, "Sōden meimoku." Original in Tokyo University Library, *Haikai san hiroku*. This work is also analyzed by Hama Rintarō, "Wazaogi no seishin," pp. 7–8.

11. I am indebted for this translation and commentary to the translations by Esperanza Ramirez-Christensen in "The Essential Parameters of Linked Poetry," *Harvard Journal of Asiatic Studies*, vol. 41, no. 2 (Dec. 1987); by Earl

Miner in *Japanese Linked Poetry: An Account with Translations of Renga and Haikai Sequence* (Princeton, NJ: Princeton University Press, 1979); and the commentary by Toshisada Nakamura, *Bashō no renku o yomu* (Tokyo: Iwanami shoten, 1985).

12. Michael Polanyi, *Knowing and Being*, p. 124.

13. Levine has enumerated several factors that may have initiated this change in communicative cultures: "Administrative needs of centralizing monarchies revived the impetus for legalistic language and led to the compilation of precise codes. Technical developments in warfare and production and the increased use of money in commerce diffused a disposition toward more precise calculation in human transactions. Ascetic Puritanism tended to promote an aseptic use of language, as in the famous "plain style" sermons of the New England divines. The ideal of sincerity came to replace a courtly ideal of grace and charm with a call for plain and direct speaking. Above all, however, it was the impressive advances in mathematics and the physical sciences that quickened an impulse toward symbolic precision. Those advances inspired many seventeenth-century philosophers to extol the benefits to be gained from recasting all language and thought into a 'mathematicalized' mode." See Donald N. Levine, *The Flight from Ambiguity: Essays in Social and Cultural Theory* (Chicago: University of Chicago Press, 1985), p. 2.

14. For their exchanges, see: Kawabata Yasunari in *Yasunari Kawabata, Rudyard Kipling and Sinclair Lewis: Nobel Prize Library*; Oe Kenzaburo, *Japan, the Ambiguous, and Myself: The Nobel Prize Speech and Other Lectures*.

15. For an overview of Kokugaku, see H. D. Harootunian, *Things Seen and Unseen: Discourse and Ideology in Tokugawa Nativism* (Chicago: University of Chicago Press, 1988).

16. Kamo no Mabuchi, "Kuni no kokoro" (ca. 1760), Kamo Momoki, editor, in *Kōhon, Kamo no mabuchi zenshū shisōhen I* (Tokyo: Yoshikawa Kōbunkan, 1942), p. 1095.

17. Kamo no Mabuchi, "Manebi no age tsuroi," in *Kōhon, Kamo no mabuchi zenshū shisōhen*, p. 895.

18. Suzuki Eiichi, "Kamo no Mabuchi no shisō: sono "ku ni no tefuri" ron o chūshin ni," in Bitō Masahide sensei kanreki kinenkai, editors, *Kinseishi ronsō jōkan* (Tokyo: Yoshikawa kōbunkan, 1984), pp. 471–473.

19. *Yamato* is the ancient name for Japan; *gokoro* can be translated as "consciousness" or "sensibility." Motoori Norinaga's prodigious classical scholarship and his careful analytical inquiries that pioneered the philological study of ancient Japanese had the ultimate goal of recovering the true Japanese aesthetic and philosophy and thus reclaiming Japanese identity. However, his philological study of Japanese classics owed not only to the scholarship of Kamo no Mabuchi but also to the methodology of the Confucian scholarship of Ogyū Sorai (1666–1728). Sorai established an influential Confucian school based upon classical Chinese philology. In other words, the analytical aspect of Motoori's scholarship had its roots in the scholarship of Ogyū Sorai, whose life was devoted to the search for the original Chinese mind, or *kara gokoro*. The richness of Japanese culture in fact stemmed from such intersections of

diverse cultural systems. For Motoori, however, even Buddhism stood outside authentic Japanese consciousness since it was an imported religion.

20. Bitō Masahide, "Sonnō jōi shisō no genkei: Motoori Norinaga no baai," *Kikan Nihon shisōshi*, vol. 13 (1980), pp. 100–114; Watanabe Hiroshi, "Michi to Miyabi," *Kokka gakkai zashi*, vol. 87, nos. 9, 10, 11, 12; vol. 88, nos. 3, 4, 5, 6 (1974–1975).

21. Of course, we should note an insight of Kanō Mikiyo regarding the double images of the Meiji emperor, "fatherly" as well as "motherly." "Omigokoro to hahagokoro: yasukuni no haha," in Kanō Mikiyo, editor, *Josei to tennōshi* (Tokyo: Shisō no kagakusha, 1979). This complexity is also discussed in T. Fujitani, *Splendid Monarchy: Power and Pageantry in Modern Japan* (Berkeley: University of California Press, 1996). See also Carol Gluck, *Japan's Modern Myths: Ideology in the Late Meiji Period* (Princeton, NJ: Princeton University Press, 1985).

Chapter 10

1. Fernand Braudel said that "If a society remained more or less stable, fashion was less likely to change. . . . Japan was also conservative. . . . For centuries, it remained faithful to the *kimono*, an indoor garment hardly any different from the present-day *kimono*." See Fernand Braudel, *The Structure of Everyday Life, Vol. 1* (New York: Harper and Row, 1981), p. 312. As the discussion in this chapter indicates, there was nothing static about Tokugawa fashion history.

2. Georg Simmel, "Fashion," *American Journal of Sociology* 62 (1904): 543.

3. Kuki Shūzō, *Iki no kōzō* (Tokyo: Iwanami shoten, 1979, originally published in 1930). See also Asō Isoji, *Iki/Tsū: Nihon bungaku kōza* (Tokyo: Kawade shobō, 1954); Nakano Mitsutoshi, "Sui, tsū, iki," in Sagara Tōru, Bitō Masahide, and Akiyama Ken, editors, *Kōza, Nihon shisō*, vol. 5: B (Tokyo: Tokyo Daigaku shuppan kai, 1984). In English, see Nishiyama Matsunosuke, "Iki: The Aesthetic of Edo," in Nishiyama Matsunosuke, *Edo Culture: Daily Life and Diversions in Urban Japan, 1600–1868*, translated by Gerald Groemer (Honolulu: University of Hawaii Press, 1997).

4. It is true that some well-known Japanese aesthetic categories (e.g., *wabi*, *sabi*, and *yūgen*) emerged during the late medieval period, but these were appreciated primarily among the upper classes. In contrast, *iki* originated among the townspeople and was perceived as a category belonging to urban commoner culture. *Iki* could be expressed by using commercially available goods that were considered fashionable.

5. See, for example, Senmoto Masuo, "Kinsei shoki no ifuku tōsei," *Nihon rekishi* 421 (1983): 54–72; Mizubayashi Takeshi, "Kinsei no hō to kokusei kenkyiū josetsu," *Kokka gakkai zasshi*, vols. 90, 91, 92, 94, 95 (1977–1982); Taniguchi Sumio, *Okayama hanseishi no kenkyū* (Tokyo: Hanawa shobō, 1964).

6. "Oan monogatari," reprinted in Miyamoto Tsuneichi, Haraguchi Torao, Higa Shuncho, editors, *Nihon shomin seikatsu shiryō shūsei*, vol. 8 (Tokyo: Sanichi shobō, 1969), p. 373.

7. Takebe Yoshito, *Kawachi momen no kenkyū* (Yao: Yaoshi kyōdo shiryō kankōkai, 1961); Takebe Yoshito, *Nihon momenshi no kenkyū* (Tokyo: Yoshikawa kōbunkan, 1985); Nagahara Keiji, *Shin momen izen no koto* (Tokyo: Chūō kōronsha, 1990); Louise Cort, "The Changing Fortunes of Three Archaic Japanese Textiles," in Annette B. Weiner and Jane Schneider, editors, *Cloth and Human Experience* (Washington, DC: Smithsonian Institution Press, 1989), pp. 377–414; Louise Cort, "Bast Fiber," in William Jay Rathbun, editor, *Beyond the Tanabata Bridge: Traditional Japanese Textiles* (Seattle: Thames and Hudson, 1993).

8. Takebe Yoshito, *Nihon momenshi no kenkyū*, pp. 123–135.

9. Wakita Osamu, *Kinsei hokenshakai no keizai kōzō* (Tokyo: Ochanomizu shobō, 1963); Takebe Yoshito, *Kawachi momen no kenkyū*.

10. Nagahara Keiji, *Shin momen izen no koto*, p. 46.

11. Hayashi Reiko, "Kinsei shakai no mensaku to mengyō," in Nagahara Keiji et al., editors, *Kōza: Nihon gijutmuno shakai shi* (Tokyo: Nihon hyōron sha, 1983); Hayashi Reiko, "Machi to mura," in Nihon sonrakushi kōza henshū iinkai, editor, *Nihon sonrakushi kōza 7: Seikatsu II, kinsei* (Tokyo: Yūzankaku, 1990); Hayashi Reiko, *Ryūtsū rettō no tanjō* (Tokyo: Kōdansha, 1995); Oka Mitsuo, "Nōson no henbō to zaigō shōnin," in *Iwanami kōza: Nihon rekishi, kinsei*, vol. 4 (Tokyo: Iwanami shoten, 1976); Nagahara Keiji, *Shin momen*; Takebe Yoshito, *Nihon momenshi no kenkyū*; William Hauser, *Economic Institutional Change in Tokugawa Japan: Osaka and the Kinai Cotton Trade* (Cambridge: Cambridge University Press, 1974).

12. Nagahara Keiji, *Shin momen*, pp. 130–158.

13. Yanagida Kunio, "Momen izen no koto," in Yanagida Kunio, *Zenshū*, Chikuma bunko edition (Tokyo: Chikuma shobō, 1990, originally published in 1924).

14. See, for example, codes in *Gotōke reijō*, no. 378 and no. 435. Reprinted in Ishii Ryōsuke, editor, *Kinsei hōsei shiryō*, vol. 3 (Tokyo: Sōbunsha, 1959), pp. 209, 232. Judging from the shogunate's clothing ordinances, the consumption of cotton – and to a lesser extent silk – clothing appears to have been widespread in both urban and rural areas by the early part of the seventeenth century. The shogunate imposed sumptuary regulations on the peasantry that forbade them from wearing silk *kimono* and defined cotton and *asa* as the proper materials for their garments. Examples of these ordinances included the laws of 1628 (fifth year of Kan'ei) and 1642 (nineteenth year of Kan'ei). The mere presence of these ordinances, in turn, suggests more widespread use of cotton among the farmers and the possibility of some townspeople and wealthy village leaders being able to afford silk.

15. Hayashi Reiko and Ōishi Shisaburo, *Ryūtsū rettō no tanjō* (Tokyo: Kōdansha, 1995), pp. 45–49; Hayashi Reiko, "Kinsei shakai no mensaku to mengyō," in Nagahara Keiji et al., editors, *Kōza: Nihon gijutsu no shakai shi*; Takebe Yoshito, *Nihon momenshi*.

16. See Oka Mitsuo, "Nōson no henbō to zaigō shōnin," in *Iwanami kōza: Nihon rekishi, kinsei*, vol. 4 (Tokyo: Iwanami shoten, 1976), p. 57.

17. Senmoto Masuo, "Kinsei shoki," pp. 54–72.

18. To specify the precise use of Japanese historical terminology, town ordinances (*machibure*) were issued by the office of the town magistrates to the residents

of the city of Edo, whereas general ordinances (*sō bure*) were issued by the Chief of Senior Councillors (*rōjū*) and intended for the whole country. The ordinances to Edo commoners (*machibure*) were distributed from the magistrate's office either directly to the chiefs of the town sections (*nanushi*) or through the senior town chiefs. Each *nanushi* wrote down the ordinances and announced them to the residents of his section. *Shōhōjiroku* is the record of town ordinances, while *Ofuregaki Shūsei* refers to the collection of general ordinances. These two sources partly overlap with one another. Aside from these two sources, I also refer to *Gotōke reijō*, *Tokugawa Kinrei kō*, and to some other collections of ordinances. Collections of legal and governmental documents include: *Buke genseiroku*, in Ryōsuke Ishii, editor, *Kinsei hōsei shiryō*, vol. 3 (Tokyo: Sōbunsha, 1959); *Gotōke Reijō*, in Ryōsuke Ishii, editor, *Kinsei hōsei shiryō*, vol. 2 (Tokyo: Sōbunsha, 1959); Maedake Hensanbu, editor, *Kagahan Shiryō* (private publication of the Maeda clan, 1931). For the collections of *sō bure*, see Takayanagi Shinzō and Ryōsuke Ishii, editors, *Ofuregaki shūsei* (Tokyo: Iwanami shoten, Kanpo-era volume 1934; Hōreki-era volume 1935; Tenmei-era volume 1935; Tenpō-era volumes 1–2, 1935). For the collection of *machibure*, see Kinsei Shiryō Kenkyūkai, editors, *Shōhō jiroku* (Tokyo: Gakujutsu Shinkōkai, 1965); Kikuchi Shunsuke, editor, *Tokugawa Kinreikō* (Tokyo: Yoshikawa Kūbunkan, 1931); *Tokugawa Jikki, Kokushi Taikei, vol. 42* (Tokyo: Yoshikawa kōbunkan, 1970).

19. *Shōhō jiroku*, p. 1, no. 4. *Tsumugi* is an inexpensive kind of silk.
20. The prohibition of imported woolen coats has nothing to do with protection of domestic industries. Japanese farmers did not raise wool-bearing sheep; the provision was intended to prevent displays of conspicuous consumption. *Shōhō jiroku*, p. 8, no. 25.
21. Moriya Takeshi, *Genroku bunka – yūgei, akusho, shibai* (Tokyo: Kōbundō, 1987).
22. N. B. Harte, "State Control of Dress and Social Change in Pre-Industrial England," in D. C. Coleman and A. H. John, editors, *Trade, Government and Economy in Pre-Industrial England* (London: Weidenfeld and Nicolson, 1976), p. 139.
23. Daniel Roche, *The Culture of Clothing: Dress and Fashion in the Ancient Regime*, translated by Jean Birrell (Cambridge: Cambridge University Press, 1994), p. 49.
24. Adam Smith, *The Wealth of Nations* (New York: Random House, 1937, originally published in 1776), p. 329.
25. Herman Freudenberger, "Fashion, Sumptuary Laws and Business," *Business History Review* 37 (1963); N. B. Harte, "State Control of Dress and Social Change in Pre-Industrial England"; Kawakita Minoru, *Sharemono tachi no igirisushi* (Tokyo: Heibonsha, 1993).
26. Harada Nobuo, "I shoku jū," in Nihon sonraku shi kōza henshū iinkai, editor, *Nihon sonraku shi kōza, vol. 7, Seikatsu [2] Kinsei* (Tokyo: Yūhikaku, 1990); Senmoto Masuo, "Kinsei shoki," pp. 54–72; Nishimura Eiko, "Edo jidai ni okeru ifuku kisei ni tsuite," *Kenkyū shūroku: Okayama daigaku* (1971): 131–154.

27. *Gotōke reijō*, p. 155, no. 279.

28. Ibid.

29. *Tokugawa Kinrei kō, vol.* 4, pp. 356–357.

30. See Ogata Tsurikichi, *Honpō kyōkaku no kenkyū* (Tokyo: Nishida shoten, 1981), p. 31.

31. The book included records dated several years later; it could therefore have been completed several years after the date of the preface, which is 1614. See Miura Jōshin, *Keichō kenmonshū*, reprinted in *Nihon shomin seikatsu shiryō shūsei, vol. 8* (Tokyo: Sanichi Shobō, 1969), pp. 471–643.

32. Ibid., pp. 561–563.

33. Ibid., pp. 562–563. The story of Ōtori's group is also recorded in a few other sources, as it involved the assassination of an official of the shogunate. Although we have no means of verifying the accuracy of Miura Jōshin's detailed description of these events, the fact that such a dramatic story was recorded by a contemporary writer with such intense interest indicates that the attitudes and conduct of the *kabuki-mono* had a certain appeal to other sectors of Tokugawa society.

34. *Kagahan Shiryō*, vol. 2, pp. 72–73. This is a reprinted collection of documents filed and preserved at the Kaga domain (the house of Lord Maeda). This arrest took place in the fifteenth year of Keichō. Even a contemporary was surprised to see the number of fatal pillars erected for the execution; the record of the Kaga *han* includes one criticism that "the number of executions is too large." The unknown writer knew that such campaigns (against *kabuki-mono*) were also conducted in Edo and Sunpu, but he maintained that the shogunate did not dare to execute such large groups of offenders in those cities.

35. Ibid.

36. *Tōdaiki*, an entry of the fourteenth year of Keichō, the second day of the fourth month. See also Ogasawara Yoshiko, "Kabuki oyobi kabukimono no kin ni okeru chūō to chihō," *Bungaku* 54 (December 1986): 152–161; Moriya Takeshi, *"Kabuki" no jidai* (Tokyo: Kadokawa shoten, 1976), p. 119.

37. *Gotōke reijō*, p. 2; *Buke shohatto* was the foundational edict of the shogunate, addressed to the *daimyo* and all the samurai population.

38. *Tōdaiki*, the entry of the eleventh year of Keichō, 1606. After the investigation, the punishment to ten *kabuki* samurai individuals was carried out in the next year. Reprinted in Nihon Shiseki Kyōkai, editor, *Shiseki Zassan 2* (Tokyo: Kokusho kankōkai, 1911).

39. *Tokugawa Kinrei kō*, vol. 1, p. 147.

40. Ibid., p. 185.

41. I discussed this case and the importance of male–male love in the samurai culture in *The Taming of the Samurai.*

42. *Tōdaiki*, the eighth year of Keichō (1603), vol. 3; reprinted in *Shiseki Zassan 2* (Tokyo: Kokusho kankōkai, 1911), p. 81.

43. Ibid.

44. Miura Jōshin, *Keichō kenmonshū*, pp. 553–554. I am referring here to the translation of this passage in Donald Shively, "Bakufu versus Kabuki,"

Harvard Journal of Asiatic Studies 18 (1955): 326–356. The reader is also referred to his other pioneering works: Donald Shively, "Sumptuary Regulation and Status in Early Tokugawa Japan," *Harvard Journal of Asiatic Studies* 25 (1964–1965): 123–164; Donald Shively, "Tokugawa Plays on Forbidden Topics," in James Brandon, editor, *Chūshingura – Studies in Kabuki and the Puppet Theater* (Honolulu: University of Hawaii Press, 1982).

45. Miura Jōshin, *Keichō kenmonshū*, p. 554. Regarding fashion and gender in Japanese history, see Takeda Sachiko, *Ifuku de yominaosu nihonshi* (Tokyo: Asahi shinbunsha, 1998).

46. Ujiie Mikito, *Bushidō to erosu* (Tokyo: Kōdansha, 1995). For an overview of male–male sexuality in Japanese history in English, see Gregory Pflugfelder, *Cartographies of Desire: Male–male sexuality in Japanese Discourse, 1600–1950* (Berkeley: University of California Press, 1999); Gary P. Leupp, *Male Colors: The Construction of Homosexuality in Tokugawa Japan* (Berkeley: University of California Press, 1995). See also my book *The Taming of the Samurai*.

47. Howard Hibbett, *The Floating World in Japanese Fiction* (New York: Oxford University Press, 1959).

48. Ogasawara Kyōko, *Toshi to gekijō* (Tokyo: Heibonsha, 1992), pp. 39–135.

49. For example, in the Kaga *han*'s record, foot soldiers and *wakatō* were allowed to use various kinds of silk materials, in addition to cotton and fiber textiles, for their costumes. For belts and collars, luxurious materials such as velvet, *shuchin*, *rinzu*, and *shusu* were prohibited. However, the servants of samurai, *komono* and *chūgen*, who were ranked lower than foot soldiers, were permitted only cotton and linen. In this way, it became clear that food soldiers and *wakatō* are the lowest ranking of the samurai but *komono* and *chūgen* were not the samurai. See the ordinance of December 25, the third year of Shōhō (1646), *Kagahan Shiryō*, vol. 3, pp. 226–228.

50. In practice, however, brothels always existed in Edo outside Yoshiwara throughout the Tokugawa period in spite of the shogunate's occasional enforcement of the law. In later years, when Yoshiwara came to be considered too pretentious, areas such as Fukagawa became fashionable centers of courtesan culture.

51. Geinōshi Kenkyūkai, editor, *Nihon geinōshi, vol. 4: chūsei-kinsei* (Tokyo: Hōsei daigaku shuppankai, 1985), pp. 283–288.

52. Moriya Takeshi, *"Kabuki" no jidai*; Cecilia Segawa Seigle, *Yoshiwara: The Glittering World of the Japanese Courtesan* (Honolulu: University of Hawaii Press, 1993).

53. Geinōshi Kenkyūkai, editor, *Nihon geinōshi, vol. 4*, pp. 286–287.

54. Donald Shively, "Bakufu versus Kabuki," pp. 326–356.

55. Saitō, Ryūzō, *Kinsei jiyō fūzoku* (Tokyo: Sansei dō, 1935).

56. The *wakashū* from the *Kabuki* theaters were often popular "kept boys," or glamorous young companions of mature men. During the early modern period, committed relationships between older men and young boys were often considered the purest form of love in the samurai community. Furthermore,

young samurai boys, dressed like women as far as their garb and hairstyles were concerned, often served a lord as personal attendants (pages). The shogunate repeatedly issued laws against "boy-crazy behavior" (*wakashū gurui*) such as the cases in May and June of the fifth year of Shōhō and May and June of the second year of Shōhō. But the shogunate's intention in these ordinances was to regulate disorderly behavior and aggressive sexual assaults on boys, not homosexuality as such.

57. The earliest surviving book that was similar to this pattern book is the two-volume *On'echō* (1661 and 1663), a sample book from the famous *kimono* shop Kariganeya. This shop, which was owned by the family of the master painter and designer Ogata Kōrin, contributed to raising *kimono* design almost to the level of a fine art. The shop's customers included the first shogun, Tokugawa Ieyasu; the second shogun, Hidetada, and his wife; and their daughter, Tōfuku Monin, who married the emperor Gomizunoo. Although the Kariganeya sample book was intended for "upscale" customers, the Hiinagata sample books were published for a general audience, an indication that a popular market for *kimono* was emerging. For examples of Hiinagata (also known as Hiinakata) pattern books, see *Kosode moyō hiinakata shūsei*, vols. 1–4 (Tokyo: Gakushū kenkyusha, 1974); Senshuoku bunka kenkyūkai, editor, *Edojidai hiinakata monyō* (Kyoto: Kyoto shoin, 1964). For the styles of Ogata Kōrin, see Tabata Kihachi, editor, *Kōrin fū hiinakata* (Kyoto: Kyoto shoin, 1964). For an overview, see also Koike Mitsue, "Kinsei nihon no fukushoku monyō," in Tanida Etsuji and Tokui Yoshiko, editors, *Ifukuron: Fukushoku no biishiki* (Tokyo: Nihon hōsō kyōkai, 1986).

58. Nagasaki Iwao, "Designs for a Thousand Ages: Printed Pattern Books and Kosede," in Carolyn Dale and Sharon Sadako Takeda Gluckman, editors, *Fashion: Kosode in Edo Period Japan* (New York: Weatherhill, 1992).

59. For a survey of literary productions referring to Echigoya, see Saitō Ryūzo, *Kinsei jiyō fūzoku* (Tokyo: Sansei dō, 1935).

60. These lists of clothing shops did not include a number of clothiers who sold only to the shogunate. Eight such suppliers existed before the Genroku era. The number of exclusive purveyors to the shogun increased to 29 during the Genroku era; these merchants did not sell *kimono* to ordinary people. In any case, however, the total number of clothing merchants indicates that the demand for clothing was considerable. See Saitō Ryūzo, *Kinsei jiyō fūzoku*, pp. 88–105.

61. Ono Takeyo, *Ryūkō no fūzoku zushi* (Tokyo: Tenbōsha, 1978), pp. 138–140.

62. Namura Jōhaku, "Onna chōhōki," in Nagatomo Chiyoji, editor, *Onna chōhōki, Nan chōhōki, Gendai Kyōyō bunko* (Tokyo: Shakai Shisōsha, 1993), p. 46.

63. This incident occurred in May 1681, according to *Tokugawa Jikki* in *Kokushi Taikei*, vol. 42, p. 413. This famous episode was mentioned in a number of contemporary essays: "Shison Daikoku bashira," in Kokusho Kankōkai, editor, *Tokugawa bungei ruijū*, Vol. 2 (Tokyo: Kokusho kankōkai, 1914), p. 484; Kato Hyoan, "Waga koromo," in *Nihon shomin seikatsu shiryō*

shūsei, vol. 15 (Tokyo: San'ichi shobō, 1971), p. 20. The story would not have been widely retold among the people unless there had been a widespread craze for fashion among the merchant class.

64. Town order, issued in February, the third year of Tenwa (1683), in *Shōhō jiroku*, vol. 1, p. 228, no. 652.

65. Ibid.

66. In addition to the regulation mentioned above, four other ordinances regarding townspeople's clothing are found in *Ōfuregaki Kanpo shūsei*, p. 487. This is ordinance no. 923.

67. Also found in *Ōfuregaki Kanpo shūsei*, p. 487, no. 925.

68. For Hinagata pattern books, see Hioki Kiyochika, *Yuzen hiinagata/Kisho fukuseikai sō sho* (Tokyo: Yoneyamadō, 1926–1927, originally published in 1688); Nakamura Yukihiko and Himo Tatso, editors, *Shinpen kisho fukuseikai sōsho, vol. 35: Shinsen Onhiinagata* (Kyoto: Rimsenshoten, 1991); Kisho fukusei kai, editor, *Ohiinagata jōge* (Tokyo: Beisandō, 1936). See also note 57.

69. Ihara Saikaku, "Saikaku Oritome," in Aso Isoji and Fuji Akio, editors, *Taiyaku Saikaku zenshū*, vol. 14 (Tokyo: Meiji shoin, 1976), p. 76.

70. Saitō Ryūzō, *Kinsei jiyō*, p. 192.

71. Yoshimune frequently used his ordinances to lecture citizens about their consumption patterns, as for example in his ordinance of May 1718: "It is outrageous that men and women's clothing is so ostentatious these days, to the point that people are concerned about their underwear." The shogun threatened lawbreakers with serious penalties: "Those who disobey this law will be arrested whenever they are found." See *Shōho jiroku*, vol. 2, p. 75, no. 1604.

72. Yokoyama Toshio, "Bunmei jin no shikaku," in Yokoyama Toshio, editor, *Shikaku no jūkyu seiki* (Kyoto: Shibunkaku, 1992), pp. 30–31.

73. Kato Hyoan, "Waga koromo," p. 44.

74. *Atsuita* is a stiff, heavy brocade that was produced in Kiryū in the same manner as the Kyoto nishijin. *Atsuita* was very much in fashion in the late Tokugawa period. Nine sun is about 27 centimeters, or 10.5 inches.

75. Yonezō was a famous *Kabuki* actor. See Otsuki Nyoden, "Edo fuzoku utsuri kawari, dai roku dan," *Edo jidai bunka* 4 (1930): 43.

76. Shikitei Sanba, *Ukiyo buro, Nihon koten bungaku zenshū* (Tokyo: Shōgaku kan, 1971), pp. 216–217. On the background of such bathhouses, see Matsudaira Makoto, *Nyūyoku no kaitai shinsho* (Tokyo: Shōgakukan, 1997); Nakamo Eizō, *Sentō no rekishi* (Tokyo: Yūzankaku, 1970); Konno Nobuo, *Edo no furo* (Tokyo: Shimchōsha, 1989). *Kamiyui*, or hairdresser shops, were neighborhood "hangouts" during this period.

77. Namura Jōhaku, "Onna chōhōki," pp. 46–47.

78. For example, Shikitei Sanba's "Ukiyo doko" ("Hair Dresser's Shop in the Floating World") recounts conversations of this type. See Shikitei Sanba, "Ukiyo doko," in Nakano Mitsutoshi, Jinbo Itsuya, and Meda Ai, editors, *Nihon koten bungaku zenshū 47: Sharebon* (Tokyo: Shōgakukan, 1971), p. 315.

79. See Saitō Ryūzō, *Kinsei jiyō*, pp. 229–230.

80. On the other hand, *iki* never assumed the status of "high culture" in the sense of being a legitimate aesthetic for honorable samurai to cultivate in their public lives. It remained the popular aesthetic of urban commoners. Some samurai, however, who were attracted to the creative lifestyle and cultural pursuits of the townspeople also appreciated and enjoyed *iki* in their private lives.

81. Shikitei Sanba, *Ukiyo buro*, pp. 216–217.

82. For an interesting discussion of the impact of indigo on everyday tastes, see Henry Smith, "Blue and White Japan," *Ukiyo-e Society of America* (May–June 1995).

83. Saitō Ryūzō, *Kinsei jiyō*; Takebe Yoshito, *Nihon momenshi*.

84. Yosano's personal letter dated the twenty-third of the second month, the sixth year of An'ei (1778). Cited in Takahashi Hiromi, *Kyoto geien no network* (Tokyo: Perikansha, 1988), p. 8.

85. Ibid.

86. Takebe Yoshito, *Nihon momenshi*, p. 165.

87. Saitō Osamu, *Proto-kōgyoka no jidai* (Tokyo: Nihon hyōronsha, 1985); Saitō Osamu, "The Rural Economy: Commercial Agriculture, By-Employment, and Wage Work," in Marius Jansen and Gilbert Rozman, editors, *Japan in Transition: From Tokugawa to Meiji* (Princeton, NJ: Princeton University Press, 1986); Satō Tsuneo, "Nōgyō gijutsu no tenkan to sonraku seikatsu," in Nihon sonraku shi kōza henshū iinkai, editors, *Nihon sonraku shi kōza*, vol. 7 (Tokyo: Yūzankaku, 1990); T. C. Smith, "Pre-modern Economic Growth: Japan and the West," *Past and Present* 60 (1973): 127–160; T. C. Smith, "Farm Family By-Employment in Pre-Industrial Japan," *Journal of Economic History* 29 (1969): 687–715; Gail Lee Bernstein, "Women in the Silk-Reeling Industry in Nineteenth-Century Japan," in Gail Lee Bernstein and Fukui Haruhiro, editors, *Japan and the World: Essays on Japanese History and Politics in Honour of Ishida Takeshi* (Hampshire, UK: Basingstoke, 1988). On the life of the working population in the city in English, see Gary P. Leupp, *Servants, Shophands, and Laborers in the Cities of Tokugawa Japan* (Princeton, NJ: Princeton University Press, 1992).

88. Ono Takeyo, *Ryūkō no fūzoku*, p. 66.

89. Nagahara Keiji, *Shin momen izen*, pp. 184–214; William B. Hauser, *Economic Institutional Change in Tokugawa Japan: Osaka and the Kinai Cotton Trade* (Cambridge: Cambridge University Press, 1974); Hosaka Satoru and Asami Takashi, "Ikki to uchikowashi," in Aoki Michio et al., editors, *Ikki 2: Ikki no rekishi* (Tokyo: University of Tokyo Press, 1981).

Chapter 11

1. One of the earliest surviving records of a publishing house comes from the shop of Nakamura Chōbei in 1608, five years after Tokogawa Ieyasu assumed the title of shogun. Another publisher has been identified by a colophon dated 1609 that reads *Honya Shinpachi* – literally, "Shinpachi's bookstore." See Nakano Mitsutoshi, *Edo no hanpon* (Tokyo: Iwanami shoten, 1995), pp. 34–35.

2. Konta Yōzō, "Genroku kyōhōki ni okeru shuppan shihon no keisei to sono rekishi teki igi ni tsuite," *Historia* 19 (1957): 48–66. Such Japanese scholars as Konta Yōzō, Nagatomo Chiyoji, Suwa Haruo, and Nakano Mitsutoshi, however, have published important monographs in this field. In English, Peter Kornicki's *The Book in Japan: A Cultural History from the Beginnings to the Nineteenth Century* (Leiden: Brill, 1998) is the most thorough survey of available works in this field. Henry Smith's essay, "The History of the Book in Edo and Paris," in *Edo and Paris*, edited by John M. Merriman, James L. McClain, and Ugawa Kaoru (Ithaca, NY: Cornell University Press, 1994), provides a comparative overview of the available data and studies in these countries.

3. See Nagatomo Chiyoji, "Kinsei gyōshōhonya, kashihonya, dokusha," in his book *Kokubungaku kaishaku to kanshō* (Tokyo: Tokyodō shuppan, 1980), pp. 42–43. Regarding bathhouses, see Imano Nobuo, *Edo no furo* (Tokyo: Shinchōsha, 1989), p. 26, and also Matsudaira Makoto, *Nyūhoku no kaitai shinsho: ukiyo buro no sutorakuchā* (Tokyo: Shōgakukan, 1997). For an overview of bathing culture in pre-modern Japan, see Susan B. Hanley, *Everyday Things in Premodern Japan* (Berkeley: University of California Press, 1997), pp. 97–103.

4. In "Hanashi no Nae," cited by Nagatomo Chiyoji, "Kinsei gyōshōhonya, kashihonya, dokusha," pp. 92–106.

5. Konta Yōzō, *Edo no honyasan* (Tokyo: Nihon hōsō shuppan kai, 1977), p. i.

6. Robert Darnton, *The Business of Enlightenment: A Publishing History of the Encyclopédie, 1775–1800* (Cambridge, MA: Belknap Press of Harvard University Press, 1979).

7. Benedict Anderson, *Imagined Communities* (London: Verso, 1983).

8. Roger Chartier, "Frenchness in the History of the Book: From the History of Publishing to the History of Reading," *American Antiquarian Society Proceedings* 97, no. 2 (1988): 302.

9. Henry Smith, "The History of the Book in Edo and Paris." The essays collected in the special issue of *Late Imperial China* 17, no. 1 (1996) are useful for comparison. They include Roger Chartier's "Gutenberg Revisited from the East"; Lucia Chia, "The Development of the Jianyan Book Trade, Song-yuan"; and Cynthia J. Brokaw, "Commercial Publishing in Late Imperial China: The Zou and Ma Family Business of Sibao, Fujian." See also Inoue Susumu, *Chūgoku shuppn bunkashi* (Nagoya: Nagoya daigaku shuppankai, 2002).

10. Elizabeth L. Eisenstein, *Printing Press as an Agent of Change: Communications and Cultural Transformations in Early Modern Europe* (Cambridge: Cambridge University Press, 1979), pp. 26, 33, 39; Elizabeth L. Eisenstein, *The Printing Revolution in Early Modern Europe* (Cambridge: Cambridge University Press, 1983).

11. Works emphasizing the technology of publishing include the studies of Elizabeth L. Eisenstein cited in note 10. See also Walter J. Ong, *Interfaces of the Word* (Ithaca, NY: Cornell University Press, 1977); Alvin Gouldner, *The*

Dialectic of Ideology and Technology (New York: Oxford University Press, 1987).

12. Since the 1970s, European specialists in the history of book publication and distribution have gone beyond recounting the introduction of technological inventions and information multiplication. Various researchers have enriched the field by focusing on the cultural *practices* related to printing and books. In France, Roger Chartier and his colleagues, influenced by the history of mentalities, have accumulated a rich collection of material on an array of topics related to the history of books from the practice of reading silently versus aloud to books on bodily discipline and state formation. For an overview, see Guglielmo Cavallo and Roger Chartier, editors, *A History of Reading in the West* (Amherst: University of Massachusetts Press, 1999). In North America, Robert Darnton has studied the intriguing world of the "literary underground" in pre-Revolutionary France, in which French printers worked both inside and outside the control and patronage of the absolutist state. Darnton's work reminds us that the history of books should be integrated within the larger organizational patterns of society, including the organization of industry, government control and patronage, and intellectual groups or institutions. See Robert Darnton, *The Literary Underground of the Old Regime* (Cambridge, MA: Harvard University Press, 1982), and Robert Darnton, *The Business of Enlightenment*. Natalie Davis argues in her pioneering essay, "Printing and the People," that the availability of printing also changed the agency of the people. She maintains that printing allowed the French Protestants in the sixteenth century to set up communication networks that opened new religious options for the people. Printing, she noted, served to "challenge traditional hierarchical values." See Natalie Zemon Davis, "Printing and the People," in her book *Society and Culture in Early Modern France* (Stanford, CA: Stanford University Press, 1965), p. 225. For a good overview of the American case, see David D. Hall, *Culture of Print* (Amherst: University of Massachusetts Press, 1996).

   Most recently, Adrian Johns's massive study of the role of books in early modern English society has challenged the position of Elizabeth Eisenstein, who stressed the significance of a technological revolution that brought standardization, uniformity, and fixity to printed media. In contrast, Johns maintains that printing was a diversified and unstable enterprise. "The very identity of print itself has had to be made" through historical contingencies in which various kinds of early modern "knowledge" were simultaneously formulated. See Adrian Johns, *The Nature of the Book: Print and Knowledge in the Making* (Chicago: University of Chicago Press, 1998), p. 2. The reader is also referred to a critique of the technology model by Michael Warner, *The Letters of the Republic* (Cambridge, MA: Harvard University Press, 1990).

13. Suwa Haruo, *Shuppan kotohajime-Edo no honya* (Tokyo: Mainichi shinbun sha, 1978), pp. 9–16.

14. Kawase Kazuma, *Gozan-ban no kenkyū: Bibliographical Study of the Gozan Editions* (Tokyo: Nihon Kosekisho kyōkai, 1970); Martin Collcutt, *Five*

Mountains: The Rinzai Zen Monastic Institution in Medieval Japan (Cambridge, MA: Council on East Asian Studies, Harvard University, 1981).

15. The Western method of movable type was not widely used outside the circles of Christian missionaries, who were eventually expelled from Japan.

16. Suzuki Toshio, *Edo no honya* (Tokyo: Chūō kōronsha, 1980), p. 26. He emphasizes 1626 as the date by which movable-type publications had been replaced by woodblock publications.

17. For example, Konta Yōzō, Suwa Haruo, and Nagatomo Chiyoji all support this view. Some researchers, however, object to the accepted view of the limitations of movable wooden type. In particular, see the works of Nakano Mitsutoshi, especially *Edo no hanpon*.

18. It is possible that the publishers considered movable type's limit of one hundred copies – assuming that modern estimates of the limit are accurate – to be inconvenient. On the other hand, few publishers could expect to sell more than a hundred copies of most titles. If a book sold a thousand copies, it was sufficiently unusual that the publisher would celebrate the event with a big "thousand copies party."

19. In the Tokugawa system, the woodblocks were inscribed by carvers who were in most cases independent craftsmen. In this system, the publisher (*han moto*) usually placed an order with a wood-carving shop, and the woodblocks that were produced then became the possession of the publisher.

20. Nakamura Yukihiko has traced the path of woodblocks once owned by a famous publisher, Hachimonji ya, through a series of trades with other publishers. See Nakamura Yukihiko, "Hachimonjiya moku hangi yukue," in *Nakamura Yukihiko Chojutsu shū* (Tokyo: Chūō kōronsha, 1983). Okamoto Suguru has studied the correspondence between a famous scholar, Motoori Norinaga, and his publisher, and he has arrived at the same conclusion. See Okamoto Suguru, "Kinsei shuppan no ichi sokumen: Motoori-ke kankei bunsho o chūshin ni,"*Kinsei bungei* 31 (1979): 49–51.

21. In the Tokugawa publishing world, the notion of paying fees for manuscripts to the authors of commercial publications was a very late innovation. Takizawa Bakin (1767–1848), a writer of popular best-sellers, claimed that he and his contemporary Santō Kyoden were the first to receive fees from publishers. It was around Bakin's time that the mass market for popular books reached full maturity; some best-selling novels sold more than 10,000 copies. There is some evidence that Ihara Saikaku also received payment for his manuscripts. See Suwa Haruo, *Shuppan kotohajime-Edo no honya*, pp. 99–103.

22. Tokugawa authors had only limited rights over their publications.

23. Buddhist temples continued to be a reliable source of business for commercial publications since the priests regularly consumed a good number of books themselves and needed a steady supply of standardized texts of Buddhist classics for distribution to their followers.

24. Graphs in figures were based on the data compiled by Morita Seigo, "Edoki shoten no hassei keikō," *Bungaku* (September 1974). See also Sakamoto Muneko. Also, see *Kyohoigo hanmoto betsu shoseki mokuroku* (Osaka:

Seibundō shoten, 1982); and Inoue Takaaki, "Kinsei shorin hanmoto no sōgyoki bunruihyō," in his *Kinsei shorin hanmoto sōran Nihon shoshigaku taikei vol. 14* (Tokyo: Seimodō shoten, 1981). There were publishing firms that published several books and then disappeared from the record. The reader is advised to note that the number of publishers in these graphs should not be taken as absolute. I am presenting these two graphs in order to illustrate the general trend of competition among Tokugawa publishers from the high rate of new entries. I could not integrate the newer research on the number of publishers in the provinces, which used different sets of data for counting the number of shops. According to these newer studies, the number of provincial publishers rose significantly toward the end of the Tokugawa period to a greater extent than this graph can show. In fact, the decline in the number of Edo publishers was probably a consequence of so-called proto-industrialization, in which the provincial towns increased their share of economic production. For an overview of Japanese provincial publishers, see Oowa Hiroyuki, "Chihō shoshi no kiso teki kōsatsu," in Asakura Haruhiko and Oowa Hiroyuki, editors, *Kinsei Chihō shuppan no kenkyū* (Tokyo: Tokyōdō shuppan, 1993); P. F. Kornicki, "Chihō shuppan nitsuite no shiron," in Yoshida Mitsukuni, editor, *19 seiki nihon no jyōhō to shakai hendō* (Kyoto: Kyoto daigaku Jinbun kagaku kenkyūjyo, 1985). For an examination of a Nagoya publishing house in English, see Matthi Forrer, *Eirakuya Tōshirō: Publisher at Nagoya* (Amsterdam: Gieben, 1985).

25. Tokugawa woodblock publishing was quite efficient, offering a fast turnaround. One record indicates that a lengthy scholarly publication by Motoori Norinaga (a famous scholar of Japanese classics) was published two months after the author gave the manuscript to a publisher. See Suguru Okamoto, "Kinsei shuppan no ichi sokumen: Motoori-ke kankei bunsho o chūshin ni," *Kinsei bungei* 31 (1979): 43–51.

26. There is a great deal of secondary literature on Japanese woodblock illustration and prints. For an introduction in English, see David Chibett, *The History of Japanese Painting and Book Illustration* (Tokyo: Kōdansha International, 1977).

27. Nagatomo Chiyoji, *Kinsei kashihonya no kenkyū* (Tokyo: Tokyōdō shuppan, 1982), pp. 11–12.

28. Other cities, first Osaka and then Edo, published similar lists, though much later. Unfortunately, these lists of books in print do not specify the number of copies of each title. We must also note that these catalogs were not exhaustive lists of all books available at the time. Furthermore, some catalog editions were supplementary to older ones, whereas others attempted to list as many titles as possible.

29. The book lists were often classified by subject. The classification of the original lists, however, is somewhat arbitrary and often misrepresented the actual content of the book. It is not difficult to arrive at different numbers of titles in each class if the class is slightly redefined. Regarding the quantitative study of *shoseki mokuroku* (book lists in print), Konta Yōzō's detailed table has been available since 1958. I used the sources for a recount focusing on the

emergence of books of civilized knowledge, applying a classification different from Konta's.

30. The limitations of the primary source material have already been noted: the catalogs were neither exhaustive nor adequately subcategorized. On occasion, books were classified inaccurately, and some famous contemporary publications never made it into the catalogs. But, in spite of these limitations, the source material is a useful general index to the major trends in Tokugawa publishing.

31. *Genroku Taiheiki*, reprinted in Nakajima Takashi, editor, *Miyako no Nishikishū* (Tokyo: Kokusho kankōkai, 1989).

32. Although the rise in publication of Neo-Confucian books is less spectacular compared with the remarkable increase in nonacademic titles, the emergence of commercial woodblock publishing in the seventeenth century coincided with a growing interest in Neo-Confucianism among the Japanese literati. Unoda Shōya remarked that "The publishing revolution, the shift from movable font printing to woodblock publishing, not only made the *Four Books* physically available to the broad reading public, but the structure of discourse itself was popularized." See Unoda Shōya, "Hankō jusho no fukyū to kinsei jugaku," *Edo no shisō, vol. 5: dokusho no shakaishi* (Tokyo: Perikan sha, 1996), p.14.

33. The term can be spelled with two different sets of Chinese ideograms.

34. Based on Nakamura Kiyozō's calculations. The reader is referred to Nakamura Kiyozō, *Kinsei shuppanhō no kenkyū* (Tokyo: Nihon gakujutsu shinkō kai, 1972), p. 37. The number of titles listed in 1754 and 1772 represents a decline from the earlier period. The smaller number of titles should not, however, be misconstrued as evidence of the decline of commercial publishing as an industry. Nakano Mitsutoshi has observed that the major Tokugawa publishers began to publish their own catalogs of titles in the eighteenth century. The general book catalog ceased publication in 1801 because "the number of published titles became so large that it was impossible for the general catalogue to cover them. After around the era of Hōreki (1751–1763), the individual publishers' catalogues flourished and gradually replaced the general catalogue." Nakano Mitsutoshi, *Edo no hanpon*, p. 194. In spite of the limitations of the mid-eighteenth-century general book catalogs, they are still useful for rough estimates of the ratios of various book categories.

35. R. P. Dore, *Education in Tokugawa Japan* (London: Routledge & Kegan Paul, 1965); R. Rubinger, "Problems in Research on Literacy in 19th-Century Japan," in Motoyama Yukihiko Kyoju Taikan Kinen Ronbun Henshū iinkai, editor, *Nihon Kyoikushi ronso* (Kyoto: Shibun kaku, 1988); Aoki Michio, "Bakumatsuki minshū no kyōiku to shikiji nōryoku," in Aoki Michio and Kawachi Hachirō, editors, *Kōza kinseishi: Kaikoku* (Tokyo: Yūhikaku, 1985), pp. 219–269.

36. The study of readership in Tokugawa Japan is a field awaiting further investigation in Japanese historiography. The following description of the Mori family's reading record is based upon the study of Mizumoto Kunihiko, "Kinsei no nōmin seikatsu – shōya no kōyūkankei kara," in Nihon sonrakushi

kōza henshū iinkai, editors, *Nihon sonrakushi kōza, vol. 7: Seikatsu II Kinsei* (Tokyo: Yuzankaku, 1990), pp. 3–26, which focuses on social networks of the Mori family; Yokota Fuyuhiko, "Ekken bon no dokusha," in Yokoyama Toshio, editor, *Kaibara Ekken-Tenchi waraku no bunmeigaku* (Tokyo: Heibon sha, 1995); and Yokota Fuyuhiko, "Kinsei minshū shakai ni okeru chiteki dokusho no seiritsu," in Edo no Shisō henshū iinkai, editors, *Edo no shisō, vol. 5, Dokushō no shakaishi* (Tokyo: Perikan sha, 1996). The latter two studies focus on the reading life of the Mori.

37. Noma Kōshin, "Ukiyo zōshi no dokushasō," *Bungaku* 26, no. 5 (1958): 63–73.
38. Noma Kōshin was the first scholar to notice the importance of the use of diaries for the study of the history of Japanese books. See Noma Kōshin, "Ukiyo zōshi no dokushasō," *Bungaku* 26, no. 5 (1958): 63–73.
39. Yokota Fuyuhiko, "Kinsei minshū," p. 56. See also his "Ekken bon no dokusha."
40. Yokota Fuyuhiko, "Ekken bon no dokusha."
41. "Mukashi gome mangoku tsū" (1725), cited by Nagatomo Chiyoji, "Kinsei gyōshōbonya, kashihanya, Dokusha: Media, Dokushosō, ba," in *Kokubungaku, kaishaku to kanshō* 45, no. 10 (1980): 104.
42. Peddlers played an important part in the history of European books. See Laurence Fontaine, "The Eighteenth Century: The Networks of Booksellers and Book Pedlars in Southern Europe," in his *History of Pedlars in Europe*, translated by Vicki Whittaker (Cambridge: Polity Press, 1996).
43. The subject matter, however, influenced the manner of advertisement. In particular, books on religion or the humanities were treated with greater respect than materials for entertainment or light reading.
44. Nagatomo Chiyoji, *Kinsei kashihonya*, p. 33.
45. For example, Nagatomo has reported that the rental fees of the Nakajin lending library in the hot spring resort of Kinosaki were about ten times higher than those of the Owariya library in Owari. See Nagatomo Chiyoji, *Kinsei kashihonya*, p. 116. On book rental shops, see Peter Kornicki, "Kashihon bunka hikaku kō," *Jinbun gakuhō* 57 (1984): 37–57, which provides a comparative overview of rental shops in various countries. See also Peter Kornicki, "The Publisher's Go-Between: *Kashihonya* in the Meiji period," *Modern Asian Studies* 14, no. 2 (1980): 330–344.
46. Nagatomo Chiyoji, *Kinsei kashihonya*, pp. 42–43.
47. In Britain, the number of commercial lending libraries had increased by 1801 to "no fewer than one thousand," according to *Monthly Magazine*. In the German-speaking regions of Europe, there was at least one lending library in operation by the 1780s and 1790s. In France, the *loueurs de livres* multiplied rapidly during the two decades preceding the French Revolution. The lending libraries symbolized the popularization of readership; middle-class readers considered them ideal sources of reading materials. They did resemble the *kashihon ya* in that the bulk of their holdings was such lighter matter as chivalric romances, ghost tales, and sentimental love stories. Unlike their Japanese counterparts, however, who were prohibited from publishing

comments on current events, the European lending libraries often circulated a variety of newspapers. The number of book rental shops in Tokugawa Japan was probably roughly comparable during the same time period. See Reinhard Wittmann, "Was There a Reading Revolution?," in Guglielmo Cavallo and Roger Chartier, editors, *A History of Reading in the West*, p. 307.

48. *Yanagidaru Meiku sen*, edited by Hideo Yamazawa (Tokyo: Iwanami shoten, 1995), p. 190.

49. Santō Kyōden, *Sōchōki*, cited in Nagatomo Chiyoji, *Kinsei kashihonya*, p. 66.

50. See Ono Takeo, *Edo bukka jiten* (Tokyo: Tenbōsha, 1992); Mizuno Minoru, "Kusazōshi to sono dokusha," in Zenkoku daigaku kokugo kokubunkai, editors, *Kōza Nihon bungaku, Vol. 8, kinsei II* (Tokyo: Sanseidō, 1969), p. 101. There are many studies on *gesaku* in Japanese. See, for example, Nakano Mitsutoshi, *Gesaku kenkyū* (Tokyo: Chūōkōronsha, 1981); Inoue Takaaki, *Edo gesaku no kenkyū, kibyōshi o shutoshite* (Tokyo: Shintensha, 1986).

51. The reader is referred to Robert Darnton's *Literary Underground of the Old Regime* for a description of the French experience, in which publishers located beyond the country's border played an important role.

52. The earliest known regulatory document was issued in Kyoto in 1657. See Konta Yōzō, *Edo no kinsho* (Tokyo: Yoshikawa kōbunkan, 1981), p. 55; Konta Yōzō, *Edo no honyasan* (Tokyo: Nihon hōsō shuppan kai, 1977), p. 65; Nakamura Kiyozō, *Kinsei shuppanhō no kenkyū* (Tokyo: Nihon gakujyutsu shinkōkai, 1972). For an interesting case study of censorship in English, see Peter F. Kornicki, "Nishiki no Ura: An Instance of Censorship and the Structure of a *Sharebon*," *Monumenta Nipponica* 32, no. 2 (1977): 153–188.

53. Reprinted in *Ofuregaki Kanpo shūsei*, p. 990, no. 2012. At this stage, however, these ordinances were primarily directed at woodblock carving shops.

54. For a survey of Oshichi's appearance in Tokugawa literature, see Takeno Shizuo, "Yaoya Oshichi denshō," *Geinō bunkashi* 7 (1986).

55. Reprinted in *Ofuregaki Kanpo shūsei*, pp. 990–991, no. 2014. On the legal documents, see note 18 in Chapter 10.

56. Ono Hideo, *Kawaraban monogatari* (Tokyo: Yūzankaku, 1960).

57. A summary translation of the code reprinted in *Ofuregaki Kanpo shūsei* (Tokyo: Iwanami shoten, 1934), pp. 993–994, no. 2020. For the nature of various legal and governmental documents of this period, see note 18 in Chapter 10. The shogunate's regulations were initially addressed only to guilds that published *mono no hon*, or "highbrow" books. In the Tokugawa scheme of classification, books reflecting the standards of elite culture were called *mono no hon*, whereas popular works – especially illustrated books – were called *sōshi*. Books of *jōruri* songs were also not considered representative of high culture, although even the samurai were often fond of them, as we have seen. These two types of books, *mono no hon* and *sōshi*, were produced by two different groups of publishers, who were usually organized into separate trade associations. In the early Tokugawa period, the shogunate did not take the *sōshi* seriously because of their mostly lowbrow content. Some of them

were simply dismissed as entertainment fit only for women and children. As a newly literate readership began to take shape, however, it was the *sōshi* that would prove to be a vital force in creating spheres of communication. Edo, a new contender in the publishing industry, was particularly quick to adapt to the popular demand for *sōshi*.

58. Yoshiwara Kenichirō, "Kansei kaikaku to Edo hangiya nakama," in *Haga Kōshirō sensei Kokikinen Nihon bunkashi kenkyū* (Tokyo: Kasama shoin, 1981), pp. 245–261.

59. Suwa Haruo, *Shuppan kotohajime-Edo no honya*, p. 171.

60. See Nakano Mitsutoshi, *Edo no hanpon*, pp. 41–42. There is an interesting side story about the use of movable wooden fonts for printing political writings. Movable wooden type – which produced print of lower quality – was sometimes used in much the same way as people now use rapid-turnaround copy shops. Books printed from movable type were not considered "real" printed books; therefore, they were usually not regulated by the authorities. Consequently, politically sensitive works were sometimes "printed" in small quantities (for example, in a press run of only ten copies) with movable type in order to avoid censorship by the publishers' guilds. See Nakano Mitsutoshi, *Edo no hanpon*, pp. 36–43.

61. Robert Darnton, *The Literary Underground of the Old Regime*, p. 21.

62. For a comparison of the position of Confucianism in Tokugawa Japan particularly with its roles in China and Korea, see the section, "Confucian and Post-Confucian Samurai" in my book *The Taming of the Samurai*.

63. Kai-wing Chow, "Writing for Success: Printing, Examinations, and Intellectual Change in Late Ming China," *Late Imperial China* 17: 1 (1996): 124.

64. Noma Kōshin has described the tight connection between oral storytelling and the popularity of *ukiyo-zōshi*, an early form of Tokugawa fiction. See Noma Kōshin, "Ukiyo zōshi no dokushasō," *Bungaku* 26, no. 5 (1958): 613–614.

65. Maeda Ai, *Kindai Dokusha no seiritsu: Chosaku shū*, vol. 2 (Tokyo: Chikuma shobō, 1989), pp. 336–337.

66. Maeda Ai, "Kindai bungaku to katsuji teki sekai," in *Kindai Dokusha no seiritsu: Chosaku shū*, Vol. 2, p. 334.

67. Yokota Fuyuhiko, "Kinsei minshū shakai ni okeru chiteki dokusho no seiritsu," p. 5.

68. Guglielmo Cavallo and Roger Chartier, editors, *A History of Reading in the West*, Introduction, p. 26.

69. Geinōshi kenkyūkai, editors, *Nihon Geinōshi* 6, pp. 36–40.

70. Moriya Takeshi, "Toshi to Geinō," in his *Kinsei geinōshi* (Tokyo: Kōbundō, 1992); Moriya Takeshi, *Kinsei Geinō kōgyōshi* (Tokyo: Kōbundō, 1985).

71. Kōsaka Jirō, *Genroku otatami bugyō no nikki* (Tokyo: Chūō koronsha, 1984), p. 131.

72. *Dangi* originated in medieval Buddhist performative preaching, but the homilies were secularized during this period, taking in moral topics outside the scope of Buddhism. There existed at that time a literary review called *Gesaku hyōban sengoku sōshi*, which focused its discussion on books derived from

dangi storytelling. See Honda Yasuo, "Kokkei bon to wagei," in Zenkoku daigaku kokugo kokugun gakkai, editor, *Kōza Nihon bungaku, vol. 8, Kinsei hen 2* (Tokyo: Sansei dō, 1969), pp. 114–122. Hiraga Gennai (1728–1779), a Renaissance man who pioneered several new genres of late Tokugawa literature and arts as well as participating in the activities of cultural circles, adapted the style and plot of *dangi* storytelling in his humorous novels. Another important subject that I cannot discuss here is *musume gidayū*, popular female narrative singing. See Kimi Coaldrake, *Women's Gidayū and the Japanese Theater Tradition* (London: Routledge, 1997).

73. Honda Yasuo, "Kokkei bon to wagei"; Inoue Mitsusada et al., *Nihon Rekishi Taikei, 3 Kinsei* (Tokyo: Yamakawa Shupponsha, 1984), pp. 1034–1035.

74. Konta Yōzō, *Edo no kinsho*, pp. 21–54; Okamoto Katsu, editor, *Baba Bunkōshū: Sōsho, Edo bunko* (Tokyo: Kokusho kankōkai, 1987).

75. Minami Kazuo, *Edo no fūshiga* (Tokyo: Kōbunkan, 1997), pp. 73–76.

76. On the study of *namazu-e*, see C. Ouwehand, *Namazu-e and Their Themes* (Leiden: Brill, 1964).

77. Konta Yōzō, "Bakumatsu masu media jijō," in Miyata Noboru and Takada Mamoru, editors, *Namazu-e* (Tokyo: Ribun shuppan, 1995). For example, according to Konta, a popular painter named Utagawa Kuniyoshi published a colorful print in 1850 entitled "Good Doctors and Dirty Patients." There was nothing explicitly subversive about the picture except the clever descriptions of several cartoon figures as patients who needed medical attention. A rumor began to circulate shortly thereafter that the comical figures of the "dirty patients" represented high officials of the shogunate. The physical characteristics of the "patients" started a guessing game about their true identities. Three days after publication, the artist's woodblock was confiscated.

Chapter 12

1. See Chapter 6 on *mibun* and *kakushiki*.

2. In Chapter 1, therefore, I consider that civility has a social function of reducing "emotional transaction cost."

3. His diary is now reprinted in Kokuritsu Shiryōkan, editor, *Yoda Nagayasu Ichidaiki* (Tokyo: University of Tokyo Press, 1985). The actual citation appears on p. 50.

4. Yokoyama Toshio, "Some notes on the history of Japanese traditional household encyclopedias," *Japan Forum (Oxford)* 1, no. 2 (1989): 248–249.

5. The term can be spelled using two different sets of Chinese ideograms.

6. Kaga Archive, Tokyo City Library.

7. The preface of *Nan Chōhōki* (The Gentleman's Treasury). Reprinted in *Onna Chōhōki, Nan Chōhōki: Gendai kyōyō bunko* (Tokyo: Shakai shisōsha, 1993), p. 198. For the list of *chōhōki*, see Nagatomo Chiyoji, "Chōhōki Nenpyōkō," *Bungaku bu ronshu* 87 (2003): 49–68.

8. *Shosatsu Chōhōki*. Photoreprint edition, *Kinsei bungaku shiryō ruijū* (Tokyo: Benseisha, 1976).

9. Other handbooks include such model letters as "a letter to acknowledge and appreciate receiving a letter," "a letter asking to borrow something," and "a letter to a person who came to visit in your absence." See *Chōhōki taizen* (the fourth year of Genroku, 1691), Kokuritsu kokkai toshokan Archive. As in many other cases, however, the model letters in this handbook were not original. They were derived from an earlier book, *Shogaku bunshō*, which had been published several years previously. In this way, the Tokugawa manuals came to be characterized by multiple copies of sources of conventional knowledge.

10. *Shorei Daigaku*. The original is in the Waseda University Library Archive, date of publication unknown.

11. The comprehensive tradition of the teachings of the original Ogasawara School is available in reprinted form in *Dai Shorei-shū, – Ogasawara ryū densho*, vols. 1–2, Shimada Isao and Higuchi Motomi, editors (Tokyo: Heibon sha, 1993). Also see Ise Sadatake's famous *Teijō zakii* (Tokyo: Heibonsha, 1985, originally published in 1843). Futaki Kenichi's detailed historical survey of the ritual manners of the medieval shoguns' court, *Chuūsei no buke girei no kenkyū* (Tokyo: Yoshikawa Kōbunkan, 1985), supplies a detailed overview of this subject.

12. Waseda University Library Archive.

13. Waseda University Library Archive.

14. Elsewhere in Western medieval law, we read that the slave who eats his master's bread cannot bear witness with his master against someone for violation of the peace. In contrast, the ritual of the Christian Eucharist symbolizes the equality of the congregation under the headship of Christ, from whom physical as well as spiritual nourishment is accepted in the actions of eating bread and drinking wine consecrated through the recital of Christ's own words.

15. Waseda University Library Archive.

16. *Shogaku bunshō narabini Yorozu shitsukekata mokuroku*, Waseda University Library Archive.

17. Norbert Elias, *The Civilizing Process*, translated by Edmund Jephcott (Oxford: Blackwell, 1982), pp. 48–56. For a recent critique, see Anna Bryson, "The Rhetoric of Status: Gesture, Demeanor and the Image of the Gentleman in Sixteenth- and Seventeenth-Century England," in Lucy Gent and Nigel Llewellyn, editors, *Renaissance Bodies: The Human Figure in English Culture, c. 1540–1660* (London: Reaktion Books, 1990). See also Harry Berger, Jr., *The Absence of Grace* (Stanford, CA: Stanford University Press, 2000).

18. *Dai Shorei-shū, – Ogasawara ryū densho*, vol. 1, p. 136.

19. Of course, there is no such thing as universal "dirt," as Mary Douglas noted in her *Purity and Danger* (London: Routledge, 1966), p. 2.

20. Kaibara Ekken, "Sanrai guketsu." See also Shimada Isao and Higuchi Motomi, editors, *Daishorei shū – Ogasawara ryū reihō densho*, and Ise Sadatake, *Teijō zakii*, which featured similar instructions. See also Inoue Tadao and Ishige Naomichi, editors, *Shokuji sahō no shisō* (Tokyo: Domesu shuppan, 1990).

21. Ise Sadatake, *Teijō zakii*, pp. 157–160.

22. Japanese books on manners occasionally listed "no-no" sequences. *Nan chōhōki*, for example, made a particular effort to translate the prescriptive Ogasawara school's text into negatives in order to make it easier for young boys to remember.

23. Steven Ozment, *When Fathers Ruled* (Cambridge, MA: Harvard University Press, 1983), p. 141.

24. "The Book of Nurture and School of Good Manners," in Frederick J. Furnivall, editor, *The Babees Book* (New York: Greenwood Press, 1969), pp. 76–79, originally published in the fifteenth century. The quotations have been translated into modern English.

25. Otto Brunfels, *Von der Zucht*, B5a–B6b. Cited by Steven Ozment, *When Fathers Ruled*, p. 140.

26. Beyond "no-no's," to be sure, physical grace had a prominent position in such Renaissance courtesy literature as Baldassar Castiglione's *Il libro del Cortegiano*. But "grace" was usually described as "an 'air,'" which shall make [the courtier] at first sight pleasing and lovable."

27. See Chapter 9 regarding the Buddhist view of the body.

28. Niimura Izuru, "Kotoba no shitsuke to kotobano tashianami," in *Niimura Izuru zenshu, vol. 2: Kokugono Kijun* (Tokyo: Chikuma shobo, 1972). Kojien provides a similar account of the derivation of *shitsuke*. See also Ishii Hisao, "Shitsuke," in Sato Kiyoji, editor, *Kōza nihongono goi* (Tokyo: Meiji Shoin, 1983).

29. See my book *The Taming of the Samurai*, pp. 299–325.

30. The idea embedded in the etymology of *shitsuke* was compatible with the Japanese medieval aesthetic that emphasizes "oneness of body and mind," as discussed in Chapter 9.

31. Waseda University Library Archive.

32. See Chapter 1 regarding "emotional transaction cost."

33. Nunokawa Seiji, *Kinsei chōnin shisō no kenkyū* (Tokyo: Yoshikawa kōbunkan, 1983); Nunokawa Seiji, *Kinsei nihon no minshū rinri shisō* (Tokyo: Yoshikawa kōbunkan, 1973).

34. Hayashi Reiko, *Edo dana hanka chō* (Tokyo: Yoshikawa kōbunkan, 1982), pp. 71–78.

35. Miyamoto Mataji, *Kinsei shōnin ishiki no kenkyū* (Tokyo: Kōdansha, 1977, originally published in 1941), p. 25, 70–91, 237–244.

36. Penelope Brown and Stephen Levinson, *Politeness: Some Universals in Language Usage* (Cambridge: Cambridge University Press, 1987).

Chapter 13

1. On the political development of regional *daimyo* polities in English, see Marc Ravina, *Land and Lordships in Early Modern Japan* (Stanford, CA: Stanford University Press, 1999); Luke S. Roverts, *Mercantilism in a Japanese Domain: The Merchant Origins of Economic Nationalism in 18th Century Tosa* (Cambridge: Cambridge University Press, 1999).

2. See Chapter 6 for a detailed discussion of this case.

3. Scc Chapter 7 for a longer discussion of Watanabe Kazan.

4. See Chapter 2.

5. For example, Sugi Hirtoshi and Tada Jinichi's studies of the *haikai* poetry networks contain examples of the complex overlapping of various networks. See Sugi Hitoshi, "Zaison bunka no kōryūken to kaisō kozō," *Minshūshi kenkyū* 45 (1993): 43–62; Tada Jinichi, "Tama chiiki no haikai kōryū ni miru zaison bunka no hirogari," *Chihōshi kenkyū* 40, no. 4 (1990). See my discussions in Chapters 8 and 9.

6. For example, see Ihara Saikaku, *Nihon eidaigura* (1688).

7. Natsume Sōseki, "Civilization of Modern-Day Japan," in *Kokoro and Selected Essays*, translated by Edwin McClellan and Jay Rubin (London: Madison Books, 1992), p. 272.

8. Ōishi Shinzaburō, *Edo jidai* (Tokyo: Chūō kōronsha, 1977), p. 66.

9. Takagi Hiroshi, *Kindai Tennōsei no bunkashi teki kenkyū* (Tokyo: Hazekura shobō, 2000).

10. Kanō Mikiyo, "Omigokoro to hahagokoro: yasukuni no haha," in Kanō Mikiyo, editor, *Josei to tennōshi* (Tokyo: Shisō no kagakusha, 1979); T. Fujitani, *Splendid Monarchy: Power and Pageantry in Modern Japan* (Berkeley: University of California Press, 1998), pp. 172–184; Carol Gluck, *Japan's Modern Myth: Ideology in the Late Meiji Period* (Princeton, NJ: Princeton University Press, 1985).

11. Emiko Ohnuki-Tierney, *Kamikaze, Cherry Blossoms, and Nationalisms: The Militarization of Aesthetics in Japanese History* (Chicago: University of Chicago Press, 2002).

12. Yamaguchi Masao, *Haisha no seishinshi* (Tokyo: Iwanami shoten, 1995).

Illustration Credits

0.1. Japan, the Beautiful, Daimler Chrysler, Japan, Inc., reproduced with permission; 3.1. *Hanami takagari byōbuzu* by Unkoku Tōgan, MOA Museum, reproduced with permission; 4.1. *Toyotomi saireizu* by Iwasa Mtabei, Tokugawa Museum, reproduced with permission; 6.1. From *Ehon kotosugai* by Jichōsai, New York Public Library, Spencer Collection, Astor, Lenox, and Tilden Foundations, reproduced with permission; 6.2. From *Dai Nihon eidai setsuyō mujinnzō*, Waseda University Library, reproduced with permission; 7.1. From *Kyōka nihon fūdoki* by Yoshima Gakutei, The British Museum, reproduced with permission; 7.2. From *Toin zukan*, New York Public Library, Spencer Collection, Astor, Lenox, and Tilden Foundations, reproduced with permission; 10.1. From *Yunazu*, MOA Museum, reproduced with permission; 10.2. *Shijō kawara yurakuzu*, Seikadō Archive, reproduced with permission; 10.3. From *Kabuki-zukan*, Tokugawa Museum, reproduced with permission; 11.3. From *Ehon sakaegusa* by Katsukawa Harushio, New York Public Library, Spencer Collection, Astor, Lenox, and Tilden Foundations, reproduced with permission; 11.4. Peddler Doll (photograph by Eiko Ikegami), 11.5 and 11.6. *Namazu-e* by Utagawa Kuniyoshi, courtesy of Rijksmuseum voor Volkenkude, Leiden; 12.1. From *Ogasawara shorei daizen*, Waseda University Library, reproduced with permission; 12.2. From *Shorei daigaku*, Waseda University Library, reproduced with permission; 12.3. From *Onna shorei ayanishiki*, Waseda University Library, reproduced with permission; 12.4. From *Daii setsuyō-shū*, Waseda University Library, reproduced with permission; 12.5. From *Edo dai setsuyō kaimaizō*, Waseda University Library, reproduced with permission; 12.6. From *Yamato setsuyō-shū shikkai nō*, Waseda University Library, reproduced with permission; 12.7. From *Dai Nihon eidai setsuyō-shū*, Waseda University Library, reproduced with permission; Plate 1. From *Ōka eika no zu* by Katsukawa Haruyuki, Tokyo Ota Kinen

437

Museum, reproduced with permission; Plate 2. From *Kabuki-zukan*, Tokugawa Museum, reproduced with permission; Plate 3. *Woman Reading a Letter* by Utagawa Kunisada, Los Angeles County Museum of Art, Etsuko and Joe Price Collection, reproduced with permission; Plate 4. *Fugaku Sanjūrokkei Gohyaku rakanji sazidō* by Katsushika Hokusai, Rijksmueum voor Volkenkunde, Leiden, reproduced with permission.

Index

Abe Yasurō, 93
addiction to performing arts, 152–153
aesthetic civility, 140
    See also artistic knowledge as civility;
        enclave identities; *iemoto* system;
        nouveaux riches; status (*mibun*)
        system of Tokugawa shogunate;
        trespassing of status boundaries
    and cultural authorities, 160–164
    need for investigation of hierarchical
        and, 324–327
    and private versus public, 140
    and standard model of propriety, 140
    use of artist names, 146–147
aesthetic Japan. *See* cultural identity of
    Japan
aesthetic quality, judgment of, 83–84
aesthetic sensitivity, 285
aesthetic sociability, 366–368
    and counter publics, 39–40
    and emotional transaction cost, 31–32
    and enclave identities, 367–368
    in enclave publics, 38–41
    Watanabe Kazan's self-assessment,
        367
    weak ties, 366–367
agency, and culture, 55–56, 58
agent of change, fashion as. *See* fashion
    politics
agents, *haikai* literary, 179–182, 186
Aizawa Muan, 215, 216
alliances, *ikki. See ikki*
allusions. *See haikai* poetry
ambiguity
    See also Kokugaku
    Japanese versus Chinese national
        identities, 232–234
    problems in political discourse,
        381–383

skirmish between Oe Kenzaburo and
    Kawabata Yasunari, 3, 231
    in tacit modes of communication,
        230–235
Amino Yoshihiko, 88–90, 96
Amorous Books (*kōshoku bon*), 299, 309
Anderson, Benedict, 290
Anderson, P. W., 52–53
anonymity, authorial, 184–186
aristocracy. *See* emperors; imperial court
artistic knowledge as civility, 140–144
    See also arts; civility; performing arts
    education of samurai, 143
    in merchant families according to
        Shōbai ōrai, 143
    rise in number of masters according to
        Kyōhabutae, 142
artists as public persons, 197–203
    and critical political consciousness, 201
    Watanabe Kazan, 198–203
arts
    See also aesthetic sociability;
        associations; communal arts and
        literature; *haikai* poetry; *iemoto*
        system; imperial court; *nouveaux*
        riches; overlapping networks;
        performing arts; trespassing of
        status boundaries; women's
        participation in arts; *Za* arts and
        literature
    collective nature of, 4, 71–75
    increasing autonomy of, 141–143
    and magical power, 108
    performance as holy act, 92–93
    for pleasure (*yūgei*), 142
    as public affair (*kuji*), 82
    as technology of transformation, 82–83
    Vincent Van Gogh's comment on
        Japanese, 19

socialization
   See also state formation, Tokugawa
   during Heian period, 84
   and isolation in *za* arts, 99–101
   in linked poetry, Sōgi's views on, 78
   during Tokugawa state formation,
     130–131
social power
   See also "Freedom and People's Rights"
     movements; "Poor People's Party"
     Rebellion; *haikai* poetry; *Kokugaku*;
     literacy; rural communities
   and complexity of networks, 209–211
   poetry, protest, and rise of, 204–220
   and village-based *ikki* organizations,
     205
social reputations, 151–152
Sōgi
   patronage by warlord Uesugi, 113
   on socialization in linked poetry,
     78
songs, *jōruri. See jōruri* songs
*Songs selected by the Ministry of
   Education,* 377
sōson (corporate village), 104
spectatorship, impartial, 26–27
standardized instruction, 168–169
standard model of propriety, 140
stanzas, associational, 228
state
   See also aesthetic sociability;
     commercial publication, regulation
     of; fashion politics; imperial court;
     Japan; nation-state; Tokugawa
     shogunate
   civility, and associational networks,
     32–33
   Habermas's view of impact on publics,
     62–63
   influence on networks and publics,
     62–64
   institutional segregation by, 32–33
state-associational network relations,
   32–33, 63, 127
state formation, Tokugawa, 127–139
   See also categorical redefinition of
     publics; enclave publics; Tokugawa
     network revolution
   control of *ikki* and *za* organizations,
     128–129
   political hierarchies and institutional
     segmentation, 128–131
   reorganization of samurai vassalage,
     128
   and socialization, 130–131
state-market relations, 34–37
   Charles Tilly's views on, 34

   institutional constraints on market,
     35–37
   socio-economic changes in early
     Tokugawa period, 34–35
status boundaries. *See* commonality; *kugai;
   mu'en;* trespassing of status
   boundaries; *yasurai hana* dances
status (*mibun*) system of Tokugawa
   shogunate, 147–149
   See also civility; commonality; fashion
     politics; *kabuki-mono*
   formal rankings (*kakushiki*), 148
   and invention of private domain,
     136–139, 145
   and participation in associational
     networks, 148–149
   and social topology, 365–366
   and sumptuary regulations, 256–257
   system of obligations, 148
   and territorial or occupational social
     groups, 148
   three dimensions of, 147–149
status of *jōruri* songs, 145
stories, folk, 92–93
*Stories of Olden Days. See Mukashi
   Mukashi Monogatari*
storytelling. *See dangi;* mixed media; *za*
   arts and literature
strangership, 26–27, 29, 160
stratification, categorical. *See* publics
strength of overlapping networks. *See*
   overlapping networks
strength of weak ties. *See* weak ties
*Structural Transformation of the Public
   Sphere, The,* 58–59
student recital, 146
subversion. *See haikai* poetry
subversion of gender roles in *Kabuki*
   theater, 263–266
subversive prints. *See namazu-e* (subversive
   prints)
subversive spirit, 323
Sugi Hitoshi, 211–212
Sukematsuya, 349
sumptuary regulations
   See also fashion contests
   Adam Smith's denunciation of, 258
   and commercial concerns, 259–260
   in comparative perspective, 257–260
   Contemporary Fashionable Patterns,
     275
   and design trends, 275
   in Edo, 274
   English, 257
   for farmers, 259–260
   and fashion politics, 255–257
   French decree regarding, 257

Other Books in the Series (*continued from page iii*)